THE SPECULAR MOMENT

Goethe's Early Lyric and the
Beginnings of Romanticism

M E R I D I A N

Crossing Aesthetics

Werner Hamacher

& David E. Wellbery

Editors

Stanford
University
Press

Stanford
California
1996

THE SPECULAR MOMENT

Goethe's Early Lyric and the
Beginnings of Romanticism

David E. Wellbery

Stanford University Press
Stanford, California
© 1996 by the Board of Trustees of the
Leland Stanford Junior University

Printed in the United States of America

CIP data appear at the end of the book

Stanford University Press publications
are distributed exclusively by
Stanford University Press within
the United States, Canada, Mexico, and
Central America; they are distributed
exclusively by Cambridge University
Press throughout the rest of the world.

for my mother,
Margaret L. Reynolds,
and in memory of my father,
Edward M. Wellbery

Acknowledgments

The first ideas for this book were sketched out during a stay at the Stanford Humanities Center in 1982–83, and the major work of elaboration was undertaken at the Wissenschaftskolleg zu Berlin during my fellowship year there in 1989–90. I am grateful to both those institutions and their respective directors, Ian Watt and Wolf Lepenies, for their support.

For their suggestive comments on portions of the book read or heard, I wish to thank John Bender, Marshall Brown, Rüdiger Campe, Hans Ulrich Gumbrecht, Rodolphe Gasché, Fritz Gutbrodt, Werner Hamacher, Andreas Huyssen, Carol Jacobs, Friedrich Kittler, Wolf Kittler, Eberhard Lämmert, Winfried Menninghaus, Inka Mülder-Bach, Rainer Nägele, Peter Pütz, Tom Saine, Helmut Schneider, Bianca Theisen, Michael Titzmann, Jürgen Trabant, Peter Utz, Hans Vaget, Rainer Warning, Marianne Wünsch, Walter Zimmerli, and Raimar Zons. Ernst Behler, Dorothea von Mücke, and an anonymous referee read the penultimate version of the manuscript in its entirety and their remarks were decisive in helping me to sharpen my argument.

Some ten years ago Klaus Weimar of the University of Zurich initiated a dialogue with me on Goethe's poetry that has been the crucible of most of the ideas in the book. During the same time, Helen Tartar of Stanford University Press has provided indispensable, detailed advice on every aspect of the writing, and her unflagging editorial commitment has sustained my belief in the project throughout. I trust it will not be felt as a diminishment of my gratitude to those mentioned above if I single out my indebtedness to these two individuals. Without their collaboration *The Specular Moment* would not have been written.

An earlier, briefer version of Chapter 1 appeared in Wilfried Barner, Eberhard Lämmert, and Norbert Oellers, eds., *Unser Commercium: Goethes und Schillers Literaturpolitik*, Veröffentlichungen der deutschen Schillergesellschaft, vol. 42 (Stuttgart: Metzler, 1984). Chapter 2 is a revised version of an article published in *Goethe Yearbook* 1 (1982). Chapter 9 represents an expansion of my contribution to David E. Wellbery and Klaus Weimar, *Goethes "Harzreise im Winter": Eine Deutungskontroverse* (Paderborn: Ferdinand Schöningh, 1984). Permission to use these materials is gratefully acknowledged.

Contents

Contents

Note on Abbreviations

For the most part, Goethe's poems are cited from: Johann Wolfgang von Goethe, *Sämtliche Werke, Briefe, Tagebücher und Gespräche*, vol. 1: *Gedichte 1756-1799*, ed. Karl Eibl (Frankfurt a. M.: Deutscher Klassiker Verlag, 1987). References to this edition are indicated as *Gedichte 1756-1799*. Other works by the young Goethe, such as reviews, dramas, essays, and occasionally versions of poems, are cited from: Johann Wolfgang von Goethe, *Sämtliche Werke nach Epochen seines Schaffens*, vols. I/1 and I/2, *Der junge Goethe 1757-1775*, ed. Gerhard Sauder (Munich: Hanser, 1985 and 1987). This edition is indicated as *Münchener-Ausgabe*. Finally, well-known works such as *Die Leiden des jungen Werther* or *Faust* are cited from the widely distributed Hamburg edition: *Goethes Werke*, ed. Erich Trunz (Hamburg: Christian Wegner, 1968). The abbreviation employed to refer to this edition is: *H. A.*, with volume and page.

Phillip Otto Runge, *Mother at the Source.*
Destroyed in World War II. Formerly
Kunsthalle, Hamburg, Germany
(Foto Marburg / Art Resource NY;
S0077061   1102.722).

PART ONE

The Specular Moment

§ 1 Idyllic and Lyric Intimacy

Modern interpretation, Carlo Ginzburg has argued in a deft essay, follows the spoor of Morelli.[1] Rather than focus on the grand themes that parade as center and essence, it seeks its clues on the periphery, among the inadvertent traces and remainders of cultural production. Morelli's major concern was to authenticate the painterly signature of the great masters, to provide accurate attributions by meticulously examining such details as the folds of ears. My own purposes here, of course, do not bear centrally on disputes regarding authorship (the corpus I shall be analyzing is, with rare exceptions, firmly affixed to Goethe's name), but I shall nevertheless begin by assuming the basic gesture of Morelli's method and attending to a collocation of marks (clues, traces) that, under scrutiny, crystallize into the signature of a historical emergence. At issue are the linguistic forms—lexical, syntactic, and rhetorical configurations—I have emphasized in the following two texts:

> 1. Ob ich Dich liebe weiß ich nicht:
>   *Seh ich nur einmal dein Gesicht,*
>   *Seh Dir in's Auge nur einmal,*
>   Frei wird mein Herz von aller Qual;
> (5) *Gott weiß, wie mir so wohl geschicht!*
>   Ob ich Dich liebe, weiß ich nicht.[2]

> Whether I love you I don't know:
> *If I see your face just once,*
> *If I look into your eyes just once,*
> My heart becomes free of all torment;

(5) *God knows what so sweetly happens to me!*
    Whether I love you I don't know.

(Emphasis added)

2. MAIFEST

    Wie herrlich leuchtet
    Mir die Natur!
    Wie glänzt die Sonne!
    Wie lacht die Flur!

(5) Es dringen Blüten
    Aus jedem Zweig,
    Und tausend Stimmen
    Aus dem Gesträuch,

    Und Freud und Wonne
(10) Aus jeder Brust.
    O Erd o Sonne
    O Glück o Lust!

    O Lieb' o Liebe,
    So golden schön,
(15) Wie Morgenwolken
    Auf jenen Höhn;

    Du segnest herrlich
    Das frische Feld,
    Im Blütendampfe
(20) Die volle Welt.

    O Mädchen Mädchen,
    Wie lieb' ich dich!
    Wie blinkt dein Auge!
    Wie liebst du mich!

(25) *So liebt die Lerche*
    Gesang und Luft,
    Und *Morgenblumen*
    Den Himmels Duft,

    Wie ich dich liebe
(30) Mit warmen Blut,
    Die du mir Jugend
    Und Freud und Mut

Zu neuen Liedern,
Und Tänzen gibst!
(35) Sei ewig glücklich
Wie du mich liebst!³

MAY FESTIVAL

How gloriously Nature
Lights up for me!
How the sun shines!
How the field laughs!

(5) Blossoms press forth
From every branch,
And a thousand voices
From the bushes,

And joy and delight
(10) From every breast.
Oh earth oh sun
Oh bliss oh delight!

Oh love, oh love,
So golden beautiful,
(15) Like morning clouds
On those heights;

You bless gloriously
The fresh field,
In blossoms' fragrance
(20) The full world.

O maiden, maiden,
How I love you!
How your eye gleams!
How you love me!

(25) *Thus the lark loves*
Song and air,
And *morning flowers*
The heaven's fragrance,

As I love you
(30) With warm blood
You who to me youth
And joy and spirit

> For new songs,
> And dances give.
> (35) Be eternally blissful
> As you love me!
> *(Emphasis added)*

The two texts are utterly familiar, so much so, in fact, that their singularity and strangeness have been almost entirely effaced. They were written during Goethe's Strasbourg sojourn of 1770–71, the period of the poet's first collaborations with Herder and of what is referred to (not insignificantly, as we shall see) as his Sesenheim idyll, an episode of amorous attachment involving a certain Friederike Brion and bathed in the 'natural simplicity' of the provincial Alsatian village where the girl, a pastor's daughter, lived. Such are the terms—the dates, places, proper names, and mythical values—out of which one of the best-known biographical anecdotes in German literary historiography is constructed. Here is one of its variants:

> At the end of March 1770, Goethe came to Strasbourg. In his turbulent, yearning soul, the elements for a new beginning were already prepared. With the Behrisch odes, written in Leipzig, he had already reached the point of speaking of his feelings in an unmediated fashion. But at that time he did not yet realize what he had accomplished, and in the *New Songs* he had fallen back into the Anacreontic mode. In Strasbourg, new experience propelled [*trieb*] him once again to speak with immediacy; his artistic power [*Kraft*] had in the meantime grown, and this time his was more than just a vague searching—thanks to Herder. In October 1770, he met Friederike Brion in Sesenheim; his capacity for love—which would remain with him throughout his life and would occasionally lead him into profound crises—was deeply touched. It drove him to express himself, and to do this he required a language that was fundamentally different from that of the current tradition. At this point he met Herder, who was in Strasbourg from September 1770 to April 1771 as the patient of an eye doctor. Constructed on a broad basis, Herder's new theory of art reflected and called for exactly what Goethe was seeking: naturalness, simplicity, feeling, force of expression, symbol. It provided him examples that pointed in this direction—folk songs, Ossian, Homer, Shakespeare—and it emphasized traits in these works which Goethe had not previously noticed. Now he overcame the last barrier that separated him from a new art, and he did it in a storm. A fortunate constellation joined together inner preparedness, soulful experience [*seelisches Erleben*], and intellectual vision, a constellation

that fit fortuitously into broader circumstances: the new generation in Germany, generally weary of the old forms, required not only a theoretician like Herder, but also a singer [*Sänger*], a youth who could shape in exemplary fashion the art that was yearned for. It was at this time that Goethe created [*schuf*] his first great poems in the new style. They became immediately known among friends and, with their publication in 1775 in the journal *Iris*, also among broader circles. . . . It was a literary revolution. With his Sesenheim Songs, and even more with the hymns that soon followed, Goethe became the most important lyric poet of the youthful generation and inaugurated a new epoch in the history of lyric poetry, much as he did for the drama and the novel with *Götz* and *Werther*.[4]

With admirable economy this narrative condenses a tenacious tradition of Goethe interpretation that is authorized, ultimately, by the poet's autobiography *Dichtung und Wahrheit* (*Poetry and Truth*, esp. Books X and XI). It rests on a psychology (and even a metaphysics) of artistic production that remains believable today only in a few isolated backwaters of literary-historical research. Like every hermeneutics of experience (*Erlebnis*),[5] the biographical interpretation of Goethe's poetry unfolded here is in essence tautological, drawing on, and reinforcing, the mythical values—'nature', 'force', 'youth', 'unmediated song'—the texts themselves set into circulation.[6] However, it is not for the sake of an easy polemic that I have cited Erich Trunz's story in extenso. Rather, I want to insist on the discursive fact with which the story attempts to grapple: that the lyric texts Goethe began to compose in 1770–71 break decisively with literary tradition, that something like *a new possibility of poetic enunciation* opens up in them. Goethe's poetry of this period not only marks an innovation in the history of German literature, it fundamentally alters the nature of poetic writing, inaugurating a type of literary discourse that, from a European perspective, can be called the Romantic lyric. The following pages seek to analyze this *discourse*, in the emphatic sense that Foucault and Kittler have lent to the term.[7] The question is how to account for its emergence without resorting to the myth of unmediated expressivity.

This is where Morelli's method of detection proves helpful. Its execution requires, as Poe demonstrated in "The Purloined Letter," a peculiarly ascetic form of attention. I therefore invite my reader to review the two poems quoted at the outset, but to hold in abeyance (to bracket, as phenomenologists say) everything the tradition of biographical interpretation has viewed as their central or essential message: the poet's spontaneous emotionality, for example, or his *Naturgefühl* ('feeling for nature'). Attend rather, like Dupin, merely to the letter of the texts, in particular to the verbal forms that have been emphasized, to their context and resonance. Then, with only these words and phrases as the horizon of your reading, consider the following two documents. They are excerpts from a collection of idylls published in 1760 by the Swiss writer Salomon Geßner (1730–88):

3.   DAMON: Hier liebe Phillis, seze dich im Klee. O könnt ich immer dich lächeln sehn, und deine Augen!—Nein, sieh mich nicht so an, sprach er, und drükte sanft des Mädchens Auge zu; Glaube, *wenn dein Blick so lächelnd mir ins Auge sieht, ich weiß nicht, wie mir dann geschieht,* ich zittre, ich seufze dann, und meine Worte stoken.

PHILLIS: Nimm, Damon, nimm die Hand von meinen Augen, denn, wenn du meine Hand in deine drükest, dann gehts mir eben so, wie fährts durch mich, *ich weiß nicht was es ist,* dann pochet mir das Herz.[8]

DAMON: Here, dear Phillis, sit down in the clover. O if only I could always see you smile, and your eyes!—No, don't look at me that way, he said, and tenderly pressed the maiden's eyes closed; Believe me, *when your glance looks so smilingly into my eyes, I don't know what happens to me then,* I tremble, then I sigh, and my words get stuck.

PHILLIS: Take, Damon, take your hand from my eyes, for when you press my hand in yours, then I feel the same thing, the way it shoots through me, *I don't know what it is,* then my heart pounds.   *(Emphasis added)*

4.   DAPHNIS: Schön ist es, wenn auf fernen Hügeln die Herden in dunkeln Büschen irren; doch schöner ists, O Chloe! wenn ein frischer Blumen-Kranz dein dunkles Haar durchirret; schön ist des heitern Himmels Blau, doch schöner ist *dein blaues Auge, wenn es lächelnd mir winket.* Ja liebe Chloe, *mehr liebe ich dich als schnelle Fische den klaren Teich, mehr als die Lerche die Morgen-Luft.*

CHLOE: . . . Ach! riefst du, die Götter sind Zeugen! ich liebe dich! ach! sprach ich, *ich liebe dich, mehr als die Bienen die Blüten, mehr als die Blüten den Morgentau.*[9]

DAPHNIS: It's beautiful when on the distant hills the flocks wander through the dark bushes; but it's more beautiful, O Chloe! when a fresh wreath of flowers wanders through your dark hair; beautiful the serene heaven's blue, but more beautiful still is *your blue eye when it winks smilingly at me.* Yes, dear Chloe, *I love you more than the quick fish loves the clear pond, more than the lark loves the morning air.*

CHLOE: ... Oh! you called out—the gods are my witnesses!—I love you! Oh! I said, *I love you more than the bees love the flowers, more than the flowers love the morning dew.* *(Emphasis added)*

What does this juxtaposition of texts by Goethe and Geßner reveal? On the negative side it demonstrates, forcefully, that Goethe's post-Anacreontic poetry did not come into being as an act of unmediated creativity, that the poetry does not simply represent an efflorescence of emotions the poet suddenly discovered within himself, that the texts cannot be construed simply as the expressions of an antecedent *Erlebnis,* either biographically or imaginatively lived. Quite the contrary, the form of discourse these texts by Goethe inaugurate, which I shall call here, in abbreviated fashion, the lyric, turns out to have a specific and describable genealogy in the Nietzschean sense of the term. The italicized verbal forms are literally traces: marks remaining from an anterior discourse from which the lyric derives. On the positive side, then, the juxtaposition of these texts by Goethe and Geßner enables us to read the fault lines of a *discursive event*: the lyric emerges across a series of borrowings and displacements, distortions and transformations, a process that in Nietzsche's genealogical theory carries the name "reinterpretation."[10]

The parent system of literary signification from which the new lyric discourse is born, represented here by the two texts of Geßner, is the sentimental idyll, a narrative-poetic hybrid that flourished in the developing bourgeois culture of the mid-eighteenth century with its pronounced (and antiaristocratic) ideology of "natural simplicity."[11] Geßner's individual contribution to the genre's history and the source, quite probably, of his considerable popularity was the attainment of an unparalleled, and yet unembarrassed, naïveté of expression. To his contemporaries, Geßner's language seemed as natural and transparent as the spring water from which his shepherds and shepherdesses took their refreshment, a pure medium in which human sentiment could be exchanged without the deflections of artifice. The idyll, in Geßner and elsewhere, is the utopia of perfect communication.[12] In Goethe's reinterpretation, this utopia is absorbed into the very movement of lyric speech.

The lineaments of this reinterpretive process come into sharper focus when we consider the continuities linking the juxtaposed texts. Their filiations are most evident, of course, on the level of linguistic surface structure. The texts employ identical lexical and syntactic forms to such an extent that a conscious and deliberate borrowing on Goethe's part seems likely. But I don't want to belabor this question of authorial intention, which is probably undecidable anyway. Far more significant from a discourse-analytical perspective is the stylistic fact to which these verbal echoes point: the stylistic register of "simple, artless speech" the lyric will exploit throughout Romanticism—the tone of common parlance Wordsworth, in the Preface to *Lyrical Ballads*, also invokes as a stylistic paradigm—is an achievement of the sentimental idyll. To be sure, the diction and syntactic ductus of Romantic song are preformed in other discourses as well, most notably in the folk song, to which I shall return in Chapter 7. It nevertheless remains a literary-historical fact that the lyric, even in the strand of its development that seems most closely entwined with music, draws some of its stylistic resources from the gentle accents of idyllic prose.

Much more has been taken over here, however, than a few surface forms or a range of stylistic selections. The two pairs of texts share as well a common thematics, a conceptual repertoire embracing such values as 'nature', 'sincere love', 'emotionality', 'simplicity'. Furthermore, their diegetic movement centers on the same event: what is narrated is always 'the recognition of mutual love' as it is jubilantly experienced within the amorous dyad. The texts are also oriented toward the same referential domain, the same slice of social life, which we can describe as the sphere of intimate emotional bonds. And finally, they affirm and reinforce the same nebulous ideological proposition: that 'love', in its true form, is equivalent to 'nature'.

Even this rapid enumeration of the similarities obtaining between the sample texts sheds considerable light on the discursive event that is my concern here. For what all these affiliations amount to globally is the fact that the lyric *seizes hold of the same cultural space*—the same sphere of practices, interactions, and meanings—as that occupied by the idyll. Both discourses, in other words, adhere to the same region of relevance, a domain I shall call here, following Niklas Luhmann, *the field of intimate communication.*[13] This is not to say that the two discourses are equivalent. On the contrary, intimate communication is susceptible to a high degree of historical variability, and the changes it undergoes are keyed to the changing forms of literary (and nonliterary) discourse that lend intimate experience its contours and codes. Goethe's texts do not simply carry the idyllic tradition forward; they decisively alter it, engendering in the process a new discursive practice and a new codification of intimate love. In this sense, the traces from which I took my point of departure indeed crystallize into a historical signature. They reveal a process of cultural transformation in which the task of organizing intimacy is passing from one discourse to another.

∼

Discursive event (Foucault), recodification (Luhmann), reinterpretation (Nietzsche): the process these quasi-synonyms designate embraces much more than a change of content.[14] To be sure, discursive mutation affects semantic organization, bringing forth new structures of meaning and reference; but it also touches on other dimensions of the communicative transaction, generating new enunciative modalities and strategies of reading, new coordinates locating the discourse in time, new criteria of authorial attribution, new intertextual networks, and new material determinations of the discursive medium. In view of this complexity (and the list I have just run through is partial), it is clear that no adequate definition of the lyric can be derived from the slender corpus of four texts I am working with here. But the juxtaposition of Geßner and Goethe does at least enable us to delineate one path in the lyric's genealogical network and thus to develop a preliminary characterization, to be expanded in subsequent analyses, of the mode of existence of these poetic texts. The task is to parse the differences between the idyll and the lyric, to discern the labor of transformation that produces the latter out of the former. The most telling of these differences seem to me to be located at the following four discursive levels: (a) pragmatic structure, (b) fictional structure, (c) temporal structure, and (d) semantic structure. I want briefly to trace, for each of these dimensions, how the lyric appropriation of the idyll reorganizes the poetry of intimate communication.

(*a*) In what is perhaps the most far-reaching departure from its predecessor, the lyric introduces a forceful innovation on the *pragmatic level of discourse*. Indeed, even where they employ identical formulations, the idyll and the lyric establish different communicational frames and instantiate, therefore, different sorts of language act. The question of pragmatic structure, of course, is a complicated one to which I shall often return. For the present, however, I shall restrict myself to a global and ideal-typical distinction in order to capture what I take to be the major thrust of the lyric innovation. The language acts we encounter in Geßner's texts, and these texts themselves, can be classified as *performed utterances*. Their

mode of address is inflected, in other words, by a certain theatricality; they
seem always to rehearse, or perform, a latent script. And just as in a
theatrical performance it is not the actor in his own person who is the
subject of the utterances, but rather the *role* he plays, so here the statements are not moored to the life of an individual. The subject of enunciation in the idyll is a *social role* shaped by the expectations of the implicit
audience before which the speech performance occurs. Hence the standardized names of the characters: Damon and Phillis, Daphnis and Chloe.
In the lyric text, however, the theatrical frame vanishes and the communicative gestures become *authentic utterances.* By this term I mean acts of
speech embedded in the speaker's existential situation and marked, therefore, by the urgency of the speaker's care (*Sorge*) in the broadest sense of
the term. Thus, the subject of enunciation is no longer a social role; it is,
rather, a *self,* which is itself at stake in the communicative action.[15]

The distinction between performed and authentic speech takes us to the
nerve of one of the lyric's most pressing internal problems: How can one
achieve authenticity of speech? How can one speak (an intrinsically repeatable and public action) in such a way as not to betray the singularity and
inwardness of the subject's experience? There will be ample opportunity in
the ensuing pages to explore the ways in which this problem ramifies—to
sound, as it were, the depths of the lyric's inner treason. And in many
respects my inquiry will be nothing other than an analysis of this subjectivity, or self, which endeavors to bring itself to speech in the lyric and for
which the lyric is the privileged linguistic mode of existence.

At this juncture, however, I merely want to note one consequence of the
ideal-typical distinction I have drawn for the global pragmatic structures
of the lyric and the idyll: the two types of language act sketched out here
elicit different interpretive strategies from the reader. The reader of a
Geßner idyll grasps the informational value of an individual utterance via
expectations of appropriateness that have their source, on the one hand, in
an antecedent knowledge of the social script being enacted and, on the
other hand, in the internal sequence of the individual idyll. Interpretation,
in other words, involves comparison with a tacitly mastered cultural
program. The reader of the lyric text operates differently. He/she understands an individual utterance by developing inferences regarding the
feelings and desires of the speaking subject; that is, through an effort of
empathetic projection.[16] The task is no longer to relate the text to a
normative paradigm, but rather to grasp, *through an act of divination,* the

subjectivity that alone gives the text its coherence. That is to say, *the authentic utterances of the lyric call forth a hermeneutics of identification* such as we find developed in Romantic hermeneutic theory from Herder to Schleiermacher, the inventor and canonizer, respectively, of the concept of divination in its hermeneutic sense.[17] Thus, the lyric appropriation of the idyll evidenced in the juxtaposed texts engenders an entirely new form of cultural communication. Textual processing unfolds no longer as the playing of a social game, but rather as the reactualization by the reader of a subjective mode of being articulated in the text.

(*b*) Along with the change in pragmatic structure that separates the two discursive forms, we can discern a shift in the *type of fictionality* manifested by the idyll and the lyric respectively. Fictional reference, after all, is by no means unchanging; even unreality has a history. Thus, in the two cases at hand the fictional structure serves a very different function, and its effects of reference are established along divergent routes. Geßner's idylls employ fictionality in order to embody, in a nuanced and condensed figuration, general social norms. The idyllic fiction, in other words, has the status of a *prototype*, a leading image expressing a social conception as to how life would be under the ideal conditions of the state of nature. It does not matter that this image is in itself impracticable, that its fictional status is generally acknowledged. The point is that the values evinced by the idyllic fiction are held to possess universal validity. In short, the idyll uses fictionality as an instructional device, a heuristic construction, the advertisement of an "ought." The lyric texts, however, dispense with this normative function; they are not at all intended to exemplify a pregiven behavioral code. Rather, the lyric image is grounded in the will or desire of the speaking subject. No longer a normative guide applicable in the arena of social contacts, the lyric fiction is in essence an imaginary anticipation, the correlate of a wish (in the Freudian sense of *Wunsch*). The function of this chimerical plenitude, as I shall often have occasion to note, is to cover a lack, to provide compensatory access to a bliss forever lost. The discursive reinterpretation I am tracing here brings forth a new species of unreality, one which is socially and psychologically effective precisely because of the ontological void at its center. The idyllic prototype is transformed into what it seems appropriate to term the *lyric phantasm*.

(*c*) The third alteration bears on the temporal structure of the two discourses. The lyric imports into the domain of intimate communication a substantially different *temporality*. The issues involved here are intricate, and I can only sketch (as with the other discursive dimensions) their barest outlines. The point of the juxtaposition, after all, is not to provide an exhaustive analysis but to open up territory for future exploration. Thus, I shall restrict my remarks to two types of temporal relation: external temporal relations, which connect the discourse to the time of its reading; and internal temporal relations, which organize the time of the discursive action itself. The movement from idyll to lyric affects both temporal dimensions decisively.

Externally, the idyllic discourse is characterized by a fundamental discontinuity between the time of its reading and the events it narrates. The idyllic action unfolds in a temporal sphere altogether separate from the time of our experience, a fabulous time that is marked as such and that corresponds to the fabulous Arcadian place in which the shepherds dwell. There is no passage from this enclosed temporal world to the "now" of reading, no bridge joining this "once upon a time" to the present. Goethe's transcription of the idyll as lyric shatters the former's temporal insularity and relocates the textual event within the temporal horizon of the reader. That is not to say that the lyric represents a world that is objectively verifiable as contemporary to the reader's experience in 1770. Its link to the present moment of reading is not chronological, but phenomenological. Indeed, the lyric event has no other time (neither an entirely fictional one, nor an objective one) than that which relates it to the *Jetztzeit*, or temporal actuality, of the reader.[18] And this is true regardless of whether the event is marked as 'past', 'present', or 'future': in fact, these temporal fields are opened up and acquire their significance only with reference to the moment of reading itself. Conversely, the *Jetztzeit* of reading is only itself disclosed with regard to the temporal determinations (the 'past', 'present', or 'future') of the lyric event. In this sense, the reading of the lyric becomes a process in which time emerges for the subject and the subject emerges in time, a movement of temporalized self-constitution, which, as we shall see, can attain considerable complexity and ambiguity.

The idyll's spatio-temporal insularity with regard to the time of reading is balanced internally by an unshakeable temporal continuity. In the idyllic world, tomorrow flows naturally from yesterday and today, and one is just as much a shepherd in the morning as in the evening. Becoming, one might say, is merely a manifestation of Being; time circles into itself according to a natural rhythm that is objectively guaranteed.[19] The lyric discourse, however, presupposes an abruptly discontinuous temporality; the lyric inevitably has an *ecstatic* character, standing out from the rest of time. In other words, the utterances that constitute Geßner's texts are embedded in a 'before' and 'after', whereas in the lyric the utterances constitute a temporal structure that exists for itself, independently of any supportive temporal context. This ecstatic structure harbors some of the genre's deepest paradoxes. In its brevity, the lyric moment seems infinitely fragile, and it is certainly incapable of generating a stable future. Yet in its intensity it seems to efface all linear time, as if its evanescence equaled eternity. There is a temporal affinity, one which Goethe will often exploit, between the lyric and a mystic rapture.

(*d*) As I have mentioned above, one of the major continuities between the idyll and the lyric is their common thematic orientation toward the categories of Love and Nature (terms I capitalize to emphasize their symbolic status[20]). Indeed, the central ideological thrust of both discourses is to establish an equivalence between these two categories, to urge that Love, in its truest form, is Nature. But this thematic and ideological continuity obtains only at a very high level of abstraction, and the two discourses in fact organize the conceptual space they share in very different ways. Goethe's lyric appropriation of the idyllic world, in other words, lends the terms Love and Nature a *new semantic structure*.

Nature can be semanticized in two ways, either as the whole of Nature or as individual natural phenomena. In the idylls of Geßner, the encompassing totality of Nature has the character of a scenic backdrop, a locale or sphere of life where the shepherds and shepherdesses abide. The inner structure of this sphere is that of an *order*: all the movements and relations it encompasses obey a *law* and an *economy*. Thus, it is easy to see why idyllic Nature is well suited for encoding behavioral norms; its lawlike rationality functions as a paradigm for rational-virtuous conduct. The semantic determination of the entirety of Nature as an ideal order draws in its wake a corresponding definition of the parts of Nature: individual natural phenomena are treated as cases of the universal law, poignant instantiations of a rational, economic principle.

The semantic organization of Nature as universal order and individual exemplification is completely abandoned in the lyric. Here Nature, in its totality, is a *productive force* or power, and as such it cannot be represented as a scene, but only as a *process*. The relationship of this force to individual natural phenomena is one of *manifestation*: these are the variable expressions of the one productive Nature, the scattered syllables, as it were, of the song that Nature brings forth. In this sense, the function of natural phenomena within the semantic system of the lyric has nothing to do with conformity to a general principle; rather, these phenomena allow the internal, hidden, animating force that Nature is to enter into the domain of appearances. Consequently, the type of grouping that allies the phenomena of Nature one to another changes as we move from idyll to lyric. In the former, a principle of classification collects and distinguishes sets of phenomena according to their external characteristics and their utilitarian functions: Geßner's Nature (like that of his contemporary Linnaeus) tends toward a taxonomical ordering. But in the lyric what draws the individual phenomena together is the fact that they point in kindred ways to the animating source whose expressions they are. The phenomena Goethe names are linked by a network of analogies which suggest an underlying unity precisely by cutting across taxonomic divisions. Finally, this shift in what one must call the being of Nature brings with it a change in the way the human subject relates to the natural world. In the idyll, it is a matter of conforming to the lawlike order of Nature, whereas in the lyric the human subject seeks to experience Nature as the productive force that dwells within both man and the cosmos.

The categories of Love and Nature are correlated in both genres, and therefore the process of semantic reinterpretation proceeds, in both cases, along similar paths. In the idyllic discourse, Love is in essence an interpersonal bond that combines social, moral, and emotional features. It is something that can be objectively identified according to behavioral criteria, as the many stagings of Love in Geßner's texts reveal. The lyric, however, negates both the sociality of Love and its objective representability. Love becomes a privileged experience—a discovery of the self in the other—which lies outside all normal discourse and social competence. Furthermore, because Love is the relation one entertains to one's most intimate self, it is not the object of the lyric discourse, but rather its Origin: the emotional movement the authentic utterances of the text endeavor to articulate.

At this point I shall break off my comparison of the texts by Goethe and Geßner. The analysis, of course, could be pursued further, taking into consideration other dimensions of the discourses exemplified by the sam-

	Idyll	*Lyric*
Pragmatic:	performed utterance	authentic utterance
	speaker as role	speaker as self
	interpretation within game framework	hermeneutics of identification
Fictionality:	fiction as prototype	fiction as phantasm
Temporality:		
internal:	continuous time	ecstatic time
external:	discontinuous	reader's *Jetztzeit*
Semantics:		
Nature:	encompassing order	underlying force
	individual examples	analogical expressions
Love:	normative, behavioral	experience of self in other

Schema 1: Structural Comparison of the Idyll and the Lyric

ple texts, such as their very different workings of rhyme, rhythm, and spatial arrangement. And the features of the two discourses my discussion has sought to characterize, which are summarized in Schema 1, could be described in much finer detail. Even a schematic account, however, renders intelligible the general thrust of the discursive shift that concerns me here. From a discourse that pertains entirely to the domain of social interaction, that stages Love within its virtual theatricality as a kind of natural etiquette, there emerges a discourse keyed to the movements of consciousness and desire, which constitute a private subjectivity in its radical inwardness. The two discourses, in other words, organize and manage intimacy in entirely different ways; intimacy has, in each, a different mode of existence and adheres to different structures of affectivity. Idyllic intimacy is located in the region of conduct and behavior, in an interpersonal domain that, however 'natural' it might appear, is governed by social norms and role expectations, indeed, constitutes the model of an ideal sociality. But the reader of the lyric is not being trained in appropriate forms of interaction with others: rather, he/she is turned toward the foyer of an inner intimacy, the site of his/her own subjective being. The socializing or acculturating effect of the lyric is not achieved in the field of conduct, but in the field of phantasms, yearnings, memories, and wishes: that is to say, in the field of the *imaginary*. Let it be said right away (I have already alluded to the matter under point [a] of the comparison) that the intimacy the lyric produces is neither homogeneous nor unproblematic. On the contrary, it is troubled by a sort of inner hiatus, by its own form of inter-, one might say; and this distance-within-proximity cannot be reduced to the fact that the lyric subjectivity appropriates itself in relation to a 'you' (the beloved/addressee). But this is a question to be explored in later analyses. For the present, I want to insist merely on the general discursive fact that the juxtaposition of Geßner and Goethe has dramatized: with the birth of lyric song out of the spirit of idyllic prose a type of communicative transaction is inaugurated that sends readers, as it were, *into and through the language of the poem in quest of their most intimate subjectivity.* This quest is possible because it has been undertaken in advance by the lyric subject, whose speech emanates from an inner origin toward which, in speaking, it seeks to return. The lyric—in the general formula of its discursive constitution—is a *path toward the Source,*[21] and this Source bears the double name of Nature and Love. My genealogical analysis suggests, in short, that lyric discourse is one in which subjectivity itself—its emergence, modulations, and crises—is being elaborated, worked out and on. The intricacies and inner tensions of this semiotic labor (and play) provide the object of study investigated in the following chapters. At this point, however, at least a provisional hypothesis can be stated: the lyric discourse that emerges in these two texts by Goethe takes effect by simulating, in the register of the imaginary, the fusion and presencing of the values Nature, Love, and Origin. The Origin or Source in question here is that of both poetry and subjectivity.

Discourse analysis construes its task as the identification of general regularities governing the production and reception of statements. It analyzes the networks that connect discourses to one another in historically specific constellations, the spheres of practice and interaction discourses organize, and the transformations discourses undergo. Thus, discourse analysis is, methodologically speaking, opposed to hermeneutics; it approaches its object of study from the outside, as an observer of the system and not as its interpreter.[22] Indeed, as I pointed out in my discussion of the pragmatic structure of the lyric, the hermeneutic position—the position of the subject which empathetically seizes the text at its point of subjective origination, the point, or moment, that Schleiermacher designated the *Keimentschluß*[23]—is itself inscribed within the discursive order. In this sense, Pierre Macherey's dictum that interpretation is always tautological, reproducing the *projet idéologique* of the discourse it attends to, is entirely apt.[24] It certainly applies to the tradition of biographically oriented, *Erlebnis*-based analysis that has, until recently, dominated Goethe scholarship.

But the generalizing movement of discourse analysis remains incomplete, especially as regards literary writing, if it is not combined with a mode of reading that attends to the specific texture of the corpus under investigation. The reason for this is that the regularities that define a discourse do not saturate its individual instances, they do not fully define *the singularity of the text,* which (inevitably?) contains moments that escape, disturb or contravene discursive regulation.[25] Such moments reveal themselves in what can be thought of as a nonhermeneutic mode of reading, a reading that attends not to the animating intention or the essential truth of the text, but rather to the dynamics of its textuality. Thus, I want to conclude this section with some specific observations regarding the two texts by Goethe from which I started out. The purpose of these remarks is to point out some of the concrete possibilities and problems of aesthetic realization opened up by the discursive event I have charted here.

Our first text (Text 1) exploits the temporal parameters of lyric discourse. It detaches a single moment (and it is worth keeping in mind that the German word for moment is *Augenblick*, literally 'eye-look') from the scenic-narrative context of the idyll, isolates that moment in such a manner that it stands out—ecstatically—from all time. This moment receives its identity from a unique event: the loving subject's look or regard into the loving regard of the beloved/addressee. By freeing up and absolutizing a momentary utterance on the part of the subject, the text speaks of—indeed, jubilantly asserts—the subject's absolute freedom: "Frei wird mein Herz von aller Qual" (4). Note that this moment cannot be fixed in terms of a precise temporal position. Is the sudden release spoken of here inferred from past experiences? Or does it occur, as in Geßner's idyllic scenario, in the presence of the beloved? Or is it a possible future event which the subject hopes and longs for? These questions are undecidable: past, present, and future shade into one another as modalities of the moment of speech or reading.

Beyond question, however, is the absolute value of the visual exchange that fills the lyric moment (it is literally an *Augenblick*) and that has absorbed into itself all the euphoric connotations of Love. The rhymed oppositional pair "einmal" / "aller Qual" (3–4) effectively reduces all other experience to an obscure, negative background against which the radiant moment of vision is semantically profiled. The lovers' look no longer functions merely as evidence on the basis of which mutual love can be inferred, as it clearly does for Geßner. Here Love *is* the look, *is* the experience of absolute specularity.

This point is lent an additional, important nuance by the line that frames the text: "Ob ich Dich liebe weiß ich nicht" (1, 6). When first encountered, the line suggests indecision, as in the paraphrastic translation: "I'm uncertain whether I love you or not." Yet so emphatic and assured are the central lines that when the initial verse returns it has acquired an altogether different interpretation. The true nature of the subject's amorous feelings (love or not love?) is no longer in question; what is at issue is the capacity of the common word *lieben*, and the common knowledge that word designates, adequately to comprehend what the subject feels. Thus, the repeated verse is indeed a frame, in the technical semiotic sense: it carves, positionally and semantically, a border between the poem's intimacy and the world of conventional mediations that surrounds it. From a social point of view, the domain of experience (the loving regard) the text cuts out appears as ignorance ("weiß ich nicht"), but internally it enjoys an absolute privilege in comparison to which all conventional classifications—love or nonlove, knowledge or ignorance— are reduced to insignificance. Hence the delicate ambiguity of line 5, which yields up two possible readings: "God only knows [that is, no one knows, it can't be known] what so sweetly happens to me" (this is the reading in terms of "ignorance"); and "Only God knows what so sweetly happens to me"—that is, the ecstatic moment of visual encounter and Love *is* divine knowledge and therefore, since divine knowledge is *per definitionem* auto-reflexive, it is knowledge, or self-knowledge, of the divine. This ambiguity only faintly shimmers forth from this brief and unassuming text, but it nevertheless suggests aesthetic possibilities Goethe's subsequent poetry will explore in all their consequences: the new lyric discourse allows the subject to identify with the divine Father, to appropriate His position of knowledge, which is the position of specular union with the beloved 'you'. Such lyric assault on paternity, however, will not always prove so easy as in these six lines of verse.

The second of our sample texts ("Maifest") allows us to follow out the ramifications of the semantic transformations discussed above. Here the radiant moment of the reciprocal amorous regard (22–24) is situated within an intensifying series that passes through two other domains:

Nature and Song. Of course, the semantic fields Nature, Love, and Song can be ascertained in the text's idyllic predecessor as well, but their transposition to the lyric alters decisively both their inner organization and their relations to one another. This can be illustrated even at the point of closest proximity between the texts:

> Ja liebe Chloe, mehr liebe ich dich als schnelle Fische den klaren Teich, mehr als die Lerche die Morgen-Luft. . . . ich liebe dich, mehr als die Bienen die Blüten, mehr als die Blumen den Morgentau. *(Text 4)*

> So liebt die Lerche
> Gesang und Luft,
> Und Morgenblumen
> Den Himmels Duft,
>
> Wie ich dich liebe
> *(Text 2, 25–29)*

In Geßner's text, the figure of comparison differentiates and hierarchizes the juxtaposed domains, in the sense of the following paraphrase: "Just as each creature—fish and bird, bee and flower—loves the vital element with which, by the Wisdom of Nature's law, it is paired, so too do I love you, with whom the same wise Providence has joined me; but our love stands higher [mehr] in the order of things." In Goethe's text, however, the simile suggests an underlying identity among all the compared entities, as in this reading: "My love for you *is* the lark's love of air and song, *is* the morning flower's love of the heaven's fragrance." This shift in semantic implication is made possible by a subtle alteration of the *tertium comparationis* around which the comparisons in each text turn. The pivot term for Geßner is a concept of 'natural belonging and providing': "As each creature belongs to the vital element in which it thrives, I belong to [that is, love] you." But for Goethe the lark loves not only the medium in which it abides, but equally the product—the aesthetic product, let us note—of its natural expressivity. This applies to the morning flower as well, for the fragrance it loves is both the atmosphere in which it flourishes and its own expressive (and again aesthetic) product. There is no distinction here between a vital element and aesthetic-expressive activity. To live, in other words, is to express; Life and Love, the very being of natural entities, vibrate from an inner Source that everywhere is one.

Such metaphorical-analogical melding of heterogeneous spheres characterizes the semantic operations of Goethe's text generally. Indeed, the overriding semantic project of the text is to establish an equivalence between the three major terms: Nature, Love, and Song (artistic productivity). This effect is achieved by using a single set of semantic features—for example, 'luminescent beauty', 'vitality', 'euphoria'—to concretize or define each of the three major symbolic values. Thus, Nature, Love, and Song become interpretants of one another: Nature is the force of Love, Love is a natural efflorescence, Song is the expression of Love, Nature is a single Song, etc. This tautological circle obviously allows for almost infinite variation. It generates a hermeneutic series each member of which endeavors to establish the essential truth of the text by privileging, or substantializing, one of its major terms. What is at stake in this poetic undercutting of culturally fixed distinctions, however, is not a propositional claim. At stake, rather, is the instance that slides beneath all the distinctions in order to constitute itself in and through this very movement: the aesthetic subjectivity that posits itself as autonomous within the text. Several factors underline the text's ultimately reflexive character: the extensive use of metaphors and similes that draw the objective world into the subjective sphere, the reciprocal mirroring that unites the loving couple, the thematization of artistic productivity that concludes the text. The text enacts what I will call an aesthetic cogito, a self-affirmation that turns back into itself and that I would epitomize with the formula: "I am in that I sing that I am." Thus, the lyric discourse opens up a space in which aesthetic subjectivity achieves autonomy in the precise sense that it gives itself its own law of being.

At this point the inner problematic of the lyric announces itself. My discussion of the first text (Text 1) showed that the enactment of aesthetic self-appropriation is set off—and thus guaranteed in its stability—by a pair of framing lines. Qua frame, these lines occupy a paradoxical position at once inside and outside the text. They carve out the infinitely slender line of a difference that, as limit, haunts the homogeneity of the poem's intimacy even as it makes that intimacy possible.[26] In "Maifest" the affirmation of aesthetic autonomy also relies on a compositional paradox, although a far more intricate one.

To grasp the issues involved here it is necessary to begin with a rough sketch of the poem's linear composition. The text divides into three sections of three stanzas. Each of these sections draws its semantic coherence from the fact that it principally thematizes one of the text's major

Strophe	Symbolic Value	Cognitive Operation
I–III	Nature	Perception
IV–VI	Love	Intellectual Grasp of Relations
VII–IX	Song	Self-Reflection

Schema 2: Compositional Structure of "Maifest"

symbolic values and that its utterances are primarily concerned with a distinct type of cognitive operation. Thus, there emerges a compositional structure that can be set out as in Schema 2. Viewed in terms of its linear unfolding, then, the text starts out in a predominantly receptive mode, oriented toward the manifestations of Nature, passes through an understanding of Love as the essential relation among entities, and culminates in a self-apprehension in which Song names the Origin of Song itself. (An increase in syntactic complexity accompanies this rather Hegelian movement.)

Clearly this linear structure alone cannot support the claim of aesthetic autonomy for the text. On the contrary, if the spatiotemporal articulation of sense were the poem's sole dimensionality, then the moment in which autonomy is finally realized (stanza IX) would be relativized by anterior moments, themselves defined by heteronomy. Autonomy would emerge out of its other and not out of itself, which is to say, it wouldn't be; its affirmation would fail. To counter this eventuality the text employs a number of devices. Each of the major compositional divisions, for example, is effaced by a sort of rhythmic and syntactic overflow, suggesting that no real division, or difference, obtains among the parts. Indeed, the basic semantic thrust of the text is to eliminate (through the repetitive use of relatively few semantic markers) the differences among the values Nature, Love, and Song. But these strategies, powerful as they are, do not suffice to solve the problem of spatiotemporal articulation precisely because the continuities they generate presuppose the differences they erase.

A simplified model can make this point clearer. Given that the strategy of the text is to efface the differences between Nature, Love, and Song, to set these terms as equivalent, the semantic purport of the text can be represented in the formula: $A = B = C$. Indeed, one could argue that this formula, emptied as it is of any residual semantic content that might resist the equation of its terms, says what the poem wants to say. It asserts complete identity. But even this semantically empty assertion of identity runs up against the problem of its *com-position*, of its textual deployment: of the differences among—the intervals between—the signs that make up its configuration. In order to state $A = B = C$ (or: Nature = Love = Song), I must at the same time *write* that $A \neq B \neq C$. The assertion of identity presupposes a difference among the terms whose identity is being asserted, and in this sense the identity posited is not, and cannot be, absolute. The only possible solution to this dilemma would seem to be the paradoxical one of eradicating the text's very inscription.

In a sense, this is exactly what happens. The text superimposes upon its spatiotemporal articulation the figure of a circle; the path forward proves to be a return to the Source. In other words, insofar as the creative principle disclosed in VII–IX generates "new songs, and dances" (33–34), it generates as well the very text we have before us, which presents itself as a song/dance for a May festival. What saves the affirmation of autonomy is the transformation of articulate sequence into teleology: the end was already there, fully present to itself, at the beginning; the text merely makes explicit in its final moment what it was all along (autonomous Song).

Familiar though this circular narrative structure is—it will come to dominate, in various forms, what is called the Age of Goethe—it is nonetheless paradoxical in the strict sense of the term. That is to say: if the autonomous self-positing of Song is true for *this* poem in the articulate movement of its reading, it is likewise false, for it implies that that movement does not in reality exist. The possibility of the song's being present here and now as what it claims to be (Song sung from the Source of Song) is its nonbeing here and now as articulate song. The speech/writing of the text betrays the very intimacy of which it speaks, and this intimacy— the sheer presence-to-itself of poetic subjectivity—can only be saved if it is located in a moment anterior or posterior to the text itself, a moment which gathers the spatiotemporal composition of the text into the simultaneity of a single creative *Keimentschluß* or, alternatively, a single hermeneutic act of empathetic restitution on the part of the reader. The lyric text, even as it aspires to the status of voice spoken from the Source, inescapably refers to an anterior moment which cannot be spoken and to a future moment which cannot be but promised. This structure of reference is the hiatus of temporality and of sense that is opened up by the text. The poem is the postponement of its origin, the origin the aftereffect of textuality. The circle of self-appropriation is severed by the utterance or inscription in which it is formulated.

If the Origin toward which the poem moves and from which it claims to sing is split by the textuality of the poem, then one can expect that this lack will have to be compensated for, supplemented, filled in; that the text, in other words, will employ an element extraneous to its logic of self-enclosure in order to guarantee the purity and intimacy that self-enclosure purports to achieve. And indeed this occurs, with a touch of irony that is structurally necessary, in the final two lines:

> Sei ewig glücklich
> Wie du mich liebst!

It is no accident that these lines have proved to be an irritation for traditional interpretations,[27] for they cannot be integrated within the teleo-logic of aesthetic self-appropriation the rest of the text strives to enact. In contradistinction to everything that has preceded them, these lines call attention to the textual—that is to say, written—status of the poem. They represent the only speech act in the poem (an illocution, apparently, of blessing) that pertains to a futurity beyond the act of speech itself. This futurity is not to be understood mimetically; it has nothing to do with the real-life behavior of the maiden/addressee (say, with her continuing affections), as is usually assumed. At issue, rather, is the future destiny (the destination) of the text itself: its reading. The final lines, in other words, are an envoi, a closing formula that sends off the poem by supplementing it with a meta-statement, an instruction on how to read the poem of which the envoi is—and simultaneously is not—a part.[28]

What is the content of this instruction, the force of this injunction to the reader? In order to receive the blessing the text proffers, in order to experience the bliss ("glücklich") and the effacement of time ("ewig") it promises, a certain reading strategy is required. The name of this mode of reading is Love ("wie du mich liebst"), in the emphatic sense the poem has accorded that term: the experience of the specular presence of the loving other, a perfect, and wordless, exchange. This Love was the Source of the poem, out of which it emerged and toward which it returned. The envoi, then, simply directs the reader to return the text to the Source from which, as text, it is cut off: "Interpret empathetically so that the text as text disappears before the phantasmatic presence of the loving soul whose flux of feeling precedes all speech. Efface the text and its time and insofar as you do this [wie du mich liebst] you will know eternal bliss." The hermeneutics of experience, with its hallucination of a poetic soul from which the text originates, has obeyed this injunction to the letter.[29]

Only now does the significance of a final difference between the juxtaposed texts become perceptible. In Geßner's idylls, both partners—Damon and Phillis, Daphnis and Chloe—have access to speech, but in Goethe's lyric texts verbal expression is the prerogative solely of the male figure. Only he can say 'I'; the female 'you' remains forever silent. This silence is a structural necessity within the discursive system of the lyric: if the female were to become one speaker among others, then she could not fulfill the function the lyric accords her. She could not, in other words, guarantee access to the Source beyond all speech. The female addressee, "Maifest" tells us, gives ("gibst," 34) the poet the generative capacity that produces genuine Song. But this gift (about which much will be said in subsequent analyses) is not instruction in verbal technique, nor does it even occur through words. It is the pure transmission of Love through the perfect medium of the loving regard. In the silence of this specularity lyric speech posits both its origin and its end.

§ 2   The Crisis of Vision

Perhaps the most intractable problem the critic dealing with lyric poetry faces is that the object of study resists, by virtue of its discursive constitution, the very project of critical construction. The lyric is a momentary and, as it were, aphoristic form, a rupture of the world of continuous speech. Criticism, however, aspires to discursive continuity, be this in the form of argument (systematic linkage) or narrative (historical linkage). Hence the critic's dilemma: either respect the singularity of the lyric text and thereby abandon the critical project of narrative-argumentative synthesis or work toward establishing such synthesis and thereby occlude the movement of self-differentiation that distinguishes every lyric text of merit. The lyric, tendentiously stated, is the genre of contingency, and of contingency, as Aristotle noted, there can be no science.

The solution to this dilemma is not to solve it at all; to accept it as a constitutive dilemma and stretch critical discourse between its horns. The first chapter drew a historical-systematic picture, moved in the direction of abstraction, and only at the end briefly focused on the specific dynamics of the two texts by Goethe that provided its occasion. The results are easily summarized: Goethe's lyric innovation derives from and transforms idyllic intimacy, constitutes a specifically lyric intimacy as the movement toward the Source of both poetry and subjectivity, figures this Source as the specular exchange with the beloved/addressee, but in the very statement of this exchange fissures the originary unity with the difference internal to articulation. To compensate any compression in that reading, this chapter attends, with a certain drive toward technical precision, to a single text by Goethe, a text contemporary with the two previously discussed. The analysis should illuminate my claims about "Ob ich Dich liebe" and "Maifest" while introducing new, and darker, complexes of significance into the overall argument.

The text in question here is, like "Maifest," among Goethe's most famous:

5. Mir schlug das Herz; geschwind zu Pferde,
    Und fort, wild, wie ein Held zur Schlacht!
    Der Abend wiegte schon die Erde,
    Und an den Bergen hing die Nacht;
(5) Schon stund im Nebelkleid die Eiche,
    Ein aufgetürmter Riese, da,
    Wo Finsternis aus dem Gesträuche
    Mit hundert schwarzen Augen sah.

    Der Mond von einem Wolkenhügel
(10) Sah schläfrig aus dem Duft hervor;
    Die Winde schwangen leise Flügel,
    Umsausten schauerlich mein Ohr;
    Die Nacht schuf tausend Ungeheuer—
    Doch tausendfacher war mein Mut;
(15) Mein Geist war ein verzehrend Feuer,
    Mein ganzes Herz zerfloß in Glut.

    Ich sah dich, und die milde Freude
    Floß aus dem süßen Blick auf mich.
    Ganz war mein Herz an deiner Seite,
(20) Und jeder Atemzug für dich.
    Ein rosenfarbes Frühlings Wetter
    Lag auf dem lieblichen Gesicht,
    Und Zärtlichkeit für mich, ihr Götter!
    Und hofft' es, ich verdient' es nicht.

(25) Der Abschied, wie bedrängt, wie trübe!
    Aus deinen Blicken sprach dein Herz.
    In deinen Küssen, welche Liebe,
    O welche Wonne, welcher Schmerz!
    Du gingst, ich stund, und sah zur Erden,
(30) Und sah dir nach mit nassem Blick;
    Und doch, welch Glück! geliebt zu werden,
    Und lieben, Götter, welch ein Glück.[1]

    My heart pounded; quickly, to horse,
    And away, wildly, like a hero into battle!

Evening already cradled the earth,
And on the mountains hung the night.
(5) Already the oak stood in a misty cloak,
A towering giant there,
Where darkness out of the bushes
Peered with a hundred black eyes.

The moon from a cloudy hill
(10) Peered sleepily out of the mist;
The winds lightly flapped their wings,
Soughed frightfully in my ears.
The night created a thousand monsters—
But my courage was thousandfold;
(15) My spirit was a consuming fire;
My whole heart dissolved in a glow.

I saw you, and mild joy
Flowed from your sweet look to me.
My heart was wholly at your side,
(20) And every breath for you.
Spring's rosy-colored light
Lay on your dear face,
As did tenderness for me, you gods!
And though hoped for, I didn't deserve it.

(25) The departure, how pressed, how faded!
Out of your glances your heart spoke.
In your kisses, what love,
Oh what delight, what pain!
You went; I stood, and looked to the earth,
(30) And gazed after you with moist regard;
And yet, what bliss! to be loved,
And to love, you gods! what bliss!

An organization of the text into symmetrical halves (*A*, stanzas I–II; *B*, stanzas III–IV) immediately suggests itself, for several reasons. First, certain syntactic features—in the broad sense, which includes suprasentential relations—point to such a division. The major break in narrative continuity occurs between II and III, and, while the sections constituted by this break are, as narratives, relatively intelligible in themselves, their linear connection is not at all apparent. Moreover, each half evinces markers of closure. *A* opens with "Mir schlug das Herz" (1) and repeats the lexeme "Herz" in its final line (16); the second half begins with "Ich sah dich" (17) and ends its properly narrative portion (i.e., everything up to the final exclamation in 31–32) with "Und sah dir nach mit nassem Blick" (30). Finally, and perhaps most importantly, the occurrence of "doch" near the end of each section allows for the perception of a syntactic diagram (*X*, doch *Y*), of which both *A* and *B* represent variants. Here, however, similarity accentuates contrast. The "doch" of the first half introduces an event within the past of the poem's narrated action, whereas the second "doch" introduces an exclamation valid for the present of the act of speech, or even for all time if the final lines are read as stating a universal truth. The "doch" segment of the first half both functions within the narrative and closes off that section of the poem. The second half, as it were, ends twice. Its narrative section ends with line 30, which marks closure by virtue of repetition, whereas the second half as a whole ends with the exclamation of lines 31–32 introduced by "doch." In this sense, the exclamation appears as an addition, a supplement, to the main body of the text. Note that the final two lines—both inside stanza IV by virtue of line count and outside it by virtue of their supplementary function—bear a structural similarity to the envoi of "Maifest." This structural analogy is reinforced by the fact that in both cases the same lexical material—"lieben" and "Glück" or "glücklich"—predominates. As I shall subsequently show, this analogy can be taken further: like the envoi of "Maifest," the *clausula* of "Mir schlug das Herz" is a point where the poem remarks its own textual status.

A global, and therefore nebulous, tonal opposition between the two halves is generated by the words "wild" (2) and "milde" (17), occurring near the beginning of each. The semantic opposition of these terms, which announce the basic emotional tenor of each section, is supported by their phonological matrices: "wil*d*" occurs with "for*t*," "Hel*d*," "Schlach*t*"; "mil*de*" modifies "Freu*de*." The signifiers themselves seem as abrupt or fluid as the atmospheric values they connote. Thus, in the secondary code (textual system) specific to this poem, "wild" and "milde" are antonyms, dividing the poetic universe as forcefully as the more apparent contrasts between aloneness/togetherness (on the narrative level) or absence of color ("schwarzen," 8)/presence of color ("rosenfarbes," 21).[2]

In addition to elements that tend to sever the poem into two syntactically similar but semantically opposed halves, the text contains signals that the two sections are united by common complexes of significance. Most notable is the repetition of the lexemes "Herz" (1, 16, 19, 26) and "sehen" (8, 10, 17, 30). The significance of these two key words is also emphasized by their compositional placement, with "Herz" occupying the first and final lines of *A* and "sehen" holding the same first and final (excluding the closing exclamation once again) positions in section *B*. Thematic continuity is also suggested by the repeated appearance of "stund" and "Erde" at both beginning (3, 5) and end (29). The large-scale organization of the text, then, results from two contravening tendencies, one dividing the text, the other pointing toward unity. As it moves from the larger patterns of organization to the details of each line, my reading of "Mir schlug das Herz" will be governed by these two, differently oriented forces. That is to say, I will attend to the factors of closure that lend each section of the poem its relative autonomy yet will endeavor to synthesize the two sections within a single trajectory of reading.

~

Perhaps the easiest approach to the first half of the poem is to start with the rather obvious observation that rhythmically, syntactically, and semantically the text readily subdivides into two-line segments. Where this internal norm is violated, a contrast is drawn and stylistic focalization takes place. For instance, it is clear that lines 21–23 must be considered as a single segment and that as a result line 24 is isolated from the body of the stanza (the exclamation "ihr Götter!" at the end of 23 serving as a demarcation). This isolation underlines the unique status of the line as a comment on the entire stanza and as the sole instance of grammatical negation in the poem, an anomaly that is by no means accidental. In *A*, a similar focalization takes place, albeit for a different reason:

> Die Nacht schuf tausend Ungeheuer—
> Doch tausendfacher war mein Mut; *(13–14)*

The effect of internal divergence in this segment (which Friedrich Jacobi, the editor of the journal *Iris*, sensed strongly when he added, as I suspect he did, the dash) derives from the adversative conjunction linking the phrases and from the comparative. Each line deals with things sharply distinguished from one another, and the segment as a whole sets these very different things into opposition. As a result, an adversary relation between night and self is foregrounded, and this affects the interpretation of the entire section. That is, in section *A* something like a conflict in which self and night play the roles, respectively, of protagonist and antagonist unfolds: lines 1–2 introduce the protagonist; 3–4 announce the appearance of the antagonist figure; 5–12 enumerate examples of the antagonist's activities; 13–14 bring the peripeteia of the conflict; and 15–16 return us to the victorious protagonist figure in a manner that echoes ("Herz," 16) his initial designation in 1–2. This deployment of the conflict across section *A* can be schematized as follows:

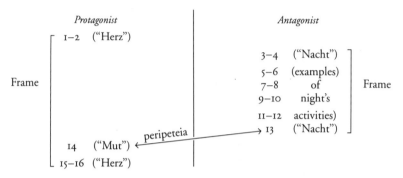

Schema 3: Conflict in "Mir schlug das Herz," Section *A*.

It must be stressed that the structuration of *A* this diagram represents is rough and provisional, accounting for little more, really, than a reader's ability to identify any given two-line segment as containing a protagonist or antagonist figure. Despite its abstractness, however, the schema does suggest a certain compositional completeness: the entire section is framed by protagonist-segments, and segments mentioning the name of the antagonist ("Nacht") frame the internal verses. Furthermore, the hypothesis that conflict serves as the central narrative function of the two stanzas taken together seems confirmed by the occurrence of the term "Schlacht" in line 2. Thus, rather than read the poem mimetically as the narrative of a night ride, as has been the practice in traditional Goethe scholarship,[3] it would seem more faithful to the compositional symmetries of the text to view its narrative content, at least in section *A*, as a kind of fantastic night battle. Such a reading, of course, presupposes that the language of the text be taken seriously in and of itself, such that, to cite just one example, what appears in the mimetically conceived narrative as a simple time marker ("it was nearly night as I departed") becomes, in the poetic reading, the introduction of the antagonist figure. In "Mir schlug das Herz"—as in all lyric texts of distinction—the linguistic texture is where the action is.

With this methodological proviso in mind, I turn to the first segment (1–2) of *A*, whose stressed syllables are:

1:	*schl*ug	*H*erz	-sch*w*in*d*	*Pf*er*d*-
2:	*f*or*t*	*w*il*d*	*H*eld	*Schl*acht

Immediately apparent is the reverse phonological symmetry of the accented syllables, by virtue of which the two lines realize an extended chiastic pattern (*a,b,c,d // d,c,b,a*). This configuration provokes a kind of cross-reading, which solicits the semantic affiliations of the paired terms. The coupling effect is especially pronounced for the verb "schlagen," where the phonological echo with "Schlacht" activates a poetic etymology. Thus, the standard syntagm "Mir schlug das Herz" becomes a metaphor for emotional turbulence and conflict, the "Herz" a "Held," which is to say, an agency defined by discord. The emotional turmoil and conflict that thus emerge as the poetic connotation of 1–2 provide the opening situation of the narrative unfolded in *A*. The narrative begins with trouble, with a state of disunity and conflict that requires resolution, and in this manner points forward toward its end, which will represent the inversion of the opening situation, alleviation of the discord. But of course this point cannot be reached until the agon or conflict is fought through, which is precisely what occurs across the verses dominated by the figure of the heart's antagonist.

The nature and cause of the inner conflict begin to emerge into view in the verses that introduce the antagonist:

> Der *A*bend *w*i*e*gte schon die *Er*de,
> Und an den B*er*gen h*i*ng die N*a*cht; *(3–4)*

As in 1–2, we find a chiasmus realized among the stressed words by virtue of phonological correspondences (with the vowels here playing the decisive role), a pattern that is supported by the mirror symmetry of the lines on the level of syntax (NP–VP // VP–NP). Thus, in "Abend" and "Nacht" we have two words for phases of the day which are mutually defined in terms of sequence: "Nacht" follows upon "Abend." With "Erde" and "Bergen" we have words for spatial entities that exist in a relationship of whole to part. More exactly, "Erde" functions within the egocentric perspectivization of the text as a collective term for 'everything as far as one can see', whereas "Bergen" signifies a member of that collection of visible things, namely, 'the periphery, the outer limit'. The figuration of the entire segment, then, involves an interaction of time and space, an interaction made possible by the verbs, which, because they require subjects semantically marked as concrete, tend to personify "Abend" and "Nacht," thereby spatializing them. The relations of before-after and visual field–periphery can therefore be superimposed on one another: "Abend" embraces the proximate field of visible space, while "Nacht" stands at that field's outer edge. (Note that this poetic figuration exactly reverses the facts of normal perceptual experience, something that interpretations of the text as the document of an actually lived experience conveniently ignore.) Due to the logic of sequence between the two agencies, the necessary implication of the spatial semantics is that soon the night itself will replace the soothingly cradling "Abend" and envelop the subject's visual field entirely.

Herein lies, I believe, the source of the negative valorization "Nacht" acquires in the course of the first section: the antagonist figure stands in for the negative effect of time, the rendering absent of the objects of experience. Lines 3–4 anticipate a temporal process that accelerates and becomes more threatening as it progresses. The inevitability of the night's advance, and of temporal loss, is emphasized in several ways: the repetition of "schon" (3,5), which even in its first occurrence hints at anxiety; the sequence "Abend" (3), "Nacht" (4), "Nacht" (13), which enacts the temporal sequence along the verbal string; the sequence "wiegte" (3), "schläfrig" (10), which accomplishes essentially the same effect. But the central point is that the negative effect of time and loss is dramatized in terms of the enfolding of the visible world by the darkness of the night. This drama, only lightly alluded to in the figuration of 3–4, is played out in the following four segments (5–12), each of which has to do with the *loss of the objects of vision.*

The four segments (5–12) that constitute the central phase of *A* can best be approached via the lines that frame them. They are preceded by the introduction of the antagonist figure in 3–4 and are followed by a second mention of this figure in 13: "Die Nacht schuf tausend Ungeheuer." Clearly line 13 functions within a series that runs from "hundert" (8) to the triumphant "tausendfacher" of 14, but beyond its effect of intensification this culminating line of the antagonist segments seems to serve a classificatory function that enables an understanding of what has gone before. That is to say, it interprets the previous verse pairs in terms of a general principle exemplified in each: "the night produces monsters." Applied to the foregoing segments, this means that loss of reality to time and darkness engenders, in the absence of visual objects, phantom objects that appear as monstrous. The "Ungeheuer" are objectifications of the protagonist's anxiety at the loss of a substantial visual world—ghosts, as it were, that lurk within absence and make that absence yet more terrifying.

In the first segment of the antagonist-series, the point of departure is a natural object, an oak:

> Schon stund im Nebelkleid die Eiche,
> Ein aufgetürmter Riese, da,   *(5–6)*

The use of the definite article implies that the oak is well known to the speaker, a familiar and reassuring landmark, perhaps. With the advance of night and time, this point of reference becomes obscured from vision. Enveloped in the night mist, it is no longer a natural object, but an unnatural and threatening one, an "aufgetürmter Riese." The pattern here is that a visible object is covered over and its shape consequently distorted. This is what happens in the fifth segment as well: a natural object, the moon, begins to be obscured from vision by clouds and mist. In this instance, however, no phantom shape is created; the light of the moon, its consoling regard, is merely weakened. The remaining segments in the group (7–8, 11–12) reveal a different pattern. The starting point is not an object ordinarily visible, but rather an invisible object or, more accurately, a nonobject. Out of this absence of visual reality, this void, monstrous, phantom beings are engendered, but they are not seen as such. Rather, they seem to haunt the nonvisible, lending it a suggestion of hidden agency which is all the more frightening for not being susceptible to objectification.

In both variants, the trial to which the protagonist is subjected is articulated in terms of the theme of vision, be it as the loss of the natural and familiar objects of vision or as the threat of the nonvisible itself. It is hardly accidental, then, that we find at the very center of this sequence two occurrences of the verb "sehen":

> Wo Finsternis aus dem Gesträuche
> Mit hundert schwarzen Augen sah.
>
> Der Mond von einem Wolkenhügel,
> Sah schläfrig aus dem Duft hervor;
>
> *(7–10)*

Apart from the locative phrases (to which I shall return), two basic oppositions emerge: one involves the subject doing the seeing ("Finsternis"/"Mond"), the other the character of the seeing ("Mit hundert schwarzen Augen"/"schläfrig"). While the contrast of 'darkness' and 'moon' is clearly a matter of the absence or presence of light, the second opposition is not entirely transparent. In my view, it works as follows: the metaphor of the moon seeing necessarily endows the moon with the semantic feature 'possesses eyes' or, in a stronger reading, makes of the moon a single eye, which would cast its light and sight onto the subject. To say that the moon is peering sleepily from behind (or over the edge of) a cloud is therefore to suggest that its metaphorical eye is closing, sees only weakly, verges on disappearance. This connotation can be brought into opposition with the "hundred black eyes" of the darkness, a contrast that reiterates and expands upon the semantic complex we have been observing all along: darkness envelops the visible world, overpowering even the one consoling source of nighttime light, the moon.[4]

A further point requires emphasis here. All the occurrences recounted in the four segments involve by implication visual experience by the subject, an experience in which vision itself undergoes a certain crisis. Yet it is not merely the world as object of vision that is being threatened, but also the world as subject of vision. The verbs of perception apply not to the protagonist, but to the things outside him, the moon and the darkness. With the waning of the moonlight, the protagonist cannot only not see anything, he cannot be seen by anything either. The only active vision his eye can find is the nonresponsive, black, and empty peering of the darkness, which, of course, is not a seeing at all. The claim "Finsternis . . . sah" is a kind of oxymoron that results from talking about the absence of vision in a code of vision. This oxymoron functions to intensify the blackness of the dark, to render "Finsternis" a *principle of darkness* rather than the merely relative obscurity of the natural night. What the self encounters during its trial of anxiety, then, is a nothingness or visual void conceived both as the absence of things to vision and as a kind of active absence or nonvision, whose (dis)embodiment is the peering dark. The threat posed by the darkness, therefore, not only affects the visible world, but also touches the protagonist with invisibility by eliminating any agency of sight that could see him and, in seeing him, confirm his identity.

The peripeteia (13–14) leads from the antagonist segments back to the protagonist, with the conjunction "doch" serving as a pivot. The battle that is being won here is, of course, not the sort that can be described in terms of blows delivered. As a battle within the self, a battle to overcome the anxiety engendered by the crisis of vision, the trial of the protagonist requires no overt action, but merely that he hold out, be willing to go however far the challenge requires. One must suffer the trauma of loss, and out of this sufferance, this anxiety-ridden crisis of the visual that shakes the subject to its core, something like a victory emerges. In this text (we shall encounter the pattern in others as well and thereby specify more closely the nature of the trauma) the turn is indicated by the shift from the hyperbolic "tausend" of line 13 to its exponential raising, "tausendfacher," in the subsequent line. At the same time, a reversal occurs on the pho-nological level, vocalically staging the transformation taking place in terms of the text's semantics:

> Die N*ach*t schuf *tau*send Ungeheuer—
> Doch *tau*sendf*ach*er war mein Mut;
>
> *(13–14)*

The anxiety is overcome and the focus returns to the protagonist-subject:

> Mein Geist war ein verzehrend Feuer,
> Mein ganzes Herz zerfloß in Glut.
>
> *(15–16)*

These verses reintroduce the protagonist figure in such a manner that the original state of trouble, intensified across the trial of anxiety, is overcome, relaxation and release replace the original torment, and the narrative sequence comes to a close. That is to say, the verb phrases "schlug" (1) and "zerfloß in Glut" (16), each considered in terms of its linguistic environ-ment, are correlated in such a way that the second can be read as the inversion of the first, the alleviation of the troubled condition of the "pounding" heart. Note in this regard that lines 15–16 themselves ex-emplify the correlation of beginning and end that marks closure and completion: the first accented word ("*Geist*") and the final one ("*Glut*") are noticeably similar in sound. (This finality is heightened by the fact that the text employs the same *g*-phoneme to construct its *clausula*.[5]) The parallel positioning of "ver*zehr*end" and "*zer*floß" clinches the phonologi-cal patterning that gives a finalizing function to these lines by foreground-ing the prefix *zer-* and actualizing its significance. Indeed, this prefix, which makes up part of the predicate applied to the protagonist-word "Herz," seems to have imprinted itself on that word. Whereas in the opening lines the *H-* of "Herz" was italicized due to the retroactive effect of "*H*eld," here the -*erz* component assumes prominence within the poetic figuration. Thus, within the textual system of "Mir schlug das Herz" the verbs "schlagen" and "zerfließen" enter into an opposition that unfolds along a series of semantic virtualities encoded in each term:

schlagen: 'articulate', 'divided', 'rigid', 'violent'

zerfließen: 'fluid', 'continuous', 'unified', 'peaceful'

Applied to the field of the emotions, such oppositions yield a global distinction between a feeling of constriction, internal division, conflict, and hardened, because threatened, self-assertion on the one hand, and a feeling of expansion, release, peace, and surrender of self on the other. These are the poles of emotion between which the poetic narrative of section *A* moves. The *fabula* structure organizing the poetic system is *the model of an emotional crisis in which anguished conflict, initiated by the experience of temporal and visual negativity, is transformed into flowing release.* One could speak here—and subsequent analyses will confirm the point—of a recuperation of poetic subjectivity through sufferance. By exposing itself to the principle of absence, to visual negativity, the subject undergoes a crisis that finally liberates it from the anguish of loss.

~

The second section of the poem begins with a radical semantic alternation, disclosing a new universe of significance. In the traditional reading, the initial phrase "Ich sah dich" (17) merely marks the point when the rider, arriving at his intended destination, first catches sight of the beloved. In other words, the phrase is trivialized, glossed as indicating merely one among an entirely predictable and natural series of causally related events, and is thereby absorbed into a verisimilar construction of the text that interprets it either as documenting an actual night ride Goethe himself undertook or as relating the fiction of such a ride. My reading, however, takes the text itself, in the density of its linguistic configurations, as the object of analysis, viewing it not as the representation of real or imagined events, but rather as a kind of dream scenario. Authorization for this procedure can be drawn from Goethe's own works. The following text, contemporary to "Mir schlug das Herz," provides a kind of synopsis of my analysis up to this point and a preview of what is to follow:

6. Ach wie sehn ich mich nach Dir,
    Kleiner Engel! nur im Traum,—

Nur im Traum erscheine mir!
Ob ich da gleich viel erleide,
Bang um Dich mit Geistern streite,
Und erwachend atme kaum.
Ach wie sehn ich mich nach Dir,
Ach wie teuer bist du mir,
Selbst in einem schweren Traum![6]

Oh how I yearn for you,
Little angel! Only in dream—
Only in a dream appear to me!
Although I suffer so much there,
In fear do combat for you with spirits [ghosts],
And awakening can hardly breathe.
Oh how I yearn for you,
Oh how dear you are to me,
Even in a troubled dream.

I must refrain here from any commentary on this text, which I have adduced merely to support the claim that "Mir schlug das Herz" can be read not as mimesis (the story of what happens when a rider visits his beloved), but as a phantasmatic scenario in which the spirits and phantoms that haunt it are to be taken seriously as the figurations of an emotional crisis and in which the beloved is not just a pretty girl, but rather the figuration of a kind of counterforce to those phantoms of absence and darkness. Such a reading of the poem as dream script will necessarily register the radical breach that separates the nonvision, or vision of absence, at the center of *A* from the 'full vision' that opens section *B*. Having passed through the crisis in such a way that the confrontation with absence eventuates in a transformed emotional state, the self is suddenly confronted with a single, privileged object of vision that presents itself to sight and returns the self's regard. *Suddenly the plenitude of vision is recovered.* Everything depends on getting clear what this recuperation of vision means.[7]

Let us first note that the third stanza never moves beyond the specular moment named in the first three words. No additional events, such as an embrace or a conversation, ensue from the initial seeing. In other words, this seeing alone constitutes the object of the stanza, and this seeing is just what the text shows it to be, namely, a perfect (and wordless) reciprocity between two selves. The first three words already contain *in nuce* the entire development that follows in the next seven lines. United by the verb "sah," the "ich" and "dich" mirror one another insofar as the "dich" is not only an object of vision but potentially a subject of vision capable of returning the first subject's regard. Indeed, precisely this is what occurs as the two-line segment (17–18) comes to an end. The "ich," initially an agent, becomes a "mich," the object of the beloved's visual response. Seeing here moves in two directions; it is a mirroring. The segment 17–18 is constituted semantically as a chiasmus: "ich sah dich" is followed by a paraphrase of the reverse statement, "du sahst mich."

This mirroring, this chiastic reciprocity, is exfoliated in the subsequent five lines (19–23), up to the expression of gratitude "ihr Götter!" In lines 19–20, as in the first three words of the stanza, the direction of the movement is toward the beloved:

> Ganz war mein Herz an deiner Seite,
> Und jeder Atemzug für dich.   *(19–20)*

The following segment reverses this direction:

> Ein rosenfarbes Frühlings Wetter
> Lag auf dem lieblichen Gesicht,
> Und Zärtlichkeit für mich,   *(21–23)*

Both groups end with similar prepositional phrases, and this points up the equivalence between the two figures referred to by the pronouns. Furthermore, both segments have the same syntactic structure: two clauses with verb deletion in the second clause. Structurally, then, the two segments recapitulate the mirroring of the stanza's first two lines. To 'see', in the sense specific to this text, is to see and to be seen, to be at once the subject and the object of vision. More radically phrased: vision here is the vision of vision; the act of seeing folds back onto itself, *sees its own seeing*.

The reciprocity that characterizes the specular moment of stanza III is not developed solely in terms of vision; it is also an emotional reflexivity. The "milde Freude" belongs not to one or the other of the two figures, but to both; each is at once the source of the other's joy and joyful, just as each is both the subject and the object of the act of vision. The same point can be made with reference to the syntagm "süßen Blick" (18), in which the metaphorically employed adjective functions to conflate the realms of seeing and feeling. This metaphorical effect is underlined by virtue of the contrasting syntagm "nassem Blick" (30), which modifies the visual regard in a strictly literal way so that the previous intertwining of vision and emotion is understood no longer to obtain. This is not the only case in which the unity and reciprocity of III yields to difference and divergence in IV.

The significance of the specular moment, its semantic range, ramifies as the details of the third stanza are compared with other points in the poem. A rather notable difference exists, for instance, between the representation of the self in III and that in I and II. Only within the specular moment is the self presented as an identity or whole ("ich"), whereas in *A* it is dispersed among its parts ("Herz," 1; "Ohr," 12; "Mut," 14; "Geist," 15; "Herz," 16). The connotation of fragmentation is heightened in *A* by the "hundert schwarzen Augen" (8), which, while not belonging to the self, nevertheless suggest violent dismemberment and the multiplication of parts.[8] The paradigmatic series that develops around the lexeme *Herz* allows for a more exact characterization of this difference. The initial usage ("Mir schlug das Herz," 1) points to internal disunity and conflict. The culmination of the *A*-sequence marks the disappearance of conflict and the dissolution of the self in an indefinite emotional expansiveness; the self in its entirety ("Mein *ganzes* Herz," 16) relinquishes its anxious self-assertion and is taken up in a fluidlike release. In the third stanza, the at first conflict-ridden, then dissolved self is constituted as a whole. The speaker finds himself as an identity in the presence of, in the responsive vision of, the beloved: "Ganz war mein Herz an deiner Seite" (19). Read as an adverb, "ganz" here points to 'total' emotional investment in the beloved (as does "jeder" in 20). Considered as an adjective, however, "ganz" demonstrates the 'unity' of self discovered through the vision of the beloved. Seeing the beloved, the protagonist finds himself: *his identity—his "ich"—is constituted within the mirroring that allows him to see himself being seen.*

We can say, then, that lines 17–23, up to the address "ihr Götter!," represent an expansion of the nuclear phrase "Ich sah dich." This syntactic and semantic exfoliation does not involve, however, a factor of temporal expansion, or sequencing, such as we find throughout the *A*-section and again in stanza IV (esp. 29–30). Everything the stanza has to say is contained within the instant of vision, the *Augenblick* that seems to constitute a self-sufficient temporality, an *ecstatic* moment defined by specularity. When the phrase "ihr Götter!" (23) introduces figures that exist outside the reciprocity between "ich" and "dich," the time of the text shifts to the present of enunciation and the final line of the stanza (24) is addressed to a 'you' (namely, the 'gods') different from the preceding seven lines. The text does not add to the specular moment, but breaks off from it to an altogether different angle of address.

Thus, whereas *A* increases in intensity across the strophic division between I and II, *B* is clearly divided at the point of disjunction between III and IV. The initial "Der Abschied" (25) of IV stands to the specular moment of III in a relation of radical discontinuity, a fact that tends to seal that moment inside the typographical space it occupies. This effect is strengthened by the fact that the transitional phase between III and IV is the interjection, which operates on another level of discourse from what precedes it. Thus, a break in the discourse and the spatial break of the strophic division intervene before the narrated events are taken up again. My claim, then, is that the major articulation of sense in *B* bears on the opposition unity/disunity. That the specular moment of III connotes unity should be clear enough from what has been said up to this point. In comparison to this emphatic identification of "ich" and "dich," everything else is *Ab-schied*, 'departure', a 'cutting-off'.

Not only does the address to the gods in 23–24 break from the specular moment on the level of discursive address, it also introduces the only instance of grammatical negation in the poem, bringing with it the moral disjunction between 'deserving' and 'not deserving'. Such logical and moral disjunctions then find their spatial counterpart in the "Abschied" that is the theme of IV. Indeed, everything points to the fact that this word marks not a conventional farewell but a separation and division of the most radical sort. Note first how the "ich" and "dich" of III, in addition to surrendering their phonological similarity, are no longer united by a reciprocal activity. Instead of shuttling back and forth between them, as if between mirrors, the text distributes the terms over different fields of the stanza, fields which abut in line 29. But precisely here, at the point of their tangency, their disunity is marked most forcefully: to each is attributed a verb semantically (not to mention vocalically) opposed to that of the other—"Du gingst, ich stund," (29)—articulating separation as a perverse verbal inflection. Similarly, in 27–28 the "Liebe" (no longer defined as something shared) subdivides into two opposed terms, "Wonne" and "Schmerz." Finally, the exclamatory syntax tends to bring disunity into the organization of the expressive plane.

To characterize III and IV in terms of the opposition unity/disunity is correct enough, but much too abstract. This opposition is developed (one could also say "interpreted," with Peirce's notion of interpretant in mind) in terms of the theme of vision. The final syntagms of the first and final lines of the *Abschied* section already indicate as much: both "trübe" (25) and "mit nassem Blick" (30) suggest a disruption of vision. But note that neither phrase entails the impossibility of vision, merely that things aren't so clear. This implication is fully ramified in the use of the verb *sehen*.

I have already alluded to the compositional significance of *sehen*. Like "Herz" in *A*, the lexeme appears in the first and final lines of the properly narrative segment. It also occurs twice in section *A*, though not in first or final position, and in this sense its distribution corresponds exactly to that of "Herz." Clearly we are dealing with one of the key words of the poem. Here, for the sake of an overview, are all of its occurrences:

1. Wo Finsternis aus dem Gesträuche
   Mit hundert schwarzen Augen sah. *(7–8)*

2. Der Mond von einem Wolkenhügel
   Sah schläfrig aus dem Duft hervor; *(9–10)*

3. Ich sah dich, *(17)*

4. ich stund, und sah zur Erden, *(29)*

5. Und sah dir nach mit nassem Blick; *(30)*

The text establishes an ad hoc verb conjugation, a poetic version of verbal inflection. Verb conjugations are themselves paradigmatic groups. Poetry not only projects preexisting (linguistically codified) paradigms onto the syntagmatic axis,[9] but creates new paradigms specific to textual systems. As this example illustrates, this is done by drawing on and displacing already-existing (codified) paradigms.

The five instances of the verb can be reduced to three classes if we presume the rule that instances of *sehen* belong in a class with all other instances occurring in contiguous propositions, a cumbersome way of stating what the eye tells us much more economically: class *a*, instances (1) and (2); class *b*, instance (3); class *c*, instances (4) and (5). Superimposed on this spatial articulation is a syntactico-semantic one: in *a* the verb is used without an object; in *b* it is used with an object in the accusative case; in *c* the verb is used with an object, but not in the accusative case. How is this to be interpreted?

I have already mentioned that instance (1) is rather odd. If we consider "Finsternis" the object of an implied act of seeing on the part of the speaker, then we can say that what he sees is invisible, is *the* invisible. No visible object presents itself, however obscurely; rather, obscurity itself is seen. I contrasted this power of the darkness with the weakness of the moonlight, pointing out that, whereas "darkness sees intensely" ("mit hundert schwarzen Augen"), the moon sees "schläfrig," weakly, its metaphorical eye closing and nearly closed. This contrast allows one to interpret "Finsternis" as an active principle that renders absent the objects of vision. In the paradigm we are looking at now, the syntax of the verb *sehen* is semanticized. In *a* the verb appears without an object; it is intransitively used. The seeing in *a* is therefore, in this regard as well, an empty affair. Especially when we compare the other members of the *sehen* paradigm, we are forced to conclude that in stanzas I and II a code of vision is manipulated in order to negate the meaning 'vision', or to figure a *crisis of vision*.

This contrasts starkly with *b*, where the use of *sehen* is transitive. Here, to be sure, the 'seeing' reaches something, establishes contact, works. Furthermore, as I have already stressed, what is seen in this transitive seeing is another, likewise transitive, seeing: the beloved's "Blick" back toward the speaker. The crisis of the *a*-group is replaced by *an absolute vision in which sight sees its own radiant luminosity*.

Now the final *c*-group: here we have *sehen* plus prepositional phrase and *sehen* plus dative object and prepositional prefix. I would suggest that the type of 'seeing' signified by these verbs falls between the 'nonseeing' of *a* and the transitive, fulfilled 'seeing' of *b*. It is a 'seeing' which has an object, but in a less sure and complete way than in *b*. In other words, the type of *sehen* signified in *c* can have an object that is known or believed to be there, but is not necessarily seen. Transitive seeing, however, is always on target, always greeted, so to speak, by its object; there is no possibility of disunity or nonconnection between act and object; it is not a matter of an intentional or purposeful looking-to-see, but of fully actual seeing, regardless of one's intentions. In the *c*-type of *sehen*, by contrast, we have an act that is separated from its object, a looking-to-see which may, or may not, be objectively fulfilled.

Arranged on a continuum, the three types can be summarized as follows: *a*, objectless nonseeing; *c*, seeing toward or after an object where a discrepancy between act and object is possible; *b*, seeing of an object that is sheerly *in actu*. This is the paradigm of 'vision' that is articulated across the text. Each member of the paradigm can be defined in terms of distinguishing features: *a* entails 'nonpresence'; *b*, 'presence'; *c*, 'undecidable, either presence or absence of the object'. More interesting, however, is to ask what other series of terms relevant to the text are grouped in homologously structured paradigms. Since we are dealing with vision, let us consider first the types of luminosity that correspond to each type of seeing. In *a* 'darkness' is unquestionably the appropriate semantic value, especially after everything that has been said regarding "Finsternis" as an active principle that, rather monstrously, renders absent the objects—and subject—of vision. In this case, then, the text makes explicit the semantic term required for its interpretation. Now if 'darkness' fits into the *a* group, then 'light' must be considered the appropriate term for *b*, if only because *a* and *b* are antonymous classes. Other aspects of the text also speak for such an attribution. Recall, for example, that what is seen in *b* is itself an act of seeing that reflects back on the first and can thus be readily conceived as a source of 'light'. Recall also that, like a source of light, the beloved conveys something that flows outward toward the "ich," at one point ("rosenfarbes Frühlings Wetter") even seeming to generate a springtime—and possibly Homeric—dawn. If we now ask what the proper semantic value for *c* would be within this luminosity code, the obvious answer would be "trübe," which the text generously supplies at 25.[10] Finally, let's consider each slot or class in terms of the subject-object relation. In *a* the grammatical subjects of the verb *sehen* are 'worldly objects' ("Finsternis," "Mond") that point toward an 'objectlessness'. That is to say—and this holds especially for the dominant figure "Finsternis"— the subject function is absorbed by an object that itself is equivalent to an undifferentiated void. In *b* we find, as is to be expected, the opposite state of affairs. Here the subject of *sehen* is indeed a subject ("ich"), but the decisive point is that the object is also a subject, the "dich" which, as has been emphasized, returns the subject's regard. How does this relation turn out in *c*? Predictably: the subject function is filled by a subject ("ich") and the object function by two concrete objects, namely "Erden" and "dir." Note that in *c* the beloved does not return the subject's regard; she is, like the other things of this earth, a concrete object potentially seen. To summarize:

Class a	*Class c*	*Class b*
absence	undecidable: presence or absence	presence
darkness	"trübe"	light
undifferentiated object (=void)	subject and object, differentiated	undifferentiated subject
nonseeing	uncertain seeing	fulfilled seeing

Schema 4: Semantic Relations in "Mir schlug das Herz"

Having sketched the system of values organized by the text-specific code of vision,[11] I will add some observations regarding the overriding structure of the *B*-section. Unlike *A*, *B* does not lend itself to structuration in terms of a *fabula*. Rather than modeling a process, it models a disjunction between sharply opposed terms: between *b* and *c*, as defined above, as well as between unity and disunity. *A*, as narrative, operates by crossing a semantic division;[12] *B* draws a semantic division. In this sense, stanza IV (25–30) has (and we begin to see how the text develops a certain self-commentary as it approaches its conclusion) its own relationship to the specular moment of III as one of its possible *denotata*. *Abschied*, as the severence of the specular dyad, is an adequate description of *B* as a whole, which is the disunity of 'unity' and 'disunity'. Furthermore, the 'division', or *Abschied*, we are dealing with is not just one among several, but is in a sense primordial. As the division between 'unity' and 'disunity'—'identity' and 'difference'—it represents the logically prior division presupposed by all other, local and specific, divisions. With Hölderlin, one could speak of this severence as the "Urtheil."[13]

These considerations make an additional connotation of IV especially intriguing. Compare the lines "Floß aus dem süßen Blick auf mich" (18) and "Aus deinen Blicken sprach dein Herz" (26). The verb *fliessen*, together with "süß" and the subject of the verb ("Freude," 17), allow us to read the unity of vision in III as "immediate communication through feeling." The positionally equivalent line in IV yields an opposed connotation: 'disunity' and 'mediate vision' appear in the semantic register of 'communication' as 'language', which is to say that the break from the specular moment involves the transition from a self-relation achieved in the mode of 'feeling' to a divided and mediated relationality that is linguistic. This connotation lends even greater appeal to the Hölderlinian term, since it locates the primordial division, or "Urtheil," in the fracture of 'feeling' by language.

The analysis thus far has produced the following structural characterization of the text: Section *A* is organized as a poetic *fabula* that models an emotional crisis in terms of a conflict between heart and night. This battle is a struggle within the self that arises out of the confrontation with what might be called an *absolute negative*, a principle interpreted in the semantics of the text by such terms as 'darkness', 'nonvision', 'absence', and 'void'. The *zerfließen* in which this *fabula* culminates leads in stanza III to the specular moment, which can be described with exactly the opposite set of terms, for example, 'light', 'immediate vision', 'presence', 'subjectivity', all of which we can subsume under the notion of an *absolute positive*.[14] However, the structure of the poem is not saturated by the opposition of an absolute negative and an absolute positive. Rather, a third term is introduced, which functions at once as *disjunction and mediation*. Only in stanza IV do we find a disjunction between subject and object, but, by the same token, only with such disjunction does mediation become necessary and possible. Section *B*, then, is internally divided: it is organized as the disjunction between the absolute positive on the one hand and disjunction/mediation on the other. Again, this scission of the poetic universe suggests the Hölderlinian opposition between "Seyn" and "Urtheil," between being in its absolute unity and being as articulated by linguistic-logical judgment.

~

One aspect of the text I have hardly touched on is its self-reflexive dimension. It is commonplace, when discussing modern poetry, to say that a poem reflects on or thematizes itself, its status, its coming into being. This habit of speech is entirely legitimate as long as the consciousness-centered or phenomenological sense of the terminology is not taken too literally. I prefer to account for the same state of affairs by saying that such terms as 'language', 'poetry', or 'this poem' appear among the terms the secondary code specific to the poem organizes. When this happens, the poem itself is one of the things the model projected by the poem takes into account. However, rather than signaling the pure transparency of poetic auto-cognition or self-reflection (as consciousness-centered theories of poetic language would have it), such remarks of the text within the text tend to disturb the homogeneity of the poem.[15]

I have said that the division between III and IV can be interpreted as the division between 'feeling' and 'language', and I based this claim on the opposition established in the text between "floß" and "sprach." Other features of IV support this reading but also, and more importantly, actualize not merely the meaning 'language' but, more concretely, 'this poem as language'. First, the exclamations in 25, 27, and 28 foreground the present of enunciation as the temporal standpoint from which the poem is uttered. Up to line 23, text and reader are absorbed, as it were, in the hallucinatory presence of the narrated past. The temporal difference between the past and the present standpoint of enunciation is veiled. Only with the exclamations, which already seal off the specular moment at the end of line 23, does the difference between the time of speech and the time of the events spoken of announce itself. This calls attention to the poem as nonidentical with its object.

A second feature of IV that tends to emphasize the status of the poem as language is the fact that the exclamations exhibit themselves as simple acts of predication. The syntax never goes beyond the attribution of a single noun or adjective; the formula is inevitably *wie* + adjective or *welch* + noun. The nouns themselves are quite abstract, a quality highlighted by their isolation from any larger syntactic or scenic context: "Liebe," "Wonne," "Schmerz." The language of the stanza, then, demonstrates itself as 'language', a term we can partially specify as implying 'abstract' and 'distinct from its object'. Of course, on two occasions stanza IV reverts to the past of the narrated action, but only to illustrate difference and separation. In 26 the emotion of the beloved no longer flows from her regard to the lover ("Floß . . . auf mich," 18), but must be read out of a language of looks, thereby acquiring the necessarily hypothetical character of an occult meaning. The same point can be made for lines 29–30: "Du gingst, ich stund" (separation takes place with the ineluctable necessity of grammar); "und sah zur Erden" (return to a mediate relationship with the world of objects, which was enveloped by night at the outset);[16] "Und sah dir nach mit nassem Blick" (the beloved assumes her place among those objects, to which the subject stands in a mediate and uncertain—Is she there? It's impossible to say—relationship).

If the meaning 'this poem as an act of language' is actualized in IV, then the meaning 'poetry as language' is likewise brought out. Furthermore, all the terms I earlier grouped under the *c*-type of *sehen* will apply to 'poetry'. This is not the only text by Goethe, after all, in which the aesthetic is located between 'light' and 'darkness': "Und was ist Schönheit? Sie ist nicht Licht und nicht Nacht. Dämmerung: eine Geburt von Wahrheit und Unwahrheit. Ein Mittelding."[17] ("And what is beauty? It is not light and not night. Dusk: a birth of truth and untruth. A middle-thing.") I want especially to emphasize the equivalence between 'poetry as language' and the term 'mediate vision', a 'looking-to-see' that may or may not find its object. Here we can say that the text models poetry as having a problematic and uncertain representational, or perhaps epistemological, status. Since the preeminent object of the poem is the beloved, the entire experience of the beloved as 'presence', 'vision', 'light', 'subjectivity', and 'feeling' is endowed with an ambiguous and questionable status. The poem cannot be apodictic about its relation to the absolute positive it purports to represent.

Such considerations allow important features of the *clausula* (31–32), which I have thus far ignored almost totally, to emerge. Often misnamed a maxim, the closing formulation proves to be in many respects a recapitulation within a reduced format of the essential features of lines 25–30. Here again the break between the past of the narrated action and the present of enunciation is dramatized, its effect heightened perhaps by the adversative "doch." Indeed, the relationship between the *clausula* and the specific event recounted in III is even more tenuous than in the other exclamations, since we are dealing with a general proposition that does not refer to any particular event. Thus, these last two lines exhibit with special force their status as 'poetry', as 'language'. But of course the formal composition of the lines is what emphasizes their 'poetic' character: the chiastic structure "Glück . . . -lieb- // lieb- . . . Glück," and the passive-active reversal of the verb. In this way, *the closing formula constitutes a structural emblem for the entire poem.* Not only does it repeat—this time obviously—the chiastic figure that organizes, phonologically, the verse pairs 1–2, 3–4, and 15–16, it also exemplifies the chiastic reciprocity of seeing–being seen that is the structure of the specular moment of III. With the final formula, the poetic devices of the preceding lines are laid bare. In particular, the specular moment, the absolute positive of the text, appears from this standpoint as the merely artful product of certain grammatical and rhetorical mechanisms.

Such, at least, is one line of interpretation a reader might legitimately pursue. A second, diametrically opposed interpretation, however, is likewise possible. The adversative "doch" marks a reversal from loss and consequent sadness—note the tears implied in 30—to a "Glück" that seems perpetually available. This "Glück" is the chiastic reciprocity of being loved and loving, now detached from any specific moment and rendered general and repeatable. In this reading, the closing formula is a consolation: that 'poetry'—which these two verses so manifestly are—maintains something of the 'love' that is the experience of presence and vision within the specular moment. If 25–30 foreground 'poetry as language' and therewith the meanings 'separation' and 'disunity', then 31–32 could be said to connote 'language as poetry', implying the consoling capacity of poetry to recapitulate on the level of generality the absolute positive of reciprocal vision.

Both interpretations are possible; neither can be chosen with certainty. But this only means that the text itself, by allowing two contradictory interpretations concerning its status, *exemplifies what it says* regarding poetry. Recall that the *c*-type of *sehen*, of which poetry is an instance, implies that the object of that 'seeing' may or may not be present, that a disjunction between act and object is possible. Thus, the text establishes a model in which poetry both appears as undecidable in its epistemological status and exemplifies such undecidability. It was to capture something of this ambiguity that I chose the modifier "specular," which connotes the immediacy of vision but also the mediate light that is received off the reflective surface of mirrors. The absolute positive of the text is specular in the sense that it is encoded as the sheer immediacy of seeing and being seen, while being made available only in its reflection in a poetic medium, the epistemological status of which is uncertain. In the *clausula*, at the very point when the poem seeks to coincide with itself and exemplify its achievement, it marks its own internal divergence.

~

At this point, a point of indecision, I shall break off my reading of "Mir schlug das Herz." No doubt more could be said about the text. Indeed, one of the paradoxes of poetic readings is that every effort to exhaust the text by meticulously attending to the threads of significance constituting its texture finally turns back on itself and reveals not interpretive mastery, but the interminability of analysis. Every subcode disclosed hooks up with other codes; every interpretive answer is the occasion of a further question. To cite merely one example, the complex that ties together the ideas of love and specularity on the one hand with the ideas of fortune or luck (alternate meanings of "Glück") and of an unearned gift of the gods on the other reveals the pressure on our text of a certain economic code. The gift of specularity as the originary exchange in which love and self-identity emerge is set into opposition with purposeful economic activity; the ecstatic moment of the reciprocal regard contrasts with the deliberate, long-term management of time; the prelinguistic flow of emotion is a kind of enriching expenditure that stands in implicit juxtaposition to a notion of parsimonious saving. We shall encounter this latent economic code in more explicitly developed form as we consider other texts from the corpus. Such texts will also provide an opportunity to ramify the reading of other aspects of "Mir schlug das Herz," such as the crisis of vision that occurs in section *A*. For the present, however, I want to emphasize the major result of the inquiry thus far. As the title of this part indicates, all three texts by Goethe analyzed here center on the same figure of visual reciprocity, a chiastically organized structure in which the poetic subject's desire finds fulfillment in the loving regard of the beloved/addressee. Their common dream, the focus of their poetic *Wunsch*, is the specular moment, which attains poetic formulation in the following lines:

> Seh ich nur einmal dein Gesicht,
> Seh Dir in's Auge nur einmal,
> Frei wird mein Herz von aller Qual;
>
> *(Text 1, 2–4)*

> O Mädchen Mädchen,
> Wie lieb' ich dich!
> Wie blinkt dein Auge!
> Wie liebst du mich!
>
> *(Text 2, 21–24)*

> Ich sah dich, und die milde Freude
> Floß aus dem süßen Blick auf mich.
>
> *(Text 5, 17–18)*

In the following chapters I shall argue that the specular moment, conceived in its full range of significance, provides a key to the epochal significance of Goethe's lyric innovation.

§ 3 Transcendental Etudes

Du mein! solch Herz darf mein ich nennen,
  In Deinem Blick
Der Liebe Wiederblick erkennen,
  O Wonne, o höchstes Glück!

You mine! such a heart I may call mine,
  In your regard
Recognize love's responsive regard,
  Oh delight, oh highest bliss!

*(Hegel to his fiancée Marie,
April 17, 1811[1])*

In the foregoing chapters, I have tried to describe with some degree of semiotic precision the placement, configuration, and resonance of the poetic locus I call the specular moment. Semiotics, however, provides only the instruments for description, not descriptive context; it is condemned, fortunately, to impurity. Thus, I must situate my readings within a particular frame of reference, organize my observations in view of an overriding schema or problem. With regard to "Maifest," for example, I referred to the project of a poetic *cogito,* a self-grounding of song; and my reading of "Mir schlug das Herz" culminated in a comparison of that text to Hölderlin's "Urtheil und Seyn," which was written in response to (indeed, on the flyleaf of) Fichte's *Doctrine of Science* (1794), the idealist transcription of the Cartesian enterprise. I have been suggesting, in other words, that the three texts in question have *a shared crux in the problem of the originary constitution of subjectivity,* a problem that has agitated philosophical reflection from Descartes and Leibniz at least to the phenomenology of Husserl. This frame of reference is by no means the only legitimate one for a reading of Goethe's poetry, and in the chapters that follow I shall press toward other analytical registers, such as psychoanalysis and social history, to which, of course, passing allusion has already been made. At least at the start of this chapter, however, I will abide in the terminological domain of the discourse on subjectivity, for it is there, I believe, that the most immediate connection can be drawn between Goethe's poetry and the philosophy and literary theory and practice of Romanticism. The Romantic corpus still offers us the most insistent and compelling discursive elaboration of the question of the subject and of its transcendental self-constitution.[2] Needless to say, my aim is not to develop a detailed history of the Romantic theory—or theories—of subjectivity. Rather, I shall pursue what might be called a strategy of rhapsodic comparison by calling attention to texts from the Romantic corpus that bear striking resemblances to those by Goethe analyzed above. In this way, Goethe's texts will assume their position within a series of cognate endeavors, a series which I believe deserves the title "transcendental études." This contextualization will begin, I hope, to disclose the forces that are at play within those texts.

A brief detour, however, is necessary in order to bring out more clearly the basis for the ensuing comparisons. It leads through a poem Goethe composed at the same time as the four with which we are already familiar:

> 7. Erwache Friedericke
> Vertreib die Nacht
> Die einer Deiner Blicke
> Zum Tage macht.
> (5) Der Vögel sanft Geflüster
> Ruft liebevoll
> Daß mein geliebt Geschwister
> Erwachen soll
>
> Es zittert Morgenschimmer
> (10) Mit blödem Licht
> Errötend durch Dein Zimmer
> Und weckt Dich nicht.
> Am Busen Deiner Schwester
> Der für Dich schlagt
> (15) Entschläfst Du immer fester
> Je mehr es tagt.
>
> Die Nachtigall, im Schlafe
> Hast Du versäumt:
> So höre nun zur Strafe
> (20) Was ich gereimt
> Schwer lag auf meinem Busen
> Des Reimes Joch.
> Die schönste meiner Musen,
> Du—schliefst ja noch.[3]
>
> Awaken, Friedericke
> Drive away the night

Which one of your looks
Makes into day.
(5) The birds' soft whisper
Calls full of love
That my beloved sibling
Should awaken

Morning's shimmer trembles
(10) With pale light
Blushing through your room
And wakes you not.
On the breast of your sister
Which beats for you
(15) You sleep ever more deeply
The more day breaks.

The nightingale, in sleep
You have missed:
So hear now as punishment
(20) What I have rhymed;
Heavy lay on my breast
The yoke of rhyme.
The most beautiful of my muses,
You—were sleeping still.

The text is imbued with the mocking playfulness and artful joking characteristic of the Anacreontic mode the previously discussed poems almost
completely abandon, and, despite certain interesting ambiguities in the
construction of the speech situation, it is too trivial to warrant much
commentary.[4] Worthy of attention, however, is the poem's basic argument:
without the animating presence of the beloved's "Blick," which is not
merely something seen, but the very source of visibility and light (1–4), the
poet is condemned to a conventional and constraining "rhyming," to a
species of poetic imitation that can bear testimony only to its own utter
inadequacy, the inadequacy of its utterance. The "freedom" of the "heart"
which "Ob ich Dich liebe" (Text 1, 4) jubilantly asserts is replaced by a
"yoke" (22), which holds the poet's "breast" (21) in harness. The poem
cannot be truly poetic, cannot join the ranks of the "new songs, / and
dances" whose emergence "Maifest" celebrates (Text 2, 33–34), precisely
because it does not usher forth from the experience of specularity. The
maiden is separated from the poet by the walls of her house and room;

asleep, her eyes closed, she is incapable of providing the ocular radiance, the light of loving subjectivity, which is the Origin of song. "Erwache Friedericke" is, as it were, a blind text, produced in the darkness which, in "Mir schlug das Herz," the beloved's luminescent regard so thoroughly dispels. Furthermore, the poem's blindness is that of writing: rather than singing in the real or virtual presence of the beloved, the poet merely inscribes the fact of her absence in a versified, awkwardly rhymed screed that will later punish her with the very lack and constraint her absence has inflicted upon it.[5]

"Erwache Friedericke" not only confirms the reading of the specular moment as the new, post-Anacreontic Source of poetic subjectivity, it also supports my arguments concerning the ambiguity of a poetic speech that seeks to return to that speechless Source. The stark and unyielding opposition we encounter between the light of the beloved's "Blick" and the darkness of a merely conventional poeticizing haunts, in a subtler fashion, the other texts as well. To render the specular moment in language is to submit it to an articulatory dismemberment and temporal deferral that fracture its essential unity. This dilemma lends "Ob ich Dich liebe," "Maifest," and "Mir schlug das Herz" their poetic tension. As the previous two chapters have shown, these texts enact the simultaneous emergence and retreat of the Source, its appearance *and* dissimulation. Thus, it is no accident that "Erwache Friedericke" so clearly foregrounds its written character in the final stanza, for it is precisely at the points where the other poems mark their textual status that their origination in specularity is problematized, their self-enclosure in intimacy broken open. Recall the framing lines of "Ob ich Dich liebe," the *envoi* of "Maifest," and the thematization of 'poetry' in the final stanza of "Mir schlug das Herz," all moments in which the texts announce, in however veiled a fashion, a discrepancy between themselves and the specular moment they claim as their truth. To be sure, the lyric speech Goethe's texts of the 1770's inaugurate delineates the path of poetic subjectivity toward its Origin, but this Origin is itself caught in a movement of return and withdrawal.

Here we have a starting point for comparison, because this formula— the return and withdrawal of the Origin—is one of those coined by Foucault to characterize "postclassical" or "modern" thought, a thought that is essentially concerned with the problem of the transcendental ground of experience, with the conditions of possibility that underlie our empirical encounters with things, our expressions, our labors, our lives in nature. The discussion of modern thought Foucault offers in *The Order of Things* has such epitomizing force and didactic power that it is worth quoting at length:

> A task is thereby set for thought: that of contesting the origin of things, but of contesting it in order to give it a foundation, by rediscovering the mode upon which the possibility of time is constituted—that origin without origin or beginning, on the basis of which everything is able to come into being. Such a task implies the calling into question of everything that pertains to time, everything that has formed within it, everything that resides within its mobile element, in such a way as to make visible the rent, devoid of chronology and history, from which time issued. Time would then be suspended within that thought, which nevertheless cannot escape from it since it is never contemporaneous with the origin; but this suspension would have the power to revolve the reciprocal relation of origin and thought; and as it pivoted upon itself, the origin, becoming what thought has yet to think, and always afresh, would be forever promised in an imminence always nearer yet never accomplished. In that case the origin is that which is returning, the repetition toward which thought is moving, the return of that which has always already begun, the proximity of a light that has been shining since the beginning of time.[6]

In Foucault's view, the lineaments of this thought begin to show themselves during the 1770's and are fully developed in the 1790's and the first decades of the nineteenth century; that is, in the intellectual and artistic upheaval we call Romanticism. My contention is that the lyric poetry Goethe produces during the 1770's is one of Romanticism's significant beginnings.[7] Specifically, the problematic of subjectivity these lyric texts explore bears important connections to the problematic of the transcendental subject, which later becomes, in the philosophy and literary theory and practice of the Romantic movement, the focal point of creative intellectual/poetic endeavor. From a chronological perspective, this thesis may seem mythical; it suggests an extravagant belief in the anticipatory force of poetic writing. In fact, though, it is an argument for strict contemporaneity. Suffice it to recall (Foucault does not mention this) that the 1770's are also known to us as Kant's "silent decade," the period following his breakthrough of 1769, during which he elaborated the problem of transcendentality that receives its first philosophical codification in the *Critique of Pure Reason* (1781). Goethe's lyric poetry constitutes a phase of literary experimentation parallel to Kant's philosophical enterprise and to that of his Romantic successors. The following comparisons endeavor to chart this dimension of the historical and cultural significance of Goethe's lyric by tracing the Romantic redaction of the figure of specularity.

~

Nowhere is the pathos of the Origin Foucault describes more pronounced than in the philosophical teaching of Johann Gottlieb Fichte, and with his work, rather than Kant's, my comparisons take their point of departure. Fichte, of course, viewed himself as the authentic explicator of Kant's system or, perhaps more accurately, as the author of the system Kant did not yet think but nevertheless, and unknowingly, presupposed. His conception of his relation to Kant was paradigmatically hermeneutic, recalling the hermeneutic dictum that one must seek to understand an author better than the author understood himself. Not surprisingly, Fichte accomplished this hermeneutic project by leading Kant's work back to the first principle, the principle of principles, the ultimate condition of possibility upon which the Kantian edifice rested and without which it would tumble not to the ground, but into its own groundlessness. Such was Fichte's project, a quest for the Origin if ever there was one, and this drive toward the Source makes of his work the philosophical analogue of the lyric problematic I have tried to thematize.

The central concept in Fichte's work is *Ichheit* (egoeity) or *Selbstbewußtsein* (self-consciousness), and even when, in the course of his philosophical evolution, this term cedes its privileged place to others (for instance: the Absolute, or Light, or God), the structure of self-consciousness remains Fichte's focus of inquiry. Nothing is easier to ridicule, of course, than a philosophy which places the *Ich*, as one loosely says, at the center of things, making of this substantialized shifter the demiurge that brings forth the world, and several of Fichte's contemporaries, most pointedly perhaps Jean Paul, took advantage of the opportunity for sarcastic caricature this concept provides. But ridicule is often the sanctuary of lazy thought. Fichte labored to come to grips with a real philosophical problem, and his efforts in this direction have recently inspired penetrating contributions to the theory of self-consciousness.[8] This problem cleaves closely to the dynamics of the lyric, and I shall therefore try to find a way to it by summarizing, in severely reduced form, two of Fichte's arguments.

(*a*) The first discloses the necessity of the principle of self-consciousness as the transcendental ground of knowledge. Consider the proposition

$A = A$, the so-called principle of identity, without which any sort of logical inquiry would collapse. No principle could be more certain. But, as Fichte points out in the *Foundation of the Entire Doctrine of Science* (1794), this principle does not stand on its own; a reflection on its structure and meaning takes us to a higher, or more primordial, principle. For what is proposed in $A = A$ is the necessary connection between the terms, so that if A, then (necessarily) A. This relation between the terms is posited, as Fichte puts it, "in and through the ego [*Ich*], for it is the ego which here makes the judgment."[9] The same goes for the subject and predicate of the judgment: regardless of whether they actually refer to existents or not, they are posited in and through the ego as the terms of the relation of identity. Thus, "it is posited that in the ego . . . there is something that is always equal to itself, always one and the same, and this absolutely posited X [the necessary relation of identity] can be expressed as: ego = ego; I am I."[10] The condition of possibility without which no thing could be thought as identical to itself is thus the identity of the ego to itself, which is to say: egoeity or self-consciousness. If there is to be knowledge, we cannot do without the *Ich* that posits itself as *Ich*.

(*b*) But—and here we come to Fichte's problem—how are we to conceive of this primordial (transcendental not empirical) self-consciousness? The inherited model for conceiving the ego's relation to itself is leaky, for according to this model (called the "reflection model of self-consciousness") the subject takes itself as an object, represents itself to itself. This model, however, presupposes what it seeks to explain insofar as the subject which would be conscious of itself by virtue of this reflexive, or representational, act must already be a self-conscious subject in order to perform that act. Or, to give the matter a different twist, in order to grasp the identity between itself as both subject and object of the reflection or representation, the subject must apply some criterion as to what is and is not itself. This criterion can only be drawn from an anterior knowledge of what it itself is: that is, from its own consciousness of self, which was, once again, what the reflection model sought to explain in the first place. As Dieter Henrich has shown with exemplary lucidity, Fichte was acutely aware of this problem. Moreover, his philosophical development can be reconstructed as a series of efforts to come to terms with this problem, to formulate a concept of *Selbstbewußtsein* that doesn't fall prey to circularity and regress.[11] Each new version of the *Doctrine of Science* brings a new formulation of what originary self-consciousness is; each moves toward the Origin, only to see that Origin withdraw.

Fichte's strategy in each of these formulations is to characterize self-consciousness in such a way that no breach is opened up between subject and object, between awareness and that which the awareness is of. In other words, it is to collapse the distance between the two elements such that they become one and the same. Hence we read in the *Second Introduction to the Doctrine of Science* (1797):

> Only through this act and solely through it, through an acting on an acting itself, which determined acting is preceded by no other acting whatsoever, does the ego come to be *originarily* for itself.[12]

Apart from any technical philosophical questions this description might raise, it clearly shows the *representational aporia* to which Fichte's strategy (and no other is available to him) leads. The ego is constituted by an act that has no object outside itself, but rather turns back on itself and is nothing other than this introverted turning. But if this is so, then the verb "acting on" loses its normal significance, since it presupposes precisely what Fichte says is not the case, namely, an object (be it a thing or another action) which functions as the target or material of the acting on in question and, of course, a subject which performs this acting on. (One might add that the concept of 'action', as distinguished, for example, from 'movement', presupposes a third term, a rule that lends the action its identity.) The equivalence posited elsewhere by Fichte between the concept "Ich" and that of "in sich zurückkehrendes Handeln" ("acting which returns back into itself") illustrates the same representational dilemma.[13] To return one must first have gone somewhere, abided, for however brief a time, in another place, but Fichte's return occurs without any interruptive departure. It is pure self-affection. The *Ich* is always at home, enfolded in self-sufficiency. However, is such a return still a return? Therein lies the problem, for if it is, it must, by the very logic of the term, open a hiatus within the intimacy of self-consciousness; and if it is not, then we still don't know, and perhaps can't know, what this originary act is. The Fichtean *Ich* acts only upon itself and is only insofar as it thusly acts, but this Origin, it would seem, escapes every effort to speak it.

Fichte nonetheless keeps trying, and the result is perhaps the most urgent and restless (homeless?) prose in the German philosophical canon.

I believe that the problems this writing endeavors to negotiate are related to the lyric problematic described in the two previous sections of this chapter. Not that Fichte's philosophy would provide the authoritative interpretation of Goethe's texts or articulate the truth which they, brilliantly but only imagistically, anticipate. My contention, rather, is that both discourses—poetic and philosophical—participate in the same *projet idéologique* (Macherey), the same quest for self-origination. If this is so, then we can expect that both discourses, at least at certain decisive points along their respective trajectories, draw on and evoke similar imaginary constructs, that they dream similar dreams, and that in these dreams a similar *Wunsch* finds the scene of its fulfillment. The following passages from Fichte's work—both bearing on the structure of self-consciousness— indicate that this is indeed what occurs:

> For according to paragraph 1. consciousness is *a positing idealiter of itself*: a seeing and furthermore a seeing of itself.
> In this remark we find the ground of the errors of all other philosophical systems, even the Kantian. They regard the Ego as a mirror, in which an image is reflected, but in their case the mirror does not itself see, and therefore a second mirror is required for that mirror, and so on. In this way, however intuition is not explained, merely a reflecting.
> The Ego in the Doctrine of Knowledge, on the other hand, is not a mirror, but *an eye*; it is a mirror which reflects itself, it is image of itself; *through its own seeing the eye (intelligence) becomes its own image.*[14]

> Knowledge is now found, and it stands before us, as an eye which rests on itself and is closed into itself. It sees nothing outside of itself, but it sees itself.[15]

These texts, both describing what Fichte calls "intellektuelle Anschauung" ('intellectual intuition'), or the act through which self-consciousness gives itself to itself, are, quite simply, *versions of the specular moment.* They imagine an intimacy of self-presence in which no relation to exteriority obtains, a unity in which, as in "Mir schlug das Herz" (Text 5), the "Ich" finds itself in a seeing of its own seeing. This is a mirroring, to be sure, but one in which the externality and representationality of real-world mirrors are eliminated. Hence the rhetorical contortions of the first passage cited: Fichte disavows the mirror relationship, which renders self-consciousness a subject-object relation (thereby leading to the infinite regress of the reflection model), and then reintroduces it by moving the mirror, as it were, to the very edge of the eye. What is seen is solely the seeing itself, nothing external to it. The self-mirroring mirror accomplishes what no real mirror can. It mirrors its mirroring, and the metaphor, consequently, self-destructs. The same can be said of the second passage: to ensure that the "eye" of the I entertains in its seeing no relation to an other, Fichte closes it upon itself so that its only object of sight is its own seeing. But is this still a seeing? Can eyes that are closed still see? Here again the Origin withdraws in the very moment it is spoken, exactly as in the poetic texts analyzed above. And for exactly the same reason.

In the texts of Goethe and Fichte, then, we find the same specular scene, the same coursing of the act back into itself, the same constitution of the I in a seeing that sees only its own vibrant visuality. And yet there is a major difference between the two versions of specularity, a difference that by no means annuls the validity of the comparison, but nevertheless requires that its nuance be marked. In the lyric variant, specularity is a scene of desire and fulfillment. There is a female figure who, in presenting herself to the male subject, gives him simultaneously his identity and the truth of his desire. This gift passes across the wordless exchange of the reciprocal regard and, received into the subject (who thereby becomes a full and identical subject), grounds his creativity, his productivity as poet. Fichte's philosophical variant of specularity betrays none of this; there is no female figure here, only eyes and light and mirrors. I would suggest that we read this difference as a discursive rule, to be precise, as a rule of exclusion. Philosophical discourse, as it shaped itself in the all-male universities of 1800, could not acknowledge that it spoke of and from desire and that this speech, therefore, figured Woman. Goethe's lyric consigns the female figure, of course, to the status of speechless Origin and mirror of the I, but philosophical discourse renders her invisible, even though she is the very source of visibility.

What happens, though, when the philosopher withdraws from his public role and seeks privately to engage the question of his Origin? He turns to poetry, as reader and writer, and allows what his bureaucratic position banished to return to him. Thus, in or around 1812, Fichte composed a sequence of three sonnets that restore to the scene of specularity what the abstractions of the previously cited passages quite literally efface. The *Doctrine of Science*, despite the technical ring of its name, turns out to be philosophy in the etymological sense of the word: love of Sophia, who appears to Fichte as the muse of astronomical knowledge. The Origin (*Ursprung*) of the I is the Eye of Urania:

Das ists. Seit in Urania's Aug', die tiefe
Sich selber klare, blaue, stille, reine
Lichtflamm', ich selber still hineingesehen;

Seitdem ruht dieses Aug' mir in der Tiefe
Und *ist* in meinem Seyn,—das ewig Eine
Lebt mir im Leben, *sieht* in meinem Sehen.[16]

This is it. Since into Urania's eye, the deep
Clear-unto-itself, blue, still, pure
Flame of light, I myself in stillness looked;

Since then this eye rests in my depths
And *is* in my Being,—the eternally One
Lives in my living, *sees* in my seeing.

~

No one could accuse Novalis of effacing Sophie. The final words of his famous fairy tale celebrate her as "Priesterin der Herzen" ("priestess of hearts").[17] She is beloved, muse, and mediator of the divine, for whom, from whom, and through whom his poetry speaks. And, not surprisingly, she always makes her appearance, presents herself, in a scene of specularity, giving the poetic subject a self-certainty and faith that dissolve even the otherness of death:

The hill [of the grave] became a cloud of dust—through the cloud I saw the transfigured features of the beloved. In her eyes eternity rested—[18]

This passage from the stunningly bold *Hymnen an die Nacht* (*Hymns to the Night*, 1800) illustrates what might be considered, at least from the perspective of this inquiry, the major discursive transformation accomplished by Novalis's poetic writing: the deempiricization (I apologize for the term) of Goethean specularity, the detachment of the specular moment from any experiential context, its firm localization within the transcendental sphere. Indeed, the *Hymnen* begin with a systematic negation of perception, of empirical vision, a gesture which has both philosophical-religious and poetological implications. This transformation or (recalling Nietzsche) reinterpretation of the specular moment inaugurates one of the major strains of the Romantic lyric, the spiritual song (*geistliches Lied*). Thus, the lines from Fichte's sonnet are unthinkable prior to the quasi-mystic re-working of specularity that is achieved in Novalis's singular poetic oeuvre. In fact, this very sonnet of 1812 can be read as a somewhat heavy-handed redaction of the final poem of Novalis's *Geistlichen Liedern* (1800), the sequence which sets the pattern for this subtype of Romantic lyricism.[19]

A further example of Novalis's philosophical-religious recodification of the specular moment is provided by the famous distich composed in connection with the novel fragment *Die Lehrlinge zu Sais* (*The Apprentices at Sais*, 1798):

> One succeeded—he lifted the veil of the goddess at Sais—But what did he see? He saw—wonder of wonders—himself.[20]

The distich confirms that the female figure only gives the male subject back to himself, that she functions—paradoxically—to veil femininity, to maintain it within the Same, to prevent its manifestation as Other. I shall try to untangle this paradox of the unveiling which veils in a subsequent phase of the argument. At present, however, I want to call attention to one final figure in the text of Novalis, which has become the very emblem of German Romanticism, the famous "blaue Blume" (blue flower) of Heinrich von Ofterdingen's dream:

> However, what attracted him with full power was a tall, light-blue flower which stood in closest proximity to the source and touched him with its broad, shining leaves. Around it there stood countless flowers of all colors, and the most delicious aroma filled the air. He saw nothing but the blue flower, and contemplated it for a long time with inexpressible tenderness. Finally he was about to approach it when all at once it began to move and change; the leaves became shinier and pressed themselves onto the growing stem; the flower bent toward him; and the flower petals displayed an open blue collar in which a tender face hovered. His sweet astonishment was growing along with the peculiar transformation when suddenly the voice of his mother awakened him.[21]

Here we have indeed an oneiric *Wunsch* and its focus is the plenitude of specularity, located—inevitably—at the Source. No doubt much that is relevant for our theme could be learned by interrogating the details of the scene: Why is it, for example, that among the plurality of flowers the dreaming subject sees only one? Is specularity linked to a singularization of the Woman, to a reduction of the multiplicity of women to the unique paradigm of the eternal feminine? And what is suggested by this growing stem, which, in turn, provokes a growing of the subject's own "sweet astonishment"? Do these swellings suggest a phallic component within the specular phantasm? Why does the transition to specularity occur as Heinrich is about to approach the flower? Is it to hold his desire within the abeyance of vision, to prevent contact with a threatening corporeality? And why does the scene finally dissolve in the voice of the mother? Could this voice have sustained the dream all along? These are all intriguing questions, questions that probably lead to the paradox of the aletheic veil alluded to above, but I want to postpone a discussion of them until they can be more richly contextualized than is possible now. My theme is still the visual figuration of the specular moment and its relation to the values of the Source and of subjectivity. For the moment, then, I shall simply constate what at this point seems hardly surprising: that the "blaue Blume"—the presiding figure at the Origin of poetic subjectivity, the *arché* that determines the poetic quest by presenting the figure of its *telos*—is also a version of specularity.

The list of citations I have just run through—and it is little more than a list—documents the insistence of the specular figure in Novalis's writing. A compelling reading of these passages would have to mobilize a good deal more evidence, to attend to the specific context of each occurrence, and to explore the nuances of their linguistic figuration. This is beyond the scope of my inquiry. Instead, I would like to call attention to some reflections by Novalis which were written in response to Fichte and which thematize in a remarkably lucid fashion what I referred to in Chapter 1 as the problem of composition or, in connection with Fichte, as the problem of representation. Both processes—composition and representation—involve setting caesurae which rift the very unity, or identity, those processes seek to convey. This is precisely what Novalis latches onto when he begins to read Fichte. Here is the beginning of his first note on the philosopher:

> In the proposition *a* is *a* there lies nothing but a positing, distinguishing, and uniting (binding) [*ein Setzen, Unterscheiden und verbinden*]. It is a philosophical parallelism. To make *a* more distinct, *A* is divided. *Is* is set up as the universal content, *a* as the determinate form. The essence of identity can only be set up in a *semblance-proposition* [*läßt sich nur in einem* Scheinsatz *aufstellen*]. We leave the *identical* in order to represent it [*Wir verlassen das* Identische *um es darzustellen*].[22]

Novalis's reflection here parallels exactly my remarks on Goethe's "Maifest," where, however, it was a matter of com-posing the radical identity $A = B = C$ (Nature = Love = Song). Indeed, one might say that Novalis's strictures on composition, or on what he calls "representation" ("auf-stellen," "darstellen," and later "vorstellen"; the key matter is the "Stelle," the place, slot, or position, which acquires its definition only from other places, slots, or positions) are more radical, since his point of departure is the proposition $a = a$, in which the signs yoked together by the logical copula are tokens of the same type. His point is that even this formulation does not succeed in representing the absolutely identical, or rather, that the very operation of representation dissimulates the identical by intro-ducing within its oneness the caesura of a difference. The identical appears as divided, severed within itself, and even the binding of the posited elements across the movement of the syntax does not erase this operation of *Unterscheiden* (differentiation, distinction). Thus, the proposition of identity is a *Scheinsatz*: the identical passes over into its semblance, and the difference between the identical and its mere semblance is produced by the difference internal to the proposition. Novalis is very clear on the source of this difference within the representation. A few lines after the quoted passage, he writes: "we represent it [the identical] through a nonbeing, a nonidentical—sign—."[23] *The sign fissures being and the identical, introduces into its perfect intimacy a nonidentity, which interrupts, as in "Mir schlug das Herz," the sheer transitivity of pure specularity.* Indeed, the sign itself *is* the nonidentical, for it can only be what it is by virtue of its difference from other signs. The sign, like the Hölderlinian "Urtheil," opens the hiatus in being.

These are heady thoughts, set down, let us remember, by a young man of twenty-two (the same age, approximately, as the Goethe of "Maifest" and "Mir schlug das Herz"). They are thoughts that, in the notes and fragments that follow in their wake, lead in all sorts of speculative direc-tions and engender a labor of terminological and conceptual experimenta-tion of extraordinary complexity. I cannot begin to trace out the paths of this thought here. Yet introducing Novalis reveals the persistence in his work of a certain constellation of values that reaches beyond his texts and constitutes an epochal discursive ordering: the discursive configuration that determines the mode of existence and inner problematics of the lyric speech inaugurated in the texts of the young Goethe. To summarize, we find in Novalis: (a) an insistence on the Origin in its absolute identity to itself as pure subjectivity and the figuration of this Origin as specularity, the perfect exchange within the intimacy of the dyad of lover/beloved; and (b) an awareness that this Origin is dissimulated, that it withdraws as soon as it is formulated, that self-identity is torn asunder by the nonidentity Novalis calls the "sign." This duality corresponds to the tension my readings sought to disclose in the lyric texts of Goethe, and the cited passages from Novalis confirm and clarify those readings. Moreover, we find in Novalis an additional theoreme which retrospectively illuminates the poems discussed in the previous two sections.

To be sure, the originary identity cannot be represented, cannot become an object of knowledge (or object in general), because the operation of knowledge/representation violates that identity. But could it be that I am given to myself in another form than self-representation, that there is, so to speak, a pre-representational and presemiotic level of experience that abides within the intimacy of the Origin? Novalis's answer to this question is affirmative, and the name he gives to this originary level of experience or self-givenness is *Gefühl* (feeling).

Consider the following argument: Philosophy, in contradistinction to all other sciences, does not deal with objects of our acquaintance. It does not deal with objects at all, but rather with what, in our learning about objects, remains other-than-objective, which is, of course, the one who learns ("der Lernende"). Now, philosophy itself is "in" the one who learns, and therefore would seem to be nothing other than self-contemplation ("Selbstbetrachtung"). This definition, however, is contradictory, since it implies that what philosophy treats is an object, which is precisely what "der Lernende" is not. What, then, is the starting point of philosophy if not the reflective (hence objectifying, representational) act of self-contemplation? Novalis's (noticeably tentative) answer is: "Es ist ein Selbstgefühl vielleicht."[24] ("Perhaps it is a self-feeling.") Feeling would be the preobjectifying and presemiotic self-givenness in which the identity of the "Ich" remains uncontaminated by difference (by the nonidentical). It would be the "Seyn" (being) which "Darstellung" (representation)— defined by Novalis as "das Nichtseyn im Seyn"[25] ("the nonbeing in being")—could never appropriate. Hence Novalis's conclusion to this argument: "Es [das Gefühl] läßt sich nur in der Reflexion betrachten—der Geist des Gefühls ist da heraus."[26] ("It [feeling] can be contemplated only in reflection—[but] there the inner spirit of the feeling escapes.")

This concept of "feeling" sheds light on the lyric problematic discussed above because the function of "Gefühl" in Novalis's text conforms exactly to the discursive ordering disclosed in Goethe's poems. "Maifest" concludes with an *envoi* which directs its reader to move beyond the text itself, to reenact the Origin from which the poem issued by reactualizing the love that Origin is. Feeling/love is the domain prior to language to which the poem gives access only by effacing its semiotic constitution or, as Novalis formulates it more emphatically, its nonidentity. The opposition feeling/language was also shown to operate in "Mir schlug das Herz" in a fashion entirely homologous to its articulation in Novalis's "Fichte Studies." Indeed, ten years before the elaboration of Novalis's reflections, Goethe published in his *Faust* fragment the following lines, in which Faust states his views on our relation to the Absolute:

> Gefühl ist alles,
> Name ist Schall und Rauch.[27]
>
> Feeling is all,
> Name is sound and smoke.

Novalis's reflections on feeling, with all their intricacy and sophistication, are nothing more than a philosophical transcription of their own discursive situation. "Gefühl" is a compensatory term: it feigns access to an Origin that is always already lost. Furthermore, we must attribute the same compensatory function to a concept of the lyric as a pure and nondissimulating language of feeling, as the music of an orality immediate to itself, as song sung from the Source of song. That Novalis held such a conception is certain.

But Novalis's thoughts on the break between the originary sphere of self-givenness in feeling and the linguistic/semiotic domain of reflection and representation also allow us to speculate on the nature of this loss and therewith to disclose the drama that lends his insistence on primordial feeling its urgency.

> Why don't we become aware [knowing] of it—because it is what makes becoming aware possible in the first place, and consequently this lies *in* its sphere—the action of becoming aware cannot therefore go out of its sphere and endeavor [want/claim] to embrace the maternal sphere.[28]

The pronoun ("it") in the first two clauses refers to what Novalis calls the "first action," that is, the primordial act of self-constitution in the prereflexive mode of feeling. Thus, a few lines prior to the quoted passage we read: "the Ego feels itself, as content." The basic argument of the passage, then, is familiar to us: the second act—the act of knowing reflection—leaves the originary sphere of feeling (first act) in order to represent it, but in doing so sacrifices the unfissured intimacy that characterizes the Ego's immediate self-relation in feeling. The argument is a variant of the one discussed in the previous paragraph. Of note, however, is the name bestowed on the Origin: "the maternal sphere," a rare, if not unique, designation in Novalis's ruminations. A proscription seems to be operative here, and that proscription, that philosophical taboo, has a sexual character: reflection must not want to embrace the Mother; feeling must remain the sole path of access to Her. Indeed, feeling is always already within Her; it is the name for the unity I have with myself within Her. Can we note in these thoughts the accents of a certain anxiety, of an urgent need to affirm that the Mother is indeed the plenitude that contains me and gives me to myself? And is it this anxiety the dream wish of specularity and primordial feeling works to assuage? The following passage—coming only a page after the word "Muttersfäre" has been inscribed—confirms this suspicion:

> To Mere Being there attaches no modification, no concept—one can set nothing at all in opposition to it—except, in a purely verbal fashion, Nonbeing. But this is a copulating little hook, which is only hung onto it pro forma—It only appears so. Grabs, however, a handful of darkness.[29]

The philosophical sense of the passage is clear: Being allows for no predications, cannot be set in opposition to any predicates which would define or modify it. Not even the opposition to Nonbeing tells us what Being is, for this predication, performed across the logical copula (e.g., "Being is opposed to Nonbeing"), is an empty verbal construct which has no conceptual content. However, to abide with the philosophical interpretation is to refuse to read the details of this passage in their excess and overdetermination. The tone and gesture of disdain here betray an anxiety they work to banish. Is it an anxiety that this "copulating little hook" ("copulirendes Häckchen") could enter into the Mother, could tear open Her plenitude, could reveal that plenitude to be merely a "darkness"? Or is it that the "copulating little hook" that is merely "hung" on the Mother reveals in its charade that she is fundamentally deprived of what that hook signifies? And, since the maternal sphere is nothing other than my unity with Her, my oneness and identity in the intimacy of feeling, doesn't this deprivation affect me as well? Furthermore, if the Mother is castrated, if there is nothing there to grasp, then the I is castrated also: it lacks full identity as the phallus-within-the-Mother, the unique object and fulfillment of the Mother's desire. Such is the loss the compensatory notion of "Gefühl" seeks to veil; and such is the darkness the sheer light of specularity attempts to dispel.

~

From the intricate philosophical reflections of Fichte and Novalis, we now turn to some literary instantiations of specularity. Beyond documenting the insistence of the specular moment in the Romantic literary corpus, these examples will also alert us to complexes of significance that, though alluded to, have remained thus far underdeveloped. My first case is a text by Joseph von Eichendorff. Eichendorff's poetry might be termed the exemplary instance of the Romantic lyric, its most accessible and popular variant. Indeed, we owe Eichendorff the poem that has, more firmly than any other, established itself in cultural memory as the very emblem of Romantic lyricism, if not of the lyric generally.[30] The text I want to discuss here lacks such canonical prestige, but has thereby preserved a degree of freshness, an ability to surprise:

DER BLICK

Schaust du mich aus deinen Augen
Lächelnd wie aus Himmeln an,
Fühl' ich wohl, daß keine Lippe
Solche Sprache führen kann.

(5) Könnte sies auch wörtlich sagen,
Was dem Herzen tief entquillt;
Still den Augen aufgetragen,
Wird es süßer nur erfüllt.

Und ich seh des Himmels Quelle,
(10) Die mir lang verschlossen war,
Wie sie bricht in reinster Helle
Aus dem reinsten Augenpaar.

Und ich öffne still im Herzen
Alles, alles diesem Blick,
(15) Und den Abgrund meiner Schmerzen
Füllt er strömend aus mit Glück![31]

THE LOOK

When you look at me out of your eyes
Smiling, as if from the heavens,
Then I feel indeed that no lip
Could conduct such language.

(5) Even if it could literally say
     What springs forth deeply from the heart;
     Silently assigned to the eyes,
     It is fulfilled all the more sweetly.

     And I see heaven's source,
(10) Which was so long closed to me,
     As it breaks in purest brightness
     From the purest pair of eyes.

     And I silently open in my heart
     Everything, everything to this look,
(15) And the abyss of my pain
     It streaming fills with bliss!

In Eichendorff's lyric poetry, the Romantic imaginary is developed in two directions, is defined by a double tendency: (a) an exploration of the dangers and delights of the perverse, an attraction toward and a flight from the mobility of desire, its perpetual meander;[32] and (b) an exploration of absence as the ground of the imaginary, a tendency to radicalize that absence into a kind of absolute withdrawal. With the latter tendency, desire no longer meanders, but rather attains to its ultimate directionality: beyond every horizon into a fulguration of being. Of these two characteristic movements in Eichendorff's writing, "Der Blick" clearly participates in the second. It follows the discursive path that in Eichendorff so often leads toward the Madonna, and not the more labyrinthine one that errs in the sphere of Venus. In doing so, it reveals very clearly what is specific to this portion of Eichendorff's *oeuvre*: the way the object of desire is hallucinated as absented, withdrawn to an infinite remove, and the way this very absence is experienced by the subject as a fulfillment. In Eichendorff's texts, the lyric phantasm acquires a peculiar vacuity, offering not the presence of an imago, but something (nothing?) free of every perceptual determination. Desire, sustained by the metaphor of flight so insistent in Eichendorff, yearns beyond the perceptual concreteness of the image toward and into an objectless radiance. The beloved object becomes, paradoxically, the absence of the beloved; fulfillment is displaced into a silence inaccessible to speech.[33] This movement is already discernible, of course, in the texts by Goethe analyzed in the previous two chapters, but in Eichendorff it is radicalized. Thus, as regards the text we have before us, it is possible to speak of an *infinitization of specularity*.

The poem is apt for my purposes because it allows me to trace a further Romantic transformation of the lyric problematic set into place by Goethe's poetic experimentation. How is the domain of specularity constructed here? As with Goethe and the Romantics generally, it is opened up in the moment when the eye of the beloved opens and fills the subject with the loving gaze. In Eichendorff's text, the force of this *Blick* is total: it dominates the entire phantasy, in which no other body part—except for a hypothetical and negated "lip" and a transparently metaphorical "heart"— is mentioned. In other words, the interest of desire here, the image in which it is invested, has nothing to do with the body of the beloved, nothing to do, in fact, with the visibly corporeal in general. As the title indicates, the specular moment is absolutized, removed from any scenic or narrative context that would allow us to construe it as tied to a concrete individual, an interpretive possibility Goethe's texts still allow. Nor do we encounter the mystical allegorization of the beloved so typical of Novalis. Here there is no 'maiden', only an abstract 'you', no face, no rosy color, no blue flame, only the sheer brightness of the look. The focus and fulfillment of poetic desire exists only as an anobjective radiance, a pure light. This is what I meant when I said that the beloved in Eichendorff is absented. She cannot give herself in a corporeal presentation, but rather is phantasized in and as the empty space of visuality itself, which her retraction from the text leaves behind.[34] In this absence, the poetic subject finds a certain safety: safety from the otherness of the female body, safety from an otherness of desire that threatens to destabilize its integrity.

The reduction of the beloved object to the single instant and instance of the "Blick" parallels the displacement of the beloved into a silence which cannot be spoken, but which nevertheless governs the poet's speech. Indeed, isn't this "Blick," around which our text is organized, introduced as a language beyond language, as a fulfillment of the communicative impetus transcending any that language could achieve (1–4)? Even were language able to name literally ("wörtlich," which in this context can also be read simply as 'in words') the 'originary' ("entquillt") emotionality the "Blick" conveys, it would still lack the para-designative 'sweetness' ("süßer") of the loving regard (5–8), the same sweetness that characterizes the beloved's look in "Mir schlug das Herz" (Text 4, 26). The "Blick" is a language prior to all language, a pure medium that realizes the three mythical values of this (and other Romantic) texts: it is the Source ("Quelle," 9) or site of an originary and unmediated emergence into presence; it is the Infinite, opening out from the eye toward an internality that outreaches, and even engenders, the heavens; and it is, finally, a Liquidity ("Strömen," 16) that absorbs all differences into the oneness of its movement and fills even the 'abyss' ("Abgrund," 15) of the subject's abandonment. The vacancy left by the withdrawal of the beloved object, but nevertheless still eroticized as the absence *of* that object, this decorporealized space of visuality, becomes in Eichendorff's text the medium of an imaginary self-appropriation that has no other content than reflexivity itself. Hence the epiphany—chiastically figured—of the third stanza:

> Und *ich seh'* des Himmels Quelle,
>
>   · · ·
>
> Wie sie bricht in reinster Helle
> *Aus dem reinsten Augenpaar.*
>
> *(9–12; emphasis added)*

The subject sees the infinite Source and the Source of the Infinite as a pure radiance that returns its own regard. Subjectivity is here constituted, exactly as in Fichte's definition, as a self-mirroring mirror, that is to say, as anobjective specularity.

~

I have called the transformation of Goethean specularity "Der Blick" exhibits an infinitization; emptied of all perceptual determination, the specular moment is transposed onto an ethereal plane (the heavens), suggesting a quasi-religious transcendence. The work of E. T. A. Hoffmann might be considered the ironic counterpart to this tendency, especially if we recall Hoffmann's own programmatic definition of irony (gleaned from the etchings of Jacques Callot) as the conflict of "human and animal" or—in a stronger but nevertheless perfectly accurate translation—of "idealization and sexuality."[35] This contention finds corroboration in two texts that narrate, albeit with symmetrically opposed results, the story of a student who becomes a poet. In these narratives, the idealized philosophical and poetic versions of specularity I have thus far discussed are opened onto another scene, as Freud would say, a scene charged with the dynamics of sexuality. Hoffmann is perhaps the first, and certainly one of the most acute, analysts of poetic writing, and his work thus provides indispensable material for our inquiry.

Anselmus, the protagonist of *Der goldene Topf* (*The Golden Jar*, 1814), is lying on a grassy riverbank outside of Dresden. It is Ascension Day, a holiday redolant with memories of childhood happiness. He set out from his student apartment in the hope of revivifying those memories and perhaps of meeting some girls, but this project—at once regressive and erotic—runs amok when he stumbles into the apple cart of an ugly old woman, spilling and squashing her wares. To be sure, this is not an unusual situation. Anselmus tends toward awkwardness, especially around girls, and he is a chronic spiller, especially of ink, which has made his chances for professional success (his aspiration is to become a clerk and to climb the bureaucratic ladder) as dubious as his amorous prospects. The encounter with the "Apfelweib" (apple-wife) condenses this double problem of eros and writing into something of a mythic curse, not merely because it alludes to the Fall, but because this woman, appearing as she does out of the "Schwarzes Tor" (Black Gate) leading from the city, confronts him with the terror of sexuality. Indeed, in her next appearance (likewise at a door) she will first horrify him with her gaping mouth—surrounded by loose skin and equipped with sharp, pointed teeth—then transform herself into a "Riesenschlange" (giant snake), which squeezes Anselmus in its coils and lays its "pointed tongue of glowing iron on his breast" so that "a cutting pain suddenly tore apart the pulsing artery of life."[36] The "Apfelweib"—at once phallic monster and *vagina dentata*—is the terrifying threat of a sexual embrace that simultaneously castrates and engulfs the male subject.

The movement of Hoffmann's narrative labors to allay this threat and thereby to allow Anselmus to accede to a happy love, as well as to the status of "Dichter" (poet). Along the way the "Apfelweib" is killed off, of course, and Anselmus learns to write without spilling his ink in uncontrolled emissions. Intricate and interesting as this narrative process is, I cannot discuss it here in any detail. Instead, I will concentrate on the first phase of Anselmus' itinerary, which occurs as he is lying on the river bank where he has sought refuge from the terrifying spillage in the mouth of the "Schwarzes Tor." In this "Paradies" of prelapsarian nature, his desire begins to assume the manageable shape that will lead to his poetic-erotic success, for the simple reason that the proper *telos* of that desire—that is, his beloved and his muse—appears to him here for the first time. The apparition begins in the medium of sound:

Da fing es an zu flüstern und zu lispeln, und es war als ertönten die Blüten wie aufgehangene Kristallglöckchen. Anselmus horchte und horchte. Da wurde, er wußte selbst nicht wie, das Gelispel und Geflüster und Geklingel zu leisen halbverwehten Worten:

> Zwischendurch—zwischenein—zwischen Zweigen—zwischen schwell-
> enden Blüten, schwingen, schlängeln, schlingen wir uns—Schwester-
> lein—Schwesterlein, schwinge dich im Schimmer—schnell, schnell
> herauf—herab—Abendsonne schießt Strahlen, zischelt der Abendwind—
> raschelt der Tau—Blüten singen—rühren wir Zünglein, singen wir mit
> Blüten und Zweigen—Sterne bald glänzen—müssen herab—zwischen-
> durch, zwischenein, schlängeln, schlingen, schwingen wir uns Schwes-
> terlein.—

So ging es fort in Sinne verwirrender Rede.[37]

Then there began a whispering and lisping, and it was as if the blossoms rang like little crystal bells that had been hung out. Anselmus listened and listened. Then the lisping and whispering and ringing became, he himself didn't know how, soft words, half blown away.

> Between and through—between and in—between the branches—be-
> tween the swelling blossoms, we swing, twist, and sling ourselves—sis-
> ters—sister, swing yourself in the shimmer—quickly, quickly up—down—
> evening sun shoots rays, evening wind hisses—dew rustles—blossoms
> sing—we move our little tongues, we sing with blossoms and branches—
> soon the stars will shine—must go down—between and through, between
> and in we sisters twist, sling and swing ourselves.—

Thus it continued in a speech confusing to the senses.

The scene is crucial for my inquiry because it is the primal scene (the *Urszene*) of the lyric. Anselmus lies on the bosom of Nature, like Goethe's Ganymed, whose poetic ascension we will encounter further on, or like Goethe's Werther, that most lyrical of novelistic protagonists. The meta-phorical structure the scene enacts is familiar from "Maifest," in which, of course, Nature manifests itself as Song. Indeed, the softly whispered and ringing words that Anselmus hears in the branches and blossoms of the elder bush beneath which he lies approximate one of the major subtypes of the Romantic lyric, the tone poem, in which semantics cedes place to a play of sounds.[38] Anselmus' poetic career is initiated, then, in a lyric experience that brings him into contact with the Origin of poetry itself, emerging out of Nature as pure sound and capturing the subject with its magical presence.

But Hoffmann's text (especially if we recall the trauma of sexuality from which Anselmus is escaping) allows us to read this aural hallucination in a different register. What is here called before the student's inner ear, surrounding and soothing him, is the voice of the Mother, a voice experienced as a continuous flow of sound, lightly varying across its hushed consonants (*sch-*) and ringing vowels (*i* and *ei*). This phantasized aural envelope, retrospectively constituted to compensate for the threat that the castrating "Apfelweib" poses, enfolds Mother and male subject in a fused unity and allows that subject to recuperate its wholeness in the reflection of an "acoustic mirror."[39] The semantics of the tone poem confirms this reading: the aurally transmitted singing of the sisters speaks of their swinging, slinging, and twisting *between* the branches, as if their aural presence could fill and efface the gaps that might possibly open up within Nature; and this singing sounds forth from and evokes the swelling plenitude of the breastlike flowers (note the phonic proximity of "Blüten" and "Brüsten"). A maternal presence is, quite literally, e*voked* here, made voice, but this is a Mother untouched by lack and therefore posing no threat (no gaping cavity, no giant phallus) to the identity of the male subject. The voice of Nature from which the lyric (conceived as the primordial form of all poetry since Herder) emerges is the phantasy of oneness, wholeness, and erotic union within the mother/child dyad.[40]

Is this union also, as indeed the texts by Novalis considered above suggest, the poetic *Wunsch* figured by the specular moment? The continuation of the passage cited leaves little doubt that this is so:

"Das ist denn doch der Abendwind, der heute mir ordentlich verständlichen Worten zuflüstert."—Aber in dem Augenblick ertönte es über seinem Haupte wie ein Dreiklang heller Kristallglocken; er schaute hinauf und erblickte drei in grünem Gold erglänzende Schlänglein, die sich um die Zweige gewickelt hatten und die Köpfchen der Abendsonne entgegenstreckten. Da flüsterte und lispelte es von neuem in jenen Worten, und die Schlänglein schlüpften und kosten auf und nieder durch die Blätter und Zweige, und wie sie sich so schnell rührten, da war es, als streue der Holunderbusch tausend funkelnde Smaragde durch seine dunklen Blätter. "Das ist die Abendsonne, die so in dem Holunderbusch spielt," dachte der Student Anselmus, aber da ertönten die Glocken wieder, und Anselmus sah, wie eine Schlange ihr Köpfchen nach ihm herabstreckte. Durch alle Glieder fuhr es ihm wie ein elektrischer Schlag, er erbebte im Innersten—er starrte hinauf, und ein Paar herrliche dunkelblaue Augen blickten ihn an mit unaussprechlicher Sehnsucht, so daß ein nie gekanntes Gefühl der höchsten Seligkeit und des tiefsten Schmerzes seine

Brust zerspringen wollte. Und wie er voll heißen Verlangens immer in die holdseligen Augen schaute, da ertönten stärker in lieblichen Akkorden die Kristallglocken, und die funkelnden Smaragde fielen auf ihn herab und umspannen ihn in tausend Flämmchen um ihn herflackernd und spielend mit schimmernden Goldfaden.[41]

"That's just the evening wind whispering to me today in regular, intelligible words."—But in that moment it resounded above his head like a third of bright crystal bells; he looked up and caught sight of three little snakes shining in greenish gold, which had wrapped themselves about the branches and stretched their little heads toward the evening sun. Then there was anew a whispering and lisping in those same words, and the little snakes slipped and caressed their way up and down through the leaves and branches, and as they moved so quickly it seemed as if the elder bush scattered thousands of sparkling emeralds through its dark leaves. "That's the evening sun which plays so in the elder bush," thought the student Anselmus, but then the bells resounded again, and Anselmus saw how a snake was stretching her little head toward him. Like an electric impulse it shot through all his members, he trembled in his inmost center—he stared upward, and a pair of dark blue eyes looked at him with inexpressible yearning, so that a completely unknown feeling of highest bliss and deepest pain sought to burst his breast. And as he continued to look into the gently blissful eyes with warm desire, the crystal bells resounded louder, and sparkling emeralds fell down upon him, wrapping him in thousands of little flames and playing in shimmering gold threads.

Werther's experience of the embracing oneness of Nature, of which Hoffmann's text is a redaction, coalesces in the vision of the "Gestalt einer Geliebten"[42] ("figure of a beloved"). This is precisely what happens here. The whispered music of Nature assumes visual form, culminating in a version of the specular moment in which Anselmus looks into the eyes of his beloved, the little snake Serpentina, as she casts her regard lovingly back onto him. The utterly fantastic character of the scene, however, allows us to read the specular phantasm in a register almost totally obliterated in all the other texts we have considered thus far. (The exception is the blue flower scene in *Heinrich von Ofterdingen.*) That is, the equation beloved = little snake, which the fiction posits, exposes the symbolic structure organizing not merely this, but all versions of the specular moment. By symbolic structure I mean—following Nicolas Abraham[43]—a significative configuration that conflates and (tentatively) resolves a subjacent conflict and thereby organizes subjects into a specific interpersonal array. The little snake eases the tension between Anselmus' desire and his fear that that desire might be fulfilled. His desire is to be one with the Mother, to know the Mother as encompassing plenitude, to see that the Mother is possessed of a phallus, to be the phallus that is the object of the Mother's desire. And his fear is that the realization of that desire will unleash a horrible punishment, that the Mother is deprived of the phallus, that he too is so deprived, that she is a giant phallic snake which will cut him apart, castrate him. (Recall the "copulating little hook" of Novalis.) The specular moment is a discourse of narcissistic identification. It urgently affirms: "Yes, you have the little phallus which I am. There is oneness and the Same. And I am one in that your oneness shines back on me." The subject constitutes itself here, in the words of André Green, as the "object of the object,"[44] as the seen of the seen. Hence the erotization of Anselmus' body, the play of little flames and sparkling threads that, as the text formulates it, electrifies him, and as psychoanalysis formulates it (hardly less mysteriously) cathects his ego. A desire is born here that stabilizes identity and orients what, in the course of the narrative, will become the writing of poetry.

Yet this desire is manageable only insofar as it remains unfulfilled, only insofar as it is circumscribed by a law and sanctioned by that law's representative. The passage mentions no third figure beyond the dyadic pair, but the effects of proscription are nevertheless legible. The snakes are firmly held in the diminutive, the heads they hold erect within the maternal sunlight are likewise qualified as little.[45] And of course a distance (the condition of possibility of specularity) always separates Anselmus and Serpentina. In fact, if we return to the lyric that the three snakes sing, we discover that it speaks, toward the end, of a law which they too must obey: a law of time which frames their play in the sunshine and constrains them with necessity ("müssen"). Indeed, Anselmus' aural-ocular tryst with Serpentina comes to an end when a "rauhe, tiefe Stimme"[46] ("rough, deep voice") is heard summoning the little snakes home. As the subsequent phases of the text make clear, this voice, which Anselmus experiences as "feindselig" (inflected with enmity) and which leaves his dream "zerrissen" (torn apart) is that of the Father, Archivarius Lindhorst.[47] This figure will eventually orchestrate Anselmus's poetic initiation and lead him to union with Serpentina as a "Leben in der Poesie"[48] ("life in poetry").

Anselmus's initiation into the life of poetry succeeds, then, because it is controlled by a benevolent father figure who structures the young man's desire by fixing it on the specular mirror of primary narcissism and by eliminating the terror of sexuality embodied in the "Apfelweib."[49] This all happens within the generic confines of what Hoffmann called the "Fantasiestück," a 'fantasy piece' which steers the problem of sexuality toward a happy outcome. This fantastic plot provides us with an analysis of the lyric which stresses its positive, productive function as a discourse that stabilizes identity by setting the subject in relation to the figure of an Origin in which the law of the Same prevails. If we move, however, to another generic frame, to the "Nachtstück" or 'night piece', we discover that this narcissistic solution to the problematic of desire and identity—the solution Romanticism generally labors to institute—is in fact extremely precarious. Thus, Hoffmann's most famous night piece introduces into the intimacy and domesticity of the specular phantasm an otherness that shatters the self and that Freud, in a great essay, called "das Unheimliche" (the uncanny).[50] In fact, "Der Sandmann" ("The Sand Man," 1816) is the countertext to "Der goldene Topf," exactly reversing the earlier story's plot structure and initiating its student-poet protagonist not into a blissful recuperation of the Origin, but into madness and self-destruction.

Thanks to the fame of Freud's essay and to the role it has played in recent theoretical discussions,[51] the text of "Der Sandmann" is sufficiently well known that I can forgo even a cursory discussion of its plot and of the psychoanalytic problematic of its reading. Yet certain features of this text pertain to the specular moment and its lyric figuration, and "Der Sandmann" submits those issues to a penetrating and disturbing analysis. Hence we find, at the very center of what Freud calls Nathanael's "narcissistic" love for the mechanical doll Olimpia,[52] a scene of specularity involving the production and reception of poetry. Nathanael is reading his works aloud to his utterly patient beloved:

> Aber auch noch nie hatte er eine solche herrliche Zuhörerin gehabt. Sie stickte und strickte nicht, sie sah nicht durchs Fenster, sie fütterte keinen Vogel, sie spielte mit keinem Schoßhündchen, mit keiner Lieblingskatze, sie drehte keine Papierschnitzen oder sonst was in der Hand, sie durfte kein Gähnen durch einen leisen erzwungenen Husten bezwingen—kurz!—stundenlang sah sie mit starrem Blick unverwandt dem Geliebten ins Auge, ohne sich zu rücken und zu bewegen, und immer glühender, immer lebendiger wurde dieser Blick. Nur wenn Nathanael endlich aufstand und ihr die Hand, auch wohl den Mund küßte, sagte sie: "Ach, ach!"—dann aber: "Gute Nacht, mein Lieber!"—"O du herrliches, du tiefes Gemüt," rief Nathanael auf seiner Stube,

"nur von dir, von dir allein werd' ich ganz verstanden." Er erbebte vor innerem
Entzücken, wenn er bedachte, welch wunderbarer Zusammenklang sich in
seinem und Olimpias Gemüt täglich mehr offenbare; denn es schien ihm, als
habe Olimpia über seine Werke, über seine Dichtergabe überhaupt recht tief
aus seinem Inneren gesprochen, ja als habe die Stimme aus seinem Innern
selbst herausgetönt. Das mußte denn wohl auch sein; denn mehr Worte als
vorhin erwähnt sprach Olimpia niemals. Erinnerte sich aber auch Nathanael
in hellen nüchternen Augenblicken, z.B. morgens gleich nach dem Erwachen,
wirklich an Olimpias gänzliche Passivität und Wortkargheit, so sprach er
doch: "Was sind Worte—Worte!—Der Blick ihres himmlischen Auges sagt
mehr als jede Sprache hienieden."[53]

But never before had he had such a glorious listener. She did no needlework or
knitting; she didn't look out the window; she fed no bird; she played with no
little lap dog, with no beloved cat; she spun out no paper cutouts or anything
else in her hand; she attempted to master no yawn with a forced cough—in
short!—for hours she looked with fixed unwavering regard into the eye of her
beloved, without budging or moving, and this love grew ever more glowing,
ever more vital. Only when Nathanael finally stood up and kissed her hand,
indeed her mouth too, did she say: "Ach, ach!"—but then: "Good night, my
dear one!"—"O you glorious, you deep spirit," Nathanael cried when back in
his room, "only by you, by you alone am I wholly understood." He trembled
with inner delight when he reflected on the wonderous harmony that revealed
itself more and more each day in his and Olimpia's spirit, for it seemed to him
as if Olimpia had spoken about his works and his poetic gift in the truly deep
sense of his inner feeling, indeed as if the voice had sounded forth out of his
own internality. And to be sure that must have been the case, for Olimpia
never spoke more than the words just mentioned. But when even Nathanael
himself actually recalled, in bright, sober moments such as in the morning
light after awakening, Olimpia's utter passivity and laconism, he nonetheless
said: "What are words—words!—The look of such a heavenly eye says more
than every language here below."

The parodistic tone of the passage should not deceive us into dismissing
the scene it narrates as an insignificant aberration, as the case of a poet
whose lack of genuine talent relieves us of taking his predicament seriously. In fact, the text gathers together nearly all the major components
of the cultural definition of poetry in terms of specularity. Olimpia's love,
revealed in the unwavering gaze of the specular regard, proves to be the
perfect interpretation for the poems Nathanael has produced, because love
is the Source of that poetry. Indeed, in a move that is by no means atypical

for Hoffmann,[54] the beloved's voice and that of the poet fuse in an orality that emerges from a single, deep internal source. Returned to its Source by virtue of the beloved's empathetic act of understanding, Nathanael's poetry is no longer exposed to the dispersion, discontinuity, and opacity to which its written character would otherwise condemn it. Olimpia's hermeneutic appropriation of his texts is total; Nathanael feels himself *wholly* understood; and in the security of this understanding he finds the wholeness of his subjectivity. Thus, the scene enacts what the *envoi* of "Maifest" could only hold out as a promise: the transformation of the text into the transparency and luminescence of specular love. Note the mimetic impossibility around which the scene is built: Nathanael reads the texts before him but at the same time, impossibly, looks into Olimpia's loving eyes as they cast his love back to him. The specular exchange takes effect, in other words, only when the blockage of the text, or more generally, of language, is effaced. It is this ob-literation of the nonidentity marked by and marking the sign (Novalis) that the quest for the Origin shaping the lyric ideology seeks to accomplish. Hence the reiteration in the final quoted sentence of the claim implied in every figuration of specularity from Goethe to Eichendorff: "Der Blick ihres himmlischen Auges sagt mehr als jede Sprache hienieden."

The specular phantasm, I have argued all along, serves a compensatory function, assuaging an anxiety incited at once by language and by sexuality. Can we discern the sexual aspect of specularity in the passage cited? It is operative in the series of negated actions that are introduced to qualify Olimpia's absorptive listening. She neither knits nor does needlework; she plays with no animals, cuts no shapes out of paper, and never has to suppress a yawn. On one level, of course, all these things she doesn't do merely signal her absolute attentiveness, contrasting her to Nathanael's real sister/beloved Klara, whose distracted listening to his poetic efforts had frustrated him in an earlier scene.[55] This aspect of the passage confirms the perfection of Olimpia's hermeneutic gifts: distraction and nonattention, which spring from the finitude marking our relation to the sign, are absent from this dream of total understanding, of an understanding that, quite literally, sees through to the poem's creative *Keimentschluß*. But this list of negative mentions (of *Verneinungen*, or denegations, in Freud's sense[56]) can also be read in a sexual register. By not sewing or stitching (archetypically feminine activities), Olimpia does nothing which could create a phallic substitute and thereby call attention to what Nathanael, to preserve his narcissistic self-constitution, must deny: the absence of the phallus, sexual difference, the otherness of femininity. By admitting no furry little animals into her lap, Olimpia hides her sex; by not yawning, she reveals no corporeal openings, no threatening oral cavities. And of course she refrains from making any threatening incisions, from cutting up pieces of paper, which could all too easily be confused with those on which Nathanael has inscribed his poems. All these no's and not's, all these things which the text says in order to say that they aren't there, all these denials must be maintained if the illusion of Sameness structuring Nathanael's self-conception is to be upheld. Compare in this connection Novalis's urgent disclaimer: no "copulating little hook" must be hung on the maternal sphere. When this occurs—and it occurs linguistically, by virtue of the logical copula—the lucent Source of specularity is occluded. One grabs only a handful of darkness.

But "Der Sandmann" is, according to Hoffmann's own generic designation, a night piece. It is informed, we might say, by the darkness of sexuality, by anarchic sexual difference. Thus, it is no accident that its sad story is presided over not by a benevolent father figure who guarantees the law of the Same, but rather by the terrifying personification of Novalis's "copulirendes Häckchen." Freud, of course, interprets the figure of Coppelius as a negatively invested father-imago whose terrifying effect on Nathanael issues from the threat of castration. And indeed, in Freudian theory, the relation between narcissism and castration is one of systematic complementarity.[57] But Hoffmann's text calls, I think, for nuancing the Freudian reading. To be sure, castration is at issue here, but not merely in the form of an imagined paternal aggression. This specification of the lawyer's (later optician's) function in the narrative economy fails to account for the copular ambiguity and nonidentity of the figure. As the shift of his name from masculine to feminine form (Coppelius/Coppola) indicates, the terror that this intruder brings into the domestic sphere is the terror of nonidentity, of a difference that is not organized into the stable role allocation of male here, female there. Hence, in the primal scene Nathanael recalls at the start of the narrative, Coppelius figures as the other of the father, that is, the mother, but a mother endowed with such phallic attributes that she/he feminizes the father. As Freud himself noted on another occasion, what engenders anxiety in the child witnessing such a scene is not the one or the other of the actors, but the spectacle's oscillating indeterminacy and the ambivalence this engenders in the child.[58] In a sense, then, Freud's reading of Coppelius/Coppola solely as castrating father itself works to stabilize the difference/indifference of the textual problematic Hoffmann works through. This interpretive divergence from the text is betrayed in Freud's misreading—his effacement of the letter—of the story's climactic scene.[59] According to Freud, Nathanael spies the lawyer Coppelius through the fateful glass and this incites his final outbreak of madness. In fact, though, he looks toward Klara—his sister/beloved and maternal substitute—and not the father but the female figure finally shatters his narcissistic identity. The source of terror here is a nonsource, an originary dispersion of sexual difference, an indeterminacy of generic (gendered) positions. This difference prior to stable opposition, which the concept of castration at once figures and dissimulates, is the uncanny. And, as if to stress this point, Coppelius himself first appears in this ultimate scene with a feminine sexual marker as a "sonderbar[er] klein[er] grau[er] Busch"[60] ("a peculiar little grey bush") in order then to rise up "riesengroß"[61] (gigantically large) from the crowd. We are back in the realm of the "Riesenschlange" (giant snake) into which the "Apfelweib" haunting Anselmus' erotic endeavors transforms herself. In contrast to "Der goldene Topf," however, there is in "Der Sandmann" no archinterpreter Lindhorst to disambiguate the difference/indifference, the anarchic symbolization, of the copular phallus by affixing it firmly to its paternal position. At least the text knew no such interpreter before Freud.

~

The tour of Romanticism in this chapter by no means exhausts the possibilities for contextualizing the poems by Goethe discussed in the first two. Indeed, it seems that every historical-cultural period in which lyric-poetic writing assumes crucial importance and in which love is submitted to reinterpretation also engages the problematics of specularity. Comparisons between Goethe and Dante, Goethe and Petrarch, Goethe and Shakespeare, Baudelaire, or Celan could prove as revealing (although, of course, revealing of different things) as the intra-Romantic comparisons worked through here.[62] But choices must be made, and, once made, we must abide their consequences. This section has analyzed, within an epochal frame, the beginning of a new form of lyric writing and has traced some of the continuities and transformations which the central figure of that mode of writing undergoes across a span of some forty-five years. To be sure, this path of inquiry has taken me some distance from Goethe's texts, but it has raised issues that will thread their way throughout the following chapters. In conclusion, let me cite a text that labors to bring Romanticism to a close. Here again we find a version of the specular moment (note lines 1–2, which forcefully recall Text 1), but, as it were, in the mode of quotation, a figure marked as passing away if not already past. What is it that shatters the dream of specularity? Quite simply this: the beloved begins to take on corporeality. More decisively, she steps out of her role as silent Origin and appropriates what Romanticism, starting with Goethe's lyric transcription of the idyll, denied her: she begins to speak. Here, then, is the fourth poem from Heine's *Lyrisches Intermezzo* (*Lyrical Intermezzo*, 1823):

> Wenn ich in deine Augen seh',
> So schwindet all mein Leid und Weh.
> Doch wenn ich küsse deinen Mund,
> So werd' ich ganz und gar gesund.
>
> Wenn ich mich lehn' an deine Brust,
> Kommt's über mich wie Himmelslust.
> Doch wenn du sprichtst: Ich liebe dich!
> So muß ich weinen bitterlich.[63]
>
> When I look into your eyes,
> Then all my suffering and pain disappears.
> When I kiss you on the mouth,
> Then I am wholly and entirely healed.
>
> When I lean on your breast,
> It comes over me like heaven's delight.
> But when you speak "I love you!"
> Then I must cry bitterly.

PART TWO

*The Sexualization
of Specularity*

§ 4   The Originary Donation

Zum Sehen geboren,
Zum Schauen bestellt,
Dem Turme geschworen,
Gefällt mir die Welt.[1]

Born to see,
Commissioned to look,
Sworn to the tower,
The World pleases me.

One way of describing the transformation of the specular moment accomplished in the texts by Novalis and Hoffmann discussed in the previous chapter is to call it a *sexualization*. Specularity absorbs into its figuration an interplay of significations that derive from a sexual-erotic register. But what does the feverishly erotic mysticism of Novalis or the lurid imagination of Hoffmann really have to do with the (apparently) spontaneous innocence of Goethe's Sesenheim songs? And, in view of this tonal or attitudinal distance between the young Goethe and his Romantic successors, is it appropriate to suggest that the psychoanalytic terminology the latters' texts elicit could be applied, without distortion, to the former's idyllic creations? In this chapter I shall show that the transformation in question—a transformation I shall call the sexualization of specularity—is already carried out in Goethe's poetry of the early 1770's and that the narcissistic complex determining the destinies of Heinrich, Anselmus, and Nathaniel structures the movement of Goethe's texts as well. The fifth chapter will then trace the ramifications of this sexual complex in Goethe's poetological thinking, particularly as regards the figure of genius.

Before engaging Goethe's texts directly, however, I will consider briefly a text by one of his major contemporaries, a text that marks a literary-historical breakthrough no less significant than Goethe's lyric innovation of the 1770's. The text I am referring to is Christoph Martin Wieland's *Geschichte des Agathon* (*History of Agathon*, 1766–67), the novel that set the paradigm for the emergent subgenre of the *Bildungsroman*. In the fourth chapter of the novel's first book (there are eleven books all told), we encounter the following narrative rendering of the specular moment:

Agathon returned the regard [*Anblik*] of this young slave with an attentiveness in which a pleasant astonishment gradually rose to the point of ecstatic delight [*Entzükung*]. Precisely these motions revealed themselves as well in the graceful countenance of the young slave; their souls recognized one another in exactly the same moment [*Augenblicke*], and seemed already to flow [*fliessen*] into one another through their looks [*Blike*] before their arms could embrace one another and their lips, trembling with delight, could cry out, "Psyche—Agathon." They remained silent for a long time; what they felt [*empfanden*] was beyond all expression; and for what purpose would they have required words? The use of language ceases when souls communicate immediately [*sich einander unmittelbar mittheilen*], see [*anschauen*] and touch [*berühren*] one another immediately, and feel more in a single moment [*einem Augenblike*] than the tongue of the muses could speak in entire years. Perhaps the sun would have passed unnoticed over their heads and returned again to the ocean without their having noticed the movement of the hours in their continuous moment/look of ecstatic delight [*Augenblik der Entzükung*], had not Agathon . . . with gentle force extricated himself from the arms of his Psyche. . . . "Time is precious, dearest Psyche," he said, "we must take charge of the moment [*uns der Augenblike bemächtigen*]."²

Note how precisely, how exhaustively, the scene gathers together the essential features of the specular moment: the recognition of mutual love in and through the reciprocal regard, the ecstatic character of the experience, the liquid flow of emotion, the effacement of time, the inaccessibility to language of this purest and richest, this entirely unmediated mode of communication. Even the economic aspects alluded to at the end of Chapter 2 are woven into the scene: only when Agathon extracts himself from Psyche's embrace and breaks from the enclosure of the specular dyad does he begin to calculate and plan, treating time as a resource.³ But beyond documenting once again the insistence of the specular moment in the literary texts of the period, we should note the placement and function of the specular scene within the overall context of the novel. In contrast to Goethe's lyric texts, which enact specularity in its momentary eruption, Wieland's narrative integrates the figure within a developmental pattern, functionalizes it within a biographical program. Thus, a brief look at the overarching narrative structure of *Agathon* can show us something the lyric texts, in their insularity, hide: the cultural efficacy of specularity as a symbolic matrix organizing identity formation. The *Bildungsroman*, in fact, is just that: a schema or program for the production of subjective identity, a codification of desire.⁴

Quickly sketched, the narrative context of the passage cited above is as follows. Agathon, the novel's protagonist, is a youth of exceptional beauty. At the beginning of the narrative, he stumbles onto a Dionysian festival (the novel is set in ancient Greece) being celebrated on an island by a group of women, who, in their frenzy, take him for the god of their cult. Only the arrival of a band of pirates, who rape the women and carry them and Agathon off as slaves, saves him from the maenads' orgiastic violence. The novel starts, then, with the terrifying threat of female sexuality, much as Hoffmann's "The Golden Jar" begins with Anselmus' encounter with the horrible "Apfelweib" in the orifice of the "Black Gate." On the ship, the pirates continue their orgy and finally fall into a drunken sleep. At this point (violent sexuality safely lulled), Agathon spies a young male slave, as attractive as himself, who turns out not to be male at all, but rather the graceful Psyche, the beloved of Agathon's adolescence. The mutual recognition of the lovers, recounted in the passage quoted above, occurs in radiant specularity.

Wieland's narrative, then, deploys the specular moment as a counter or check against a sexual turbulence (recalling the Latin *turbus*, meaning 'crowd') that threatens his corporeal integrity, the beauty of his bodily self-image. The source of this apotropaic efficacy resides in the symbolic structure of the specular figure, a structure I shall begin to explicate by considering the layers of significance condensed in the beloved object, Psyche. She is, first of all, not entirely a "she." In this, her first appearance in the novel, she masquerades as a young male slave, as Agathon's *semblable*. The love crystallized in the specular encounter obeys the law of the Same. Second, she is Agathon's first, his primordial love. Their acquaintance derives from the period of his primary (and parentless) socialization into the Delphic religion. Throughout the novel, Agathon will recall this childhood phase as a kind of paradise and as the wellspring of his truest, most intimate identity, particularly emphasizing the living wholeness of the religiously interpreted universe in which he moved, a universe animated and held together by a world-soul (= psyche). The primal love that is ecstatically recuperated within the specular moment, then, is the male child's attachment to the figure who lends unity and identity not only to him, but to the entire cosmos and makes that cosmos the mirror of his own inwardness. Finally—and this is only revealed at the novel's end—the amorous bond to Psyche is incestuous: she is, in fact, his sister. This feature lends the figure of the specular dyad both its danger and its socializing force. In fact, these two aspects are inextricably entwined: the incest prohibition, which has its source in a law external to the specular dyad, forces the internalization of the transgressive amorous attachment, its installation within the subject where it can function as the noncorporeal paradigm of his desire, the Psyche whom the Eros that Agathon is will ceaselessly pursue.

To summarize, Wieland's text (published in 1767, three years prior to Goethe's Sesenheim poems) situates the specular moment within a program of psychosexual socialization. Experienced within the field of alienation (recall that Agathon is a captive of the pirates, a slave, a commodity), the ecstatic encounter takes the male subject out of real time, governed by economics, and—as if it were an anamnestic umbilical cord—allows him to recover his unity with the Origin, with a primordial, childhood love governed by the law of the Same, a love in which his own inmost identity (his psyche) is constituted in the reciprocal regard exchanged with his familial counterpart. The specular moment, as we saw earlier, is a narcissistic scenario. Agathon's socialization (his *Bildung*) commences when his desire is fixed on the mirror of primary narcissism, the mirror which endows him with the schema of his own identity.[5]

One more component of Wieland's model needs to be set into place. Precisely because Agathon's attachment to Psyche is incestuous, it must not be realized, must not pass over into the domain of the corporeal. Were this to happen, the paradise of childhood and the oneness of identity that paradise guarantees would be shattered. The novel illustrates this by introducing a snake into the garden: the priestess of the Delphic temple who, in violation of her office, attempts to seduce the young Agathon and, to accomplish this end, arranges for Psyche's removal. In fact, the priestess is nothing other than the corporeal stand-in for Psyche: her name—Pythia—is a transform of the girl's own, a fatal transform that renders the psychic beloved as sexual temptress and snake (python). The fall into sexual attachment and transgression is thus doubly motivated, on the one hand by the corporealization of the psychic image, on the other by a confusion on the level of the signifying name.[6] Both of these hazards to amorous stability will have to be brought under control.

Were the mastery of the seductive woman to occur right away, of course, there would be no novel. Agathon escapes the coils of Pythia's plot only to fall into a subtler entanglement. In league with the Sophist Hippias, a merchant of appearances and signifiers, the exquisite hetaera Danae succeeds in seducing the young man. She accomplishes this by assuming the lead role in a dance first performed by a girl named—what else?—Psyche. The dance enacts the story of Daphne and Apollo, the story, that is, of an ever receding, unreachable object of desire. By inserting herself into the symbolic position of Psyche/Daphne, Danae manages to deflect Agathon's amorous longing from the noncorporeal image of his sister onto the sensuous reality of her own body. Duped by this substitution of the female body/signifier for the ideal signified, Agathon falls into erotic error. The transgression involved is not merely that of an illicit affair (Wieland thoroughly ironizes any moralistic objections that might be raised at this level), but rather the fundamental transgression that occurs when the narcissistic investment in the beloved *semblable* of childhood is no longer contained by the law.

The law in question is that of the Father, the law proscribing incestuous union and thereby establishing the psychic imago within the subject's internality. In the final book of the novel, Agathon encounters the personal instantiation of this law, the arch-interpreter who disambiguates the confusion of bodies and signifiers and retrieves for him the truth of his childhood attachments and beliefs. The arch-interpreter's name is—recall Hoffmann's Archivarius Lindhorst—Archytas, the lawgiver and wise ruler of the Republic of Tarent, the friend of Agathon's deceased father who becomes the ideal father to whose symbolic-political position Agathon will eventually accede. In the home of Archytas (that is to say, under his supervision) Agathon is reunited with Psyche, but only to learn that their union can never take place in the real domain of corporeal particularity. Archytas explains that Psyche is Agathon's sister (which is to say, he installs the law prohibiting incest) and that she has married his own son (which is to say, she is now his daughter). Agathon's socialization thus achieves completion not through the outright renunciation of Psyche, but through the internalization of his love for her. The corporeality of the sister is negated (surrounded by the Father's "No!"), while the ideal sister is preserved as soulful meaning, elevated to a level of generality or conceptuality, where she remains the amorously invested image of Agathon's subjective identity. *Bildung* is nothing other than this internalization of the Origin under the auspices of the paternal law.

The Agathonian schema of socialization will remain essentially intact throughout the development of the *Bildungsroman* in Romanticism: in Goethe's *Wilhelm Meisters Lehrjahre* (*Wilhelm Meister's Apprenticeship*, 1794), Novalis's *Heinrich von Ofterdingen*, and, as we have seen, in that condensed *Bildungsroman* of poetic initiation, Hoffmann's "The Golden Jar." We are dealing with a pattern of symbolic organization that does not belong to one author or another, but rather has a transindividual validity within the culture. Nevertheless, there is one major difference between Wieland's *Agathon* and its successors (at least those named here): whereas the latter all center on the Mother as the object of primary identification, Wieland introduces the Sister. It would seem that in 1767 the maternal imago had not yet achieved the centrality that accrues to it in the 1790's. The first version of *Agathon* is characterized, in fact, by a thoroughgoing effacement of the Mother. Agathon's own mother, Musarion, dies before the story begins, and Archytas is a widower. In the authorized edition of the novel Wieland published in 1794, however, all this is changed. First, Psyche, married to Archytas's son, bears children. Second, Agathon's beloved Danae shows up in Tarent, having renounced her hetaeran ways and dedicated herself to a life of chaste virtue. With her arrival, a final transformation of the beloved image occurs:

> Her [Danae's, although she has changed her name to Chariklea] most pleasant activity was to help Agathon's sister in raising her three daughters, over whom the Graces had poured all their gifts. Without noticing it, she became accustomed to regarding these lovely children as her own. The children grew up in the conviction that they had two mothers, and Psyche took the greatest delight in maintaining their young hearts in this pleasant error that made of her and her friend a single person.[7]

The young hearts of the children—their desire—are oriented during this phase of primary socialization by an image of Danae and Psyche as one. Returning to Tarent after a journey, Agathon himself comes to occupy the children's perceptual-imaginary standpoint. As the novel's last page tells us, he "made no distinction" ("machte keinen Unterschied") between Psyche and Danae.[8] What was excluded from symbolization in 1767 now forms the novel's final tableau: psychic *semblable* and corporeal object of desire are fused into a single ethereal image, the apotheosis of the Mother.

The promotion of the Mother to the status of predominant imago and idealized focus of identification that takes place between the first (1767) and final (1794) versions of Wieland's *Agathon* (a similar purification of the maternal role can be traced between the two versions of Goethe's *Wilhelm Meister*[9]) parallels a general sociocultural process occurring during the last third of the eighteenth century. As several historical investigations have demonstrated, this period witnesses a consolidation of the symbolism of the family around the Mother, who assumes control of the child's primary socialization.[10] This development, in fact, produces the concept and experience of childhood in its modern sense. Shaped by the tender guidance of the Mother, charged with the emotionality of the intimate bond with her, and protected from the constraints and the tumble of public life, childhood becomes a kind of affective cocoon that the adult subject retrospectively invests as the site and source of its most intimate identity. Adulthood, in fact, is often sensed as exile from this paradisiacal state and the poetic imagination becomes a means for recovering that state, an anamnestic umbilical cord. This is the sociocultural frame of the sexualization of specularity. Perhaps for the first time in the history of Europe, the poetic imagination draws its energies from the domain of infantile sexuality.

Let us imagine a text that would exactly confirm the thesis we have derived from *Agathon*, and in particular from the placement of the specular moment within its program of *Bildung*. Our hypothetical text would have the following characteristics. (a) It would locate the source of imagination ("Phantasie") in the enclosure of the mother/child dyad. Indeed, it would radicalize this notion of dyadic oneness, figuring it as the containment of the male child within the Mother's body ("im Mutterleib"). (b) It would reveal the narcissistic investment that characterizes this phase, an investment through which the child becomes the little phallus within the Mother (the little "Pipi"). (c) To support this phallic identification, the fantasy in question would equip the subject with other phallic attributes, say, a gun (not as traditionally phallic as a sword, but having the advantage of connoting 'explosive discharge' ["Geschoß"]). (d) Thus equipped, the subject would carry out some sort of phallic adventure, such as the penetration of a dragon's belly ("Bauch"), and earn for itself the predicate of manhood ("Mann"). (e) In addition to its phallic component, the fantasy would also contain a specular scene, an encounter with a beloved who seems to be the solar source of light ("Sonnenschein"). In this scene, the specular union with the beloved would pass over into a liquid-oral register as she transmits to him the glow ("Glut") of his desire. (f) Finally, our hypothetical text would mark the fact that its fantasy is lost, that the subject only retrospectively constitutes the paradisiacal country ("Land") of childhood, that the path back ("der Weg dahin") cannot be found.

Just such a text, in fact, was composed by Goethe in 1774 or 1775. As its title suggests, it is a commentary on a historical *novum*, on a transformation in the mode of being of the imagination. Since this text perfectly conforms to the predictions listed above,[11] I will cite it without commentary, merely marking the features (a) through (f) in its margin:

8. DER NEUE AMADIS

Als ich noch ein Knabe war
Sperrte man mich ein
Und so saß ich manches Jahr
Über mir allein
(a)   Wie in Mutterleib.

Doch du warst mein Zeitvertreib
Goldne Phantasie
Und ich ward ein warmer Held
(b)   Wie der Prinz Pipi
Und durchzog die Welt.

Baute manch Crystallen Schloß
Und zerstört es auch
(c)   Warf mein blinkendes Geschoß
(d)   Drachen durch den Bauch
Ja ich war ein Mann!

Ritterlich befreit ich dann
Die Prinzessin Fisch
Sie war gar zu obligeant
Führte mich zu Tisch
Und ich war galant.

Und ihr Kuß war Himmelsbrot,
Glühend wie der Wein
Ach ich liebte fast mich tot
(e)   Rings mit Sonnenschein
War sie emailliert.

Ach wer hat sie mir entführt?
Hielt kein Zauberband
Ihr verrätrisch Fliehn?
Sagt, wo ist ihr Land
(f)   Wo der Weg dahin?[12]

THE MODERN AMADIS

When I was still a boy
They shut me in

And so I sat for years
Wrapped in myself alone
(a) As if in the womb.

But you were my amusement
Golden Fantasy
And I became a warm hero,
(b) Like Prince Pipi
And wandered throughout the world.

Built crystal castles
And destroyed them too.
(c) Cast my shining shot
(d) Through the dragon's belly.
Yes, I was a man!

Courtly I freed then
Princess Fish.
She was, oh, so obliging,
Led me to her table,
And I was gallant.

And her kiss was heaven's bread,
Glowing like wine—
Oh, I loved till I nearly died—
(e) All around with sunshine
Was she glazed.

Oh, who stole her from me?
Did no magic bond restrain
Her treacherous flight?
Tell me, where is her land,
(f) Where is the path that leads there?

~

There is something suspiciously mechanical, I admit, about my use of "Der neue Amadis": it demonstrates rather too easily the general sociohistorical thesis regarding the linkage of poetic imagination to infantile sexuality and thereby transforms the poetic text into banality. In defense of this reductive critical gesture, however, it should be noted that the text itself evinces a reductive, banalizing tendency. "Der neue Amadis" is, in fact, a caricature: it maintains a satiric distance from its central problematic (the sexualization of specularity); its symbolization is deliberately simplistic and underdetermined, obeying the rigid formula $x = y$; its lexicon is mockingly parodic.[13] In fact, the real interest and energy of this text lie not so much in the act of saying as in the act of denegation (Freudian *Verneinung*) it performs. By naming the speaker a "modern Amadis," Goethe equates him with a literary figure who since Cervantes has signified vacuous fictionality, a fantasy life that has no connection with reality. It is as if the title were to proclaim: "What follows here is a pathology, a curiosity of the day, and has no connection with me." The body of the poem continues this strategy on another semantic plane by suggesting that the narcissistic subject is simply someone who never matured. In other words, the poem relies on an implicit value of 'manhood', a value that inevitably requires stabilization through acts of rejection and denial.

"Der neue Amadis" reveals, then, that a lyric text which merely reproduces social codifications pays for such conformity with triviality. The sociocultural frame sketched out with regard to Wieland's *Agathon*, in other words, is not a generative matrix capable of determining texts of poetic merit, and when such determination does occur, the result is aesthetically disappointing. This is not to say, of course, that poetic writing occurs independently of the codes and practices that constitute its context. On the contrary, precisely these codes provide the raw material of poetic production. But the poetic text achieves its status as poetic by fracturing them, carrying them to extremes, exposing their inner contradictions. The relation between poetic text and cultural context is not one of reproduction, but rather of excess: in its overcoding, in its surabundance of signification, the poetic text destabilizes normative linkages of meaning, disfigures standardized images, and reveals new possibilities of symbolization. Thus, rather than repeating the familial code, the finest of Goethe's texts experiment with it, submit it to a kind of trial in which its inner tensions are explored and brought to a breaking point. In this process, the agon inhabiting symbolization is suffered; the pathos of the speaking being becomes legible.

Nowhere is this clearer than with regard to the sexualized specular structure. To begin examining this, let us look at a text whose tonality and affective timbre depart from all the texts by Goethe considered thus far. Like "Der neue Amadis," it is not a great piece of poetic writing; its execution is deliberately casual, even careless; its point, in every sense of the word, blunt. No doubt this is why the poem has received little attention. But in its double promiscuity of craft and content, the text does engage central issues of the young Goethe's writing, and it does so with an obviousness that we can gratefully exploit.

9. AUF CRISTIANEN R.

Hab oft einen dummen düstern Sinn
Ein gar so schweres Blut,
Wenn ich bei meiner Cristel bin
Ist alles wieder gut.
(5) Ich seh sie dort, ich seh sie hier
Und weiß nicht auf der Welt
Und wie und wo und wann sie mir
Warum sie mir gefällt.

Das schwarze Schelmen Aug dadrein
(10) Die schwarze Braunen drauf,
Seh ich ein einzigmal hinein
Die Seele geht mir auf.
Was sie so gar einen süßen Mund
Liebrunde Wänglein hat.
(15) Ach und es ist noch etwas rund
Da sieht kein Aug sich satt.

Und wenn ich sie denn fassen darf
Im lüftgen deutschen Tanz
Da gehts herum da gehts so scharf
(20) Da fühl ich mich so ganz
Und wenn's ihr tummlig wird und warm
Da wieg ich sie sogleich
An meiner Brust in meinem Arm
Ist mir ein Königreich.

(25) Und wenn sie liebend nach mir Blickt
Und alles rings vergißt
Und dann an meine Brust gedrückt
Und weidlich eins geküßt
Das lauft mir durch das Rückenmark
(30) Bis in die große Zeh
Ich bin so schwach ich bin so stark
Mir ist so wohl so weh.

Da möcht ich mehr und immer mehr
Der Tag wird mir nicht lang
(35) Wenn ich die Nacht auch bei ihr wär

Davor wär mir nicht bang.
Ich denk ich fasse sie einmal
Und büße meine Lust
Und endigt sich nicht meine Qual
(40) Sterb ich an ihrer Brust.[14]

ON CRISTIANE R.

I often have a dumb dark sense
A much too sluggish blood;
When I'm with my Cristel
Everything is good again.
(5) I see her there, I see her here
And don't know in this world
And how and where and when she—
Why she pleases me so.

Her black, rascally eye there,
(10) The black eyebrows above,
If I look in just once
My soul opens up.
What a sweet mouth,
Such love-round cheeks she has.
(15) Oh, and there is something else round,
No eye can gaze there enough.

And when I'm allowed to take hold of her
In the airy German dance,
It spins around, it moves so swiftly,
(20) Then I feel myself so whole.
And when she gets dizzy and warm,
I cradle her right away
On my breast, in my arms,
It's a king's realm to me.

(25) And when she lovingly to me Looks
And forgets everything around,
And then pressed to my breast
And given a rich kiss,
Then it courses through my spine
(30) Right into my big toe,
I'm so weak, I'm so strong,
To me such bliss, such ache!

> Then I would like more and still more,
> The day doesn't seem long to me,
> (35) If I were also with her for the night
> I wouldn't be afraid.
> I think I'll take hold of her sometime
> And pay for my desire
> And if my torment then didn't end
> (40) I'd die at her breast.

Obvious, first of all, is the close connection between the figuration of this text and that of the three poems by Goethe discussed in the first two chapters. Compare, for example, the neutralization of knowledge hinging on the threefold repetition of the verb "wissen" in "Ob ich Dich liebe" (Text 1) with what occurs in lines 6–8. Or note the proximity between the central specular phase of that poem and the specular exchange we encounter here in lines 11–12. Recall, finally, the experience of wholeness attained in "Mir schlug das Herz" (Text 5, 19), which has its counterpart here in the line "Da fühl ich mich so ganz" (20). Clearly our text is a reworking of the same imaginary material we found in the Sesenheim songs.

This redaction, however, does not leave the central poetic locus of those songs unchanged. In "Auf Cristianen R." the specular moment initiated by the verb "Blickt" (25), capitalized in the manuscript, passes over into a corporeal and sexual rendering that skirts the obscene. Before addressing this transformation—the sexualization of specularity—directly, we should note the cultural context within which this eroticization is accomplished. The scenic frame of the poetic fantasy is mentioned in line 18: "Im lüftgen deutschen Tanz." We are dealing not with the folk dance that is the background of "Maifest" (Text 2), but rather with a specifically modern dance, the German waltz, historically the first social dance in which a full corporeal embrace is permitted, which removes the dancing dyad from the group and accords it full autonomy. It would be hard to imagine a cultural practice that more pointedly exemplifies the general transformation of love taking place in the last third of the eighteenth century, the process Niklas Luhmann calls the separating out (*Ausdifferenzierung*) of intimacy, its crystallization into an autonomous functional sphere within the social system.[15] Thus, it is no accident that in the novel by Goethe that Roland Barthes rightly saw as the broken encyclopedia of Romantic love the same dance provides one of the key events binding the protagonist to the *imago* of his beloved.[16] Note that on that occasion the dance stimulates the same sense of "world loss" as in the poem ("und alles rings vergißt," 26):

> Nie ist mir's so leicht vom Flecke gegangen. Ich war kein Mensch mehr. Das liebenswürdigste Geschöpf in den Armen zu haben und mit ihr herumzufliegen wie Wetter, daß alles rings umher verging, und—Wilhelm, um ehrlich zu sein, tat ich den Schwur, daß ein Mädchen, das ich liebte, auf das ich Ansprüche hätte, mir nie mit einem andern walzen sollte als mit mir, und wenn ich drüber zugrunde gehen müßte.[17]

> Never before did I move so lightly. I was no longer a human being. To have the dearest creature in my arms and to fly about with her like a storm so that everything around us disappeared, and—Wilhelm, to be honest, I swore in that moment that a girl that I loved and on whom I had claims would never waltz with anyone other than me, even if it would mean my end.

Needless to say, *Die Leiden des jungen Werther* (*The Sorrows of Young Werther*, 1774) has none of the sexual explicitness of "Auf Cristianen R."; the novel's hero writes his letters and experiences his love under the strictest self-censorship, a censorship marked here in the dash that breaks off the narrative account of the dance at precisely that point where the poem spills over into graphicness. But we can nevertheless assume that it is the eroticized atmosphere of the new dance form from which the novel here draws its transgressive energy, and which prompts Werther's jealous oath. Indeed, just three years prior to the publication of *Werther* the sexual connotations of the waltz could still be registered as a scandal, as the following passage from Sophie LaRoche's novel *Geschichte des Fräulein von Sternheim* (*History of Miss Sternheim*) reveals. The speaker (rather, the author of the letter) is the hypermoral Seymour, who must look on as the rakish Prince dances with the novel's heroine:

> The deepest pain was in my soul when I heard her sing and saw her dance the minuet with the Prince and others. But when he embraced her around her body [*um den Leib faßte*], pressed her to his breast [*an seine Brust drückte*] and hopped along at her side in the amoral, obscene German whirlwind dance with an intimacy that ripped apart all the bonds of decorum—my quiet melancholy was transformed into burning rage.[18]

A strongly marked sexual connotation inheres, then, in the cultural frame of the "German dance," a dance of two (as opposed to a group dance), a dance of the embrace (as opposed to a dance of pose, greeting, constellation), a dance of intimacy (as opposed to theatrical display). Goethe's poem brings this connotation to the foreground and exploits it for its own ends. How? Through a comic treatment in which the technique of corporeal specification predominates. Just as the eye of the beloved here becomes a "Schelmen Aug" (9), the text in general has something "schelmisch" about it, a rascally tonality. The poem, quite simply, is an off-color joke.

In Freud's analysis, such jokes (the tendentious *Zote* or dirty joke) are a device for obviating the socially and culturally imposed censorship regarding matters sexual. They accomplish this end through the techniques of *Witzarbeit*, principally that of substitutive displacement:

> The dirty joke becomes witty [*witzig*] and is only tolerated so long as it is witty. The technical means it uses in most cases is allusion, that is: the substitution of something small [*Ersetzung durch ein Kleines*], something located in a distant connection, which the listener reconstructs in his mental representation [*Vorstellen*] as a full and direct obscenity. The greater the disproportion between what is directly given in the dirty joke and what is necessarily excited in the listener, the more elegant [*feiner*] the joke becomes, and the higher it can hazard its way [*sich hinaufwagen*] into proper society [*gute Gesellschaft*].[19]

Certainly the major thrust, so to speak, of our text is to affront the moralized discursive space Freud calls "gute Gesellschaft," and it does this precisely through the obviousness of its displacements. Hence its rascally tone, its antic jocularity. But the text employs displacements nonetheless, either through circumscription (the unmentioned breasts whose fullness exceeds—and here the ocular passes over into the register of orality—every demand for satiety, 15–16) or through substitution ("große Zeh" for "erection," 30). Insofar as the text employs such techniques of *Witz*, insofar as it operates with a displaced obscenity, it is conditioned by the force of social-moral censorship. Indeed, as a joke it has—this is the lesson of Freud—such censorship as one of its constitutive moments.

I will return shortly to this question of censorship, of the intervention of a social Other, but first I want to look more closely at the restructuring process that takes place when the specular moment is sexualized. Here are the decisive lines:

> Und wenn sie liebend nach mir Blickt
> Und alles rings vergißt

> Und dann an meine Brust gedrückt
> Und weidlich eins geküßt
> Das läuft mir durch das Rückenmark
> Bis in die große Zeh   *(25–30)*

The union of lover and beloved within the dance, the union that in the earlier texts was solely an exchange of looks, solely specular, is here structured as a line of communication, of transmission, running from the maiden to the speaker. The stages through which this communication passes are arranged in the following sequence:

maiden——"Blick"——corporeal contact ("an . . . Brust gedrückt")——kiss——path through "Rückenmark"——"große Zeh"

Summarily paraphrased, the sequence is, of course, banal and puerile: "When I dance with her and look into her eyes, when I squeeze her and give her a kiss, it makes me so hot that I get a hard-on." The strategy of affront this text practices is to solicit from the reader this all too obvious reconstruction of "full and direct obscenity" (Freud). But, if we remain at this level of paraphrase, allowing the lurid fruits of our reconstruction either to titillate or to embarrass us, the joke will really be on us; we will remain its captives, which is to say the captives of the code of sexuality it sets into place. This is the situation of traditional Goethe criticism with its uneasy tolerance of the young Goethe's excesses. To move beyond this form of uncomprehending comprehension requires that we consider the erotic sequence around which the poem is organized not as a paraphrasable content, but rather as a symbolic structure and operation.

Perhaps the best way to start an analysis of the sexual mini-myth the stanza unfolds is to note that its narrative syntagmatics almost exactly conforms to that of classical erotic poetry, which inevitably and by explicit convention follows the recipe: *visus, allocutio, tactus, basium, coitus.*[20] The classical sequence charts a strategy of seduction, a method of conquest; its terminus is the sexual possession of a woman conceived as other, a figure who may or may not resist, whose defenses must be broken down. One might say, then, that Goethe's text transforms this structure in such a way as to eliminate its martial connotations. In "Auf Cristianen R." we are no longer dealing with a series of calculated steps viewed from the detached (though not dispassionate!) standpoint of the connoisseur, no longer with an *ars erotica*, a technique, but rather with the sudden emergence of desire across a chain, let us say, of automatic "firings."

The sequence isolated above, then, represents the internalization of the classical erotic schema, its removal from the observable and social domain of seduction and its relocation within the subject, where it produces the truth of the subject's desire.[21] Note in this regard the alterations the classical sequence undergoes: the moment of *visus*, which is traditionally a kind of sighting, is drawn into the internality of the specular *Blick*; the moment of *allocutio* falls away, in conformity with everything that has been said above regarding the silence and asociality of the specular exchange; and finally the moment of *coitus* is postponed and the text pauses at what might be termed the extreme point of desire. This desire itself, in the sweet agony of unfulfillment, is the text's real focus of interest, not the accomplished erotic conquest. This point becomes forcefully clear if we recall what was obvious from the beginning: that the path running from the maiden across look, embrace, and kiss to the "große Zeh" is a path of communicative transmission. What is communicated along this path is precisely the desire which the toe/erection at once expresses and bears witness to. (Note here that the meaning 'erection' is doubly marked, primarily through the "große Zeh," and secondarily because "Rückenmark" connotes 'manly rigidity'. As it were, the entire body becomes turgid; the toe is merely the tip, the extremity, of a corporeal erection.) The maiden gives something to the subject, and this act of giving, this originary donation, is a charge, in the double sense in which we say a battery is charged (energy transfer) and a committee is charged (symbolic transfer of power). The communication within the sexualized specular moment is a flow of energy that empowers the male subject, gives him the gift of the phallus.

The loins of our text, its slightly obscene central lines, bear, then, a symbolic operation of some complexity, an operation that structures the field of sexuality according to a specific array of cultural values. (This suggests that Freud's "full and direct obscenity" is not the truth of the joke-text, but merely one of its effects.) No doubt these values are closely connected with the general recodification of intimacy that is taking place in the late eighteenth century, with the implosion of the family onto the parent/child nucleus, and with the production of infantile sexuality in reformist pedagogy from Rousseau on. From this perspective, the difference between the sequence of sexual charging Goethe's text enacts and the seduction sequence of classical erotic poetry is especially interesting. In the latter, the phallus, as the mark of sexual/martial power, is, as it were, an a priori of maleness, and the woman is merely the object on whom that power is exercised. In Goethe's text, however, the phallus is received as a gift emanating from a female source. His reinterpretation (in Nietzsche's sense once again) of the classical erotic schema—a schema which, of course, was still operative in the Anacreontic poetry of the mid-eighteenth century—amounts to nothing less than a matrilinear recoding of sexuality.

In view of the readings worked out in the first two chapters, this is hardly surprising. The specular moment inevitably figures the female as Source; in addition to its ocular exchange, it involves a flow of liquidity and energy between "Ich" and "Du"; and this exchange is also a gift: "Die Du mir Jugend / Und Freud und Mut / / Zu neuen Liedern, / Und Tänzen gibst!" (Text 2, 31–34; emphasis added). Moreover, the texts by Novalis and Hoffmann figuring specularity prompted the suspicion that the spec-ular moment can be read as a narcissistic self-investment enfolded within the mother/child dyad and having the phallus as its phantasmatic center. "Auf Cristianen R." not only confirms that to compare Goethe's texts with those of his Romantic successors is pertinent, it also demonstrates that the sexualization of specularity accomplished in early texts by Goethe con-forms to a similar, narcissistic pattern. It is no accident, then, that in the poem at hand the speaker's entire body is charged; the narcissistic *Wunsch* of auto-engenderment is the dream that I am—not that I merely have—the phallus.

The transformation of the specular moment I am tracing here—its sexualization—brings to the fore the phallic component that earlier Goe-thean examples of specularity kept submerged. This shift, this rendering explicit of sexuality, has a further consequence: it shatters the idyllic sense of fulfillment that characterized the Sesenheim songs. Just as Agathon's pristine love of Psyche bends toward transgression as soon as the beloved object assumes corporeality (Pythia, Danae), so too in Goethe the inno-cence of "Maifest" becomes problematic when the question of a real sexual union arises. Thus, at exactly the moment the word "große Zeh" is mentioned, the narrative of communicative charging breaks off and the divided condition of blocked desire seizes semantic control:

> Ich bin so schwach ich bin so stark
> Mir ist so wohl so weh!   *(31–32)*

This unfulfillment is the crux of the poem, the axis around which it turns from the obviousness of its joking to the mystery of its end.

To chart the angle of this poetic turn, it is helpful to compare the text once again with the version of specularity we find in "Ob ich Dich liebe" (Text 1). That poem embeds the specular moment within a conditional when/then construction: "when I see you, then my heart is freed." "Auf Cristianen R." unfolds as an expansion and variation of this syntactic structure (which, as we shall discover in the next chapter, Goethe also relies on in "Künstlers Morgenlied"):

> Wenn ich bei meiner Cristel bin
> Ist alles wieder gut. *(3–4)*
>
> Seh ich ein einzigmal hinein
> Die Seele geht mir auf. *(11–12)*
>
> Und wenn ich sie denn fassen darf
> Da gehts herum . . . *(17, 19)*
>
> Und wenn's ihr tummlig wird und warm
> Da wieg ich sie sogleich *(21–22)*
>
> Und wenn sie liebend nach mir Blickt
> Das läuft mir durch das Rückenmark *(25, 29)*

This set of conditional constructions forms the syntactic scaffolding of the poem, which thus progresses as an intensifying series of partial fulfillments, euphoric events that repeatedly occur. But in the final stanza, the when/then formula (which now must be translated if/then) operates along a different vector, evoking an unreal or counterfactual condition:

> Wenn ich die Nacht auch bei ihr wär
> Davor wär mir nicht bang. *(35–36)*

And this counterfactual is followed by the thought of a future possibility, the realization of which seems more than unlikely:

> Ich denk ich fasse sie einmal
> Und büße meine Lust *(37–38)*

This alteration of the syntactic figure from a real to an unreal conditional abruptly halts the accumulation of intensity achieved across the first four stanzas and, in doing so, splits the universe of the poem. Whereas the first part of the text offers us the homogeneous world of the events prior to and within the dance, the final stanza projects a world which is sheerly an object of thought, bifurcating the text into two opposed semantic subdomains (say, real vs. wished for). Clearly, some sort of interruption, blockage, or deflection has occurred. But why? And what is its agency?

An answer to these questions emerges when we consider the following juxtaposition:

> Und wenn ich sie denn fassen darf
> Im lüftgen deutschen Tanz   *(17–18)*
>
> Ich denk ich fasse sie einmal   *(37)*

The dance—recall the erotic connotations of the waltz—is a sociocultural sphere in which the normally proscribed embrace (*fassen*) is allowed to take place symbolically. Within this space, the subject can claim union with the beloved and the gift of the phallus; it can regress, in the fantasy sustained by the dance's movement and corporeal contact, to the original event of that donation, that specular charge; and in doing so, it can attain to the status of an autonomous lawgiver: "Ist mir ein Königreich" (24). The dance is the space where the world, as a field of alterity, responsibility, heteronomy, disappears—the space of the absolute dyad. Indeed, Werther and Lotte, to recall the other dancers that appear in this early phase of Goethe's oeuvre, even come to occupy their own cosmos ("herumzufliegen wie Wetter").

But this fulfillment is only a symbolic achievement, circumscribed and tolerated by the very force of social normativity (and censorship) that prevents its translation into action. Thus, Werther soon encounters the raised finger of authority; the voice of a social "No" names the man to whom, by law, Lotte is bound. And this "No" (the *non du pere*, as we know from Wieland[22]) is marked in our text in the modal auxiliary "darf" that qualifies the verb of erotic embrace ("fassen"). However intensely the dancing subject might fancy itself a king, the law that determines its desire comes from elsewhere. Circumscribed from without, the specular fantasy is also fractured within, inscribed with the force of negation. In "Auf Cristianen R.," the fissuring power lurking in the word *darf* emerges in all its virulence in the final stanza, which splits the poem's semantic universe in two. This process of semantic incision, let us recall, begins to show itself in the antonyms of the fourth stanza's final two lines ("schwach"/"stark"; "wohl"/"weh"). That is to say, at precisely the moment ("große Zeh") when the subject claims for itself the status of the phallus, the social Other forcefully asserts its constraint, displacing the coital union onto a sheerly optative plane and bending the jocularity of the text toward an almost Petrarchan tonality (love as a torment unto death) in the final two lines. From the standpoint of social and moral normativity, the phantasm of the phallic self is both transgressive and regressive, as is a poetic practice that simulates and stimulates that phantasm. The specular union with the beloved is, without question, a station on the amorous itinerary of the Romantic subject, but a station where that subject is forbidden to abide. The attachment must be severed (like the universe of our poem), and the subject, untethered, must begin its peregrinations through loss (cf. "Der neue Amadis"). The poetic subject becomes a wanderer, a pilgrim, seeking an Origin, the primordial donation, that always lies in the unreachable depths of the past.

~

In the circle of "sensitive souls" (*Empfindsamen*) with which Goethe associated in 1772 in Darmstadt and Homburg, the poet called himself "wanderer" and "pilgrim." The group included Goethe's closest male friends at the time, Herder and Johann Heinrich Merck, Herder's fiancée Caroline Flachsland, and a small number of other figures, including a lady-in-waiting from the Homburg court named Luise Henriette von Ziegler. This last was known in the circle, which had developed its own alternative onomastics, by the name of Lila, and it was to her that Goethe, following his departure from Darmstadt to Wetzlar, sent three poems, each of which was addressed to one of the ladies of the group. By far the most accomplished of these three poems is the one addressed to Lila herself. Since traditional Goethe scholarship has left the poem relatively untouched, offering no more, really, than an identification of the real-life Lila and the inevitable note that the tower mentioned in the text refers to the tower of the Homburg castle, I shall attend to its poetic figuration in some detail. As I hope to show, the text is imbued with the sexual problematic that emerges within the sexualized specular moment.

10. PILGERS MORGENLIED
an Lila

MorgenNebel, Lila,
Hüllen deinen Turm um.
Soll ich ihn zum
Letzten mal nicht sehn!
(5)   Doch mir schweben

Tausend Bilder
Seliger Erinnerung
Heilig warm um's Herz,
Wie er so stand
(10) Zeuge meiner Wonne,
Als zum ersten mal
Du den Fremdling
Ängstlich liebevoll
Begegnetest,
(15) Und mit einem mal
Ew'ge Flammen
In die Seel' ihm warfst.

Zische Nord
Tausend schlangenzüngig
(20) Mir ums Haupt!
Beugen sollst du's nicht!
Beugen magst du
Kind'scher Zweige Haupt,
Von der Sonne
(25) Muttergegenwart geschieden.

Allgegenwärt'ge Liebe!
Durchglühst mich,
Beutst dem Wetter die Stirn,
Gefahren die Brust,
(30) Hast mir gegossen
In's frühwelkende Herz
Doppeltes Leben,
Freude zu leben,
Und Mut.[23]

PILGRIM'S MORNING SONG
for Lila

Morning clouds, Lila,
Cover your tower;
Will I not see it
This last time!
(5) But there hover
A thousand images
Of blissful memory
Holy, warm about my heart,

How it stood so
(10) Witness of my delight,
When the first time
You encountered,
Frightened, loving,
The stranger,
(15) And all at once
Cast eternal flames
Into his soul.

Hiss, North Wind,
Thousand snake tongued,
(20) Around my head!
You shall not bow it!
You may bow
The heads of childish branches,
Separated from the sun's
(25) Maternal presence.

All-present Love!
You glow through me,
You turn my brow against the weather,
My breast against dangers.
(30) You have poured
Into the early-wilting heart
A double life,
Joy to live,
And courage.

The text deploys a rigorously symmetrical but intricately entwined skein of correspondences that begins to emerge into view when we consider its large-scale compositional patterns. On the temporal plane, the poem is spoken out of a moment of departure, a "last time" ("zum / Letzten mal," 3–4), which hesitates at the point of severance between past and future. (Note how the temporal cut of the departure is enacted in the line division that splits the temporal marker.) From within this moment, which is one of acute crisis, the subject recalls a point of origin, a "first time" ("zum ersten mal," 11) enclosed within the unity and oneness of its sudden apparition ("mit einem mal," 15). (This moment of origination, standing out, in its temporal self-enclosure, from the rest of time, is a version of the specular moment; its "einem mal" repeats that of "Seh ich nur einmal dein Gesicht, / Seh Dir ins Auge nur einmal"; Text 1, 2–3.) The memory—and this text encapsulates a whole theory of memory, of "Seliger Erinnerung" (7)—of the first time enables the subject to return to the present of departure, but now with a resolve and assurance that make possible mastery of the initial crisis (18–25). Following this passage from present to past (origin) and back to the present, this exercise in crisis management, the third stanza maintains itself in an eternal present, a perpetuity, which knows itself as having derived from the originary event and which extends forward toward the challenges of the future. That is, the poem closes by assuming a supratemporal perspective, by taking up a position within the domain of the universal in which all the temporal dimensions, sundered by departure at the beginning of the text, are knit together.

The compositional precision of the text is also revealed in the deployment of general thematic material. Thus, the first four lines speak of a threat to the subject, a threat figured as a visual blockage ("nicht sehn," 4) and caused by the intervention of a "meteorological instance" ("Nebel," 1). The next four lines, introduced by the pivot word "Doch" (5), register a resistance to that threat, a resistance that stems not from the subject's own agency, but rather from the thousand images of blessed memory that warm—thereby countering the connoted coldness of the weather—his heart. There follows a third section, consisting of nine lines, that recalls the content all those images convey, the singular event they refer to and bring back. This nine-line phase is the axial segment of the text, its turn from crisis to resolve. Thus, the next four lines (18–21) recur to the theme resistance to threat, with the threatening meteorological agency now exhibiting a more virulent form (the "North Wind," 18) and with the resistance itself now emanating from the subject's own manly uprightness (21). Another four-line segment then states once again the theme of threat in departure with which the poem began. Here, however, that threat is displaced onto a group other than the subject. It affects only the "childish branches" (23) cut off or 'de-parted' ("geschieden," 25) from the "maternal presence" of the sun (24–25). The text then concludes with a nine-line section, its third stanza, which at its very center (30) refers back to the event recounted in the nine-line axial phase of the first stanza and extracts the supratemporal meaning of that event for the subject. The poem is thereby sealed off with an auto-interpretation that relocates the remem-

Section	Number of Lines	Theme	Temporality
A-1 (1–4)	4	threat	
			present of departure
B-1 (5–8)	4	resistance	
C-1 (9–17)	9	specular encounter	past moment of origin
B-2 (18–21)	4	resistance	
			present of departure
A-2 (22–25)	4	threat	
C-2 (26–34)	9	specular encounter interpreted	synthetic time

Schema 5: Structure of "Pilgers Morgenlied"

bered event at its center in the dimension of the universal. This compositional structure is shown in Schema 5.

The process this schematic model of the poem's composition begins—but just begins—to suggest reveals that "Pilgers Morgenlied" is not exhausted by simple referentiality, that it is not merely a document of some purported biographical incident. Rather, the compositional structure exhibits the blueprint of a symbolic process, a process organized according to a chiastic pattern (*A*-1, *B*-1, *C*-1, *B*-2, *A*-2), with a recapitulation of the axial *C* segment in the final stanza. Moreover, the process that unfolds across this chiastic armature draws on and ramifies certain *symbolic constants* of Goethe's early poetry generally. Thus, it could be shown that the text works through some of the same imaginative material as "Wandrers Sturmlied," in which the subject about whom certain figures 'hover' ("umschweben") likewise experiences an internal warmth, in which the antagonist is meteorological in character, and in which an inner "Glühen" provides the basis of the subject's self-assurance. (See Chapter 5.) Perhaps even more remarkable are the filiations that link this text to "Mir schlug das Herz" (Text 5). In that poem, too, we encounter the terms "Freude," "Mut," and "glühen" (nominalized as "Glut"), central to Goethe's poetic lexicon; and the tower of "Pilgers Morgenlied" is echoed, or anticipated, in the figure of the "aufgetürmter Riese" (Text 5, 6). In fact, both texts share the same general processual structure: the initial threat or crisis of vision associated with a departure; the specular encounter alleviating that threat; and the final *Aufhebung*—in the threefold Hegelian sense of negation, elevation, and preservation—of the specular structure within the element of universality.

In view of these constants we might say that, rather than providing the source of the poem, the biographical details (the Homburg tower, the person named Lila) are utterly secondary. Like the *Tagesreste* (remainders from the day's experience) in Freud's dream analyses, they are meaningful only insofar as they are functionally integrated into the text's symbolic complex, only insofar as they can be invested so as to figure elements of the text's conflictual desire. Not that every text says the same thing. Variations, shifts of emphasis, even reversals of valorization are possible. For instance, the tower in "Pilgers Morgenlied" is not, as in "Mir schlug das Herz," a threatening agency, but rather the object to which the threat, marked in both texts by "Nebel," is directed. The invariant element tower—an element occurring also in the poem "Auf dem See" ("On the Lake") and in the lyrical essay "Von deutscher Baukunst" ("On German Architecture"; see Chapter 5)—allows for both positive and negative investments much as the snake in Hoffmann's "The Golden Jar" is both the diminutive "Schlänglein" with which the male subject narcissistically identifies and the "Riesenschlange" that terrifies the subject with the threat of castration. But the biographical reading not only reduces the text to the expression of a punctual occasion and thereby blocks an analysis of the overriding regularities elaborated in and governing Goethe's poetic production; by attaching the poetic elements univocally to a real-world referent, it furnishes them with a stability and identity that obscures their essential lability and multivalence, their essential non-essentiality, one might say, the surabundance of significance that disperses their noematic core. A cigar or tower, to be sure, is sometimes just a cigar or tower, but not in a poetic text of this caliber and disseminating energy.

My reading, then, pursues a double task: to describe the overriding symbolic structures "Pilgers Morgenlied" shares with other texts in Goethe's corpus and to unleash from its referential mooring the play of significance the text sets into motion. I start with the tower and its penumbra of associations. In poetic readings, the free associations Freud elicited from himself and his patients must be extracted from the text and from its intertexts. The tower is covered by the "morning clouds" (or fog), and its nonvisibility is experienced by the subject as a threat. This "um" ('around') endows the tower with a semantic marker of centrality, a marker it shares with the "Herz" ('heart') of line 8 and with the "Haupt" ('head') of line 20. The heart returns in line 31, where it is described as having been—prior to the assurance and self-certainty the subject has acquired in the course of the text—"frühwelkend" ('early wilting'). This qualification associates the heart with plants, which make their appearance in the text as the saplings implied in the phrase "Kind'scher Zweige" ('childish branches,' 23). These branches, too, have a "Haupt," but one which, unlike that of the poetic subject, "bows" under the assault of the threatening meteorological instance. All these associative paths—and, of course, others could be followed—turn back into each other and knot into certain groupings and juxtapositions:

(a) the tower, marked by centrality and verticality, threatened by a meteorological agency that surrounds it, rendering it invisible . . .

(b) the heart—the center of the poetic subject—which was once wilting (that is, lacking in vital force), which furthermore is now warmed because surrounded by images . . .

(c) the "Haupt," which is either upright (sharing the verticality and centrality of the tower) or bowed (as in wilting), that is, either possessed of manly rigidity in the face of the meteorological threat which surrounds it or childishly yielding to that threat . . .

Can there be any doubt that the series "Turn"–"Herz"–"Haupt"–'tree'– 'poetic subject' also includes the element 'phallus'? The answer, of course, is no, but only if the term 'phallus' is understood as a symbolic position defined by its function in relation to the other positions in the series. The text does not refer to sexuality as if to an anatomical domain; rather, it organizes sexuality, inscribes it within a code of values, institutes it by establishing its myth. The phallus is not the truth of the text, it is a component of its lie.

To trace further the intricacies of the sexual myth condensed in the text, it is useful to refer back to the discussion of "Auf Cristianen R.," where, of course, similar cautions regarding referential paraphrase were raised. That text enacts a matrilinear encoding of sexuality, an encoding revealed in the sexualized specular moment as a gift of the phallus from the beloved to the amorous subject. This gift allows the subject to claim for itself the status of the phallus, to assert its identity as an erect phallic self, which assertion, however, immediately calls forth the intervention of a social Other not actually figured in the text but nevertheless legible in the severence of the poem's semantic universe. In "Pilgers Morgenlied" we encounter a similar pattern, although with two significant variations: first, the antagonistic Other appears within the textual figuration as a "meteorological instance"; second, rather than ending in a state of unresolved anguish, the text seems to work through to an affirmative solution of its problematic. These two factors, along with the matrilinear code the two texts share, allow us to perceive the specific contours of the sexual myth it creates. That myth, in a word, is one of castration.

Consider the threat of nonvisibility articulated at the outset of the text:

> Morgen Nebel, Lila,
> Hüllen deinen Turn um.
> Soll ich ihn zum
> Letzten mal nicht sehn!
>
> *(1–4)*

The tower is Lila's, a metonymy of her presence, and its invisibility aggravates the anguish of departure: such is the reading in the semantic register 'the pilgrim's wanderings', the isotopy suggested by the title. But what is a departure? Is it not the repetition of a primordial crisis of separation, of a paradigmatic experience of severence that is reenacted every time a subject is torn from a beloved object or place? This is precisely what the end of the second stanza suggests in its evocation of the heads of the childish branches, which bow before the threatening onslaught of the north wind because they are "Von der Sonne / Muttergegenwart ge-schieden" (24–25). The separation from Lila, figured in the invisibility of the tower (so that not even the metonymy of her presence is visually available to the subject), reenacts the child's severence from the Mother. A third instance seems to have imposed itself between mother and child, blocking the light of her solar presence, the light that gives growth and life—and therefore uprightness—to the branches of the tree.

But this severence allows for a second reading. If the tower is hers—Lila's—in other than a metonymic sense, if it belongs to her as an attribute of her being, then its invisibility marks a crisis of a different sort: the discovery that she (Lila, the Mother) does not possess, or no longer possesses, the phallus. This discovery on the part of the male child, combined with an experienced or remembered threat that bears on its own sexual explorations, coalesces into what Freud refers to as the "infantile sexual theory" of castration, the potentially terrifying idea that this difference where sameness was assumed, expected, and wished for is the result of a punishing intervention.[24] Exactly this complex is legible in Goethe's text with its invisible tower, its intervening Other, its acute anxiety.

The explanatory myth of castration in Freud's theory is the complement to the child's narcissism, to its investment in a phallic version of self-identity, to its insistence on the law of the Same. The poetic locus of this narcissism is the specular moment, especially its sexualized or phallic variant, as in the phantasm of an erect phallic self in "Auf Cristianen R." (not to speak of Hoffmann and Novalis). Thus, it is no accident that, in the nine-line axial phase of the text's first stanza, the subject recovers from the initial threat by remembering the unity which presided prior to the break of departure. Here is the content of the subject's blessed memory:

> Wie er so stand
> Zeuge meiner Wonne,
> Als zum ersten mal
> Du den Fremdling
> Ängstlich liebevoll
> Begegnetest,
> Und mit einem mal
> Ew'ge Flammen
> In die Seel' ihm warfst.
>
> *(9–17)*

Here are all the elements of specularity: the ecstatic moment of encounter, the symmetrical structure pivoting around the revealing phrase "Ängstlich liebevoll" (the anxiety signals an element of transgression), the phenomenon of energy transfer that charges the subject with the "flames" of life and desire. And, as the focus of the specular exchange, we find, of course, the erect "Turn": "wie er so stand / Zeuge meiner Wonne." Is this her (Lila's) tower, as the anaphoric reference back to the opening lines would seem to indicate, or the speaker's, who, after all, experiences delight and receives into his "soul" (later interpreted as "heart," 31) the energizing flame? The answer is both. The fantasy effaces sexual difference with the hallucination of the maternal phallus that the subject longs to be.[25] Note especially the circulation of meaning set into motion by the word "Zeuge": First of all, as "witness" the tower sees everything; it is both subject and object of vision and light, which links it, of course, to the maternal sun named at the end of the stanza. Second—and this is also suggested by its status as "witness"—it bears testimony or provides a symbolic guarantee. Finally, because of its echo of the verb "zeugen," it alludes to generative-procreative power. The phallic tower is at once source and object of vision, symbolic testimony, and generative force, and in this functional conflation it holds the subject's fascination as the center of the specular phantasm.[26] Furthermore, the threat of castration figured in the other portions of the text is directed precisely at these three functional domains: first, the meteorological Other negates the visibility of the tower, its effect of visual presence; second, it assaults the symbolic testimony of uprightness, the rigidity that, as it were, stands in for manliness; and finally it attacks the principle of generativity, bringing about in those who remain dependent on the Mother a sort of saplessness, a wilting. Nothing could more elegantly reveal the complementarity of narcissism and castration than this perfect symmetry.[27]

There is a further aspect of Freud's theory of (the infantile theory of) castration which illuminates our text. In his note on Medusa, Freud showed that symbolizations—and we might add, poetic textualizations—of castration simultaneously represent several conflicting aspects of the complex and that, even as they have a terrifying effect, they also have a consoling one. They simultaneously affirm and deny castration, acknowledging the absence of the phallus, conflating this absence with the female genitals, while pluralizing the phallus and affirming its manly rigidity. To view the Gorgon is to experience the terror of her severed head and of the female sex, but at the same time to deny this horrifying vision in the rigidification of the body as stone.[28] I believe that this sort of interplay can be remarked in Goethe's text as well, which evokes Medusa in the lines: "Zische Nord / Tausend schlangenzüngig / Mir ums Haupt!" (18–20). The shifting, indeed contradictory logic of symbolization can be observed here in the migration of Medusan connotation among the three actants of the poetic scenario. By virtue of predication, the thousand snake tongues belong to the meteorological antagonist figure, but since these tongues would hiss "around my head," they serve to identify the poem's protagonist, the speaking subject, with the Gorgon's detached and snake-extruding head. Finally, via the numerical term 'thousand', a Medusan signification is attached to the beloved female object, the first encounter with whom the subject remembers in "A thousand images . . . Holy, warm about my heart." The poetic textualization, then, condenses all the positions within the castration scenario and sets them into an oscillating play of affirmation and denial. Within this play there is no certainty as to who is castrating and who is castrated, who is male and who female, who is self and who is other. This is the difference/indifference of sexuality I discussed in connection with Novalis and Hoffmann, the uncanny movement of the text that eludes the stability of identity and opposition.

"Pilgers Morgenlied," as I mentioned earlier, reworks the imaginary material of "Mir schlug das Herz." In both poems, an initial anxiety is coupled with departure and a threat to visibility; both assuage this anxiety by evoking the specular moment; and both conclude by preserving the specular encounter on the level of generality. In view of these similarities, a rereading of "Mir schlug das Herz" in terms of the problematics of narcissism and castration suggests itself. Recall that "Mir schlug das Herz" begins at a temporal threshold:

> Der Abend wiegte schon die Erde,
> Und an den Bergen hing die Nacht;
>
> *(3–4)*

The verb "wiegen" (cradle) can be read as evoking the childhood experience of going to sleep, a reading supported by the later occurrence of "schläfrig" (sleepy), the term that qualifies the moon's regard. The anxiety the poem unfolds across its first section, in other words, is that of the child exposed, abandoned to absence, to the night's darkness. This anxiety concretizes itself in the following figuration:

> Schon stund im Nebelkeid die Eiche,
> Ein aufgetürmter Riese, da,
> Wo Finsternis aus dem Gesträuche
> Mit hundert schwarzen Augen sah.
>
> *(5–8)*

Note the spatial specification that at once bridges and is broken by the separation between lines 6 and 7: "there," in the very place "where" darkness peers out of the bush, the "towering" tree rises up like some gigantic monster. This conflation of the threatening tower with the darkness within the bush, of phallic monstrosity and the vision of the female sex as absence, is a transform of the castration scenario played out in "Pilgers Morgenlied." The spatial conflation accomplished by the deictic gesture ("there"/"where") enacts a confusion of sexual markers (male/female, castrating/castrated) analogous to the uncanny movement of Medusan signification. Both texts, then, uncover a level of what might be termed anarchic symbolization: the dimension of an immemorial difference that shatters the subjective self-certainty based on the stability of the visual world.

In his study *Inhibition, Symptom, and Anxiety*, Freud writes: "In repression, the decisive fact is that the ego is an organization whereas the id is not; the ego is precisely the organized part of the id."[29] Ego organization, related to subjective self-certainty, relies on the repression of a fundamental disorganization. Anxiety appears when this disorganization announces itself, and in Freud's analysis this occurs first in the experience of separation and object loss, secondarily in castration anxiety.[30] Freud's argument can be applied to the two anxiety-ridden poems "Mir schlug das Herz" and "Pilgers Morgenlied" in the sense that both link anxiety to separation and departure, both imagine a scenario of castration, and both reveal, in the interstices of that scenario, a fundamental disorganization threatening subjective identity. The threat involved is inevitably figured as a loss of vision, as a disturbance of perception, and the reason for this is that perceptual representation is the medium in which ego organization is achieved. Again Freud: "The first condition of anxiety that the ego itself introduces is therefore anxiety at the loss of perception, which is equated with the anxiety of object loss."[31] Subjective identity, perception, self-representation as guaranteed by the perceived object (primarily the mother): this is the nexus of the specular moment. Both poems find in this poetic locus the Origin of poetic subjectivity. At the same time, however, both texts reveal that this Origin is, as Freud says, only a part ("Anteil"), that it is limited, and that this limit—this *limes* or wall—is porous to a dimension of alterity and difference that, anarchically, resists representational stability.

Even as the figure of castration shatters the self-certainty of narcissism and erupts with the uncanny difference/indifference of sexuality, it serves a restabilizing and socializing function. To pass through the crisis of the castration complex is, so to speak, to reduce the unmanageable complexity and dispersion of sexuality to a limited oppositional pair. Castration disguises or dissimulates the uncanny mobility and confusion of identity it sets into motion. As Jean Laplanche, synthesizing Freud and Heidegger, has argued, the infantile theory of castration is a way of mastering anxiety by providing that anxiety a concrete object and therewith a sort of intelligibility.[32] This domesticating function emerges clearly wherever we see the figure of castration assume the shape of a narrative, wherever it becomes a narrative operator in the formation, the *Bildung*, of the subject, wherever it casts the *angoisse* of alterity into the past and turns the subject toward a future. And, of course, "Pilgers Morgenlied" performs precisely this sort of narrativization. Recall the poem's temporal structure: spoken from a moment of departure and severence (the severence, perhaps, of time itself: "zum / Letzten mal," 3–4), it remembers an originary moment, and by doing so, by repeating the primordial donation of phallic identity in the inwardness of "Erinnerung," at once repels the anxiety of separation and affirms its necessity. This working through of the castration anxiety then discloses a futurity for the subject, which is evoked in the third stanza. The simultaneous separation from and preservation of the specular moment, this *Aufhebung* of the Mother's solar presence, is accomplished through a dual movement. On the one hand, the poetic subject, emerging from the remembered experience of specularity, appropriates for itself the male value of upright or heroic fortitude by casting off its anxiety onto an other: the sapless and clinging child, feminized by virtue of its adherence to the Mother. This gesture establishes a stable opposition between the realms of male and female and draws a narrative path of maturation leading from the latter to the former. The subject is now in a position to shift its narcissistic identification with the Mother onto an identification with a male antagonist figure, an equal against whom it will test itself on the field of destiny and whose desire it will simulate on the field of adult sexual love.

The second stabilizing operation guarantees the subject's accession to the dimension of the universal. The initial addressee, Lila, bound to particularity and corporeality by the force of the proper name, becomes in the second stanza the general term "Liebe" (26); the "Muttergegenwart" (25) to which the "childish" (the not-yet-manly) anxiously cling, becomes the "Allgegenwart" (26) of conceptuality, always accessible to the subject precisely because it is the element of subjective internality. The narrativization of the castration complex thus offers a consoling promise: renounce and you shall have, not in the dimension of the real, but rather in the dimension of meaning. In this dimension, time is no longer severed, but rather synthesized in the unity of a synoptic temporal consciousness. Lila's tower, through the very movement which casts off its female corporeality and particularity, has become the idea around which a male sociality can be organized. We are not far from the "Turmgesellschaft" (tower society) of Goethe's *Wilhelm Meisters Lehrjahre* (*Wilhelm Meisters Years of Apprenticeship*), the novel that, along with Wieland's *Agathon*, established the generic paradigm for the *Bildungsroman*.

§ 5 Genius and the Wounded Subject of Modernity

Goethe's poetry of the 1770's exhibits a strong affective investment in the theme of 'genius', a theme that is likewise prominent in his poetological and critical writings of the period. The term, of course, is not unique to Goethe; it possessed a banner function in the work of the *Sturm und Drang* and, beyond that local German movement, in Pre-Romantic and Romantic writings produced throughout Europe. One need only think of Edward Young's influential *Conjectures on Original Composition*, of the Kantian dictum that "beautiful art is the art of genius," or of the first French copyright law, proclaimed with revolutionary pathos by the National Assembly in its meeting of July 19, 1793, which based intellectual-literary property in "the rights of genius."[1] From Addison's 160th *Spectator* article to the aesthetic theory of Schopenhauer—that is, for more than a century—the term genius is ubiquitous in discourse on literature and art. Moreover, with few exceptions its penumbra of associations remains constant throughout the period: genius is the capacity of original artistic (or more broadly, cultural) production; the genius does not create according to prescribed rules, above all doesn't imitate; the genius is closely tied to nature. However outmoded the notion seems today, there can be little doubt that, for the Age of Goethe, 'genius' was a term charged (in the full sense of the word) with significance.

Despite its ubiquity, and despite extensive scholarship on the term, we really know very little about what genius is. To claim, as Jochen Schmidt's recent *History of the Thought of Genius 1750–1945* does for the young Goethe, that genius is "the all-powerful psychic force of the creative human being,"[2] merely reproduces, tautologically, the discourse it seeks to interpret. This repetition assumes the form of a hypostasis: it posits genius as a substance, an energy, or an anthropological fact and thereby assumes that Goethe's use of the term, whether in a poetic or in a quasi-theoretical context, adequately captures a real state of affairs. There are real psychic, social, and cultural issues at stake in Goethe's invocation of the concept of genius, but I question whether these issues can be grasped by reading the concept in a directly referential fashion. A more productive approach might be to consider genius as a *symbolic position* and to elaborate its charge of significance—the investment it attracts—by attending to its functional placement within a discursive constellation.

As I shall endeavor to show for the young Goethe, the symbolic position of genius is related to the complex of sexualized specularity. It does not coincide entirely with that complex, but overlaps with it at certain decisive points that, not accidentally, occur mainly in lyric texts or in reflections on artistic production pertaining to lyrical writing. Leaving aside the broader context within which the concept of genius is articulated in the late eighteenth century, we will focus here on Goethe's specific use of the term during the first half of the 1770's, when in his work the figure of genius acquires a symbolic valence that can only be called extremist. Goethe thinks (and writes) 'genius' through to its end, to the point where it comes to designate the auto-production of poetic subjectivity.

To begin to unravel the determinants and inner tensions of this symbolic position, it is useful to start with a simple and rather conventional passage:

11.   Wir glauben überhaupt, daß das Genie nicht der Natur nachahmt, sondern selbst schafft wie die Natur. Da fleußt eine eigene Quelle gleich der anderen, aber nicht nach ihr gemacht, sondern wie sie aus dem Felsen geboren,—laßt die Springwerke nachahmen![3]

In general we believe that genius does not imitate nature but rather itself creates like nature. One unique source flows there equal to another, but not made in its afterimage, rather like them born out of the cliffs,—let the fountains imitate!

The juxtaposition of genius and imitation, the rejection of a notion of artistic production as the replication of an ontic array, is conventional. Rather than taking the created world as a prototype to be copied, the genius brings forth out of himself (as we shall see, the masculine pronoun is fully appropriate here) his own creation. Equally conventional, especially in German invocations of genius, is the polemical jab at the culture of the ancien régime, whose decorative and effete waterworks are referred to in the closing phrase. The obviousness of these motifs, however, should not obscure the problematic, even aporetic, character of the concept of genius invoked in this passage. The genius is the figure who *occupies the standpoint of the origin*. Imitation is foreign to him. Indeed, even the foreign is foreign to him: genius is inevitably *native*. But how can this radical originality be conceived if not through reference to another origin that serves as its paradigm? On this question all the rhetorical contortions of the passage hinge: the very gesture that asserts radical originality reintroduces, through particles such as "like" and "equal to," a mimetic relationship to an anterior paradigm. Hence the denial that follows immediately upon the comparison ("but not made in its afterimage"), a denial belied by the simile that succeeds it. In the end, the affirmation of genius must be stabilized by casting off the problem of constitutive mimesis onto an other: the manifestly derivative fountains of the aristocratic garden.

The paradox of a mimesis that denies mimesis, of an originality that is attained by imitating an antecedent origin, alerts us to the fact that the concept of genius is not without its internal agon. In order to occupy the position of genius, I must displace the one who occupies that position before me, a usurpation which appears irenic only as long as the mimetic competition is played out in the relative innocence of such particles as "like" and "equal to," only as long as the original position is held by an abstractly creative nature. This will not always be the case. As soon as the origin becomes personified, as soon as the problematic of genius is nested in an actantial configuration, the element of conflict comes to the fore.[4]

The first, and still rather abstract definition of the symbolic position 'genius' as the existence who occupies the origin ramifies in various directions. The position condenses several layers of significance, and individual passages invoking it inevitably draw their resources from more than one semantic register. Thus, in Text II we encounter a recurrent topos in the discourse on genius, a topos that will prove to be especially important in its lyric figurations. The genius, as source emerging into being (or "born") from between the cliffs, is *originary liquidity*. I would caution against immediately translating this metaphor into a conceptual meaning, as if its function were merely to stand in for some psychological state such as creative vitality. The figure of "liquidity" introduces into the discourse on genius a range of significant possibilities that go well beyond such a simple substitution. The flow of liquid is an unbroken movement, a movement that suffers no articulatory incisions or caesurae. It is the paradigm of pleasure and fulfillment; it is a form of expressivity; it is common to water, semen, paint, and ink. All of these semantic values contribute, as other texts make clear, to the definition of genius. Moreover, as we have seen, especially in "Mir schlug das Herz" (Text 5), liquidity is a semantic value that inheres within the specular moment, where it characterizes the prelinguistic flow of emotion ("joy") between lover and beloved, the absolute unity of feeling that is the origin of poetry and subjectivity. This suggests that the origin the genius occupies also bears an erotic signification, that the symbolic position of genius is the site of a sexual union.

Among the texts on genius that weave an especially rich semantic skein are those Goethe devoted to Strasbourg Cathedral, "Von deutscher Baukunst" ("On German Architecture," 1772) and "Dritte Wallfahrt nach Erwins Grab im Juli 1775" ("Third Pilgrimage to Erwin's Grave, in July 1775"). In the first of these, we encounter the following passage:

12. Schädlicher als Beispiele sind dem Genius Prinzipien. Vor ihm mögen einzelne Menschen, einzelne Teile bearbeitet haben. Er ist der erste aus dessen Seele die Teile, in Ein ewiges Ganze zusammen gewachsen, hervortreten.[5]

More damaging to the genius than examples are principles. Prior to him individual human beings might have worked out individual parts. He is the first out of whose soul the parts, grown together in One eternal whole, emerge.

The unbroken liquid flow, the genial expenditure, creates. What it creates, what it pours itself into, is *whole* ("ganz"). This insistence on the value of wholeness constitutes a third dimension of the symbolic position: genius is the force of unification, the animating energy that guarantees the oneness (note the capitalization of "Ein") of its products and that produces only products which are one. Such oneness is not a matter of numeration (parts and fragments can be counted easily enough), not a unity imposed from an external perspective. Rather, it is a unity from within, a wholeness that radiates outward from an *undivided point—or act—of conception.*

A passage from the second text on the cathedral allows us to define this wholeness-producing act more precisely. The initial addressee is the cathedral itself, praise of which, however, soon slides over to praise of the genius-creator.

13. GEBET

Du bist Eins und lebendig, gezeugt und entfaltet, nicht zusammengetragen und geflickt. Vor dir, wie vor dem Schaum stürmenden Sturze des gewaltigen Rheins, wie vor der glänzenden Krone der ewigen Schneegebürge, wie vor dem Anblick des heiter ausgebreiteten Sees, und deiner Wolkenfelsen und wüsten Täler, grauer Gotthard! Wie vor jedem *großen Gedanken der Schöpfung*, wird in der Seele reg was auch Schöpfungskraft in ihr ist. In Dichtung stammelt sie über, in krützelnden Strichen wühlt sie auf dem Papier Anbetung dem Schaffenden, ewiges Leben, umfassendes, unauslöschliches Gefühl des, das da ist und da war und da sein wird.[6]

PRAYER

You are One and living, engendered and developed, not compiled and stitched together. Before you, as before the foam-storming crash of the powerful Rhine, as before the shining crown of the eternal snowy mountains, as before the view of the tranquilly spread out lake and your cloud-cliffs and desolate valleys, gray Gotthard!, as before every *great thought of creation*, there becomes active in the soul what in it too is creative force. It stammers over into poetry, in scribbled lines it twists on paper praise to the creating One, eternal life, encompassing, ineradicable feeling of the One who is and was and will be.

The wholeness characterizing the product of genius derives from the undivided nature of the creative act, an act depicted here according to (but not entirely according to) the model of procreation. Genius *engenders* ("zeugen"); its product emerges as if from a natural birth and possesses, therefore, the oneness and life characteristic of an organism. The undivided act of conception is at once cultural (spiritual, artistic) and natural (biological). The symbolic position of genius is located at the intersection of these two semantic spheres.

We are dealing here not with facts (that is, with "real" intellectual and procreative conception), but with discursive facts: with concepts of conception defined by their intratextual functions and by their functions within adjacent discourses. Thus, it is no accident that the symbolic position of genius is associated in Text 13 with birth and biological engenderment. The relation to this domain inheres in the etymology of the term 'genius' and belongs to the earliest determinations of the figure. Genius is inevitably *natal*. For the Romans, the genius is the god who engenders the individual, or who attends at the individual's birth, or is itself born with the individual; in all cases, it adheres to the individual as a kind of protector, a tutelary guide.[7] This is not to say that Goethe's use of the term derives entirely from the Roman tradition, of which, of course, he was aware. On the contrary, his writing on genius displaces the traditional semantics, bending it away from a focus on the die-cast of birth (genius as the figure of contingent destiny) toward an insistence on procreation as inseminating act, as undivided and autonomous production.

Hence the opposition that governs the opening of Text 13: the genius engenders; he does not sew or suture, does not stitch together parts or fragments already given, merely simulating a unified creation, but simulating it in such a way that the scissions—like scars—show through. This verb of 'stitching' ("flicken") occurs as well in "On German Architecture," where it derisively qualifies the Franco-Italian bricolage of classical architectural forms in opposition to the original (native) German architecture manifest in Erwin von Steinbach's Strasbourg Cathedral.[8] Stitching is what one is left to do *after* the demise of traditions; it starts in a condition of historical ruination, of domination by the inherited fragments of a past that is not one's own (not native).

The opposition between "zeugen" and "flicken," therefore, points to a national-historical dimension of the term 'genius', a semantic register I shall return to shortly. In formal terms, if the genius doesn't stitch, it is because, as *forma formans*, as sheer act, he is himself not sewn or sutured. The force (and organ) of genial production is unwounded, knows no internal severences. In view of the historical connotation just alluded to, this reading of the term "flicken" raises the question: Is the undivided, unwounded force of genius possible in modernity, in the present out of which Goethe's texts are written? Or is modernity, at least a certain predominant form of modernity, the condition of ruination and scission, and the modern subject, therefore, inevitably wounded? By referring to himself as a "geflicktes Schiffchen"[9] ("stitched-together little boat"), the speaker of the "Baukunst" essay suggests an affirmative answer to the latter question.

Before following out these threads of significance—the questions of historical foundation, of wounding and modernity—let us look at some further aspects of the "prayer" that is Text 13. Originary liquidity appears in the reference to the "foam-storming crash of the powerful Rhine." This river-source (rich in national-historical connotations) belongs to a landscape easily recognizable as the topography of the sublime. Indeed, in the poem "Harzreise im Winter" (see Chapter 9), the river's "Sturz," or 'crashing fall', signals the moment of sublime inspiration and poetic ascent to the mountain peak, the seat of the divine (alluded to in our text as the austere "gray *Gott*hard"). This linkage between genius and sublimity, like that between genius and procreation, is traditional. In a passage that was important for Goethe, Horace defined the style of Pindar, a major prototype of the sublime genius, with exactly this figure of the surging mountain stream.[10] If the symbolic position of the genius is defined as the standpoint of the origin, then this standpoint can be attained only (or at least in most cases) by an elevating flight of inspiration.

This correlation of genius with sublimity contains two interesting features. First, the topography of the sublime introduces into the discourse on genius a semantics of *verticality*. Second, it allows the position of genius to be specified as the *position of the divine Father*. In and through his sublime ascent, the genius attains to the paternal standpoint of God, becomes, as the tradition has it, a *homo secundus deus*, with the decisive difference, however, that the *secundus* falls away.[11] In the most extreme formulations of the young Goethe, it is clear that the genius is the figure who *displaces* God by usurping His position. Text 13 shows this forcefully. The cathedral, rather than glorifying a superior God, becomes equivalent to the most immense *"thought of creation,"* and its genial creator, therefore, the object of prayerful reverence. The discourse on genius is an assault on Christianity.

This it must be. The Christian God, who created man in His image, thereby condemned mankind to imitation. (I will return to this point in Chapter 8, in connection with the ode "Prometheus.") If the genius occupies the origin, then he can achieve this position only by appropriating for himself the attribute of divinity. Only through this ultimate mimesis can the law of mimesis be overcome:

14. Du hast dir das herrlichste [Denkmal] errichtet; und kümmert die Ameisen, die drum krabeln, dein Name nichts, hast du gleiches Schicksal mit dem Baumeister, der Berge auftürmte in die Wolken.

    Wenigen ward es gegeben, einen Babelgedanken in der Seele zu zeugen, ganz, groß, und bis in den kleinsten Teil notwendig schön, wie Bäume Gottes; wenigern, auf tausend bietende Hände zu treffen, Felsengrund zu graben, steile Höhen drauf zu zaubern, und dann sterbend ihren Söhnen zu sagen: ich bleibe bei euch, in den Werken meines Geistes, vollendet das begonnene in die Wolken.[12]

You erected for yourself the most glorious [memorial], and if your name is of no concern to the ants that crawl around it, then you have the same destiny as the architect who towered up mountains into the clouds.

> To only a few has it been given to engender a Babel thought in the soul, whole, great, necessarily beautiful to the smallest part; to even fewer, to encounter a thousand willing hands to dig out the foundation of cliffs and magically to raise steep heights upon it, and then dying to say to their sons, "I remain among you, in the works of my spirit; complete what was begun into the clouds."

Babel, the emblem of blasphemous hybris, is here affirmed. The genius of Erwin von Steinbach ascends to the cloudy heights and attains to equivalence with the divine creator of the mountains.

Note, in connection with this heretical assault on paternity, the semantics of verticality that runs through the text: towered-up mountains, the tower of Babel, the trees of God. Note also that the aim of this upward striving is meteorological in nature: Erwin von Steinbach's Tower of Babel has its goal in the clouds that surround the mountains of the divine creation. All of these figures—tower, tree, and meteorological Other—are familiar to us from "Pilgers Morgenlied" (Text 10). Viewed in relation to that text, they reveal that the concept of genius also includes a phallic component. This is not at all surprising, of course, given the insistence on procreative generation ("zeugen"; a term also liminally present in "Pilgers Morgenlied") in both Texts 13 and 14. In fact, one of the features that distinguishes Erwin in the text just cited (14) is that he is a father who lives on in his sons, a successful progenitor. His work—his tower, his tree—perpetually engenders. In view of this complex, we can further specify the symbolic position: *the genius is also the existence who identifies with—who is—the phallus.*

Rather than consider further evidence for the phallic interpretation of genius at this point, let us consider a semantic register to which I alluded above in passing: the national-historical (but not nationalist) dimension of genius. This aspect assumes prominence in the great figures of the past: in Erwin von Steinbach, the inventor of a German style of architecture; in Homer, Pindar, Mohammed, Caesar, Shakespeare, and (unfortunately) Ossian. One common way Goethe represents the historical significance of the genius is through the figure of the wanderer. Imagine life as a kind of spatiotemporal stretch, a field of possibilities, challenges, dangers, and conflicts through which no a priori route is given. The task, then, is to find a way through this unformed turbulence, to chart a livable pattern of human existence, and this the genius does. Hence the peripatetic semantics of Goethe's early essay in praise of Shakespeare: Shakespeare is the "greatest of wanderers"; he moved through life as if with "seven-league boots"; his "gigantic steps" astonish us; and our souls are made fiery and great when we regard even one of his "footprints."[13] The governing concept is that of unprogrammed semantic endowment. In the absence of transcendently guaranteed structures of meaning, the genius establishes a historically binding interpretation of what it is to be human; he is the progenitor of an immanent and yet totalizing shape of symbolization. The genius *carves a path* through life, *writes the law* of a historical-cultural tradition.

The definition of the genius as the originator of historically innovative semantic structures bespeaks a concept of history as immanent development through time, a concept that crystallizes, of course, in the historico-philosophical theories produced from the latter part of the eighteenth century into the nineteenth (in Germany, from Herder to Hegel). One feature of the late-eighteenth-century reconceptualization of history is immediately relevant here. In Goethe's use of the genius figure we can note a recurring temporal structure that is a variant of the general *Verzeitlichung* (temporalization) of experience that the emergent historico-philosophical discourse codifies.[14] This structure valorizes the past and the future at the expense of the present. The genius is either the figure who *was* or the figure who *will be*; his place is not in the present.

For the past, such figures as Erwin von Steinbach and Shakespeare serve in Goethe's texts as exemplars of bygone grandeur. Genius as future possibility is most often evoked in the figure of the 'youth' ("Jüngling") to come.[15] The present—the modern world—is consistently construed as the era that has forgotten the genius and his accomplishments (see Text 14), or, worse yet, as the era that, by virtue of its artificiality, abstract rules, and fashionable borrowings, has made genius impossible. *Modernity is the wound of genius.* In this sense, the present is what one must break with in order to make possible a future genius, the author of a new, and native, law. The best way to do this is to renew contact with past genius and to draw therefrom the energy required for the creation of a future that is one's own. In its temporal structure, then, the discourse on genius swings back and forth between the anamnesis of a lost origin and the invocation of a perpetually imminent originality. It is at once nostalgic and utopian, and in both of these shadings sharply critical of modernity.

At this point it is useful to look back at the determinations of the symbolic position of genius touched on thus far. The genius, I have argued (in a slightly different order), is the figure that:

(1) occupies the origin;
(2) expresses itself in an expenditure of liquidity;
(3) engenders by virtue of its unfissured, unifying procreative power (cf. "zeugen");
(4) gives human life an individual historical law;
(5) supplants the divine Father;
(6) identifies with the phallus.

Although only partial and still quite abstract, this list confirms the claim that genius is not an anthropological fact, not a creative psychic energy inaccessible to further analysis. On the contrary, the six determinations of the figure systematically cohere; they play into one another, articulate in different registers an affine logic. Genius *is* this logic, this interplay of symbolic valences. If we take originality (1) as defining genius in its most general form, then we can say that such genial originality is imagined in the realm of natural phenomena as the emergence of liquidity (2) and in the biological domain as procreation (3), an idea that, of course, is intimately related to the phallus (6). But the phallus is not merely the agency of biological engenderment; it is likewise the attribute of the Father (5), the source of a liquid expenditure (2), the mark of oneness and identity (3), and the sign of authority that characterizes the law (4). Traditionally, of course, the laws of human culture were grounded in the transcendent origin occupied by the divine Father. If the genius takes on the position of cultural originator, then he must assume the Father's position, either through identification or usurpation (5). He must become his own Father, produce himself out of himself, occupy the position of origin in its most radical sense. The genius is the figure of auto-origination, which is to say, the figure of an impossibility. For the young Goethe, the site where this impossibility takes place is art.

~

Several of Goethe's lyric texts from the early 1770's stage the logic of genius sketched out above. For example, the three poems Goethe selected to lead off the collection of lyric poems he compiled in Weimar, probably in 1778,[16] work through the problematics of genius with particular intensity. Moreover, along their sequence one can observe something like a rearticulation of the logic of genius, a transfiguration of its symbolic structure. The first text in the series is one of Goethe's most famous poems, a text often considered emblematic for what is referred to as the *Geniezeit* (period of genius).

15. MAHOMETS GESANG

Seht den Felsenquell
Freudehell
Wie ein Sternenblick!
Über Wolken
(5) Nährten seine Jugend
Gute Geister
Zwischen Klippen im Gebüsch.

Jünglingfrisch
Tanzt er aus der Wolke
(10) Auf die Marmorfelsen nieder
Jauchzet wieder
Nach dem Himmel

Durch die Gipfelgänge
Jagt er bunten Kieseln nach,
(15) Und mit frühem Führertritt
Reißt er seine Bruderquellen
Mit sich fort.

Drunten werden in dem Tal
Unter seinem Fußtritt Blumen
(20) Und die Wiese
Lebt von seinem Hauch.

Doch ihn hält kein Schattental
Keine Blumen
Die ihm seine Knie umschlingen
(25) Ihm mit Liebesaugen schmeicheln
Nach der Ebne dringt sein Lauf
Schlangewandelnd.

Bäche schmiegen
Sich gesellig an
(30) Nun tritt er
In die Ebne silberprangend

Und die Ebne prangt mit ihm
Und die Flüsse von der Ebne
Und die Bäche von Gebürgen
(35) Jauchzen ihm und rufen: Bruder!
Bruder nimm die Brüder mit!
Mit zu deinem Alten Vater
Zu dem ewgen Ozean
Der mit weitverbreiten Armen
(40) Unsrer wartet
Die sich ach vergebens öffnen
Seine Sehnenden zu fassen
Denn uns frißt in öder Wüste
Gier'ger Sand
(45) Die Sonne droben
Saugt an unserm Blut
Ein Hügel
Hemmet uns zum Teiche!
Bruder!
(50) Nimm die Brüder von der Ebne
Nimm die Brüder von Gebürgen
Mit zu deinem Vater mit.

Kommt ihr alle!—
Und nun schwillt er
(55) Herrlicher, ein ganz Geschlechte
Trägt den Fürsten hoch empor
Und im rollenden Triumphe
Gibt er Ländern Namen, Städte
Werden unter seinem Fuß.

(60) Unaufhaltsam rauscht er über
Läßt der Türne Flammengipfel
Marmorhäuser eine Schöpfung
Seiner Fülle hinter sich.

Zedernhäuser trägt der Atlas
(65) Auf den Riesenschultern, sausend
Wehen über seinem Haupte
Tausend Segel auf zum Himmel
Seine Macht und Herrlichkeit.

Und so trägt er seine Brüder
(70) Seine Schätze seine Kinder

Dem erwartenden Erzeuger
Freudebrausend an das Herz.[17]

MOHAMMED'S SONG

See the cliff spring
Joy-bright
Like a star's glance!
Above the clouds,
(5) Nourished his youth
Good spirits
Between cliffs in the bush.

Youth-fresh
He dances out of the cloud
(10) Down onto the marble cliffs,
Rejoices again
Toward heaven.

Through the mountain corridors
He chases after bright-colored pebbles,
(15) And with the early steps of a leader
He tears his brother springs
Along with him.

Below in the valley grow
Flowers beneath his footsteps
(20) And the meadow
Lives from his breath.

But no shadowy valley holds him,
No flowers,
Embracing his knees,
(25) Flatter him with eyes of love;
To the plain his course presses,
Wandering snakelike.

Streams press
To join him.
(30) Now he enters,
Resplendently silver, the plain,
And the plain is resplendent with him,
And the rivers of the plain
And the streams from the mountains
(35) Rejoice and call out: Brother!

Brother take your brothers with you!
With you to your Ancient Father,
To the eternal Ocean,
Which with arms spread wide
(40) Awaits ours
That, oh, in vain open
To grasp his yearning arms,
For in the desolate desert we are eaten
By greedy sand.
(45) The sun above
Sucks our blood.
A hill
Dams us to a pond!
Brother!
(50) Take the brothers from the plain
Take the brothers from the mountains
Along with you to your father.

Come all of you!—
And now he swells
(55) More gloriously, an entire race
The prince carries upward
And in rolling triumph
He gives names to lands; cities
Come into being under his foot.

(60) Without stopping he rushes past,
Leaves the towers' peaks of flame,
Marble buildings a creation
Of his abundance behind him.

Atlas carries houses of cedar
(65) On his giant shoulders; roaring
Above his head there wave
A thousand sails toward heaven:
His power and glory.

And so he carries his brothers,
(70) His treasures, his children
Toward the waiting progenitor,
Joy foaming to his heart.

The text draws on and ramifies nearly all the determinations of the
symbolic position mentioned above: the genius-stream springs from an

origin; it is a flow of liquidity; the path it carves (note the references to footsteps in lines 15, 19, and 59) is an individual historical law (the Islamic religion) around which a civilization is organized; the stream's expenditure is procreative, engendering natural richness (18–21), cultural splendor (60–63), and "children" (70), even an entire "race" ("Geschlecht" 55); and of course the stream's overall trajectory aims at identification—or merging—with the Father (71–72). Only the phallic component of the genius position receives no easily recognizable figuration. Given this nearly complete inflection of the genius paradigm, it is easy to understand why critics have viewed this text as an expression of Goethe's belief in the force of genius or even of his own sense that he himself was such a genius.

But things are not this straightforward. The poem is imbued with difficulties and tensions that mark the symbolic position of genius with discrepancy. This can be seen by considering the relation between the act of utterance (*énonciation*) and the statement uttered (*énoncé*). If we take the speaker of the poem to be Mohammed (a reading strongly suggested by the title), then the statement can be thought of as describing an ideal form of subjectivity (the genius-stream), which Mohammed wants to be, but, wanting to be, isn't. If, by contrast, we follow the drama fragment *Mahomet*, in which the poem appears with slight variation as a choral hymn of praise sung by Mohammed's daughter and son-in-law,[18] the same break between utterance and statement emerges, with the difference, however, that in this case Mohammed, or an idealized version of Mohammed, is located on the side of the statement. To put this another way, in both readings the genius is designated as a "he," not an "I," and is therefore held at an unbridgeable distance from the speaking subject. Moreover, read in the context of the dramatic action (insofar as it can be reconstructed), the hymn of praise is tinged with irony. It is sung to the prophet at the point when he has just been poisoned (poison is a kind of antiliquid), at the point of imminent death, so that its assertion starkly contradicts the reality posited by the dramatic plot. Rather than speaking the truth of Mohammed's destiny, the chorus sung by Ali and Fatema expresses their own deluded wish, their own impossible desire. This dramatic tension between finitude and the longing for transcendence is also inscribed within the poem.

The fundamental discrepancy characterizing the relation between utterance and statement comes to the fore in other aspects of the text, which we will consider later. Internally, the articulation of the *énoncé* is accom-

plished through the ramification of a single metaphor equating the movement of the stream with the process of religious-historical foundation. So
salient is this metaphor that every critic who has written on the poem has
noted it; paradoxically, though, its very salience has blocked detailed
investigation of its structure and function. Note first of all the general
semantic effect achieved through the overriding metaphorical strategy: the
fusion—the identification—of the semantic domains of nature and culture. The poem posits a world in which these domains are continuous, in
which no scission divides them. Genius is the figure that brings identity to
the world, the world's healing redeemer.

Of course there is, rhetorically speaking, nothing especially convincing
about such an abstract metaphorical equation. To gain persuasive force, it
must be demonstrated, made to show forth, endowed with what rhetori-
cians called *enargia*, the effect of perceptual immediacy. This is achieved
through a double movement. First, semantic features drawn from common knowledge about streams and religious civilizations (such as that of
Islam) are projected from one domain onto the other and vice versa,
setting into motion a process of semantic exchange. Predicates belonging
to the stream (e.g., that of carrying ships, 64) are ascribed to the religious
founder, and predicates belonging to the religious founder (e.g., that of
heaven-directed enthusiasm, 11–12) are ascribed to the stream. This process of predicate exchange alters (in the second movement of the rhetorical
demonstration) the semantic structure of the terms equated. Each metaphorical predicate steers the interpretation of the subject term to which it
is attributed by selecting from that term's repertoire of semantic virtualities
certain ones for actualization. Remaining with the examples that have
been mentioned, to say that a religious founder carries ships is to foreground the idea that religious founders are the animating spirits of a
civilization and that civilization extends itself through marine trade. Likewise, to say that a stream joyously shouts toward heaven is to focalize the
idea that a surging mountain stream sprays upward when it strikes rocks.
In short, the metaphorical attribution promotes to semantic prominence
features of the subject term that confirm the legitimacy of the attribution.
The persuasiveness of the metaphor, its evidentiary force, derives from this
delicate labor of semantic interweaving, from a process closely akin to
what Goethe derisively called "flicken" (Text 13).

But the decisive feature of the text's metaphorics is that the two metaphorically related terms (stream / religious founder) each assume, alter-

nately, the positions of vehicle and tenor. This mode of figuration is a *specular metaphorical structure*: a structure whose elements represent one another like mirror reflections. Thus, the poetic metaphor frees itself from reference to something given prior and external to it and becomes a semiotic relation that grounds itself (engenders its terms). In and through its specular metaphorics, the text of genius throws off the fetters of mimetic or representational dependency and posits itself as absolute.

The interwoven metaphorical and nonmetaphorical predications do not simply assume the structure of a list or description, but are themselves narratively organized. This process of narrativization reveals especially clearly, I believe, the drama inherent in the symbolics of genius. The narrative trajectory of "Mahomets Gesang" is patent. The poem relates the career of the genius-stream from the potentiality of youth to the accomplishments of manhood. The hero fulfills the mission that was already inscribed in his first appearance, and of course is duly celebrated. (Note the semantic arc extending from "Himmel," 12, to "Himmel," 67.) The question is: What is the content, or purpose, of this mission? To found a civilization, of course. But what is the founding of a civilization? What kind of act is that? What sort of logic—what sort of narrative logic—does it obey?

At this juncture, it is helpful to recall the Lotmanian model of narrative structure I alluded to in my remarks on "Mir schlug das Herz" (Text 5). According to Lotman, narrative is constituted as the crossing of a semantic border, as the transgression of a limit separating opposed semantic spaces. This operation is typically figured as a topographical transport: a protagonist (the hero) moves from one domain to a second—semantically opposed—domain. Since the border between these two domains is a culturally ratified division (a kind of positive law), it marks the site of the narrative conflict, the place where the hindrance or antagonist appears. Applying this model of narrative to "Mahomets Gesang," we might ask: What are the opposed semantic spaces whose opposition is neutralized and transformed ("revolutionized," one might say) by the movement of the narrative subject? Furthermore: What is the nature of the conflict (agon) that develops at the point of transgression? To answer these questions is to disclose some of the symbolic labor performed by the figure of the genius.

The trajectory of the genius-stream's movement is meticulously delineated: from the mountains (1–17), through the alpine valley (18–27), across the plain (28–63), and toward the ocean (64–72). But the opposition mountains/ocean is, taken literally, too trivial to generate the kind of poetic energy this text evinces. The salient opposition is categorical rather than geographical. The mountains from which the genius-stream is born belong to the domain of nature, and the genius-stream's accomplishments in the plain (the fruits of his "triumph," 57) are clearly cultural. The border the hero crosses is that between nature and culture; the genius is the figure who, by carving out his narrative trajectory, unites—or, in an extended, transitive sense of the term, identifies—these two domains.

This is by no means a trivial task, and every reading of the poem that takes it as simply expressing Goethe's belief in the natural basis of cultural production remains blind to the poetic difficulty of the text. In fact, the genius-hero runs up against two barriers that threaten to divert him from his narrative trajectory and block the accomplishment of his semantic project. These obstacles mark the points of conflict in the text. The major conflict is unfolded across the sixth stanza, which is, compositionally speaking, the central and longest stanza, and which, topographically speaking, marks the stream's movement from the mountains and their valleys to the plain. This, of course, is the border between nature and culture, and it is therefore no accident that the stanzas preceding the sixth have natural phenomena as their semantic focus, whereas the stanzas following the sixth enumerate principally civilizational accomplishments. By attending to the border crossing between the mountains and the plain, and especially to the conflict, or obstacle, that emerges there, we should be able to uncover the logic—the narrative logic—of the act of founding a civilization.

The name of the border (and the name of the law which prohibits its crossing) is finitude. This is made clear in the appeal to the genius-stream by the weaker brother streams: they are separated from the "Father" (37), the river of rivers or "eternal Ocean" (38); their desire to embrace and be embraced by the infinite is blocked (39–42). The agency of this blockage is figured in the text's topographical code:

> Denn uns frißt in öder Wüste
> Gier'ger Sand
> Die Sonne droben
> Saugt an unserm Blut
> Ein Hügel
> Hemmet uns zum Teiche!   *(43–48)*

Entering the plain, the streams are no longer sustained by the "natural" surge of their alpine origin; they are consumed and dissipated by the dryness, evaporated by the sun's heat; their natural energy is dessicated by a kind of parasitism. This is indeed the point where nature reaches its border, where it runs up against the limit of its own internal lack. Death— the destiny of all merely natural beings—is the name of this lack. The hill that dams (and damns) the rivers, transforming them into still ponds, is the hill of the grave. Beneath the word "Teiche" (pond) the shadow word "Leiche" (corpse) makes itself silently heard.

The culture hero—the genius-stream—compensates for the lack within nature (death). This is his triumph, his victory in the agon of finitude:

> Kommt ihr alle!—
> Und nun schwillt er
> Herrlicher, ein ganz Geschlechte
> Trägt den Fürsten hoch empor
> Und im rollenden Triumphe
> Gibt er Ländern Namen, Städte
> Werden unter seinem Fuß. *(53–59)*

The foundational act that brings forth civilization out of nature obeys the logic of supplementarity,[19] fills in the gaping deficiency of nature by aligning individuals (and death always and only strikes individuals) to the collective unity of the "Geschlecht," the species, race, culture, or political entity which becomes the subject of history. Death is annulled through the endowment of meaning, through the inscription of the law and the names that give the community its historical self-consciousness.

Not every cultural supplement of nature's lack works, however. On the contrary, since Rousseau at least, European consciousness has been acutely aware of the blood-letting side of culture, its devitalizing effects. Culture can degenerate into senseless repetition, empty imitation, superfluous and suffocating ornamentation; in short, it can become the negation of nature. Of the many passages by Goethe that illustrate this awareness the following sentence is especially revealing: "Uns kommt jede Portraitverzierung vor, wie Moos und Wispeln, die dem Baume die Kraft aussaugen"[20] ("The ornamentation of portraits seems to us to be like the moss and little plants that suck out the force of the tree"). As ornament, the cultural supplement reveals its degenerative potential. The scribble of decoration, the parergonic addition, is as parasitic as the sun that draws off the rivers' liquidity.

It disperses the concentrated individuality of the portrait, saps the power of the (phallic) tree. There are, then, two deaths the genius must overcome, one natural and the other cultural, and both these deaths guard the border that separates the mountains from the plains. The genius is a hero precisely because he overcomes both these lethal obstacles. He compensates for the lack within nature through his act of cultural foundation, to be sure, but he does so in such a way that the life of nature is preserved and in turn compensates for the lack within culture.[21]

Note the implications of this logic. The identity between nature and culture, which it is the function of genius to guarantee, does not derive from what might be called linear or material continuity, from an uninterrupted emanation. Such continuity is broken by the doubly determined death at the border between the mountains and the plain. The genius crosses this border by supplementing the lack within nature (death) with culture and at the same time supplementing the lack within culture (nonnatural death) with nature. Through this operation, each of the opposed terms stabilizes itself through the other, each functions as the crutch or prosthesis of the other, and the relation primacy/secondariness is replaced by one of double secondariness. The act of genius establishes the continuity of nature and culture by aligning the two domains in a structure of *reflexive supplementarity*.[22] Moreover, this structure repeats, and validates, the metaphorical structure of the text; the genius, as we have seen, is the figure in whom nature is metaphorized as culture and culture is metaphorized as nature. Reflexive supplementarity, however, not only organizes the narrative and tropological structures of the text internally, it also determines the relation of these two textual strata to one another. The narrative itinerary of the genius is the unfolding of the metaphorical equation and the metaphorics of genius is the condensation of its narrative itinerary. In short, the symbolic figure of genius obeys, at every level of its textualization, a grammar of specular exchange.

This analysis of the figurative logic of 'genius' can be more precisely specified through a semantic analysis. Let us say that one of the basic components of 'nature' is the semantic term 'Life' ('vital force') and that this term stands in opposition to (is the logical contrary of) the semantic unit 'Meaning'. Whereas 'Life' has its being sheerly *in actu*, in the unfolding present of its vital existence, 'Meaning', as ideality, is susceptible to repetition and can therefore be transmitted as cultural tradition. By adding to each of these opposed terms their respective contradictory terms

('Non-Life' and 'Non-Meaning'), we can derive a logical matrix or semiotic square to model the semantic structure the text figuratively and narratively deploys.[23]

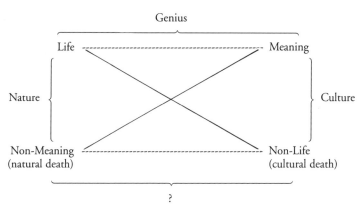

Schema 6: Semantic Structure of "Mahomets Gesang"

The schema makes clear the ambiguity inherent in the terms 'nature' and 'culture'. 'Nature', in other words, can be positively valorized insofar as it entails the presence of vital force or creative energy ('Life'), but it also carries a shadowy, threatening signification, precisely the death ('Non-Meaning') that marks the limit of all merely natural beings. And of course 'culture' too bears a double signification: it is at once the 'Meaning' that supplements the natural lack, thereby making historical tradition possible, and the cultural death ('Non-Life') that renders artifacts empty repetitions, dead letters, parasitic ornaments. From this point of view, the mediation between 'nature' and 'culture' the genius accomplishes appears as a selection and an exclusion. Selected are the two oppositional terms of the top horizontal axis, 'Life' and 'Meaning', terms the genius aligns in a relation of mutual—or specular—supplementarity. What the myth of genius excludes, however, is the bottom axis containing the negative terms of natural and cultural death. This suppression of significant values is achieved through the dual operations of metaphorical and narrative figuration discussed above. These operations produce the phenotypic aspect of the myth of genius, the semantic structure of which the semiotic square models.

Genius is not a substance or anthropological fact, but a symbolic position. The schema makes this point forcefully clear by showing how the term 'genius' is situated within a differential array of values, how it is generated from an elementary combinatoric. Perhaps the most interesting implication of the analysis, however, bears on what might be termed the inverse double of 'genius', the 'anti-genius' implied by the very constellation of terms that lends 'genius' its semantic determination. I have marked this position (the lower horizontal axis) with a question mark, thereby indicating that it receives no explicit designation or figuration in the text of "Mahomets Gesang." It is the unspoken of the text, the blocked term. Despite this suppression of a semantic term, it is possible (even requisite) to speculate what term might occupy this position, and the candidate I would tentatively put forward is the term "Gift," 'poison'. The drama fragment *Mahomet* foresees that the prophet will die by poison, and poison, as noted above, is a kind of anti-liquid, bringing death where the genius-stream brings life. Poison combines natural and cultural features, derived as it is from the realm of natural substances but likewise marked by the cultural features of deception and malevolent intent. 'Poison' is, then, the other of 'genius', an other which is not external to the heroic, life-bringing figure, but rather is something like its systematic complement. What is repressed in the text of "Mahomets Gesang" (although perhaps not completely repressed, as we shall see) is precisely this complementarity: the recognition that the healing or redemptive force of genius is inevitably touched by its own poisonous other.

The second obstacle to the genius-stream's trajectory, the second potential deviation from his path, precedes the agon occurring at the plain's edge. It is located within the still natural domain of the "Tal" ("valley," 18), within a sort of cleavage or fold of nature. Here are the decisive lines:

Drunten werden in dem Tal
Unter seinem Fußtritt Blumen
Und die Wiese
Lebt von seinem Hauch.

Doch ihn hält kein Schattental
Keine Blumen
Die ihm seine Knie umschlingen
Ihm mit Liebesaugen schmeicheln
Nach der Ebene dringt sein Lauf
Schlangewandelnd. *(18–27)*

The threat here is that of an embrace that remains within nature, of a seduction that tempts the genius-hero to abide within nature's "shadowy valley." Clearly an erotic force (a desire), the genius runs the hazard of erotic captivation, as if he were the beautiful Adonis tempted away from his manly duties by the kindred beauty of Aphrodite, but only to suffer the feminized death of enfoldment in the cabbage leaves.[24] Love here is a kind of natural entrapment, an enslavement to the Mother that blocks maturation to adult male (cultural) accomplishment. Were the genius to yield to the allure of the clinging "Schattental," he would regress to the space of his first youth, the likewise cleft and shady place ("Zwischen Klippen im Gebüsch," 7) where he was "nourished" ("nährten," 5). The gate through which such regression would pass is narcissistic captivation, the flattering "Liebesaugen" of the flowers that bend toward their specular image in the stream.

Implicit in this first challenge to the genius and in his diegetic surmounting of it is what might be called a critique of natural paradise, perhaps also a critique of Rousseau, who was often misread in Germany as advocating a return to nature. The genius must leave this domain, must make his way toward the plain, where the earnest challenge of death and cultural labor awaits him. In short, the genius must fall from the false paradise of maternal enclosure. And the final line and word (a Goethean neologism) of the passage just cited, the line that names the stream's movement as it escapes the natural entrapment and heads toward the plain of culture, bears the serpentine trace of this fortunate fall: "Schlangewandelnd." Perhaps this trace, marking the genius's departure from the Mother, also connects up with what I referred to above as the repressed term of the text: the poison the genius necessarily bears with him, his own inverse double. The fact that this poisonous marker occurs at the point of severence from the feminine suggests that a certain alliance obtains between the two terms, as if the problem of negative complimentarity (genius/poison) were also the problem of a certain repressed or marginalized dependence on the maternal sphere. As the figure of autogeneration, the genius must be conceived as motherless: "Doch ihn hält kein Schattental."

In addition to the obstacle of death (both natural and cultural), then, the genius must overcome the prior threat of specularity. But this seems paradoxical. Specularity, I have argued, is the very structure of genius. This is certainly correct here, for the first sentence of the text, the sentence that proclaims the origin of the genius-stream, its emergence into presence, is organized according to the chiastic pattern of seeing and being seen that is common to all instances of the specular moment:

> *Seht* den *Felsenquell*
> *Freudehell*
> Wie ein *Sternenblick*!
> *(1–3; emphasis added)*

From "Seht" to "-blick," pivoting around the alliterative and rhyming terms "Felsenquell" and "Freudehell," the opening lines structure the epiphany of genius as specular exchange. Moreover, the self-enclosure of specularity is enacted by the poem as a whole, not merely in the metaphorical and narrative features described above, but also in the relation between the poem's beginning and its conclusion:

> Dem erwartenden Erzeuger
> Freudebrausend an das Herz.
> *(71–72)*

The "Freude" of the origin is recovered at the end, which itself is nothing other than the point of origin, the position of the "Erzeuger," the divine procreator. The text carves a circle (much like "Maifest," Text 2), a circle within which nature and culture flow, streamlike, into one another.

It seems clear, then, that specularity has two forms, or that it is an intrinsically ambiguous structure. On the one hand, it can signal dangerous captivation within the natural sphere, narcissistic entrapment, a return to the origin that is sheerly regressive. (This hazardous aspect of specularity is fully developed in the ballad "Der Fischer," which I shall discuss in Chapter 7.) On the other hand, specularity is a progressive return to the origin, a mediated, teleological closure, a structure of identity that is achieved not by going back to the natural source, but by passing the limits of nature and at the same time preserving nature within the cultural domain. The first version is marked as maternal, the second is authorized by a paternal instance. The first is immediate and intuitive, the second dialectical, in the technical sense of the word. The genius returns to the origin, to be sure, but only after having freed himself from maternal attachment. He returns, in other words, to—and as—the Father. In "Mahomets Gesang," the symbolic position of genius unfolds as the myth of auto-engenderment, of self-fathering.

That is why the position of genius is the position of the phallus. As I mentioned at the outset, the phallic component of the symbolic position is not especially prominent in this poem. Nevertheless, near the end of the text, where the glory of the genius is proclaimed, a semantics of verticality is erected. First we read about "der Türne Flammengipfel" (61), a formulation that descriptively captures, as commentators have remarked, the reflection of the sun's rays on the towers. But the same formulation poetically fuses, as they have failed to note, the ideas of tower and mountain peak, familiar as emblems of genius from the essay "On German Architecture" (Text 14), with the flames of erotic energy. This poetic condensation is soon followed by mention of the "Zedernhäuser" (64), which read descriptively are the ships carried by the river, but read intertextually with the Bible allude to the "trees of God" ("Bäume Gottes," Text 14) that likewise figure Erwin von Steinbach's towering construction.[25] Finally, the genius-stream becomes a mountain god, an "Atlas" with "Riesenschultern" (64–65), as if to prepare his return (as Father) to his mountain origin. The function of all these vertical signs, these towers, trees, and mountains, is to bear testimony and witness. And this, as we know from the tower of "Pilgers Morgenlied" (Text 10), is a phallic function. In "Mahomets Gesang," the phallic markers testify to two things: the (pro)creative "abundance" of the genius ("Schöpfung / Seiner Fülle," 62–63) and his "power and glory" ("Macht und Herrlichkeit," 68). The allusion to the divine Father of Christianity is flagrant. (The phrase "Macht und Herrlichkeit" cites the Lord's Prayer.) The phallic testimony proclaims—blasphemously—that the genius has attained, perhaps usurped, the Father's position, has become the One "who is and was and will be" (Text 13).

Having noted this cluster of phallic markers at the poem's conclusion, let us return for a moment to the genius-stream's triumph in the agon of finitude. At the point where the natural and cultural antagonists of death are overcome, at the point where the scattered and dissipating individual streams are gathered into the unity of a species or community, the text proclaims:

> Und nun schwillt er
> Herrlicher, ein ganz Geschlechte
>
> *(55–56)*

The interruption of the overarching syntactic structure effected by the break between lines 55 and 56 produces a kind of counter-text, in which the word "Geschlecht" functions syntactically in apposition to the genius-stream and semantically to designate the male sexual organ. The triumph of the genius-stream is signaled by this "glorious" or "lordly" ("*Herr-licher*") swelling of a sex that is "whole" ("ganz"). The instance that authorizes the law and anchors the names of communal identity is thus the phallic marker of oneness and wholeness. The myth of genius is the myth of this singular, phallic sex. For this reason, the myth requires the occlusion of the two terms conflated in the word "Schlangewandelnd": 'poison' and the 'feminine'. We will return to this aspect of the myth later on.

Genius is a figure of desire, in both senses of the genitive: in the subjective sense, because it bespeaks a desire for genius, a desire to identify with, or assume, the genius's position; in the objective sense, because what is desired is itself a desire, an ideal desire, a desire that is originary, self-identical, and knows no scissions. This objective desire appears in all the figurations of genius: as phallus, as joyous expenditure of liquidity (cf. "Freudebrausend," 72), as the Father, as cultural foundation continuous with nature, as auto-engenderment or self-origin. And the subjective desire is what, out of lack, speaks of these figures, but, because it speaks, fails to coincide with them. Speech divides us from the genius by dividing us.

Another aspect of the text points in the same direction. The trajectory of the genius, I have shown, returns to the origin, has the origin as its end. The text itself, however, cannot accomplish such circular closure. It can only refer to the natural origin (the time of conception and nourishment within the Mother) as that which *was* ("Nährten," 5), and to the unification with the Father-progenitor as that which *will be* ("erwartenden," 71). The text, in other words, is spoken from a present that is open and incomplete, no longer and not yet. As text, it severs the specular enclosure that nevertheless serves as its paradigm of meaning production. This temporal break is recapitulated on the level of perception: the origin of the genius figure—his conception and prenatal nurturing—takes place "Über Wolken" (4), above the clouds that always block, in Goethe's poetry, the paternal instance from view; and the end—the reunification with the "Erzeuger"—is also located in a nonperceptible beyond, the ever receding horizon of the ocean. The subjective desire that speaks in Goethe's poetry of genius (and in his discourse on genius generally) cannot coincide, temporally or perceptually, with the objective desire it longs to identify with. It can only recall or promise it. The genius himself is always past or future, always beckoning. Hence the sole line in the text that seems to be spoken by the genius-stream: "Kommt ihr alle!—" (53).

~

Of Goethe's poems of the 1770's, the Pindaric ode "Wandrers Sturm-lied" ("Wanderer's Stormsong") is perhaps the most recalcitrant to inter-pretation. Richly and often obscurely allusive, syntactically twisted and formally complex, it demands, preliminary to a disciplined reading of its poetic structure, a philological apparatus that would itself fill numerous pages. Therefore I shall restrict my comments to a few passages, treating even these selections only briefly. What follows, then, is not a reading but a concatenation of glosses, which necessarily neglects the considerable scholarship that has built up around the poem and that has successfully clarified many of its opacities.[26] But this neglect may turn out to be an advantage. As yet, scholars have not managed to disclose the motivational complex that governs the text's progression, the pattern of its semantic interlacing, the play of its affective investments. To use a distinction employed by Walter Benjamin, they have attended to the mythological aspect of the text, its citation of traditional motifs, but have failed to grasp its poetic *mythos*, its 'law of identity' (*Identitätsgesetz*).[27] The symbolics of genius traced out in the foregoing provides, I believe, a way into this *mythos*, which, as I shall show, achieves poetic integration in the form of conflict.

The poem's first stanza:

> 16. Wen du nicht verlässest Genius
>   Nicht der Regen nicht der Sturm
>   Haucht ihm Schauer übers Herz.
>   Wen du nicht verlässest Genius
>   Wird der Regenwolk
>   Wird dem Schlossensturm
>   Entgegen singen
>   Wie die Lerche
>   Du dadroben.[28]

> Whomever you don't abandon, Genius,
> Neither rain nor storm
> Breathes shuddering fear over his heart.
> Whoever you don't abandon, Genius,
> Will against the raincloud
> Will against the hailstorm

Sing like
You, lark,
Up there.

In a tone whose urgency seems an effort to assuage anxiety, the poem commences as an invocation of the genius as the figure who could protect the wanderer (the poem's speaker) against the hazards of the storm. What is the logic of this appeal? The most obvious answer, of course, is that genius is traditionally a protective agency, the minor deity who accompanies the individual from birth, and Goethe's text certainly draws on this inherited conception. But to abide at this level of reading is to miss the drama that begins to unfold with the poem's introit, a drama that emerges clearly as soon as we consider the passage in terms of the symbolic constants that govern this phase of Goethe's oeuvre. I made the same methodological point above with regard to "Pilgers Morgenlied" (Text 10), and indeed that text, perhaps more than any other, sheds light on the passage before us now. In "Pilgers Morgenlied" the poetic subject is confronted by a meteorological other—the clouds blocking the subject's vision, the coldness of harsh weather, the cutting north wind—whose threat is most acutely felt at that moment when the subject claims for itself the position of the phallus. Other texts (such as "Mahomets Gesang") have led to a reading of 'genius' as the figure who displaces the Father-God and successfully identifies with the phallus. Combining these two dimensions of signification, it is an easy inference that genius is a form of subjectivity that can meet, and overcome, the terrifying meteorological violence, that can resist the force of symbolic sanction. Exactly this ramification of the figure of genius is explored in "Wandrers Sturmlied." As if to quiet its trepidation, the poetic subject insists: so long as the protective figure of the genius accompanies me, so long as I coincide with that figure, I have nothing to fear; my song will sing its triumphant opposition to the paternal-meteorological threat; and I will ascend like a lark (which is to say, conveyed by my own singing) to heavenly heights. Genius would give the poetic subject the capacity to "sing against" ("Entgegen singen," 7), to mount a sort of lyric rebellion, an assault on the paternal instance of the law.

A subsequent passage designates the divinity lurking behind these meteorological phenomena as Jupiter, the Father-God:

(71) Warum nennt mein Lied dich zuletzt?
      Dich von dem es begann,

Dich in dem es endet
Dich aus dem es quillt
(75) Jupiter Pluvius!
Dich! dich strömt mein Lied,

(71) Why does my song name you last?
You from whom it began,
You in whom it ends,
You from whom it springs forth,
(75) Jupiter Pluvius!
You! you my song streams,

Here the full reach of genial ambition becomes apparent. It is not merely a question of courageously surmounting the threat posed by the "Sturmatmenden Gottheit" ("storm-breathing god," 93). Rather, the poetic subject would coincide with that divinity; its song would be the creative flow of liquidity that originates and ends with the "pluvian" (rain-making) god. More than this: that god would be the transitive product of the song's streaming, which is to say, of course, that the poetic subject would usurp the paternal position, becoming, qua genius-singer, the origin of the origin, the creator of the creator. This is the definition of genius familiar to us from "Mahomets Gesang," with the crucial difference, however, that the "storm-song" is spoken in the first person.

Were liquidity the only semantic register defining the symbolics of genius in "Wandrers Sturmlied," the text would be a simple variant of "Mahomets Gesang." But the mimetic competition that characterizes the drama of genius is enacted with other gods and within other semantic fields as well. The poem's second stanza reads:

(10) Den du nicht verlässest Genius
Wirst ihn heben übern Schlammpfad
Mit den Feuerflügeln.
Wandeln wird er
Wie mit Blumenfüßen
(15) Über Deukalions flutschlamm
Python tötend, leicht, groß
Pythius Apollo.

(10) The one you don't abandon, Genius,
You'll lift above the muddy path
With wings of fire.

> He will move
> As with flowery feet
> (15) Above the sludge of Deucalion's flood,
> Killing the python, lightly, greatly,
> Pythius Apollo.

The poetic genius identifies—mimetically and competitively—not only with the rain god Jupiter, but also with the god of the sun—of heat and light and form—Apollo. Following the flood (the father-god's liquid surge that washed Deucalion onto the Parnassian mount), he would, like the god Apollo who rules that mountain, separate form from nonform, kill the python with graceful grandeur, bring forth a world of beauty. This form-giving capacity is figured in a semantics of 'heat' and 'verticality': the "Feuerflügeln" that would lift the genius-poet above the muddy (formless, mixed, undifferentiated) remains of the flood. In "Mahomets Gesang," the semantics of 'fire' was lightly touched on in the phrase "der Türne Flammengipfel" (Text 15, 61), the phallic testimony of the genius's triumph. In "Wandrers Sturmlied," however, the idea of fire (including related notions such as warmth and glowing heat) is articulated across the entire text, entering into opposition with the liquid aspect of the genius problematic. With respect to the text's repertoire of divinities, this opposition is reflected in the pair Jupiter versus Apollo.

The split in "Wandrers Sturmlied" between the semantics of liquidity and that of fire introduces a new form of conflict into the drama of genius, a conflict that integrates the text's allusive threads in the structure of a poetic *mythos*. True genius is defined here by a double task: it must maintain itself in the pluvian flood (in the violence of the storm) and at the same time endow the world with Apollonian form. The manic-depressive cadence of the poem, its oscillation between enthusiasm and deflation, derives from the fact that the speaker, the subject aspiring to the symbolic position of genius, cannot do both. He fails in the Apollonian aspect of his task, and his is a failure of desire.

Recall that we are on Parnassus, the mountain of Apollo and his Muses.[29] Speaking from this position, the poet claims parity with the python-killing god, endeavors to usurp the god's position as lord of the Muses, whose circular dance is centered on his warmth:

> (23) Wen du nicht verlässest Genius
> Wirst im Schneegestöber
> (25) Wärmumhüllen,

Nach der Wärme ziehen sich Musen
Nach der Wärme Charitinnen.

Umschwebt mich ihr Musen!
Ihr Charitinnen!
(30) Das ist Wasser, das ist Erde
Und der Sohn des Wassers und der Erde
Über den ich wandle
Göttergleich.

(23) Whomever you don't abandon, Genius,
You will in the swirling snow
(25) Protect with warmth;
To warmth are drawn the muses;
To warmth are drawn the charites.

Hover about me you muses!
You charites!
(30) That is water, that is earth,
And the son of water and of earth
Above whom I move
Equal to a God.

To grasp what is at stake in this seizure of Apollo's position, it is useful to compare this passage with a similar one in "Pilgers Morgenlied" (Text 10). There the female figure comes to the wanderer in a thousand images that hover about his heart, exactly as the muses do here (see Text 10, 5–8), and there too this circulation of female images is characterized by warmth. A slight, but decisive difference, however, obtains between the two texts, a difference in directionality that marks a major transformation of semantic values. In "Pilgers Morgenlied," the warmth proceeds from the female figure to the poetic subject, whereas in "Wandrers Sturmlied" the poetic subject, appropriating the position of the sun god Apollo, is *himself the source* of warmth. The full significance of this transformation for the problematic of genius becomes clear when we recall that the female figure (the beloved) in "Pilgers Morgenlied" endows the speaker with the erotic energy that allows him manfully to meet the threat of the meteorological other. This "originary donation" is also figured in a semantics of warmth:

und mit einem mal
ew'ge Flammen
in die Seel' ihm warfst.
(Text 10, 15–17, emphasis added)

In "Wandrers Sturmlied," the male genius does not receive his warmth from a female figure. Rather, it is an attribute of his being, and it draws the female (the Muses) to him. The genius, in the figuration specific to this text, is the existence *who does not borrow his desire*. He is himself originary, self-identical desire, the source and center of life-giving, formative warmth. This relocation of the origin of desire finds its expression on the cosmic level as well: "Pilgers Morgenlied" figures the "sun" as "maternal presence": "der Sonne / Muttergegenwart" (24–25); in "Wandrers Sturmlied," however, the sun is male, the radiant god Apollo.

To pursue this comparison one step further, in "Pilgers Morgenlied," the gift of warmth—flames, glowing ("Glut," 27), life—proceeding from the female/mother to the poetic subject finds its realization in the tower. The primal donation is the gift of the phallus, a gift the poetic subject at once renounces and preserves in its passage through the drama of castration. In the background of the castration drama there lurks, obscure and terrifying, a figure of monstrosity: Medusa, "thousand snake tongued" (19). Seen in this context, the identification with Apollo "Wandrers Sturmlied" attempts (unsuccessfully, as we shall see) acquires a further motivation. Since Apollo does not derive his desire from the Mother, but rather is himself the autonomous source of desire (the sun), he need not fear the monstrosity of sexual difference/indifference. This deviation from the paradigm established in "Pilgers Morgenlied" motivates the onomastics of our text. "Pythius Apollo"—the name announcing his first appearance in "Wandrers Sturmlied"—designates the god as snake killer, the slayer of the monster emerging from the storm.

The conflict organizing the *mythos* of "Wandrers Sturmlied," therefore, is played out on the field of desire. Apollo does not derive his desire from the Mother. Without mediation, without the support of any other or outside, he—Apollo—is the phallus. It thus follows from the text's law of identity that, at the very point when the mimetic competition with the sun god reaches its highest agonistic pitch, it is articulated in a phallic semantics of warmth, centrality, and verticality:

> Weh! Weh! Innre Wärme
> (60) Seelen Wärme,
> Mittelpunkt!
> Glüh entgegen
> Phöb Apollen.
> Kalt wird sonst

(65) Sein Fürstenblick
Über dich vorübergleiten,
Neidgetroffen
Auf der Zeder Grün verweilen
Die zu grünen
(70) Sein nicht harrt

Oh! Oh! Inner warmth,
(60) Soul warmth,
Midpoint!
Glow against
Phoebus Apollo.
Otherwise coldly will
(65) His princely regard
Glide past you,
Envy struck
Linger on the cedar's green
Which to grow green
(70) Doesn't wait for him

Envy is the mimetic affect par excellence. To envy an other is to see in the other what I would be, but am not: a full subject, independent, enclosed in self-identity. This is what the speaker aspires to here: to glow outward from an undivided center, to glow autonomously without any support from an other, and to show this undivided glow in the upright testimony of the cedar tree upon which Apollo's regard enviously lingers. In "Mahomets Gesang," the cedar—the vertical, evergreen tree of god—bore witness to the triumph of genius, and my reading of that witness function as phallic is confirmed by the recurrence of the tree in this passage. To compete with Apollo, to seek to earn his envy, is to aspire to the position of the phallus, to wish to outglow or "glow against" the solar deity. Apollo is the phallic sun, the source of the world's glowing warmth, its order (he is a prince), and its differentiations (he eliminates monstrosity and rules the circular dance of the Muses). And he is all this *without himself being differentiated,* without reference to an other from whom he would borrow the force and luminosity of his desire. The position of Apollo toward which the poetic subject's ambition is directed is the position that *escapes castration.* Genius would be the successful attainment of that position, which is why genius is impossible for the speaking being.[30]

All the motivational strands of the poetic *mythos* I have traced out thus far are drawn together in the final stanza:

Wenn die Räder rasselten
Rad an Rad, rasch ums Ziel weg
Hoch flog
Siegdurchglühter
(105) Jünglinge Peitschenknall
Und sich Staub wälzt'
Wie von Gebürg herab
Kieselwetter in's Tal,
Glühte deine Seel Gefahren Pindar!
(110) Mut!—Glühte?—
Armes Herz!
Dort auf dem Hügel
Himmlische Macht
Nur so viel Glut
(115) Dort meine Hütte
Dort hin zu waten!

When the wheels rattled
Wheel to wheel, rapidly away to the goal,
Up flew
From victory-glowing
(105) Youths the whip's lash
And dust rolled
As down from the mountains
The gravel storm rolls into the valley;
Your soul glowed against dangers, Pindar!
(110) Courage!—Glowed?—
Poor heart!
There on the hill
Heavenly power,
Just enough glow—
(115) There my hut,
To wade there.

Pindar, the paradigm of poetic genius, withstands the violent conflict figured here in the chariot race, the turbulence of which is in turn compared to the downward crash of a mountain storm. This storm is a raging mountain river, pushing gravel before it. To sing the race is therefore to attain, in the rush of poetic language, the status of the storm-breathing god Jupiter. (The passage alludes, of course, to Horace's praise of Pindar's sublime style, pouring from his mouth like a mountain stream.)

Thus, Pindar accomplishes what the speaker of "Wandrers Sturmlied" aspires to: he outdoes Apollo by identifying with the God of originary liquidity. (See lines 71–77, cited above.) And his triumph occurs precisely on the field of conflict occupied by Apollo, the Pythian games named for their founder, the snake-slaying god. Of course, the precondition of this poetic victory is the inner "Glut"—the force of autonomous desire—for which Apollo is the paradigm. This desire allows Apollo to master the flood and to slay the Pythian monstrosity. The same desire allows Pindar to maintain himself in the turmoil of the Pythian games, to transform the rolling turbulence of the race into a poetic form that earns, if not the envy, at least the respect of the sun god: the testimony of his poetic achievement, as we know from Horace, will be the wreath woven from the leaves of the laurel tree, the evergreen tree of Apollo's desire.

The turn to Pindar in the final stanza, then, is a tactic in the poet's mimetic competition with Apollo. Pindar's triumph demonstrates the possibility, human and poetic, of earning the sun god's recognition and of attaining the position of genius. But the emulation of the Greek singer, the paradigm of genius, fails. The Pindaric tone legible in the enjambed syntax, the bold comparisons, and the allusions of the strophe's first half collapses, and the second half of the strophe mimics the exhausted panting of the all-too-human wanderer seeking shelter from the storm. What is the reason for this breakdown of the emulative poetic gesture? Here, once again, are the decisive, failure-enacting lines:

> Glühte deine Seel Gefahren Pindar!
> Mut!—Glühte?— *(109–10)*

The arc of the Pindaric period is broken by repetition, by a doubling that, even as it reproduces the first term, differs from it. This repetition affects the verb "glowing" that names autonomous desire, the force with which the poet aspired to combat Apollo ("Glüh entgegen / Phöb Apollen," 62–63) and with which Pindar masters the turbulence of the chariot race. Returning, the verb appears as its own echo, split by duplication, and the question mark that succeeds its second occurrence diverts its reference away from a thematic intentionality toward an intentionality that, as in a citation, has the word itself as its target. This shift accentuates the tense of the verb, foregrounds the idea of pastness, and thereby marks the difference between the time of Pindar's glowing triumph and the present of the act of speech. A law of temporal alterity and historical distance enforces itself here in the very movement of the text. To imitate genius—and this, of course, is what not only the final stanza, but the entire poem, as Pindaric ode, undertakes to do—is only to aggravate the wound of separation from it. Genius is always past or future (Pindar was the singer of triumphant youth), never present. Perhaps this wound of nonidentity (of noncoincidence with genius) is legible in the dash that breaks the syntax at the very moment the verb of desire recurs: "Mut!—Glühte?—." And perhaps the nonidentity that emerges from the attempt to repeat the achievement of genius also echoes the melancholy question: "Glühte . . . Pindar! / Mut—Goethe?"

Whether or not one chooses to accept such a reading of the text's graphics and phonics, this much is clear: the mimetic competition with Apollo has ended in failure. The initial identification with the python-slaying god who moves lightly and gracefully "above the sludge of Deucalion's flood" (15) splits apart, and the speaker is left to "wade" ("waten" parodistically echoes the Apollonian "wandeln," 13) through the formless mud toward his hut. There, like the peasant from whom he distinguished himself in an earlier passage, he will find the "umwärmend Feuer" ("fire warming round," 43) from which to *borrow* the glow that he lacks. Thus, the phrase "Himmlische Macht" ("Heavenly power," 113), which marks the center of the strophe's second half, enacts a gasp of surrender. It addresses Apollo, whose priority the poetic subject must finally acknowledge. Apollo, the solar phallus, the slayer of monstrosity, the undifferentiated source of form and differentiation: this is the impossible position of genius.

~

Modernity is the wound of genius. This statement characterizes a historical semantic structure. The discourse on genius that develops across the eighteenth century is oppositionally organized, drawing from the agon it stages the instruments of a global critique. In the terms of Niklas Luhmann and Peter Fuchs, the concept of genius projects an extra-social standpoint from which the social system is able to observe itself.[31] Genius is a device of discourse, naming the other of contemporary society in terms of which that society can be evaluated and criticized. From this perspective, society, in its modern form, appears as the negation of genius, the stifling of genial productivity, and precisely this feature of modernity, according to the discourse on genius, condemns it. I have touched on some of the commonplaces of this condemnation: modern culture is shackled by abstract rules, fashionable borrowings, empty conventions; commercialization throttles creativity; and when a genuine artistic product does emerge, it is immediately set upon by parasitic reviewers and critics. A bit later I shall add a further predicate to this catalogue of negativity: modernity is the age of writing and print, that is, of scriptural impoverishment, alienation, and reification of emotional experience and expressivity. Edward Young's *Conjectures on Original Composition* assembles all these critical motifs in a fashion that remains compelling, in Germany as well as England, at least till the end of the 1780's.

But the notion that modernity inflicts a wound on genius is more than an exorbitant metaphor for the impersonality and the debilitating effects of such macro-processes as the formation of a literary market and a literary public sphere. It also applies—I am tempted to say literally—to the process of individual subject formation. The modern subject is a wounded subject, a subject that cannot attain to the status of genius precisely because it is divided from itself, and therefore from genial wholeness and self-identity, by an internal cleft, a painful incision. The wound modernity inflicts, in other words, is castration. Hence the phallic component of the figure of genius. As the being who identifies with—who is—the phallus, the genius serves as the paradigm of unsevered fullness and subjective unity against which the modern condition of scission can be measured. As in the case of narcissism and castration (and for the same reason), we are dealing with a relation of systematic cohesion, of symbolic complementarity. The myth of genius has as its inverse double the myth of castration.

To make this claim concrete I will consider in detail one further lyric text by the young Goethe ("Künstlers Morgenlied"), the third poem in the sequence that opens the collection of 1778. Before doing so it is useful to stress certain implications of the two foregoing analyses. In "Mahomets Gesang" (Text 15), the myth of genius, at least on the level of the *énoncé*, seems to succeed: the poem completes a circular itinerary in which the genius-stream folds back on its own origin and achieves the status of auto-originating subject. The genius's act of self-fathering, however, can only be realized through a double repression: on the one hand, a repression of the complementary term to genius, of its shadow or inverse other, the semantic value 'poison'; on the other hand, a devalorization or marginalization of the feminine or maternal values associated in the text with a false version of specularity. Note that these two exclusions leave their trace in the same word, the strongly focalized "schlangewandelnd" (27), marking both the

severence from the natural-maternal sphere and the complementary relation between the genius-stream and the snake's lethal venom. "Schlangewandelnd" functions, one might say, as an Oedipal limp, the mark of an
inherited flaw. The conclusion of that text likewise reveals that the banishment of the feminine does not occur without remainder. As the stream
approaches the heart of the "waiting progenitor" (71–72), as the expectation of the "joy foaming" ("Freudebrausend," 72) union reaches its peak, it
is said that the stream "carries" or bears its "children" ("tragen," 69–70),
a term suggesting pregnancy. The genius-stream has internalized the
feminine function it initially appeared to have transcended. In its self-
conception as phallic, self-fathering subject, it remains dependent on,
beholding to, a certain conception of the female or Mother.

Thus, the phallic myth of genius, as "Mahomets Gesang" inflects it,
requires the repression of the other sex (one might say: of the otherness
of sex). Similar implications follow, but more blatantly, from my discussion of "Wandrers Sturmlied." There poetic aspiration is directed toward
Apollo, the figure of autonomous desire, the solar phallus who does not
borrow his desire from an other, but rather is himself the source of all
desire. It is this self-generating desire that enables Apollo to slay the
pythian monstrosity (again a snake) and to order the feminine Muses in
their circular array. But the poet's—the modern subject's—attempt to
usurp Apollo's position, unlike that of Pindar, the singer of the Pythian
games, fails, leaving him to wade through the sludge (impure mixture) and
to borrow his warmth from an external source. He is condemned to a
condition of alterity and secondariness, a condition that appears historically and poetically as the differential repetition separating him from
Pindaric originality.[32]

The troublesome figure, then, the figure who hampers the modern
subject and prevents it from achieving the status of (phallic) genius, is
feminine. If the modern subject is castrated, it is because of a certain
dependence on, or imbrication with, a female instance. Castration is the
mark of an alterity within the subject, an alterity that derives at once from
the otherness of sexual difference and from the otherness immanent to the
order of signs. This reading is confirmed by the major dramatic text
Goethe completed during the early 1770's.

Of course, I cannot develop here a full analysis of *Götz von Berlichingen*,
but a thumbnail sketch of its symbolic network should suffice to substanti-
ate my claim. The drama stages the historical demise of a sociocultural

order based on immediacy, trust, orality, and male rule, the demise also of a certain form of subjectivity as embodied by the play's eponymous hero. Götz, however, is not defeated by forces that are entirely external to him. To be sure, the drama deploys a reticulated set of oppositions contrasting the last knight with the emergent social order of mediation, deception, and writing that ultimately eradicates his world, but this oppositional schema (which has until recently governed the interpretation of the drama[33]) is complicated by the fact that Götz himself is marked by the very disunity and artificiality against which he stubbornly protests. Götz is a wounded subject. He has lost his right hand, the hand of trust, of love, of martial execution, and wears in its place an iron prosthesis that imports an element of death, disunity, and mediation into his every gesture. The iron hand is the structural analogue of the poison term "schlangewandelnd" in "Mahomets Gesang." And of course poison, administered by the female figure Adelhaid (the mistress of deception who also administers the modern state) plays a decisive role in the dramatic plot. In short, the seed of Götz's undoing—the force of modernity that finally disaggregates his world—is castration, and this force of castration is linked at once to the semantic register of poison (deception, writing, deadening abstraction) and to that of the feminine. *Götz von Berlichingen* is the counter-text to "Mahomets Gesang." Rather than founding a civilization, Götz fails to transmit himself, fails to father successfully. His feminized son, who no longer speaks and acts according to the code of knighthood, does not receive the paternal word.[34] Only by setting down on paper his memoirs— that is, by accepting the supplement that was his undoing and writing, like Rousseau, against writing—does the last knight outlive himself.

Preparatory to looking at "Künstlers Morgenlied" I will adduce one further text that correlates modernity with the wound of castration, the lyric fable "Der Adler und die Taube" ("The Eagle and the Dove"). Here are its opening lines:

> 17. Ein Adlerjüngling hob die Flügel
>   Nach Raub aus;
>   Ihn traf des Jägers Pfeil, und schnitt
>   Der rechten Schwinge Sennkraft ab!
> (5) Er stürzt' herab in einen Myrtenhain,
>   Fraß seinen Schmerz drei Tage lang,
>   Und zuckt' an Qual
>   Drei lange, lange Nächte lang;

Zuletzt heilt' ihn
(10) Allgegenwärtger Balsam
Allheilender Natur.
Er schleicht aus dem Gebüsch hervor,
Und reckt die Flügel, ach!
Die Schwingkraft weggeschnitten![35]

An eagle-youth raised his wings
After prey;
A hunter's arrow hit him, and severed
The sinewy force of his right wing!
(5) He plunged down into a myrtle grove,
Ate his pain three long days,
And twitched in agony
Three long, long nights along;
At last he was healed by
(10) The all-present balm
Of all-healing Nature.
He crawls out of the bush,
And stretches his wings, oh!
The force of swinging flight cut away!

The eagle's fall into the myrtle grove is its fall into modernity, into the false idyll of eighteenth-century Anacreontic fashion. Soon enough it will encounter the cooing doves emblematic of Anacreontic eroticism's cuddly titillations, who preach the Enlightenment doctrine of "Glückseligkeit" ("happiness," 35), a synonym, in this text, for "Genügsamkeit" ("comfortable self-satisfaction," 46). The poem elaborates, in other words, an easy polemic against the literary fashion of the day, drawing the lesson that the eagle's aspiration has lost its cultural meaning. In individuals who still hold to that aspiration, it remains only as an object of "mourning" ("tieftraurend," 18). These opening lines, then, establish the narrative etiology of the eagle's unhappy sojourn on an Anacreontic earth. The cause of the eagle's doleful condition—what condemns him to modernity—is nothing other than a wound.

A dramatic agon weaves through these lines. The eagle is a topos of genius, of the most sublime flights of inspiration, of poetic ascent to the divine—Jupiter's eagle, the eagle of Pindaric song. The "Raub" (prey) it seeks, then, is no ordinary eagle's food, but rather equivalence with the heaven's lord: a "Raub" in the sense of the English cognate 'rob', a theft, a usurpation. This youth would raise his wings—the bodily member expressive of his desire—to seize the position of the sun. And of course this member, uplifted in rebellious challenge, receives the laceration that cuts off the "force" ("Kraft") of flight. But who is the eagle's antagonist? Who is the "hunter" whose arrow interrupts its ascent? I would suggest that it is the very god whose solar position the eagle seeks to usurp, the divine hunter known for the lethal accuracy of his arrows, against whom the eagle-hunter would compete. Apollo, the "himmlische Macht" (Text 16, 114) to whom the poet of "Wandrers Sturmlied" finally succumbs, the solar phallus, inflicts the castrating wound. Note in this connection the following richly allusive detail. The text specifies that the arrow severs the "sinewy force" ("Sennkraft") of the eagle's wing. The word "sinew" ("Senn-" is a variant of "Sehne") also refers to the string of a bow, and perhaps also to that of a musical instrument. With his own divine bow/ lyre (the traditional Apollonian attributes), Apollo lacerates the wing/ bow/lyre/phallus of genial ambition. Such is the causality the text posits for the modern condition of poetry. Modernity is the wound of genius.

Finally, it should be remarked that the text submits the figure of castration to a certain doubling. The effects of the wound are mentioned at two points: in line 4, which depicts the actual severence of "Der rechten Schwinge Sennkraft" by Apollo's arrow, and in line 14, which relates the eagle's discovery that its "Schwingkraft" is "weggeschnitten." It is as if castration occurred twice, initially as the trauma of the sudden cut and later as the retrospective consciousness that the debilitating incision has taken place. Between these two moments a maternal/female instance intervenes: "all-healing Nature," whose "balm" soothes the wounded eagle's agony to such a degree that, emerging from the protective "Gebüsch" (almost as if it were being born), it has forgotten that Apollo's arrow has lamed its wing. Only when it tries to stretch its wing again does it sense not the pain of the wound, but the pain—"ach!"—of having been wounded. The awareness that it cannot coincide with the sun, that it cannot, as the genius must, identify with the solar phallus, in short, the knowledge of castration, is linked here to a dependency on the Mother. The Mother is the instance who assuages the wounded subject's pain and at the same time mediates a consciousness of woundedness; she is the figure both of restored (imagined) fullness and of lack.

These observations on wounding set the stage for the third major lyric text dealing with the problematic of genius:

18. KÜNSTLERS MORGENLIED

Ich hab euch einen Tempel baut
Ihr hohen Musen all
Und hier in meinem Herzen ist
Das Allerheiligste.

(5) Wenn Morgends mich die Sonne weckt
Warm froh ich schau umher
Steht rings ihr ewig Lebenden
In heilgem Morgenglanz

Ich bet hinan und Lobgesang
(10) Ist lauter mein Gebet
Und freudeklingend Saitenspiel
Begleitet mein Gebet.

Ich trete vor den Altar hin
Und lese wie sich's ziemt
(15) Andacht liturgscher Lektion
Im heiligen Homer.

Und wenn der in's Getümmel mich
Von Löwenkriegern reißt
Und Göttersöhn auf Wägen hoch
(20) Rachglühend stürmen an

Und Roß dann vor dem Wagen stürzt
Und drunter und drüber sich
Freund Feind sich wälzen in Todesblut
Er sengte sie dahin

(25) Mit Flammenschwert der Heldensohn
Zehn Tausend auf einmal,
Bis dann auch er gebändiget
Von einer Götterhand

Ab auf den Totenrogus stürzt
(30) Den er sich selbst gehäuft
Und Feinde nun den schönen Leib
Verschändend tasten an.

Da greif ich mutig auf und faß
Die Kohle wird Gewehr
(35) Und jene meine hohe Wand
In Schlachtfeld Wogen braust.

Hinan hinan! es heulet laut
Gebrüll der Feinde Wut
Und Schild an Schild und Schwert auf Helm,
(40) Und um den Toten Tod.

Ich dränge mich hinan hinan
Da kämpfen sie um ihn
Die tapfern Freunde, tapferer
In ihrer Tränenwut.

(45) Ach rettet! Kämpfet rettet ihn
Ins Lager bringt ihn rück
Und Balsam gießt dem Toten auf
Und Tränen Toten Ehr.

Und find ich mich zurück hierher
(50) Empfängst du Liebe mich
Mein Mädgen! Ach im Bilde nur
Und so im Bilde warm!

Ach wie du ruhtest neben mir
Mich schmachtetst liebend an
(55) Und mir's vom Aug durchs Herz hindurch
In Griffel schmachtete

Wie ich an Aug und Wange mich
Und Mund mich weidete
Und mir's im Busen jung und frisch
(60) Wie einer Gottheit war.

O kehre doch und bleibe dann
In meinen Armen fest
Und keine keine Schlachten mehr
Nur dich in meinem Arm.

(65) Und sollst mir meine Liebe sein
Alldeutend Ideal
Madonna sein ein Erstlingskind
Ein heiligs an der Brust

Und haschen will ich Nymphe dich
(70) Im tiefen Waldgebüsch
Ein geiles Schwänzgen hinten vor
Die Ohren aufgereckt

Und liegen will ich Mars zu dir
Du Liebes Göttin stark

(75) Und ziehn ein Netz um dich herum
Und rufen dem Olymp

Wer von den Göttern kommen will
Beneiden unser Glück
Und solls die Fratze Eifersucht
(80) An Bettfuß angebannt.[36]

ARTIST'S MORNING SONG

I have built you a temple
You high Muses all,
And here in my heart is
The holiest of all.

(5) When in the morning the sun awakens me
Warm, joyful, I look around;
You stand in circle, you eternally living ones,
In holy morning radiance.

I pray upward, and song of praise
(10) Most pure is my prayer,
And joy-ringing play of strings
Accompanies my prayer.

I step before the altar
And read, as is fitting,
(15) The devotion, a liturgical lesson
In holy Homer.

And when he me into the tumult
Of lion-warriors tears
And gods' sons on chariots high
(20) Press on, storms glowing with revenge,

And horse then falls beneath the chariot
And above and below each other
Friend, foe, twist in the blood of death;
He burned them down,

(25) With flaming sword the heroes' son,
Ten thousand all at once,
Until he too, mastered
By the hand of a god,

Falls upon the pile of dead
(30) That he heaped up himself,

And the foe now his beautiful body
Touches in desecration.

Then I take up and grasp
My charcoal as a weapon,
(35) And on my high wall
Splash the waves of the battlefield.

Upward, upward! Loudly roars
The foe's howling rage,
And shield to shield and sword on helmet,
(40) And about the dead one, death.

I press upward, upward
Where they battle for him,
The brave friends, braver still
In their tearful rage.

(45) Oh save! Fight, save him,
Back to the camp return him,
And pour balm over the dead one
And tears of honor to the dead.

And when I find myself back here
(50) You receive me, love,
My maiden! Oh, only in image
And thus in image warm!

Oh, how you rested next to me,
Looked at me, loving, with desire,
(55) And from my eye through my heart into
My pencil it desired.

How I on eye and cheek
And mouth revelled,
And it was young and fresh in my breast
(60) Like a god.

Oh, return and stay then
Close in my arms,
And no, no more battles—
Just you in my arms.

(65) And you shall be to me my love,
All-interpreting Ideal,
A Madonna be, the first child,
A holy child at her breast.

> And I will seize you as nymph
> (70) In the deep forest bush
> A horny tail behind, in front
> Ears sticking up
>
> And as Mars I will lie with you,
> Strong, you goddess of love,
> (75) And pull a net about you
> And call to Olympus
>
> Whoever among the gods shall come
> Envy our happiness,
> Even should it be the grimace of jealousy
> (80) Spellbound at the bed's foot.

In this text, which was first published as the end piece to a miscellany of remarks on art and criticism entitled *Aus Goethes Brieftasche* (*From Goethe's Briefcase*, 1776) and can therefore be considered to have a programmatic status, the threads of significance I have been tracing here, including the major conflicts, come together and find a provocative resolution. The poem divides into five sections of four stanzas each. The first section (stanzas I–IV) narrates the artist's daily ritual (the if/then structure suggests a repeated practice): the vision of the eternally living forms (the Muses) in the morning sun, joyful prayer, worshipful reading in Homer. Here I want to remark the implicitly blasphemous conflation of artistic and religious registers of significance centering on the repeated occurrence of the term "holy" ("heilig"). The attribution of this term shifts from the heart of the speaking subject (3), to the sun's morning radiance (8), to the genius-poet Homer (16). Beneath the continuity of these ascriptions, the contours of a conflict are legible. The poet claims sacred power—indeed, the most sacred power ("das Allerheiligste," 4)—for himself, but this claim is immediately countered by the reference to the "heilgem Morgenglanz" (8). Who is the holy center of the muses' circular array, the speaker or the sun, the poet or Apollo? This, of course, is the question raised by "Wandrers Sturmlied," and there can be little doubt that "Künstlers Morgenlied" repeats the essential conflict of that poem. Hence the turn to Homer at the close of this first section and the predication of sacredness to him: Homer—like Pindar in "Wandrers Sturmlied"—would provide the guarantee that poetic genius is possible, that the speaking being can assume the standpoint of sacred centrality and rule, from the position of the god Apollo, the harmonious dance of the Muses.

The second section (stanzas V–VIII) enacts the movement of an identificatory reading of the *Iliad*, in particular the scene of Patroclus's death in the battle before the gates of Troy. The language of turbulent battle, both in its lexicon and in its enjambed syntax, echoes that of the Pindar stanza of "Wandrers Sturmlied" (supporting the reading of Homer in this text as a parallel figure to Pindar). In both cases, the proof or demonstration of genial accomplishment is to have mastered, through poetic depiction, the elemental violence of a battle or competition. The genius-artist is caught up in an agon analogous to the one he represents. And, as in "Wandrers Sturmlied," the divine figure of Apollo plays a key role in the drama of artistic ambition, for the "hand of a god" (28) that lames Patroclus, taming his wild ambition, is, of course, that of the sun god.[37] The mimetic competition with Apollo, latent in the first section, thus emerges with full virulence as soon as the poet attempts to appropriate the position of genius via his identificatory reading of Homer. In fact, what occurs here is a failure of identification with the precursor poet, or perhaps a slippage of identification away from Homer to the figure of Patroclus.

This is why, in the third section (stanzas IX–XII), the speaker takes up his own "weapon" (34), the charcoal drawing instrument with which he enters the Homeric battle scene. Here to draw is to fight, to attempt to wrest beauty of form ("den schönen Leib" of Patroclus, 31) from the violence and amorphous turbulence of the scene, and, more specifically, from the violation of a desecrating wound. Everything hinges on the redemption of the hero's beautiful body because the speaker's own corporeal integrity, the oneness and identity of his bodily self-image, is also at stake. Artistic production, far from being the outpouring of creative energy interpreters have consistently read into this text, is a desperate effort of self-restitution, an effort to save one's identity as harmonious, unitary bodily schema before an onslaught of forces that threaten it with dismemberment.

But Patroclus, lamed by Apollo, is not retrieved. The third section breaks off the Homeric identification at the point of the speaker's plea to bring the fallen warrior "back" ("rück") to the "camp" (or perhaps "bed": "Lager," 46), a call that apparently goes unanswered. The fourth section (stanzas XIII–XVI) then opens with the speaker's finding himself "back here" ("zurück hierher," 49). This movement from the epic register of martial conflict to the thematic realm of erotic love ("Liebe," 50) repeats a gesture of generic self-differentiation traditional in the lyric throughout antiquity. The lyric poet, as opposed to his epic counterpart, sings not of the glories of battle, but rather of the sweeter glories of amorous experience. This generic opposition (through which Sappho, for instance, claims superiority to Homer[38]) is figured in Goethe's text in the contrast between the historical painting of the Homeric scene (which the speaker-artist fails to complete) and the painting of his beloved "maiden" (51) that stands complete in his atelier.

Or is it a completed painting? This, of course, is the accepted interpretation of the word "Bild" (51), and I see no reason to reject it out of hand. I would remark, however, that the word "Bild" can be read in a second way, namely, in the sense of 'imaginary or remembered image'. This reading fits better with the details of the text, for if we take stanza XIV as relating the contents of the "Bild," as the introductory particle suggests, then we would have to conclude that it is a most unlikely painting indeed. That stanza names an event that took place between the lovers: how the maiden, lying on the bed next to the speaker, looked desiringly into his eyes, and how this desire passed through his eye and heart and into his artist's pencil. Even if we avoid altogether the erotic reading of this exchange (which it is possible only counterfactually to do), we would still have to conclude that the "Bild" represents the event prior to the execution of a painting (the preparation, say, of the "Griffel"). What is remembered or imagined here—what is phantasized—is the emergence of a condition of artistic readiness (the pencil infused with desire), a condition that has its source in the erotic charge (note the parallels to "Auf Cristianen R.," Text 9) transmitted to the artist by his beloved.

This reading has the additional advantage of making sense of the transition to the fifth section of the poem (stanzas XVII–XX). Were the beloved to return, were the condition of artistic preparedness reestablished, then the speaker could transform that condition into art; that is, into the three possible paintings imagined in succession across the four stanzas: a Madonna and Child, a Nymph and Faun, and finally, significantly elaborated across two stanzas, a Venus and Mars. Not only would these paintings emerge out of the loving encounter with and embrace of the beloved, their contents would be translations of that encounter into various religious and mythological motifs. The imagined artworks, in other words, would function as identificatory schemata in which the artist reconstitutes and celebrates a primal fantasy: the fantasy of his own constitution as erotic-artistic subject in the loving eyes of his "maiden" and in the primordial donation of desire and artistic capacity (the "Griffel") that flows from that specular regard.

Overall, then, the text juxtaposes two types of artistic identity formation, the epic-heroic paradigm of the *Iliad* (sections two and three), to which the artist proves unequal, and the primal fantasy of love (sections four and five), in which some measure of success is achieved. This juxtaposition of artistic models provides the grid for a historical reflection on the nature and possibilities of art in modernity. While Homeric grandeur (like the poetic achievement of Pindar in "Wandrers Sturmlied") proves to be no longer attainable, the lyric paradigm of love discloses the basis for a specifically modern form of artistic achievement. Such are the contours of the text's overarching argument. A closer examination of the poetic figuration will enable us to see how the reconceptualization of genius "Künstlers Morgenlied" performs is linked to the sexualization of specularity.

I have already remarked that the battle scene echoes the Pindar stanza of "Wandrers Sturmlied," which draws its poetic resources from the characterization of Pindar's sublime style presented in Horace's Ode IV, 2. The shift from Pindar to Homer, however, decisively alters the poetic rendering of the genius problematic by enhancing the possibilities for dramatic specification. In other words, whereas the turbulence of the Pindaric race remained internally undifferentiated and the competition with Apollo was only allusively evoked by the thread of significance leading out from the Pythian games and the poetic laurel, here we have identifiable actors—Patroclus, Apollo, Hector—locked in a deadly fight. Here the failure to attain genius resides not merely in the speaker's inability to repeat the achievement of his genius-precursor; rather, that poetic failure is acted out in the conflict of the epic characters. It is not sufficient to say, as interpreters of the poem have done, that this portion of the poem bespeaks an intense or enthusiastic reading of Homer. The point is that the Homeric text is read as a figuration of the agon of genius, as if Homer had anticipated, in the dynamics of the epic scene, the impossibility of later poets' matching his achievement. For Goethe, the Homeric text not only represents the Trojan War with incomparable artistic power, it also stages its own resplendent victory over any subsequent poetic endeavor that seeks to equal its triumph.

Hence the identification with Patroclus, the Greek hero debilitated by Apollo and subsequently slain and defiled by Hector. Note the development of this identification. Out of the undifferentiated turbulence of the battle ("Freund Feind sich wälzen in Todesblut," 23), the singular hero rises up, his gesture held in the epic praeteritum, glowing flamelike against the background of the numberless vanquished:

> Er sengte sie dahin
>
> Mit Flammenschwert der Heldensohn
> Zehn Tausend auf einmal,   *(24–26)*

The figure of Patroclus serves to demonstrate the (human poetic) possibility of surviving the violence, the possibility of form-giving mastery, of self-generated identity. But exactly this is the prerogative of Apollo. Thus, the claim of genius invested in Patroclus immediately elicits the sun god's intervention:

> Bis dann auch er gebändiget
> Von einer Götterhand   *(27–28)*

Recall the lesson of "Der Adler und die Taube," that the wound of genius is struck by Apollo. Here the stanza extends from "Flammenschwert" to "Götterhand," from the glowing instrument and testimony of Patroclus's ephemeral victory, held, of course, in his hand, to the hand of the radiant god who wounds him in the very moment he rises up to claim that victory. In "Wandrers Sturmlied," too, the competition with Apollo ("Glüh entgegen / Phöb Apollen," Text 16, 62–63) was played out in a semantics of heat, and ultimately it was a lack of heat ("Glühte?," 110) that marked the collapse of poetic ambition. Here the seme of 'fiery desire' is attached to the "Flammenschwert," the sole descriptive feature of Patroclus. This sword of desire, held high in self-affirmation, is the phallus. Apollo's blow—like his arrow in "Der Adler und die Taube"—inflicts the wound of castration.

The crisis fantasy of castration becomes, as it were, allusively explicit at the point when Patroclus, like the eagle, "falls" ("stürzt"):

> Ab auf den Totenrogus stürzt
> Den er sich selbst gehäuft
> Und Feinde nun den schönen Leib
> Verschändend tasten an.   *(29–32)*

The allusion here is to Hector's violent act following the stunning of Patroclus by Apollo, and it is important to recall exactly what this act was. Here is A. T. Murray's prose translation of the passage from the *Iliad*:

> But Hector, when he beheld great-souled Patroclus drawing back, smitten with the sharp bronze, came nigh him through the ranks, *and smote him with a thrust of his spear in the nethermost belly, and drave the bronze clean through*; and he fell with a thud, and sorely grieved the host of the Achaeans.[39] *(Emphasis added)*

The "beautiful body" torn open and desecrated, the phallic schema of corporeal oneness shattered: such is the significance of castration. Castration is a kind of semiotic catastrophe in which the phallic symbolization of the self breaks apart. The myth of genius, which is nothing other than the myth of phallic self-generation and identity, culminates in a scene of mutilation and wounding.

The violation of Patroclus—and this violation alone—motivates the artist-speaker's active intervention in the epic scene that the poem's third section unfolds:

> Da greif ich mutig auf und faß
> Die Kohle wird Gewehr
> Und jene meine hohe Wand
> In Schlachtfeld Wogen braust.
>
> *(33–36)*

The full weight of this motivation deserves to be stressed. The artist's entire effort, as he takes up the charcoal and wildly draws, is directed at redeeming the "beautiful body," at saving it from profanation or desecration. And he has every reason for wanting to do so, since this desecration would destroy his own self-conception, posited at the beginning of the text (as I remarked, in implicit affront to Apollo) as "das Allerheiligste" (4). Thus, with the precision of its deictic gesture ("Da," in other words: "there, at the point and moment of violation"), Goethe's text proffers an astonishing definition of art: artistic activity functions as a defense against the threat of castration; art is the attempt to maintain (to hold on to, as one holds something in one's hand) a paradigm of self-identity, the corporeal schema of phallic oneness figured in the hero's beautiful body. But not only the artist's self-representation is at stake here: castration, as semiotic catastrophe, threatens the order of representation in general, the very possibility of ordering a world of beautiful appearances, the possibility of creating a world whose forms shine forth in Apollonian light. The shattering of the phallic self—the wounding of genius—is also the destruction of the world of aesthetic presence embodied in the Homeric epic.

The end of section three, with its plaintive "Ach rettet!" (45), suggests that, in this text at least (that is, in contrast to the *Iliad*), no redemption of the beautiful body occurs. Homeric genius, which would successfully rival Apollo, has become a historical impossibility. Thus, the historical painting that would imitate the Homeric scene and present the glory of Patroclus's body remains an abandoned sketch. But this failure is signaled in a second way. The weapon the artist takes up (in his hand) is a "Kohle" (34), the charcoal employed to sketch out in colorless black lines the skeleton of a painting that, of course, is never realized. The poetic significance of this word derives from its contrast with the term designating the weapon Patroclus bears in his hand: in a reversal that achieves the utmost in cutting irony, the text moves from the burning "Flammenschwert" of ancient heroism to the burned-out "Kohle" of modernity, from the radiant phallic sword that would challenge Apollo to the charcoal stub of the modern subject.

The reading of the poem's Homeric sections articulated here can be supported through reference to other texts, most notably, of course, *Die Leiden des jungen Werther*, the most extensive artistic engagement with Homer in this early phase of Goethe's career. Indeed, one way of looking at that novel is to see it as exploring the question: What happens when the subject denies castration? For there can be little doubt that Werther's entire imaginative labor is directed toward restoring a world lost to the semiotic catastrophe castration is.[40] And of course a certain reading of Homer—an idyllic reading that systematically avoids the violence of the *Iliad*—sustains this phantasmatic project. But to develop an analysis of the novel that would concretize these claims would lead me too far away from the trajectory of my argument. I will therefore cite another text by Goethe from the early 1770's that, I believe, confirms my construal of "Künstlers Morgenlied." In a review of a scholarly edition of Homer Goethe writes:

> Homer—doch so übersetzt, kommentiert, extrahiert, enucleiert, so sehr verwundet, gestoßen, zerfleischt, durch Steine, Staub, Pfützen geschleift, getrieben, gerissen.[41]

Homer—but so translated, commented, extracted, enucleated, so very wounded, struck, his flesh ripped open, dragged, driven, torn through stones, dust and puddles.

Exactly the strategy I attributed to "Künstlers Morgenlied" is employed here. Just as the Patroclus scene served as a cipher for the failure of the modern artist attempting to imitate the Homeric epic, in this passage Achilles' desecration of Hector's body figures the destiny of the Homeric text at the hands of modern translators and commentators. In both cases the artistic *corpus* is submitted to a violent wounding and desecration; in both, modernity fails to reproduce the aesthetic presence of the Homeric world. Moreover, what is involved in the passage from the review is clearly a semiotic catastrophe: a kind of linguistic violence, disintegration, and scattering set into motion by a reflective culture of bookish scholarship. Recall that the same deadening bookishness appears in *Werther*, in the hated figure of the new pastor's wife, who assiduously studies the modern theological writings of "Kennikot, Semler, and Michaelis."[42] It is no accident that this woman mediates one of the novel's major figurations of castration: the cutting down of the ancient nut trees, the counterparts to the cedar "trees of god" that rise up in Goethe's texts on genius.

   The lesson that Homeric art, the art of self-fathering genius, the art that shines in the Apollonian light of presence, is shattered in modernity and that this shattering is the catastrophe of the phallic subject is only half the story "Künstlers Morgenlied" relates. The final two sections of the poem develop an alternative paradigm of art based not on the heroic Homeric model, but rather on the model of intimate love. This new type of art, at once lyric and modern, will provide an *instrument* (the reason I emphasize this word will become clear in what follows) with which Apollo can be successfully rivaled.

   Recall once again "Der Adler und die Taube." I remarked that in that text the castration of the eagle occurs twice, first in the scission of the wing by Apollo's arrow, then in the eagle's awareness of its wounded condition following its healing by a maternal nature. The figure of this healing is the "balm" ("Balsam," Text 17, 10) administered by the female instance. Insofar as it remains attached to the Mother, insofar as it owes its health to a feminine-natural donor, the eagle cannot attain the heights of genial artistic accomplishment. This means that it must remain in mourning, that it must turn unproductively within itself, for the only alternative to the Apollonian model of art the text offers is the utterly insufficient one of Anacreontic titillation. Like "Der Adler und die Taube," "Künstlers Morgenlied" images the healing of the wounded body as the effect of a soothing "balm" ("Balsam," 47) and the site where this restoration of the body would take place is the "Lager," from a Homeric perspective the "camp" of the Greeks, but from a modern perspective the soft "bed" of love. For it is "love" ("Liebe," 50) that receives ("Empfängst," 50, which also suggests 'conceives' in the procreational sense) the wounded artist when he "finds himself back here" (in his atelier, in the present of modernity). Up to this point, therefore, the two texts run entirely parallel. But "Künstlers Morgenlied" then takes a radically different and more positive line of development from that followed out in "Der Adler und die Taube." The reason for this difference is that "Künstlers Morgenlied" knows another kind of love (and hence another kind of art) from the insipid Anacreontic variety. The matrix of this modern form of love and art is sexualized specularity.

I cite once again the opening stanzas of the poem's fourth section:

> Und find ich mich zurück hierher
> Empfängst du Liebe mich
> Mein Mädgen! Ach im Bilde nur
> Und so im Bilde warm!
>
> Ach wie du ruhtest neben mir
> Mich schmachtetst liebend an
> Und mir's vom Aug durchs Herz hindurch
> In Griffel schmachtete   *(49–56)*

Could the configuration here be more familiar? Compare the passage with "Pilgers Morgenlied," in which the crisis of nonvision that threatens the subject unable to perceive the tower is overcome by consoling "Bilder / Seliger Erinnerung" that hover "holy, warm" about its anxiety-ridden heart (Text 10, 6–8). In "Künstlers Morgenlied," too, a remembered-imagined "Bild" generates in the devastated subject (the "Kohle" has failed to flame) a warmth, as if that "Bild" could provide an alternative—milder, sweeter, more lyrical—to the Apollonian sun. Moreover, the content of the image is introduced, just as in "Pilgers Morgenlied," by an extended "wie" clause that relates the originary event of the specular encounter. Finally, in both texts the focus of the specular fantasy is phallic: in one the standing tower ("Zeuge meiner Wonne," Text 10, 10); in the other, the artist's instrument, infused with desire. The specular fantasy elaborated in the second of the quoted stanzas likewise resembles that of "Auf Cristianen R." (Text 9), in which a line of communication runs from the eye of the beloved through embrace, kiss, and spine to the big toe of the poetic subject. Exactly such a path of transmission is traced out here from the "Aug" through the "Herz" and into the "Griffel."

These similarities with "Pilgers Morgenlied" and "Auf Cristianen R." allow us to conceptualize the resolution "Künstlers Morgenlied" finds for its agonistic artistic problematic. Genius is autonomous desire, self-fathering, identification with the phallus. Thus, where genius succeeds, as in "Mahomets Gesang," the subject's imbrication with the feminine must be repressed: the genius-stream leaves the maternal valley of specularity behind. But in fact this repression is a preservation or internalization of the feminine. Where the subject endeavors to deny outright and totally its dependence on the feminine and thus to achieve equivalence with the solar phallus Apollo ("Wandrers Sturmlied," "Der Adler und die Taube," the Homer sections of "Künstlers Morgenlied"), *the irreducible debt of the modern subject to the Mother* and hence the otherness of sexual difference return as the catastrophe of castration.[43] "Künstlers Morgenlied" resolves this dilemma, as it were, by accepting the debt, by abandoning the poetic aspiration to Apollonian grandeur and drawing its resources instead from the infinite plenitude of the Mother. In my reading of "Auf Cristianen R.," I argued that that text performs a matrilinear recoding of sexuality in which the desiring subject is constituted in and through the Mother's primordial donation of the phallus. If "Künstlers Morgenlied" fantasizes the same scene of energetic-symbolic charging, it is because that text locates the origin of art, and of aesthetic subjectivity, in the same maternal gift. The "Kohle" burned to deadened blackness by the Apollonian fire becomes the artist's "Griffel," alive with the desire it has received within the specular regard.

The figure of an artistic instrument charged with desire is not unique to "Künstlers Morgenlied." We encounter it in a passage from the Sulzer review of 1772, in which the transition from amateur ("Liebhaber") to "Künstler" is characterized as the point where "die Seele mit einflösse ins Instrument"[44] ("the soul would flow into the instrument"). And in the "Baukunst" essay from the same year, the following passage occurs:

wenn dann männlicher, die gewaltige Nerve der Begierden und Leiden in deinem [the addressee here is the "Knabe," the youthful artist of the future] Pinsel lebt, du gestrebt und gelitten genug hast, und genug genossen, und satt bist irdischer Schönheit, und wert bist auszuruhen in dem Arme der Göttin, wert an ihrem Busen zu fühlen, was den vergötterten Herkules neu gebar; nimm ihn auf, himmlische Schönheit, du Mittlerin zwischen Göttern und Menschen, und mehr als Prometheus leit er die Seligkeit der Götter auf die Erde.[45]

when then the powerful nerve of sufferings and pains lives in your paintbrush, when you have striven and suffered enough, and enjoyed enough, and you are satiated with earthly beauty, and worthy to rest in the arms of the goddess, worthy to feel at her breast what gave birth anew to the deified Hercules— accept him then, heavenly Beauty, you mediator between the gods and human beings, and more than Prometheus let him conduct the bliss of the gods onto the earth.

Isn't this the wish that finds the scene of its fulfillment in "Künstlers Morgenlied," with its love-charged instrument, its soothing rest in the arms of the beloved, its rebirth (recall the word "Empfängst," 50) as a god ("Und mir's im Busen jung und frisch / Wie einer Gottheit war," 59–60)? The idea of artistic rebirth, especially, is central to both the essay and the poem, an idea that, of course, is inseparable from the matrilinear recoding of the artistic origin. The artist returns to the origin, to his birth as subject, but also achieves, in and through this recovery of the Source, the status— in particular the bliss—of a divinity.

A passage from *Des Künstlers Erdewallen* ("The Artist's Sojourn on Earth," 1773) provides a further variant of this sexualized specular scenario:

> 19. Meine Göttin deiner Gegenwart Blick
>   Überdrängt mich wie erstes Jugendglück
>   Die ich in Seel u. Sinn himmlische Gestalt
>   Dich umfasse mit Bräutigams Gewalt
>   Wo mein Pinsel dich berührt bis du mein
>   Du bist ich bist mehr als ich ich bin dein
>   Uranfängliche Schönheit Königin der Welt![46]

> My goddess, the regard of your presence
> Overwhelms me like youth's first happiness,
> You whom in soul and sense, heavenly figure,
> I embrace with the force of a bridegroom.

Where my brush touches you you are mine
You are I, are more than I, I am yours,
Primordial beauty, queen of the world!

The love-based model of art, like that of self-fathering genius, is a model of artistic self-generation, the difference being that the autonomous paternal instance is replaced by the maternal gift and the reciprocity of the specular regard. In fact, what we have here is an endless circularity and exchange: recalling the event that gave birth to him as artistic subject (the Mother's primordial donation of desire), the artist recreates or reenacts that event with his charged instrument and thereby constitutes the Mother as she constitutes him. The artistic act simulates an erotic union with the Mother, whose issue is the artist reborn as erotic-artistic subject, and so on endlessly.

In the passages cited from the *Baukunst* essay and *Des Künstlers Erdewallen,* the artistic act is figured in three registers of significance: the relation between mother and child, sexual union, and rebirth as a god. "Künstlers Morgenlied" realizes each of these conflated semantic domains serially in the motifs of the three paintings imagined across the poem's concluding section. Madonna and Child, Nymph and Faun, and Venus and Mars are differently nuanced permutations of a single matrix, sexualized specularity. Pride of place is given to the motif of the mother/child dyad, which restores to the artistic subject, figured, of course, as the "Erstlingskind" (67) at the nurturing maternal breast, the attribute of sacredness that had been threatened with castrating desecration. The phallic series running through the entire text ("Flammenschwert," "Kohle," "Griffel") culminates in the naughtily explicit "Schwänzgen" and the "Ears sticking up" (71–72) of the faun. But the most pointed demonstration that the matrix of specularity provides a genuine, even superior alternative to Apollonian art occurs in the motif of Venus and Mars. The artist assumes not only the role of Mars, but also that of Vulcan, who, netting the lovers in their illicit embrace, calls the other Olympian gods to laugh at them. Not that the artist figures himself as cuckold: this aspect of the mythologeme is entirely absent. Rather, the demonstrative gesture of Vulcan, the exhibition of the lovers' embrace, is functionalized, and the force of the demonstration is to awaken "envy" ("Beneiden," 78) on the part of the jealous onlooker. Not just any onlooker: as Hans Vaget has shown, the passage from the *Odyssey* Goethe's text alludes to here makes it unmistakable that the god held in thrall by the mimetic desire of envy is none other than Apollo.[47] Thus, where the poetic subject of "Wandrers Sturmlied" fails in his effort to leave Apollo "neidgetroffen" (Text 16, 67), "envy-struck," by the phallic, evergreen uprightness of the cedar tree, the subject of "Künstlers Morgenlied" succeeds. The text imagines a form of art that rivals the Apollonian paradigm; with his maternally endowed instrument, the artist steals the prestige of the solar phallus.

One final component of the *matrilinear recoding of art* performed by "Künstlers Morgenlied" needs to be set into place. This is the status of the term "Bild," which both explicitly and implicitly governs the final two sections of the poem. Extending the reading of this word in its initial occurrence (51–52) as remembered-fantasized image (as opposed to finished, material painting), I would suggest that the apostrophe to the "maiden" that opens stanza XVI ("o kehre doch und bleibe dann," 61) is directed not at the maiden qua real, bodily person, but rather at the imagined maiden, the maiden as "Bild." This is implied by the fact that the "Bilder" whose motifs are listed across the poem's final section are not real paintings, but rather images that would come into being were she to return and stay. The beloved object, in other words, is decorporealized; her being is that of the imagination (*Einbildungskraft*) itself. The maternal source of modern art is not the real mother, but the Mother as *Phantasie*.[48]

This means, of course, that love-based art is inevitably marked by an awareness of its own fictionality, its status as "Bild." Thus, the Love who receives and conceives the artistic subject ("Empfängst," 50) does so *only* within the imagination: "Ach im Bilde nur" (51). But to promote such negativity to the status of the poem's sole message would amount to a massive historical distortion. Decorporealization lends the Mother her generative power as the source of artistic productivity: "Und so im Bilde warm!" (52). As "Bild," the Mother becomes an infinite semantic resource, the "Urbild" (cf. "Uranfängliche Schönheit" in Text 19) of all artistic "Bilder," transforming herself across such artistic motifs as Madonna and Child, Nymph and Faun, Venus and Mars. She is the reference, the meaning, the key to all artistic images, liminally present in all of them, captured by none. "Künstlers Morgenlied" designates this semantic plenitude as "Alldeutend Ideal" ("All-interpreting Ideal," 66). As the quantifying prefix indicates, we are dealing here with the domain of universality, with the element of internality. *This universalized imaginative function is the matrix of modern art.*

To conclude this reading of "Künstlers Morgenlied," I want to step back from the poem a bit and consider what might be termed its discursive ramifications. The text inscribes the program of a new form of aesthetic theorizing, a program which is actualized in the philosophical discourse on art that emerges in the last decade of the eighteenth century in the wake of Kant's *Critique of Judgment* (1790). Speaking very broadly, this discourse comprises two essential components: a philosophical-historical construction of modernity and a theory of the (autonomously) productive imagination. In "Künstlers Morgenlied" these two discursive components, perhaps for the first time, enter into the specific alliance that characterizes post-Kantian aesthetic theory.

As regards the first, the poem deploys a classical strategy of generic self-definition (based on the homology lyric : epic :: love : war) in order to position itself historically vis-à-vis the paradigm of Homeric art. A certain historical self-consciousness, in other words, inheres in, and emerges from, the text's fundamental rhetorical gesture. From this perspective, "Künstlers Morgenlied" can be read as a response to the *querelle des anciens et des modernes*, which anticipates the philosophical-historical justification of modern art elaborated in post-Kantian aesthetics.[49] As in Schiller's *On Naive and Sentimental Poetry* (1796), the lack that distinguishes the modern aesthetic subject from its ancient counterpart (and Homer, of course, is Schiller's privileged exemplar of the naive artist) becomes an advantage, one Goethe conceives as 'love' and Schiller qualifies with the predicates 'freedom' and 'progressivity'.

But the text from the canon of post-Kantian theory that reveals the most striking similarities to the implicit aesthetics of "Künstlers Morgenlied" is Wilhelm von Humboldt's treatise *On Goethe's Hermann und Dorothea* (1799). Goethe's bourgeois epic, which Humboldt submits to a minute analysis, is the poet's second extended literary response to Homer (the first, as mentioned above, being *Werther*). Thus, Humboldt's subject matter quite naturally leads him to reflect on the difference between ancient (Homeric) art and Goethe's modern aesthetic practice, or rather to *construct* this difference as a schema of self-definition for modern consciousness.

We can observe Humboldt's differential schema at work in the following passage.

> Whoever reads *Hermann und Dorothea* during hours when his heart is open to the effect of the poet must undeniably concede that there reigns here another spirit than in the works of the ancients. He will find this spirit to be not exactly

greater and better, but different and equally excellent; he will feel himself not more powerfully attracted, but more inwardly penetrated.[50]

A modern form of aesthetic excellence that does not surpass that of the ancients (is not "greater" or "better"), but rather must be judged on an entirely different evaluative scale: this too is the thesis of "Künstlers Morgenlied," which abandons the (impossible) mimetic competition with Homer and Apollo in order to take up a position on an alternative field of artistic achievement, the gentler "Lager" of love. And Humboldt's conception of the difference between the ancient and modern aesthetic domains as that between 'power' ("mächtig") and 'inwardness' ("innig") likewise parallels the Goethean opposition between 'martial-heroic' and 'amorous' modes of art. Interestingly, Humboldt also articulates the ancient/modern difference in terms that bear on the question of sense perception: "If the ancients tend more toward the depiction of nature in its sensuous splendor and grandeur, he [Goethe] inclines more toward displaying the internality of humanity."[51] The modern poet cannot achieve an art of "sensuous splendor and grandeur," cannot, in the terms of "Künstlers Morgenlied," produce an artistic world that shines forth in Apollonian radiance. Thus, the god withdraws from the world of aesthetic objectivity and becomes a function within the subject's psychic economy. Humboldt's formulation of this historical-aesthetic displacement reads as follows: "Thus, what the ancients sought beyond the limits of the earth on Olympus, our poet is required, in order to remove it from the everyday circle of events, to submerge in the equally hidden depths of our emotionality."[52] Aesthetic transfiguration is no longer possible as the apotheosis of the solar deity, but only within the embrace of the goddess, the specular union in which the aesthetic subject is reborn as a god.

The governing historical conception here is clearly one of internalization: art no longer strives to exhibit the sensuous world in the power of its fulguration, but rather articulates an inwardness that is the very source of our 'humanity'. The Olympian gods become figures within an autonomous "language of phantasy," which is how Karl Phillip Moritz redefined mythology in his ground-breaking treatise of 1795.[53] At this point, then, the schema of historical differentiation intersects with the notion of the productive imagination. As I suggested with regard to "Künstlers Morgenlied," modern art earns its legitimacy vis-à-vis its classical predecessor by drawing on the *universal imaginative function* of the "Bild." But what is the structure of this formative capacity? How does the imagination in fact operate? Again, Humboldt's treatise on Goethe offers illuminating suggestions, not only because it works out a detailed theory of the artistic *Einbildungskraft* or *Phantasie*, but also, and especially, because it addresses this theme from a pragmatic perspective. Humboldt's concern, in other words, is to show how the aesthetic construct elicits imaginative activity from the recipient. Thus, his analysis reveals with remarkable perspicacity the movements of an innovative form of reading, the form of reading opened up as a historical possibility through Goethe's lyric experimentation.

The productive imagination, as Humboldt describes it, is not merely the spontaneous faculty for the production of quasi-visual forms. It is that, to be sure, but this imaginative productivity is motivated, driven: it is oriented by a *desire*. Through his own (similarly oriented) imaginative achievement the poet "fills" ("erfüllt") the imagination of the reader with "an infinite yearning for ever new connections, ever new flights" such that it "swells to merge with" ("entgegenschwellen") the poem's "resonances" ("Tönen").[54] Note especially that the desiring imagination is not oriented toward something external, but rather finds its fulfillment in the exercise of its own productivity, in a process of ongoing transformation. That is to say, desire here is desire for the production of the image itself, an image that is constantly being reformed within a self-sustaining process. It would seem, then, that the autonomous imagination, as Humboldt conceives it, draws on what I referred to above as an infinite semantic resource: the matrix of specularity.

This reading is confirmed by another passage in which Humboldt analyzes the reader's imaginative response to Goethe's text. After discussing the scene between Hermann and his mother in which the mother successfully interprets her son's inwardness (his love for Dorothea), Humboldt notes that, attending to this scene, readers will naturally recall 'moments' ("Augenblicke") from their own experience and that these remembered moments enter into the imaginative constitution of the aesthetic object:

> Instead of abandoning Hermann and giving ourselves over to our memories, it is he alone who is present before our eyes; but at the same time those memories swell our breast and fill our heart; we are not conscious of them individually but their effect is alive in us and transfers itself onto the object.[55]

The verbs of 'swelling' and 'filling' repeat those in the passage on the desiring or yearning imagination cited previously, but here the mechanism of that desire is described more precisely. In its constitution of the aesthetic object—the object that, qua image, would fulfill its desire—the imagination is sustained and energized by unconscious memory traces. The memories involved here are not merely fragments of earlier perceptual experiences (as in pre-Kantian theories of the re-productive imagination); rather, they are scenes of interaction (note: between mother and son!), scenes in which desire is at once awakened and finds its fulfillment. To designate this process Humboldt employs the term "übertragen," for which various English equivalents suggest themselves: 'transport', 'translate', 'metaphorize'. In my rendering I have selected 'transfer' in order to evoke, at the risk of anachronism, the Freudian notion of transference. For the imagination operates in Humboldt's description very much like the mechanism Freud too called "Übertragung": it constitutes the aesthetic object as a screen onto which are projected unconscious schemata of interaction, themselves derived from earlier experiences.

Traditional interpretations conceive of the productive imagination—the centerpiece of post-Kantian aesthetics—as a transcendental demiurge that authors a creation ex nihilo, as the capacity of the subject to create absolutely, without pregiven pattern, without rules of procedure other than those it gives itself.[56] Following Humboldt, I want to claim (less spectacularly, but I think more interestingly) that *the imagination is the capacity of transference.*

This definition immediately gives rise to an objection: if the imagination is essentially transferential, if it brings forth the aesthetic object as the image of antecedent experiences, then its functioning could hardly be called productive or autonomous, precisely the predicates that post-Kantian theory most consistently and adamantly ascribes to it. The advantage of the traditional interpretation is that, by presupposing an authorizing subject, it can account for the attribution of autonomy. To meet this objection it is necessary to render the concept of *Übertragung* more precise. Transference is not an activity performed by a subject that is, as it were, completely *itself* (self-identical) and that imports *real* experiences into a fictional construct which would merely reproduce them; such an operation would obey the mimetic logic of original and copy and could hardly be thought of as autonomous production. Rather, we must endeavor to think of the transferential operation of the imagination as taking place *prior to the constitution of the subject,* as a process of *originary transference* through which the subject emerges in its identity. To put this another way:

the "experience" or "Augenblick" which the subject of the aesthetic experience recalls and transfers onto the aesthetic object is itself an experience of transference, the experience of the specular moment in which the subject emerges in and through an exchange of qualities, most notably the quality of subjecthood itself. Nothing—no subject, no experienced object—precedes transference. *Übertragung* is originary self-affection by, or within, the specular image.[57] The aesthetic imagination, absorbed in the image it produces, repeats and externalizes this primordial oscillation. In his essay on Falconet (one of the pieces included in "Aus Goethes Brieftasche"), Goethe formulates this transferential process from the perspective of the painter: "Nimm jetzo das *Haften* an Einer Form, unter *allen* Lichtern, so wird dir dieses Ding immer lebendiger, wahrer, runder, es wird endlich du selbst werden."[58] ("Consider now *fixed attention* to a *single* form, in *all* lightings, then this thing becomes for you ever more alive, truer, rounder; finally it will become you yourself.")

I conclude, then, with this definitional proposal: aesthetic-imaginative experience, as it is first disclosed in Goethe's lyric poetry of the 1770's and is codified in the philosophical theory of the 1790's, is *recursive transference*. In both its productive and receptive aspects, art becomes the transferential reenactment of an originary transference, the stage upon which the transferential process of subject constitution is infinitely rehearsed. This definition explains why the imagination is driven by a desire which it itself fulfills: *it is a desire for the experience, or assurance, of subjecthood*, the desire that first came alive and found its satisfaction in the specular regard. And it explains furthermore why the Mother is the matrix of modern art, its inexhaustible semantic resource, its "Alldeutend Ideal" (Text 18, 66): the Mother occupies the opposite pole (the complementary position) within the transferential structure in which the subject is constituted. The transferential imagination is the medium in which subject and Mother emerge and exchange their attributes, indeed, their identities; it is originary oscillation. To cite once again "Des Künstlers Erdewallen" (Text 19):

Wo mein Pinsel dich berührt bis du mein
Du bist ich bist mehr als ich ich bin dein
Uranfängliche Schönheit Königin der Welt!

PART THREE

The Myth of
Lyric Voice

§ 6 Primordial Orality

Specularity, the transferential imagination, anamnesic contact with the Origin: these terms are components of the myth of the lyric that begins to emerge around 1770. The most prominent feature of this myth is its pursuit of the poetic essence in an "*arché* beyond discourse," to recall the phrase introduced by Wilfrid Sellars in his critique of the philosophical "myth of the given."[1] Hence the predominantly visual character of the figure of specularity, which, of course, stages an aesthetic myth of the given, of what I have called a primordial donation, the gift of the Mother's luminescent presence:

> Meine Göttin deiner Gegenwart Blick
> Überdrängt mich wie erstes Jugendglück
>
> *(Text 19)*

A presence that sees, a seeing or look that is the very form of presence, and as such divine, an originary (first) bliss: such is the prediscursive fulguration of subjectivity in which Goethe's lyric texts seek their ground. This chapter examines the linguistic correlate of this ground or, to put the matter another way, the specific "orientation toward language" that allies itself with the rooting of the lyric in specularity.[2]

In pursuing this line of inquiry, I take my cue from a creative reader of Goethe who, in addition to writing his own *Faust*, was also a poet of the narcissistic moment of seeing oneself seen. In a note from 1918, Paul Valéry offers the following definition of the "veritable poetic principle":

> I believe that this principle is to be sought in the voice and in the *singular*, exceptional union, difficult to prolong, of the voice with thought itself. To give

to the act of voice a sort of life of its own, autonomous, intimate, impersonal—
that is to say, personal-universal (as opposed to personal-accidental), to make
of the word a resonator of the spirit, that is, *of the entirety of the perceived and
perceiving*, passive and responding,—such is the end, the desire, the sign, the
commandment.[3]

The lyric is oriented toward language as voice, as intimate resonance, a
medium that vibrates forth from the irreplaceable singularity of the speaking body but at the same time merges with conceptuality (thought) such
that the utmost in tonal personality coincides with universality. The
lyric is the voice set free ("autonomous"), no longer an instrument, no
longer the accident of idiosyncrasy, but rather a unique form of spiritual-
corporeal life. I have nothing to add to Valéry's principle except to
historicize it. My argument is that the *absolutization of the voice*—the
semantic-conceptual effect produced when Valéry writes, without further
qualification, "la voix"—is disclosed as a historical possibility during the
last third of the eighteenth century. This voice, in other words, did not
always exist, is not an anthropological given, but rather becomes historically accessible only during the era that, not accidentally, itself produced
the concept of anthropology. The "desire" and the "commandment" that
conspire to render the voice the end of lyrical writing take shape within a
particular cultural constellation. Valéry's definition is a last redaction of a
Romantic myth.

In the German-speaking world this myth begins with Herder, whose
Treatise on the Origin of Language (1772) celebrates the originary song of
human speech:

> There all of nature sang and resounded in advance: and the song of the human
> being was a concert of all these voices insofar as his understanding needed
> them, his feeling seized them, his organs were able to express them.—There
> was song, but neither the song of the nightingale, nor Leibniz's musical
> language, nor the animal's cry of feeling: expression of the language of all
> creatures, within the natural scale of the Human Voice![4]

Two aspects of this passage deserve emphasis. First, the isolation of the
human voice from all other significant or expressive sound systems. Voice
is not merely a capacity learned through imitation of the animals (the
singing nightingale), nor a tonal calculus indifferent to its embodiment
(Leibniz's music), nor the unmediated expression of our animal suffering
(the cry), but rather a unique insertion, as it were, into the chorus of

natural sounds, a specifically human capacity inseparable from our rationality and sensibility, indeed the very medium in which rationality and sensibility are realized. That is to say, the human voice is an autonomous instance; it introduces into the world an expressive *novum* that obeys its own inner dynamic and exhibits its own unique productivity. Let us call this feature the *personality* of the voice, its anthropological specificity.

The second aspect of the passage I want to stress involves the translational capacity of the voice. Although only one voice within the chorus of resounding nature, the human voice has the capacity to translate (and in translating to transform) the various sounds of nature into its own tonal currency. It is the unity of all natural voices, their concert. This capacity extends even to nontonal features of the natural world. Herder's theory of hearing as the middle sense—the mediator that unites all other sense impressions into the coherent shape of an integral human experience—renders audition the very existence of reason.[5] Everything the human being sees, feels, smells, and tastes has an inwardly audible tonal correlate, which in turn can be transformed into a voiced expression. Let us call this omni-translational capacity of the voice its *universality*, its complicity with the concept. The thrust of the cited passage, then, brings us very close to Valéry's conception of the lyric voice as the personal-universal. And this is not surprising insofar as what Herder describes is nothing other than primordial human *Gesang*.

This song, in which language, world, and even the subject have their origination, belongs to the past. What separates modernity from the world of promordial orality, Herder makes clear in his treatise "Ueber die Würkung der Dichtkunst auf die Sitten der Völker in alten und neuen Zeiten" ("On the Effect of Poetry on the Customs of the Peoples in Ancient and Modern Times," 1778), is the cultural caesura introduced by the printing press: "Now [that is, following Gutenberg's invention] the poet wrote; previously he sang."[6] With utter simplicity, the sentence states one of the governing (symbolic) oppositions of Herder's writing. Throughout his work, condemnations of the culture of writing and print provide the counter-theme to his celebration of the anthropological miracle of voice and ear. And around this opposition other, homologous pairs cluster: artificiality vs. naturalness, reflexivity vs. immediacy, rule-governed vs. spontaneous cultural production, market vs. expressive community, abstract vs. concrete, to mention just a few. This axiology, which is closely connected to the problematic of 'genius', informs much of the poetological thinking of the late eighteenth century. The condition of its emergence is the rapid expansion of the literary public sphere during the same period, a development that has received considerable attention in recent research.[7] The cultural context in which voice emerges as the desire and commandment of the lyric is effectively dominated—that is to say, structured—by the media of writing and print.

From this perspective, an interpretation of Herder's valorization of the voice as a compensation for a lost oral culture seems attractive. To be sure, one of Herder's major achievements as a critic—the revaluation of folk poetry—betrays strong nostalgic tendencies.[8] Such an interpretation fails to distinguish, however, between the actual dynamics of oral exchange in preliterate societies and that imagined in Herder's texts. This point emerges clearly from an examination of Herder's introduction to his edition of *Volkslieder* (1778–79), in which Homer is extolled in the following terms:

> He did not sit down on velvet in order to write a *heroic poem* in twice twenty-four songs according to Aristotle's rule or, if the muse so wished, beyond the rule, but rather sang what he had heard, represented what he had seen and vitally seized hold of: his rhapsodies did not remain in book shops and on our rags of paper, but rather in the ear and in the heart of living singers and hearers, out of which they were much later collected and finally, buried beneath glosses and prejudices, came to us. Homer's verse, as encompassing as the blue heaven and communicating itself in such myriad ways to everything that dwells beneath it, is not the hexameter of schools and art, but rather the meter of the Greeks that lay ready in their pure and subtle ear, in their resounding language, and waited, as it were, like a plastic clay for the figures of gods and heroes. Infinite and untiring it flows in gentle cascades, in repeating epithets and cadences, such as the ear of the people loved [*wie sie das Ohr des Volks liebte*]. These features, the agony of all translators and epic poets, are the soul of its harmony, the soft cushion [*sanfte Ruheküssen*] of rest, that at every line's end closes our eyes and puts our heads to sleep so that they might awaken to new vision with every new line and not tire of the long way.[9]

Herder is historically such a decisive and influential critic not because of the accuracy of his observations and judgments, but because he formulated a new *imaginary of language and literature*. Homeric song, as Herder construes it, has nothing to do with oral culture in the technical sense of the term. There is no mention, no perception, of the noisy give and take of preliterate cultural production, of its ritualistic features, its problems of memory and storage, its necessary redundancies, its laborious construction of tradition. The voice of Homer is no real voice burdened by limitations of volume and projection, and his listeners are no real bodily assembly, galvanized by corporeal proximity. Finally, there is no mention of the rigorous discipline (the mnemotechnics, the schooling of the voice, the training in set forms) characteristic of oral cultures; it is as if everything ushered forth spontaneously. In short, orality does not occupy a place in the world, is not a technology of the word. To the contrary, Homer's voice and song go directly to the heart and ear of his auditors without ever passing through an exteriority, and these auditors are the sheer internality of their attentive listening. Herder imagines the collectivity of oral culture as a single individual that, in the inwardness of its audition, hears its own voice, the originary song of its language.

Two operations, then, produce the value of *primordial orality* that Herder's text endows with such mythical dignity: a singularization of collectivity and an internalization of sound. The group becomes an individual subject attentive to the movements of its own inwardness. Both of these operations come together in the phrase "wie sie das Ohr des Volks liebte": the people as a single ear affectively bound to the gentle cascades of voice that resound within it. At this point, the imaginary character of Herder's concept of orality—the phantasmatic scene it evokes—profiles itself most clearly. We are dealing with an intimate emotional tie, with the love of an individual subject for the voice that vibrates within it, and in particular (as the cited passage goes on to say) for the soul whose audibility, whose very existence, that voice is. Any remaining doubts as to the private, individual, and inward nature of this primordial orality, this circuit of voice and ear, are dispelled by the transformation of the soul into a "soft cushion" that soothes us (with this pronoun Herder slides back into the contemporary world) into sleep. The rhapsode's performance before his assembled listeners has become a lullaby sung to a child.[10] The "gentle" ("sanft"; one might also translate "tender") cadences the ear so loves emanate from a maternal instance. Primordial orality is the voice of the Mother. As such it becomes, to cite Valéry once again, the desire and commandment of the lyric.

Before attending to this scene of mother and child, let us consider how Herder's text on Homer confronts the question of writing. The issues involved can be most readily elicited by looking at a second dimension of the linguistic-literary imaginary this text sets into place. Homer's verse, we read, is "as encompassing as the blue heaven"; infinite and untiring, it "flows in gentle cascades." The tropes here adumbrate the mythical topography of the civilizing river familiar to us from "Mahomets Gesang" (Text 15): the heavenly Origin, the flow of originary liquidity downward from the mountains, communication of the divine to all who dwell within the compass of its historical law. The force of orality carries the life of nature into the cultural domain and thereby establishes the identity of a historical subject, a *Volk*.[11]

Note that the communicated content of Homer's language is neither the hierophany of the gods nor the sudden glory of the heroes (both of which are reduced to secondary status), but rather the Greek language itself "resounding" ("klingend") in the "pure and subtle ear." Homer qualifies as a genius because he made the originary song of the Greek language audible and thereby enabled the collective subject of the Greek people, within the immediacy of primordial orality, to hear itself singing, to experience its auto-constitution as the personal-universal voice. But the comparison with "Mahomets Gesang" draws out a darker, more troubling aspect of this passage. Recall that the most strenuous semiotic labor in that poem occurs at the point of narrative transition from nature to culture, the point at which the genius-stream runs up against the blockage of death—natural death on the one hand and cultural death (parasitism, ornamentation, dessication) on the other. Herder's account of the destiny of Homeric song meets with similar difficulties, which show themselves most forcefully at the point where Homer's voice passes into the region of writing.

Herder works through this decisive transition in the first large rhetorical period of the quoted passage. Through the initial half of the period, the opposition between voice and writing is held in firm control. Homer did not write from a velvet seat (connotation: 'social hierarchy', 'decadent luxury'), nor according to prescribed rules (connotation: 'reflexivity', 'abstraction', 'heteronomy'). No, he sang. And what Homer sang was immediate to his ear ("was er gehöret") and to his eye ("was er gesehen"); in short, he sang 'what he . . . vitally seized hold of' ("was er . . . lebendig erfaßt hatte"). "Lebendig" (alive, vital) is the key word here (and one of the most positively charged lexemes throughout Herder's writings): the word for presence, immediacy, movement, a word intimately linked to the verb of flowing ("fließen") that subsequently defines Homer's verse. Up to this point, then, the text operates with an easy juxtaposition of Homeric song (vital, experientially saturated, spontaneous, etc.) and modern poetry (decadently luxuriant, reflective, unfree, etc.). This juxtaposition cannot be maintained, however, when Herder turns to the problem of diachronic transmission. And turn to this problem he must, for Homer himself (the biographical person) is outlived by his song. The possibility of this survival, of the song's repetition beyond the animating presence of the living poet, cannot be thought without introducing—into the very flow of Homeric voice—the deadening effects of writing.

This occurs in the period's second half. The conceptual strain that contorts this passage shows itself most evidently, I think, in the redundancy of the word "living." The adjective specifies nothing about the terms of which it is predicated. (Dead singers and hearers, after all, do not recall anyone's rhapsodies.) Within Herder's ideological project, however, the term serves a necessary connotative function. It asserts, or insists, that a kind of remaining ("bleiben") is possible other than the commercialized and raggedly material (and, by implication, dead) storage of cultural knowledge exemplified by writing and books. To claim that the singers and hearers of Homer's verses were living, in other words, is to establish a semantic barricade that protects the vitality of orality from the lethal effects of writing. It is no accident that this threat emerges with regard to the problem of transmission. Transmission rests on the possibility of repetition independent of the animating presence (the life) of the speaker, a possibility constitutive of every linguistic utterance but most flagrantly evident in writing. The fact that Homer's song can be repeated therefore implies that it is not merely the pure flow of living voice, that the death writing is inhabits that song from the outset. This is the implication Herder's repetition (!) of the term "living" seeks to deny. Yes, he urges, a living repetition is possible, a kind of cultural remaining that survives natural death (the death of Homer, the individual) without surrendering the pure vitality of voice and succumbing to the cultural moribundity of script.

Similar exertions directed at saving voice from the morbid contamination of writing inflect the rest of the passage. The collection ("gesammlet") of the Homeric rhapsodies, for example, is said to occur only much later ("spät"). Why? Because this act of collection renders stationary the flowing (and therefore living) movement of primordial orality, freezes that movement in order to store it within the perduring framework of an archive. As an operation of cultural transmission, then, collecting is closely related to the material reserves of book shops and rags of paper, which, according to Herder's wish, have nothing, nothing at all to do with the living voice of

Homeric song. Moreover, this operation, as the close of the period indicates, makes inevitable the piling up of written commentary ("glosses and prejudices") that has effectively buried Homer's voice, deadened it, rendered it inaudible to the modern ear. The adverb "spät," therefore, works to hold the act of collection at a distance from the origin, to pretend that collection, with all its lethal consequences, is entirely exterior to primordial orality. But Herder's apotropaic manoeuver only half succeeds. Via the phrase "out of which" ("aus denen"), the act of collection penetrates into the very life of voice, stilling its movement at the source. That is to say, in this odd, impossible idea of collecting out of the ear and heart (for these, surely, are the referents of "denen") the predicate of 'static remaining', which was supposed to distinguish writing from the living flow of voice, becomes a semantic component of the concept of voice itself. Such is the implication the notion of cultural transmission (of repetition and remaining) bears: death dwells within the living voice. And it is this implication that Herder's writing works to suppress.

This passage on Homer allows us to see that the concepts of voice and writing in Herder's texts, and in the late eighteenth century generally, do not simply refer to facts, but rather function within a mythical constellation that organizes the perception of facts. Within this myth, primordial orality is the operator of a seamless transition between nature and culture, the guarantee that a mode of cultural transmission free of the deadening effects of writing is possible. The problem of cultural transmission, however, presents itself not only at the level of large-scale historical traditions, but also at the level of individual development. Each human subject must find a path of access from the state of nature into which it is born to the state of culture in which its natural deficiencies (so prominent in Herder's conception of the human being as a creature of lack) are compensated by a system of meanings. The medium in and through which this transition is accomplished is, once again, the voice:

> The nursing infant that stammers its first words repeats with this stammering the feelings of its parents and swears, with each early stammering through which tongue and soul form themselves, to render these feelings eternal, as truly as it calls them his father- or mother-language. Throughout its life these first impressions of its childhood, these images from the soul and heart of its parents, will live and act within it: together with the word the entire feeling that early overflowed its soul will return: with the idea signified by the word all of the associated ideas that then lay before it in its morning-view into the

realm of creation—they will return and act more powerfully than the pure and clear central idea itself.[12]

Three ideas are intertwined in this passage. First, Herder clearly conceives of orality as the medium not merely of the tongue's training, but of the formation of the soul. Subjectivity emerges within the audibility of the voice. This implies (second idea) that the voice is the carrier of what might be termed an ontogenetic semantics: into adulthood it maintains a link to the experience of language acquisition and to the familial network of feelings, symbolic positions, and perceptual colorings that characterized that experience. We might say that language in Herder takes on a personal-historical density, that it bears the sedimentations of childhood experience even into the phase in which such experience is forgotten; in short, that my language is so entwined with my childhood that it remembers more than I do. These two linked notions are important, of course, in understanding the emergence of the lyric. The lyric is the form of language use in which the anamnesic potential of language is actualized, in which the formation of the soul in the movements of the voice is recapitulated, in which the resonant traces of childhood impressions shaped within the familial network of symbolic positions become audible once again.

The third idea of the passage is not explicitly mentioned but concerns the overall point of Herder's remarks, their function within a larger context of argument. Herder wants to claim that the transition from nature to culture the nursing infant negotiates is itself a natural event, more precisely, that it obeys a natural economy.[13] The economy in question (the economy that structures the entirety of Herder's argument in the *Treatise*) is that of lack and supplement. As a sheerly natural being, the human infant is poorer and weaker that any of the animals. But this weakness is itself the condition of strength, for nature supplements the instinctual poverty of the human creature with the richness of education, development, culture, and community. And the instrument through which this process of natural supplementation occurs is language, the orality through which the child internalizes the "feelings of its parents" and therewith shapes its "tongue and soul."

This point is crucial in understanding how the concept of primordial orality functions in Herder's theory and in particular in seeing who the agent of this orality actually is. The transition from nature to culture is smooth and continuous; it is accomplished not by the violent imposition of an arbitrary law as in Rousseau, but by what Herder calls the "economy of the nature of human kind."[14] Here is another look at this economy:

> The woman, in nature so much the weaker part, must she not accept the law from the experienced, providing, Language-forming man? Yes, if it be called law what is merely the mild benificence of instruction? The weak child, so literally called immature, must it not accept language, since it enjoys with it the milk of its mother, the spirit of its father? And must not this language be rendered eternal if anything is to be rendered eternal? Oh, the laws of nature are more powerful than all the conventions which cunning politics concocts and the wise philosopher claims to enumerate! The words of childhood—these our early playmates in the dawn of life! with which our entire soul formed itself—, when will we fail to recognize them, when will we forget them? Our mother language was simultaneously the first world we saw, the first sensations we felt, the first activity and happiness we enjoyed.[15]

The deficiencies of the natural creature do not run up against a heterogeneous law of culture which would press the infant into conformity; rather, they are compensated by a gentle benevolence, by a sort of loving care that the economy of nature guarantees. The man, as the stronger, language-shaping agency, conveys his law (if this protective charity be called "law") to the woman, who in turn transmits it to the child. The child, then, is twice removed from the violence of the law, first by the father's love of the mother, and then by the mother's love for the child. Especially this latter love—the maternal donation through which the child receives its first language—can be stylized as "natural." The infant passing into culture drinks in the mother's voice like milk from her breast. The maternal voice (a liquidity) nurses the child and thereby transforms creaturely poverty into cultural abundance. Primordial orality is the voice of the Mother, the medium of a natural culturation. And the meaning carried in what I referred to above as the ontogenetic semantics of language—the meaning reactualized in the lyric—is the affective cocoon that unites mother and child. This is why the poetry of Homer is a lullaby whose tender cadences are beloved to the ear.

We are now in a position to see the mythical function of Herder's concept of primordial orality. Primordial orality—the Mother's voice—is the natural supplement, the instrument that enables the transition between the state of natural lack and that of its cultural supplementation without departing from the realm of nature. In this sense, the concept of primordial orality (in homology with the concept of genius) serves to ground culture in nature, in a nature, however, that is loving, gentle, maternal. But myths are not simply chimeras; they are maps for organizing reality and for mediating its contradictions. Thus, by the time Herder's century had come to an end, his concept of the maternal voice had become a program of socialization. The influential Swiss pedagogue Johann Heinrich Pestalozzi, in a treatise entitled *On the Sense of Hearing with Respect to Human Cultivation Through Tone and Language* (1803–4), offers young mothers the following advice:

> Bring forth tones, clap, beat, pound, speak, sing,—in short resound to the child so that it adheres to you, so that it loves you; let high grace flow from your lips; please the child through your voice as no one pleases it, and don't think that you would require art in order to do this; don't think that you would even have to know how to sing. The loving sweetness [*Lieblichkeit*] of speech that comes from the heart is of much more value for the cultivation of your child than any art of song, in which in any case you would stand far behind the nightingale.[16]

No art (in Herder's terms, no convention or law) is required for the process of culturation. Rather, the entire linguistically organized world "flows," as Pestalozzi puts it, with a verb that is familiar to us, in tones from the mother to the child. The task the pedagogue prescribes for mothers, in other words, is that of simulating the Natural Mother, of instantiating her tender love, and of communicating this love in the sweet cadences of her voice. This act of transmission, moreover, has no other effect than to awaken love in the child, to bind the child affectively to the first sweet tones it heard, through which its soul shaped itself. The maternal voice is the donation of desire.

Culturation through the maternal voice produces the Romantic subject. A little-known text by the painter Phillip Otto Runge, whose remarkable *Mother at the Source* appears at the beginning of this book, documents this. The text in question is a lyric entitled "Die Töne" ("The Tones"), which opens with an evocation of the past time when the speaker lived "Freudevolle Stunden / Auf der Mutter Erde Schoß" ("Joyful hours / In the lap of Mother Earth"). What filled these hours and shaped the speaker's desire were the sounds this Mother sang to him:

> 20. Lag so still für mich allein
> Unter Schatten, dunkeln Büschen,
> Vor mir Wasser, Wies' und Hain,
> Hört' im Rohr die Lüfte zischen,

(5) Höre, wie der Vogel singet,
       Daß der hohle Wald erklinget—
       Horch, Trompeten nun aus Weiten,
       Näher holder Töne Gleiten—
       Und die Abendsonne sinkt.
(10) O nach diesen, diesen Tönen
       Möcht ich immer satt mich sehnen![17]

       Lay so still alone with myself
       Beneath shadows, dark bushes,
       Before me water, meadow, grove;
       Heard in the reeds the winds' whisper;
(5) Hear how the bird sings,
       So that the hollow forest resounds—
       Hark, trumpets now from afar,
       Closer the gliding of sweet tones—
       And the evening sun goes down.
(10) Oh to these, these tones
       I want always to yearn to repletion.

Recall here the speaker of Goethe's "Der neue Amadis" enclosed "Über
mir allein, / Wie in Mutterleib" (Text 8, 4–5); recall the maternal "Schattental" of "Mahomets Gesang" (Text 15, 22). Runge fills the natural-
maternal enclave with sound and in doing so recapitulates Herder's description of the natural economy of socialization. Even the distancing of
the paternal law that characterized Herder's text finds an echo here in the
commanding trumpets heard from afar—post horns or hunters' horns perhaps, perhaps the signal of some regal procession, and in any case marked
as 'masculine' and 'authoritative'—while nearby sweet tones "glide" in a
sort of prearticulate cascade. And just as Pestalozzi urged mothers to
impart their love to their children through tones so that the child's soul
lovingly attaches itself to them, here too the subject is bound by an infinite
yearning for the loving soul that first made itself audible as artless, natural-
maternal song. Runge's text makes clear why, as Valéry claimed, voice is
the desire and commandment of the lyric.
       The late-eighteenth-century valorization of voice is allied with a recon-
ceptualization of music. The Romantic shift from painting to music as the
privileged artistic paradigm has often been commented upon and is closely
linked to the promotion of the lyric (the type of literary communication
most closely bound to music) to equal status with the epic and the

drama.[18] This elevation of music within the system of the arts is accompanied by a reconceptualization of music in terms of voice. The voice (and the modulations of emotion it carries) becomes the primordial instance of musical expression. Thus, for Herder music and language have a common origin in the *Gesang* of primordial orality, a view he shares with Rousseau.[19] And not only Rousseau: in the field of music theory generally the eighteenth century witnesses a paradigm shift that removes music from the Pythagorean domain of mathematical proportionality (cf. Mattheson's *Der vollkommene Capellmeister*) and artful virtuosity (cf. Gluck's operatic reform) in order to relocate it within the sphere of human emotionality.[20] By the century's end, the linkage between music and language through the voice is a musicological truism: "The universal communicability of the charm of music resides in the tones through which human affects tend to express themselves. The tone of our voice in speaking (especially where nature hasn't been entirely suppressed by culture) is a more or less distinct expression of our emotional state, a weaker or livelier sign of the attitude (*Gesinnung*) which lies at the basis of our words."[21] This emotionalization, naturalization, and anthropologization of music finds its technological support with the development of the clavichord, that instrument capable of reproducing the most subtle modulations of affect without severing them in an articulate series.[22] By 1800 the stage is set—theoretically, instrumentally, and poetically—for the emergence of the Romantic *Lied*.

I began these remarks by citing Valéry's definition of the lyric principle as voice. It seems appropriate to close with a sentence from Valéry's successor as the leading aesthetic critic writing in the French language. In his essay on the Romantic *Lied*, Roland Barthes endeavors to define the phantasmatic structure that sustains and is sustained by the genre's fusion of lyric voice and music. His speculations, formulated with the unique combination of passion and precision that characterizes all his critical work, illuminate remarkably, as the following consideration of texts by Goethe will confirm, the cultural definition of the lyric in terms of primordial orality. Barthes's central thesis is: "For *to sing*, in the romantic sense, is this: fantasmatically to enjoy my unified body."[23] This dream of oneness the *Lied* affords, a dream that constantly appears and retreats, is the oral/aural version of specularity.

~

The text from Goethe's oeuvre that most radically fuses the lyric and orality is not a lyric poem strictly speaking, but an excerpt from the drama fragment *Prometheus* (1773), one of the boldest compositions from this phase of Goethe's career. The drama's first act opens with a scene of imminent rebellion. Prometheus stands on the threshold of a deed that will transgress the divine law emanating from the will of his father, Zeus. Exactly what this rebellion consists in becomes clear only in the course of the drama: Prometheus intends to give life to the statues he has sculpted and therewith to bring forth a race (humanity) that would live outside of Olympian rule. It is important to note the precise legal definition, as it were, of the transgression Prometheus plans. Zeus does not object to the act of artistic creation per se, nor even to the hyperbolic form of artistic creation Prometheus aspires to, in which the artistic products become living (human) beings. He merely insists that this artistic production take place under his own aegis, so that the life of the created beings would derive, ultimately, from him, and these beings, along with their artist-maker, would abide within the compass of his command. At issue, then, is the law—the *nomos*—of art. Prometheus cannot accept the subjugation of his artistic productivity to a higher (legal-political, theological, paternal) instance. He aspires to the position of ultimate, autonomous creator, a position familiar to us as that of genius.

In the first act, this rebellious intention is formulated across three dramatic exchanges, of which the third proves decisive. In the initial dialogue with Mercury, the emissary of the Olympian ruler Zeus, Prometheus refuses to heed the god's command. The subsequent dialogue with his brother, the cautious Epimetheus, reveals Prometheus's democratic (or bourgeois) convictions in that he rejects an offer to rule the earth as a sort of feudal lord, an option that would still leave the hierarchical principle of Zeus's law intact. Both these exchanges serve only to stiffen Prometheus's intransigence; the dramatic situation of imminent rebellion remains unchanged. The titan continues to will autonomous artistic production, an art in which humanity would fashion itself beyond the limits of the Father's law. How could this goal be achieved? How is an art independent of the Father, a self-fathered art, possible?

The third dialogue, this time with Zeus's daughter Minerva, provides an answer. Indeed, the dialogue is itself the answer in that it is the first interlocution in the drama that does not occur in Zeus's name. Both Mercury and Epimetheus, after all, come as the Father's delegates, mediating his will, conveying his proposals for compromise. But Minerva approaches Prometheus on her own:

21. PROMETHEUS: Du wagst es meine Göttin?
   Wagest zu deines Vaters Feind zu treten!
   MINERVA: Ich ehre meinen Vater
   Und liebe dich Prometheus.[24]

   PROMETHEUS: You dare, my goddess?
   Dare to step over to your father's enemy!
   MINERVA: I honor my father
   And love you Prometheus.

Two bonds, honor for the father and love for the father's son (her brother), determine Minerva's position, and they are mutually exclusive. Thus, the very act of approaching Prometheus, in obedience to her attachment to him, skirts transgression. Not that Minerva comes out of a spirit of rebellion, which in this text is a strictly masculine prerogative; she clearly hopes to find a solution to the conflict that divides Prometheus and Zeus, and thus divides her. In this sense her role is an utterly familiar, and familial, one: it is the role of Hermann's mother, the role of Wilhelm Meister's mother, of Heinrich von Ofterdingen's mother, indeed of countless mothers in classical-romantic literature. In short, Minerva is the figure who elicits and understands the movements of Prometheus's most intimate internality because, as we shall see, she is the source of that internality.

Of course, Minerva is not actually (that is, within the dramatic fiction) Prometheus's mother, but she appears in what will become the mother function, much as Psyche in Wieland's *Agathon*, likewise a sister, is transformed into a maternal imago in the final version of the novel. At this historical juncture (1773), the mother function is not yet firmly attached to the biological mother; the role can still be occupied by the sister, by an older woman (cf. the female friend of Werther's youth), by a beloved (cf. Werther's Charlotte, Lila of "Pilgers Morgenlied," the "beloved" of "Künstlers Morgenlied," Faust's Gretchen). At stake here is a symbolic position (the Mother writ large) and not a biological or biographical fact. This symbolic position enables an art outside the regime of the paternal law, for in the course of the dialogue Minerva will be persuaded to conduct Prometheus "zum Quell des Lebens all" ("to the source of all life," 200), to the originary liquidity that will enable him to animate his statues. Access to the source of autonomous art passes, in this text as in "Künstlers Morgenlied," through the maternal instance.

The dialogue between Prometheus and Minerva is hardly a dialogue. Following the initial exchange just cited, Minerva remains essentially silent while Prometheus addresses her in three large waves of speech: a reflection on the meaning of their relationship prompted by her declaration of love for him (100–133); a rehearsal of his labors under the gods' rule (135–66); and finally a description, soon intensified to an apostrophe, of his sculptures (167–86). Prometheus, that is to say, does not speak so much with her as before her; suasion occurs not through the give and take of argument, but rather through the evocative force of a language in which the subject utters its own history, its own desire. To put this in generic terms, the goddess/sister is less a dramatic agent than an ideal lyric addressee, the figure in whom the speaker's surge of words is absorbed into the silence of a perfect (hermeneutic) understanding. That such comprehension has indeed taken place is indicated, on the level of the dramatic plot, by the scene's conclusion: Minerva agrees to take Prometheus "zum Quell des Lebens all," the site where his art, otherwise "gebunden . . . von Leblosigkeit" ("tethered . . . by lifelessness," 194–95), will come alive.

The generic slide from a dramatic to a lyric register shows most clearly in the first and the last of the three waves of speech distinguished above; here we shall only consider the first half of the former in any detail. This passage, in conformity with its generic drift toward the lyric, evinces a certain inward concentration and self-isolation. It is one of the most remarkable moments in Goethe's lyric corpus:

> (100) PROMETHEUS: Und du bist meinem Geist
> Was er sich selbst ist.
> Sind von Anbeginn
> Mir deine Worte Himmelslicht gewesen!
> Immer als wenn meine Seele spräche zu sich selbst!
> (105) Sie sich eröffnete
> Und mitgeborne Harmonien
> In ihr erklängen aus sich selbst.
> Das waren deine Worte.
> So war ich selbst nicht selbst,
> (110) Und eine Gottheit sprach
> Wenn ich zu reden wähnte,
> Und wähnt ich eine Gottheit spreche,
> Sprach ich selbst.
> Und so mit dir und mir

(115) So ein so innig
      Ewig meine Liebe dir.

(100) PROMETHEUS: And you are to my spirit
      What it is to itself.
      From the beginning
      Your words have been heaven's light to me!
      Always as if my soul spoke to itself!
(105) As if it opened up
      And harmonies born with it
      There reverberated of themselves.
      Those were your words.
      Thus I myself was not myself,
(110) And a divinity spoke
      When I imagined speaking,
      And when I imagined a divinity spoke,
      I spoke myself.
      And so with you and me
(115) So one, so inward
      Eternal my love to you.

As mentioned, this speech responds to Minerva's simple statement: "I love you," and its seventeen lines can be taken as an explication of the relation "Liebe," which, not surprisingly, is their final noun. Yet the passage adds a new dimension to the figuration of specular love we have been examining in that it formulates the primordial exchange in terms of language. This would seem to contradict my argument regarding the essentially pre-linguistic, prearticulate character of specularity, but the converse is true. We are dealing here with a language prior to language, an originary language that knows none of the opacities and inertness of ordinary linguistic exchange, a language that resounds within an absolute inwardness and unity.

To see this, it is useful to contrast the concept of language imagined in the passage with other types of linguistic behavior. Communicational dialogue, for example, presupposes the ability of the speaking subject to distinguish its use of the first-person singular pronoun from that of its interlocutor and to distinguish itself, as speaking subject, from the content of its utterance. Both of these premises of practical communication are eliminated here. The speech exchange Prometheus invokes is not an exchange *between* differentiated subjects *about* a third thing, or topic.

Rather, "Ich" and "Du," as agents of speech, are indistinguishable, bound
in an undifferentiated intimacy. Moreover, the speech of Prometheus/
Minerva has no identifiable—that is to say, separable—semantic content.
It is a pure resounding ("erklängen aus sich selbst"), and this resounding of
harmonies is nothing other than the soul of the speaking subject ("als
wenn meine Seele spräche zu sich selbst"). The primordial ("Anbeginn")
language Prometheus recalls (in a memory, an anamnesis of the origin) is
one in which addresser and addressee, utterance and propositional content, are one ("So ein so innig"). That is to say, *the differences constitutive of
normal communication are absorbed into an unsevered unity.*

The language prior to language that Prometheus introduces as the
extended interpretant of the term "Liebe"—a language that is not about
love, but rather is love itself, and as such the origin of the self—is
primordial orality. Thus, the passage employs the central motifs characterizing the late-eighteenth-century mythologization of orality. The language of Prometheus/Minerva is music ("Harmonien," "erklängen"), or
rather, since we are still dealing with speech and not, say, an instrumental
performance, the coincidence of music and language as song. Moreover,
this voice emanates from the Mother (Minerva is a maternal function) and
enfolds the dyadic pair within the unity of an aural envelope. Not that the
Mother is a speaking subject in the sense of an intending agent who would
use the first-person singular pronoun as a self-distinguishing marker.
Rather, the voice of primordial orality speaks, as it were, through her,
resounding out of her and thereby giving birth ("mitgeborne") both to the
"soul" of Prometheus and to her as the Mother. To phrase the matter
theologically: in the beginning was not the Word of the divine Father, but
rather the auto-originating ("erklängen *aus sich selbst*") voice that constitutes the mother/child dyad.

Prometheus's speech accomplishes a *matrilinear recoding* of the symbolic
paths of authorization that link language to its originating instance.
Therefore, the symbolic operation performed here is continuous with (a
variant of) the matrilinear recoding of art discussed above in connection
with "Künstlers Morgenlied" (Text 18). This is why the dialogue (which is
not really a dialogue) between Prometheus and Minerva is itself the answer
to the question of how an art outside the Father's law is possible. By
returning with Minerva to the embrace and birth of primordial orality,
Prometheus discloses the principle of autonomous artistic production.
The voice, as auto-origination, is the "Quell des Lebens all" (200). More-

over, the passage also accomplishes a matrilinear recoding in the domain of sexuality akin to that elaborated in the burlesque poem "Auf Cristianen R." (Text 9). The voice, in other words, is the *primordial maternal donation* in and through which the subject receives the truth of its desire. This is revealed not only by the fact that the evocation of primordial orality occurs as a response to and explication of the word "Liebe," but also, and more flagrantly, by the fictional context of the drama. For when Minerva leads Prometheus to the "Quell des Lebens all," an event that takes place offstage, in the silence between the drama's two acts, she is taking him to the scene of their erotic (incestuous) union. It is no accident, then, that the sculptures-become-human of the second act refer to Prometheus as "father."

We are now in a position to define more precisely the aesthetic imagination, previously characterized as transference, as originary self-affection, the medium in and through which subject and Mother emerge as an oscillation of identities. It is language prior to difference, a language in which "Ich" and "Du" coincide, in which the utterance is indistinguishable from the statement; it is voice, pure and primordial orality. In analyses to which I am indebted in a measure beyond the capacity of footnotes to indicate, Jacques Derrida has argued that such a concept of the voice as originary self-affection is a recurrent and insistent figure of thought throughout the Western philosophical-linguistic tradition, especially within the subject-centered philosophical discourse of modernity (Rousseau, Husserl).[25] Most pertinent to my argument is Derrida's limited epochal construction, his contention that the modern notion of founding subjectivity rests on a phonocentric myth, the myth of the phenomenological or, as I shall call it, transcendental voice as subjective presence-to-self in the immediacy and transparency of the *s'entendre parler*.[26] This pertinence derives from historically specific, interdiscursive connections. The *Prometheus* fragment represents, after all, Goethe's major literary altercation with Rousseau (as mediated by Wieland). Moreover, I have insisted all along, especially in Chapter 3, on the filiations between Goethe's lyric and the philosophical problematic of transcendental subjectivity. Finally, the development of language and music theory in the late eighteenth century, as sketched out above, confirms the thesis regarding the modern valorization of voice. Kittler's work, in many respects a historical concretization of Derrida's argument regarding phonocentrism, has disclosed the network of pedagogical and familial discourses (as in, for example, Pestalozzi's treatises) that made the theoretical prestige of orality a reality of socialization. By 1800, Prometheus's birth out of the maternal voice becomes an institutionalized strategy of subject formation. Thus, Derrida's analysis of phonocentrism allows me to expand and render more precise my characterization of the lyric discourse that emerges in Goethe's texts of the 1770's. The passage from *Prometheus* discussed here—a passage that in its pronominal play enacts transference—suggests a possible reformulation of the entire complex established across my earlier chapters in terms of primordial orality: *the lyric is the cultural-discursive site in which the transcendental voice—as language prior to language, as the origin of subjectivity within the maternal matrix—is rendered imaginatively accessible.*[27]

I want to stress the theoretical status of this definition: it formulates not what the lyric (or Goethe's lyric) *is* in itself, but rather the *myth of itself* that the lyric projects. As such, it is the counterpart to the historical myth of modern art sketched out in the previous chapter with regard to "Künstlers Morgenlied," to the familial-sexual myth of the maternal donation of desire, to the myth of the specular moment. Indeed, I have endeavored to show across my entire argument the way in which these mythical codes or registers play into and intertwine with one another. The methodological lesson I draw from Derrida's work, then, is that discourses require analysis in terms of the *strategies of self-grounding* through which they stabilize themselves. The lyric myth of the transcendental voice is one such strategy.

To argue that the type of orality projected in the lyric is the transcendental voice enables us to distinguish the specifically lyric medium from others, most obviously, of course, from a poetic practice in which the orientation toward language is directed at inscription per se. (Within the general field of inscription, further distinctions would have to be made, say, between mannerist lettrism and modernist *écriture*.) But it is insufficient to say that the lyric is essentially voiced (as opposed to written); indeed, the statement is potentially misleading. For the voice in question here is not the empirically audible utterance of the spoken word, not a voice that is a medium for face-to-face exchange. To put this another way, it is not the oratorical voice of rhetoric, not the voice as an instrument of performance. To see this, one need only reflect on the fact that oratorical orality is inevitably situational, locked into the spatiotemporal particularity of empirical context. Even when the oratorical text is written down and therefore can be transported beyond its context of production, it nevertheless continues to refer to that context, and such reference is an irreducible component of its functioning. This oratorical constellation—a representative subject role acts out a spoken utterance addressed to a particular audience—defines a large proportion of the poetic texts produced prior to Goethe's lyric innovation, prior, let us say, to Romanticism.

But if the orality of lyric discourse is not the empirically audible utterance, what is it? It is—the definition tells us as much—an idealized orality, an orality that was never spoken or heard, that, paradoxically enough, achieves its purest form as silence: the transcendental voice. This implies that the lyric voice is not situational; it is everywhere, and therefore nowhere in particular. One can reverse the previous formulation and say that the idealized orality of the lyric is oral ideality, a nonparticular and therefore nonempirical medium that remains ever itself, infinitely accessible and reproducible. This, indeed, is the crux of Derrida's analysis: the theoretical privilege of the voice derives from its complicity with idealization, with the production of meanings, or idealities, that can be infinitely reactualized or rendered present.[28] Goethe's term for this mode of being is "allgegenwärtig" (all-present), a compound that binds the universal logical quantifier to the attribute of unmediated self-givenness. Hence the lines from "Pilgers Morgenlied": "Allgegenwärt'ge Liebe! / Durchglühst mich" ("All-present love! / You glow through me," Text 10, 26–27). The passage from *Prometheus* has instructed us that this "love"—specularity, transferential imagination, origin of subjectivity and poetry—is also the transcendental voice as the identity of "Ich" and "Du," utterance and statement, in the inward resounding of the soul. It is no accident, then, that Minerva responds to Prometheus's evocation of primordial orality with the line: "Und ich dir ewig gegenwärtig" ("And I eternally present to you," 117). Prometheus himself soon specifies that this presence (of her to him, and therefore of himself to himself) within the transcendental voice eludes situational limitations: "Abwesend auch mir immer gegenwärtig" ("Even in absence always present to me," 123). The self-authorizing myth of the transcendental voice lends the lyric, as Valéry also noted, an index of universality.

I want to pursue one step further the logical implications of the line "Abwesend auch mir immer gegenwärtig." Elliptically, the line says that Minerva (her love, her voice) is present even under the condition of absence. That is, she can be *either* present *or* absent in one sense, but in another she is always present. The antinomy that structures the line does not oppose presence and absence as simple alternatives. Rather, it opposes the kind of presence that characterizes the transcendental voice to the alternative presence/absence; it claims that the transcendental voice is immune to this difference.

The consequences of this claim become apparent when one reflects that the opposition presence/absence relentlessly organizes two vast domains of human existence: empirical experience on the one hand, and language on the other. The opposition governs empirical experience in the sense that such experience is bound to the limitations of space and time. Whatever object is present here and now can, at another place and in another moment, be absent. Thus, empirical objects are notoriously haunted by instability; they cannot provide a secure basis for a self-conception. Precisely this problem is worked through in the opening monologue of Goethe's dramatic fragment *Mahomet*, alluded to above in connection with my reading of "Mahomets Gesang" (Text 15).[29] In that monologue, the prophet turns successively to three empirical correlates of his internality, a star, the moon, and finally the sun, and each proves inadequate because it withdraws into absence. Belief cannot be grounded in spatiotemporal objects precisely to the degree that these are not, in the terms of the *Prometheus* text, "ewig gegenwärtig." Thus, Mohammed concludes his monologue by affirming the "liebendes Herz" ("loving heart") as the only possible mode of access to the eternal creator, a solution to his crisis of belief that is obviously akin to the "Liebe" uniting Prometheus and Minerva.

The sense in which language is submitted to the opposition presence/absence is equally obvious: every linguistic sign functions by virtue of its difference from other signs, which it is not; signs, in other words, are diacritical. Hence we say that linguistic elements are discrete, cut by the alternating pulse of the difference between present and absent terms. As I have already mentioned, the transcendental voice imagined in the text from *Prometheus* is a language in which the differences constitutive of communication are abolished: speaker and addressee, utterance and statement are one. Precisely such an elimination of differences is posited in another passage on language (such passages are relatively rare) by Goethe:

22.   Der verheißene Geist erfüllt die versammelten Jünger mit der Kraft seiner Weisheit. Die göttlichste Empfindung strömt aus der Seel in die Zunge, und flammend verkündigt sie die großen Taten Gottes in einer neuen Sprache und das war *die Sprache des Geistes.* . . .

Mehr als Pantomime doch unartikuliert muß die Sprache gewesen sein. Paulus setzt die zur Empfindung des Geists bewegte Seele dem ruhigen Sinn entgegen, nebeneinander vielmehr, nacheinander! Wie Ihr wollt! Es ist Vater und Sohn, Keim und Pflanze. *pneuma! pneuma!* was wäre *nous* ohne dich![30]

The prophesied spirit fills the assembled disciples with the force of its wisdom. The most divine feeling streams from the soul into the tongue, and, flaming, it proclaims the great deeds of God in a new language, which is *the language of the Holy Spirit.* . . .

The language must have been *more than pantomime and yet unarticulated.* As regards this feeling of the spirit, Paul opposes the moved soul to the quiet mind, or rather he places them next to one another, in succession! As you please! It is a matter of father and son, seed and plant. *Pneuma! Pneuma!* What would *nous* be without you!

At issue here, of course, is the speaking in tongues that characterizes the miracle of Pentecost: a language in which subjects themselves do not speak, but rather are spoken by the Holy Spirit, a language that communicates itself immediately to the feeling soul. This language is conceived as *prearticulate*; it "streams" as an originary liquidity (and fire) from the soul to the tongue. The originary, prearticulate language of the soul that Goethe reads into the Pentecostal miracle occupies the same systemic position as the primordial orality in which the soul of Prometheus is born (with the difference, of course, that the *Prometheus* passage is matrilinearly encoded, whereas the biblical commentary remains within the sphere of a patrilinear-Christian authorization). As the ideal of language prior to difference and articulation, the lyric would be the form of language in which something like the Pentecostal miracle is achieved in modernity, a speaking of the soul to the soul, a speaking in which, as in the passage from *Prometheus*, the soul (*pneuma*) is born.

Thus, the lyric maintains an essentially negative relation both to empirical experience and to ordinary language, and furthermore, it derives its legitimacy from this negative relation. This qualification of lyric discourse contradicts two commonly held views regarding Goethe's poetry: that it stems from and is oriented toward occasions of personal (which is to say: empirical) experience, and that such experiences find an adequate linguistic expression in the poems themselves. My thesis is that Goethe's lyric poetry understands itself as a translation—and as such inadequate—from a domain of experience (specularity) and a medium of expression (the transcendental voice) that are nonempirical and nonlinguistic. The lyric, in other words, refers to a site of *presence* ("ewig gegenwärtig"), with which, qua language, it cannot coincide.[31] Thus, the language of the lyric (not to speak of its writing) is obliged to self-negation: to be what it claims to be (namely, language spoken from a Source that is prearticulate) the lyric must efface the very differences that constitute it as a linguistic artifact. The speech of Prometheus illustrates this structure of immanent self-negation especially clearly insofar as it evokes the transcendental voice through a systematic denial of differences.

The myth of the transcendental voice also projects a model of lyric reception. It situates the text within the framework of an implicit narrative that maps out an ideal pragmatics. This narrative unfolds in three stages: (a) the text springs from the Origin; (b) as text, it exists in a state of alienation; (c) the act of reading and of empathetic comprehension frees the text from its alienated condition by returning it to the Origin. Goethe's lyric texts, in other words, cannot be adequately characterized as sheer expression, pragmatically empty and self-sufficient. Rather, they emplot the story of their own hermeneutic redemption.

The narrative of origin, alienation and return is realized through the maiden/beloved's double function as the Source of the poem and as its recipient or addressee.[32] The dramatic action of *Prometheus* illustrates this pragmatic plot: Minerva is at once the Source of the transcendental voice and the agency who, after hearing his invocation of this voice, gives life to Prometheus's death-tethered artistic products by bringing them to the "Quell des Lebens all." In a further text by Goethe, the receptive role of the beloved is similarly developed in terms of the theme of 'voice'.

23. AN LINA

Liebchen, kommen diese Lieder
Jemals wieder dir zu Hand,
Sitze beim Klaviere nieder,
Wo der Freund sonst bei dir stand.

(5) Laß die Seiten rasch erklingen,
Und dann sieh ins Buch hinein;
Nur nicht lesen! immer singen!
Und ein jedes Blatt ist dein.

Ach, wie traurig sieht in Lettern,
(10) Schwarz auf weiß, das Lied mich an,

Das aus deinem Mund vergöttern,
Das ein Herz zerreißen kann!³³

TO LINA

Little dear one, should these songs
Ever return to your hand,
Then sit down at the clavichord,
Where the friend was accustomed to stand beside you.

(5) Let the strings hastily resound,
And then look into the book;
Only, don't read! always sing!
And every page is yours.

Oh, how sadly in letters,
(10) Black on white, the song looks at me
That from your mouth can deify,
Can tear open a heart!

The text was composed for the edition of *Göthe's neue Schriften* (*Goethe's New Writings*) published in 1800, where it appears in the section "Lieder" ("Songs"). In the final, authorized edition of Goethe's works (the so-called *Ausgabe letzter Hand*) it is the final text in the subsection of his poetry entitled "Lieder." The reason this contextualization is important is that it allows us to classify "An Lina" as a meta-*Lied*, a song about songs, a poetic theory of what poetic singing is. In this sense, the reading of the poem is severely curtailed if one refers its scenario exclusively to the practice of singing poetry to musical accompaniment. Rather, this situation of *Geselligkeit* (sociability) provides something like a narrative scaffold that charts out the destiny of song from origin to end. The Origin: lover and beloved united within musical orality (4); the End: the songs' return to the scene of their production where they are animated by the beloved's look (not her readings!) and by her voice, a voice that has the power to transfigure the lover, to deify him (11). And stretching out between this ideal past and ideal future, the nonlife of the songs as writing and as print ("Lettern," 9): the state of mournful alienation and loss ("traurig," 9) from which only the voice of the Origin can redeem them. The pragmatic constellation we encounter in "An Lina" corresponds to that of "Maifest," which figures the specular exchange with the beloved as the primordial donation of the force of song and which concludes with an envoi instructing the beloved to return the text to this Origin in 'love': "Sei ewig glücklich / Wie du mich liebst!" (Text 2, 35–36). Only in a reading qualified as 'loving' can the text find redemption from the state of alienation characterizing its linguistic, and preeminently its written, existence. This love, far from being an empirical fact about this or that person's feelings, is the originary sphere from which the poem emerged in the first place: specularity, the maternal gift, the transcendental voice.

~

To conclude these remarks on Goethe's lyric figuration of orality, I want to attend to a text that, to my mind, is one of the poet's most intriguing achievements:

24. AN DEN GEIST DES JOHANNES SEKUNDUS

  Lieber, heiliger, großer Küsser,
  Der du mir's in lechzend atmender
  Glückseligkeit fast vorgetan hast!
  Wem soll ich's klagen? klagt ich dir's nicht!
(5) Dir, dessen Lieder wie ein warmes Küssen
  Heilender Kräuter mir unters Herz sich legten,
  Daß es wieder aus dem krampfigen Starren
  Erdetreibens klopfend sich erholte.
  Ach wie klag ich dir's, daß meine Lippe blutet,
(10) Mir gespalten ist, und erbärmlich schmerzet,
  Meine Lippe, die so viel gewohnt ist
  Von der Liebe süßtem Glück zu schwellen
  Und, wie eine goldene Himmelspforte,
  Lallende Seligkeit aus und einzustammeln.
(15) Gesprungen ist sie! Nicht vom Biß der Holden,
  Die, in voller ringsumfangender Liebe,
  Mehr mögt haben von mir, und mögte mich Ganzen
  Ganz erküssen, und fressen, und was sie könnte!
  Nicht gesprungen weil nach ihrem Hauche
(20) Meine Lippen unheilige Lüfte entweihten.
  Ach gesprungen weil mich, Öden, Kalten,
  Über beizenden Reif, der Herbstwind anpackt.
  Und da ist Traubensaft, und der Saft der Bienen,
  An meines Herdes treuem Feuer vereinigt,
(25) Der soll mir helfen! Wahrlich er hilft nicht
  Denn von der Liebe alles heilendem
  Gift Balsam ist kein Tröpfgen drunter[34]

TO THE SPIRIT OF JOHANNES SECUNDUS

Dear, holy, great kisser,
You who in thirsting, breathing
Bliss almost preempted me!
To whom should I complain, if I didn't complain to you!
(5) To you, whose songs like a warm cushion [kissing]
Of healing herbs lay down beneath my heart,
So that it once again from the cramped stiffness
Of earthly doings recovered beating.
Oh how should I complain to you, that my lip is bleeding,
(10) Is split open, and hurts terribly,
My lip, that is so used to
Swelling with love's sweet happiness
And, like a golden, heavenly gate,
To stammer out in babbling bliss.
(15) It's sprung! Not from the bite of the dear one,
Who, in full, round embracing Love,
Would like to have more of me, and would like to kiss
Me altogether, and to gobble me up, and as much as she could!
Not sprung because after her breath
(20) Unholy air desecrated my lips.
Oh sprung because the autumn wind grabs
Me, barren and cold one, through biting frost.
And here is juice of grapes, and juice of the bees,
United at my hearth's faithful fire,
(25) That's supposed to help me! Truly it doesn't help.
Because of love's all-healing
Poison balm in it there's not a drop.

As my maladroit English rendering makes clear, the text presents even the
translator attempting merely a prose paraphrase with insuperable difficulties. Puns such as the play on "kisses"/"cushion" (5), lexical and syntactic
deformations, the nominalized adjectives, and, above all, a jogging rhythm
and intricate sound texture bind the poem to the language of its invention.
This attachment to the mother tongue, moreover, is far from fortuitous;
the imaginary terrain this text charts out is that of poetic orality.

Here, as so often, compositional structure provides a useful point of
departure. The poem's twenty-seven lines parse into three rhetorical-
thematic sections of unequal length. The first eight lines invoke the spirit

of Johannes Secundus as the predecessor most appropriate to receive the poet's complaint. That complaint (the poet suffers from a wounded lip) unfolds across the fourteen-line middle section. Finally, in the concluding five lines, the poet explains why the means he has at his disposal to assuage his wound, namely wine and honey warmed at his fire, provide no comfort.

The most obvious figure of coherence holding together this rather loose compositional scaffold is the opposition between the first and third sections established by the repetition of the participle "heilend" ("healing," 6, 26). The spirit of Johannes Secundus (1511–36), author of the Neo-Latin poem cycle *Basia* (*Kisses*), is apostrophied as an effective healing force, whereas the wine and honey available to the poet in his present situation are not. This opposition varies a figure employed in "Wandrers Sturmlied." There the summoned genius is said to "spread its woolen wings" beneath the wanderer, warming him in the stormy night (Text 16, 19), much like the "warm cushion / Of healing herbs" beneath the poet's heart in this text. The echo suggests that the spirit of Johannes Secundus has a function analogous to that of a genius or tutelary deity. Moreover, the speaker of "Wandrers Sturmlied" rejects as insufficient the poetry of his century modeled on that of the wine-chanting Anacreon and the "bienensingenden" ("bee-singing," Text 16, 97) Theocritus. Likewise, in our text the wine and honey warmed by the homey fire (the same external source of borrowed heat and borrowed desire the speaker of "Wandrers Sturmlied," in his poetic failure, must resort to) are judged inadequate to heal his wounded lip. One final intertextual connection: in "Der Adler und die Taube," the eagle's wounds are soothed (although insufficiently and ambiguously) by "Allgegenwärtger Balsam / Allheilender Natur" ("all-present balm / Of all-healing Nature," Text 17, 10–11). In the present case, healing does not occur because not even a drop of "love's all-healing . . . balm" (26–27) is contained in the wine and honey. It seems clear, then, that "An den Geist des Johannes Sekundus" performs a condemnatory gesture vis-à-vis eighteenth-century Anacreontic poetry similar to those enacted in the two poems of failed genius. The text works through a problematic bearing on the (contemporary) impossibility of a certain kind of poetic achievement. Thus, it is no accident that the motifs of 'wounding' and the 'meteorological antagonist' play a central role in the text's motivational complex.

By calling on the "spirit" of Johannes Secundus, on his genius, the poet seeks relief from his present situation, which we can provisionally define as the absence of love. Love's soothing force is not available to him, merely honey and wine. The appeal to the Neo-Latin precursor, then, rests on the presupposition that his spirit or genius animates a poetry invested with the healing power of love. Indeed, recalling the text on the Pentecostal miracle, we might say that Johannes Secundus's poetry is a gift of tongues in which love translates itself immediately into language. In other words, this poetry, like the primordial language of Prometheus and Minerva, knows no difference between utterance (oral production) and statement (the theme of love). Johannes's poems are not about love, but rather themselves realize erotic bliss; they are, as their title indicates, "kisses" (*Basia*), the healing "Küssen" ("cushion"/"kissing," 5) that releases the poet's heart from its cramped stiffness and allows it the *jouissance* of liquid pulsation. In comparison to this eroticized orality (and oralized eroticism), the artificial gratifications of wine and honey are mere palliatives.

But the orality that provides the imaginative focus of "An den Geist des Johannes Sekundus" must be rigorously distinguished from the primordial voice recalled in Prometheus's speech to Minerva. We are dealing here neither with the birth of the soul nor with the audition of an inner music. The poetic language imagined here does not resound in an inner ear, is not the subjective presence-to-self of the *s'entendre parler*. Orality in this text is something both more primitive and more corporeal. It is the site of a remarkable conflation in which the functions of Love (kissing), Life (breathing, eating, drinking), and Language (poetry) intermix. The text conducts us to a scene that cannot be figured visually, a scene that is therefore no scene at all, prior to audition and specularity, prior to the oneness of subjecthood. The bliss evoked in the Secundus poem is the pleasure of oral gratification, of a production and consumption whose organ is the breathing, eating, drinking, speaking mouth.

Thus, the poems of Johannes Secundus are characterized as "thirsting" or "craving" ("lechzend," 2), "breathing" ("atmender," 2), "bliss" ("Glückseligkeit," 3). And it is this fusion of vital-linguistic functions that the poet's own lip, during a time indefinitely past, was accustomed to:

> Meine Lippe, die so viel gewohnt ist
> Von der Liebe süßtem Glück zu schwellen
> Und, wie eine goldene Himmelspforte,
> Lallende Seligkeit aus und einzustammeln.
>
> *(11–14)*

Speaking here is breathing ("aus und ein-"), tasting ("süß"), and loving, in the full, that is, coital, sense of the word; the lip becomes a phallus, swollen with the love that it speaks, breathes, and tastes. Note especially the verbs designating this linguistic production: "lallen" and "stammeln" refer not to semantics, not to the field of idealities, but rather to corporeal production, the singsong and repeated syllabic bursts of sound that lips, tongue, teeth, and oral cavity conspire to shape. And the verses themselves, in their irregular rhythm, phonically mimic in their accented words this babbling oral pleasure: "Lippe"-"Liebe"; "schwellen"-"lallen"; "süßtem Glück"-"Seligkeit"; "Himmel"-"stammeln."

Note that this mimicry has the status of a memory; it recalls an experience now lost to the poet, whose present situation, and desolation, is defined by the absence of love. And since orality, in this text, is the primordial zone of love, the separation from the beloved manifests itself most forcefully there, at the oral aperture:

> Ach wie klag ich dir's, daß meine Lippe blutet,
> Mir gespalten ist, und erbärmlich schmerzet,
>
> · · ·
>
> Gesprungen ist sie!
>
> · · ·
>
> Ach gesprungen weil mich, Öden, Kalten,
> Über beizenden Reif, der Herbstwind anpackt.
>
> *(9–10, 15, 21–22)*

Like the eagle of "Der Adler und die Taube," the poet is cut off from the fulfillment of his aspiration by a wound, an incision performed by the meteorological agency that in "Pilgers Morgenlied" (Text 10) threatened the poetic subject with castration. Certainly a reading of the lip's wound as 'castration' is justified here as well insofar as this lip figures as an organ that swells with "love's sweet happiness" (12). Such a reading, however, must also endeavor to specify the distinctive inflection the figure of castration receives here. In "An den Geist des Johannes Sekundus" the threat does not emerge in response to a preeminently visual-specular identification with the maternal figure, which is at the same time an identification with the phallus. Rather, it is directed at the lip as the organ of an undifferentiated sexual-linguistic-alimentary bliss. Castration here 'splits' ("spalten") the lip and thereby splits these functions from one another. The wound that pains the poet is his separation from the unity of language and instinct. Precisely this severence, however, constitutes language as a structure of semiotic mediation.

To see this point, it is useful to recall Herder's interpretation of the origin of human language in the treatise that, as noted above, valorizes orality as audibility (and thus as intelligibility). In the famous scene depicting the first human linguistic utterance, Herder juxtaposes the human stance vis-à-vis the primordial object of linguistic designation—in Herder's text, a female sheep—to two others, that of the hungry predator (wolf or lion) whose alimentary instinct compels it to consume the object, and that of the rutting ram, whose sexual instinct likewise thrusts it upon its white, soft, and woolly partner. The human being, in contrast to these two natural figures, is characterized by an instinctual lack; no particular appetite determines the human relationship to the ewe. In the space of this lack ("Mangel") the supplement, the specifically human supplement, of language emerges, a system of audible signs.[35] The story Herder tells, it is clear, conforms to a moralizing design, attests to the triumph of human freedom and reflection over the quasi-mechanical forces of instinct. The speaking being ("der Mensch") celebrates the extrication of his language from the crude sensuousness ("Sinnlichkeit") of alimentation and sexuality with the aureole of successful sublimation.

Goethe's text views this process from a less moralizing angle: the leap from the prelinguistic stage of alimentary-sexual babble to the stage of linguistic designation results from a violent cut, the caustic bite of the meteorological antagonist to which the subject, barren and cold ("mich, Öden, Kalten," 21) for lack of inner heat, can provide no resistance. I suspect that this implicit critique of moralization, and not its flagrant eroticism, has made this text such a scandal, even to its author. Herder's edifying account locates the fact of violence exclusively on the side of instinct and lets language unfold in a thoroughly irenic sphere. In "An den Geist des Johannes Sekundus," by contrast, language itself is the trace of a violent incision, of castration. To speak, as Herder says human beings do speak, requires a lip that bleeds, that is split open and hurts terribly. The price of sublimation is a wound.

What is truly surprising about this text, however, is not the figure of castration, whose agency is the antagonistic weather that Goethe, and the eighteenth century, saw as the enforcer of conscience.[36] Its remarkable and singular feature is the figuration of the maternal sphere from which the subject is severed. In all the poems examined thus far, this sphere is structured according to the schema of specularity, the eroticized regard in which the subject sees itself being seen and receives through this visual exchange the gift of its desire. Recall the example of "Künstlers Morgenlied," in which this primordial donation becomes the matrix of modern art:

> Ach wie du ruhtest neben mir
> Mich schmachtetst liebend an
> Und mir's vom Aug durchs Herz hindurch
> In Griffel schmachtete   *(Text 18, 53–56)*

Specularity, in other words, is always a scene, a spatial array opened before the eye (and the "I"). Its distinguishing feature is a certain distance within unity, a decorporealization that guarantees stability and identity. The foundational function of the specular figure derives from its visual character, from the prestige of perception as the medium in which the subject sees itself being seen. To call this Origin 'voice' in the sense of inner audition and transparency (as in the text from *Prometheus*) does not significantly alter this structure. We are still dealing with a medium of idealization, with the presence of the subject to itself, with an acoustic mirror. But in "An den Geist des Johannes Sekundus" the machinery of idealization—distance, decorporealization—disappears. Neither the soul nor its delegates the eye and the ear function here as the organ of contact with the Mother, but rather, and exclusively, the mouth.

The verbs "lallen" and "stammeln," which define the mouth's linguistic production, recall both infantile babble (see Herder's text on the nursing infant) and drunken speech, the speech, that is, of a mouth full of liquid pleasure. If specularity and the transcendental voice figure the Origin of the subject in the luminescence and transparency of the primordial exchange with the Mother, then this poem recalls a form of contact with the Mother that is prior to this Origin, a formless form of contact that resides solely in the eroticism of the lips and the oral cavity:

> Nicht vom Biß der Holden,
> Die, in voller ringsumfangender Liebe,
> Mehr mögt haben von mir, und mögte mich Ganzen
> Ganz erküssen, und fressen, und was sie könnte!   *(15–18)*

The paradigm of love evoked here does not coalesce into an object relation and does not, therefore, install an image of subjective identity. Quite to the contrary, the eroticism of the mouth morcellates, disperses, and consumes the subject. Note especially the line break that pivots around the inflection of "ganz" first as nominalized adjective, then as adverb. In several of the previously analyzed texts this word of 'wholeness' signals the poetic subject's self-appropriation within the specular moment (see, for example, Text 9, 20: "Da fühl ich mich so ganz," and especially Text 15, 54–55: "Und nun schwillt er / Herrlicher, ein ganz Geschlechte"); in other texts the same word marks the originating, procreative capacity of the genius. "Ganz," in short, is a qualifier of self-identity, a term that refers to the 'phallic' morphology of unsevered oneness. Here, however, self-totalization passes immediately over into a total disidentification, an oral consumption that bites apart the subject's swelling, loving lip.

This poem, singular in Goethe's lyric corpus, imagines an orality that is, strictly speaking, unimaginable, a primitive orality that, to use the language of the eighteenth century (Herder's language), remains on the level of alimentary-sexual instinct. (Note that the verb "fressen" employed here refers to 'animal' as opposed to 'human' eating.) This instinctual sphere is by no means free of violence; Goethe is far from positing a pristine natural domain to which the harsh intervention of culturation (castration) would come from the outside. In this sense his text is not a simple reversal of Herder's valorization. Rather, the alimentary-sexual-linguistic orality evoked in the poem combines pleasure and violence; it is intrinsically ambivalent. And this ambivalence extends to the directionality of the oral activity, in which to kiss is to be kissed, to eat is to be eaten.[37] There is a strong suggestion here that oral pleasure and oral anguish, at their extremes, coincide.

This brings me to one final intricacy of the text. As we have seen, the poet laments his severence from the domain of love conceived as the unity of alimentary, sexual, and linguistic functions, a severence enforced by the splitting of his lip. But not merely the fact that his lip is wounded occasions his lament; what seems to frustrate him is that this wound was inflicted by the cold wind and the biting frost. The wound of castration could have—but didn't—come from the beloved: "Nicht vom Biß der Holden." Instead, it came from the "beizenden Reif." This juxtaposition carries a double implication. On the one hand, it suggests that the meteorological violence is merely a pale and, as it were, banal repetition of what would have been a truly ecstatic wounding, the erotic bite of the female, and that this trivialization, so dessicated and cold, is the actual loss the poet complains about. It irks him not merely that he is wounded, but that he is wounded in such an undignified, perhaps unheroic, way, that, severed from the beloved, he lacks the inner heat ('desire', 'poetic creativity') to combat the meteorological antagonist. The comic tonality of the text derives primarily from this path of reading, which is also related to disdain for the century's wine-and-honey concept of poetic-erotic pleasure.

At the same time, however, the juxtaposition implies that the wound I am calling 'castration' *could have been* inflicted by the female, indeed that the female's bite is the very paradigm of that wound ("beizen"/"Biß"). Moreover, since this bite would split the male subject's swelling phallic lip and morcellate the wholeness of phallic identity, the unavoidable implication is that the female mouth executing the bite is both an oral and a vaginal cavity, *vagina dentata*. In this sense, "An den Geist des Johannes Sekundus" would seem to confirm what I argued earlier in connection with such texts as "Wandrers Sturmlied" and "Der Adler und die Taube": that the castrating wound is associated with the feminine, that the feminine is an essentially ambiguous figure, wounding and healing at once. (The fact that these texts are related to our poem in other registers supports this comparison.) Moreover, in my reading of "Mahomets Gesang" I suggested that 'castration' is avoided through a double repression, on the one hand of the 'feminine' and on the other of the term 'poison'. These references illuminate the final lines of our text, in which the poet complains that the wine and honey at his disposal contain not a drop of "der Liebe alles heilenden / Gift Balsam." Love is at once "poison" and "balm"; the feminine is at once the paradigm of castration and the figure of plenitude who promises to assuage its wound.

I have stressed throughout this discussion of "An den Geist des Johannes Sekundus" that the poem is a kind of *hapax legomenon* within Goethe's lyric corpus, a singular instance that breaks with the pattern of his other lyric texts. No other poem by Goethe refers to a dimension of language so primitive, so material and subjectless, as this one. Likewise, no other poem (at least from this phase of Goethe's writing) accords the female figure so much initiative as an erotic agent. The function of the beloved here is not to endow, through the sweetness of her regard or her voice, the loving male subject with the gift of desire; rather, her desire emerges in all its corporeal specificity: "mögte mich Ganzen / Ganz erküssen, und fressen, und was sie könnte!" But this double deviation (toward a materialism of language and an active female eroticism) confirms the systematic coherence of Goethe's lyric writing. It reveals the essential ambiguity of the female figure, and the essential ambivalence of the love that becomes the principle of Goethe's artistic production. As long as she is held in the distance and decorporealization of specularity, the female can function as the donor of desire, selfhood, and creativity, can assuage the wound of castration by offering the subject a stabilized phallic self-image. But beneath or behind this image function of the beloved, as it were, there lurks another female or maternal figure, a figure who can't be seen in the transparency of the specular regard or heard in the inner audibility of the soul's music, a figure who threatens the subject's integral wholeness. Wherever this figure makes her presence felt—as the anarchic Medusan signification of "Pilgers Morgenlied," as the pythian monstrosity of "Künstlers Morgenlied," as the repressed female "poison" of "Mahomets Gesang"—she appears as a snake. "An den Geist des Johannes Sekundus" makes this ambivalence vis-à-vis the feminine explicit. The "Biß der Holden" is also a snake's bite, severing the phallic lip. 'Love'—the *Urwort* of Goethe's lyric innovation—is split by what Freud called a *Gegensinn*: "Gift" and "Balsam" in one.[38]

§ 7 Primordial Song

One of the principal sites in which the myth of primordial orality finds expression is the critical discourse on folk poetry that emerges in the 1770's. Again Herder is the decisive figure, fashioning through both his published collections of folk poetry and his theoretical writings the concept of a "poetry of the peoples" (*Volkspoesie*), which radically altered the axiology of the eighteenth-century literary system. The close connection between the concepts of folk poetry and primordial orality—epitomized, for example, in the title of the 1807 edition of Herder's folk-song collection, *Stimmen der Völker in Liedern* ("Voices of the Peoples in Songs"),[1] hardly requires demonstration here. Suffice it to recall that the mythologization of Homeric voice from which I derived the central motifs of the myth of primordial orality occurs in the introduction to Herder's 1779 edition of folk songs. The classification of Homer as *Volksdichter* suggests how capacious Herder's notion of folk poetry was, embracing everything from Shakespeare to the songs of the Greenlanders. The decisive criterion is not primitive or unschooled circumstances of production, but the critic's intuition that something originary—the living poetic voice—achieves articulation, becomes audible, in the texts exhibited as examples. Folk poetry presented itself to the eighteenth-century imagination as primordial song, as much the creator of its *Volk* as its product.

In the decades following Herder's first anthology, of course, the concept of folk poetry increasingly narrowed its scope to a national field of reference, as revealed in the canonical Romantic collection published in 1805 by Achim von Arnim and Clemens Brentano, *Des Knaben Wunderhorn* ("The Youth's Horn of Wonder").[2] Whereas Herder, with enlightened universalism, wanted to make "the living voice of humanity"[3] audible, his Romantic successors were more attuned to the authentic expression of a German inwardness. But the medium of this inwardness remained orality, as Goethe's notoriously distanced review of the *Wunderhorn* reveals. The best fate this volume could meet with, Goethe suggests, would be to find its home on the pianos of amateur and master musicians, where its songs would blend with traditional and new melodies. Then follows a dubious compliment that varies the wish the poet had expressed for his own "Lieder" in "An Lina" (Text 23): "If under such conditions these songs were carried from ear to ear, from mouth to mouth, by their own element of sound and tone, if they gradually returned enlivened and glorified to the people [*Volk*] from which they had as it were in part originated, then one could say that this little book had fulfilled its purpose and could now be lost as a written and printed book because it had passed over into the life and cultivation of the nation."[4]

The skeptical edge implicit in this surmise should not obscure the fact that Goethe was a key figure in the promotion of an emphatic notion of the folk song. Not only did he collaborate early on with Herder, collecting songs from Alsatian mothers for his convalescent mentor, his own poetic production of the 1770's includes some of the most enduring recreations of the folk-song tone in the German language. Such was Goethe's preeminence that Arnim and Brentano lavishly dedicated *Des Knaben Wunderhorn* to him. In doing so, as Ernst Beutler has shown,[5] they paid homage to the captivating spell Goethe's early poetry had exerted on their own imaginations. One of the most intriguing testimonies of this influence is a letter Brentano wrote to Arnim in 1801 while traveling on the Rhine: "When I arrived on top at the outlook point, my heart was moved and I was inspired as never before, and I sang with reverence: 'I am the king of Thule.'"[6] The statement, whether a fully accurate report or not, bespeaks more than appreciation for poetic accomplishment.

One of the claims made in the first chapter was that Goethe's reinterpretation of the idyll invents a lyric discourse that draws on the deepest resources of subjectivity and in turn makes those resources available to empathetic reenactment by the reader. The evidence of Brentano's letter suggests that this occurs most forcefully in texts that, generically and stylistically, connote an archaic poetic practice. Such texts are not experienced as historicizing imitations that mark a distance to their prototype even as they simulate its form. Rather, they are read, heard, memorized, and sung as the renewed emergence of poetry in its purest, which is to say originary, state. In Goethe's romance, composed probably at the time of his own Rhine journey in 1774, Brentano finds a vehicle of ecstatic identification, an identification not so much with the poem's title figure as with the poem itself. As it were, Goethe's poem infiltrates Brentano's voice, dictates itself to the young poet and calls forth in him a history and a desire that he recognizes as his own.

In this chapter, I want to explore the textual basis for such an identification by inquiring what it is that sings in the songs, romances, and ballads that Goethe composed in the tone of the folk song during the 1770's. The texts selected to pursue this question are the three Brentano acknowledged as his favorites: in addition to "Der König in Thule," "Heidenröslein," dating from the beginning of the decade, and "Der Fischer" ("The Fisherman"), probably composed in 1778. Along with "Der Erlkönig," which I shall not attend to here, these texts embody Goethe's contribution to the lyric myth of primordial song.

25. HEIDENRÖSLEIN

> Sah ein Knab' ein Röslein stehn,
> Röslein auf der Heiden,
> War so jung und morgenschön,
> Lief er schnell es nah zu sehn,
> (5) Sah's mit vielen Freuden.
> Röslein, Röslein, Röslein rot,
> Röslein auf der Heiden.
>
> Knabe sprach: ich breche dich,
> Röslein auf der Heiden!
> (10) Röslein sprach: ich steche dich,
> Daß du ewig denkst an mich,
> Und ich will's nicht leiden.
> Röslein, Röslein, Röslein rot,
> Röslein auf der Heiden.
>
> (15) Und der wilde Knabe brach
> 's Röslein auf der Heiden;
> Röslein wehrte sich und stach,
> Half ihr doch kein Weh und Ach,
> Mußt es eben leiden.
> Röslein, Röslein, Röslein rot,
> Röslein auf der Heiden.[7]

HEATH ROSE

A youth saw a little rose standing;
Little rose on the heath,
Was so young and morning-lovely.
He ran quickly to see it close up,
(5) Saw it with much joy.
Little rose, little rose, little rose red,
Little rose on the heath.

The youth said: "I'll break you,
Little rose on the heath."
(10) Little rose spoke: "I'll prick you,
So that you'll forever think of me,
And I don't want to suffer it."
Little rose, little rose, little rose red,
Little rose on the heath.

(15) And the wild youth broke
The little rose on the heath;
Little rose resisted and pricked,
But no "woe" and "oh" helped her,
She just had to suffer it.
(20) Little rose, little rose, little rose red,
Little rose on the heath.

Perhaps no poem of Goethe's is, to paraphrase Herder's remark on Homer, so loved by the German ear as this song, recalled either in its linguistic musicality or in Schubert's setting. The intense affective attachment the poem attracts focuses especially on what might be called its aura of purity. As regards both its title figure (nature's uncultivated rose, synecdoche of Nature herself) and its own apparent artlessness of execution (which Herder called its "Kinderton"[8]), the text functions as an emblem of innocence. Its fascination derives from its air of virginity, and this no doubt for the very reason that the story it tells is that of virginity lost.

Which brings me to the problem of reading this text. Objects of the strong affection we call love tend, as Freud often noted, to be overvalued ("überschätzt"). We treasure them (the noun "Schatz" in German means 'treasure' and is also an appellation for a beloved), shield them from criticism, preserve them in their perfection and wholeness—in their innocence. Thus, the tradition of Goethe criticism has for the most part held "Heidenröslein" at the safe distance of fond adoration, rigorously obeying the taboo against analytically penetrating its pristine simplicity. Clearly, this attitude—it is the attitude of Valentin toward his sister Gretchen in *Faust*—is no longer tenable. But likewise untenable is the opposite stance, the hermeneutic pathos of Faust himself, which dreams of violating the poem's innocence, of lifting its veil in order to possess the naked truth at its center. The phantasm of virginity is the phantasm of its violation. The delicate task this text poses to a critical reading is to find a position external to this alternative, a position from which the systematic interplay of purity and desecration—the interplay the text itself stages—can be observed.

Let us start, then, as neutrally, as technically, as possible by reconstructing the poem's narrative movement. The story the text tells, like all narratives in their overriding macrostructure, consists of three phases: (1) an initial state; (2) an action effecting a transformation of the initial state; and (3) an outcome or state resulting from the action. In "Heiden-röslein," this structure parses as follows.

Phase 1. The first stanza establishes the opening situation as a state of proximity ("nah," 4) and equilibrium (both the youth and the rose are standing) in which the central activity is that of seeing. Through the terms "jung" and "morgenschön" (3) this state accumulates connotations of 'pristineness': it is as if just born, not yet tainted by time and the accumulated duplicities of reflective culture, untouched, as we say. The world evoked in this stanza resembles that unfolded across the entire text of "Maifest" (Text 2), which includes within its more expansive lexicon of 'natural innocence' all three of the connotational markers ("morgen-," "schön," "jung") employed here. And of course the central event of "Maifest" is likewise a seeing that communicates joy ("Freude") to the poem's male figure. In view of this convergence between the two texts (not to speak of "Mir schlug das Herz," Text 5), we can designate the first narrative phase of "Heidenröslein" the "innocence of specularity."

Phase 2. The second phase of the narrative, articulated across stanzas two and three, enacts the severance of the original unity. This disjunction is the actual event of the narrative, its border-crossing or movement from one state to a second, semantically opposed state. Note that the inception of the narrative movement alters the temporal structure. The specular encounter of the first narrative phase culminates in an action (if such poised stasis can be so termed) of indefinite duration ("Sah's mit vielen Freuden," 5). The second phase, however, unfolds across a series of punctual, temporally discrete moments, so that the two narrative phases are opposed as 'timelessness' is to 'sequence' or 'succession'. Moreover, the three occurrences of the verb "sehen" in the first phase are replaced by the three (repeated) verbs "sprechen," "brechen," and "stechen," which mark the events of the second. The rhyme that links these three verbs effects their semantic fusion such that 'speaking' in this text becomes a cognate of 'breaking' and 'pricking'. The speech of stanza two, that is, is already the act of violent breaking that shatters the unity of specularity, much as Werther's effort to describe his visual impressions of natural self-sufficiency leaves those very impressions "zerstückt" ("broken into pieces").[9] Finally, the fracture of specularity the second phase of the narrative accomplishes is a wounding painful to both the youth, who gets pricked, and the flower, which, of course, is broken. On a preliminary reading, then, the first two stages of the narrative revolve around the accompanying oppositional schema.

Phase One		*Phase Two*
unity	vs.	severence
timelessness	vs.	sequence
vision	vs.	language
joy	vs.	pain

Schema 7: Narrative Movement of "Heidenröslein"

Phase 3. The first two phases of the narrative exhaust the three stanzas of the text. No fourth stanza follows to depict what happens after the rose is plucked and the youth is wounded by the thorn. It would seem, then, that the poem is, narratively speaking, fragmentary, incomplete, that it does not carry out the basic three-phase narrative schema from which we took our point of departure. But in fact this is not so, and to see why is to begin to gain acquaintance with the poem's remarkable artistry. Although not scenically realized, as the other two are, the third phase of the narrative, the state following the narrative event or border-crossing, is mentioned in the text, and this mention occurs as a prediction.

In stanza two, the heath rose warns the youth that the act of breaking will result in a pricking that in turn will cause the youth perpetually to recall the lost flower: "Daß du ewig denkst an mich" (11). Note that this line—this threat, warning, or perhaps even curse—occupies the exact center of the text, and this because, as we shall see, it speaks the very law of the poem itself. The act of breaking—the attempt to move beyond specularity and to seize and possess the object of vision—will eventuate in a recurrent, obsessive memory that haunts the youth's future. It is important to stress the temporal intricacy of this prediction (or curse). From within the enclosure of the narrative past, the text projects a future state that is nothing other than the *return*, as memory, of this past. As I mentioned, this future state is not presented as a scene, but it remains a crucial component of the text's narrative significance in that it represents the narrative outcome, the state achieved following, and as a result of, the transgression of phase two. Although not narrated, this phase is nevertheless enacted and its enactment is the very performance—the speaking or singing—of the poem. *The poem itself is the return of the memory of the heath rose.*[10]

This elementary narrative analysis reveals what previous interpreters of the poem have failed to grasp: "Heidenröslein" tells the story of its own constitution as poetic phantasy. In the song itself, the rose returns as primordial phantasy, the phantasy of an original rupture, or articulation, the phantasy of the loss of vision in language such that that vision only comes back, glimmers forth out of memory, in order to suffer once again its loss. The poetic phantasy is nothing other than the return of this loss, the flare-up of a wound ('prick'), the repetition of a severence ('breaking'). To put this another way, the phantasizing subject is the subject condemned to repeat this trauma, to "forever think of me." It is bound for all time to a vision of unity and timelessness that reappears only to shatter again and again. Moreover, this story of the constitution of poetic phantasy motivates and lends semantic pertinence to the text's most prominent formal feature. The refrain, recurring at the end of each stanza and partially realized in each stanza's second line, functions to dramatize the return, incessant and obsessive, of the rose as memory. The trait that lends the text its compositional law and most clearly marks it as folk song, as primordial song, becomes the trace of the text's rootedness in loss.

The narrative movement I have constructed in terms of the register of poetic phantasy is imbricated with and derives its energy from a sexual dynamics. Here the focus lies, of course, on the connotations of the breaking of the flower, the ensuing pricking, and the element of blood, unmentioned but forcefully implicit in the narrative scenario, especially because of its association with the color term "rot." In other words, the text draws, massively and obviously, on the iconography of defloration. The central phase of the narrative figures an act of sexual aggression in which the maiden gets pricked in the moment when the flower of her virginity is plucked.

At this point, it would seem, we have destroyed the poem's appearance of innocence, discovering beneath its metaphorical veil a scenography of rape. As I suggested at the outset of my remarks, however, such hermeneutic pathos of truth, rather than explicating the movement of the poetic phantasy, merely reproduces it. That is not to say that the text has nothing to do with defloration; rather, that defloration is itself a phantasmatic event.

The best way to get at what I mean by this somewhat enigmatic statement is to call attention to the operation of reading involved here. The text, after all, does not say that the youth pricks the flower, but rather exactly the reverse. In other words, in order to generate the signified 'defloration' we must reattribute agency and redirect the action. Of course, such adjustments of the manifest text, as Freud showed in his *Traumdeutung*, are entirely legitimate, merely reversing the process of *Entstellung* (distortion) that produced the oneiric or, in the case at hand, poetic figuration. There can be no argument but that the entire poetic context, not to mention the force of colloquial usage, supports this semantic alteration. As I said, the iconography of defloration here is massive and obvious. The text, I want to claim, *urges* us to read its literal sense metaphorically as the story of the violation of female virginity carried out by a male agent; the *Wunsch* it stages is that the reading in terms of defloration be its one true reading. By pretending to hide its truth, the text elicits the hermeneutic operation that answers its desire.

To insist, as this text does, on a particular metaphorical reading is to block—to expel or repress—alternative readings. Is another semantic construction than that of defloration nonetheless possible? Consider once again the metaphorical vehicle: the "Knabe" is pricked, suffers a wound, and this wound is a punishment for his illicit attempt to possess the female object of desire presented to him within the unity of specularity. Unmentioned in this scenario is the corporeal site where this wound is inflicted, an element so tacitly assumed, so much a component of the narrative frame, that one easily forgets to ask after its identity. The youth's finger, the corporeal extremity that grasps the rose's thorny stem, receives the laceration; the member that would pluck the flower is itself cut open. And this is why the text works to ensure the reading of defloration: because the very scene that prompts that reading can also be read as a figuration of 'castration'.

Yet castration is no more the truth of the text, no more its hermeneutic center, than is defloration. The two readings are complementary. The poetic phantasy is not a metaphorical veil that at once hides and reveals a stable meaning; rather, it is the site where complementary meanings cross one another, pass over into their mirror inversions. This movement can be schematized, or graphically dramatized, as in the accompanying diagram.

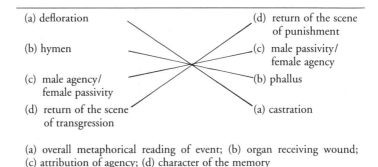

(a) defloration   (d) return of the scene
                                       of punishment

(b) hymen   (c) male passivity/
                                       female agency

(c) male agency/   (b) phallus
    female passivity

(d) return of the scene   (a) castration
    of transgression

(a) overall metaphorical reading of event; (b) organ receiving wound;
(c) attribution of agency; (d) character of the memory

Schema 8: Poetic Phantasy of "Heidenröslein"

The complementarity of the two readings illustrated by the schema reveals that the sexual content of the poetic phantasy is not a content at all. Rather, sexuality here is a movement of transposition between terms, a transference, an instability of role allocation. The poetic phantasy is sexual to the degree that it stages the interplay of the two readings, an interplay in which defloration is the metaphor of castration, and vice versa. In his discussion of the trope of metaphor, Aristotle distinguishes between the process through which meaning is transferred (*epiphora*) and the product of this process, the renominalized meaning (*metaphora*).[11] Applying this distinction here, one could say that a hermeneutic reading seeks to stop—to freeze or fix—the epiphoric movement by privileging, and insisting on as true, a single metaphorical product, be it defloration or castration. The text itself not only complies with this hermeneutic gesture, it elicits it. The innocence of the text, inviting interpretive penetration, is in fact an elaborate seduction.

To make this point another way, the two narrative scenarios are not the truth of the text, not a meaning that it hides behind a veil of apparently innocent figuration. (This would be an all-too-comfortable, all-too-hermeneutic account.) Rather, both narrative scenarios—castration and defloration—are stabilizations of the essential ambivalence that sexuality, in this text and perhaps not only in this text, is. Both are mythic accounts that press into a framework of intelligibility what in fact shatters (fractures, breaks open) the contours of stabilized meaning. As such, they at once reveal and dissimulate a semiotic crisis, a movement of differentiation and indifferentiation, that can no longer be thought of as a determinate content. On the one hand, the perfection of virginity is ruptured; on the other hand, the oneness of the narcissistically cathected phallic self is severed. Virginity and the phallus are mirror images of one another (recall that our starting point was the innocence of specularity). What is at stake in their respective violations, then, is the undoing of the identity for which each term—virginity and phallus—provides a schema. This text ties the origin of (poetic) phantasy to the emergence or outbreak of sexuality, to be sure; but this is because phantasy is an oscillating figuration in which the essential ambivalence of sexuality returns and, returning, makes its indeterminacy felt.

One of the issues at stake in the interplay of complementary readings constituting the poetic phantasy is that of subjective identity. The hypostasis of a single metaphorical reading stabilizes identity by establishing firm role allocations. Thus, in the interpretive construction of the story as one of defloration, male and female are opposed to one another as 'agency' and 'passivity'. This role allocation dissimulates the sexuality of the phantasy conceived as the epiphoric movement between these two poles. Sexuality *is* this movement, *is* the labile difference/indifference of male/female, active/passive, pleasure/pain. And in this sense, sexuality disidentifies the subject and exceeds the limits of fixed role attributions. The version of the text I have cited here betrays the process of dissimulation through a minute grammatical distortion. In the third stanza, at the point where the act of breaking/pricking is accomplished, the text reads:

> Röslein wehrte sich und stach,
> Half ihr doch kein Weh und Ach,
> Mußt es eben leiden. *(17–19)*

One might describe the symbolic process enacted across these lines as a disarming of the female/rose: her capacity to act aggressively ("*weh*rte" and "st*ach*") is transformed—through what might be termed a consonantal amputation—into her helpless cry ("Weh" and "Ach") and her resultant passivity ("leiden") is pronounced a matter of necessity ("mußt"). This symbolic removal of the rose's thorn (of its capacity to play the role of phallic aggressor) is supported by the use of the feminine dative pronoun "ihr," which is grammatically incorrect insofar as its apparent referent ("Röslein") is neuter. The problem is that the correct form, the neuter dative pronoun "ihm," would have introduced a semantic ambiguity since it is indistinguishable from the dative masculine form. Grammatical propriety, in other words, would have left indeterminate whether it is the "Knabe" or the female/rose whose "Weh und Ach" is so ineffectual here and who assumes the passive role. The grammatically deviant pronoun eliminates this semantic ambiguity and thereby dictates the role allocation of 'female sufferance'.[12]

To see how the narrative analysis of the poem into three movements fits into this discussion of the sexual dynamics operative in the text, it is useful to recall the ambiguity of the specular figure, and in particular that of its feminine pole. The female/mother is both the donor of the phallus who heals the wound of castration and the instance that threatens the subject with castration. In "Heidenröslein," this ambiguity is transferred onto the figure of the virgin (the rose), who combines both passivity and threatening aggressivity.[13] This instantiation of the bivalent female pole of specularity as virgin leads to the complementary images of speech/writing (phase 2) as either defloration or castration. We might say that the text projects two interpretations of poetic subjectivity (or authorship). In the former, the moment of 'speech' and 'fracture' becomes an act of sexual aggression: poetic writing is stylized as violent and authoritative inscription on the virginal female body, which presents itself within the specular image. In the latter reading, the same moment becomes the severence of the phallic oneness of identity attained within the specular exchange, the loss of that identity in castration. The memory that returns to the poet and constitutes the refrain of his song rehearses both these events, both his act of transgression and his punishment. In this apparently innocent folk song, the poet writes his own ambivalent relation to writing and to the feminine, a relation that, in both respects, is sexual in the sense I have tried to lend that term here.

〜

26. ROMANZE

Es war ein König in Thule
Ein' goldnen Becher er hätt
Empfangen von seiner Bule
Auf ihrem Todes Bett.

(5) Den Becher hätt er lieber,
Trank draus bei jedem Schmaus
Die Augen gingen ihm über,
So oft er trank daraus.

Und als er kam zu sterben
(10) Zählt' er seine Städt' und Reich'
Gönnt alles seinen Erben
Den Becher nicht zugleich.

Beym hohen Königsmale
Die Ritter um ihn her
(15) Im alten Vätersaale
Auf seinem Schloß am Meer.

Da saß der alte Zecher
Trank letzte Lebens Glut
Und warf den heil'gen Becher
(20) Hinunter in die Fluth.

Er sah ihn sinken, trinken
Und stürzen tief ins Meer;
Die Augen thäten ihm sinken,
Trank nie keinen Tropfen mehr.[14]

ROMANCE

There was a king in Thule;
A golden cup he had
Received from his beloved
On her death bed.

(5) The cup he held most dear,
Drank from it at every feast;

His eyes overflowed,
As soon as he drank from it.

And when he came to die
(10)   He counted his cities and realms,
Granted all to his descendants,
The cup not so quickly.

At the king's high meal,
The knights all around him
(15)   In the ancient hall of the fathers
In his castle on the sea—

There sat the old reveller,
Drank a last time life's glow,
And threw the holy cup
(20)   Down into the flood.

He saw it sink, drink,
And fall deep into the sea;
His eyes sank closed;
He never drank no drop more.

Like "Heidenröslein," this ballad (or romance) is a predominantly narrative text, but, rather than concentrate on a single moment, the narrative of "Der König von Thule" (as the text is titled in other variants) unfolds across a long duration, a duration that coincides, I shall argue, with the course of an entire lifetime. Another way of conceptualizing this difference between the two texts is to say that the poetic resonance of "Heidenröslein" derives from its concentrated figurality, whereas "Der König von Thule" produces its semantic multivalence extensively. The key elements of the poem accumulate significance by moving across a succession of positions, by sequentially changing places. One could speak here of a poetics of exchange.

The easiest approach to the text, therefore, is to follow out its narrative sequence, not by simply (although the act is never a simple one) retelling its story, but by commenting on it, inscribing its margins with a series of glosses that locate semantically the various positions the narrative passes through. The first stanza introduces the cup ("Becher") as a metonymy for the beloved. Its significance for the king stems from the fact that it comes from her, and, like a memento, it will accompany the king after his separation from her, recalling her to him, evoking her presence in absence.

This process of metonymization is crucial to the logic of the text. Rather than metaphorically semanticizing the cup (for example, by introducing a descriptive value such as 'feminine roundness'), the poem invests it with significance by marking its passage from one hand to another, by charting the movement of this singular gift. The meaning of the cup is established laterally rather than vertically; it has, at this point at least, no semantic depth or density. The cup is, then, a *symbol,* recalling the ancient notion of symbol as a material item passed from hand to hand in order to betoken an interpersonal bond. "Der König von Thule" dramatizes a process of symbolic exchange.

The symbolic act delineated in the first stanza has a directionality: the cup (no doubt a formal drinking cup, a chalice) is a 'gift' given by the beloved to the king. The bond between beloved and king—the bond attested to by the symbol—is that between donor and receiver, a relationship, fundamentally, of debt or obligation. This suggests that the debt will have to be repaid, the gift returned, which, of course, is what happens at the poem's, and not just the poem's, end. But there is more to be said about the act of giving, above all, that it occurs at the moment of the beloved's death. The establishment of the symbolic bond coincides with the severance of the physical bond between king and "Bule," with the end of their corporeal embrace. Thus, the opening stanza structures the emergence of the symbol according to the equivalence:

$$\text{separation from} \quad = \quad \text{gift of the}$$
$$\text{beloved body} \qquad\qquad \text{symbol}$$
$$\text{(death)}$$

The bed of love becomes a "Todes Bett," and the natural, physical union is succeeded by a state of symbolic union. The king maintains his attachment to the body of the beloved—and recalls the bond of debt that links him to that body—through the symbolic cup.

Can we speak here of the birth of the subject (the king) in its separation from the natural/female body? Certainly the analyses carried out in the previous chapters would buttress such a reading. The beloved's gift to the king corresponds to what I have called a maternal donation. Moreover, the bed of love and death could also be glossed as the site of a birth, which, after all, is a severance of the corporeal union of child and mother.[15] Finally, since the poem ends with the king's death, it prompts a retrospective reading of the opening stanza as birth. With the gift of the symbol the king is born as subject, which is to say: born as one who lives indebted to the maternal donation that gave him—what else?—himself. The subject becomes subject, becomes what the language of idealism calls a For Itself (*Für Sich*) and this text calls a king, at the moment when a death severs the bond of nature and replaces it with a symbolic linkage.

The second stanza establishes the cup as the king's favorite object, establishes his affective attachment to the cup. But it also adds one further semantic determination to the "Becher": its function as a vessel out of which the king drinks. Now this may seem an utterly trivial, mimetically or naturalistically motivated detail, without poetic relevance. But through the function of drinking, a function that will return, the value of 'liquidity' familiar from other texts enters into the poem's semantic repertoire. Indeed, so central is this complex drinking/liquidity to the poetic figuration that it saturates, as it were, the entire field of the king's life activity. His story contains no adventure, no military victory, no examples of wise governance, but just this one, iterated act: his drinking out of the cup on the occasion of every feast. Once the second stanza recounts this about him, nothing more remains to be told, and the third stanza abruptly turns to the moment when the king comes to die. Hence the later characterization of the king as "Zecher" (17), which more strongly focalizes the idea of drinking than the English equivalent "reveller." The story the romance narrates consists just of these three moments: the gift of the cup; drinking; death. Clearly, to grasp the logic (or economy) of this story it is necessary to analyze more closely what the act of drinking involves.

We are told that the king drinks from the cup at every feast, that drinking, in other words, is a repeated action in 'high', 'official', or 'ceremonial' circumstances, circumstances that have no other purpose than the celebration of the king himself, of his kingship. This is not simply a pleasurable imbibing, nor a sheerly practical quenching of natural thirst, it is a ritual activity. In his festive drinking the king commemorates the symbolic bond represented by the cup, recalls the gift of the cup and the relation of debt that links him to its donor, the dead beloved.

We are also told (somewhat later) that what the king drinks on these ritual occasions is "Lebens Glut" ("life's glow," 18).[16] Since a narrative frame of alcohol-laced feasting ("Schmaus," "Zecher") surrounds this bit of information, it presses upon us a reading of "Lebens Glut" as a metaphor for wine, a metaphor which foregrounds a well-known property of wine, namely that it engenders in the one who drinks it a sense of glowing vitality. But such a reading operates far too mimetically or naturalistically for this text and above all ignores the ritual character of the narrative frame. Much more interesting (because it engages more complexly with the text's semantic network) is a reading that moves in the opposite direction: the wine presupposed by the narrative frame is the metaphorical vehicle and the metaphorical tenor is life's glow. The fact that the vehicle (wine) goes unmentioned indicates that, from the standpoint of the king, it has passed over into and been effaced by the tenor. Metaphorical mediation (vehicle standing in for the tenor) succeeds so thoroughly that it is no longer mediation, but rather the full and immediate presence of the tenor itself—of life's glow. Since the drinking is a ritual activity, and since it occurs as the king prepares for death (this feast of the fifth stanza is a final feast, a "last supper"), I feel justified in calling this metaphorical process a *transubstantiation*: the scene of the feast, that is to say, reinscribes the Holy Communion; ritual usage transforms the metonymic symbol into metaphorical presence. Thus, it is no accident that the line following the mention of "Lebens Glut" specifies the cup as "heilig" ("holy").

But "Der König von Thule" alters—decisively—the theological script of the communion. After all, the king's ritual drinking does not commemorate the death and resurrection of Christ (and the gift of eternal life), but, rather, the death of the beloved and her gift to the king. The divine love of the Father, whose only Son died so that we might live eternally in Him, is here replaced by a love stemming from a 'female', 'corporeal', and 'natural' instance. In this sense, the poem conforms to the pattern pointed out in previous analyses: the matrilinear encoding of desire, of art, of language. Moreover, the phrase "Lebens Glut" (with its semantic markers 'vitality', 'fiery heat', and 'liquidity') recapitulates the essential elements of what I have called the primordial maternal donation. To cite merely one example ("Pilgers Morgenlied"):

> Allgegenwärt'ge Liebe!
> Durch*glühst* mich, ('fiery heat')
>   . . .
> Hast mir *gegossen* ('liquidity')
> In's frühwelkende Herz
> Doppeltes *Leben*, ('vitality')
> *(Text 10, 26–32; emphasis added)*

The gift of the cup marks the debt of the king (of the subject) to a natural-maternal figure in that it recalls another, and more fundamental gift: the gift of inner life, of desire, in short, of love. The subject is born as subject in the moment when the natural nexus of this love is severed (by death) and replaced by a symbolic nexus (betokened by the cup). Exactly this severance constitutes the subject's debt. The Mother/beloved must be lost so that the subject can live, but at the same time the life of the subject is oriented (or given meaning) by the symbol that links and separates it to/from the absent female figure.

When the king performs his act of ritual drinking, two things happen: (1) he takes in the "Lebens Glut" of the primordial maternal donation; and (2) his eyes overflow with tears. By drinking from the cup, the king reenacts the primordial donation of life's liquidity, indeed, reenacts it so intensely that this liquidity is rendered transubstantially present within the ritual. Drinking, the king takes into himself not the blood of Christ, but the liquidity of natural/maternal vitality. Turning to the second aspect, we encounter the other side of the symbolic bond: the tears—a marker, most obviously, of sadness, mourning, loss—recall the element of debt, recall, in other words, that severance from the maternal sphere (the death of the beloved) is the precondition of the king's subjecthood. Thus, the ritual drinking fuses the aspects of gift and debt, of transubstantial presence and absence or separation. The symbol—and the relationship of exchange it commemorates—is intrinsically bivalent.

This bivalence of the symbol profiles itself especially clearly when we consider that the two aspects of the ritual are condensed in the semantic feature of 'liquidity'. Drinking, the king takes into himself the "Lebens Glut," contains the glowing liquidity within the differentiation of his individuality. With the king's weeping, however, this same liquidity surges up from within him and overflows the container he, the king, is. The gift recalled by the symbolic cup is the gift of the king's own subjecthood. Just as the cup contains the liquid within the contours of its formal differentiation, the subject contains the liquidity of life while differentiating itself from life. The symbol, condition of possibility of subjecthood, separates and differentiates. But exactly this severance (the 'death' the symbol also recalls) constitutes the moment of debt and thereby evokes the necessity of repayment. The tears that overflow their containment within the subject suggest that this repayment will occur when differentiation ceases, when the vital liquidity is no longer contained within the contours of individuality and both subject and symbol are reabsorbed by the undifferentiated flow of life from which they were separated.

The third stanza adds a further semantic determination to the cup. Or rather, it negates one: the "Becher" is not an object of value among others; it cannot be transferred, circulated, inherited. Another way of putting this is to say that the cup is priceless; its value (for the king) does not translate into the universal currency of money. Thus, when the king counts his cities and realms, he does not include the cup among these quantifiable entities. Nor does he pass it on to his heirs: the cup cannot be disappropriated. This negative determination of the cup can be translated into positive terms. Let us say that the domain to which all the king's possessions except the cup belong, the domain over which he rules as king, is the domain of universal exchange. The items that fall within this domain are measurable according to a system of equivalence (counting) that functions independently of the particular person who owns them at any one time. Thus, they can be traded, bought, sold, and inherited. The cup is an object passed from one instance to another, it has symbolic value, and it involves an element of debt. Nevertheless, it does not fall within the domain of universal exchange. To localize the transaction involved in the gift of the cup, therefore, we must posit a second domain, a domain of *singular exchange*. The cup/symbol can only be passed once, can only move between these particular individuals. It is a nonexchangeable, and therefore singular, symbol.

What is it, in the final analysis, that I have received in a transaction of exchange (gift and debt), but that is nevertheless not something I possess and can pass on, say, to my heirs? The answer, of course, is: my own singular identity. The gift of the cup is the singular exchange through which the king receives—what else?—himself. He does not possess the cup as in a relation of ownership, nor does he rule the cup in the sense of legalized, and therefore transferable, governance. Rather, he relates to the cup through the singularity of his existence (which is why the cup is given to him at his birth as subject and why, as we shall see, it dies with him as well). The cup is the *singular symbol* which differentiates individual identity. And the pact that symbol betokens pertains to no one but the 'I' which it holds in this unique relation of gift and debt. "Der König von Thule" confronts us with the remarkable paradox of a law that applies to just one case.

There is more to be said about the status of this singular symbol, but at this point I want to turn to the fourth and fifth stanzas, which introduce the narrative moment of the cup's return and hence of the repayment of the symbolic debt. These two stanzas, despite the punctuation mark that closes off the first, form a syntactic unit, the fourth stanza merely providing, adverbially, the location from which the act of throwing the cup, as depicted in stanza five, occurs. Thus, a spatial opposition of 'high' vs. 'low' is installed in the text:

> Beym hohen Königsmale (13)   vs.   Hinunter in die Fluth (20)

The essential matter here is to note how the vertical polarization 'high' vs. 'low' is articulated with a gender opposition. The high is encoded as the realm of 'masculine authority', of kingship ("Königsmale"), hierarchy ("Die Ritter um ihn her," 14), paternal tradition ("Vätersaale," 15). This leads to a semanticization of the 'low' as 'feminine' and 'maternal': the "Meer" (16)—this "Fluth" (20) of undifferentiated liquidity—is the *mère*.

Interlaced with this dominant homology, a second set of equivalences makes itself felt across the two stanzas. The masculine or paternal sphere not only stands above the maternal sea, it is 'surrounded' by it. Thus, what might have seemed a superfluous listing of descriptive details assumes an important semantic function: the "Schloß" (16) marks the first line of differentiation from the sea; within the castle is the ancient "Vätersaal" (15); within this hall is the circle of knights (14). And, of course, at the center of this circle stands the king, performing his last act of ritual drinking, which is to say: celebrating one final time the containment of liquidity within his differentiated individuality. The spatial organization of the masculine domain as a series of concentric circles dramatizes the figure of *differentiation through containment* that is so central to the function of the cup as singular symbol.

Since the final stanza gathers together all the semantic determinations of the cup mentioned thus far and brings them to their logical conclusion, I will not comment on it at any length. Suffice it merely to list the major functions actualized at the text's conclusion:

(a) The king, born with the gift of the cup, dies.
(b) The symbolic debt incurred with this gift is repaid.
(c) The original separation from the female/liquid sphere is succeeded by a final reunification.

(d) Differentiated individuation figured as the containment of liquidity is reabsorbed in undifferentiation.

(e) The male/paternal/social domain yields to the sphere of the female/maternal/natural.

Note that the capacity of the final stanza to evoke these registers of meaning derives from the process of positional exchange that organizes the poem's repertoire of significant elements. What the king received, he now gives back. What the cup contained now contains the cup. The eyes that had overflowed with tears now sink fully into liquidity. The last line of the poem adds an almost comic twist to this set of reversals. On the one hand, the double negative is a formulation in colloquial or "unschooled" speech (the sort appropriate for this folk ballad or romance) of the fact of the king's death. Thus, the line can be read: "the drinker never drank another drop again." But if one presses the significance of the double negative a bit, it is possible to derive an alternative reading: "he evermore drank every drop, or all drops." Drowned (like the cup), the dead king takes in the entirety of life's liquidity, much as this liquidity drinks him in. The realm to which he returns together with his singular symbol knows no differentiation, no droplets of water. And it likewise knows no agents or objects: drinker and liquid have become one forevermore.

In "Der König von Thule," Goethe reactivates an archaic poetic form, but the mythic tale his ballad unfolds rests on a peculiarly modern semantic structure. To see this point, it is useful to return to the notion of the singular symbol that characterizes the function of the text's central element, the cup. The singularity of the symbol derives from the fact that it stands outside (and in opposition to) all the tokens, all the items of property, that circulate within the domain of universal exchange. That is to say, the function of the cup within this text—and the function of the text itself considered as the myth of the cup—is to differentiate something that the system of universal exchange alone cannot indicate, isolate, and stabilize: the individual identity which is uniquely mine. The fact that the singular symbol is required in order to fulfill this function lends the text its historical index.

For centuries, European culture had relied on two systems of universal (symbolic) exchange to identify individuals: the stratification of society locating individuals within a hierarchical system of differences (estates, etc.) and the system of religious symbols securing individuals within a theological or metaphysical schema. Where these two (overlapping and mutually supportive) systems are in place, there is no identity problem, and hence no need for the singular symbol. There is no authentic identity, uniquely mine, which would exist outside the genealogical position I am born or adopted into and the metaphysical position I am baptized into. The eighteenth century witnessed the collapse of these two codes of identity conferral and therefore the emergence of (the problem of) authentic individual identity. Social stratification gave way to functional differentiation, with the result that social status was pluralized and relativized and therefore lost its capacity to define who one is. Likewise, the binding force of religious symbolism became attenuated so that, at least for educated groups, it could no longer serve to ground identity in the metaphysical individuality of God. The individual was left without a firm social or metaphysical anchorage, without a universal symbol that would fix its identity. Hence Goethe's famous dictum: "Individuum est ineffabile."[17] Within this context (which was really an absence of context, a kind of symbolic vacuum), several cultural innovations of the eighteenth century became intelligible as attempts to solve the problem of identity circumscription. The cult of friendship that emerged around mid-century, for example, can be seen as an effort to construct a limited, alternative sociality that could ratify individual identity. Pietism reinscribed the language of religious selection as personal experience. The Enlightenment cultivation of sympathy (perhaps the fundamental anthropological value of the century's middle decades) linked individual affective experience to the encompassing unity of a generalized humanity. Only at the century's end did a stable solution to the problem make its appearance and find an institutionalization that still remains in force today: the idea of *Bildung* as the educative process actualizing universal human potentialities within the variety of individual life histories.

These historical developments are sufficiently well known, I trust, that even the summary sketch I have provided here will suffice to evoke a background against which the significance of "Der König von Thule" stands out.[18] The text intervenes in the historical-discursive constellation bearing on individual identity in two ways. First, it declares as irrelevant to the question of identity the two systems of universal symbolism—social hierarchy and religion—that had traditionally served to ground individuality. The paternal realm of kingship, domination, genealogical position, and possession—in short, the entire nexus of relations within which the

king would be located in a stratificational system of social differentiation—
is reduced to the domain of expropriable or exchangeable goods, and
religious symbolism is not even mentioned. It is as if the entire social-
religious world had been rendered a matter of economics, of the count-
able, thereby leaving the individual without a symbolic mooring. Second,
to compensate for this massive evacuation of significance, the singular
symbol is introduced. This symbol, figured in our text as the cup, organizes the two transitions that human individuality necessarily negotiates:
birth and death. The king, one might say, is not born into a paternally
defined lineage from which he draws his proper name; rather, he is the
son—exclusively—of the beloved. (This matrilineage is marked in the
rhyme "Bule"/"Thule.") And the king's death is neither his entry into
the pantheon of historical-genealogical memory nor his rebirth in God,
but rather his reabsorption by the natural-maternal sphere from which he
had separated himself. Thus, "Der König von Thule" carves out a remarkable, and historically innovative, definition of the self's inner core of
identity. This definition, enacted across the text's logic of exchange, states
simply: *I am my love, my desire.* What constitutes my essence and engages
me at the level of my singular existence is my love for the maternal beloved
from whom I was severed, whose presence I seek to reinvoke, and to
whom, in death, I return. Recall Goethe's formulation in the early letter to
Cornelia glossed in Chapter 5: I am, and will always be, the child of the
Mother, to whom 'love' binds me in a relation of irrevocable obligation
("Schuldigkeit").

Given this reconstruction of the text's twofold historical gesture, I can
amplify my reading of the ritual drinking that plays such a central role in
the elaboration of the poetic myth. As we have seen, the text consigns the
domain of religious symbolism to irrelevance. Such symbolism no longer
provides an adequate anchorage for individual identity, no longer gives
meaning to the events of birth and death, no longer relates life to its divine
Source. And yet the religious symbolism is not simply negated. The king's
drinking constitutes a ritual act in which the wine is transubstantially
metaphorized into the "Lebens Glut" of the primordial donation. Thus,
one of the central components of the historically defunct religious code
(the Holy Communion, wine as the blood of Christ) is reactualized and
integrated within the context defined by the singular symbol. That symbol, to put the matter another way, displaces the universal religious symbol
and at the same time assumes its prestige and efficacy. The labor of

reinterpretation (in Nietzsche's sense) this text accomplishes could hardly be more audacious: the ritual drinking that constitutes the ceremony of the singular symbol usurps the authority of the Mass.

This brings me to my concluding hypothesis regarding "Der König von Thule." The historical phenomenon of the late eighteenth century whose cultural-discursive position corresponds to the element of ritual drinking in this text is nothing other than the production/reception of art. To be more precise, the myth of the singular symbol this text elaborates across its patterns of exchange is *the myth of autonomous art.* It is important to specify that the term "myth," as employed here, designates a program that organizes information by integrating it within an array of symbolic positions between which relations of equivalence and opposition, paths of derivation, substitution, and transformation are carved out. In this sense, myths do not (passively) reflect reality, they (actively) systematize it by establishing the network of reference (what Heidegger called the *Verweisungszusammenhang*[19]) within which objects and activities, and even subjects, acquire their positional significance.

The institution of autonomous art, which, as noted in Chapter 5, achieves philosophical codification in the 1790's, conforms with remarkable congruence to the textual system of "Der König von Thule." It is the frame of a repeated activity (ritual) that grounds individuality by linking it to an innovative symbol. This symbol, singular in the sense that it is not determined by any universal code (social, religious, or normative aesthetic), derives metonymically from the deepest resources of subjectivity, and brings these within the containment of its formal individuation. Aesthetic practice, in both its productive and receptive aspects, thus becomes a kind of secular communion in which the inner life of the subject is experienced as a metaphorical presence. This inner life derives, ultimately, from the earliest experiences of childhood and is nothing other than the love received through the primordial maternal donation. On this reading, of course, autonomous art is anything but functionless. Quite the contrary, it is a system of symbolic exchange that produces an extremely important cultural artifact: the modern individual.

A reading of this sort cannot be verified with absolute certainty, but its plausibility can be heightened by citing other texts from the same authorial or epochal corpus that corroborate some of its semantic inferences. "Der König von Thule" is clearly related to "Künstlers Morgenlied" (Text 18) and the drama fragment *Prometheus* (Text 21), both of which center on the figure of the primordial maternal donation and both of which have art as their thematic focus. But "Der König von Thule" deviates from these texts in its elaboration of the problem of exchange. To show that the linkage between the semantic elements art / maternal donation / exchange is a possible—or grammatical—one within the symbolic system of the corpus, we need to invoke a text that makes this linkage explicit. Such is the opening monologue of the drama *Des Künstlers Erdewallen,* a text cited in part earlier as Text 19. In the monologue, the artist addresses his painting of Venus Urania, first recalling the primordial donation which his act of painting (with the phallic "Pinsel") reinstantiates, then turning to the lamentable fact that he will have to sell the painting in order to feed his children: "Und ich soll dich lassen für feiles Geld—" ("And I am supposed to give you up for lousy money—," 10). This contrast between the primordial exchange constituting the artist's identity and the type of exchange carried out with the universal equivalent of money then ramifies into the following consoling reflection (the addressee is still the painted Venus Urania):

> Du gehst in eines Reichen Haus,
> Ihn in Kontribution zu setzen,
> Und ich trag' ihnen Brot heraus.
> Und er besitzt dich nicht, er hat dich nur,
> Du wohnst bei mir, Urquell der Natur,
> Leben und Freude der Kreatur!
> In dir versunken
> Fühl ich mich selig an allen Sinnen trunken.
>
> *(20–27)*

> You'll go into a rich man's house,
> To force him to a contribution,
> And I'll carry them [the children] bread back out.
> And he doesn't own you, he merely has you;
> You live with me, primordial source of nature,
> Life and joy of all creatures!
> Absorbed in you
> I feel myself blissfully drunk in all my senses.

Here we find variants of all the elements of "Der König von Thule," with the painting assuming the position of the cup. As singular symbol, the painting cannot be disappropriated or translated into the universal currency of money; the painting is the metonymy of the maternal-natural source that gives life to all creatures; viewing the work issues in a state of intoxication in which the source is rendered metaphorically (transubstantially) present. Even the death of the king—his sinking with the cup into undifferentiated liquidity—finds its counterpart in the word "versunken," which marks the absorption of aesthetic experience. In short, both "Der König von Thule" and *Des Künstlers Erdewallen* divide the subject between two economies: the singular exchange that grounds individual identity and the universal exchange that is limitless alienation. The eighteenth century replaces the symbolic systems of social stratification and religion with the opposed, but interlaced codes of art and money. This recodification of individual identity is what sings in the primordial song of "Der König von Thule."

~

27. DER FISCHER

Das Wasser rauscht', das Wasser schwoll,
Ein Fischer saß daran,
Sah nach dem Angel ruhevoll,
Kühl bis an's Herz hinan:
(5) Und wie er sitzt und wie er lauscht,
Teilt sich die Flut empor,
Aus dem bewegten Wasser rauscht
Ein feuchtes Weib hervor.

Sie sang zu ihm, sie sprach zu ihm:
(10) Was lockst du meine Brut
Mit Menschenwitz und Menschenlist
Hinauf in Todesglut?
Ach wüßtest du, wie's Fischlein ist
So wohlig auf dem Grund,
(15) Du stiegst herunter wie du bist,
Und würdest erst gesund.

Labt sich die liebe Sonne nicht,
Der Mond sich nicht im Meer?
Kehrt wellenatmend ihr Gesicht
(20) Nicht doppelt schöner her?
Lockt dich der tiefe Himmel nicht,
Das feucht verklärte Blau?

Lockt dich dein eigen Angesicht
Nicht her in ew'gen Tau?

(25) Das Wasser rauscht', das Wasser schwoll,
Netzt' ihm den nackten Fuß,
Sein Herz wuchs ihm so sehnsuchtsvoll,
Wie bei der Liebsten Gruß.
Sie sprach zu ihm, sie sang zu ihm;

(30) Da war's um ihn geschehn:
Halb zog sie ihn, halb sank er hin,
Und ward nicht mehr gesehn.[20]

THE FISHERMAN

The water murmured, the water swelled;
A fisherman sat beside it,
Watched his pole in total calm,
Cool right to his heart;

(5) And as he sits and as he listens,
The flood divides itself;
Out of the flowing water murmurs
A moist woman.

She sang to him, she spoke to him;
(10) Why do you tempt my brood
With human wit and human cunning
Up into death's glow?
Oh, if you knew, how the little fish feels
So pleasureful on the ground,
(15) You'd climb down here just as you are,
And only then become healthy.

Doesn't the dear sun refresh itself,
And the moon as well in the sea?
And doesn't their face wave-breathing
(20) Turn doubly beautiful there?
Doesn't the deep heaven tempt you,
The moistly transfigured blue?
Doesn't your own face tempt you
Down here in the eternal dew?

(25) The water murmured, the water swelled,
Wet his naked foot;
His heart grew full of yearning,

As at the greeting of his beloved.
She spoke to him, she sang to him;
(30) Then he was done for:
She half pulled him, he half sank down,
And was never seen anymore.

If we assume that the transformation of generic constraint into inventive freedom is an index of artistic maturity, then this text, the third in Brentano's personal canon, certainly demonstrates how early such maturity came to Goethe. Probably composed in 1778, on the cusp, that is, of the poet's thirtieth year, the poem evinces an artistry so confident that it can realize itself without a trace of self-assertion, disappearing beneath the tonal simplicity of the ballad yet eliciting from that genre's formal resources unheard-of subtlety and complexity of thought. Alembicated reflection blends with the effortless flow of the ballad's narrative, fusing popularity and accessibility with high artistic ambition in a manner that seems as if designed to embody Kant's definition of the poet: "The poet announces merely an entertaining play of ideas, but so much comes out of that play for the intellect that it is as if he intended merely to pursue the business of that cognitive faculty."[21]

To illustrate this masterfully inconspicuous artistry while finding an ingress for a reading of the text, let us look at this pair of lines:

Labt sich die liebe Sonne nicht,
Der Mond sich nicht im Meer?

(17–18)

Because it is actualized so variously, the phonic ordering of these lines, albeit rigorous, falls unobtrusively on the ear. The consonantal echo of "*Labt*" in "*liebe*" is subdued nearly to the point of indiscernability by virtue of the fact that the meter, nudging the line's first accent toward "sich," effectively robs the alliterative head-word "Labt" of its intonational stress, and hence of perceptual prominence. Similarly, the dilation of the monosyllabic verb ("Labt") in the bisyllabic adjective ("liebe") veils with variation the near consonantal identity of the two words. In contrast to this surreptitious alliteration, the pairing in 18 ("*Mond*"/"*Meer*") presents a sharply etched profile due to the metrical, morphological (both words are nouns), and positional (first and last accented slots) parallelism that supports it. As for the assonance "sich"/"nicht," it eludes the rigidification of rule by moving from extreme position (first and last metrical accents) in 17 to middle position in 18, where only one of the words bears metrical stress. Taking these three phonic pairings together, we can say that the cited lines offer themselves to auditory experience as:

(a) a sharply contoured alliteration ("*M*ond"/"*M*eer") heard
(b) against a diffuse, receding background alliteration ("*L*a*b*t"/ "*l*ie*b*e") and
(c) accompanied by an assonance ("s*ich*"/"n*ich*t"), the vehicles of which move toward merger at line-center.

Note that a semantic shape begins to shimmer forth from this auditory configuration. The foregrounded alliteration "*M*ond"/"*M*eer" functions as a phonic diagram of the event the verses describe, the reflection of the heavenly bodies on the surface of the water. At the same time, the softer background alliteration adds to this focal notion of mirroring a connotative penumbra derived from the semantic virtualities of "Labt" and "liebe." Thus, the sound texture takes on a suggestive, even seductive force, subtly infusing the reflection of the heavenly bodies on the water's surface with the more compelling attractions of a regenerative oral-erotic bliss.[22] Moreover, the centripetal movement of the assonance charges this beckoning suggestion with a kind of narcissistic thrall, as if what the water's mirror offered were self-possession of the ego ("s*ich*"/"n*ich*t").[23] But to insist on these semantic inferences as certain would amount to a hermeneutic indiscretion of the sort Goethe, with his famously trivializing gloss on the poem, sought to prevent.[24] The point is that the constructions of meaning only vibrate forth from the phonic texture, that they flee hermeneutic fixation, and that this seductive semblance of sense is what an adequate reading of the poem must endeavor, tactfully, without interpretive urgency, to observe.

Of course, the semantic configuration attributed to the two lines cited—the mirror of specularity, oral-erotic union, liquidity, narcissism—engages arguments developed throughout this book. My reading of "Der Fischer" will certainly have to explore these linkages. I will come back to these central lines via a detour, however, one that passes first through an examination of certain important, though neglected, compositional features.

The poem's four stanzas can be divided into two groups according to whether they are spoken by the narrator or by the female figure that emerges from the water:

Stanza:	I	II	III	IV
Speaker:	Nar.	"Weib"	"Weib"	Nar.

This arrangement lends the text a chiastic structure ($A_1/B_1/B_2/A_2$), which is not surprising in that Goethe often employs chiastic schemata to figure specularity. Recall in this connection the compositional structure of "Pilgers Morgenlied" (Text 10), which I represented as: $A_1/B_1/C_1/B_2/A_2$, with an interpretive recapitulation of the chiastic axis as C_2. In "Der Fischer" the pattern is at once less complex, involving fewer units, and more clearly contoured insofar as the units are demarcated as stanzas. Of course, this delineation is not entirely pure. The first line of stanza II—"Sie sang zu ihm, sie sprach zu ihm:"—is still spoken in the third person, from the standpoint of the narrator. Moreover, the same line, with verbs reversed, recurs in the narrator's stanza IV. Note further that line 1, initiating the narrator's stanza I, reappears as the opening line of stanza IV: "Das Wasser rauscht', das Wasser schwoll" (1, 25), so that it acquires, beyond its expressed significance, a positional connotation as the narrator's refrain, as the signature affixed to "his" stanzas. A similar function must be attributed to the line: "Sie sang zu ihm, sie sprach zu ihm:," the only line in the text besides the narrator's refrain that is repeated. But, of course, the repetition of this female refrain does not occur at the head of the female figure's second stanza, but within the narrator's stanza IV. As a result, the rule of strophic division (narrator: I and IV; "Weib": II and III) is doubly violated, first because a line occurring within a female stanza is spoken by the narrator, second because a line falling within the narrator's stanza IV belongs to the female stanza.

This slight disturbance of the compositional symmetry seems hardly worth noting until one remarks that the line in question—"Sie sang zu ihm, sie sprach zu ihm" (9 and, with verb reversal, 29)—is the single line in the text that thematizes speech or song as such. Where it is a matter of speech/song in this text, difficulties arise, difficulties that bear precisely on the attribution of agency to speech/song. The questionable line marks a certain interference of the narrator's and the woman's speech, an undecidability as to who is speaking here, or to whom the speaking belongs. And this undecidability quickly suffuses the entire text, since the maverick line names just what the text itself is, a singing and speaking. Note further that the narrator's refrain, structured exactly like that of the female figure (i.e., two clauses with subject repetition and verb variation), depicts the movement and sound of the element out of which the "Weib" emerges. Hence the repetition of the sounding verb in the lines marking her first appearance: "Aus dem bewegten Wasser *rauscht*/ Ein feuchtes Weib hervor" (7–8). One might say that she is already there in the "Rauschen" with which the narrator onomatopoetically designates the sound of the water. And, if we take her singing and speaking to be (among other significations, of course) the aural effect of the water, then the two refrains—"Das Wasser rauscht', das Wasser schwoll," and "Sie sang zu ihm, sie sprach zu ihm"— approach synonymy. Again we encounter an interference of the two speakers, a sort of connotational slide that blurs the distinction between them.

This recalls the *Prometheus* fragment, in which primordial orality manifests itself precisely as the indiscernability of voicing agency:

> Das waren deine Worte.
> So war ich selbst nicht selbst,
> Und eine Gottheit sprach
> Wenn ich zu reden wähnte,
> Und wähnt ich eine Gottheit spreche,
> Sprach ich selbst.   *(Text 21, 108–13)*

Of course, the confusion of voices in "Der Fischer" is not urgently thematized as in the *Prometheus* fragment; it is almost imperceptibly enacted in the connotational slide initiated by the text's slight deviation from its own internal norm. But for the very reason that it is stated less overtly and without the pathos of the earlier text, indeed, for the very reason that it is not stated, in the strict sense of the term, at all, the effect of confusion in "Der Fischer" is all the more unsettling. Whatever Prometheus might say about the merger of voices in the sphere of primordial orality, it is nonetheless clear that *he*, with all the insistence of the first-person singular personal pronoun, is saying it. As we have seen, Prometheus's anamnesis of the oral origin functions to ground his subjective self-certainty and therewith his claim to autonomous artistic production. In "Der Fischer," however, an impersonal narrative voice—a voice of which it might be said, must be said, that it is "Kühl bis an's Herz hinan" (4)—is infiltrated by another voice that returns out of the depths of aural memory, much as modern poetry, in this text, opens itself to the voices of an archaic form (the folk ballad). And if we assume, as Goethe would, that the ballad is the primordial poetic form, enclosing like an egg the potentialities that

realize themselves across literary history as epic, drama, and lyric,[25] then
we can say that this receptivity, this affectability by an other, allows the
originary voice of poetic signification—"Sie sang zu ihm, sie sprach zu
ihm"—to enter into, captivate, and merge with the poet's voice. Poetry
here is hetero-affection, the usurpation of voicing agency by an archaic
song that rises up (demonically, ghostlike) from the past; it is a kind of
ventriloquism, a possession.[26] Can it be accidental that poetry so conceived draws its narrative motif from the mythic tradition involving
elemental spirits which couple with human beings in order to steal their
souls (their voicing agency)?

A hypothesis is emerging here, which can be expressed as the homology:
poet (or narrator) : the voice of a poetic past :: fisherman : singing female
figure. Phrased differently, the story "Der Fischer" tells reflects the constitution of the text as art ballad. If one presupposes such a structural relation
between the text and its diegetic material, then it is possible to read certain
statements that apply within the latter as comments on the problematic of
the text itself. From this perspective, the question of uncertain agency
elicited from the compositional deviations and with reference to the
complex of primordial orality becomes thematic in the poem's penultimate
line: "Halb zog sie ihn, halb sank er hin" (31). To test this hypothesis
requires a closer look at the text's narrative movement.

Before doing so, however, some preliminary methodological remarks
are necessary. As was pointed out in Chapter 2, poetic narrative is distinguished from other sorts, both pragmatic and fictional, by the fact that
recountings of the narrated story are of practically no analytic use. Of
course, no analysis of, say, the *Iliad* that relied solely on an English prose
retelling of the events at Troy could provide an adequate description of
Homer's artistry, but it could nevertheless disclose essential aspects of the
epic. The reason for this is that a constitutive feature of nonpoetic narrative is that it operates with a sphere of noematic objects (actors, actions,
scenery, etc.) that is separable from (although, in the case of fiction,
entirely given through) the language that refers to it. These noematic
objects are themselves significations and thus susceptible to structuration
of the sort carried out by narratologists interested in the *fabula*-level of
the text. Poetry, however, deploys its significations without reference to
noematic objects; it constitutes a purely noetic universe in which, as I
phrased it in Chapter 2, the linguistic texture itself is the action.[27] This
does not imply that the concepts of narratology are irrelevant to poetic

analysis; indeed, several of the readings carried out in the previous chapters would have been unthinkable without instruction from such theoreticians as Lotman and Greimas. The point, rather, is that in poetic narrative the elements and relations that make up the *fabula*-structure are not found at the level of noematic objects (which doesn't exist), but at the noetic level, nested in the linguistic texture itself. Which is to say that a parsing of the narrative movement "Der Fischer" articulates must take as its point of departure, and as its point of arrival, the interlacings of the poem's words.

To make this point more specific, call to mind the basic narrative model of two opposed states mediated by a transformative action (border-crossing). As with several texts discussed in earlier chapters, this model works quite well for "Der Fischer." Indeed, the positioning of the narrator's refrain emphasizes the structural feature of semantic opposition by providing a background of similarity, hence comparability, against which the differences constitutive of the opposition emerge all the more forcefully. That is to say, stanza I embodies the initial state, the incipience of the narrative action, and stanza IV the final state, the action's product or result. Now it is possible, of course, to derive from these two stanzas propositions descriptive of noematic objects and to note the contrasts between them. One might say, for example, that in stanza I the fisherman is outside the water, in stanza IV he is in the water; or that in stanza I he is alive, in stanza IV he is dead. Such descriptions of state, however, are not only massively banal, they are potentially erroneous. Note, for example, that stanza IV does not say explicitly either that the fisherman goes into the water or that he dies. The phrase "sank er hin" does not necessarily mean either of these, and to assume that it does is to occlude other possible readings.

Yet it would be absurd to deny that such constructions of a noematic order—the sort of constructions one undertakes in the comprehension of nonpoetic narratives—cannot be carried out. They can, and with a considerable degree of consensus among readers. Insofar as we read the text as *poetic* narrative, however, these noemata will not provide the principal target or object of our intentional attitude, and that is to say that they will function not as noemata at all, but, rather, as shadings, more or less prominent, of the semiosis. With respect to the just-mentioned example: 'death' is not *what* the poem tells with the phrase "halb sank er hin"; the poem does not relate a fact about a fictionally posited world at all. Rather, 'death' is one virtual signification of the phrase, a connotation and not an event. This point has validity for the entire text of "Der Fischer": there is here no basic story, no literal referent, no ground-level concatenation of facts *about which* this text would be.[28]

To the degree that the narrative model with its opposed states and mediating transformation is relevant to the text, then, it appears as a structural schema that informs the linguistic texture, shapes the verbal interlacings into overriding patterns. An especially prominent marker of such shaping emerges in the contrast "ruhevoll" (3) vs. "sehnsuchtsvoll" (27). Against the overdetermined relation of similarity that joins the terms (they are positionally, morphologically, and syntactically equivalent), the components (here nominalized) "Ruhe"/"Sehnsucht" emerge as a forcefully informative opposition. One way of conceiving the antonymous relation between these terms is to think of "Ruhe" ('peace', 'quiet', 'composure') as that toward which "Sehnsucht" ('yearning') is directed. This allows for an encoding of the polarity as, respectively, 'feminine' vs. 'masculine': the peaceful self-containment of the woman and the urgent longing of the man to enter into precisely that state of inner peace. Just such a code is operative, for example, in Friedrich Schlegel's novel *Lucinde*.[29] Goethe's use of the opposition in "Der Fischer" is related to this Romantic code, but also deviates from it. Thus, it is clear that the "Sehnsucht" emerging in line 27 defines the amorous desire of the masculine fisherman; its outbreak, after all, is qualified by the simile "Wie bei der Liebsten Gruß" (28). But it seems doubtful that "Ruhe" names the state of quiescent self-sufficiency toward which "Sehnsucht" is directed. On the contrary, the "Ruhe" at the poem's outset seems to function more as a suppression of "Sehnsucht," a precariously held composure out of which the subject can (and indeed, in the course of the narrative transformation, will) be drawn. "Ruhe" is not the polar opposite of "Sehnsucht," as in Schlegel's myth of gender, but the tenuous control, perhaps the willful ignorance or forgetting, of "Sehnsucht," which, despite the denial of its efficacy, nevertheless threatens to resurge. "Ruhe" is the state that is overwhelmed by "Sehnsucht." The initial and final narrative states here are opposed as 'tenuous control' and 'loss of control'.

The opposition "Ruhe"/"Sehnsucht" ramifies as one considers the poetic context in which each term appears. Context, of course, is not a given, but a matter of selection, and we shall soon see that the poem offers several different contextualizations for its elements. For the present, however, I shall stipulate the context of the terms under discussion to be the lines in which they occur together with the two immediately preceding lines. Thus, our original opposition expands to:

> Das Wasser rauscht', das Wasser schwoll,
> Ein Fischer saß daran,
> Sah nach dem Angel ruhevoll,   *(1–3)*
>
> vs.
>
> Das Wasser rauscht', das Wasser schwoll,
> Netzt' ihm den nackten Fuß,
> Sein Herz wuchs ihm so sehnsuchtsvoll,
>
> *(25–27)*

The sentential function of the term "ruhevoll" is to qualify an act of seeing, the object of which is the fishpole ("Angel"); "sehnsuchtsvoll," by contrast, modifies the growing—the desiring dilation—of the heart. That is to say, what is called "Ruhe" in this text rests on the gap between a subject and the object of its activity, on a differentiation or separation, a cognitive distance. This is an intentional looking-to-see of the sort encountered near the end of "Mir schlug das Herz" (Text 5), that is, a relation to objectivity in general. The sentential context of "Sehnsucht" eliminates such distance; instead of directedness toward an object outside the subject, the line evokes a movement of expansive yearning that is located at the very center of subjective life ("Herz"). The opposition between "Ruhe" and "Sehnsucht" thus ramifies into a contrast between a controlled relation of distance toward an external object on the one hand and the seizure of the subject at the heart of its being on the other, in short: distance vs. fusion, control vs. possession, separation vs. infiltration.

Let us try now to gauge the poetic weight of the two lines that precede the verses. "Ein Fischer saß daran": the line positions the fisherman at a point next to, but nevertheless not merging or overlapping with, the water; it dramatizes spatially the aspect of separation, hence distance, but at the same time indicates that this distance is minimal, the control it guarantees precarious. The corresponding line of stanza IV: "Netzt' ihm den nackten Fuß," marks the crossing of the distance between fisherman and water, the abolition of the distinction between them. The terms from which we began ("ruhevoll" and "sehnsuchtsvoll") both function within a rhyme that links them to the narrator's refrain, in particular, to that refrain's last word, "schwoll." In the first stanza, the semantic effect of the rhyme is one of juxtaposition; while the water murmurs and swells ("schwoll"), the fisherman looks quietly ("ruhevoll") toward his "Angel," the utilitarian instrument he interposes between himself and the water. The corresponding rhyme in stanza IV, however, transforms the antonymous relation "schwoll"/"ruhevoll" into one of synonymity. Indeed, if we recall that "sehnsuchtsvoll" modifies a verb ("wuchs") that is virtually a semantic cognate of "schwoll," then the synonymous tendency of the rhyme becomes all the more apparent. In comparison to "ruhevoll," "sehnsuchtsvoll," with its expanded (and lexicalized: "Sucht" is a compulsion, a passion, a disease) middle syllable, enacts dilation (growing, swelling). Thus, via the synonymous rhyme "schwoll"/"sehnsuchtsvoll," the water floods the subject, infusing the heart with the ebullition of desire.

The syntactic structure of the three-line segments cited also dramatizes, or poetically enacts, the liquefaction of the subject. Note in this connection that the narrator's refrain in stanza I forms a unit complete unto itself. Line 1, that is to say, "contains" the water, its sound and swelling, within the limits of the verse, and the second line turns to a different agent, the fisherman, who occupies his own subject position within the proposition (he "sat"). In IV, however, the water spills over the limits of the stanza's first line and usurps the syntactic case-function of agency in the second. Whereas the fisherman in I is the subject of an action that holds him at a minimal distance from the water, in IV he has become the recipient of an action (wetting) performed by the water. But this overspill is only syntactically an action. Semantically it is devoid of the intentionality, the directedness, that the concept of action requires. We might call it a passion: it happens to the subject, overwhelms it, but itself has no agency. Much the same is true of line 27: the expansion of the heart is involuntary, a sufferance. The phrase occurring somewhat later in the stanza, "Da war's um ihn geschehen" (30), with its impersonal subject ("es") and its verb of 'happening' ("geschehn"), captures this usurpation of agency in the event of passion with laconic precision.

I remarked above that poetry, as this text conceives it, is hetero-affection, a possession (in the sense that one is possessed by a demon). The narrative opposition, the ramifications of which we are tracing out here by cross-reading stanzas I and IV, semiotically works through exactly such a process. An *Other*—the water, its sound, its erotic fluidity—invades the fisherman, extinguishes his agency, overwhelms the "Ruhe" of his self-control with "Sehnsucht." This invasion of subjectivity by otherness—an otherness that is not that of an object, but rather the subversion of the subject-object relation—is the source of the text's uncanniness. *Das Unheimliche*, as Freud learned from Schelling, is the murmur of an alien presence at the heart of what is most intimately familiar, oneself.[30]

This reference to Freud, hence to the question of the text's relation to sexuality, brings me to the detail of the "Angel" (fishpole). Because of their obtuseness, their recalcitrance to any sort of reading beyond a purely referential construal, such trivial items often bear a strong affective charge. The reader suspects that the detail means something, and all the more so for the fact that he/she cannot figure out what that something is. The only available hypothesis is the mimetic one (It's just a fishpole!), but that hypothesis is irritatingly unsatisfactory. The way to lift this blockage is to contextualize the element in question, to see it not as the mimetic banality it seems to be, but as a relational entity (as the component of a structure). I have already remarked on the function of the fishpole as the object of the fisherman's act of seeing and thus as a component of his precarious "Ruhe." But the word is polycontexturally determined (that is, overdetermined) and stands, in addition to its sentential function, in the following opposition:

Sah nach dem Angel ruhevoll,

(3)

vs.

Netzt' ihm den nackten Fuß,

(26)

My proposal, then, is that "Angel" and "Fuß" can be read in relation to one another (or cross-read) in such a way as to exfoliate their semantic-poetic function. This proposal is not original with me. In a brief, dense commentary on "Der Fischer" that has, to my knowledge, gone unnoticed in the scholarship on the poem, the psychoanalyst Georg Groddeck unhesitatingly asserts: "The fishpole—note the peculiar masculine form Goethe employs—is immediately recognizable as a symbol of the male member [*des Gliedes*], and the quiet coolness [*das ruhevoll Kühle*] of the fisherman demonstrates how alien sexual excitation [*Erregung*] is to him."[31] A bit later (his commentary moves linearly through the poem), Groddeck glosses the "foot": "In the subsequent lines symbol hooks up with symbol, the naked foot, which is wetted, is the phallus, the growing [*Wachsen*] of the heart, the ever-stronger swelling-up [*Anschwellen*] of an erection."[32] This reading, it seems to me, is at once utterly compelling and utterly inadequate.

Groddeck's intuition hits the mark insofar as it is based on a recognition of the similarity relation, the equivalence, between the two details. First of all, the sense of obtuseness I attributed above to the "Angel" also strikes me, although slightly less forcefully, as a quality of the element "Fuß." Both have that mute opacity that attracts affective investment, provoking, and at the same time blocking, the ascription of meaning. On closer inspection, this sense of dumb thereness can be seen to derive from the anomalous status of the two elements within their poetic environs: "Angel" and "Fuß" are the only units in the two stanzas semantically marked as 'material', the only elements that do not belong either to the water or to the internality of the fisherman; they are, in short, the only things mentioned. This semantic coloration of conspicuous or startling thingness, the pull of the two words toward material particularity, lends them a nuance of 'obscenity' of exactly the sort that might stimulate the attribution of the signification 'male member' or 'phallus'.[33] Which brings me to the second probable textual motivation of Groddeck's interpretation: the foot is specified as being "naked" ("nackten"), that is to say, unclothed, exhibited to sight, hence 'obscene'. By virtue of the parallelism of the terms, this quality of obscenity migrates retrospectively to the fishpole. And indeed, if we look at the immediate context of that term, we discover that this migratory connotation has indeed arrived. As it were, the phrase "*nach dem* Angel" prospectively echoes the phrase "*nackten* Fuß." Paronomastically, the fishpole too is naked, although its nakedness, disguised as preposition and article, has yet to emerge in full flagrancy.[34]

Intertextual relations within the corpus also lend credence to Groddeck's interpretation. Consider in connection with the "Angel" the opening lines of "Jägers Nachtlied" ("Hunter's Nightsong") together with the reformulation of those lines in the revised version of the poem entitled "Jägers Abendlied" ("Hunter's Evening Song"):

> Im Felde schleich ich still und wild,
> Lausch mit dem Feuerrohr,[35]

> Through the field I sneak still and wild,
> Listen with my fire-pipe [musket],

> Im Felde schleich' ich still und wild,
> Gespannt mein Feuerrohr,[36]

> Through the field I sneak still and wild,
> Tensed (cocked) my fire-pipe,

Since the poet himself placed the second variant in close proximity to "Der Fischer" (a single poem separates them) in the 1789 edition of his collected works, *Goethes Schriften*, a cross-reading of the texts seems warranted. In fact, the similarity of the poems is patent. Both in the hunter's songs and in "Der Fischer" we encounter a male figure in search of natural prey (hunter/fisherman) and the instrument or weapon employed in the pursuit is focalized (gun/fishpole).[37] The reason these two variants corroborate Groddeck's interpretation of the "Angel" is that they demonstrate the possibility of metaphorizing the weapon as an extension of the hunting subject's internality, as an index or expression of the condition of desire. Thus, in the first variant, the hunter listens—note that the same verb ("lauschen") designates the angler's aural attentiveness in "Der Fischer" (5)—with, or perhaps through, his musket, a notion that is carried here by the pun "Rohr"/"Ohr" ("pipe"/"ear"). The musket, in other words, is an extension of the body, a member, mobilized to readiness. In the second variant, the verb of audition (along with the glaring pun) is replaced by the participle ("Gespannt"/"tensed"), which names both the firearm's readiness and the subject's emotional-corporeal tension (desire). From this perspective, it seems entirely legitimate to read the fisherman's "Angel" as a bodily extension, with the difference, however, that it is not charged with energizing expectancy.[38] Finally, the intertextual reference supporting Groddeck's reading of "Fuß" hardly requires mention here. It is the "große Zeh" ("big toe") of the burlesque poem "Auf Cristianen R." (Text 9), the corporeal extremity, a part of the foot, that indicates the charge of desire, the maternal donation of the phallus. To be sure, "foot" triggers its sexual connotation less overtly than "big toe," save that it bears the sexualizing predicate of nakedness. There can be no question, I think, but that Groddeck's 'phallic' intuitions are validated by the Goethean corpus.

Why, given all these grounds for agreement, do I find Groddeck's interpretation so inadequate? Because his notion of the symbol invariably obeys the simplistic substitutional rule $x = y$. Whatever element (x) in the poem strikes him as requiring the attribution of meaning (and those elements are usually nouns taken in isolation from their syntactic function) he replaces with a term (y) that refers to an anatomical domain. The result is a crudely lurid little anecdote about flaccid or erect members, a puerile tale Groddeck takes to be the real truth referred to by the text. Thus, the error of his method, despite the effort to penetrate the text's verisimilar surface and find access to its symbolic depth, coincides with that of the most trivial mimetic reading. He construes the text as referring to a sphere of noematic objects, as telling a story that unfolds in an existent (even if only fictively existent) world. Although some of Groddeck's intuitions are remarkably acute, what he makes of them is, poetologically speaking, primitive and banal.

If we assume, as indeed all the points of agreement with Groddeck enumerated above compel us to do, that both "Angel" and "Fuß" figure a 'phallic-sexual' component, then a major difference between the two figurations immediately appears. With the "Angel," sexuality is displaced outside the self, presents itself as an object of vision; it doesn't bear any intrinsic, natural, or corporeal connection to the subject. Thus, the figure of the "Angel" is split by a dual reading: it acknowledges sexuality (the fishpole does, after all, connect the subject to the water) while denying it (the fishpole is other than the subject, an object out there). The sexuality that is relevant to this text is not a referent (Groddeck's 'male member'), but rather *the very structure of the figuration*. One could characterize this structure as censorship, which by forbidding public acknowledgment necessarily lets such acknowledgment slip through. This censorship is the correlate of the precarious control signified in the fisherman's "Ruhe." Its play of suppression and revelation, hiding and exposure, is likewise a feature of the disguised nakedness of "nach dem," which is why the rhythmical anxiety of those two words is brought under control when "Angel" is pronounced. The "Ruhe" of the fisherman is already a form of sexuality, but a sexuality dissimulated, projected outside the subject in the guise of objectivity. The subject maintains its composure as subject, holds onto its agency, only by denying the otherness that threatens to flood the self at its heart.

This inundation occurs at the other pole of the narrative opposition, via the "Fuß." Like the fishpole, the foot is a metonymy of the subject, but a metonymy of a different sort. The semantic line of connection is no longer that between an entity and a second entity located next to it, say, a utensil. Rather, the connection is immediate and natural, therefore more obvious, "naked." And just as the spatial position of the fisherman in stanza I can be read as dramatizing the structure of the metonymic fishpole (proximate but nevertheless separate), so too in stanza IV the immediate corporeal connection that supports the metonymic linkage foot-to-fisherman is reflected in the abolition of the distance separating the fisherman and the water. In fact, the corporeal-metonymic transfer suffuses the entire scenography: the water, murmuring and swelling, wets the foot; the foot is corporeally linked to the heart; the heart grows yearningly, hence swells, hence is swollen by the water. To speak here of an "erection," as Groddeck does, is both right and wrong. Wrong insofar as what is meant is an anatomical reality which the critic or analyst would exhibit as the true referent of the text. Correct insofar as the connotation "erection" introduces into the text the dual idea of upsurging sexuality on the one hand and turgidity on the other. The verses themselves, infused with a significance that flows through their metonymic ductwork, perhaps through their metrical feet, become erect, charged with liquid. Once again, the sexual content of the verses is not a noematic object or referent, and therefore not a content at all, but the structure of the figuration itself. Sexuality, at first dissimulated and contained in the metonymy of displacement, now overflows the text in the process of corporeal-metonymic transfer.

Although I have as yet discussed the second halves of stanzas I and IV only in passing, it seems advisable to pause for a moment and review the ground that has been covered. The accompanying schema summarizes the oppositional pairs constitutive of the initial and end states of the poetic narrative.

Stanza I: Initial State	*Stanza IV: Final State*
"Ruhe"	"Sehnsucht"
tenuous control	loss of control
subject-object relation	possession of subject
distance/delimitation	fusion/infiltration
antonymous rhyme	synonymous rhyme
"schwoll"/"ruhevoll"	"schwoll"/"sehnsuchtsvoll"
spatial separation	spatial overlapping
"daran"	"netzt"
syntactic containment of water in line 1	water syntactically overflows containment in line 1
agency/intentional action	agency relinquished/event of passion
"Angel"	"Fuß"
metonymy as displacement/separation	metonymy as connection/transmission
censorship	nakedness
"nach dem"	"nackten"

Schema 9: Oppositional Pairs in "Der Fischer"

From this synoptic representation the overriding tendency of the component oppositions emerges into view, a tendency I shall call the *subversion of
the subject*. The narrative elaborated in the poetic texture of "Der Fischer"
involves the undermining of agency, of the delimitation and distance that
make agency possible, of a structure of figuration (metonymy by proximity) that operates through displacement and denial (censorship), hence
of a controlled relation ("Ruhe") to sexuality. This subversion is an erasure
of limits, be they compositional, syntactic, spatial, figural, or semantic.
The final state of the narrative, the accomplished subversion, thus appears
as an *unbordering*, an abolition of distinctions enacted at various levels of
the text, an overflow.

This characterization of the general oppositional structure inflected in
"Der Fischer" immediately raises the question: What is it that brings about
the narrative transformation leading from initial state (delimitation) to
final state (unbordering)? What accomplishes the subversion of the subject? The answer one feels compelled to reach for, of course, is the "Weib,"
but this answer, although correct enough, is dangerously close to being
false insofar as it suggests that the "Weib" is an autonomous being, existing
independently within the fiction. Clearly, however, the most prominent
feature of the "Weib" is that she is a fantastic being, a creature of myth or
superstition, and this feature is internal to her significance in the text. This
point can be formulated in terms of a generic distinction. Whereas a folk
ballad, because it participates in a socio-symbolic context organized by
myth and superstition, might very well posit such a "Weib" as a fictively
real being, Goethe's art ballad makes this fictional (mythical, superstitious)
character of the figure a component of the figure's significance. At issue in
the poem is not the "Weib" per se, but rather her generation, her production as illusion.

The mechanism of this production begins to profile itself in the second
half of stanza I, in the lines that introduce the "Weib" into the text:

> Und wie er sitzt und wie er lauscht,
> Teilt sich die Flut empor,
> Aus dem bewegten Wasser rauscht
> Ein feuchtes Weib hervor.   *(5–8)*

The mythological function of the water sprite, this spirit of the aqueous
element, is to couple with a human male and through this erotic embrace
to steal his soul, hence his life, his agency. Hers is a vampiric love, much

like that which Goethe, some four years after composing "Der Fischer," attributed to himself:

> Bin so in Lieb zu ihr versunken
> Als hätt ich von ihrem Blut getrunken.[39]
>
> In love to her I am so sunk
> As if from her blood I had drunk.

In "Der Fischer" as well the action of the vampiric lover will eventuate in a sinking, a liquid absorption. But the point I want to make here bears on the first line of the cited passage, a line that seems to have no other function than to mark the time of the sprite's appearance: she comes "as" the fisherman is sitting and listening.[40] If, however, one leans a bit on the particle "wie," it can be read as indicating not merely time but also aspect. The appearance of the "Weib" occurs not only while the fisherman sits and listens, but also as a function of his sitting and listening. She is a projection of the fisherman, an externalized likeness ("wie"), a figuration that arises as a result of his cognitive attitude.[41]

This attitude is defined by the line's two verbs. Sitting has already been glossed as the verb marking the fisherman's proximate distance to the water, to its sound and swelling. The line's second verb, "lauschen," signifies more than a passive hearing; it indicates an effort of auditory fixation, an attempt to localize a target or object, as in the usage encountered in "Jägers Nachtlied" ("Lausch mit dem Feuerrohr"). Of course, such listening has nothing to do with the methods normally employed in fishing, but this violation of mimetic veracity, far from being a defect, triggers the poetic significance. To say that the sprite appears as the fisherman sits and listens is to say that she appears as a result of his endeavor to discriminate an object that holds the undifferentiated murmur of the water at a distance and allows him to relate to it within the domain of representation. Paradoxically, the most flagrantly fantastic or mythological element in the text—the sprite—results from the application to the water's turbulent murmur of the very operation that guarantees cognitive mastery. This fisherman will not be drawn to his death by a "Weib," but rather by his own imaginary projection.

The subsequent lines of the cited passage make this clear. Whereas at the outset the water is an undifferentiated sound and swelling, it now divides ("Teilt sich die Flut empor"). The repetition of the sounding verb "rauschen" in 7, a verb that also lightly connotes 'intoxication', 'sexual excitement', has already been noted. Whereas this verb previously indicated the auditory effect of the water, it has now acquired a prefix that transforms sound into vision. "Hervor" places the "Weib" within the field of manifestation, makes of her an opposite of the fisherman, an object present before him. (The feature of visual presence connoted by the prefix "hervor" is heightened by virtue of its reversal in the corresponding line of the fourth stanza ["Und ward nicht mehr gesehn," 32].) The activity of "lauschen" thus succeeds in soliciting from the "Rauschen" a target of attention; the subversive hetero-affection of sexuality is rendered as a relation to objectivity; the subject understands the water by pressing it into conformity with its own cognitive structure. But precisely this cognitive operation, this fishing expedition that seeks to capture the water as an object of knowledge, produces the fantastic figure of the sprite. The delusion here is the very attempt knowingly to seize, to arrest, to objectify. And this attempt will prove to be the subject's undoing.

This reading of the "Weib," though strongly divergent from traditional commentary on the poem,[42] finds corroboration in a reading of the middle stanzas (II and III), in which the transformation converting the narrative's initial state (delimitation) into its final state (unbordering) is accomplished. Such a reading should demonstrate that the structure of projection determines the entire process of seduction, that the sprite's promise to the fisherman is that he will find in the waters of sexuality nothing but himself.

The most salient feature of the middle stanzas is that they are a citation. Their truth value, therefore, is suspended, and attention is directed away from a sphere of referents toward the formulation itself. Of course, dialogue, hence quoted speech, is a traditional trait of the ballad, but Goethe does not simply adopt this formal characteristic, he remotivates it, endows it with a poetic function specific to this text. The sprite's seventeen lines of speech display, disclose to inspection, the very mechanisms of speech that produce the aqueous world's allure. To ignore this fact (as virtually every interpreter of the poem has), to attempt to penetrate through the surface of this language and embrace the water's depth of meaning, is to repeat the fisherman's error. By citing the sprite's utterances, the text stages its own misreading, a misreading that consists in forgetting the techniques of suasion. The subversion of the subject—the transformative process that converts the narrative's initial state into its final one—is accomplished in this text through the seductions of rhetoric.

To call attention to the citational quality of the sprite's speech is to raise the question of who, or what, is being cited here. I have already noted that the attribution of agency to speech is problematic in this text, but now the difficulties appear even more grievous. For example, in view of the hypothesis that the "Weib" enters the text as a projection of the fisherman's cognitive attitude, it follows that her speech is in some sense his, that it echoes his epistemological stance. Moreover, if we consider that the singing and speaking of the sprite emerge from the sound of the water, then the citation could also be called a *translation*, indeed a treasonable translation that recasts the undifferentiated aqueous murmur into an intelligible statement. The otherness of the water and of sexuality thereby becomes the Same; hetero-affection is domesticated as meaning. Finally, if we read the text as remarking its own constitution as art ballad, as indeed we must, then the cited song can be read as displaying the seductive allure of an archaic poetic voice, an allure that consists precisely in the fact that it tempts one to translate that voice or to hear it as the echo of one's own. Note that these three readings are supported by the female refrain. In its first occurrence (9), the order of the verbs suggests a movement from sound to sense: "Sie sang zu ihm, sie sprach zu ihm." When the refrain returns near the poem's end, however, this hermeneutic directionality is reversed—"Sie sprach zu ihm, sie sang zu ihm"—suggesting the reabsorption of intelligibility in the medium of sound.

I want to reserve these questions bearing on the status of the sprite's speech for later treatment and consider now the rhetorical mechanisms that speech deploys. The passage is articulated across an intensifying series of six illocutionary units, the first of which is an interrogative:

> Was lockst du meine Brut
> Mit Menschenwitz und Menschenlist
> Hinauf in Todesglut? *(10–12)*

The argumentative cunning of this question lies in the fact that its available answers (e.g., "Because I'm a fisherman and that's what fishermen do") are irrelevant. Such answers contain no information not already obvious and cannot, therefore, function as answers at all. But, although unanswerable in the usual, informative sense, the question nonetheless (indeed, all the more so) continues to exert its interrogative force. This force can be described as the demand that the one receiving the question fill in the lack whose existence the question, as question, presupposes. Since this can't be done, since an informative answer is unavailable, the fisherman has no alternative but to seek that lack in himself. The unanswerable question of the sprite, in other words, compels the fisherman to regard his entire sphere of activities as deficient. This suggestion of deficiency is also conveyed by what might be called the lexical presuppositions of the phrasing, the derogatory accent that falls on "Menschenwitz und Menschenlist," the stylization of angling as a murderous activity ("Todesglut"). Qua recipient of the question, the fisherman is forced *to call himself into question.* The demand that issues from the Other (here instantiated by the "Weib," but, of course, her status as source of the speech is problematic), this hetero-affective incitement, opens an internal discrepancy within the subject, divides the subject within itself. Despite its overtly tactical manifestation in the text, the rhetoricity of the sprite's speech is not a facultative level of language use superadded to ordinary speech, but rather emerges with the subject's relation to language as the *summons of an impossible reply.*

The second illocutionary unit of the sprite's speech, the unit that completes the first of her two stanzas, is formed as an assertion in the mode of a counterfactual condition:

> Ach wüßtest du, wie's Fischlein ist
> So wohlig auf dem Grund,
> Du stiegst herunter wie du bist,
> Und würdest erst gesund. *(13–16)*

One way of describing the effect of the opening rhetorical ploy is to say that by placing the subject internally in question it gives rise to a condition of nonknowledge; divided from itself, the subject doesn't know itself. The second illocutionary move builds on this effect by positing the existence of a knowledge which the addressee doesn't possess. The state of self-discrepancy is thus recoded as a condition of unnecessary lack, as a temporary and corrigible defect. Moreover, since to know how the fish feels in its pleasureful existence is equivalent to feeling that pleasureful existence oneself, the knowledge posited by the verb is a self-knowledge, a self-feeling, untouched by discrepancy. The very same voice that in its hetero-affective summons divides the subject also generates the image of an undivided, whole and healthy ("gesund") state of subjective being. That is to say, it transforms the lack it implants within the subject into a desire oriented toward the fullness of identity, the completeness of self.

Consider somewhat more closely the relation between these two states—divided and undivided—as it is formulated across the logic of counterfactual condition and consequence. To know "how pleasureful it is to/for the little fish" is just to be the little fish as it is to/for itself. However, were one this, then the consequence that the sprite draws from the counterfactual condition, namely that the fisherman would "climb down here just as you are" would not hold. For in that case the fisherman would precisely no longer be "just as you are," nor would he have to climb down (since he would already be at the "Grund"). Being something cannot be a motivation (or reason) for becoming that very something. The function of the qualification is to call attention to *the contradictory structure of the desire* that emerges from the sprite's speech. The desire to be completely oneself, whole and healthy, as the sprite promises, is the desire to be other than oneself (other than divided) and yet still oneself; the desire to be what one is not (whole and healthy) and yet to remain the self one is ("wie du bist").[43] If the rhetoricity specific to the first segment of the sprite's speech is the summons of an impossible reply, the second phase—which replies to that summons, but contradictorily, hence impossibly—is *the enthymeme of desire.*

To summarize: the first stanza of the sprite's song and speech (stanza II of the poem) discloses a primordial rhetoricity of song/speech, a rhetoricity that is not a matter of artful technique, although it is the source of all poetic art. This rhetoricity, as summons of an impossible reply and enthymeme of desire, situates the subject vis-à-vis language as a divided subject for whom the promise of wholeness is only the aggravation of division.

The four illocutionary units of stanza III form a series of rhetorical questions:

> Labt sich die liebe Sonne nicht,
> Der Mond sich nicht im Meer?
> Kehrt wellenatmend ihr Gesicht
> Nicht doppelt schöner her?
> Lockt dich der tiefe Himmel nicht,
> Das feucht verklärte Blau?
> Lockt dich dein eigen Angesicht
> Nicht her in ew'gen Tau? *(17–24)*

Rhetorical questions, particularly rhetorical yes/no questions such as these, are powerful suasive devices because they suggest that a genuine alternative as to their answer (yes or no) exists while at the same time presupposing, and thereby rendering inescapable, either assent, as in this case, or dissent. The respondent is thus placed in a position—an obviously contradictory position—where free assent is compelled. The fisherman has no choice but to choose "yes!" as the answer to all the sprite's questions. Now assent, certainly one of the basal components of language use, is a complicated matter, but whatever one might say about its intricacies, it seems incontrovertible that it relates conation (desire, will) to a proposition. To assent to a proposition is to declare oneself *for* that proposition, to commit oneself. Assent, in other words, involves identification with something: the 'I' that assents, that says "yes," identifies with, wills for itself and as its own, the I-position of the assenter. With my assent I declare my identity with the one who says "yes," who wills for himself—myself—that such and such be the case. Thus we see the force of the sprite's rhetorical questions: they compel the fisherman's assent to, his identification with, his own desire; they make his free assumption of his subject position inescapable. What shimmered forth as an unreal condition in the enthymeme of desire is now affirmed by the subject as its own. The subject addressed by language has no choice but freely to choose—to identify itself with—the subject position language delegates to it. Let us call this dimension of the song's rhetoricity *the paradox of identity*.

This analysis, which applies to the force of the rhetorical question in general, allows us to discern the sequential logic of the four individual questions the sprite poses. They fall into two groups. The first two questions bear, in their propositional content, on the sun and moon, which are said to quench themselves in the sea and whose face (a singular term about which more will be said) turns upward from the water's surface with redoubled beauty. The second pair pertains to the fisherman himself, in particular to his attraction by—hence his desire for—something, namely the deep heaven and its water-transfigured blueness on the one hand and his own face as reflected by the aqueous mirror on the other. That is to say, the series builds toward the rhetorical question that compels from the subject free assent to its own desire for itself, that compels its identification with itself as the subject of its desire. This ultimate solicitation of self-identification is prepared by a mediating image that offers the fisherman the paradigm of another self, that of the sun and moon. Thus, the sequential arrangement of the four rhetorical questions obeys the logic of the enthymeme. It presents the image of an other (the sun and moon) which the fisherman is to imitate in order to enjoy his own self un-dividedly. Only by identifying himself with (assenting to) an other can he be the self he desires and for that very reason he can only ever be other than the self he desires. The rhetoricity of the sprite's speech thus compels the subject to an impossible, but ineluctable, identification.

Thus far I have focused on the rhetoricity of the text as an illocutionary dimension and have all but ignored its elocution, the figurations the sprite deploys. But clearly the figurative dimension of her speech and song intensifies its seductiveness, its attractive pull, by charging the impossible object of desire with a dense cluster of connotative values. In my opening remarks on lines 17–18, I elaborated the way in which such suggestive appeal emerges from the song's phonic texture. This analysis could be extended to the entire passage, which is phonically among the richest and most intricately organized in Goethe's poetic oeuvre. Suffice it to note, by way of example, the alliterative and assonantial glide that moves through the counterfactual conditional assertion: "wüßtest," "wohlig," "wür-dest";[44] "Grund," "herunter," "gesund." Indeed, these verses, with their vocalic interplay of 'high' and 'low', enact the very 'descent' to the ground they thematize. On the level of syntactic figuration one could cite the parallelism that organizes the two sets of rhetorical questions in stanza III: the first question in each pair involves two different grammatical subjects ("Mond"/"Sonne"; "Himmel"/"Blau") sharing the same verb ("Labt sich"; "Lockt"); the second question is formed with a single, and indeed nearly the same, grammatical subject ("Gesicht"; "Angesicht"), as well as with verbs that bear the same directional prefix ("Kehrt . . . her"; "Lockt . . . her"). Such syntactic symmetry allows the two pairs to appear as mirror images of one another and thereby supports the fisherman's iden-tification with himself as with the sun and moon. In short, a pervasive structural tendency of the sprite's song is to generate iconic relations between the phonic and syntactic levels on the one hand and the semantic level on the other. Lines that speak of reflection themselves reflect, and thereby reflect themselves. This is to say that the object of desire the song semantically proffers, the tantalizing wholeness of self-reflection, is simu-lated by the song itself. The song that calls forth desire presents itself as the object of that desire, promising its captivated auditor: I am nothing but the mirror, the echo, of your self.

My opening discussion of lines 17–18 argued that their phonic-lexical patterning evokes a regenerative oral-erotic bliss ("Labt sich . . . liebe") tinged with narcissistic appeal ("*sich nicht*"). This connotational cluster recurs throughout the sprite's song. The semantic strand of 'regeneration' begins with the promise of a becoming healthy or whole ("würdest . . . gesund," 16), continues through the intensified beauty ("doppelt schöner," 20) of the reflected heavenly bodies, appears subsequently in the moist transfiguration of the sky ("feucht verklärte," 22), and culminates in the promise of an "eternal dew" ("ew'gen Tau," 24)—a matinal, liquid cleansing that would know no end. The leading idea seems to be that of a rebirth, a new origination into a higher, transfigured, and intensely beautiful state of being. More prominently featured in the song is the isotopy of 'erotic embrace,' which is dramatized in the figure of the sun (feminine) and moon (masculine) quenching themselves in the sea and thereby becoming one face ("ihr Gesicht," 19), as if the differences of time (day/night) and sex were overcome in the unity of a single body. Indeed, we are impelled—not the least by the text's set of background beliefs regarding elemental spirits and their seduction of humans—to read the entire scenario of the song's presentation as the initiation of an erotic embrace. What is the "Weib" offering the fisherman if not herself? What is submersion in the waters out of which she comes and which she personifies if not entry into her? And who, finally, is this "Weib" of the waters, who speaks of all who dwell within her fluidity as her "Brut" (10), if not the figure of the Mother? We have seen that the narcissistic tinge of lines 17–18 suffuses the song, impressing itself on the phonic and syntactic structures and finally receiving direct expression in the concluding lines: "Lockt dich dein eigen Angesicht / Nicht her in ew'gen Tau?" (23–24). Thus, the figurative tapestry of the song interweaves numerous threads, now promising rebirth and transfiguration, now a return to the enclosure of the Mother's liquid body, now alluding to a coital union, now to a narcissistic rapture. This condensation and crossing of diverse, but related semantic networks in the articulation of its figures, this fugue of penumbral wish scenarios, constitutes one of the most suggestive aspects of the song's rhetoricity.

The final aspect of the song's figurality to which I want to call attention, an aspect perhaps even more seductive than connotative evocation, is its capacity for semantic reversal. Such reversal occurs both extensively across the text and intensively in single words. A notable example is the movement from "Was lockst du" in the first line the "Weib" sings to "Lockt dich . . . nicht" (21), repeated in the song's final two rhetorical questions. The song converts the one who lures into the one who is lured, fisherman into prey. A similar reversal governs the directional prefix "her." In its initial use (20), this designates movement upward from the water toward the fisherman; in its second use, however, it designates the downward pull of the water's attraction. On the surface of the aqueous mirror the highest thing, heaven, becomes the deepest ("der tiefe Himmel," 21); the most ephemeral thing, dew, eternal ("ew'gen Tau," 24). But the boldest cases of such reversal are the song's two neologisms, "Todesglut" (12) and "well-enatmend" (19), metaphorical compounds that not only reverse the semantic valence of their individual tenors, but also stand to one another in a relation of reverse symmetry.

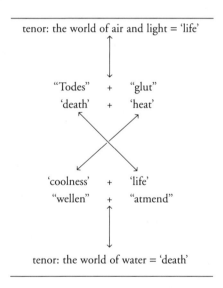

Schema 10: Metaphorical Symmetries and Reversals in "Der Fischer"

In the fluid medium of the sprite's singing, even the most drastic of human certainties are dissolved. The power of her song transforms 'life' into 'death' and 'death' into 'life.' For a suasive speech capable of such sleights of hand, convincing a fisherman that he should identify with a little fish, that, in the truth of his identity, he *is* that little fish, is child's play, a simple figural substitution that operates via the equivalence 'pursuer' = 'pursued.' But of course the juxtaposed metaphorical compounds provide more than one example among others of rhetorical power; they are the very emblem of the song itself as rhetoricity unbounded by reference, and for that reason all the more compelling. There can be no doubt that the chiastic reversal of semantic values accomplished by the metaphors—both externally with regard to their tenors and internally with regard to the position and valence of their vehicular components—enacts the inverse symmetry (left-right exchange) of mirror reflections. Once again the allure of watery reflection—hence of erotic union, regeneration, narcissistic self-love— *about which* the song speaks thematically, proves to be the figuration of the song's poetico-rhetorical force. *The song is the abyssal mirror—reflection reflecting reflection—of a language, a poetry, a rhetorical suasion that functions independently of any fixed order of referents.* If what is meant by "meaning" is a transitive relation, however complexly established, between signifying elements on the one hand and signifieds (concepts or entities) on the other, then the sprite's song, strictly speaking, means nothing. And every interpretation of the song that attributes to it a hermeneutic or symbolic depth, that reaches beyond its surface to seize its truth, repeats the fisherman's error. Even the claim that the song means itself, a claim I have skirted on several occasions, goes wrong, succumbs to the abyss of self-reference. For this 'itself' to which, according to such a construal, the poem refers, has no substantial content that could stabilize, or noematically moor, transitive meaning. The 'itself' of the song is not a stable self, but the reflection of a reflection, the figure of a figure, the echo of an echo.

As a whole, the sprite's song raises three interlocking claims.

1. The sprite's song is the citational demonstration of a rhetoricity unbounded by reference and meaning, abyssally reflecting its own reflection. The Kantian distinction noted above between poetry, as a forthright play of ideas yielding more than the intellect expected, and rhetoric, as a deceptive ploy that promises the intellect something in order to subvert its proper operation, does not apply. There is here no bifurcation of poetry and rhetoric, because what is at issue is not an artful, hence optional, technique that could be distinguished from the sincere or natural use of language. At issue is not rhetoric as a learnable skill, but rather a primordial rhetoricity, a rhetoricity that emerges with the origin of language.[45]

This conception arises from the dissonant combination of contextual frames evoked by the sprite's song. On the one hand, her singing stages the eighteenth-century fascination with the emergence of language out of nature; it dramatizes the becoming-meaningful of natural song, *Naturpoesie*, in short, primordial orality. On the other hand, the sprite's text (in contradistinction, for instance, to "Heidenröslein" and "Der König von Thule," which simulate 'naturalness' throughout) is an overt staging of rhetorical technique. Thus, primordial song is here endowed with all the attributes of artfulness; the distinction between the natural and the artificial is neutralized in a conception of arch-rhetoric. Recalling the cynical ease with which Gorgias transformed any and all semantic units into their contraries (much as the sprite does with such terms as 'life' and 'death'), one might mark this tension by saying that "Der Fischer" enacts a conception of poetry as originary sophistry.

2. To say that this sophistry is originary is to say that it is not facultative, not corrigible or avoidable. No subject position is available from which it could be unmasked and condemned. Rather, the rhetoricity staged in the sprite's song—as summons of an impossible reply, as enthymeme of desire and paradox of identity—calls forth the subject in its aporetic and inescapable position as subject of/to language. It commits the subject to an impossible narcissism, to a desire-for-self that is subverted in its very accomplishment. The narcissistic entrapment is as ineluctable as the sophistry that elicits it. Thus, the narrative transformation from delimitation to unbordering that I characterized above as the subversion of the subject is carried out here by a rhetoricity that simultaneously constitutes and deconstitutes, that renders impossible the very quest it sets in motion. Moreover, just as there is no subject position from which the originary rhetoricity of language could be refused, there is likewise no subject position from which that rhetoricity issues. The "Weib" is not the agency of this speech, but one of its effects, a making of a face upon the water no less projective than the fisherman's narcissistic mirroring. She is nothing, means nothing, but hovers above the abyss of her own auto-citation: prosopopoeia of prosopopoeia. One could speak of the emergence of the two subject figures—the subject which desires itself in language and the subject which promises that desire's fulfillment, fisherman and sprite—as a transcendental semblance (*transzendentaler Schein*), that is, as an illusion produced by the conditions of possibility of subjectivity per se. One could

speak this way, were it not that the song's rhetoricity escapes reduction to the immanence of the subjective sphere.[46] Exerting its force as hetero-affection, it opens a relationality to otherness that precedes and is the condition for both self and other. It is a voice without agency, an echo without origin, and yet it is that which calls me to my agency and fixes my desire on the origin. Goethe's text echoes this echoic voice throughout its seductive phonic texture, but also gives it a name. It is the name of that which opens the fisherman's tale and which returns as refrain to draw that tale to an end; the name of that out of which the "Weib" emerges and into which she disappears. *Rauschen*: onomotopoeia of primordial rhetoricity.

3. With the sprite's song, the text stages the complex of specularity examined throughout this book. The 'regenerative' strand of the song's connotative tapestry hooks up with the figure of 'artistic rebirth' at the end of "Künstlers Morgenlied" (Text 18) and with the vision of the artist as a reborn Hercules that concludes the essay "Von deutscher Baukunst."[47] The chiastic reciprocity between "Ich" and "Du" of "Maifest" (Text 2) and "Mir schlug das Herz" (Text 5), the sexualization of specularity in "Auf Cristianen R." (Text 9) and "Pilgers Morgenlied" (Text 10), the dream of maternal enclosure in "Der neue Amadis" (Text 8), the exchange of identity within the sphere of primordial orality in the *Prometheus* fragment (Text 21), the 'liquidity' of the maternal donation in "Der König von Thule" (Text 25)—all these aspects of the specular complex are alluded to in the sprite's song. But that song does not simply *use* these elements, instantiating a further variant of the lyric myth of auto-engenderment; it *mentions* them. That is the force of the term "staging" here: the sprite's song at once doubles the central figures of Goethe's lyric myth and neutralizes their force. It displays them *as* figures and thereby resists their affective pull. By virtue of this minuscule shift from use to mention, the project of lyric self-grounding in specularity that governed the movement of the earlier poems is exposed to a reading as text. "*Der Fischer*" *is Goethe's reading of his own previous lyric production.* In this reading, the Source (of poetry and subjectivity) is rethought as the delusive effect of a primordial rhetoricity without origin; the hermeneutic quest the earlier poems both performed and elicited appears as (unavoidable) misreading; and the dyad of specular reflection collapses into an abyss of self-reference.

These three claims take on greater plausibility when one considers an aspect of the sprite's song that has as yet remained unremarked. As we have seen, the citation of the song is also the citation of a diegetic frame, a storied context, within which that song is sung. This frame is constituted by the myths of elemental spirits the text alludes to, the stories of the Loreleis and Undines who will later populate the Romantic lyric. But this archaic—hence 'natural,' 'unschooled,' 'oral'—strain is fugally juxtaposed with one of the most artfully playful texts in the 'high' European literary tradition, a text that is itself a 'belated' and 'learned' redaction and that transforms the myths it draws on into such a tour de force of suave artificiality that it has come to epitomize indulgent literariness and fashion. Just as Goethe's *Kunstballade* subverts the opposition between an originary 'poetry of nature' and a late, deceitful poetry of 'rhetorical artfulness' by staging the origin as rhetoricity, it likewise reinscribes the archaic mythical complex within the framework of Ovid's *Metamorphoses*.[48] That is to say that Goethe's reading of his own lyric myth displays that myth—the myth of specularity—as a redaction of the story of Narcissus and Echo. Of course, interpreters of the text have recognized the narcissistic aspects of "Der Fischer," but this shimmering adjective usually functions merely as an allusive gesture uncertainly hovering between Ovid and Freud and is applied solely to lines 23–24 ("Lockt dich dein eigen Angesicht / Nicht her in ew'gen Tau?").[49] These lines, to be sure, constitute the most obvious reference to Ovid's tale, but by no means the only one. Consider the following.

(a) Ovid's Narcissus is a hunter, and it is during a chase that he encounters first Echo and then the reflective pool that will be his undoing; this narrative situation Goethe rewrites as angling.

(b) Ovid's Narcissus is characterized—this is the flaw that leads to his demise—by a cold pride that makes him immune to the amorous appeal of both youths and girls ("sed fuit in tenera tam dura superbia forma, / nulli illum iuvenes, nullae tetigere, puellae" ["and yet that slender figure / Of proud Narcissus had little feeling / for either boys or girls"; III, 354–55]); Goethe's reformulation of this untouchability is "Kühl bis ans Herz hinan" (4).

(c) The scenario of hunting allows Ovid to epitomize Narcissus's dilemma in terms of a reversal of the positions 'pursuer'-'pursued' ("petit, petitur," III, 426); Goethe translates this as "lockst du" / "Lockt dich."

(d) Ovid's Narcissus sees the reflection of his eyes as twin stars ("spectat humi positus geminum, sua lumina, sidus" ["Flat on the grass he lay to

look deep, deeper / Into two stars that were his eyes"; III, 420]); Goethe cites these heavenly bodies as "Sonne" and "Mond," intensifies the reversal of 'above' and 'below' that Ovid's stress on Narcissus's prone position on the earth captures, and echoes the doubled oneness of the twins in the singular "Angesicht" of the reflected heavenly bodies which is said to be "doppelt schöner."

(e) Ovid's Narcissus sees his face as upturned and striving upward from the wave to meet his own lips ("nam quotiens liquidis porreximus oscula lymphis, / hic totiens ad me resupino nititur ore" ["Weeping / I've seen great tears flow down your face; I bend / My head toward you, you nod at me"; III, 451–52]); Goethe weaves this upturned face into the figure of the heavenly bodies, forgetting neither the wave ("wellenatmend") nor the stress on directionality ("Kehrt . . . her").

(f) Finally, Ovid narrates Narcissus's doleful end by having death close the eyes of the youth and thereby extinguish the love that had existed only in vision ("lumina mors clausit" ["death shut fast the eyes that shone with light"; III, 503]); Goethe too marks the end as end of vision, but—for reasons still to be explored—renders the event in the passive: "Und ward nicht mehr gesehen" (32).

Against the background of these citations, the transformative gesture of Goethe's reading—the promotion of Echo to a position of centrality—forcefully stands out. Ovid's text weaves the tale of Echo's unrequited love for Narcissus around the story of the youth's specular captivation like an ornamental garland, suggesting a parallelism between the two plot lines but nevertheless distinguishing them. Goethe's text redeploys sequence as simultaneity: vocal and visual reflection, echoing and mirroring, are synthesized in and as the sprite's song. *The visual captivation becomes a function of auditory captivation, the narcissistic complex a function of rhetoricity.* Not only does Echo, in her return as sprite, sing the song that instigates narcissistic passion, that song itself becomes the narcissistic mirror. Thus, the sprite's song takes on all the paradoxical features of aqueous specularity that Ovid exploits with such virtuoso wit: "ista repercussae, quam cernis, imaginis umbra est: / nil habet ista sui"; ("He loved the image that he thought was shadow, / And looked amazed at what he saw—his face"; III, 434–35). The shadow of a reflection without substance, without an itself: this abyssal structure characterizes the sprite's song. The "Weib" whose song is quoted into the text of "Der Fischer" is, literally, the prosopopoeia of a prosopopoeia (Echo). In Goethe's text, the origin of poetry—of language and song—is the rhetoricity of a voice that has no origin, no subject, no meaning: reflection without end, the echo, literally, of an echo.

The disclosure of the intertextual relation to the *Metamorphoses* not only confirms the reading of the sprite's song as echoic rhetoricity, it also allows us to begin to develop the issues necessary for an evaluation of the poem's end with its connotations of 'suicidal death.' By virtue of its Ovidian intertext, the poem can be said to operate within a complex in which voice, echo, and literary citation are tied together. Now, exactly the same complex forms an essential network in Goethe's novel of suicidal passion, *The Sorrows of Young Werther*, where, however, the intertext is not Ovid's poem but *The Songs of Ossian.*[50] In *Werther*, the complex is linked with inconsolable mourning, or melancholy; the passages from *Ossian* Werther translates enter the novel as the voice of dead bards lamenting the lost voices of other deceased heros and bards, a virtual echo chamber of mourning. The effect of this echoic voice on Werther and Charlotte, as it returns in Werther's recitation of his translations, is worth recalling:

> Die Bewegung beider war fürchterlich. Sie fühlten ihr eigenes Elend in dem Schicksale der Edlen, fühlten es zusammen, und ihre Tränen vereinigten sich.[51]

> The movement [emotional convulsion] of both of them was terrible. They felt their own misery in the fate of the noble ones, felt it together, and their tears united.

The echoic song echoes within the two lovers ("Elend," "Edlen"), instigating an identification with the dead that passes over into liquid union. This mournful aspect does not seem immediately relevant to "Der Fischer" until one recalls that Echo, in the Ovidian text, is the very voice of mourning. This would suggest that the rhetoricity of the sprite's song, in addition to everything that has been said about it up to this point, is also imbued with loss, that its attractions are those of death, or of a liquid-born identification with the dead.

A passage from a letter by Goethe often cited in connection with "Der Fischer" can help us to develop this point. On January 17, 1778, the body of Christiane von Laßberg, who out of unrequited love had taken her life in the Ilm River, was found near Goethe's house, a copy of *Werther*, it is

reported, in her pocket. Two days later Goethe wrote to Charlotte von
Stein that he had spent the previous evening hollowing out a secluded
memorial to the deceased girl in the rocks or cliffs ("Felsen") overlooking
her last paths and the place of her death. At first aided by another, he
finally carried on the work alone, remaining at his labor of mourning until
the return of the girl's hour of death. Goethe remarks the return of that
fatal hour as follows:

> Orion stand so schön am Himmel als wie wir von Tiefurth fröhlich heraufrit-
> ten. Ich habe an Erinnerungen und Gedancken just genug, und kan nicht
> wieder aus meinem Hause. Gute Nacht Engel, schonen Sie sich und gehn
> nicht herunter. Diese einladende Trauer hat was gefährlich anziehendes wie
> das Wasser selbst, und der Abglanz der Sterne des Himmels der aus beyden
> leuchtet lockt uns.[52]

> Orion stood as beautifully in the heavens as when we rode so joyfully up from
> Tiefurth. I have quite enough memories and thoughts, and can't go out of the
> house again. Goodnight, angel, restrain yourself and don't go down. This
> inviting sadness [mourning] has something dangerously attractive like the
> water itself, and the reflection of the stars of heaven that shines forth from both
> lures us.

As has often been noted, the passage contains both lexical ("herunter,"
"locken") and imagistic material (the reflection of the heavenly bodies)
also found in "Der Fischer." Indeed, so evident is their similarity that the
letter can be adduced as evidence of the poem's approximate date of
composition. In the context of the present argument, however, a more
intriguing feature of the passage is the logic of the equation established
between mourning and water. Both are dangerously attractive and seductive, to be sure, but the point of Goethe's remark is not simply to note this
similarity. Rather, he derives the attraction common to mourning and
water from the fact that both show forth the "Abglanz der Sterne." This
idea seems rather peculiar. In what sense does one 'see' something in one's
mourning? What possible connection could there be between mourning
and an act of vision?

These questions remain a mystery until one realizes that they are
irrelevant, that the axis of the comparison is not vision at all, but mediality.
Goethe doesn't see the real stars replicated in his "Trauer" (an absurd idea);
rather, his "Trauer" transforms those stars into reflections of something
absent (the night, now past, of the joyful ride from Tiefurth). Mourning is

a reflective surface akin to the water which beckoned Christiane von Laßberg to her suicide because it *de-realizes*, ontologically hollows out, whatever returns within it. This force of de-realization is the *tertium comparationis* operative in the passage. The essential feature of whatever shines forth from the reflective medium is its ontological detachment from any original. "Trauer" reflects not the entity, but its absence, its death; it is the medium in which death returns and tempts us with an impossible identification. Goethe's discovery, then, bears on the autonomy (independence from a referent) and the thanatopic character of reflective media as the ontological source of their incitement to identification. Note that this holds for the water as well. What attracts us on its surface is not the heavenly body duplicated there, but rather the "Abglanz" itself, which is to say, something that has no itself.

Exactly this de-realization, this absence of any source or referent, of any ontological mooring, characterizes the sprite's song. It is pure "Abglanz." And when one recalls that Goethe, in his work of mourning, had hollowed out ("ausgehölt") a place for the dead girl's memory in the cliffs, the pertinence of this correlation becomes clear. The rocks and cliffs are the dwelling place of Echo and resound with her inconsolable lament. Conceived as auditory medium, "Trauer" would be an echoic voice that derealizes in and through its resounding. We cannot even say that the voice that echoes in our mourning is the voice "of" the one lost; the possessive of agency (e.g., "her" voice) no longer has any meaning. Mourning is the voice not of the dead, but of death. As if to confirm this reading Goethe concludes the letter with a shift from the visual to the tonal register. Since the suicide, he reports, his youthful companions from Weimar have become timid and superstitious, only daring to go out at night near his house if there are at least three of them. His comment on this anxiety: "eben die Saiten der Menschheit werden an ihnen gerührt, nur geben sie einen rohern Klang"[53] ("the same strings [as on a musical instrument] of human existence are struck [set into vibration] in them [as in us], they just give off a cruder sound"). The crude tone of superstitious anxiety, the finer tone of mourning: both are audible reverberations, echoes, precisely, of nothing, the sound of loss.

If "Der Fischer" melds popular superstitions about elemental spirits that seduce human beings and draw them to their death with the high literary tradition of the *Metamorphoses*, it is because in both the originary rhetoricity of a 'soulless' medium finds expression, a rhetoricity of pure and

abyssal "Abglanz" and echo. As we have seen in the analysis of the fourth
stanza's initial lines, the erotic effect of this rhetoricity is to liquefy the
subject, to extinguish in a corporeal-metonymic overflow the differences,
delimitations, and objectifications that hold the subject at a distance from
sexuality. The echoic character of this rhetoricity, traced along other paths
of reading, is openly stated in the concluding line of this segment. The
suffusion of the heart occurs: "Wie bei der Liebsten Gruß" (28). The
speech and song of the "Weib," prior to which there is neither speech nor
song, is already the similitude of another word, the proffered greeting that
holds the beloved in imminence. But this erotological rhetoricity is also
thanatological, the impossible identification with the beloved object it
elicits is also an identification with death. Hence the 'suicidal' connotation
of the poem's concluding four lines:

> Sie sprach zu ihm, sie sang zu ihm;
> Da war's um ihn geschehn;
> Halb zog sie ihn, halb sank er hin,
> Und ward nicht mehr gesehn.   *(29–32)*

As mentioned in the discussion of poetic narrative, the death of the
fisherman is not a basal fact reported in the text to which various nuances
of meaning are then added. Rather, it is a connotation, a significant
shading. The point of this distinction is not simply that the death is
indirectly stated, although this is true in the sense that this word is not
mentioned, nor even that other interpretations of the fisherman's 'sinking,'
such as 'erotic surrender,' are possible, although this is also true. Instead,
'death,' insofar as the term bears relevance to this text, is not something we
can talk about as if we already knew what it is. No less than the other
connotations the text evokes, death will find its significance only in the
context of a reading.

We can begin to stake out the territory of such a reading by picking up
an earlier remark on the significance of the verb "geschehn" in the second
of the cited lines as marking an event that overwhelms the subject. To be
sure, this line registers the perlocutionary effect of the sprite's speaking and
singing, notes the fact that her song succeeds in breaking down the
fisherman's last bastion of resistance. But this perlocution does not merely
happen to him, leaving him otherwise as he was. Rather, the event
"finishes him off," as we say, or "does him in." These English colloquial-
isms, which attempt to approximate the nuance of finality carried by the

phrase "um ihn geschehn," are inaccurate to the extent that they suggest an agency which does the "finishing." But of course there is no such agency here except for the impersonal dummy subject "es," a syntactic filler semantically tautological with the predictate of 'happening'. The fisherman is done in because he is absorbed in a sheer eventfulness in which he disappears as subject. This event is nothing other than the accomplishment of identification with the song itself, an impossible identification since it does not allow the fisherman's subjecthood to be preserved. To descend downward ("stiegst herunter") and at the same time to maintain identity ("wie du bist," 15) is attainable only within the phantasm produced by the enthymeme of desire. Once this phantasm becomes event, once the subject enters the mirror of water and song, it is no more. This is part of the force of the particle "Da": at the moment of the sprite's speaking and singing, as a result of that speaking and singing, but also 'there', in that speaking and singing, the subject is done in.

I have already noted the reversal of directionality that occurs in the repetition of the female refrain, the movement from a hermeneutic directionality (from "sang" to "sprach"), suggesting the auditor's production of meaning, to a directionality that reabsorbs intelligibility into sound. The disappearance of the fisherman, in other words, is likewise the end of all the narcissistic projections with which the subject seeks to find itself in the sheer otherness of the reflective medium. Thus, whereas the first occurrence of the female refrain opened up the space of a translation (and misreading) of the song, here no effort at making sense follows. The hallucination of the 'content' of the song withdraws, and only the singing remains. This is also indicated by the fact that the line from the first stanza to which the repeated refrain is narratively opposed is exactly the line from which the fisherman's projections take their point of departure: "Und wie er sitzt und wie er lauscht" (5). Thus, the only action that remains for the subject to perform is that of sinking, which, of course, is not an action at all, but a passive yielding with which the subject is drawn into the song to the point of rhyming with it ("sang"/"sank"), becoming its echo. The pronoun "ihn" designating the fisherman's position as the object of the song's attractive pull is rewritten as the directional particle "hin" (note the symmetry of the letters: "ih"/"hi") that gestures toward the point of his extinction, his entry into the echoic mirror.

We are beginning to see that the connotations 'death', 'suicide', and 'erotic embrace' function in this text as synonyms for the limit, the *end* (in

both senses of the word) of narcissistic representation. They mark the
point at which narcissistic desire, achieving its fulfillment, extinguishes
itself, the point of passage into the water, the mirror, the song. This is why
the text concludes with another citation of Ovid: the final line ("Und ward
nicht mehr gesehn") refers, as noted above, to the closing of Narcissus's
amorous eyes by death, erases the projectional space that opened before
those eyes. But Goethe's passive rendition also generates a slight ambiguity
by virtue of the fact that the predicate of 'no longer being seen' that fills the
poem's final line derives its subject from the previous line, where, however,
two subjects are available: "Halb zog sie ihn, halb sank er hin." Thus, it is
not entirely clear that the fisherman alone disappears from sight; it could
also be sprite and fisherman together, now united and therefore governing
a singular verb ("ward").[54] The two halves that constituted the unbridgeable division, the impossible identification, of the mirrored self—"Fischer"
and "Weib," subject and reflection—become one at the moment when
vision is annihilated. This reading, which strains the grammar of the text
in order to do justice to its gestural quality, is warranted by Ovid's text, in
which Narcissus says to his beloved image: "nunc duo concordes anima
moriemur in una" ("but as it is, we two shall die together in a single
breath"; III, 473). In a single breath (verse) and with a singular verb,
Goethe's text stages the end of the narcissistic phantasm as the vanishing of
its figures. The connotations of 'death' and 'erotic union' function in this
text as possible names for this vanishing point. What 'dies' here at the very
moment it attains erotic union with itself in the "anima una" of the final
line is narcissistic self-representation.

There is a hint of 'miraculousness' in this vanishing, and to gauge its
significance we must turn yet again to Ovid's poem. When Narcissus's
sisters arrive to perform funeral rites for him, his body is inexplicably
nowhere to be found ("nusquam corpus erat," III, 509). Goethe's final line,
with its gesture of sudden disappearance, cites this magical vanishing of
the youth's remains. And that is to say that it alludes to the magic of poetry
itself, for, of course, the disappearance of the youth's body in Ovid is the
counterpart to the metamorphosis of Narcissus into flower and of myth
into name with which the Latin poet signs his own literary achievement.
In Goethe's text, however, nothing follows upon the disappearance, no
white-petaled flower stands as a memorial sign of the fisherman's destiny,
no botanical emblem recalls the poet's own metamorphic gift. The line
"Und ward nicht mehr gesehn" relinquishes its hold on the figures of

narcissistic desire and in the same breath lets go of itself. The 'death' of the fisherman—more precisely, his disappearance as visible entity—is, simply and yet astonishingly, the end of the poem that bears his name as its title. At this limit point, the poem coincides with itself, performs exactly what it says, its cessation.

Of course, "Und ward nicht mehr gesehn" also cites a balladesque formula of closure. In its ordinary usage, the formula refers to the supraindividual context of transmitted stories in which the ballad participates. Its function is to state, "Here the tradition has nothing more to say; no further sagas about the hero exist; no other witnesses to his exploits have left behind their accounts." Goethe's citation of the formula, complexly crossed with Ovidian echoes, redirects this reference away from a tradition existing outside the poem toward the poem's very movement. The implicit subject of the verb of "seeing" is no longer the group of witnesses and anonymous singers from whom the reports of the ballad's narrated events and hence the ballad itself are inherited, but rather the one in whom and for whom the poem has called up its repertoire of figures: the listener who, sitting coolly at the source of poetry, is captivated by its echoic rhetoricity. Thus, Goethe's text radically reinterprets the historicity of the generic prototype it draws on. The historicity proper to ballads is the self-transmission, realized in and through recitation, of a narrative tradition, the becoming-present of a storied past that situates the community in relation to an event located in time, even if this time is only vaguely defined as "long ago." "Der Fischer" too involves the return and repetition of something deeply past, but what returns is a primordial evocative-suasive power that has no temporal location, be it mythical or empirical. Once again the homology which set the agenda of my reading—poet (or narrator) : the voice of a poetic past :: fisherman : sprite's song—makes its pertinence felt. Like so many of the texts analyzed in previous chapters, "Der Fischer" carves its path toward the Source of poetry and subjectivity, but in its citational reading of that quest for the Source it discloses the effects of art's primordial sophistry, stages the subversive, erotico-thanatological call, the seduction, that art originally is. Not, it seems to me, in order to criticize or repudiate that call, since that would be to renounce the "Saiten der Menschheit" within us, but to let it—citationally—happen. The origin of poetry returns in "Der Fischer" as something (nothing) radically nonoriginal: the hetero-affective rhetoricity of an echoic medium, an otherness of voice without semantic substance or agency, the pure semblance of a vocal "Abglanz." Strictly speaking, this text has no meaning that could stabilize its identity. The semantic ground ("Grund," 14) of the poem, with its seductive allure, dissolves in an abyss of self-reference. The site in which, in the course of its reading, "Der Fischer" assumes its umbral shape is the space of its difference to itself opened in and through its echoic auto-citation.

PART FOUR

Poetic Vocation

§ 8 Hermeneutics and the Origin of Humanity

28. PROMETHEUS

Bedecke deinen Himmel, Zeus,
Mit Wolkendunst,
Und übe, dem Knaben gleich,
Der Disteln köpft,
(5) An Eichen dich und Bergeshöhn;
Müßt mir meine Erde
Doch lassen stehn,
Und meine Hütte, die du nicht gebaut,
Und meinen Herd,
(10) Um dessen Glut
Du mich beneidest.

Ich kenne nichts ärmers
Unter der Sonn' als euch, Götter!
Ihr nähret kümmerlich
(15) Von Opfersteuern
Und Gebetshauch
Eure Majestät,
Und darbtet, wären
Nicht Kinder und Bettler
(20) Hoffnungsvolle Toren.

Da ich ein Kind war,
Nicht wußte wo aus noch ein,
Kehrt' ich mein verirrtes Auge
Zur Sonne, als wenn drüber wär'

(25) Ein Ohr zu hören meine Klage,
Ein Herz wie mein's,
Sich des Bedrängten zu erbarmen.

Wer half mir
Wider der Titanen Übermut?
(30) Wer rettete vom Tode mich
Von Sklaverei?
Hast du nicht alles selbst vollendet,
Heilig glühend Herz?
Und glühtest jung und gut,
(35) Betrogen, Rettungsdank
Dem Schlafenden da droben?

Ich dich ehren? Wofür?
Hast du die Schmerzen gelindert
Je des Beladenen?
(40) Hast du die Tränen gestillet
Je des Geängsteten?
Hat nicht mich zum Manne geschmiedet
Die allmächtige Zeit
Und das ewige Schicksal,
(45) Meine Herrn und deine?

Wähntest du etwa,
Ich sollte das Leben hassen,
In Wüsten fliehen,
Weil nicht alle
(50) Blütenträume reiften?

Hier sitz' ich, forme Menschen
Nach meinem Bilde,
Ein Geschlecht, das mir gleich sei,
Zu leiden, zu weinen,
(55) Zu genießen und zu freuen sich,
Und dein nicht zu achten,
Wie ich!¹

PROMETHEUS

Cover over your heaven, Zeus,
With cloudy murk,
And exercise yourself, like a boy
Beheading thistles,
(5) On oaks and mountain peaks;

You must let my earth
Stand anyway,
And my hut, which you didn't build,
And my hearth,
(10) For the glow of which
You envy me.

I know nothing more impoverished
Beneath the sun than you, gods!
You feed miserably
(15) On sacrificial taxes
And the breath of prayers
Your majesty,
And would starve, were
Not children and beggars
(20) Hopeful fools.

When I was a child,
Didn't know where in or out,
I turned my confused eye
Toward the sun, as if above it were
(25) An ear to hear my lament,
A heart like mine,
To take pity on one so distressed.

Who helped me
Against the Titans' excess?
(30) Who saved me from death,
From slavery?
Didn't you accomplish everything yourself,
Sacredly glowing heart?
And you glowed young and good,
(35) Deceived, thanked for your salvation
The sleeping one up there?

I should honor you? Why?
Did you ever lighten the pain
Of the one so burdened?
(40) Did you ever still the tears
Of the one so afraid?
Wasn't what forged me into a man
All-powerful time
And eternal destiny,
(45) My lords and yours?

Did you perhaps imagine,
I would hate life,
Flee into deserts,
Because not all the
(50) Blossom-dreams of youth bore fruit?

Here I sit, form human beings
After my image,
A race that will be equal to me,
To suffer, to weep,
(55) To take pleasure and feel joy,
And not to respect you,
Like me!

   This text, perhaps more so than any other in Goethe's oeuvre, is held to
epitomize the virulent rebelliousness and uncompromising literary ambition of the Sturm und Drang and has, as a result of this exemplary status,
attracted an unusually rich interpretive literature.[2] The reading elaborated
here unfolds as a dialogue with this interpretive tradition, which is to say
that it marks out disagreements, alternative accentuations, within a sphere
of general consensus. In particular, I maintain, in conformity with the
view commonly held in the research, that the poem engages with the
problematics of genius, indeed, that it is a poetic figuration of what genius
is. My argument picks up, therefore, on themes developed in Chapter 5,
but approaches them from an angle determined by the specificities of this
text's semantic gesture. For example, the opposition between nature and
culture around which my reading of "Mahomets Gesang" (Text 15) is
organized goes entirely unmentioned, along with such cognate issues as
the concept of supplementarity. Yet the fact, stressed in Chapter 5, that the
symbolic position of genius implies an assault on and usurpation of the
divine paternal principle has unmistakable salience in the "Prometheus"
ode. One might say that the two poems explore opposed, but systematically related aspects of the genius complex; "Mahomets Gesang" is a song
of religious founding, "Prometheus," a poetic antihymn that dismantles a
religious order. This feature of the text—its critique of religion—occupies
the focal point of my analysis.[3]
   The accentuation of the poem's critique of religious orthodoxy begins
with the major Enlightenment *homme de lettres* in the German-speaking
world, Lessing. Composed in 1774,[4] the poem circulated in manuscript
among a select few of Goethe's acquaintances, including Friedrich Hein-

rich Jacobi, who showed it to Lessing during a visit in 1780. In the conversation that ensued, Lessing remarked: "The point of view from which the poem is taken, that's my own point of view. . . . The orthodox concepts of divinity are no longer for me; I can no longer abide them."[5] Two aspects of Lessing's spontaneous, personal, but nonetheless acute appraisal guide my commentary on Goethe's text. First, I take the notion that the poem embodies a point of view (*Gesichtspunkt*) to imply that a principal task in reading the poem is the discrimination of the speech act, or complex of speech acts, the poem stages. Speech acts, after all, are positional utterances, produced within a situation which, through their implicative structure, they themselves organize; they are the linguistic embodiments of interactional or communicational perspectives. Second, Lessing's sense, registered in the phrase "no longer" (*nicht mehr*), that this point of view bears a temporal index raises for me the issue of the immanent historical structure of the poem, its chronotypic character.[6] My inquiry, then, does not so much bear on the question of how the poem relates to the historical world which sponsored it (say, to the intellectual and artistic ambience of the Sturm und Drang), but rather endeavors to disclose the historical relations within which the text, as dramatized act of speech, positions itself and, importantly, its audience. One could say that the orientation of my reading is structural rather than diagnostic, that I conceive the text as a reticulated rhetorical-semantic network rather than as an expressive symptom, and that this emphasis marks my divergence from most of the interpretive literature.[7]

Nonetheless, the path of my commentary crosses lines of thought traced out by my predecessors. One intersection in particular requires explicit mention. The reason that "orthodox concepts of divinity" are no longer valid within the world of the "Prometheus" ode is that the point of view the ode dramatizes involves a certain theory—the term, I shall contend, is entirely appropriate—of the emergence of such concepts. This theory, glimpsed by several interpreters, is most cogently formulated by Jochen Schmidt: "Thus the 'divine' is dependent on human beings. It is the product of their projective phantasy."[8] My claim in what follows is that this projective theory of religion is a component of what I describe as the *hermeneutic* standpoint assumed in Prometheus's speech. This standpoint situates both poetic persona and audience within a specific relation to the gods and to history, a relation I read as the figuration of poetic vocation.

My starting point is the aspect of the text most consistently ignored by interpreters, its global organization, its overriding figures of coherence. Two patterns collaborate to determine the poem's large-scale articulation of sense. First, despite its thoroughgoing confrontational pathos, the text exhibits a tripartite rhetorical structure that can be parsed as follows: stanzas I and II address themselves to the present situation and perform what, in illocutionary terms, can be classified as a condemnation or denunciation of the gods generally and, of course, preeminently of Zeus; stanzas III through VII, by contrast, recall a series of past events and thereby profile themselves as an essentially narrative phase; finally, the concluding stanza VIII turns toward the future, declaring the speaker's (Prometheus's) resolve to fashion a human race that will no longer heed, as he no longer does, Zeus's authority. This deployment of illocutionary blocks allows us to discern the *essentially juridical thrust* of the poem's rhetoric; the tripartite structure echoes the sequence of 'accusation', 'narration', and 'call to judgment' that traditionally organizes forensic argumentation. Far from being an unmediated expression of rebellious fervor, the text (the work, let us remember, of a young lawyer) unfolds a legal demonstration, prosecutes a case against Zeus and his entourage, indeed, as we shall see and as Lessing already saw, against the very belief in a transcendent deity.[9]

The second pattern with which the text operates and which serves as the principal organizing matrix of its semantics is narrative in character. The poem relates, obliquely to be sure, the story of a 'maturation', of a movement from the state of 'childhood' ("Da ich ein Kind war," 21) to 'manhood' ("Hat nicht mich zum Manne geschmiedet," 42); the protagonist, the subject accomplishing this narrative *parcours*, is, at least on a first level of reading, the speaker of the poem, Prometheus. It is important to note, however, that this narrative model charts not merely the development of an individual life but also the course of history conceived as the progressive appropriation of freedom by mankind. The poem, in other words, elaborates a conception of history as a process of *emancipation*, and in this respect it configures the fundamental historico-philosophical schema of the Enlightenment (*Aufklärung*).[10]

A more precise description of these two encompassing structures, rhetorical 'prosecution' and narrative of 'maturation', will be required in order to reconstruct the positionality or, in Lessing's terms, *Gesichtspunkt* of the Promethean speech act. But even this brief, abstract sketch brings out the crucial fact that the rhetorical and narrative patterns interlock with one another according to a logic of mutual containment. The retrospective account of childhood belief and youthful disappointment is a component of the prosecutory speech in the sense that that speech makes its case through a narrative mobilization of evidence. But the story that narrative tells—the saga of emancipation culminating in mankind's liberation from Zeus—has not yet, in the moment it is told, come to an end; full emancipation has not yet been achieved. In this sense the narrative contains the speech as one of its moments, indeed as the decisive moment in which the final break with the past is achieved and the advent of a humanity unconstrained by the authority of the thundering god disclosed. The speech in which Prometheus recalls the history of his unjust bondage becomes the vehicle through which he finally frees himself, and mankind, from that bondage. *The poem itself accomplishes the process about which it speaks; as act of speech it realizes the emancipatory program of Enlightenment.* The long-range goal of my reading is to show how this autological structure, the self-inclusion of the poem within its own constructed world, determines the concept of poetic vocation the text embodies.

Before addressing this question of poetic vocation directly, however, it is necessary to develop a sense of the specific way the text draws on the Prometheus mythologeme. Who is Prometheus here? How does the text rework the mythological tradition surrounding this figure? We can begin to answer these questions by tracing the implications of the spatial semantics articulated across the magnificent first stanza. The most obvious feature of this semantic structure is the opposition between "heaven" as Zeus's domain ("deinen Himmel," 1) and "earth" as Prometheus's world ("meine Erde," 6). But far more is accomplished here than a constative description of spatial borders. The use of the possessive pronoun "meine" carries the performative force of a declaration of ownership and authority; Prometheus, in violation of an antecedent allocation of proprietary rights, claims the intramundane sphere as his own. The opposition established between "your heaven" and "my earth" transforms the inherited spatial configuration in which heaven and earth are united within a vertically structured hierarchy governed by the divine will, remaps the theological-cosmological schema of authority epitomized, for example, in the Lord's Prayer: "Thy kingdom come, Thy will be done, on earth as it is in heaven."

In this sense, the (illocutionary) act of seizure through which Prometheus lays claim to the terrestrial realm is itself the theft foreseen by the

mythologeme; more accurately, the poem deploys the mythological element of theft as a figure for the act of spatial-proprietary recoding it
accomplishes. This is why the severance of the earthly domain from
heaven is accompanied by a charting of the former according to a pattern
of concentric inclusion, replacing the vertical-hierarchical order of orthodoxy with a set of horizontal relations. From the extreme points of the
visible earth ("Erde," 6), the stanza moves toward a spatial nucleus:
initially to the hut ("Hütte," 8), which, as the first human artifact created
independently of the gods, alludes to Prometheus's mythological role as
the 'founder' of human civilization; then to the center of the hut, the
hearth ("Herd," 9), the glow of which ("Glut," 10) attracts Zeus's envy.[11]
The fire within the hearth, of course, refers citationally to what, according
to the mythologeme, Prometheus stole from Zeus, but it refers to it not in
order to stage yet another variant of the mythological story. On the
contrary, the fire per se is of no interest here; its function is to figure
metaphorically what might be called *the energetic principle of centrality* on
which the new structure of authority affirmed in Prometheus's speech
rests. This figural function of "Herd" and "Glut" becomes fully manifest
when, at the center of the poem's central stanza,[12] the "heilig glühend
Herz" (33) is named. The metaphorical vehicle borrowed from the myth
slides via paronomasia ("Herd"/"Herz") and morphological variation
("Glut"/"glühend") into its tenor. In this way, the mythological figure
'theft of fire' finds its authentic interpretation: the hermeneutic truth of
the theft is the displacement of the extramundane god as the sacred center
of the world and the assumption of that central position by the Promethean subjectivity that establishes itself in the course of the poetic act of
speech. The authority of divinity is usurped by the self-positing, autonomous subject, which is to say, by the "Ich" that, with the last word of the
text, designates itself as the paradigm of a godless, hence free, humanity.

    As this preliminary analysis demonstrates, the aim of the text is not to
represent one or another of the events that constitute the Prometheus
mythologeme. These events (e.g., 'theft of fire') may indeed be alluded to,
but this occurs in order to solicit from them their true meaning (the 'glow'
of subjectivity). That is to say, the text both interprets the inherited myth
and calls attention to this interpretive act. The focus of the text is not the
mythical figuration itself, nor the meaning it attributes to the myth, but
rather the *difference* between them, as well as the *hermeneutic process* that
mediates this difference.[13] At the same time, the text that carries out this

hermeneutic operation presents itself as spoken by Prometheus; the Titan himself lays bare the true meaning of his own story. Once again we encounter the structure of self-inclusion noted with regard to the text's overriding patterns of organization. The text interprets the Prometheus mythologeme as a figure for interpretive activity and in doing so autologically observes its own labor of observation.[14]

One reason that the essentially hermeneutic character of the Prometheus figure has gone unremarked in the secondary literature, I think, is that critics have generally misconstrued the illocutionary force of the first stanza. The matter is sufficiently important to warrant a somewhat technical discussion. A point of consensus among interpreters of the poem, at least those who address the matter at all, is that the speech act accomplished in the first stanza, in particular lines 1–5, is a command that Prometheus directs to Zeus.[15] However, the speech act Prometheus performs here ("Bedecke deinen Himmel, Zeus," 1), although grammatically an imperative, does not at all meet the prerequisites for the illocutionary act of commanding or ordering. One of the conditions constitutive of the illocutionary sense of a command is that the speaker desires what he/she commands to happen. But Prometheus, of course, does not seek to instigate the execution of the actions—the covering of the heavens, the violent lashing of trees and mountain peaks—his speech act anticipates. It would be pointless, even disadvantageous, hazardous, for him to order Zeus to whip up a turbulent storm. The illocutionary force of the imperative here, rather than that of a command or order, is that of a *parodied command*, a speech act that has an altogether different character, above all a different set of presuppositions, than its nonparodistic counterpart. One employs this type of speech act in circumstances in which one is confronted by a threat. The speaker deflects or neutralizes the threat by simulating a command in which the threatened action appears as the object of the speaker's will. This parodied command is then usually followed up by an assertion of one's invulnerability, as if to say: so little does the action you threaten endanger me that I order you to do it. Thus, the basic schema of the parodied command can be exemplified as follows: "Go ahead and do it! You can't hurt me." The illocutionary sequence realized across the first stanza conforms exactly to this pattern.

The reason an accurate specification of the illocutionary act is important to a reading of the first stanza is that the presuppositional structure of the speech act is an aspect, indeed a decisive aspect, of its perspectival sense (what Lessing called its *Gesichtspunkt*). Two components of this structure are especially relevant here. First, the parodied command is *a response to an antecedent threat*. That is to say, insofar as Prometheus parodistically commands Zeus to summon up a storm, to exhibit his might in a meteorological display, he is disarming a threat that had previously terrorized him. The second component involves the attainment of a certain *type of insight*. In and through the parodied command Prometheus indicates not only that he is no longer afraid of the threatened action, but also that he now sees through the action, that he understands it to have been a tactic of intimidation. The stanza as a whole, then, registers both a certain history of fear and an insight into the causes and effects of that fear. The speech act is not an impertinent command (such would amount to a puerile gesture of rebellion inappropriate to the aesthetic and intellectual stature of this text), but rather an apotropaic device through which the subject wards off a past anxiety. Parodistically, Prometheus overcomes his own terror vis-à-vis the meteorological display of violence that had previously held him in thrall. And in doing so, he frees himself from his dependence on the god—Zeus, the thunderer—whose authority rested entirely on the efficacy of the threat.

The disclosure of the parodistic structure of the Promethean illocution reveals why the text operates, as noted above, with a historical component, that is, with a retrospective account of what preceded the speech act itself. The world the poem evokes does not begin at the moment the poem's utterance takes place, but extends backward to a past, a pretime of anxiety and intimidation from which the speech act itself frees the speaking subject. In this sense, the poem positions itself as the peripeteia of the history it at once recounts and participates in. The text dramatizes a moment of hermeneutic insight that enables the subject not only to conquer its fear, but to realize that precisely this fear was the precondition for the order of domination represented by Zeus, or for that matter by any supramundane divine instance. This is why the overriding illocution of the stanza, the parodistic command, is the vehicle for a reorganization of the spatial distribution of authority. Prometheus steals the divine fire and asserts his proprietary rights over the terrestrial domain at the moment when he realizes that a storm, far from being a sign of divine omnipotence, is, well, just a storm.

At the center of the parodied command we encounter a simile that reveals the precise hermeneutic character of the Promethean insight.

Zeus's meteorological demonstration of might, were it to occur, would be tantamount to a boy's acting out his dream of soldierly glory: "dem Knaben gleich, / Der Disteln köpft" (3–4). The simile has been consistently understood as a diminishing caricature with which Prometheus ridicules Zeus by equating his stormy theatrics with the harmless play of a youth. This reading is certainly correct, but it doesn't go far enough. In addition to marking the speaker's disdainful attitude, the simile thematizes its own status as a figure of speech, that is, as a trope that establishes a relationship of similarity between two entities. This is the text's central hermeneutic claim: the thundering god is not only "dem Knaben gleich" in the sense that his power is as diminutive as that of a play-acting boy, but also in the sense that the very image of power embodied in the meteorological show *is a metaphorical projection of a childish consciousness.*[16] It is the childish consciousness which previously was seized with terror vis-à-vis the natural phenomenon of the storm and which, as a result of that terrified state of mind, posited Zeus as the omnipotent agent of cosmic violence. The text exposes, then, the workings of a linguistic-poetic mechanism through which an immature consciousness externalizes its anxiety and in doing so creates the divine order to which it submits itself.[17] The Promethean theft of the divine fire is nothing other than the hermeneutic realization that Zeus, the father god, is a metaphorical hypostasis produced in response to such prodigious, awe- and fear-inspiring natural events as thunder and lightning. Hence, it is not a theft at all, but, rather, the reappropriation of the capacity of metaphorical creativity which was Prometheus's all along. Prometheus's interpretation of the figure of Zeus turns out to be a self-interpretation.

The hermeneutics of divinity elaborated in the first stanza is ramified in the second, the penultimate line of which picks up, with its mention of "Kinder und Bettler" (19), the idea of a childish consciousness implicit in the simile of the boy beheading thistles.[18] The conjoined nouns do not identify two discrete groups, but instead two aspects of humanity in general insofar as it practices religious rites devoted to a transcendent deity, a humanity the final line of the stanza designates as "hopeful fools" ("Hoffnungsvolle Toren," 20).[19] The notion that the gods come into being as a result of metaphorical self-projection thus undergoes a double expansion. First, whereas stanza I locates the source of the metaphorical hypostasis in the affect of fear, stanza II stresses hope as the motivation for religious belief. Second, the biographical idea of 'childhood' is reinscribed in economic terms ('beggar'). The childish consciousness that produces the gods out of its anxiety is an impoverished consciousness that foolishly hopes for relief from its need and deprivation and therefore projects the supramundane agency which would provide such relief. Hence the assertion that there is nothing more impoverished ("nichts ärmers," 12) beneath the sun than the gods: dependent on the beggarly consciousness of a needful humanity, indeed itself nothing but the projection of that need, divinity derives its wealth from those who have no wealth to offer. This economy of reproductive lack is worked out in the middle lines of the stanza in terms of a nutritional metaphor. If the gods "feed" ("nähret," 14) their majesty on the sacrificial taxes and breath of prayer offered them by beggars, it follows that they are nourished precisely by those who are themselves in need of nourishment. The handout they receive (the substanceless taxes and breath) is nothing but the deluded plea for a handout by an impoverished humanity not yet aware of the fact that the real source of abundance lies within itself and not in the heavens. Just as for Hegel the truth of the master is the slave upon whom the former is dependent for recognition, so here the splendor of the gods, their majesty, is the inverted projection of an inadequate self-consciousness.[20]

As this analysis of stanzas I and II reveals, two levels of significance come together in the figure of Prometheus. (1) Prometheus is the figure for the human capacity of linguistic-metaphorical projection. In this sense, he is the creator of Zeus, but this act of creation, born of fear vis-à-vis the prodigious violence of nature and hope that the anguish of need might be alleviated, is carried out without self-awareness, which means that the divine order, although empty of substance, appears to the creative subject as the very paradigm of the real. (2) Prometheus is the figure for the human capacity of hermeneutic insight. He interprets the mythical constellation (the divine order) as the objectification of his own anxiety-ridden, hope-driven, in short 'childish' or 'beggarly' affectivity and thus discloses the 'truth' or 'meaning' of that metaphor, namely the very Promethean subjectivity, the capacity of metaphorical projection, which unconsciously produced it. Between these two levels of significance a temporal or historical relation obtains. The hermeneutic act (2) is that through which the Promethean subject grasps the true nature of its own past and thereby emancipates itself from the self-delusion (1) that characterized this past. Hence, it is the peripeteia of the subject's history, the moment in which the subject hermeneutically appropriates the truth of its anterior projections such that it can now, from this moment into the future, self-consciously exercise its own creativity. But in order for the hermeneutic act to carry conviction, it must be shown by virtue of what process the subject performing that act was able to free itself from self-delusion and attain the level of hermeneutic insight to which it lays claim. This is why stanzas I and II, which I characterized above in the terms of juridical rhetoric as an accusation, are followed by a narrative phase, an account of the sufferance that has led up to the present moment of speech. The arraignment of Zeus, as we have seen, bears on the nonexistence of the god. The narrative component of the juridical argument will validate the accusation by recalling the experiences that prove the delusive character of belief.

~

The consensus in the research on Goethe's "Prometheus" ode, as mentioned at the outset, has it that the text embodies the concept of poetic genius current in the literary-historical phase of the Sturm und Drang. Stated this abstractly, the thesis is unobjectionable, although I would argue that 'genius' is in fact not a concept at all, but a multivalent symbolic position, and that the usual construal of the genius figure as representing an anthropological capacity of creativity is both tautological, in that it merely repeats the claim of the discourse analyzed, and oversimplifying, in that it misses the complexity and internal conflict characteristic of Goethe's theoretical and poetic texts that explore the genius problematic. The readings elaborated in Chapter 5 speak to this debate. My argument here bears on a subsidiary issue, namely, that the understanding of the "Prometheus" ode in terms of the concept of poetic genius is supported by a particular contextualization of the poem, its placement within a series of eighteenth-century texts that likewise refer to the mythological figure of the Titan. This contextualization, first mapped out in 1910 by Oskar Walzel in a book entitled *The Prometheus Symbol from Shaftesbury to Goethe*,[21] continues to set the agenda for discussions of the poem today.[22] Of course, it would be absurd to deny that comparing Goethe's text to others which also draw on the Prometheus mythologeme (especially, I would add, to texts by Rousseau, Wieland, Herder, and Goethe himself[23]) can be illuminating. My contention, rather, is that the series of texts first identified by Walzel is not the only series within which the "Prometheus" ode can be located, indeed that it is not even the most pertinent or revealing series. I want to suggest, in other words, a recontextualization of the poem that discloses paths of reading alternative to the (ultimately

rather vague) *communis opinio* according to which Goethe's poetic reworking of the Prometheus mythologeme reflects the hyperbolic notion
of creativity associated in the secondary literature with the figure of
genius.[24]

Goethe's text participates in (that is to say, both conforms to and
deviates from) an intertextual network that in the eighteenth century
possessed the consistency of a discourse; it engages in an ongoing discussion defined by specific objects, cross-references, analytical positions, and
argumentative strategies. Once this fact is realized, the accusation leveled
at Zeus in the first two stanzas of the ode can be seen to be woven of
commonplaces. The discourse in question is the theory of mythology and
pagan religion elaborated in the writings of the Enlightenment phi-
losophes. As Frank Manuel, the preeminent historian of this discourse, has
shown in *The Eighteenth Century Confronts the Gods*,[25] the Enlightenment
replaced the philological and etymological monuments of baroque erudition regarding mythology (as represented, for example, by the Jesuit father
Athanasius Kircher) with a theory of religious origins that was articulated
in three variants: a euhemerist historical theory that interpreted the gods as
actual persons who, because of some major accomplishment such as an
invention or heroic deed, were subsequently apotheosized; a deist theory
of natural religion that posited an innate monotheistic belief and thus
treated polytheism, as well as much of Christian orthodoxy, as a fall away
from the natural and true religious conception; and a psychological theory
that endeavored to explain the origin of the gods and of religious belief in
terms of the affective economy of primitive man. Goethe's "Prometheus"
ode is tributary to the last-mentioned school.

The cornerstone of the psychological theory (we can recognize here the
scenario limned in the opening stanza of "Prometheus") is already in place
in Pierre Bayle's *Various Thoughts on the Comet* (1680): "Thunder filled
men with great terror because in their ignorance of rational causes they
could only interpret the horrendous sounds as indications of a god's
wrath."[26] More influential than Bayle during the eighteenth century was
Bernard Fontenelle, whose *History of Oracles* (1686) and *Discourse on the
Origin of Fables* (1724) provided the conceptual armature for subsequent
theories of primitive mentality. In the same year as Fontenelle's *Discourse*,
the ethnographic equation between ancient paganism and primitive superstition was solidified in Joseph François Lafitau's *Manners of the American Savages Compared with Manners of the First Age*, and a year later

perhaps the greatest work in this discursive tradition (which, however, it transcends in several respects), Giambattista Vico's *The New Science*, appeared in its first edition, achieving its final form nineteen years later, in 1744. Vico's dense, boldly speculative work found in the subsequent decade its symmetrical counterpart in the pellucid, provocative, and short treatise entitled "The Natural History of Religion" which David Hume published in his collection of *Four Dissertations* in 1757.

The discursive tradition continued through the 1760's: parts of Hume's treatise were incorporated into the text by Charles de Brosses to which we owe the concept of fetishism, *Of the Cult of the Two Fetishes, or the Parallel Between the Ancient Religion of Egypt and the Present Religion of Nigritia* (1760), and in 1766 Diderot wrote a supportive preface to the posthumous work of Nicolas-Antoine Boulanger, *Antiquity Revealed Through Its Customs, or A Critical Examination of the Principal Opinions, Ceremonies, and Religious Institutions and of the Politics of the Different Peoples of the Earth*, in which geological evidence is adduced to support a variant of the fear theory. By the time Goethe composed the "Prometheus" ode in 1774, the anti-Christian potential of the discourse on the origin of the gods was being vigorously exploited in atheistic tracts by Baron de Holbach such as *Sacred Contagion: or, the Natural History of Superstition* (1768), *The System of Nature, or, Of the Laws of the Physical World and the Moral World* (1770), and *Common Sense: Ideas about Nature Opposed to Supernatural Ideas* (1772). The first chapter of *Contagion sacrée*, the full title of which pays homage to Hume, informs us, as Bayle already had, that terror motivates religious superstition.[27]

The discursive consistency of the Enlightenment theory of divine origins derives from at least the following seven features, all of which but the last bear obvious relevance to Goethe's text.

(a) An ethnographic and life-historical framing of the question of religious origins in terms of an equation between primitive mentality (as described in the travel literature from the New World), childhood mentality (which, of course, is one of the great themes of the eighteenth century) and the mentality of the ancients: the narrative organization of "Prometheus" as a movement from 'childhood' to 'manhood' derives from the widely accepted thesis that myth is born of the childhood of humanity.

(b) A causal hypothesis according to which fear vis-à-vis incomprehensible prodigies of nature (violent thunderstorms, earthquakes, volcanoes,

etc.) led to the postulation of a divine agency responsible for and expressing its anger through those phenomena: the meteorological demonstration
of divine might that Prometheus's parodied command evokes cites the
major topos of the terror-inspiring natural event.

(c) A figurational hypothesis according to which the gods are formed by
projecting anthropomorphic features onto the unknown: this notion of
projection motivates Goethe's use of the simile "like a boy / Beheading
thistles" and is most explicitly developed, as we shall see, in stanza III.

(d) A network of references to antecedent authorities, in particular to
the authors of classical antiquity—Lucian, Lucretius, Sextus Empiricus,
Cicero—in whose work the fear theory and the critique of religious
practices are preformed: Goethe's reliance on Lucian conforms to this
convention of citation.[28]

(e) A dual pathos of unveiling and critical exposure on the one hand
and of emancipation on the other: the polemical thrust of these texts,
obviously shared by the "Prometheus" ode, is to free man from his
delusions.

(f) A tendency to overflow, implicitly or explicitly, the thematic limitation to polytheism and ancient myth and to subvert aspects of Christianity: Lessing, of course, recognized this aspect of Goethe's poem very
clearly.

(g) A circumscription of the observer's or analyst's standpoint according to the opposition 'enlightened' mentality vs. 'primitive' ('superstitious') mentality: this is the aspect of the discourse that Goethe most
decisively transforms.

The elaboration of these seven discursive components constitutes what
Manuel calls "one of the great intellectual revolutions of the age,"[29] and
Goethe's "Prometheus" ode, I will claim, belongs among the most significant contributions to this revolution. If this contextualization of the poem
is accepted, however, then clearly the interpretation bearing on the concept of productive artistic genius must be modified so as to accommodate a
hermeneutic dimension (critique of antecedent religious belief). My commentary on the poem's first section laid the groundwork for such an
argument.

To solicit the specificity of Goethe's text within its discursive context,
however, closer comparisons are required. In terms of intellectual and

literary stature, the two works that equal Goethe's are those by Vico and Hume. Vico's passionately felt vision of the *giganti*, who imagine that their Jove "by the whistling of his bolts and the noise of his thunder was attempting to tell them something" and thus cast their eyes to heaven for the first time, calling the god into being, anticipates remarkably the violent storm of Goethe's first stanza.[30] But Vico's theory of providence bears little relevance to the "Prometheus" ode, and in the eighteenth century the *New Science* was little known outside Italy. For these reasons, Hume's "Natural History," which enjoyed an international reputation, provides a better point of comparison. Moreover, certain facets of this essay prove highly suggestive for a reading of the "Prometheus" poem.

Hume's argument rests on a distinction between the question of religion's foundation in reason on the one hand and the question of its origin in human nature on the other. Regarding the first, Hume declares adherence to the "primary principles of genuine Theism and Religion," according to which the "whole frame of nature bespeaks an intelligent author."[31] Of course, precisely this teleological argument is demolished in the profoundly ironic *Dialogues Concerning Natural Religion*, written contemporaneously with the "Natural History" but published only after Hume's death, and in fact the profession of theism is merely a device for disencumbering the inquiry into religious origins of dogmatic contentiousness. The issue that interests Hume is not doctrine, but human nature, the psychological and affective economy with regard to which religion can be said to have a describable "natural history." At the same time, the methodological separation of truth and history has substance for Hume's historical account. True religion presents itself only to philosophical contemplation informed by a knowledge of the intricate interconnections among natural phenomena and by abstract ratiocination, luxuries of a secure existence not available to primitive man. Hence the absurdity of the concept of a naturally or originally true religion. Theism is the privilege of a civilizationally advanced age, and even then it is attained by relatively few.

Hume's central thesis, then, is that religion originates as a derivative or, as he writes, "secondary" (107) phenomenon, that there is no religious instinct or innate religious intuition, but instead a history which, due to specific conditions of existence and by virtue of specific affective and cognitive mechanisms, can occur, and has occurred, along various itineraries. The central conditioning factor for the generation of religious concepts, in Hume's view, is the unyielding exigence of primitive life. Besieged by the pressing demands of his needful condition, the "barbarous, necessitous animal" man was at the "first origin of society" (111) lives in an agitated sense of his own endangerment. He is, in a strong inflection of the term, preoccupied by a perpetually urgent concern for his immediate future, and this future-oriented alertness to possible threats, this unceasing attention to the problem of survival, determines the affective economy out of which belief is born. Hume's innovation vis-à-vis both his ancient and his eighteenth-century predecessors is to identify the sponsoring passion of religious concepts not merely as fear, but also as hope. The "Dissertation on the Passions" (also published in *Four Dissertations*) points out the affinity of these two future-directed affects, their tendency to slide into one another, and the "Natural History" ascribes to them joint, if slightly unequal, responsibility for the emergence of the gods. In Hume's delicately poised prose: "Agitated by hopes and fears of this nature, especially the latter, men scrutinize, with a trembling curiosity, the course of future causes, and examine the various contrary events of human life. And in this disordered scene, with eyes still more disordered and astonished, they see the first obscure traces of divinity" (116).

Hume's argument regarding fear and hope (as opposed to merely the former) suggests a strong affinity to the "Prometheus" ode insofar as the accusation of Zeus and his entourage is structured in terms of the identical affective pair. The parodied command of the first stanza exposes the antecedent terror that instigated belief in the god and the denunciation of the second stanza declares the gods' dependence on the necessitous existence of "Hoffnungsvolle Toren." Nor is this the only point of tangency between the two texts. Hume's characterization of the eye that first discerns divinity as "disordered" resembles Goethe's "verirrtes Auge" (23) in stanza III and the gesture of looking toward the heavens that stanza narrates likewise appears to echo Hume's projectionist account: "The absurdity [of the tendency among mankind to conceive all beings like themselves] is not less, while we cast our eyes upwards; and transferring, as is too usual, human passions and infirmities to the deity, represent him as jealous and revengeful, capricious and partial, and, in short, a wicked and foolish man, in every respect but his superior power and authority" (118). Moreover, Hume's construction of the natural history of religion notes that fear and hope are typically awakened by alarming exceptions to the normal course of things, by prodigious natural events such as "storms and tempests" (114), and that religious sacrifice amounts to a pseudo-economic transaction, a "mercenary devotion" (148) akin to Goethe's "Opfersteuern" (15). But these points are not unique to Hume, and it is therefore impossible to decide, in the absence of other philological evidence, whether the scene of religious origins Goethe's text adumbrates derives from a reading of the "Natural History" or from a reservoir of anonymous discursive commonplaces, some of which, of course, were invented by Hume. The coupling of fear and hope (including the slight weighting of the former) strikes me as the most forceful evidence of Hume's influence, whether direct or indirect, focused or diffuse, on Goethe's text.[32]

One of the most remarkable features of the "Prometheus" ode—a feature that I have yet to discuss in any detail—is the fact that it deploys a pagan mythologeme in the service of a religious critique aimed not only at the Greek conception of Zeus but also, still more devastatingly, at Christianity. This is an issue that I will take up subsequently; I mention it here merely to make the point that Hume's "Natural History" bears cognate implications. One of Hume's major contentions, developed roughly across the second half of his essay, is that contemporary Christianity is as much suffused with superstition as ancient or primitive polytheism. Since the two belief systems are equally deluded, the question that arises in comparing them is not which is truer, but which is more beneficial to human life. Hume identifies certain aspects of polytheism that qualify it as the preferable religion. Polytheism allows for several gods, even foreign gods, and is therefore more conducive to tolerance. It encourages heroic virtues rather than the self-abasement typical of Christian saints, and, being less dogmatic, it is less inclined to absurdity. The heathen gods are more on a par with man. They too obey destiny (an idea that Goethe likewise cites[33]), and man can even contend with them, ward them off. Finally, polytheistic belief is worn lightly (Hume even calls it a type of atheism): its tales are entertaining; it is "a true poetical religion" (162). In short, Hume's view that the mythological world order is both less invasive and more enlivening than the superstition-ridden Christianity of eighteenth-century Europe opens up the possibility that mythologemes of polytheism be employed to dismantle what Lessing called the "orthodox concepts of divinity." This critical potential residing in the Enlightenment discourse on religious origins is exploited in Goethe's poem.

However compelling, the recontextualization of the "Prometheus" ode with regard to Hume and the Enlightenment discourse on religious origins calls forth an important objection: Goethe's text is, after all, a poem, not a theoretical or critical tract, and it is therefore separated from the context in which I have placed it by a considerable discursive divide. This objection in fact formulates a task of inquiry. We need to ask how it was possible that the figures of thought endemic to the Enlightenment mythographic discourse were redeployed in a poetic text and in what ways that discourse was altered by such redeployment. The question is: What is the specificity of Goethe's poetic transformation of the discursive tradition he draws on? The path toward an answer to this question leads via Herder.

Among Herder's papers is a series of notes from 1766 that consists in a chapter-by-chapter summary of Hume's "Natural History."[34] These notes mark one of the most significant gates through which Hume's thought entered the intellectual milieu of the German-speaking lands. Like his teacher, Kant, Herder experienced Hume's work as a kind of conceptual ferment, and in the years immediately following his reading of the "Natural History," he undertook a reworking of Hume's argument that decisively shifts its theoretical accents. Several texts document this process, the most significant of which, at least in relation to Goethe's "Prometheus" ode, is the fragmentary "Essay Toward a History of Lyric Poetry."[35] There can be no doubt that this text, although it doesn't explicitly name the Scottish philosopher, transfers Hume's hypothesis regarding the origin of polytheism (which is to say, of religion in general) to the historiography of poetry. Herder's essay elaborates a natural history of poetry that ascribes to the lyric the same scene of origination Hume had evoked for religious concepts. Hence the following summary statement of Herder's thesis:

> Everything taken together, one sees: sacred poetry sprouted from the ground of the primitive [raw] mode of thought, beneath the shadow of ignorance, driven forth by fear and hope; it *painted actions*, was intended to *save from evil destinies*, and through *flattery to gain good fortune*; an origin which is appropriate to the beginning of peoples, to the history of human intellect, and to the majority of cases.[36]

Herder's divergence from Hume involves, then, a reformulation of the question asked. At issue is no longer the invention of what Hume called religious principles (essentially, conceptions of divinity), but the emergence of a form of discourse. The constitution of the gods occurs within a particular type of linguistic address: "Now, the first prayers must have been *songs*."[37] Religious conceptions are the creations of an originary poeticizing, of a primordial lyric form, a "Gesang an die Götter" ("song to the gods") that Herder calls "Hymnus" ("hymn").[38]

Of course, Herder's reinterpretation is prepared in Hume's text, which adduces "the frequency and beauty of the *prosopopoeia* in poetry" as evidence of the "universal tendency among mankind to conceive all beings like themselves,"[39] but in fact the two writers employ radically heterogeneous concepts of what poetry is. Hume thinks of poetry as a fanciful entertainment, a charmingly artful discourse that pleases because it gives free play to the psychological mechanism of anthropomorphic projection. The poetry Herder thematizes, however, is the originary language in which the religious self-understanding of a people (*Volk*) is articulated. Thus, an evaluational shift begins to profile itself in Herder's text: the originary scene, which for Hume is the birthplace of superstition out of hope and fear, acquires the dignity of poetic achievement. Noting that the depiction of the gods and nature in the earliest texts always tends toward "living action,"[40] Herder makes a concession hardly imaginable in the discourse of Enlightenment mythography: "Hier hat der Ursprung der Dichtkunst freilich vieles vor uns voraus"[41] ("In this regard to be sure, the origin of poetry is a great deal ahead of us"). From the perspective of Herder's inquiry, such negative categories as error, need, and ignorance, in terms of which Hume and his predecessors unmasked religious origins, recede into irrelevance, and primitiveness becomes the guarantee of a vital, experientially rooted poetry before which modern poetic art pales. Similarly useless in Herder's view is the category of morality: primitive poetry is "not moralistic, but merely sensate,"[42] a linguistic formation in which the affective-perceptual complexity and richness of immediate experience achieves objectification as song.[43]

The poeticization of the origin is accompanied in Herder's early texts by a second displacement that bears both on the constitution of the object examined and on the analytic standpoint of the observer. The findings of the Enlightenment mythographers, Hume included, pertain to misrepresentations—for example, the use of anthropomorphic metaphors, which can be recognized as such because they deviate from a representation of the world held to be timelessly true, even if it took time and reflection to discover it. From this perspective, all myths and superstitions can be said to be the same; they all document identical mechanisms of misrepresentation. To be sure, the myths of various peoples reveal traits (contents) peculiar to them alone, but these are the result of accidental factors and therefore without intrinsic interest. With Herder, however, precisely these individual features, in their internal coherence, become the focus of the analysis. The task is no longer to identify mechanisms of deviation from the truth, but to grasp the individual forms of poetic self-articulation that various myths evince. Note that this perspective contains a universalist component, precisely the capacity of poetic self-articulation, but the decisive feature of this capacity is that it is inevitably realized in historically individuated formations through which alone it can be apprehended. Rather than enumerating mechanisms of misrepresentation from an external perspective, then, Herder endeavors to understand from within characteristic actualizations of a subjective capacity. His is a hermeneutic-historical enterprise.

A second fragment from the late sixties entitled "Von den ältesten Nationalgesängen"[44] ("On the Oldest National Songs") already reveals the directions that Herder's hermeneutic-historical reinterpretation of Enlightenment mythography will take in the ensuing decade. Once again, the starting point is a theory of the affective actuation of religious concepts, this time with explicit reference to Hume,[45] and Herder's insistence on the poetic form of these concepts is equally clear. But the thematic center of the sketch is the gradual formation of individual national identities within the medium of poetic "Urkunden,"[46] a term that combines the notion of foundational historical document with that of sacred authority. To sense the resonance of the term, one need only recall that the title of perhaps Herder's greatest work of interpretation, *Aelteste Urkunde des Menschengeschlechts*[47] (*The Oldest Document of the Human Race*) employs it to designate the account of Creation in the Book of Genesis. In fact, "On the Oldest National Songs" is one of the first in a series of preliminary essays that eventually achieved completion with the publication of the first volume of *The Oldest Document* in 1774, the year the "Prometheus" ode was composed.[48] As noted previously, the Enlightenment theory of mythology and superstition tends to spill over into a critique of Christianity. Much the same can be said of the hermeneutic-historical transformation of this discourse in Herder's early work, with, however, an important restriction: the critical edge of the Enlightenment theory, its pathos of demystification, is gradually replaced by what might be termed an anthropological affirmation. For Herder, all the "Nationalgesänge," all the mythic "Urkunden," document the marvel of human self-creation in poetry.

With this sketch of Herder's reinterpretation of Hume, the problem involved in my recontextualization of Goethe's "Prometheus" ode with regard to the Enlightenment theory of religious beginnings is solved. Once the scene of the origin is viewed as a poetic act, the discursive divide between theory and poetry becomes irrelevant. Thus, Goethe's text can be conceived as assuming a position between Hume and Herder: with the former, it shares the critical, antiorthodox impetus of the Enlightenment discourse on myth, the commonplaces of which it repeats; with the latter, it construes myth as the poetic self-articulation of mankind. Recalling Herder's designation of the originary lyric form as "Hymnus," one could say that Goethe's text is an "Anti-Hymnus,"[49] a song that repeats the gesture of the first religious hymns, but does so in such a way as to dismantle the superstitious content of those hymns and to disclose and appropriate hermeneutically the capacity of poetic self-formation to which they testify. Hence the dual significance of the Prometheus figure as: (1) the child Prometheus, who, actuated by the passions of fear and hope, poetically constitutes the mythological order; (2) the man Prometheus, who poetically interprets those delusions and thereby establishes a new "Urkunde des Menschengeschlechts" grounded in subjective autonomy. Such is the poetic vocation the "Prometheus" ode, or anti-hymn, claims for itself.

The specificity of Goethe's text is revealed by comparing it not only with the discourse on mythology that preceded it, but also with subsequent developments. Here I can only refer in passing to two texts that strike me as especially relevant. The first of these is Karl Phillip Moritz's *Doctrine of the Gods* of 1795.[50] At first glance, Moritz's little book hardly seems a theoretical contribution, consisting as it does of a simple retelling of various stories of the gods, but in fact the theoretical importance of the work is considerable. To see this point, one need only compare Moritz's text with Benjamin Hederich's *Complete Mythological Lexicon* in the edition of 1770, the reference work from which Goethe undoubtedly drew most of the details of the Prometheus mythologeme he alludes to in the ode. Whereas Hederich's work is a dictionary, each entry of which lists the various etymologies of the gods' names, their genealogies, the events associated with them, possible historical sources for the myths, and the diverse meanings (allegorical significations) attributed to them, Moritz's *Doctrine of the Gods* treats ancient mythology as an autonomous "language of phantasy."[51] Mythology is extricated from the bookish world of erudition and relocated within the human psyche. The myths no longer appear as a haphazard collection of vehicles for the signification of physical, historical, moral, or theological meanings; they in fact have no meaning extraneous to their own articulation as an imaginary language. This view is close to that of Herder, who repudiated the decoding of mythology with reference to extra-mythological meanings and attempted to grasp its incipience in the historical experience of a nation or people. The decisive difference between Herder and Moritz is that for the latter the historicity proper to myth is internal to myth itself. His *Doctrine of the Gods*, that is to say, not only retells the various myths, but also integrates them within an overriding narrative. The "language of phantasy" that mythology articulates has the form of a single story that progresses from obscure and formless beginnings to the beautiful individuality of the Olympians, then recedes into the shapelessness of night and death. Mythology, in this totalizing view, is a unified narrative that reflects the *morphogenesis of subjectivity*, and each of the various mythologemes marks a distinct phase of this morphogenesis.

Moritz's interpretation of myth as charting the history of self-becoming casts a retrospective light on the "Prometheus" ode in that Goethe's rendering of the mythologeme endows the figure of Prometheus with a certain awareness of myth as reflecting the history of the subject (a point to which I shall return). Thus, it is not only due to Moritz's personal admiration of Goethe that he cites the "Prometheus" poem in its entirety in the *Doctrine of the Gods*, but also to call attention to the fact that the text registers a particular phase within the narrative of individuation he is unfolding.

Moritz's aestheticizing account of mythic history, however, lacks the critical edge and emancipatory pathos that characterizes Goethe's reworking of the Prometheus figure and that derives, as we have seen, from the Enlightenment discourse on myth. This dimension of the problematic returns only much later in the lectures entitled *Philosophy of Mythology* that Schelling first delivered in Berlin in 1842.[52] Schelling's tautegorical notion of mythical meaning, the notion that myth signifies not something extraneous, but the very process that brings it forth, bears an obvious similarity to Moritz's conception (though Schelling does not cite him). In fact, Schelling's entire philosophy of mythology can be conceived as an idealist reworking of Moritz's narrative account, with the difference that the narrative totalization undertaken assumes world-historical dimensions.[53] Ancient myth and the Christian revelation are integrated by Schelling into a three-stage process at the end of which philosophical religion stands as the final manifestation of the truth of God. I cannot discuss here the elaborate metaphysical doctrine of potencies or the theory of unconscious production upon which Schelling's theory rests. The single point I want to make is that the origin of myth conceived by the Enlightenment theoreticians, the anthropomorphic projection of the gods actuated by fear and hope, becomes for Schelling the positional act (*Setzung* in the language of idealist philosophy) performed by the transcendental subject, which, across the entire history of myth and religion, gradually comes to a realization of its own identity with the divine principle. The dynamic internal to myth, which for Schelling is the inner truth of history itself, is the overcoming of myth.

It would, of course, be absurd to argue that Goethe's "Prometheus" ode rests on a historico-philosophical construction as metaphysically saturated as Schelling's *Philosophy of Mythology* or that his text in any way shares the idealist-Christian standpoint of the lectures. But a comparison between the two texts is nonetheless illuminating, insofar as Schelling's construction, like Goethe's, is based on the notion of a reappropriation of the subjectivity alienated from itself by its own mythic self-understanding. Within this schema Prometheus assumes a key functional position: "Prometheus is the thought in which mankind, after it had brought forth the entire world of the gods out of its internality, returning to itself became conscious of itself and of its destiny (the unhappiness of belief in the gods [*das Unselige des Götterglaubens*])."[54] In this passage, Schelling attributes to a mythological figure not only a particular role within myth, but an awareness of the mythological process. The Promethean rebellion is directed against the order of myth itself, so that Prometheus becomes, as Hans Blumenberg points out, the prefiguration of the philosophical interpreter in whom the truth of myth is disclosed.[55] For Goethe too, as we have seen, the figure of Prometheus bears a dual significance, hermeneutically disclosing the truth of the very mythological order it adheres to. In both cases, the mythological figure is endowed with a critical consciousness of the historical process it participates in, and this position—at once inside and outside the myth—endows both poem and philosophical interpretation with a kind of paradoxical intricacy. However, a major difference between Schelling and Goethe must also be remarked. Schelling's Prometheus remains chained to the rock of his agony. He grasps the nature of the theogonic process, but this realization only eventuates in suffering, and it remains to another mythological figure (Heracles) and ultimately to other, postmythological realizations of divinity (first Christianity, then philosophical religion) to liberate him. Goethe allows Prometheus to free himself and, in doing so, to free mankind from what Schelling calls "das Unselige des Götterglaubens." The act accomplishing this historical emancipation from myth is the Promethean "Anti-Hymnus," the peripeteia of history.

~

Returning to the text after this excursus, I will begin my remarks on the middle or narrative section by considering certain numerical regularities governing the arrangement of stanzas within the poem as a whole. Such regularities, as I will show in the following chapter with regard to "Harzreise im Winter" ("Hartz Journey in Winter"), can bear a semantic function insofar as they point to specific relations of similarity and juxtaposition. The compositional patterning of the "Prometheus" ode does not organize the deployment of meaningful units in as rigorous a manner as in "Harzreise im Winter," but it does exhibit a certain semantic-rhetorical blocking (in the sense that one blocks the movements of the actors when staging a drama), the precision of which has gone unnoticed in the research. The distribution of lines per stanza in the poem is as follows:

I	II	III	IV	V	VI	VII
11	9	7	9	9	5	7

No thoroughgoing regularity seems to govern this allocation of number of verses to stanzas. To be sure, three stanzas of nine and two stanzas of seven verses occur, suggesting a rule of recurrence, but the first and penultimate stanzas are without numerical parallel. If we consult an earlier version of the text, however, the deviant character of stanzas I and VI dissolves. In that version, line 8 above ("Und meine Hütte, die du nicht gebaut") is written as two lines:

> Und meine Hütte
> Die du nicht gebaut,[56]

Whatever the motivation for combining the two lines into one (perhaps the relative clause was felt to carry too little semantic weight to warrant an independent line, perhaps the intention was more tightly to fuse the semantic unit 'hut' with its qualification[57]), it is clear that the alteration sacrificed a highly visible pattern of line-to-stanza distribution. With its extra line, that is to say, the earlier version exhibits the following arrangement:

I	II	III	IV	V	VI	VII
12	9	7	9	9	5	7
(5 + 7)						

Viewed in this way, the poem consists of five-line, seven-line, and nine-line units, all of which are repeated at least once, and which can be seen to configure in two ways. With regard to the rhetorical parsing sketched at the outset, the narrative block (stanzas III–VI) appears as an expansion of the accusation (I–II) formed by splitting apart the seven- and five-line components of stanza I and setting them at the beginning and end of the segment, and by reiterating the nine-line unit:

accusation: $(5 + 7) + 9$

narrative: $7 + 9 + 9 + 5$

A second numerical correlation can be seen to obtain between the beginning and end of the entire text:

Stanza I	Stanzas VI & VII
(5 + 7)	5 + 7

This sort of salient correlation encourages a comparison (cross-reading) of the units involved, and, indeed, beginning and end prove to be related to one another in other respects, as we shall see.[58] The numerical patterning, while not yielding a univocal compositional structure, does predispose the reading of the text along definite lines. The hinge of the two different configurations noted here is stanza VI, which from one perspective is joined with the three stanzas preceding it to form the narrative unit of the text, and from another perspective is linked with the final stanza to constitute a conclusion that is the symmetrical counterpart of the opening stanza. Stanza VI simultaneously belongs to two different compositional blocks; its compositional function is thus determined (hence overdetermined) by two different sets of relations.[59] Reading the text as a palimpsest in which the stanzaic composition of the earlier versions shows through allows us to identify patterns of arrangement that, were the version of 1789 considered in isolation, might have gone unperceived. In particular, it enables us to see that, contrary to the traditional view according to which the ode dispenses with symmetrical patterning for the sake of expressive immediacy, the text complexifies composition, generating a polyvalent determination of its units.[60]

Compositional precision will prove to be a characteristic of what I have been calling the narrative block of the poem as well, but before laying out the symmetries involved in that section we must acquire a more textured sense of what is being narrated here, and how. Stanza III initiates this portion of the rhetorical argument:

> Da ich ein Kind war,
> Nicht wußte wo aus noch ein,
> Kehrt' ich mein verirrtes Auge
> Zur Sonne, als wenn drüber wär'
> Ein Ohr zu hören meine Klage,
> Ein Herz wie mein's,
> Sich des Bedrängten zu erbarmen.
>
> *(21–27)*

The stanza forms a single syntactic unit that arrays three semantic components: an act (the turning of the confused eye toward the sun); a condition prompting that act (the helplessness of childhood); and a motivation for the act (the—of course, erroneous—supposition that above the sun a kindred being exists that would take pity on and therefore alleviate the anguish of the distressed child). The delineation of act, condition, and motivation provides an analysis of mythical meaning entirely in conformity with the eighteenth-century discourse on the origin of the gods. The turning of the eye toward the sun is not a singular event, but a paradigmatic gesture epitomizing the child's stance in the world, literally its *Gesichtspunkt.* This standpoint can be called belief in the existence of a supramundane ("drüber") divine being. By figuring belief narratively, Prometheus construes the god as the product of an operation he himself, as child, performed. The action of turning the eye toward the sun is the action through which the god is constituted, thereby instituting the theological relation as a perduring structure of dependency; it inaugurates a historico-philosophical chapter—call it the theological epoch—in the history of mankind.[61]

The time-marker of the sentence ("Da ich ein Kind war") hooks up with the phrase "Kinder und Bettler" (19) in the penultimate line of the preceding stanza, indicating that what that stanza describes as a group condition—the inadequate consciousness of a childish and impoverished humanity—is now being integrated within a narrative, that is to say, historical, account. However, the conditioning factor Prometheus recalls is not merely the abstractly defined situation of childhood, it is also a state of nonknowledge ("Nicht wußte," 22), and in particular a nonknowledge as to where to go ("wo aus noch ein," 22). The latter phrase signifies, of course, an anxious disorientation, a state of desperate distress of the sort often characterized in English as "not knowing where to turn." This is why the final line of the stanza describes the troubled child as the "Bedrängten" (27).[62] It is important to note, however, that the phrase figures this distress in spatial terms, thereby connecting with the spatial semantics remarked with regard to the first stanza. Not knowing "wo aus noch ein," the child is confronted with a disorganized space. It has no bearings, no orientation or reference point, and this lack of spatial order is precisely the condition that prompts or necessitates the projection of the god. That projection, therefore, is not merely delusionary, it is also functional; it endows the chaotic world with a spatial order, centers that world in the supramundane deity 'above the sun,' and thereby allows the projecting subject provisionally to manage its distress.[63] In this sense, the god posited as dwelling above the sun is, as the second stanza states (the contrast should not go unnoticed), "unter der Sonn'" (13), a functional unit within the earthly field of human activity. The hermeneutic insight into the conditions of production and the functional efficacy of the mythic order is thus equivalent to a remapping of the semantics of space, exactly the operation that, as we have seen, is carried out in the movement of the first stanza from "Erde" to "Hütte" to "Herd."

The third component of the stanza's analysis of mythic meaning bears on the hypothesis that motivates the constitutive act of belief, the projective glance heavenward. Prometheus's act rests on the supposition that above the sun there is an ear to hear (and, implicitly, a being to respond to) his lament, that there is a heart like his to take pity on his distressed condition. By marking this assumption, the narrative points up the fact that the act of belief obeys a logic of similitude. Of course, in speaking of logic I am not implying that the act constitutive of belief follows from an inferential process; there can be no question but that, arising as it does from anguished duress, the upward look is an unreflective movement. The

point, rather, is that the act is not random, that it is grounded in human
nature, that it conforms to what Hume called the "universal tendency
among mankind to conceive all beings like themselves, and to transfer to
every object, those qualities, with which they are familiarly acquainted,
and of which they are intimately conscious."[64] Prometheus, representative
of the childhood of man, is most intimately conscious of his eye, his ear,
his heart, and it is this set of features he attributes to the world's ruler above
the sun. The process of anthropomorphic projection implied in the simile
of the boy beheading thistles here finds its retrospective, hermeneutic
explication.

The stanza specifies that the anthropomorphic hypothesis draws on two
features of the human being. First, the act constitutive of divinity, the act
figured as an upward turning of the eye, is likewise the projection of "an
ear to hear my lament." The idea here is not that the anguished child first
supposes that there exists such an ear and then directs its lament toward it,
but, rather, that the speech act of lamenting constitutes the god as its
implicit auditor. We have already seen, with regard to the simile of the boy
beheading thistles, that the hermeneutics of divinity the text develops
includes a linguistic component; the passage before us, however, makes
clear that the operative similitude of the projective hypostasis (what might
be called the originary metaphor) is drawn from the communicative
structure of language, from the presupposition of an existent addressee
that is implied in every act of speech. One could speak here of a thetic
force that inheres within the apostrophe to the god, of a vocative power
that, as "Hymnus" or "Gesang an die Götter" in Herder's terminology,
summons the god into being and institutes the theological schema. This
notion bears important consequences for the text as a whole, suggesting
that humanity, as long as it directs its lament toward a supramundane
being, has not found its proper addressee, that the emancipation of
humanity can only occur through a poetic act in which humanity addresses, and in so doing constitutes, itself. The action through which
humanity will be created, called into being as a free humanity, is an act of
speech.

The second feature to which I want to call attention is the heavenly
'heart' presupposed in the act of belief. The function attributed to this
heart is that of taking pity or, in a translation that is more faithful to the
Goethean term "erbarmen" (27), of showing mercy. As Conrady has

pointed out, this term bears a strong Christian connotation and therefore
hints that the divinity dismantled in this text is not only Zeus, but likewise
the Christian god.[65] This, of course, was the thrust of Lessing's contention that "orthodox concepts of divinity" are no longer valid from the
Gesichtspunkt the poem assumes, and my earlier reference to the vertical-
hierarchical order of space embodied in the Lord's Prayer, that order which
the Promethean speech act overturns, also touched on the anti-Christian
isotopy of the text. But I want to postpone discussion of the question of
Christianity until we reach the final stanza and accentuate instead the fact
that the similitude projected in the act of belief bears on the organ, the
heart, that figures the center of Promethean subjectivity. The god is, as
noted earlier, a distorted self-representation, a misconstrual of the true
nature of human autonomy. The heart projected 'above the sun' is in
truth—but a truth falsely understood—the heart of humanity.

If we take these two aspects of the theological hypothesis together—the
misdirection of address and the misapprehension of the heart—the internal coherence of the poetic argument emerges into view. For what happens
in the course of the narrative is that Prometheus's own heart becomes the
addressee of the poem: "Hast du nicht alles selbst vollendet, / Heilig
glühend Herz?" (32–33).[66] The task the poem sets for itself is not merely to
eliminate the orthodox concepts of divinity, but also to disclose a mode of
speech in which humanity addresses itself, as it were, heart to heart. To
achieve this mode of address is the aim of the Promethean program. The
ambition of the poem before us is to turn history around by establishing a
post-theological language in and through which an emancipated mankind
would call itself into being. In this sense, the poem would be the peripeteia
in the history of humanity, the self-appellation of mankind.

The question of poetic address is clearly a central one, but we are still
concerned with the structuration of the poem's narrative segment. As we
have just seen, stanza III figures the act of projection that constitutes
childish belief and thereby installs the initial phase—the epoch of theological dependency—within the narrative process that the text as a whole
articulates. The final phase of the narrative, a state that can only be
projected as a futurity, is the epoch of an autonomous humanity. The
speech act carried out in the poem marks the turning point of this saga of
emancipation insofar as it discloses the hermeneutic truth of the theological delusion, thereby freeing mankind from that delusion, hence to itself.

But this peripeteia does not enter the world of the text miraculously. It is prepared, or perhaps earned, across a temporal process, and this process— the intermediate phase between childhood and emancipatory act—is related in the remainder of what I have been calling the text's narrative component (stanzas IV–VI). Rather than recounting a chronological series of events, the text unleashes a cascade of (mostly) rhetorical questions that refer to a reservoir of remembered occurrences without any effort to fix the temporal location of, or causal connections among, those occurrences. This strategy has to do with the juridical function of the narrative component. The rhetorical aim here is to prove the legitimacy of the accusation and, since that accusation bears precisely on the nonexistence of the god, past events are cited only insofar as they demonstrate the anti-theological claim.

A cursory glance at the three stanzas suffices to discern the thoroughgoing parallelism of their organization. Stanza IV opens with two questions that are variants of the same type (both are who questions; both demand the negative answer "no one"). These are followed by a negatively formulated question that requires the answer "yes." And this is succeeded by a question that asks of its addressee (the "heart") whether it performed a particular action, namely the deluded "glowing" of gratitude to the sleeping god. Altogether, then, stanza IV deploys three types of question in a series that can be abbreviated as: *A A B C*.

Turning now to stanza V, we encounter in the opening line two brief interrogatives that anticipate and dispense with a possible objection: "Ich dich ehren? Wofür?" (37). The first question suggests that a doubt or worry, the recollection of an obligation perhaps (e.g., "But you should honor Zeus!"), has intervened, slightly eroding the affirmation attained in and through the first cascade of questions. To vanquish this doubt, a second series follows, filling the rest of stanza V and proving—again, in the sense of juridical demonstration—that there is no reason (no "wofür") that would justify honoring the god. This second group of rhetorical questions exactly conforms to the pattern established in stanza IV: two questions instantiating the same type (both formulated with interrogative inversion: "Hast du," both requiring a negative reply), then a negatively posed question eliciting the response "yes"—a concatenation that can be rewritten according to the abbreviation employed above as: *A A B*. Compared to the preceding stanza, then, stanza V seems to be missing a *C*-type question, a question that asks of its addressee whether it carried out a deluded

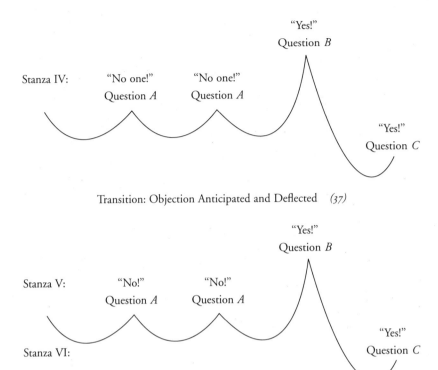

Schema 11: Affective Movement of "Prometheus," Central Stanzas

action. But, of course, precisely this question is supplied by stanza VI, thereby completing the parallelism.[67]

Parallelism is not just ornamentation, it is the organizational network of poetic significance,[68] the path traced out by the poet's semiotic labor. Viewed globally, the two parallel series of questions can be conceptualized as the graph of a repeated affective movement: an accumulation of intensity across the two *A* questions with their negative (hence rejecting) answers; a leap to the *B* question, which in both of its instances opens with an anomously long line (32; 42) and which elicits an affirmative response ("yes"); and finally a rapid decline in intensity in the *C* question, a post-epiphanic relaxation of tension, as it were, that in both instances involves a tone of ridicule. The intonational arc carved out in these two series carries the demonstrative force of the Promethean speech act.[69] Recall the juridical function of the narrative: to prove that the accusation of nonexistence is justified, to assemble its evidence in such a way that nagging doubts are vanquished and the audience is converted, brought to the point of accomplishing a certain act of judgment. To attain this goal, the text traces the score of an incantation, a kind of anti-prayer that conducts the one performing it through a sequence of cognitive-affective stages: a preparatory cleansing (A-A) that casts off antecedent expectations and false claims, the affirmation of and identification with a central proposition (B), and finally, from the elevated perspective of this identification, a backward glance toward an antecedent delusion that now seems risible (C). To speak here of emotion-laden language, as critics tend to do,[70] not only blurs the differentiated semiotics of pathos the text works through, it fails to grasp the character of the text's rhetorical gesture. This is not an instance of emotional expressivity, but a spiritual exercise, a *rite de passage*, an initiation, say, into autonomy.

The ritual or initiatory process derives its efficacy not only from the intonational arc that channels its pathos, but also from the events from the subject's past it invokes. Here too the sequence of rhetorical questions betrays a discernible logic. The *A*-questions, which I described as a preparatory cleansing, lead the subject through a kind of cathartic reliving of antecedently experienced suffering: first, through the battle with the Titans (28–29) and the threat of death and slavery (30–31); second, through the burden of pain (38–39) and the tears of anguish (40–41). The child's torment (we are still within a narrative that began "Da ich ein Kind war," 21) is summoned from the depths of memory, but returns in such a way that the no-longer-child finds the strength (or is called to that strength by the form of the questions) of negation. What is negated is the delusion that accompanied those childhood sufferings: that there exists a divine agency who would aid or redeem one, who would alleviate one's pain and still one's tears. Remembered anguish functions within the *rite de passage* as an instrument of disillusionment (which is why it serves, within the overriding juridical structure, as proof of the accusation bearing on the nonexistence of the god). This is why I called the cathartic reenactment of suffering preparatory: the negation of the prior belief in an external source of support and comfort *enables the subject to accept its suffering as the irrefutable evidence of its own inner resources.*

Precisely this act of acceptance is accomplished at the two affective-intonational peaks of the rhetorical series with what I have called the *B*-type questions:

Hast du nicht alles selbst vollendet,
Heilig glühend Herz? *(32–33)*

Hat nicht mich zum Manne geschmiedet
Die allmächtige Zeit
Und das ewige Schicksal,
Meine Herrn und deine? *(42–45)*

These two segments constitute, as it were, the heart of the poem, and it is therefore worthwhile to unravel carefully the threads of significance that come together here. First, their formulation as rhetorical questions elicits—and this is central to their effect—an affirmative response. There is no way around the internal pronunciation (silently, accompanying the reading of the lines) of the answer "Yes!" The two questions, that is to say, prompt an act of assent, an identification with the speaker position that affirms their propositional content. They call forth the subject's commitment to the proposition, or the assumption (in the sense that one assumes, takes on, a responsibility) of the truth of the proposition.[71] And it is this feature—that they elicit an act of affirmation, the appropriation of a truth as one's own—that makes them the turning point of the *rite de passage*, the point, that is to say, of conversion, in which the initiand sees and declares the truth of his own identity.

But what is the character of this truth? The feature that determines the semantic gesture of the two propositions affirmed is that their viewpoint is retrospective, that they characterize a sequence from the standpoint of its completion. The accomplishment of everything by the heart and the forging of Prometheus into a man (as opposed, of course, to the child he was at the outset of the narrative) have already occurred in the moment they are named as such; they are perfected actions, in the grammatical, tense-related signification of the term. We can say, then, that the two summary characterizations endow the events recalled in the preparatory phase of the exercise with narrative coherence; they subsume those events beneath an overriding concept of action, refigure them as a meaningful process, lend them an intelligibility *post festum*. Once the delusions regarding past suffering have been cathartically cast off, the truth of that past can be appropriated and affirmed. The conversion the text enacts is a moment of hermeneutic anagnorisis, the recognition that the heart, as the center of Promethean subjectivity, was the sole agency of the antecedent process, the recognition that the pain one has suffered has in fact shaped one into a man. Prometheus, whose own speech conducts him to the point of affirmation, is in fact carrying out an interpretation of his own past, which is to say, a self-interpretation.

It is therefore no accident that this phase of the text involves a dense cluster of allusions to the Prometheus mythologeme. The reference to "der Titanen Übermut" (29), perhaps also to the threat of 'death' and 'slavery' (30–31), likely cites the episode recounted in Aeschylus's *Prometheus Bound*, in which Prometheus, siding with Zeus in the rebellion against Chronos, survives the vengeful wrath of the Titans.[72] Note, however, that the allusion draws not on the entire narrative context (which, of course, would make no sense, given that Zeus does not exist), but solely on the aspect of 'violent conflict,' which stands in—*pars pro toto*—for the diverse forms of youthful anguish. The function of the allusion is not to represent a definite scene, but to employ the mythological element as a figure for a universal dimension of experience, in this case the fact of suffering. This tendency toward a universalizing interpretation of the mythologeme becomes fully manifest in the second passage through the phase of recalled events, which dispenses altogether with citational references to the Prometheus story, thematizing instead the general human experience of pain and tears. As regards the "Heilig glühend Herz" (33), I have already remarked that it recalls (via "Herd" and "Glut" in stanza I) the Promethean theft of divine fire. Indeed, the very address to the "glowing heart" is the hermeneutic truth of the mythological theft, the point at which Prometheus appropriates for himself, or affirms, the creative force of his own subjectivity. A similar function must be attributed to the line: "Hat nicht mich zum Manne geschmiedet" (42), which alludes to one of the most salient elements in the mythologeme, Prometheus's punishment for his various transgressions against the divine order (e.g., the theft of the fire, the sacrificial deception). The mythical punishment evoked by the literal sense of the word "geschmiedet" (Vulcan forges a chain with which Prometheus is bound to the rock) is interpreted as a metaphor for the shaping force of maturation; far from being a meaningless sufferance imposed by a wrathful god, the experience of pain and anguish is affirmed as that which forges men out of children.[73] Across all these allusions a single strategy is sustained: the poem interprets the myth as documenting the "history of the feeling of all human beings,"[74] and it does so in such a way that the hermeneutic process itself, the solicitation of a universal human sense from the mythological figures, becomes the focus of attention. This configuration is what I referred to earlier as the text's autological structure: the text interprets Prometheus as the figure of interpretation, hence of the very operation the text itself performs.

The autological reading of the text is supported by a final, intricate, richly suggestive allusion that allows us to discern the poetic unity of the two affirmations. The verb "schmieden," in addition to its association with the punishment of Prometheus, refers to the art of metallurgy, the extraction of metal from ore, and the fashioning of both practical and aesthetic artifacts. This art, called "Schmiedekunst," belongs among the inventions ascribed to Prometheus by the mythologeme,[75] and it seems indisputable that the poem, with the line "Hat nicht mich zum Manne geschmiedet" (42), weaves this thread into its texture of significance.[76] If one follows out the implications of this allusion, however, one cannot avoid the inference that the agent who forges Prometheus into manhood is none other than Prometheus himself.[77] Once this implication is seen, the internal relation between the two *B*-questions, hence between the two central affirmations of the poem, becomes strikingly clear. Read in terms of the isotopy established by the metallurgical allusion, the "Heilig glühend Herz" (33) figures both the fire-purified ore ("das glühende Erz," one could say in German[78]) and the artisan who purifies and fashions that ore into the shape of an identity ("alles selbst vollendet," 32). Thus, the hermeneutic anagnorisis achieved in the text's central affirmations is the disclosure of the identity that subtends the diverse features of the inherited mythologeme. The metonymic chain of mythic elements is absorbed in a substratum of meaning such that Prometheus occupies simultaneously the position of the ore that is purified, of the fire in which it is smelted, of the metal that is extracted and shaped, and of the artisan/artist who carries out (on himself!) this entire process, a process which is nothing other than his own history. Prometheus makes sense of his past (of his myth) by understanding it as the history of his self-making, a history that includes, as its peripeteia, this very act, dramatized in the poem, of interpretive self-appropriation. The two moments of hermeneutic anagnorisis coalesce in a single, autological figure. The conversion point of the *rite de passage* coincides with the interpretation of the Prometheus mythologeme as the story of subjective self-formation within the earthly parameters defined by time and destiny.[79]

This reading of the metallurgical allusion bears two consequences that set the agenda for further exploration of the poem. First of all, it is clear that the text operates with *paradoxical figures*: whether it is a question of an

artisan who manufactures himself or of a mythological figure that interprets the very myth within which it assumes a position, the text points to a
complex in which elements that are mutually exclusive in either a logical
or a phenomenological sense attain equivalence. In the second place, the
figuration of Prometheus as an artisan producing himself clearly bears a
relation to the aspect of the mythologeme accentuated in the final stanza,
the idea that Prometheus created man by shaping and firing figures out of
clay. A major task of my commentary on the conclusion of the text will be
to describe how these two dimensions—paradoxicality and the creation of
man—intertwine.

At this point, however, a last, brief note on the narrative section of the
poem. The final (or C-type) question in the first of the two parallel series
clearly exhibits the tendency toward ridicule remarked above. From the
elevation of insight and affirmation attained in the apostrophe to the
"Heilig glühend Herz" (33), the belief previously held by the child appears
as sheer naïveté ("jung und gut," 34), a ridiculous self-duping about which
one now, from the standpoint of manhood, can only laugh. Hence the
unmistakably parodistic tone of the first C-question: the caustic rhyme on
transcendence ("Betrogen . . ." / "da droben," 35–36), the derisive caricature of the god as the "sleeping one." (The parodistic accent becomes more
pronounced if one hears in the word "Schlafenden" the echo of the word
"Schaffenden" [creating one], a nominalized participle Klopstock, for
example, uses to designate the Christian God.) The function of this phase
within the *rite de passage* is clear; the surest guarantee that one is free of
one's delusion (or of any state one endeavors to leave behind) is being able
to laugh at it. Just as tragic catharsis prepares the way toward insight, satiric
catharsis succeeds it. Much the same can be said of the second C-question,
posed in stanza VI, in which the tone of derision is equally prominent. At
the same time, however, the second C-question allows us to discern that
the parallelism it completes supports a semantic opposition bearing on the
temporal reference of the two beliefs being ridiculed. In the first case, the
delusive belief is youthful gratitude offered with regard to events that have
already taken place (survival in the conflict with the Titans) and is
therefore a false construal, now understood as risible, of what happened in
the past; but in the second case the delusion thematized and laughed at is
an expectation: that Prometheus would hate life and flee into deserts once
his flowery dreams were disappointed. The narrative segment of the text
thus achieves closure by raising the question of the future. And this is why

the stanza that marks this closure—stanza VI—is structurally ambiguous, not only rounding out the rhetorical parallelism unfolded in the stanzas that precede it, but also joining with the stanza that follows upon it to form the numerical counterpart (5 + 7) of the poem's beginning. The conclusion of the text, the stanzaic pair VI–VII, is the site where the advent of a post-theological epoch, the final chapter in the history of emancipation, is announced.

~

Let me begin a discussion of the ode's concluding stanzas by citing a variant from 1778:[80]

> Wähntest etwa
> Ich sollt das Leben hassen
> In Wüsten fliehn,
> Weil nicht alle Knabenmorgen
> Blütenträume reiften.
>
> Hier sitz ich, forme Menschen
> Nach meinem Bilde,
> Ein Geschlecht das mir gleich sei
> Zu leiden, weinen,
> Genießen und zu freuen sich
> Und dein nicht zu achten
> Wie ich! *(46–57)*

I have already stressed the compositional linkage between the two stanzas that derives from their numerical symmetry (5 + 7) with the poem's introit and lends them salience as a significant cluster. I would amend this observation by arguing that they constitute a rhetorical unit as well, that they carve out a single gesture of speech. The discrimination of this rhetorical gesture sets the stage for a reading of the poem's closure in which the strands of argument developed in the preceding sections come together.

The rhetorical coherence of stanzas VI and VII stems from the fact that they form a two-part response to an unspoken objection. The poem exhibits a markedly dialogical character in that it anticipates, cites in advance, a foreign utterance, in terms of which it positions itself. Recall that a similar point was made with regard to line 37, in which the question "Ich dich ehren?" must be read as the preemption of a warning intervention such as: "But you should honor Zeus!" In stanzas VI and VII, the worried intervention can be imagined as something like: "But you are destroying belief, the very thing that gives us hope and assuages our fears. And once that belief is destroyed, life isn't worth living." The rhetorical gesture of Prometheus's reply to this timorous word of caution can be dramatized with the following paraphrase:

VI: Did you really imagine I would hate life, etc., if my youthful dreams were disappointed?
VII: On the contrary, here I sit and form men, etc.

The first component of the reply (stanza VI) dismisses the implicit objection or cautionary word by characterizing it as a deluded expectation, the fear that the shattering of Prometheus's youthful dreams would lead him to turn away from life. The tone of ridicule remarked above is all the more flagrant in the version cited here, in which the youth's belief is parodied with the monstrous compound "Knabenmorgen/Blütenträume" (49–50).[81] It is as if a final trepidation, the anxiety that a world without the gods would be unlivable, were being overcome.[82] With the second part of the reply (stanza VII), Prometheus sketches the future he imagines for himself and for the mankind he creates, and this sketch is meant to contrast sharply with the vision of a desolate and hated life projected in the unspoken warning. Hence the opposition between the infinitive verbs in the two stanzas: on the one hand, "das Leben hassen / In Wüsten fliehn" (47–48); on the other hand, "Zu leiden, weinen, / Genießen und zu freuen sich" (54–55). Prometheus counters the trepidatious warning by asserting that the state succeeding upon the demolition of youthful phantasies is not the abnegation of life, but the embrace and affirmation of its alternating pulse of anguish and joy.[83]

This reading of the rhetorical unity of stanzas VI and VII as the reply to an implicit, but silently formulated objection does not, of course, exhaust the poetic resources of the poem's conclusion, but it does bring me to one of the decisive features of that conclusion in that it compels me to face an issue that I have been circumventing all along, the status of the poem's addressee. The question posed in stanza VI ("Wähntest du") seems to be addressed, like the questions immediately preceding it in stanza V ("Hast du"; "Hast du"), to Zeus. However, given that the nonexistence of the god has been so thoroughly demonstrated, this reading makes no sense at all. The text appears to be mired in a contradiction between its communicative structure (in which Zeus figures as the addressee) and its argumentative purport (according to which Zeus is a mere projection). If, however, we draw out the implications of the fact that the questions apparently addressed to Zeus are responses to silently formulated objections, which those questions either follow upon or anticipate, then the contradiction evaporates. For these objections, these words of warning to Prometheus, can have no other source than in Prometheus himself, or more precisely, in the dimension of Prometheus's psyche in which a residual belief in the theological delusion continues to exert a cautionary influence. In stanzas V–VII, that is to say, Prometheus is in dialogue with his own lingering trepidation, with an internal resistance that holds him back from full affirmation. The strategy he employs to vanquish this trepidation is to set up Zeus as a kind of dummy addressee, whose warnings can then be dispensed with through the process of legal demonstration the text unfolds.

We can rephrase this point by saying that the address to Zeus in stanzas V–VII is a parodistic address through which Prometheus contends with, and surmounts, his own fear. Once the issue is formulated this way, the overriding unity of the poetic act of speech emerges into view. Recall what was said above regarding the illocutionary structure of stanza I: that it is a parodied command through which Prometheus vanquishes his anxiety, the very anxiety out of which he had metaphorically projected the god. The same parodistic tone is legible in the opening lines of stanza II, in which the vocative "Götter!" can be read, and therefore must be read, as citational parody (i.e., "you so-called gods!"). Throughout, Prometheus's speech is parodistic, addressing the god it shows to be nonexistent. Moreover, the reason this parodistic strategy makes sense is that the metaphorical projection that originally constituted the god is grounded, as noted above, in the communicative structure of language: "als wenn drüber wär" / Ein Ohr zu hören meine Klage" (24–25). Hence the strategy of the anti-hymn: by addressing the god, Prometheus's speech repeats the vocative projection that called the god into being, but, in doing so, parodistically empties the vocative of its thetic force and exposes the god as what he was all along, a nonbeing whose only hold on existence is the aberrant metaphor of mankind's hope and fear.[84]

This brings me to a decisive juncture in my reading. In view of the parodistic character of the text, it is clear that the traditional understanding of the poem as sheer expressivity anchored in the self-certainty or emotionality of poetic subjectivity collapses. But the question is: how can the text be viewed otherwise? How can we construct an adequate text-model of the "Prometheus" ode?[85]

My answer to this question runs along the following lines. Dialogically constituted, the poem is the site of a contention or an altercation (in German I would say *Auseinandersetzung*) between two discourses: on the one hand, an antecedent discourse grounded in fear and false hope, the discourse of myth and religious orthodoxy; on the other hand, a discourse of emancipation in which humanity realizes its autonomy. The first of these two discourses is the linguistic sedimentation of a prehistory that, despite the erosion of accumulated disillusionments, continues to exert a hold on the subject. The second discourse is yet to be achieved; it has an irreducibly future character. The two discourses correspond to the initial and final phases of the emancipatory narrative which the text recounts and in which it assumes the function of peripeteia. The project of the poem is to work through the altercation, that is, internally to dismantle the discourse of myth, to negate its thetic investments, to loosen its hold on the subject, and to do this in such a way that out of the labor of negation a new discourse emerges in which subjectivity acknowledges or recognizes itself. This task is accomplished through the interaction of the four strategies delineated in the course of my reading.

(a) A *legal strategy*, which organizes the rhetorical disposition of the entire text and which works toward a crisis point, a moment of decision, in which the antecedent discourse of belief is cast off and the emancipatory discourse accepted.

(b) A *parodistic strategy*, which cites the antecedent discourse of belief, including its vocative angle of address, but in such a way as to empty that discourse of its substance and validity.

(c) A *ritual strategy*, carried out in the poem's middle section, which conducts the subject through an initiatory process involving the stages of cathartic purification, affirmation, and retrospective ridicule.

(d) A *hermeneutic strategy*, which discloses beneath the delusions of the antecedent discourse of belief both the preconditions (childhood fear and hope) and the mechanisms (metaphorical projection) that produced those delusions and thereby reveals the truth of that discourse, which is the auto-production of the subject across the history of its self-fashioning.

The four strategies are components of an overriding pragmatic (in the semiotic sense of the term) transaction. The jury which Prometheus's prosecutory speech brings to the point of judgment, the audience before

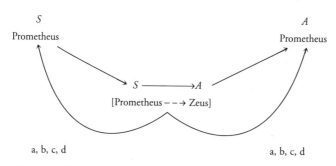

Schema 12: Communicative Relations in "Prometheus" (I)

which the parody is performed, the initiand whom Prometheus conducts through the rite of passage, and the truth disclosed in the hermeneutic process are all one and the same: Prometheus as the addressee of his own act of speech. That is to say, by simulating a speech directed to Zeus, Prometheus establishes, enters into, a communicative relation with himself. The altercation worked through in the text is the production of a new communicative structure out of the mythic discourse in which speech is directed toward the god. The child's vocative appeal, born of anxiety and hope, is thus transformed into the self-appellation of the Promethian heart, a process that can be modeled as in Schema 12.

I particularly want to emphasize the paradoxical character of this text-model. Ordinarily, communicants preexist the communicative transaction, but in this case the authentic speaker and addressee come into being in and through the labor that detaches the subject from its mythical identity and frees it to self-acknowledgment. Prometheus, in the truth of his identity and self-appellation, is the product of the discourse he produces. Once this is seen, the remarkable consistency of the poem, its thoroughgoing formedness, emerges into view. The pragmatic paradox of a speech act that engenders its communicants reflects the autological contorsions that my reading has repeatedly pointed out: the self-inclusion of the speech act as the peripeteia of the narrative it recounts; the hermeneutic paradox of a figure that interprets the very myth in which it functions as a figure; the metallurgical paradox of an artisan who forges himself out of himself. At every level— pragmatic, narrative, hermeneutic, figurative—the text twists into autoreferential structures in which inside and outside, meta- and object-language, producer and product, coincide.

We can agree with the traditional reading of this text as a programmatic declaration of artistic autonomy, but with this important modification: *the "Prometheus" ode stages autonomy as a paradoxical configuration.*

My starting point for the elaboration of this text-model was the rhetorical structure of the poem's closure (stanzas VI and VII), to which I want to return now in order to test the model as a protocol for reading. Of course, the poem's final stanza is the phase of the text in which interpreters have located the clearest declaration of the notion of artistic genius. "The point of Goethe's early Prometheus reception," Blumenberg writes, "lies in the workshop icon as it is related to aesthetic genius."[86] The phrase "workshop icon" refers to the fact that Prometheus's self-description in the final stanza ("Hier sitze ich, forme Menschen") alludes to the aspect of the mythologeme according to which the Titan formed mankind out of clay. The specification that Prometheus carries out this formative labor while sitting in all probability derives from a pictorial representation (hence icon) mentioned in Hederich's lexicon.[87] What could be a more appropriate figuration of genius as creative force than this image of Prometheus diligently shaping humankind? This interpretation only gains in plausibility when one remarks that the lines evoking the workshop icon also allude to the account of the Creation of man in Genesis:

> Hier sitz ich, forme Menschen
> Nach meinem Bilde,
> Ein Geschlecht das mir gleich sei
>
> *(51–53)*

Und GOTT sprach: Lasst uns Menschen machen, ein Bild, das uns gleich sei, . . . Und GOTT schuf den Menschen ihm zum Bilde, zum Bilde GOTTes schuf er ihn.

A more grandiose affirmation of genius would be difficult to imagine. Prometheus "transposes . . . the biblical idea of man's likeness unto God [*Gottesebenbildlichkeit des Menschen*] onto the domain of his own creativity."[88] Such is the central thesis of the traditional interpretation: as the representative of artistic or poetic genius, Prometheus is claiming to create works of art in which the represented figures possess the full vitality of real human beings. In this respect, his artistic products are analogous to God's creation of the natural world and, in particular, of man.[89]

Three types of objection can be made to this traditional interpretation.

(1) An aesthetic objection: if all that is meant by the notion of genius is that artistic production is analogous to Creation in the sense that it brings forth, for example, dramatic figures who strike us as lifelike, then that notion amounts to nothing more than a triviality inflated by hyperbole. Such self-important nebulousness could hardly provide an appropriate closure for a poem as intensely and intricately thought through as the "Prometheus" ode. (2) A logical objection: If divine creation is a metaphor for the type of artistic production carried out by the genius, then the notion of genius is contradictory. Certainly, a central component of that notion is the idea of originality, but if the artistic genius replicates an antecedent act of creation, namely God's, then he remains an imitator who draws the model of his production from an external paradigm. To put this another way, the concept of genius the traditional interpretation attributes to the text is essentially a theological concept organized according to the schema prototype/image that underlies the biblical account of Creation. (3) A methodological objection: The traditional interpretation operates with a substitutional model of signification, moving immediately from image (the workshop icon) to meaning ('creativity'), and ignoring precisely the relations that determine the specificity of the poetic text, namely the linguistic figuration of the passage in question and the relations obtaining between that passage and other parts of the text. This threefold critique of inherited views of the poem sets the agenda of a reading. The task is to develop a conception of the poem's closure that (1) is faithful to the internal rigor of the text and (2) breaks with the (contradictory) theological notion of genius. The method (3) for elaborating such a conception is to trace the relational network that determines, and overdetermines, poetic signification.

A useful starting point is the numerical correlation (5 + 7) between the closing stanzaic group (VI and VII) and the poem's first stanza. The compositional parallelism of beginning and end elicits a cross-reading of the two portions of the text, which, as it turns out, are characterized by a twofold lexical convergence. The compound "Knabenmorgen/Blüten-träume" (in the earlier version of these stanzas) echoes the phrase "dem Knaben gleich" (3), and Prometheus's assertion in stanza VII that he forms human beings after his own image—"Ein Geschlecht, das mir gleich sei" (53)—echoes the particle of comparison from that line. Thus, the focus of the two retrospective references from the end of the poem to its beginning is the same: the simile which dramatizes the anthropomorphic projection of the god. This implies that the conclusion of the poem is, in a sense to be specified, a transformation of that original projective act.

But beginning and end interlock in a second, more subtle way that has to do with the workshop icon of stanza VII. An unmentioned, but nonetheless implicit and therefore poetically pertinent, element in the scenario of Prometheus's forming of human beings is clearly the kiln in which the clay figures are fired. A possible name in German for such a kiln or oven is "Herd," precisely the element in stanza I that names the energetic nucleus of the Promethian world. At the very least, this correlation indicates that the workshop icon is anticipated by and answers to the accusation of Zeus performed across the first stanza, that it develops figural possibilities implicit in that phase of the text.

But we have also seen that the "Herd" (with its "Glut") is interwoven with the "Heilig glühend Herz" (33) addressed at the poem's center, suggesting that the image of Prometheus molding and animating his human figures signifies his endowing them with the "Glut" of his "Herz" (a notion that will have to be specified). Moreover, precisely this series of elements—"Herd," "Glut," "glühend Herz"—pertains to the metallurgical dimension of the mythologeme alluded to in the line: "Hat nicht mich zum Manne geschmiedet" (42), and, once this connection is taken into consideration, the astonishing internal consistency of the entire text makes itself felt. For clearly, the idea of smelting, purifying, and shaping metal bears a close kinship to the idea of forming ceramic statues out of clay. Thus, the function of the workshop icon is, at least in part, to resume the paradoxical figure of metallurgical self-fashioning that integrates all the allusions to and interpretations of the Prometheus mythologeme. The moment of hermeneutic anagnorisis in which Prometheus grasps the truth of his own myth as the history of self-fashioning is restated at the poem's conclusion, but restated in such a way that the formative act now acquires a universal validity, bearing not on Prometheus alone, but on mankind.

The relational significance of the final stanza, then, is determined by its reference to two complexes: (a) via the terms "Knabe" and "gleich" to the complex of 'projection', which is central to the Enlightenment critique of religious belief; (b) via the series "Erde," "Herd," "Glut," "glühend Herz," and "geschmiedet" to the figural complex of 'self-fashioning', which is the hermeneutic truth of the Prometheus mythologeme. The notion that unites both complexes is obviously the idea of 'creation': on the one hand, the creation of the god, on the other hand the self-creation of the Promethean subject. It strikes me as a forceful indication of the poetic rigor of this text that these two 'creational' complexes provide the context for an allusion to the account of Creation in the Book of Genesis. We are now in a position to gauge the force of that allusion.

Read in terms of the complex of projection, the allusion can be said to accomplish a subversion of the biblical text it cites, a hermeneutic destruction or demythologization of the *schema of imitation* on which the account of the divine creation of man rests. By virtue of the reference (via "gleich") to the simile of stanza I, the theologeme of man's likeness to God is parodistically reversed: it was not God who created man, but rather man who, caught in his fear-stricken, hope-driven, "childish" state, created God through an act of metaphorical projection. God the Creator does not exist, He is merely the product of the poetic figuration through which man attempts to manage the affective turmoil his primitive situation causes him. This is the point where the anti-Christian isotopy of the text comes most flagrantly to the fore. Goethe adapts the Enlightenment discourse on religious origins in such a way as to mobilize its anti-orthodox potential and to focus that potential on the central question of man's secondary status, his position as image ("Bild") of a divine prototype.[90] Note that this disclosure of the projective mechanism underlying the biblical conception of man's derivative position vis-à-vis God is accompanied by a reinterpretation of the Prometheus mythologeme, according to which Prometheus created man in the image of the gods.[91] Precisely the concept shared by Bible and myth, the mimetic definition of human being, is the concept the poem, by fugally juxtaposing the biblical allusion and the workshop icon, hermeneutically overturns. The issue at stake in the citational gesture, and in the problematic of genius, is mankind's originality, its independence of a prototype which it would merely copy, its unprecedented character.

But this reading, it will be objected (and rightly so), does not avoid the theological contradiction. Even if it is granted that the final stanza applies the Enlightenment notion of projection to the biblical account of the Creation of man, it nevertheless remains true that Prometheus claims to form mankind after his image, a race, species or type (*Geschlecht*) which would be like him. Thus, with the very gesture that subverts the theological model, that model is reinstated, exerting its thrall all the more forcefully for the fact that it possesses the allure of emancipation. The artistic genius who claims for himself the position of creator is still a miniature version of God. This objection, which is important and compelling, can only be overcome if it can be shown that the premise on which it rests does not hold. That premise is that the lines "Hier sitz' ich, forme Menschen / Nach meinem Bilde, / Ein Geschlecht, das mir gleich sei," envision an act of creation proceeding according to the schema prototype/copy, the schema, as I have called it, of imitation. But if this is so, then we must ask: With which of his own features Prometheus endows his creations? There is only one available answer to this question, and it derives from the second 'creational' complex contextualizing, and therefore determining the significance of, the biblical citation. This is the figural complex that extends from the workshop icon back to the "Herd" and "Glut" of stanza I, from there to the "Heilig glühend Herz" at the poem's center, and from there to the metallurgical dimension of the mythologeme, of which the icon is a figural variant. *Prometheus's formative act gives mankind the capacity of self-fashioning.* Hence it is not a creation according to the schema prototype/copy at all, but a genuine alternative to the biblical or theological model. Prometheus frees humanity to its originality, forms humanity such that humanity forms itself.

The traditional interpretation of the workshop icon as an analogue of the biblical concept of Creation goes wrong not only because it is theological, but also because it is materialistic. The assumption is that that icon— the picture of Prometheus shaping human figures out of clay—delimits the concept of 'forming' according to what might be termed a model of plastic production in which an artisan gives contour to a pliable material. Within the parameters of this model, of course, there is no possibility that the beings created could be said to form themselves; the formative agency, the artisan, stands outside his creation (much as God does in the biblical conception), and whatever qualities that creation has apart from the givens of the base material are the work of the artisan and not of the created beings. Thus, to break with the theological conception of genius as a miniature God requires that we break with the plastic notion of artistic production. And this, of course, is just what the text has done. The reworking of the metallurgical register of the mythologeme forces the image of artisanship—Prometheus smelting and shaping the glowing ore he himself is—to the point at which the logic of the image collapses into the paradox of self-fashioning. My claim is that this applies equally to the workshop icon, which is a variant of the metallurgical figure: the aspect of the mythologeme according to which Prometheus creates mankind out of clay is cited at the poem's close in order to be replaced with a concept of the artistic production of a humanity that produces itself. The fact that this concept is paradoxical, far from being a deficiency of the poem, attests to the depth and perspicuity of thought this text achieves.

The reading I am developing, by departing from the theological-materialistic schema of artistic creation, ascribes greater ambition to the poem than the traditional interpretation allows. That interpretation construes the workshop icon as a modest repetition of the biblical text. The modesty involved here consists in that Prometheus's claim to "form human beings" is restricted to the field of art: this is not the actual creation of man, interpreters argue,[92] but an analogue (hence repetition) of divine Creation within the aesthetic sphere. Now there can be no doubt but that this modesty is appropriate in a certain sense. In the first place, the world of the text already includes human beings (e.g., "children and beggars," which is to say, a humanity devoted to a supramundane god); moreover, were the poem to claim for itself full equivalence with divine Creation, it would dissolve into hubristic phantasy and disqualify itself from serious attention.

But need one be quite this modest? Is it really necessary to restrict Prometheus's assertion that he is forming humankind to the (tame but nevertheless still theological) idea that he is creating artworks in which human figures attain a lifelike fullness or in which his own inner life is externally manifested? These questions, I believe, can be answered in the negative; the text is in fact far less modest in its aspiration than its interpreters maintain. That is to say, I believe it is possible to read the Promethean claim to an act formative of humanity in a literal way: this poem purports genuinely to bring forth humankind, and not only artistic figurations of humankind. The crux of the matter is how one defines the humanity Prometheus claims to form. Not, certainly, in the sense of a natural (physical or biological) being, a definition that is not only absurd in the context of the poem, but also utterly inadequate as a concept of the human. Rather, the humanity this text claims to fashion is a humanity that fashions itself, a humanity that exists precisely to the extent that it acknowledges itself as forming itself, an autonomous humanity, hence a humanity that no longer conceives itself according to the theological schema (cf. "dein nicht zu achten," 56).

If my argument thus far holds, then a reading adequate to the text must meet three criteria. It must develop a notion of artistic genius: (1) that does not conform to the theological or materialist model; (2) that makes sense of the claim that Prometheus produces mankind; and (3) that is characterized by the paradoxical structure of autonomous self-forming. These three requirements are fulfilled by a notion of genius and of artistic production that is linguistic in character. The medium in which both the self-formation of Prometheus and the self-formation of mankind are accomplished is the language of the very poem we hold before us, the anti-hymn that at once retracts the original poetic projection of the god and establishes a new poetic *Urkunde* of mankind. The lines that constitute the so-called workshop icon: "Hier sitz' ich, forme Menschen / Nach meinem Bilde, / Ein Geschlecht, das mir gleich sei," mark, in this reading, the point of the text's self-designation. They refer (autologically) to the speech act accomplished through the inscription of the text and their claim is that this speech act forms a self-forming humanity.[93] The humanity Prometheus produces is not a represented figure within an artwork and certainly not a material statuette, but rather a *Geschlecht* that brings itself forth, comes into being, by entering into a self-relation established in and through the poem. Thus, the function of the workshop icon is to open the internal pragmatics of the text onto an external pragmatic frame: *the humanity named in the final stanza is the implicit addressee of the poem.* Resuming the text model elaborated earlier, we can say that the poem's paradoxical structure (Prometheus is the product of the discourse he produces) is the text-internal version of the text-external paradox of a self-forming humanity.

The "Prometheus" ode dramatizes the speech in which humanity, addressing itself as self-fashioning, fashions itself. With this assumption by humanity of its own truth, history reaches its peripeteia. The text hovers at the apex of this peripeteia, calling humanity to the judgment (in the juridical sense) through which it would freely constitute itself, but without any guarantee that this summons of humanity to self-acknowledgment will be realized. This is why the closure of the text turns toward the future, expressing the intention to form humanity, perhaps even the process of this formation, but not its completion. Precisely because it foresees an addressee that is self-forming, the text can only proffer the possibility of humanity. In this sense, the "oldest document of the human race" this text purports to be—the foundational document of humanity—registers not a fact, but an event that ever remains in imminence. The hermeneutic

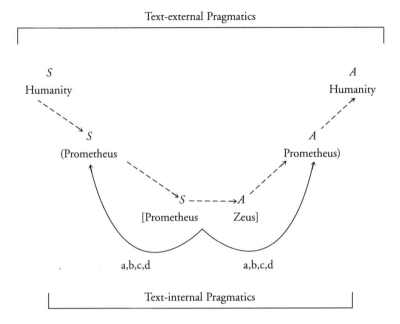

Schema 13: Communicative Relations in "Prometheus" (II)

anagnorisis in which humanity attains to the truth of its past has its basis in a future that can never be reduced to a positive state of affairs. True to the etymological sense of his name, Prometheus *foresees* humanity. The linguistic act in and through which humanity as such emerges is the promise that humanity will be.

Genius, in the definition this text elaborates, is the originality of humanity. It is the name for the fact that humanity as such has no antecedent ground, be it natural or divine, that it owes its being to no external agency, that it conforms to and copies no prototype of perfect being. Genius is the poetic autonomy of mankind, the unprecedented linguistic act through which mankind produces itself in the discourse it produces. This is why the "Prometheus" ode, which is, together with "Mahomets Gesang," Goethe's most accomplished textualization of genius, carves out its *topos* in the shape of a paradox. *Paradox is the form of originality.*[94]

It strikes me as one of the most compelling indications of this poem's acuteness of thought that it concludes with what might be termed the primitive instance of this paradoxical structure. The final line of the text

("Wie ich!") does not assert that the beings Prometheus forms would be copies of the substance he is, but, rather, that those beings—humankind—come to their subjectivity by employing the same linguistic form through which Prometheus assumes his identity as speaker of the poem. As the deictic element which identifies the speaking subject, "ich" marks the irreducibly linguistic locus of subjectivity in general. The first person singular pronoun points, in each instance of its use, to this particular individual who speaks, and yet to no individual in particular.[95] Only by assuming the role of the "ich" do I become the subject I am, and the act through which I thus fashion myself implies a "du," to which it attributes the capacity to speak "wie ich," to take on in turn the role of speaking subject which "ich" designates. The "ich," shifting between individual and class (or *Geschlecht*), is the genius of humanity in that it marks the *origo* that accomplishes itself each time language is spoken.[96] The poetic vocation this text accepts as its own is to call humanity to its originality, to the paradoxical movement of self-fashioning that coincides with the origin of language.

~

The reading elaborated here attempts to do justice to the internal consistency of this text, its intricacy and density of thought. Only by engaging with the text in terms of its figural logic and stringency of form, it seems to me, can we apprehend its self-differentiation, the specificity of its poetic achievement. This is not to say that the text bears no relation to other texts from the same corpus; on the contrary, one of the major contentions of this study is that Goethe's poetry of the 1770's evinces a systematic coherence, that it draws on a set of symbolic constants, which individual texts both cite and transform. I will therefore conclude this chapter by briefly indicating lines of filiation that link the "Prometheus" ode to texts discussed in previous chapters.

An obvious starting point is Goethe's encomium to Shakespeare of 1771. I called attention in Chapter 5 to the peripatetic image of the "wanderer's footsteps" so prominent in this speech, arguing that the figure conveys the notion of semantic innovation—the carving out of an unprecedented historical law—which is a central feature of the complex of genius. The pertinence of this aspect of genius to the "Prometheus" ode is evident insofar as the poetic vocation the text claims for itself is precisely the institution of a new "oldest document of the human race." But a comparison of the two texts is also revealing in other respects. As is well known, the Shakespeare speech mounts a harsh polemic against the derivative character of French classical theater, its adherence to the classical dramatic unities of time, place, and action. The most interesting feature of this polemic with regard to the "Prometheus" ode, however, is that it exhibits traces of the Enlightenment critique of polytheism, in particular as that critique is reworked in Herder's reception of Hume. Greek tragedy, Goethe notes, originated in a ritual context, it was the "Intermezzo eines Gottesdienstes" ("intermezzo of a religious service"),[97] and represented to the Greek people (*Volk*) the great actions of the fathers. The aesthetic and historical legitimacy of Greek tragedy is grounded in this religious context, within which the drama functioned to forge the bonds of the community and to awaken elevating thoughts in the minds of its audience. Although there can be no doubt that Goethe's evaluation of Greek drama is generally positive, there is nevertheless an unmistakable nuance of criticism in the phrase "intermezzo of a religious service," as if to say that the tragedy of Sophocles, however immense his achievement, remains tied to a system of religious belief that is no longer tenable. And this limitation becomes a bondage when it is adopted, as in the case of the French theater, as a paradigm for poetic writing in modernity. Part of the motivation for Goethe's praise of Shakespeare, then, derives from a historical assessment of the English playwright as having broken with a theological conception and grounding of art.

The anti-theological dimension of Goethe's advocacy of Shakespeare is forcefully evident in the following contrast:

> Schäckespear, mein Freund, wenn du noch unter uns wärest ich könnte nirgend leben als mit dir, wie gern wollt ich die Nebenrolle eines Pylades spielen, wenn du Orest wärst, lieber als die geehrwürdigte Person eines Oberpriesters im Tempel zu Delphos.[98]

> Shakespeare, my friend, if you were still among us I couldn't live anywhere except with you, how much I would like to play the secondary role of Pylades, if you were Orestes, far more than the honored person of the high priest in the temple at Delphi.

Shakespeare's drama here functions as the paradigm for an extra-religious art, an art that is no longer devoted to a divinity (Apollo) but takes effect within the sphere of human solidarity (friendship, as between Pylades and

Orestes). The genius, which Shakespeare certainly exemplifies, is defined as the one who frees art from religious subservience and appropriates it for mankind.

The stage is set for a comparison of Shakespeare with Prometheus:

> Laßt mir Luft daß ich reden kann!
> Er wetteiferte mit dem Prometheus, bildete ihm Zug vor Zug seine Men-
> schen nach, nur in *Kolossalischer Größe*, darin liegts daß wir unsre Brüder
> verkennen; und dann belebte er sie alle mit dem Hauch *seines* Geistes, *er* redet
> aus allen, und man erkennt ihre Verwandtschaft.[99]

> Give me air so that I can speak!
> He [Shakespeare] competed with Prometheus, shaped as he did his human
> beings trait for trait, but in *colossal dimensions*, which is why we don't recognize
> our brothers, and then he animated them all with the breath of *his* spirit, *he*
> speaks out of all of them, and one recognizes that they are familially related.

This passage, Goethe's earliest reference to Prometheus in the context of a poetological argument, bears a twofold pertinence to the "Prometheus" ode. In the first place, the focus of the comparison is Shakespeare's creation of dramatic characters, which are (one must assume) of such human vibrancy that the poet can be said to compete with and outdo Prometheus's creation of mankind. My argument with regard to the "Prometheus" poem was that the workshop icon is not limited to the production of lifelike dramatic characters, that Prometheus's formative act in fact fashions mankind, and this thesis seems to me to find support in the Shakespeare speech. For Goethe's concern in the cited passage bears not merely on the immanent dramatic world of Shakespeare's plays, but also on the effect this world has on the reader. And this effect is, precisely, to disclose our bond to, our solidarity with, the characters who populate the plays; hence the claim that they are our "brothers." The pragmatic thrust of Shakespeare's work is to summon us to our humanity, to our brother-hood with the beings who act out their destiny within the post-theological universe of the drama. The second point to be made here is that the figure of Prometheus is accorded secondary importance. Goethe's claim is that Shakespeare outdid Prometheus exactly to the degree that he did not rely, as Prometheus did, on someone else (Minerva) to infuse his creations with life. Shakespeare *himself* (note Goethe's emphases) animated his human beings, and he did so through the language with which he endowed them. The post-theological act of creation accomplished by the genius is conceived in linguistic terms. Moreover, this gift of language attributed to the artistic genius reaches beyond the dramatic works themselves and touches the reader, eliciting a desire to speak, freely to articulate one's experience. This is why the passage is introduced by the exclamation: "Laßt mir Luft daß ich reden kann!" The superiority vis-à-vis Prometheus Goethe attributes to Shakespeare bears on the fact that Prometheus is not yet seen as the founder of a language of mankind, exactly the function the ode will accord him some three years later.

The Shakespeare speech also allows us to position the "Prometheus" ode in relation to the poems of failed genius discussed in Chapter 5: "Wandrers Sturmlied" (Text 16), "Der Adler und die Taube" (Text 17), and the Homeric section of "Künstlers Morgenlied" (Text 18). In all three of these texts, the figure aspiring to genius is defeated or wounded by virtue of the conditions of modernity within which it finds itself, and in all three texts the antagonist to whom the genius succumbs is Apollo. As we have just seen, the significance of Shakespeare for Goethe derives from the fact that his works break with the classical-religious paradigm of art, that they institute an artistic sphere of human solidarity no longer oriented toward the supra-human god of aesthetic harmony. From this perspective, the failure of genius in the three poems can be seen to derive from the fact that those texts remain attached to the Apollonian paradigm, that they accord the artist at best the status "eines Oberpriesters im Tempel zu Delphos." Recall in this connection the aspiration of the poetic subject in "Wandrers Sturmlied":

> Umschwebt mich ihr Musen!
> Ihr Charittinnen!
> Das ist Wasser, das ist Erde
> Und der Sohn des Wassers und der Erde
> Über den ich wandle
> Göttergleich. *(Text 16, 28–33)*

The son of the water and the earth, above whom the speaker claims to move with godlike, Apollonian grace, is the human being, precisely the figure Prometheus forms out of clay (earth and water). The genius of "Wandrers Sturmlied" has not accepted his modernity, he strives for a supra-human position and therefore is condemned to defeat in the mimetic rivalry with the god. The difference between the figuration of genius in "Wandrers Sturmlied" and that in both the earlier Shakespeare speech and the later "Prometheus" ode, then, is the difference between a theological and a human conception of the place of art. This difference can be gauged in terms of the central figure of "Glut," the fiery glow of subjectivity. In "Wandrers Sturmlied," the measure of this poetic glow is still Apollo: "Glüh entgegen / Phöb Apollon" (Text 16, 61–62), a standard which Pindar could equal, but which the wanderer, to whom divine, Apollonian inspiration is historically inaccessible, cannot meet. In the "Prometheus" ode, however, the "Glut" of poetic production is the "Heilig glühend Herz," the hermeneutic truth of human self-formation that underlies the delusive mythic conception.

We have also seen that Goethe's texts find a way out of the dilemma of failed genius by disclosing an alternative model of art no longer organized according to the Apollonian paradigm. This model, elaborated, for example, in the final sections of "Künstlers Morgenlied," locates the origin of artistic production in the specular exchange with the beloved, a scene of artistic coitus and rebirth in which the poetic subject receives the primordial donation of its desire. The competition with Apollo can be won only on the condition that the poetic subject does not lay claim to the self-generated "Glut" of the solar god, but rather draws the source of its creativity from the specular matrix of 'love'. This complex, I have argued, is the figurational nucleus of Goethe's lyric and it is articulated across his entire poetic production from 1770 on. Perhaps the most revealing example in the context of the present argument is "Pilgers Morgenlied" (Text 10), which retrospectively characterizes the specular donation in terms that bear an obvious relevance to the "Prometheus" ode:

> Allgegenwärt'ge Liebe!
> Durchglühst mich,
> Beutst dem Wetter die Stirn,
> Gefahren die Brust,
> Hast mir gegossen
> In's frühwelkende Herz
> Doppeltes Leben,
> Freude zu leben,
> Und Mut. *(Text 10, 26–34)*

The "Glut" that enlivens the "Herz" and enables the subject to resist the threat of the meteorological antagonist—all elements that recur in the "Prometheus" ode—is figured here as the gift of the feminine figure encountered in the specular regard, the same figure who in "Künstlers Morgenlied" charges the artist's "Pinsel" with the symbolic-energetic capacity of aesthetic productivity. But the "Prometheus" ode makes no reference to the scene of primordial specular donation. The question is: Why is this so?

The answer that strikes me as the most compelling draws its justification from the Shakespeare speech. As noted above, the difference between Shakespeare and Prometheus that Goethe stresses in that text has to do with the fact that Shakespeare himself gave life to his creations whereas Prometheus still remained dependent on a divine figure—Minerva—to animate his humanlike statues. Moreover, the life with which Shakespeare endows his figures is the spirit of his language. Both these aspects of the comparison between Shakespeare and Prometheus come together in the drama fragment *Prometheus* that preceded the composition of the ode. In that text, it is Minerva who endows the sculptures with life by conducting Prometheus to the "Quell des Lebens all" (Text 21, 200), which is to say that the drama still conceives of Prometheus's creation of humankind as internally deficient, much as the Shakespeare essay does. But the drama also draws, as we have seen in Chapter 6, on the complex of specularity, and in fact lends that complex a unique inflection. The dialogue between Prometheus and Minerva recalls the specular donation of 'love' as the gift of language:

> Das waren deine Worte.
> So war ich selbst nicht selbst,
> Und eine Gottheit sprach
> Wenn ich zu reden wähnte,
> Und wähnt ich eine Gottheit spreche,
> Sprach ich selbst.
> Und so mit dir und mir
> So ein so innig
> Ewig meine Liebe dir. *(Text 21, 108–16)*

Thus, exactly the feature of Shakespeare's art in which Goethe locates the English poet's superiority to Prometheus—the fact that he animated his artistic products, and therewith mankind, with his language—finds its analogue in the *Prometheus* fragment in the dual function of Minerva: she both gives life to Prometheus's statues and gives Prometheus the gift of primordial orality within the specular exchange. In the "Prometheus" ode, however, there is no longer a Minerva figure; indeed, the entire cumbersome theological framework of the drama fragment is abandoned. And this means that Prometheus can now equal Shakespeare's achievement: he can bring forth an art in which the formation of humanity coincides with the origin of language. The Prometheus of the ode has internalized the specular donation of language that the drama works through in the dialogue between Prometheus and Minerva. As it were, the later version of the Prometheus figure carries the results of the specular exchange within his "Heilig glühend Herz," and this incorporation of the primordial donation enables Prometheus to become the genius of human originality.[100]

This brings me to a final intertextual connection. I have contended that the appropriate contextualization for the "Prometheus" ode is the Enlightenment discourse on religious origins as it is interpreted in Herder's reflections on the origin of myth and poetry from the late 1760's and early 1770's. Herder's work also provides compelling evidence in support of the linguistic inflection of the figure of genius I have attributed to Goethe's poem. Indeed, the claim that the singular, unprecedented character of human existence is rooted in language, that language is the very imprint of the human *Geschlecht*, is the central thesis of Herder's *Treatise on the Origin of Language*. Herder's break with prior thinking on this issue consists in conceiving of the origin of language not as the fruit of divine instruction, nor as the exercise of a naturally endowed capacity, but as the emergence of an irreducibly human relation to the world. And it is precisely at this point of emergence, the point at which the human being seizes the first linguistic feature (*Merkmal*) and thereby produces itself as human being, that Herder locates the figure of Prometheus: "The focal point at which Prometheus's heavenly spark ignites in the human soul is disclosed—with the first feature of recognition [*Merkmal*] language came into being."[101]

Whether or not this allusion to Prometheus motivated Goethe to transform the linguistic problematic of the drama fragment, in which language derives from the specular donation, into that of the ode, in which Prometheus, like Shakespeare, is the sole figure of poetic self-fashioning, need not concern us here. The point, rather, is that both Herder's treatise and Goethe's ode attribute to the figure of Prometheus the identical significance, and for this reason the cited passage deserves to replace Shaftesbury's notion of the artistic genius ("a second Maker, a just Prometheus under Jove") as the motto for Goethe's text.[102] The spark of divine fire with which Prometheus gives life to mankind is, according to Herder, the invention of language. The brilliance of Goethe's poem is that it thinks through the complexity of this inaugural act as a question of poetic form. The "Prometheus" ode is the paradoxical enactment of human original-ity, the self-fashioning of mankind in the medium of poetic language. Through its hermeneutic appropriation of the origin as the poetic consti-tution of humanity the poem accomplishes the peripeteia of history, promises humanity to itself as the imminent truth of its most ancient past. Such is the poetic vocation the "Prometheus" anti-hymn assumes as its calling, its responsibility.

§ 9   The Sublime

The poetic vocation envisioned and enacted in the "Prometheus" ode is the declaration of autonomy. Poised at the peripeteia of history, where it hermeneutically discloses the truth of the mythic past as the promise of a self-forming humanity, the poetic utterance becomes the paradoxical figure through which humanity freely constitutes itself. The relation thereby established between poet and audience on the one hand and the gods on the other is essentially negative ("Und dein nicht zu achten, / Wie ich!," 56–57); the radical originality of humanity is the sphere of independence from the false (mythic as well as orthodox Christian) god, whose authority derived from the projections of fear and hope. This critical definition of humanity, a transformation of the Enlightenment critique of superstition, is irrevocable. Once the step beyond the pale of orthodox religious conceptions is taken, once the delusive nature of inherited religious investments is realized, there is no return to the shelter of traditional belief. *Faust*, stemming from the same period as Goethe's initial reworking of the Prometheus myth, counts as the major document of this homelessness in European literature.

Nevertheless, the question remains whether a conception of the human grounded in autonomy can contend with the desolation of the post-theological condition. As we have seen, in the "Prometheus" ode the threat of such desolation appears as the desert ("Wüsten," 48) of a hated life ("das Leben hassen," 47), but appears only to be cast aside in the poem's final promise to form a humanity that embraces the alternating pulse of vital anguish and joy. The assurance of Prometheus—an assurance Goethe's letters show to have been hard won[1]—is that auto-constitution, as the form of human originality, can overcome the misery of spiritual barrenness. The text I shall consider in this chapter, "Harzreise im Winter" (1777), suggests, however, that the formal (negative) definition of humanity elaborated in the "Prometheus" ode does not sufficiently sustain a meaningful life, that the self-forming 'I' does not provide an adequate basis for human community. This is indicated by the fact that, in the later text, Goethe returns to the landscape of desolation and to the hate of life that poisons its inhabitant, now figured as the "Durstenden / In der Wüste" ("the one who thirsts / In the desert," 49–50). But rather than dismissing the anguish of such spiritual abandonment as a delusion, the text poses the alleviation of that anguish as the very task it seeks to accomplish. The poetic vocation worked through in "Harzreise im Winter" is to mark out a new configuration of poet, audience, and the gods, a configuration grounded in a poetic revelation of the divine.

29. HARZREISE IM WINTER

Dem Geier gleich,
Der auf schweren Morgenwolken
Mit sanftem Fittich ruhend
Nach Beute schaut,
(5) Schwebe mein Lied.

Denn ein Gott hat
Jedem seine Bahn
Vorgezeichnet,
Die der Glückliche
(10) Rasch zum freudigen
Ziele rennt:
Wem aber Unglück
Das Herz zusammenzog,
Er sträubt vergebens
(15) Sich gegen die Schranken
Des ehernen Fadens,
Den die doch bittre Schere
Nur Einmal lös't.

In Dickichts-Schauer
(20) Drängt sich das rauhe Wild,
Und mit den Sperlingen
Haben längst die Reichen
In ihre Sümpfe sich gesenkt.

Leicht ist's folgen dem Wagen,
(25) Den Fortuna führt,
Wie der gemächliche Troß
Auf gebesserten Wegen
Hinter des Fürsten Einzug.

Aber abseits wer ist's?
(30) In's Gebüsch verliert sich sein Pfad,
Hinter ihm schlagen
Die Sträuche zusammen,
Das Gras steht wieder auf,
Die Öde verschlingt ihn.

(35) Ach wer heilet die Schmerzen
Des, dem Balsam zu Gift ward?
Der sich Menschenhaß
Aus der Fülle der Liebe trank!
Erst verachtet, nun ein Verächter,
(40) Zehrt er heimlich auf
Seinen eignen Wert
In ung'nügender Selbstsucht.

Ist auf deinem Psalter,
Vater der Liebe, ein Ton
(45) Seinem Ohre vernehmlich,
So erquicke sein Herz!
Öffne den umwölkten Blick
Über die tausend Quellen
Neben dem Durstenden
(50) In der Wüste.

Der du der Freuden viel schaffst,
Jedem ein überfließend Maß,
Segne die Brüder der Jagd
Auf der Fährte des Wilds,
(55) Mit jugendlichem Übermut
Fröhlicher Mordsucht,
Späte Rächer des Unbilds,
Dem schon Jahre vergeblich
Wehrt mit Knütteln der Bauer.

(60) Aber den Einsamen hüll'
In deine Goldwolken,
Umgib mit Wintergrün,

Bis die Rose wieder heranreift,
Die feuchten Haare,
(65) O Liebe, deines Dichters!

Mit der dämmernden Fackel
Leuchtest du ihm
Durch die Furten bei Nacht,
Über grundlose Wege
(70) Auf öden Gefilden;
Mit dem tausendfarbigen Morgen
Lachst du in's Herz ihm;
Mit dem beizenden Sturm
Trägst du ihn hoch empor;
(75) Winterströme stürzen vom Felsen
In seine Psalmen,
Und Altar des lieblichsten Danks
Wird ihm des gefürchteten Gipfels
Schneebehangener Scheitel,
(80) Den mit Geisterreihen
Kränzten ahndende Völker.

Du stehst mit unerforschtem Busen
Geheimnisvoll offenbar
Über der erstaunten Welt,
Und schaust aus Wolken
(85) Auf ihre Reiche und Herrlichkeit,
Die du aus den Adern deiner Brüder
Neben dir wässerst.[2]

HARZ JOURNEY IN WINTER

Like the raptor,
Which on heavy morning clouds
Resting with gentle wing
Looks for prey,
(5) May my song soar.

For a god has
Drawn in advance
The path of each individual,
Along which the fortunate one
(10) Fast to the joyful
Goal runs;
But whomever misfortune

Has constricted the heart,
He strains in vain
(15) Against the limits
Of the venerable thread,
Which the bitter scissors
Cut just once.

Into the tremble of brush
(20) The wild animal withdraws,
And with the sparrows
The rich have long since
Sunk into their swamps.

It's easy to follow the wagon
(25) That Fortuna leads,
Like the comfortable crowd
On paved pathways
Behind the train of the prince.

But off to the side, who is it?
(30) In the bushes his path is lost,
Behind him the branches
Snap together,
The grass rises up again,
The barrenness swallows him.

(35) Oh, who will heal the pain
Of the one for whom balm became poison?
Who drank hatred of mankind
From the fullness of love!
First despised, now despising,
(40) He secretly consumes
His own worth
In insufficient self-hunger.

Is there in your psalter,
Father of love, a tone
(45) Audible to his ear—
Then refresh his heart!
Open his clouded regard
Onto the thousand springs
Next to the one who thirsts
(50) In the desert.

You who create so many joys,
To each an overflowing cup,
Bless the brothers of the hunt
On the path of the wild animal,
(55) With youthful high spirits
In joyful pursuit of the kill,
Late avengers of the damage
Against which in vain for years
The peasant has defended himself with clubs.

(60) But the solitary one clothe
In your golden clouds,
Wrap round with evergreen,
Until the rose ripens again,
The moist hair,
(65) Oh love, of your poet!

With the dawning torch
You shine to him
Through the paths by night,
Over groundless ways
(70) On barren fields;
With the thousand-colored morning
You bring laughter into his heart;
With the searing storm
You carry him upward on high;
(75) Winter streams rush from the cliffs
Into his psalms,
And into an altar of dearest thanks
For him the snow-hung brow
Of the feared peak is transformed,
(80) Which with rows of spirits
Intuiting peoples wreathed.

You stand with undisclosed breast,
Mysterious, revealed,
Above the astonished world,
(85) And look out from the clouds
Onto its empires and glory,
Which you from the veins of your brothers
Beside you water.

Because it was composed in connection with a journey Goethe undertook to the Harz mountains in December 1777, during which he auda-
ciously climbed the peak of the so-called "Brocken," interpretations of this
text have typically been organized along biographical lines.[3] This is not
an itinerary I shall follow here, my concern being—as throughout this
study—with the objectivity of the text, the internal logic of its figuration,
the validity of its poetic statement. There can be no doubt, of course, that
Goethe invested his ascent of the legendary mountain (legendary because
the "Brocken" was thought to be the site of satanic celebrations as in the
"Walpurgisnacht" scene of *Faust*) with great personal import, but to view
the text exclusively in terms of its references to the events of that journey is
to impoverish its poetic significance. A similar point was made in connection with "Pilgers Morgenlied" (Text 10), a text that bears notable similarities to "Harzreise im Winter." From a poetic point of view, biographical references are analogous to the "Tagesreste" absorbed into the fabric of
a dream; their function is not to refer to particular entities or events, but to
provide the raw material shaped in the labor of oneiric or poetic figuration.
Even a biographer will have to take the difference between poetry and life
into account; for the critic interested in the specifically poetic valence of
the text, however, that difference is an a priori of inquiry.

I therefore begin with the feature of the text that most clearly indicates
its distance from the registration of biographical fact: its formalization, the
numerical regularities that determine its spatiotemporal organization. As
noted with regard to the "Prometheus" ode, the function of such patterns
is to establish relations of equivalence (similarity and opposition) among
stanzas and stanzaic groups considered as global rhetorical-semantic units,
to render salient the contours of the poem's composition. In "Harzreise im
Winter," there appears to be no rule governing stanzaic composition, as
the juxtaposition of sequential position (Roman numerals) and line count
within the stanzas (Arabic numerals) reveals:

I	II	III	IV	V	VI	VII	VIII	IX	X	XI
5	13	5	5	6	8	8	9	6	16	7

We should not conclude from this lack of a single, transparent principle of
arrangement, however, that the question of numerical ordering is of no
importance. On the contrary, the absence of a single rule of composition
makes any notable regularities all the more informative. In addition, as the

"Prometheus" ode instructed us, the use of a relatively "free" numerical arrangement allows for a complexification of composition that overdetermines the positional significance of individual stanzas.

The most prominent numerical correlation within the text as a whole obtains between stanzas V, VI, and VII on the one hand (6 + 8 + 8 = 22 lines) and stanzas IX and X on the other (6 + 16 = 22 lines). This equivalence, once perceived, calls attention to other similarities, both semantic and syntactic in character, between these two phases of the text. For instance, each of these sections draws its overriding thematic unity from the fact that it focuses on an isolated figure cut off from the context of an encompassing social sphere: in the case of the first group, the outsider ("abseits," 29) or marginalized melancholic, in the case of the second, the "solitary one" ("den Einsamen," 60), who also bears the title of "poet" ("deines Dichters," 65). As regards the syntax, each section is introduced by the disjunctive conjunction "aber" (29, 60), which strongly marks a turn in the movement of the poetic meditation. Such swerves of thought illustrate the original meaning of the poetic term "strophe," and the use of the conjunction here suggests that the two phases of the text it introduces cohere as strophic units. In the classical poetics of the higher (especially Pindaric) ode, such units were juxtaposed as strophe and anti-strophe, and we can infer that a cognate type of compositional contrast is being employed in "Harzreise im Winter," which recalls the Pindaric tradition in other respects as well. Thus, the cross-reading of the two numerically equivalent sections not only leads to the identification of similarities on the global semantic and syntactic levels, but against the background of these kinships important differences emerge into view and arrange themselves in a pattern of inverse symmetry:

Stanzas V-VII	*Stanzas IX-X*
the outsider whose 'path' is 'lost' *(30)*	the solitary one (poet) who finds a 'way' where there is none *(68–69)*
prayer for a 'psalm' *(43–46)* (plea or request)	'psalms' realized *(75–76)* (fulfillment of request)
'balm' becomes 'poison' *(36)* (negative transformation)	'fear' becomes 'thanks' *(77–78)* (positive transformation)

The poet of stanzas IX and X is the counter-figure to the marginalized outsider of stanzas V–VII; their respective destinies are keyed to one

another in such a way that the negative condition of the outcast is
alleviated in and through the poet's ascent. Thus, the central semantic
operation that occurs between these phases of the text is one of reversal:
loss becomes discovery, a prayer for a form of religious-poetic speech (a
psalm) is answered with the event of that speech. One of the major tasks
that a reading of this poem must accomplish is to delineate the character of
this semantic reversal by exploring the poetic intricacies of these two
phases of the text.[4]

A second numerical relation that underlines an important semantic
convergence is that between the first and final stanzas. Their line count
differs (5 vs. 7), but due to their location at the structurally most prominent or weighted points of the text, beginning and end, they attract the
same sort of comparative reading as the numerically equivalent groups just
discussed. Both of these stanzas, of course, require a detailed examination
of their respective figural complexities; at this point in my commentary,
however, I am only concerned with the most general semantic relations
that connect them one to another. Globally considered, the first stanza
states a problem and the final stanza indicates that that problem has been
solved. The problem in question is poetic in character: the poet wishes
that his song might soar like the "Geier" (1), that he might attain to a
standpoint of elevation and to a viewpoint that affords the visual reach
("schauen," 4, is the key verb in this regard) that is associated with a
position on high. In the final stanza, this standpoint has been achieved; the
poetic problem stated at the outset has found a solution: the "journey"
("Harzreise") which the poem narrates has brought the speaker to the
heights he had aspired to, allowing him to identify with the visual perspective (the verb "schauen" returns, 85) such heights afford.

Taken together, the compositional relations thus far discerned enable us
to identify two major semantic processes operating in the text: a movement from beginning to end that converts a poetic problem into a solution
and an internal transformation through which a negative state of affairs
involving an outsider figure is reversed in a series of statements bearing on
the figure of the poet. There is, of course, every reason to suspect that this
internal transformation is an important factor in the achievement of a
successful solution to the poetic problem stated at the beginning, that the
realization of the poetic aspiration is brought about in and through the
process figured in stanzas IX–X. The precise nature of the connection
between the two overriding semantic processes, however, remains unclear,

as does the import of the poetic problem adumbrated in the first stanza. Some insight into these open questions can be gained by attending to the relations among the other stanzas, thereby amplifying our sense of the poem's composition.

Stanza II, because it is linked to the opening stanza by the conjunction "denn" (6), seems to provide a motivation for the poetic aspiration with which the text begins. Of course, the explanatory gesture of the conjunction is accompanied by an effect of semantic opacity due to the shift from a relatively personal ("mein Lied," 5) and topographically concrete mode of discourse to a generalizing and impersonal tone ("Jedem," 7), which draws its points of reference from an allegorically inflected scenario of antiquity (the chariot or foot race as the path of life). This discursive shift from the personal to the universal lends the text its seriousness, its claim to the level of communal validity which its generic antecedents (the higher ode, the hymn, the psalm) would lead one to expect. The poetic wish stated in stanza I is the response to a problem situation that transcends the individual and affects mankind in general. The second stanza sets out this problem situation in terms of the categories of fortune ("der Glückliche," 9) and misfortune ("Unglück," 12): the universal, human issue that motivates the poetic aspiration is the fact that fortune and misfortune are distributed arbitrarily; that individuals are at the mercy of a destiny that operates independently of their will and reason and that seems to result from the antecedent decision of a "god" ("Gott," 6).

The problem situation defined in stanza II in terms of the abstract opposition "Glück"/"Unglück" undergoes in the subsequent stanzas a process of figural concretization. This seems especially clear in the case of stanza III, in which the "Sperlinge" (21) and the "Reichen" (22) exemplify the fortunate, while the "Wild" (20), which has only the underbrush to protect it from the harshness of winter, typifies misfortune. Particularly noteworthy here is the blending of the spheres of 'nature' and 'society': the natural distribution of benefits that provides the sparrows with a comfortable winter home is recapitulated on the social level, where it is the wealthy who enjoy warmth and secure shelter. Destiny, defined in stanza II as the arbitrary distribution of "Glück" and "Unglück," is conceived here as the repetition within the social domain of the natural principle of a predetermined (cf. "Vorgezeichnet," 8) and fixed allocation of advantage. This conception of destiny will ramify as the text progresses and various social equivalents of the unfortunate "Wild"—namely, the outsider figure of stanzas V–VII and the "peasant" (59) of stanza VIII—make their appearance on the text's stage. At this point, however, I want to stress another feature of stanza III, the fact that it also stands in an obvious numerical and semantic relation to stanza I. The sparrows, which live in groups and sink downward into the warm mud, are opposed to the "Geier," which, of course, is a solitary bird that lives on high. The three opening stanzas, then, form a compositional triptych:

I	*II*	*III*
5 lines	13 lines	5 lines
"Geier"		"Sperlinge"
	"Glück" vs.	"Sperlinge"/"Reiche"
	"Unglück"	vs. "Wild"

Poetic aspiration and motivation thus cohere in a single compositional figure. As noted previously, that aspiration achieves its fulfillment in the final stanza and this fulfillment is brought about by the transformation of the outsider's desolation accomplished in and through the poet's ascent of the mountain (bringing him to a position on high). If we compare the numerical arrangement of the opening triptych with the major phase of the poet's ascent (stanza X) and the poem's concluding stanza, we again find an instance of numerical symmetry:

Stanzas I-III	*Stanzas X-XI*
5 + 13 + 5 = 23 lines	16 + 7 = 23 lines

As in the "Prometheus" ode, the positional significance of a stanzaic unit is determined, hence overdetermined, by its placement within two compositional patterns. Stanza X belongs simultaneously to the group IX–X, which is the symmetrical counterpart of the group V–VII, and to the group X–XI, which answers the opening configuration of stanzas I–III. This dual ordering not only exemplifies the compositional precision and complexity of the text, it also indicates that stanza X, which is the longest in the poem, is the axial phase of the text, the site of its most arduous semiotic labor.

The complexification of compositional patterning is, in fact, a pervasive feature of this text, a feature that embeds each stanzaic unit within a network of multiple cross-relations. For example, stanza III, in addition to occupying a position within the introductory triptych, can also be read as yoked by opposition to the stanza that follows it. Both stanzas III and IV consist of five lines, but the former focuses on a 'natural' space (although the comparison with the wealthy evokes the return of the rich to the city for the winter), whereas the latter clearly attends to events in the urban domain. The same compositional mobility applies to stanza IV. Not only can it be linked with stanza III, but it can also be read as a further concretization of the "Glück" theme of stanza II insofar as the wagon the prince's adherents follow is steered by the goddess Fortuna. Thus, the "comfortable crowd" (26) proves to be a variant of the fortunate sparrows and wealthy, with whom it shares not only movement toward warm quarters, but also the semantic marker 'many'. It is hardly surprising that the speaker, who identifies with the solitary "Geier" and who later stylizes himself as the "Einsamen" (60), abjures this cohort of courtly acolytes.

This reading of the mobile composition of the poem's opening four stanzas also enables us to see their connection with the unit V–VIII, which centers on the figure of the outcast. While stanza IV offers another and, as it were, more perniciously self-seeking version of the sparrows and the wealthy,[5] stanzas V–VII are devoted to a human counterpart of the unfortunate "Wild" (20). Compare:

> In Dickichts-Schauer
> Drängt sich das rauhe Wild,   *(19–20)*
>
> In's Gebüsch verliert sich sein Pfad,
> Hinter ihm schlagen
> Die Sträuche zusammen,   *(30–32)*

Once again natural and social categories overlap. The individual cast off from the community into a misanthropic "abseits" (29) is reduced to the status of the wild animal. This enables us to see, at least in outline, why the poetic ascent of stanzas IX–X is the reversal of the outsider's condition: by internalizing and positively transforming the fate of the outsider, the poet negates the arbitrary distribution of fortune and misfortune which stanza II identifies as the motivation for his aspiration to ascend to the standpoint on high.

The position of stanza VIII between the symmetrical groups V–VII and IX–X marks it as the initial turning point of the text. Here, for the first time, a negative condition is alleviated. The peasant, I have already

remarked, is a further concretization of the theme of misfortune, as the
following juxtaposition reveals:

> Wem aber Unglück
> Das Herz zusammenzog,
> Er sträubt vergebens
> Sich gegen die Schranken
> Des ehernen Fadens,   *(12–16)*

> Dem schon Jahre vergeblich
> Wehrt mit Knütteln der Bauer.   *(58–59)*

Furthermore, that which, due to conditions that are primarily social, the
peasant in vain seeks to ward off is a natural antagonist, the "Wild" (54),
which bears the same name as the figure of misfortune encountered in
stanza III. The peasant is reduced to the status of the beast against which
he struggles in order to protect his crops, his livestock, and his family. His
conditions of existence are equivalent to those of the harried natural
creature. But the point of the stanza, of course, is that this quasi-natural
destiny, which is in fact not natural or fixed at all, is here being overcome.
The "brothers of the hunt" (hunting in the eighteenth century was a
privilege of the nobility, which is why the peasant is limited to the use of a
club) do not remain within the city, do not follow the train of Fortuna, but
venture out in order to relieve the peasant in his plight. (This alleviation of
the peasant's hopeless condition is an incidental result of the hunt, but it is
clearly the aspect the text stresses as the hunt's principal legitimation.)
Stanza VIII, in other words, relates an instance of the negation of destiny
through concerted human action. The "Brüder der Jagd" (53) accomplish
in terms of external factors what the poet in stanzas IX and X achieves in
terms of a complex set of internal factors.

This account of the poem's compositional structure delineates only the
most general semantic relations among the stanzas considered as global semantic units. As such, it remains abstract and requires exfoliation through
a detailed reading of the poetic figuration. Nevertheless, an outline of the
poem's argument has begun to take shape. Its basic components are
deployed as follows:

I. Statement of poetic aspiration.

II. Motivation of this aspiration in terms of the problem of 'destiny': the
predetermined and unalterable distribution of "Glück" and "Unglück."

III. Concretization of the abstract opposition "Glück"/"Unglück" in terms of the "sparrows" (= "rich") and the "wild animal."

IV. Further concretization of the "Glück" theme in terms of the courtiers who follow Fortuna in order to win the favor of the prince.

V–VII. Concretization of the "Unglück" theme in terms of the outsider figure; extensive development of semantic values surrounding this figure.

VIII. Alleviation of external "Unglück" through the collective action of the hunters.

IX–X. The poet's ascent transforms the negative situation of the outsider into a positive situation; alleviation of internal "Unglück."

XI. Indication that poetic aspiration as stated at the outset has been realized.

~

The compositional structure delineated in the foregoing can be thought of as the spatiotemporal scaffold of the text, a deployment of certain thematic complexes in multiple patterns of semantic relation, a blocking out of the poem's most general configurations of significance. As such, it highlights important features of the poem's shape (features that have gone unnoticed in the research) and indicates the stringency of its formalization, but it does not by any means provide an adequate reading. On the contrary, the conspicuously linear character of the compositional figure sketched above belies what is perhaps the most striking feature of this as well as other major lyric texts, its plurivocal character, or what Karlheinz Stierle, in an important theoretical study of the lyric, has called the "simultaneity of divergent contexts."[6] To grasp the poetic character of the text, it is necessary to develop a model of the poetic figuration that takes into account the density and suggestiveness of its texture.

A lyric text can be thought of as drawing together several semantic structures in such a way that they interact with and modify one another. Poetic writing is a labor of condensation (*Verdichtung*) that intricately interweaves strands of significance. I call these strands "schemata" and mean by that term a slightly altered version of the Kantian notion. Schemata lack the richness and detail of individual perceptions, though they certainly play a crucial role in molding and rendering intelligible what we perceive. They are repeatable and therefore general, but do not possess the abstractness and conceptual neatness of categories. Schemata are applied to actual experience and make that experience manageable, yet

they are not fixed and are subject to experiential correction and amplifica-
tion. Not all schemata are structured alike, as we shall see, and even a
single schema can be employed in different ways—for instance, involving
more or less specification—on different occasions. Schemata are culture-
specific structures that organize the storage of knowledge in memory and
the application of that knowledge to present occasions. It has been shown
that, without a notion such as that of schema, it is impossible to account
for the way individuals understand texts, that texts function in part by
activating schemata that structure, at a level superior to that of linguistic-
grammatical patterns, what the text is about.[7] The "divergent contexts"
that in Stierle's view converge or undergo condensation in the lyric are
various cultural-cognitive schemata which the text jambs. Whereas the
linear unfolding of a communicative or pragmatically oriented message
specifies a single schema, the lyric message joins several together in a fugal
array. In this way, the lyric acquires remarkable semantic richness, albeit at
the cost of easy intelligibility.

    In "Harzreise im Winter," several schemata are interwoven with one
another, but for the purposes of this analysis I shall concentrate on what I
take to be the six major ones:

       1. Poetry
       2. Path
       3. Hunt
       4. Liquid
       5. Perception/Cognition
       6. Religion

Each of these six terms can be considered as the title of an encyclopedia
entry in which a body of cultural knowledge is stored in a loosely structured fashion; or as the title of a network of terms that specify the head
term by indicating semantic components, prominent associations, discursive contexts, etc.[8] Note that the cultural encyclopedia does not include
only high or dignified knowledge: familiarity with the possible permutations of the path schema is just as essential to an understanding of
"Harzreise im Winter" as is an acquaintance with the schemata of religion
or poetry.[9] Note further that the schemata are of different types. Liquid,
for example, is an object schema that can be concretized in terms of
different subschemata (e.g., 'water', 'wine') and integrated into different
contexts (e.g., the context of natural phenomena or the context of the act

of drinking). Hunt, by contrast, is an action schema that includes, in addition to various actantial roles (e.g., 'hunter', 'hunted'), typical sequences of component actions (e.g., 'pursuit', 'confrontation', 'capture', 'kill'). Finally, the schemata entertain an important relation to what is called intertextuality, since to actualize a schema is to actualize another text, or tradition of texts, in which that schema bears an important function. Schemata presuppose textual performances for their production, maintenance, and evolution, and textual performances presuppose schemata for their generation and interpretation.

Of course, one might object that Kant himself did not count aesthetic representations as schematic. In his view, the application of schemata obeys rules determined by a concept, whereas the specificity of aesthetic representations resides precisely in the fact that they cannot be subsumed beneath a single concept. My argument is that the schematic representations characteristic of our practical, communicative speech do not disappear in aesthetic texts, but, rather, are enriched by virtue of their being interwoven with other schemata in such a manner that no single schema dominates. (Another way of formulating this point is to say that poetic texts do not serve to represent a noematic object; this is the vocabulary I employed in my discussion of "Der Fischer" in Chapter 7.) The points of condensation or conjuncture at which multiple schemata are activated by the text can be called textual figures, in a broad sense of the term that includes the tropes and other semantic figures as well as syntactic, rhythmical, and phonological configurations. In a poetic text, both semantic schemata of the sort I have been discussing and schemata of syntactic relation and perceptual (including auditory) form are entwined in such a way that the imagination plays, in Kant's sense, back and forth among them.[10] Such imaginative play is the experience of poetic texture and the task of analysis is to discern the networks constitutive of the poem's textural surface, to chart the space and the dynamics of the poem's significance.

With this elementary analytical vocabulary (schema/figure) in place, I want to return to the opening stanza:

> Dem Geier gleich,
> Der auf schweren Morgenwolken
> Mit sanftem Fittich ruhend
> Nach Beute schaut,
> Schwebe mein Lied. *(1–5)*

The poetry schema is activated here not only through explicit mention ("Lied"), but also by allusion to the high poetic genres of the ode and hymn in which the metaphor of poetic flight is a standard formula for visionary inspiration. Of course, in that tradition the object of comparison is usually the eagle, which in our text has been transformed into a "Geier" (not a vulture). This shift introduces what might be called a tendency toward historical specification: this text does not claim merely to belong to the Pindaric tradition of exalted, visionary poetry, but to realize that tradition in the context of a local topography (the Harz mountains) and a local ornithology (the "Geier"). By rooting his aspiration in a particular landscape and historical moment, the poet endeavors to overcome the empty conventionalism that shackles so many eighteenth-century efforts at Pindaric loftiness. In addition to triggering the poetry schema, the term "Geier" participates in a forcefully marked alliterative and assonantial coupling: "*Gei*er"/"*glei*ch." Later in the text, this pairing of the conventional metaphor with a pronounced phonological schema will return when the idea of poetic inspiration is figured through related combinations such as "*g*efürchteten *G*ipfels" and "*Gei*sterr*ei*hen," which thus appear as echoes of the opening line. But the solitary bird of prey, again via poetic tradition, is also a metonymy for its master, the master god (Zeus/Jupiter). Thus, the bird points by contiguity to a godhead conceived as 'ruler' or 'sovereign power', and it is this sense of 'god' that marks the text's first employment of the religion schema. Line 4, which identifies the bird as a hunter and as a creature that sees far and acutely, brings two others of the schemata enumerated above, hunt and vision, into the stanza's figuration. Finally, if we consider that the title of the poem ("Harz*reise*") evokes the path schema, then the density of this initial phase of the text makes itself felt: all but one of the six major semantic schemata—liquid—are woven into the tapestry of the poem's introit. On the other hand, it is precisely this schema that determines the final line, indeed the final word ("wässerst," 88) of the text.

Three comments are required here. First, the densely woven textual figure of the poem's first stanza (and first sentence) evokes the schemata with a specific focus or perspectivization. For instance, the hunt schema is not actualized in a manner that foregrounds all of its components; rather, the text mentions a specific actor within that schema (the hunter) and a specific moment within the sequence of episodes that, according to cultural knowledge, constitutes a hunt. Thus, the perspectivization of the

hunt schema the text offers at this point holds open a number of virtualities which can be thought of as questions the text may, or may not,
answer: What will be the hunter's prey? Will the hunter find its prey? Will
a strike or capture take place? Or will the prey escape? As we shall see, these
questions will indeed find answers, but in the oblique mode of signification peculiar to lyric "anti-discourse."[11] For the moment, however, I want
to emphasize that the initial marking of the hunt schema engenders a sense
of narrative expectancy, a sort of alertness on the part of the reader to
possible itineraries of diegetic realization, and that this orientation toward
the future is a component of the first stanza's significance. Second, it
should be remarked that the semantic schemata are interwoven with and
embodied in perceptual patterns. In this connection, I already called
attention to the prominent combination of alliteration and assonance in
the first verse. Another compelling arrangement involves the distance, in
terms of stanzaic position, that separates "Dem Geier gleich" (1) from its
syntactic complement, "Schwebe mein Lied" (5). This distance seems to
bear a dual function, at once marking a disjunction between the poet and
the goal of his aspiration and highlighting, due to the inserted relative
clause that suspends syntactic closure, the significance of 'hovering' intrinsic to the verb "schweben." Thus, the stanza as a whole is a gestural sign
that enacts both the distance intrinsic to the poet's desire and the state of
suspended motion that is an aspect of the desired condition. Finally, we
should note a certain semantic tension inherent in the opening figuration.
On the one hand, the allusions to the sovereign god of power, to his bird,
to the aspect of the hunt, imbue the stanza with an aura of 'threat' that is
also meteorologically figured in the "heavy morning clouds" (2); on the
other hand, the bird's wing is said to rest "gently," perhaps "tenderly"
("sanftem," 3), suggesting a scenario of caring or loving contact, as in a
protective embrace or caress. This affective or tonal dissonance, in which
authority and love, masculine-paternal and feminine-maternal aspects,
coincide, charges the poetic aspiration with a subliminal agenda. Part of
what the poet undertakes to do through his ascent is to disclose the
internal relation, or harmony, of these dissonant values.

   Analysis is concerned not only with the interaction of schemata within
local textual figures, but also with the play of variation to which the
individual schemata are submitted as the text unfolds. The schemata,
as paradigmatic complexes, are projected, true to Jakobson's definition,
across the syntagmatic axis, generating the tension between simultaneity

and sequence that is characteristic of poetic texts. Take, for example, the hunt schema. As we have seen, it is actualized in the first stanza, where the "Geier," at once a metaphor of poetic inspiration and a metonymy of the godhead considered as sovereign power, is also described as a hunter scanning the depths for prey. This focalization of the hunt schema, as mentioned, holds open several possibilities for ramification, such as the naming of a specific prey or the development of an action sequence. The text does not realize these possibilities by narrating the further story of the "Geier," but rather by making its way through a series of different figures that, while bearing no direct connection to the "Geier," are nevertheless actualizations of the identical schema. The first of these figures appears in stanza III:

> In Dickichts-Schauer
> Drängt sich das rauhe Wild,
>
> *(19–20)*

Here we encounter a vaguely defined creature whose withdrawal into the underbrush and above all whose fear ("Schauer") suggest a reading as 'potential prey'. The first stanza shows us the hunter on high, at once awesome and serene like the god to whom it is related by contiguity, while the third stanza affords us a glimpse of the hunted below, enclosed upon itself in terror. At the same time, of course, this "Wild" represents, within the natural realm, one of the victims of destiny whose plight defines the problem situation the poet hopes to alleviate. It is for the sake of the hunted that the poet aspires to the standpoint of the hunter.

This movement between the hunter and the hunted characterizes the poetic meditation throughout. Thus, the outsider figure of stanzas V–VII, whom we have already identified as a counter-figure for the poet, reveals certain characteristics of a creature preyed upon. Like the "Wild" of stanza III, this human victim withdraws into the underbrush, where he exercises a self-destructiveness ("Zehrt er heimlich auf / Seinen eignen Wert," 40–41) reminiscent of a wounded animal. Of course, the outsider's position is the result of social and psychological factors, not of a naturally established predatory relationship; the employment of the hunt schema here, in contrast to the first two instances, is metaphorical. In the subsequent activation of the schema, however, the poetic reflection focuses on an actual hunt and, whereas in the previous two instances the fear on the part of the hunted was foregrounded, the hunt of stanza VIII proves to be a positively valued event, relieving as it does the miserable plight of the peasant. The reason for this is that the peasant himself is one of the exemplars of "Unglück," an individual whose social conditions of existence reduce him to the status of the very "Wild" which is his natural antagonist.[12] The hunters, for whose success the poet prays, mediate between the fortunate and the unfortunate, bridge their quasi-natural separation and thereby mitigate the suffering that had seemed a product of destiny.

The final evocation of the hunt schema is linked with the figure of the poet in the decisive phase of his ascent and occurs in a most indirect manner. I have already mentioned that this moment—the arrival of the poetic inspiration hoped for at the outset—echoes on the phonological plane the poem's first line:

> Dem *Gei*er g*lei*ch *(1)*
>
> des *g*efürchteten *G*ipfels *(78)*
>
> Sch*ei*tel,
> Den mit *Gei*ster*ei*hen *(79–80)*

All of the echoing terms are related to the mountain peak in its frightening aspect, which itself is a metaphor for the godhead to which the "Geier" metonymically refers. But the decisive allusion to the "Geier" occurs in the lines:

> Mit dem beizenden Sturm
> Trägst du ihn hoch empor;
>
> *(73–74)*

Referentially, the lines make no sense; a storm would ordinarily impede ascent and certainly not "carry him upward on high." Such vertical transport could only occur if some agent of the godhead such as the "Geier" would seize the poet and lift him aloft. And, of course, this is precisely what happens: the verb "beizen," which designates the "searing" effect of the storm on the wanderer, is also a technical term from the jargon of hunting and signifies the action through which a bird of prey ("Beizvogel") seizes its victim. At the very moment when the 'storm' of poetic inspiration (a connotation to which I shall return) takes hold of the poet, the hunting bird grasps its prey and bears it upward. Recalling that the "Geier" is a variant of the eagle of Zeus, we can perceive a further dimension of this activation of the hunt schema: like the mythological figure of Ganymede, the poet is being carried to the godhead by the emissary bird, an allusion that transforms the terrifying aspect of the hunt into an act of love.[13] This activation of the hunt schema also enables us to discern the specific relation between the poet and the outsider. The poet redeems the outsider by placing himself in the latter's position, by assuming the role of victim or object of prey and exposing himself to the hunter's act of seizure. And in doing so, he overcomes the fear surrounding the divine figure and reveals the terrifying strike to be an act of love. The poet's ascent is a substitutional self-sacrifice out of which a new subject and a new vision of the divine emerges.

The hunt schema, then, begins as an oscillation between the poles of 'awesome hunter' and 'terrified hunted' in order finally to focus on two acts of hunting, two interventions of the hunter in the life of the hunted. The first of these is the ostensible subject matter of stanza VIII, while the second is evoked through phonological echoes and the double-reading of the verb "beizen," but in both cases the hunt appears as a redemptive act. Articulated with this pattern of variation are the patterns formed by the sequential variations of the other five schemata. In their branchings and crossings, the six schemata constitute the symbolic network of the text. Of course, I cannot describe this network in all its ramifications here, although in the next section of my reading I will show how its strands come together at a particularly dense poetic locus. But it is worthwhile to consider, even if only in a sketchy manner, one further schema in order to gain a sense of how it interconnects with the hunt schema just described.

The characteristic feature of the religion schema that the text successively focalizes in its movement from beginning to end is that it does not rely on, or accept as definitive, any single religious tradition or belief system. Rather, the text exemplifies a strategy vis-à-vis inherited religious discourses that can be described as the mis-en-scène of an evolution in religious attitude. In other words, the schema of religion is activated across a series of displacements that alter the relation between the religious subject and the religious object. It is important to note that these changes affect both terms of the relation. It is not a matter of acquiring an improved understanding of an object that remains the same; rather, the movement from one religious attitude to another is accompanied by a change in the object as well. Indeed, one way of charting the coming-to-awareness of religious consciousness the text dramatizes is to note the transformations the concept of 'god' undergoes along the course of the poet's journey.

1. The first stanza, as we have seen, figures the godhead metonymically via the "Geier" and, it should be amended, the ominous "schweren Morgenwolken" (2). To this figuration of god as allmighty and threatening sovereign, the second stanza adds the notion of the god as the ruler of human destiny. (We can note in passing how this particular religious conception is linked with the schema of the path, here concretized as the "Bahn," 7, or allegorical racetrack of life's fortunes and misfortunes. This path-related figure connects the religious conception with the problem situation motivating the poet's search for a path in the mountainous winter landscape.) Together, then, the two stanzas—from the reminiscence of Zeus's eagle to the allusion to Atropos ("die doch bittre Schere," 17^{14})—focalize a Graeco-Roman god who arbitrarily rules over human destiny. This conception of god returns in stanza IV as the conventionalized personification "Fortuna" (25), whereby the goddess herself is less important than the practice of aristocratic favor-seeking for which she provides ideological legitimation. The hierarchical social order, with its arbitrary distribution of benefits, is a variant of the religion of destiny and, as such, a component of the problem situation the poet sets out to alleviate.

2. In stanza VII, we encounter a god whose traits are clearly Judaeo-Christian. The allusion to the psalms and to the Old Testament story of Hagar, the banished mistress of Abraham whose exile figures the situation of the outcast, reveals this god to be a "Vater der Liebe" (44) who intercedes in the life of the suffering individual. This is the god who manifested his loving care to Hagar by bringing forth springs of water in the desert of her abandonment, much as the poet requests here. It is important to note, however, that this god, although called upon, does not actually enter the text; there is no indication that the poet's prayer on behalf of the outsider is answered, that the "Father of love" actually comes to the aid of the tormented and melancholic misanthrope. In other words, the allusion to the Old Testament god, or, more generally, to the Judaeo-Christian god, marks a certain historical distance between the traditional religious conception and the present situation of the poem. The revelation does not occur as a miracle in the desert, but must wait for the poet's ascent.

3. The eighth stanza specifies its god in the following terms:

> Der du der Freuden viel schaffst,
> Jedem ein überfließend Maß,   *(51–52)*

As is frequently the case, the figuration of the god is linked to the liquid schema, here through the qualification "overflowing." Of course, the god who created the wine this overflowing cup metonymically refers to is of Graeco-Roman origin. But the obviously metaphorical function of the second line suggests a reading of the figuration as what might be termed a naturalized Dionysius/Bacchus, a vital, spontaneous force that expresses itself in joyful activity. The divine here is a natural energy and joyful expenditure, which animate human collectivity and thereby, albeit incidentally, alleviate the peasant's misery. One could speak of a pre-ethical divinity, a natural exuberance, to which the poet accords—with the phrase "Fröhlicher Mordsucht" (56)—ironic recognition. The fusion of the spheres of the divine and of nature that occurs in stanza VIII can therefore be seen to contrast with the higher, ethical, and 'loving' vision of a natural divinity achieved by the poet himself.

4. Finally, in stanza XI (I shall attend to the decisive stanzas IX and X subsequently) we encounter a god that cannot be identified in terms of any traditional religious context. This new god—new because "unerforscht" (82)—represents an activation of the religion schema unique to this text, a god the knowledge of which is attained in and through the course of the text itself; a god revealed, as we shall see, through poetic insight.

As this brief and very general account shows, the text articulates what might be called a poetic phenomenology of religious consciousness, a passage through a series of, in Hegel's phrase, "Gestalten des Bewußtseins" ("configurations of consciousness"), each describable as a particular relation between religious subject and object. The initial phase (1) marks the problem situation of the text: a god of destiny who, in his sovereign indifference to human suffering and in the violence of his interventions in human life, divides humankind into fortunate and unfortunate. The stanzas focused on the figure of the outsider—an exemplary case of the misfortune destiny parcels out—turn in prayer to the traditional god of the Old Testament (2), only to discover the absence of that god in the present. The prayer is the attitude of a divided consciousness that can only register the impossibility of the very redemptive act it invokes. In the third phase (3), divinity is characterized as the energizing surabundance of natural vitality, a god of 'life' considered in its pre-ethical sense of exuberant force. For those involved in the frenzy of the hunt, the religious attitude is equivalent to identification; the "brothers" are sustained and driven by the passion of their joyful, but murderous, pursuit. For the poet, the attitude toward this religion of nature remains distanced, ironic recognition. Finally, the text figures a religious attitude toward the Absolute (4) that comes into being as a result of the poet's ascent to the heights of vision. The decisive "Erfahrung" ("experience") of consciousness, to employ once again a term from Hegel's *Phenomenology*,[15] is elaborated in stanzas IX and X. Here the central transformation of religious attitude takes place: fear (78) becomes thanks (77) and the ancient religious vision of the peoples (81) is revealed in its true, nonsuperstitious form. This is, of course, also the moment when the hunter descends from the sky in order to seize its prey and bear it upward.

~

Everything points to the decisive character of stanzas IX and X: there the ascent to which the poet aspires in the opening stanza occurs; there the negative condition of the outsider is systematically reversed; there the epochal transformation of religious consciousness is accomplished. Exactly this is suggested by the spatial coding of the text. By carving his path through a territory culturally marked as wild exteriority or otherness, the poet seeks a new foundation and spiritual meaning for the community.[16] A meaning earned outside the social sphere, however, cannot be rendered in the language of quotidian affairs. The poetry of sublime inspiration, whose tradition defines the vocation of "Harzreise im Winter," inevitably transgresses the limits of intelligibility. This discursive excess, often acknowledged in predicates of difficulty, opacity, even madness, is the zone of poetic originality to which a reading must endeavor to find access. The task and obligation of reading is not to restate what the text says, but to remark its untranslatability.

Paradoxically enough, precisely this, discursively speaking, wildest phase of the text—stanzas IX and X—has been most assiduously submitted to mimetic taming, not the least by Goethe himself.[17] The premise of this domestication is that the text, especially in these two stanzas, relates the story of the poet's actual (or imaginatively recalled) ascent of the "Brocken," amplifying this account with certain ideal or symbolic meanings. I shall not repeat here the general arguments against such narrative constructions made in Chapters 2 and 7. Suffice it to note that any construal of a verisimilar narrative will distort certain facts regarding the text, for example that the poet does not climb the mountain at all, but is "carried upward." This is not to say that the notion of journey suggested by the title "Harzreise im Winter" bears no significance whatsoever, merely that the text is not the depiction *of* a journey. The suggestions of spatial movement through a landscape are actualizations of one of the text's semantic schemata (the path schema) and, although this schema plays a role in stanzas IX and X, it by no means constitutes the intentional object of that portion of the text. Nor do I wish to claim that the question of narrative structure is irrelevant; on the contrary, it is precisely here that the text exhibits its most clearly defined narrative contours. But in order to grasp the narrative significance of the passage, it is necessary to abandon the mimetic model and move to a somewhat higher level of abstraction.

The narrative pattern that "Harzreise im Winter" at once conforms to and modifies—this seems to me incontrovertible—is that of the 'quest'. In quest narratives, a narrative subject or 'protagonist' sets out to acquire an 'object of value' that is essential to the community. Along the way, he encounters an 'antagonist' who endeavors to block acquisition of the valued object, and in doing so threatens the life of the protagonist. Overcoming the antagonist is the test of the protagonist's heroism, a trial that can only be mastered through the intercession of a helper-figure or "adjuvant" who provides instruments, often magical, as well as knowledge indispensable to the success of the project. Once the object of value is attained and brought to the community, the lack caused by the original removal of that object is filled, the communal disequilibrium or malaise corrected, and the hero duly applauded.[18] Stanzas IX and X mark the peripeteia of just such a quest narrative, as revealed by the two types of interaction registered there. First (60–74), the poet enters into a relation with the figure "Liebe," to whom he prays for an intervention that can be called 'protective' or 'sustaining', and who responds to this prayer with a series of actions that guide, encourage, and transport him. (I have formulated this description as neutrally as possible in order to elicit the functional characteristics of the interaction.) "Liebe," in other words, is the "adjuvant," the helper whose support ensures successful completion of the protagonist's (the poet's) mission. The second phase of interaction (75–81) relates the poet to the mountain, and at this point Goethe transforms the traditional model of quest narrative. The mountain embodies a syncretism of actantial roles: it is at once the 'antagonist' (insofar as the winter landscape both terrifies the poet and hinders his ascent) and the 'donor' or 'source' of value, the figure who endows the object of the quest with its charge of significance. And what is this object that the protagonist seeks and eventually acquires? It is precisely the knowledge that the mountain is in fact not the frightening antagonist it originally seemed to be, but rather the very source of the valued object the poet brings to the community. In other words, the object the poet sets out to wrest from the antagonist is the poetic vision or cognition that reveals the mountain in its true nature. The narrative structure that organizes "Harzreise im Winter" is the story of the quest for the poetic vision the poem itself embodies.

This account of the narrative structure of stanzas IX and X as the peripeteia of a quest narrative has several advantages. It allows us to see, first of all, what might be termed the ethnological rootedness of the text, its employment and transformation of a pervasive mechanism of cultural sense-making. In "Harzreise im Winter," Goethe employs the model of the redemptive quest as a structural metaphor of poetic vocation. Thus, the various actantial roles that inhere in the quest model are no longer filled by substantial beings that have an independent existence within the narrative world; the interactions organized by the quest model involve internal, psychological factors, and the quest itself is essentially a reflective process, an inner trial. The hypothesis likewise brings to light important features of the text's overriding coherence. Quest narratives inevitably work toward the elimination of a deficiency in the community, and, as we have seen, "Harzreise im Winter" poses a communal or generally human problem, the arbitrary character of destiny, as the motivation for the poet's aspiration. Moreover, the ascent of the poet is compositionally situated in such a way that it reverses an especially grievous example of harsh destiny, the condition of the outsider. Since destiny is in essence a religious conception, the poet's project can be described as the search for an alternative religious revelation, for a vision in which the deity no longer appears as the all-powerful, terrifying sovereign who arbitrarily distributes punishment and misfortune. Precisely such a vision, I have argued, occupies the functional slot 'object of value' within the quest narrative the text unfolds. A third advantage of the hypothesis is that it provides a structural scaffold in relation to which other features of the text can be accorded a systematic position. In particular, the quest hypothesis raises two major questions: (a) What is the peculiar efficacy of "Liebe" in this text that enables it to assume the role of "adjuvant"? (b) What is the precise nature of the insight that transforms the mountain from an antagonist into

a source of value? These questions set the agenda for my reading of stanzas
IX and X.

The semantic structure of the term "Liebe" is determined by its mediating or auxiliary function in the narrative, a function that lends the term a
peculiar ambiguity. The character of this ambiguity, which is also legible in
the oscillation of the term between a subjective ('love for') and objective
('beloved object') signification, makes itself felt in the type of figuration
employed here. Because Love appears in the narrative role of the "adjuvant," it undergoes a certain degree of personification. However, this
personification remains strangely airy, bodiless: the addressee "Liebe" is
not defined in terms of such qualities as 'beauty' or 'grace', but merely by
the verb phrases designating the actions she is to accomplish. Of course,
due to the motivation of grammatical gender, Love is characterized as a
female being, but at no point does she acquire the solidity of a particular,
or even idealized, female image. The personification employed here, in
other words, is minimal; the figure is stripped of all corporeality so that
only the semantic marker 'animate', which accrues to it by virtue of its
syntactic position as agent, prevents it from being more than an abstraction.[19] Love, in this text, is a persona without a visible mask, an agency
without spatiotemporal location. This seems to me to be decisive: *the
situation out of which the poet speaks is the vacancy left by the withdrawal of
the real, corporeal woman.* This vacancy is filled by the animate abstraction
Love, the invisible agent of the actions that enable the poet to survive the
harsh exigencies (the antagonism) of the winter landscape and to realize
his poetic aspiration.

The minimal or limit personification of "Liebe" in "Harzreise im
Winter" is not a deficiency of the figure, but the very condition of
possibility of its efficacy. To see why this is so, it is useful to recall two texts
discussed in previous chapters. Consider first of all this series of excerpts
from the dialogue between Prometheus and Minerva (Text 21):

Ewig meine Liebe dir.   *(116, spoken by Prometheus)*

Und ich dir ewig gegenwärtig.   *(117, spoken by Minerva)*

Abwesend auch mir immer gegenwärtig.   *(123, spoken by Prometheus)*

Here the term "Liebe" undergoes a process of de-empiricization such that
it comes to figure 'eternal presence', a presence, that is to say, that makes
itself felt even in the empirical absence of the beloved object. As I argued in

Chapter 6, this 'love' derives from the originary donation experienced within the sphere of primordial orality, the linguistic variant of the specular moment. And this suggests, of course, that the figure of the poet in "Harzreise im Winter" has internalized (as I also contended with regard to the "Prometheus" ode) that specular donation, so that now, in the situation of extreme desolation, he can summon that donation of 'love' and draw sustenance from its 'presence even in absence'. This reading is lent support by the second text I want to adduce here, a text which might be called the paradigmatic poem of the specular gift, "Pilgers Morgenlied" (Text 10). The final lines of that poem, which I have cited on several occasions, are especially relevant to the question of personification:

> Allgegenwärt'ge Liebe!
> Durchglühst mich,
> Beutst dem Wetter die Stirn,
> Gefahren die Brust,
> Hast mir gegossen
> In's frühwelkende Herz
> Doppeltes Leben,
> Freude zu leben,
> Und Mut. *(26–34)*

Both "Pilgers Morgenlied" and "Harzreise im Winter" operate with the triangular configuration of wanderer, bad weather, and the sustaining force of love. And, as noted in Chapter 4 with regard to the former text, that force derives from the decorporealization of the beloved, the transformation of the particular addressee "Lila" into the universal term "Liebe." This animate abstraction (or minimal personification) becomes the medium of an "Allgegenwart" that enables the poet to withstand the threat of the meteorological antagonist. Both the pilgrim of "Pilgers Morgenlied" and the poet of "Harzreise im Winter" attain to a desire that is unbounded by attachment to corporeality, a sublimated love that proves to be, in the case of the latter, the resource of poetic achievement.

The relevance of these comparisons becomes clearer when we take into account what might be termed the contrastive function of the figure of Love within the text's overriding compositional arrangement. Certainly one of the defining features of "Liebe" in this text is that her actions systematically reverse the situation of the outsider, as the following juxtaposition reveals:

den umwölkten Blick *(47)*	hüll' In deine Goldwolken, *(60–61)*
Ins Gebüsch verliert sich sein Pfad *(30)*	Leuchtest du ihm/ Durch die Furten bei Nacht/ Über grundlose Wege *(67–69)*
die tausend Quellen (invisible) *(48)*	Mit dem tausendfarbigen Morgen (visible) *(71)*
So erquicke sein Herz! *(46)*	Lachst du in's Herz ihm; *(72)*

As we have seen, the task which the poet sets out to accomplish is, at least in part, to alleviate the condition of the outsider, to assume his position of acute desolation and to live through this desolation in such a way that it is overcome. The reason that he succeeds in this task is that he is aided by Love. Her actions transform the negatively inflected beclouding of the outsider's vision into a protective golden nebula, disclose the path that the outsider has lost, reveal the plenitude of a thousand colors where the outsider sees only desert, suffuse the poet's heart with the refreshing joy which the outsider so desperately lacks. Thus, what qualifies "Liebe" for the role of "adjuvant" within the poet's quest is the capacity to transform the situation of the outsider. And this implies that, if we are to grasp the efficacious character of Love in this text, we shall have to delineate more precisely the nature of the outsider's condition.

The obvious starting point for such an inquiry is the etiology of the outsider's melancholy. His doleful state stems from the fact that he is a disappointed lover, as indicated in the lines:

> Ach wer heilet die Schmerzen
> Des, dem Balsam zu Gift ward?
> Der sich Menschenhaß
> Aus der Fülle der Liebe trank! *(35–38)*

In "Harzreise im Winter," love possesses a double efficacy. It is both the force that, in its withdrawal, transforms infinite fullness into hate and desolation and the force that, in its sublimated return, transforms loss and despair into the experience of unlimited abundance. This antithetical meaning (*Gegensinn*) of the primal word (*Urwort*) of Goethe's lyric has solicited my attention on several occasions, most notably in connection with a text other traces of which (e.g., the verb "beizen") "Harzreise im

Winter" bears. I am referring, of course, to the concluding lines of "An den Geist des Johannes Sekundus":

> Und da ist Traubensaft, und Saft der Bienen,
> An meines Herdes treuem Feuer vereinigt,
> Der soll mir helfen! Wahrlich er hilft nicht
> Denn von der Liebe alles heilendem
> Gift Balsam ist kein Tröpfgen drunter *(Text 24, 23–27)*

The outsider, one could say, occupies the negative pole of love's antithetical sense, and this has forced him into the exile of his misanthropy. But the remarkable feature of the figuration of the outsider (a feature also highlighted by its echo of "An den Geist des Johannes Sekundus") is that it is so thoroughly imbued with the liquid schema: the "balm" of love has become "poison" for him and out of love's fullness he has "drunk" hate of mankind. Thus, according to the figural logic of the text, the outsider, because he imbibed the bitter beverage of loss, is entrapped in a situation characterized by the 'absence of liquid' and by a kind of destructive, even auto-destructive, orality:

> Die Öde verschlingt ihn. *(34)*

> Zehrt er heimlich auf
> Seinen eignen Wert
> In ung'nügender Selbstsucht. *(40–42)*

> Neben dem Durstenden
> In der Wüste. *(49–50)*

This negatively inflected liquid-oral complex is one of the most insistent in Goethe's writing of the 1770's. Recall the plight of the "brother streams" in "Mahomets Gesang":

> Denn uns frißt in öder Wüste
> Gier'ger Sand
> Die Sonne droben
> Saugt an unserm Blut
> Ein Hügel
> Hemmet uns zum Teiche! *(Text 15, 43–48)*

In the reading elaborated in Chapter 5, I glossed this dessication of the streams as the death that marks the border between nature and culture. Descending from the mountainous region and entering the plain, the

streams experience the limit of their natural existence and must be re-
deemed by the genius-stream, which carries them across the flatlands of
culture. This death is figured in terms of both the desert's barrenness and
an oral consumption, precisely the features that characterize the situation
of the outsider. Moreover, if we recall that the streams suffer this disaster of
dryness and orality at that moment when they depart from the maternal
vale, then another text suggests itself for comparison:

> Zische Nord
> Tausend schlangenzüngig
> Mir ums Haupt!
> Beugen sollst du's nicht!
> Beugen magst du
> Kind'scher Zweige Haupt,
> Von der Sonne
> Muttergegenwart geschieden.
> *(Text 10, 18–25)*

One must not be led astray here by the variant functions of the sun in this
text and in the passage just quoted from "Mahomets Gesang." In "Pilgers
Morgenlied" (from which, of course, the cited lines are taken), the sun
figures the "maternal presence" and it is the absence of her warmth that
causes the sapless bending of the "childish branches." These children, cut
off from the enlivening presence of the Mother, are plagued by an internal
dryness that corresponds to the dessication of the brother streams. And
here too we encounter a threatening orality in the thousand snake tongues
of the Medusan north wind (to which the branches, implicitly, succumb).
In "Pilgers Morgenlied," omnipresent or universal love ("Allgegenwärt'ge
Liebe") stands in opposition to the "Muttergegenwart" of the sun, the
absence of which leaves the childish branches to wilt in their internal
dryness and to suffer the lashing snake tongues of the north wind. Just this
is the outsider's situation: his liquid-oral desolation is a childish condition,
an internal clinging to the maternal presence, to the corporeality of the
beloved object, a fixation which, in the absence of that object, is transformed into the phantasm of barrenness and oral destructiveness. This
reading of the outsider's situation as essentially childish is supported by a
passage from the "Prometheus" ode's 1774 variant:

> Wähntest etwa
> Ich sollt das Leben hassen

In Wüsten fliehn,
Weil nicht alle Knabenmorgen
Blütenträume reiften. *(46–50)*

The elements of the 'desert' and of 'hate' that characterize the outsider figure in "Harzreise im Winter" are likewise components of the figuration here (the aspect of destructive oral consumption, however, is omitted), and the disappointment that motivates their appearance is specified in terms of childhood wishes, just as the saplessness of the branches in "Pilgers Morgenlied" is caused by their childish adherence to the maternal presence of the sun. The decisive difference between the "Prometheus" ode and "Harzreise im Winter" is that the earlier text dismisses the disappointment of the child as an insignificant threat. The autonomy of self-fashioning is sufficient to overcome the desolation that follows upon the experience of loss. But in "Harzreise im Winter" the alleviation of this desolation is the very vocation of the poet, and he accomplishes this mission due to the intervention of Love. Thus, the passage just cited from the "Prometheus" ode is echoed not only in the description of the outsider's condition ('desert' and 'hate'), but also in the prayer directed to "Liebe":

Umgib mit Wintergrün,
Bis die Rose wieder heranreift,
Die feuchten Haare,
O Liebe, deines Dichters! *(62–65)*

In "Harzreise im Winter," Love provides a compensation for the absence of a blossom that ripens. That is to say, in the terms of the "Prometheus" ode, that she overcomes the child's disappointment by filling the emptiness (the desert) and transforming the hate that the shattering of childish "blossom-dreams" leaves in its wake.

What is to be learned from this network of cross-references? First of all, of course, the general point that Goethe's major lyric texts of the 1770's draw on and vary a cluster of symbolic constants, figurational complexes that recur from poem to poem. The semantic configurations of Goethe's poetry reveal a systematic coherence that traditional biographical interpretations have occluded. In addition to this general claim (which is a governing thesis of this study), the series of passages adduced here enables us to specify the nature of the outsider's condition. The doleful state of the outcast—his entrapment in the desert of abandonment, his tormenting

phantasies of destructive oral consumption—derive from an unsuccessfully negotiated socialization. The outsider's melancholy is the introjection
of the loss of the corporeal presence of the Mother, an identification with
the abyss of absence such that the Mother returns as the negative phantasm of dryness and omnivorousness.[20] And this is why Love, as minimal
personification and animate abstraction, systematically transforms the
outsider's condition. "Liebe"—the addressee of the poet's prayer—is the
sublimation of the specular donation, desire detached from a corporeal
referent, the Mother as the universalized medium of a "Gegenwart"
immune to the alternation of empirical presence and absence. In a letter he
wrote to Charlotte von Stein on the anniversary of his journey to the Harz
mountains, Goethe invented a neologism that we can gratefully employ as
an analytical term to designate the function of Love in the poem. He
speaks there of the "übermütterliche Leitung" to which he owed the
success of his hazardous ascent of the "Brocken."[21] A more precise description of Love's invisible agency in "Harzreise im Winter" could hardly be
imagined. *Whereas the outsider is consumed by the negative phantasm of the
absent corporeal Mother, the poet finds a path through the desolation of absence
with the help of a "supramaternal guidance."*

In the course of my meander through the texts that are connected by
strands of figuration to "Harzreise im Winter," I have ignored a decisive
point, the fact that the poem accords the condition of the outsider, in
addition to its life-historical etiology, a religious significance. Consider the
final portion of the prayer the poet directs on the outsider's behalf to the
"Vater der Liebe":

> Öffne den umwölkten Blick
> Über die tausend Quellen
> Neben dem Durstenden
> In der Wüste. *(47–50)*

The schemata of perception-cognition ("Blick") and liquidity ("tausend
Quellen") are entwined here with the schema of religion. Of course, in
both "Mahomets Gesang" and "Prometheus" the desolation of the desert
bears a religious connotation, but here the religious reference points
toward a particular Biblical episode: the situation of the outsider recapitulates that of the banished beloved Hagar or, perhaps more pertinently, that
of her child Ishmael. This reference introduces a dual significance into the
text. On the one hand, a figure of threatening paternal authority (Abra-

ham) casts its shadow over the outcast's despair. On the other hand, the figure of a "Vater der Liebe" who reveals his infinite abundance in the liquid flow of the thousand springs is evoked as the divine agency who would alleviate the outsider's barren condition of abandonment. But the point of the passage, as I argued above, is that the prayer to this traditional divinity remains unanswered, that the inherited religious code no longer provides a symbolic form adequate to the task of disclosing the infinite liquid gift of the divine. This is why the poet must assume the position of the outsider, take on the terrible distress of spiritual desolation. The poet's vocation in "Harzreise im Winter" is to achieve a poetic-religious vision that redeems the outsider whose ear and heart the Old Testament psalms ("Psalter," 43) no longer, or at least uncertainly, reach; to invent a new psalm—precisely the poem we hold before us—that would disclose in the historical present the overflowing surabundance of divinity; to transform the terrifying shadow of the threatening Father into a figure of love. For this reason, he is sustained in his poetic-religious project by the invisible agency of Love. In "Harzreise im Winter," Love, the supramaternal guidance, possesses a cognitive efficacy as the medium of a poetic vision of the Absolute.

Thus far my reading of the term "Liebe" has focused on its contrastive function vis-à-vis the situation of the outsider, a function illuminated by adducing a series of other texts from Goethe's lyric corpus that draw on related figurational complexes. This reading can be confirmed and amplified by considering the series of actions attributed to "Liebe" during the phase of the poet's ascent. The verbs denoting these actions fall into two groups: a synonymical pair ("hüllen," 60; "umgeben," 62) that signifies a gesture of protective embrace; and an intensifying series ("leuchten," 67; "ins Herz lachen," 72; "emportragen," 74) that moves from the purely visual through emotional participation to physical movement. (Note that, as the intensity of these actions increases, the metaphorics becomes bolder and more innovative and a referential or mimetic reading, therefore, increasingly irrelevant.) Through the protective gesture signified in the first group, the term "Liebe" acquires a connotation of the 'maternal', whereas the second series suggests a scale of intensifying pathos culminating in the seizure and transport, the sublime ecstasy, of the poet. A second semantic level of these actions becomes apparent when we consider the instruments with which Love carries them out. These form a text-specific paradigm, in Jakobson's sense of the term:

1. Goldwolken (61)
2. Wintergrün (62)
3. dämmernden Fackel (66)
4. tausendfarbigen Morgen (71)
5. beizenden Sturm (73)

This collection of instruments through which "Liebe" exercises her invisible agency—especially if we take the "dawning torch" (no. 3) to connote the predawn light—suggests a reading of "Liebe" as Nature, for certainly Nature is the sole agent that could be said to employ these things as her instruments.

If we take a closer look at this paradigmatic series, however, an especially subtle aspect of the poem's artistry emerges into view. The five terms tend to coalesce into certain subgroups. The compounds "Goldwolken" and "Wintergrün," for example, form a conspicuous chiastic pattern on both the graphic-phonological and the semantic levels:

"*Gold*wolken"   "*Winter*grün"
color word + meteorological word   meteorological word + color word

Likewise, the formations in numbers 3–5 bear an obvious morphological similarity (adjective + noun), with the present participles in 3 and 5 serving as a frame that surrounds and isolates the grouping. Semantically, however, this second group lacks cohesion: whereas both "dämmernden Fackel" and "tausendfarbigen Morgen" suggest predominantly visual phenomena with a 'pleasant' and 'gentle' connotational nuance, the "beizenden Sturm" has nothing visual about it and tends toward a 'violent' connotation. That is to say, the paradigmatic series is constructed in such a way as to include the "searing storm" on the level of syntax and morphology, but to exclude it on the level of semantics.

This contradiction between syntax and morphology on the one hand and semantics on the other takes on further significance when we consider the overriding narrative structure of the passage. The lines

Mit dem beizenden Sturm
Trägst du ihn hoch empor;   *(73–74)*

mark the transition between the protagonist's interaction with the helper-figure "Liebe" and his interaction with the mountain. Thus, lines (75–76), which follow the upward movement, mark the point of contact between the poet and the mountain, the point at which the mountain streams pour into the psalms. But, semantically, the "searing storm" seems to be an aspect of the mountain, even though the action of carrying upward is attributed to "Liebe," so that here too a dissonance between syntax and semantics is audible. We have also seen that these verses mark the moment at which the hunter-bird descends and seizes its victim, an act of violence that proves to be an act of love.[22] This, I believe, explains the syntactic-semantic tension of the lines: they enact the moment at which the cognitive efficacy of "Liebe" as the medium of poetic inspiration overcomes the antagonistic and frightening appearance of the mountain/divinity and discloses its 'loving' character. As it were, the supramaternal presence that sustains the poet in his journey enters into and transforms the violent image of austere paternity. The strike of the "Geier" is thus experienced as a tender ("sanft," 3) caress. And this feminization or maternalization of the mountain, hence of the terrifying, paternal divinity, makes possible the reception of the liquid gift of the divine: "Winterströme stürzen vom Felsen / In seine Psalmen" (75–76).

This reading of the transitional status of the anomalous lines is confirmed by the numerical structure of stanza X, the axial stanza of the poem. The first seven lines of the stanza (66–72) pertain to the actions of Love; the final seven lines (75–81) focus on the mountain. At the exact center of these two symmetrical groups, the point of their tangency, the anomalous line-pair—syntactically a function of Love, semantically a function of the wintery alpine landscape—occurs. One can safely say that these lines represent the moment of maximum poetic intensity in the text, the point at which morphology, syntax, semantics, numerical composition, and figuration (the hunter's strike) enter into an untranslatable poetic complex. Certainly it is no accident that these lines also figure the 'flight' of sublime poetic inspiration.

In fact, the poetic significance of Love's manifestations in this phase of the text is established through reference to utterly conventional topoi. For example, the poet addresses Love with these words:

> Mit der dämmernden Fackel
> Leuchtest du ihm
> Durch die Furten bei Nacht,
> Über grundlose Wege
> Auf öden Gefilden; *(66–70)*

Count Friedrich Leopold zu Stolberg, in a poetic apostrophe to "Begeisterung" ("Enthusiasm"), employs nearly identical figures:

> Flammenatmend erhellst du Abgründe vor mir her,
> Deine wehende Fackel zeigt und gebeut mir Flug![23]

> Flame-breathing you illuminate the abysses before me,
> Your flickering torch shows and commands me to flight!

An even more obvious reference to conventional attributes of high poetic inspiration occurs in these lines:

> Umgib mit Wintergrün,
> Bis die Rose wieder heranreift,
> Die feuchten Haare,
> O Liebe, deines Dichters! *(62–65)*

The passage alludes, of course, to the laurel wreath that traditionally designates supreme accomplishment in the high, serious, idealizing lyric genres; the poet's request of Love is that she provide him the means—the inspiration—to achieve the evergreen crown. But even as we take account of this conventional allusion, we should note its remotivation in terms of the text-specific network of semantic values. The word "Wintergrün" is not simply a signal exhausted by its function of referring to the traditional code of poetic rank (for this purpose "Lorbeer" ["laurel"] would have done just as well); it also hooks up with the problem of 'presence' and 'absence' that we have identified as central to the semantics of "Liebe" in this text. That is to say, "Wintergrün" suggests the presence of vital energy ("-grün") even under conditions of absence and desolation ("Winter-"). In this sense, the term does not just mean 'inspiration', it rethinks the question of what inspiration can be. What animates the poet who must undertake his "Harzreise" under the harsh conditions of "Winter" is the 'presence even in absence' that Love is, a desire purified of its attachment to a corporeal referent, a supramaternal guidance that, with its torch, illuminates a path through the "öden Gefilden" of loss.

 We are now in a position to offer a synthetic answer to the question from which we took our point of departure. The efficacy that qualifies "Liebe" for the function of narrative "adjuvant" in the poet's quest derives from the fact that "Liebe" maintains a link to the lost presence of the 'beloved' (the Mother, Nature, the Source of vitality). In its decorporealized form, Love is the trace of the beloved. This is why the poet is the counter-figure to the outsider. The latter's melancholy condition is haunted by the negative phantasm of the Mother/beloved as barren desert and destructive orality, a phantasm that responds to and, as it were, memorializes the child's trauma of severence. What the outsider lacks is the "Ton" (44) of a psalm that would disclose the infinite abundance and overflow of divine love even in this situation of acute deprivation. This traditional religious tone has become inaudible, the outsider cowers in the shadow of a forbidding paternal imago, gnaws on the negativity of his unfortunate destiny. But the poet receives this "tone" through Love's intercession, for it is precisely at the point in the text at which the actions of Love manifest themselves (stanza X) that the poet's speech assumes the syntactic ductus of the Old Testament psalms. *As supramaternal guidance, as presence even in absence, "Liebe" is the sublimation of the originary donation and therewith the ontological form of poetic speech.* The condition for the emergence of "Love," then, is the detachment of desire from its exclusive reference to the beloved body, a process that involves renunciation, to be sure, but a renunciation that is not experienced as deprivation or punishment. On the contrary, once this sublimation is accomplished, the "Liebe" that is thereby released penetrates and transforms the austere and threatening figure of the father/god who seemed to enforce that detachment with such impersonal violence. Thus, the harsh winter landscape of the mountain sheds its frightening physiognomy (and its narrative role as antagonist), the hunter's deadly strike becomes an act of love, and infinite loss is transformed into the surabundance of the divine gift. In this sense, "Harzreise im Winter"—drawing on poetic resources accumulated across Goethe's lyric writing of the 1770's—elaborates what can be called a poetic religion of "Liebe."

I turn now to the next phase of the poet's quest, the phase in which the helper-figure "Liebe" is replaced by the complex figure of the mountain, at once the antagonist and the donor of value. Two events are related here, the first of which establishes the contact between the poet and the mountain:

> Winterströme stürzen vom Felsen
> In seine Psalmen, *(75–76)*

This passage, like the ninth and tenth stanzas generally, derives its significance from the contrast it marks to the situation of the outsider in stanzas V–VII. Whereas there the poet prayed for a psalm ("Ist auf deinem Psalter, / Vater der Liebe, ein Ton / Seinem Ohre vernehmlich," 43–45) that would reveal to the outsider the infinite surabundance of the divine ("die tausend Quellen," 48) even in radical desolation, here the "psalms" are actually called into being in such a way that the liquid outpouring enters into and achieves equivalence with the religious-poetic speech of the poet. Thus, the line pair marks the achievement of a new psalm, the poet's own, a psalm that accomplishes in the modern landscape of desolation what the Old Testament psalms did for an earlier age but are no longer capable of, the revelation of divine liquidity.

This revelation follows immediately upon the figure of poetic transport in which the poet is carried aloft by the eagle/"Geier," subliminally echoed in the "beizenden Sturm" (73). That "*St*urm," syntactically an instrument of Love, alliteratively reappears in the downward rush ("*st*ürzen) of the "Winter*st*röme," such that the semantic fusion of Love and mountain is underlined by the phonological repetition. The upward directionality of the sublime elevation is met by the downward directionality of the liquid cascade. As the poet is lifted toward divinity by the force of poetic inspiration, divinity descends into his poetic speech. The poem itself, then, becomes the site in which the supramaternal guidance merges with the paternal divinity, in which the "tone" of a "Vater der Liebe"—no longer that of the Old Testament, but a divinity unique to this text—once again becomes audible. This vision of divine surabundance is likewise related to the "overflowing" joy ("überfließend," 52) that animates the brothers of the hunt. The pre-ethical exuberance of natural energy that incidentally alleviates the material distress of the peasant corresponds to an ethical outpouring of liquidity that redeems the outsider's condition of spiritual abandonment.

At the same time, these verses exhibit an extraordinary degree of poetic freedom. They resist referential interpretation, transgress the limits of verisimilitude, and thereby emphasize the independent legitimacy of poetic speech. Any attempt to moor the poetic statement here to an empirical experience, to explain the figure in terms of a mundane event (for example, by arguing that the poet, while climbing the mountain, sees the downrushing streams and is thus inspired to sing his psalms), must be rejected as utterly artificial. For this reason, a biographical construal of the lines that links them to Goethe's ascent of the "Brocken" is entirely out of place. Such a derivation of the figure misses the essential issue, that the autonomy of poetic cognition is here being thematized. In fact, the text cites at this point a topos of poetic inspiration that can be traced back at least to Horace's famous characterization of Pindar's style (Ode IV, 2[24]) and that in the eighteenth century remained a standard reference. For instance, Stolberg cites the topos in his essay "On Enthusiasm" when he characterizes the most sublime poetic spirits as "alpine regions . . . where a rushing mountain stream crashes down into the lonely valley."[25] The following verses by Johann Peter Uz likewise offer an apt comparison:

> Mit sonnenrothem Angesichte
> Flieg ich zur Gottheit auf! Ein Strahl von ihrem Lichte
> Glänzt auf mein Saitenspiel, das nie erhabener klang,
> Durch welche Töne wälzt mein heiliger Gesang,
> Wie eine Fluth von furchtbarn Klippen,
> Sich strömend fort und braust von meinen Lippen![26]

> With sun-reddened visage
> I fly upwards to the divinity! A ray of its light
> Shines on my lyre, that never resounded more sublimely,
> With what tones my sacred song rolls,
> Like a flood from frightening cliffs,
> Streaming onward and rushes from my lips!

Uz's employment of the Horatian topos of sublimity highlights, by contrast, the boldness and precision of Goethe's lines. In "Harzreise im Winter," the difference between the domains of nature and poetry, which Uz's simile maintains, is eliminated: the mountain streams actually pour themselves into the psalms. In other words, in the lines that announce the furor of highest poetic inspiration the mimetic or referential restrictions of normal discourse are abandoned. The power and abundance of the Absolute, in its liquid gift, and the poetic-religious speech of the "psalms" enter into a relation of radical metaphorical identity.

The intensity of the poetic inspiration produces, in the subsequent lines, a transformation in the poet's attitude toward the mountain peak:

> Und Altar des lieblichsten Danks
> Wird ihm des gefürchteten Gipfels
> Schneebehangener Scheitel,
> Den mit Geisterreihen
> Kränzten ahndende Völker. *(77–81)*

In my remarks on the compositional structure of the text, I noted that the transformation accomplished here reverses that which takes place in the case of the outsider ("dem Balsam zu Gift ward," 36). In this sense, the cited lines represent the turning point in the overriding narrative structure of the text, the point at which the feared antagonist is transformed into the donor of value, the point at which the problem of destiny, which congeals into the image of an all-powerful god that arbitrarily and violently metes out punishment, is alleviated. It does not suffice, however, to consider these lines solely in terms of their narrative function. An adequate reading of the passage must attend to the precise relational character of the elements that pivot around the verb "werden" in order to delineate the significance of the poetic insight (narratively speaking, the 'object of value') attained here.

The syntactic construction of the passage yields the following global opposition:

Schneebehangener Scheitel des gefürchteten Gipfels	vs.	Altar des lieblichsten Danks

Both poles of the transformative process are occupied by metaphorical figurations, but the structure of the figuration in each case is different. The genitive construction on the left side metaphorically relates two nouns to one another. That is, the phrase "Schneebehangener Scheitel" is a metaphor that captures the external appearance of the "Gipfel" or mountain peak. This metaphor, however, is not exhausted by its descriptive function. Since the term "Scheitel" (the upper outline of the head) is a particularizing synecdoche (*pars pro toto*) of a humanlike being, the metaphor generates a personifying effect, figures the mountain as a massive physiognomy, and this personification retrospectively lends the participle "schneebehangen" the metaphorical significance of aged (hung with white hair, perhaps a beard). The righthand member of the opposition likewise places the mountain into a metaphorical relationship with another noun. In this case, however, we are no longer dealing with a metaphor *in praesentia*. (That is, in I. A. Richards' terminology, the tenor is not mentioned). Whereas the metaphor on the left side of the opposition oscillates between a literal and figural understanding of a concrete object and its personification, the metaphor on the right side of the opposition eliminates the concrete object or referent altogether. This difference in the structure of the two metaphors is also evident in the *tertium comparationis* around which they are respectively organized. On the one hand, the "Gipfel" is identified with an animate being on the basis of shared perceptual features;

the figuration operates here in the domain of external appearances. The shared features in terms of which the metaphor mountain = "Altar" operates, however, are no longer sensate attributes; the mountain doesn't look like an altar, rather it assumes a position within the life of the subject that is functionally equivalent to that of an altar. Thus, the transformation through which the negative situation of the outsider as well as the religious conception of a frightening god who rules over destiny are overcome is *a transformation in the structure of figuration itself.* The looming alpine physiognomy is a projection of the subject's fear that realizes itself as perceptual presence in which vehicle (mountain) and meaning (antagonist, threatening divine-paternal agency) are fused in an *imaginary* personification. With the reception of the divine gift—the flow of liquidity into the psalms—this mask (persona) is dissolved. The mountain no longer imposes itself in terms of its perceptual presence, but is defined as a *symbolic* token (the altar) within a network of relations.[27]

But the global opposition between the two types of metaphor embraces as well a number of suboppositions that contribute to the production of significance accomplished in these lines. The cross-reading that moves between the two oppositional poles does not merely attend to the total metaphorical construction of each, but also to the individual components that, by virtue of their syntactic parallelism or semantic resonance, are set into antonymous relations with one another. Thus, an opposition between "Gipfel" and "Dank" assumes salience due to the fact that these two terms are syntactically the genitive object, and this syntactic parallelism underlines the semantic features of the two terms that polarize them or harness them in an antithesis: in the case of "Gipfel" the class definition 'concrete, external object', in the case of "Dank" the class definition 'internal attitude toward another subject'. Whereas the meaning of the term 'mountain' can only be specified in terms of physical and perceptual categories, the concept of 'thanks' must be explicated in terms of social relations. And this brings us to a second notable subopposition that forms itself along the axis of 'subjective attitude'. The concept of 'fear' ("gefürchteten") emerges into the foreground on the left side of the opposition, while on the right side the concept of 'thanks' ("Dank") occupies the focus of attention. Again, the symmetrically opposed semantic features of the juxtaposed terms are promoted to salience: 'prospective' and 'retrospective', 'involuntary' and 'voluntary', 'naturally given' and 'socially determined'. Finally, the object of fear, the personified mountain peak, is explicitly mentioned, whereas the recipient of the 'thanks' is not. The only qualification of 'thanks'—the term "lieblichst"—points back to the subject from whom the gratitude emanates.

To gauge the significance of this oppositional network, one must recall the overriding discursive context in which it is developed. In my remarks on the religion schema, I argued that lines 77–79 dramatize an epochal transformation of religious consciousness. Thus, the oppositional network can be conceived as contrasting two types of religious attitude: each side of the global opposition represents a specific relation between religious subject and object and the various suboppositions bring to light different aspects of this attitude. For the sake of simplicity, I shall call the earlier religious attitude "Religion *A*" and the latter "Religion *B*." The transformation that leads from one to the other can then be represented schematically:

	Religion A	Religion B
subjective attitude	Fear:	Thanks:
	prospective	retrospective
	involuntary	voluntary
	natural	social
type of object	external, concrete	no object outside the subject; religious attitude related back toward subject
type of representation	imaginary: personifying, based on perceptual features	symbolic: relational, based on functional features

Schema 14: Religious Transformation in "Harzreise im Winter"

The poet attains the goal of his quest when he strips the mountain of its antagonistic appearance and grasps its significance for him and for the community as the source of value. In doing so, he transforms a religion grounded in fear vis-à-vis a phantasmatically distorted (personified) object into a religion of thanks, the object of which acquires its meaning only by virtue of its systematic position. This transformation of a religion based on imaginary representation into a religion based on symbolic relations necessarily implies a shift in the immanent poetics of the text from a poetry of the 'visible' to a poetry of the 'invisible'. Symbolically organized relations such as those of 'giving' and 'thanking' are not sensuously perceptible, and the tokens employed to designate these relations do not derive their efficacy from their perceptual features. Thus, the vision or cognition achieved in the course of the poet's quest proves to be one that is situated beyond the compass of the visible world and the linguistic meanings that refer to that world. This is the programmatic reason for the text's transgression of the restrictions of mimetic discourse. The sublime style, concretized in a singular, untranslatable textual figure, is the only mode of discourse adequate to the transphenomenal reality of religious symbolization.

What is this Other to whom the subject relates first in the mode of fear, then in the mode of thanks? Needless to say, it is not merely the mountain in its natural givenness that engenders the subject's anxiety, but the mountain as the phantasmatically projected face of something faceless: on the one hand, 'time' and 'death' (hence the 'aged' quality of the personification), on the other hand, the 'paternal authority of the Law'. The religion of fear (and of destiny) projects a god in which death and sovereignty are condensed in the terrifying physiognomy of a punitive paternal authority.[28] In the religion of thanks, however, this personification dissolves, the Other relinquishes its character as phantasmatic object and becomes the law of an invisible ethical bond. The religious celebration is conducted with symbolic tokens (the altar) and commemorates (gives thanks for) the institution of the communal religious law as a divine gift. Such is the poetic insight attained in and through the quest and proclaimed in the psalm this text purports to be. *It is an insight into the nonobjectival character of the Other, the vision (but, of course, a nonperceptual, sublime vision) of the Other as the ethical relation of gift and gratitude that is the foundation of communal solidarity.*

The reading of the poet's quest I have elaborated implies a contextualization of "Harzreise im Winter" in terms of the problematic of the sublime. I cannot review here the history of transformations this concept undergoes during the eighteenth century and must restrict my remarks to a single comparison. Goethe's poetic reworking of the tradition of sublime poetry marks, I will claim, one of the earliest instances of what might be termed the subjective interpretation of the concept, the interpretation that achieves its definitive philosophical explication in Kant's *Critique of Judgment* (1790). Among the natural phenomena to which Kant attributes the effect of sublimity—"bold, overhanging, and, as it were, threatening cliffs, thunderclouds towering up in the heavens,"—we can recognize features of the poem's mountainous topography.[29] Of course, for Kant these awe- and fear-inspiring natural phenomena are not the object of the sublime experience, but the suggestive perceptual occasions that set in motion a movement of the imagination through which is disclosed a capacity within us superior to the external violence of nature. That is to say, for both Kant and Goethe the sublime involves a movement that takes as its point of departure an external, phantasmatically distorted and hence fear-inducing object in order to conduce us to the recognition of an inner faculty. The pertinence of this comparison between Goethe and Kant emerges all the more forcefully when one considers how the latter conceives of the religious significance of the sublime:

> The human being who actually fears . . . is not at all in a state of mind to admire divine grandeur, for which a mood of peaceful contemplation and an entirely free judgement are required. Only when he is conscious of his sincere, god-pleasing attitude do those effects of might serve to awaken in him the idea of the sublimity of this being insofar as he recognizes in himself a sublimity of attitude appropriate to that being's will and thereby is elevated above the fear of such effects of nature, which he does not see as outbreaks of that being's rage. . . . Only in this way is religion distinguished internally from superstition, which is grounded in the spirit not by respect for the sublime, but by fear and anxiety vis-à-vis an over-powerful being to whose will the terrified human being sees himself subjected without according it high esteem: from which then, to be sure, nothing but favor-seeking and flattery instead of a religion of good conduct in life can arise.[30]

To free the "terrified human being" from fear vis-à-vis an "overpowerful being," that is, from a religion of "superstition," is precisely the aspiration of the poet in "Harzreise im Winter," an aspiration that is realized in the transformation accomplished in stanza X. Goethe's text instantiates a poetics of the sublime that accomplishes a revolution of religious attitude through which the harshly punitive god of destiny is replaced with the divine gift of the communal ethical bond.

Goethe's poetics of the sublime in "Harzreise im Winter" is illuminated by one further aspect of Kant's analysis. According to Kant, the experience of the sublime involves a failure of the imagination to produce a circumscribed, hence quasi-perceptual, objectival presentation, a failure, however, that makes sensible the nonempirical character of the free rational will.

For this reason the pleasure of the sublime in nature is only *negative* (in contrast to which that of the beautiful is *positive*), namely the feeling of a deprivation of the freedom of the imagination by the imagination itself insofar as it is purposefully determined according to another law than that of its empirical use. In this way it acquires an expansion and power which is greater than that which it sacrifices, the ground of which, however, is hidden from it, instead of which it *feels* the sacrifice and deprivation and at the same time the cause, to which it is subjected.[31]

The movement from an empirical use of the imagination to a use that obeys a nonempirical law, which Kant here attributes to the sublime experience, corresponds to the movement described with regard to Goethe's text as a transition from an imaginary mode of figuration, which produces a perceptually instantiated personification, to a symbolic mode, in which the poetic figuration articulates a relational structure inaccessible to sensuous intuition. The interesting feature of Kant's account, however, is that he conceives of this transition in terms of the notion of sacrifice, a notion that casts light on the overriding structure of Goethe's text. As I suggested earlier, the poet redeems the outsider by assuming his position, by submitting himself to the terror of abandonment and sacrificing himself on the terrified outcast's behalf. If we follow Kant's analysis, we can say that this sacrifice bears on the empirical use of the imagination, on the dual phantasm of the barren and omnivorous Mother and the threatening, punitive Father that holds the outsider in thrall. The poet exposes himself to the mountain's terrifying physiognomy, offers himself to the strike of the divine hunter, but only in order to experience this sacrifice as the emancipation from those fear-instilling phantasms. For Kant, this sacrifice of the imagination is precisely what demonstrates, makes sensible, the higher, moral law to which it submits. For Goethe, the same sacrifice involves the transcendence of a mimetic or empirically oriented mode of poetic discourse and the achievement of a sublime style that establishes itself as an untranslatable poetic sign.

These similarities between "Harzreise im Winter" and Kant's analysis enable us to register the specificity of Goethe's poetic elaboration of the sublime. For Kant, the decisive reference point of the sublime experience is the moral law, hence the freedom of reason ("Vernunft"), which consists in its autonomous submission to that law. The sublime movement is brought about when the violence ("Gewalt"[32]) with which reason asserts itself upon our natural-sensuous being is suffered by the imagination, at which point the very failure of the imagination to produce a quasi-perceptual presentation becomes a negative presentation of the suprasensuous character of the moral law and of the freedom of practical reason. This moment corresponds in Goethe's text to the vertical transport of the poet:

> Mit dem beizenden Sturm
> Trägst du ihn hoch empor;
>
> *(73–74)*

But, as we have seen, the agency of this transport is "Liebe," which, by virtue of the syntactic-semantic tension of these lines, enters into and transforms the threatening landscape of the mountain and renders the violent strike of the hunter an act of tenderness. Thus, whereas for Kant the sublime involves the determination of the imagination by the suprasensuous ("übersinnlich"[33]) law of moral reason, for Goethe the sublime ascent is made possible through the intercession of Love as the sublimated trace of the maternal presence. This seems to me to be the decisive difference between Kant and Goethe. For the former, the foundational ethical relation disclosed in the sublime experience is that between the rational subject and the law; for the latter, that relation is the bond of gift and gratitude, the paradigm of which is the primordial donation of love. What Kant calls "das Übersinnliche" is for Goethe, less austerely, "das Übermütterliche."

~

Before turning to the final stanza of "Harzreise im Winter" to examine the strategies employed there to achieve closure, the poem's sense of an ending, I want to take a brief look at the final two lines of stanza X, which were ignored in the preceding discussion. These two lines build an important transition to the poem's conclusion.

As we have seen, the narrative process unfolded in stanzas IX–X produces a complex semantic alteration, the transformation of a 'religion of fear and superstition' into a 'religion of thanks'. The relative clause that rounds out stanza X appends to this opposition a second contrast: the poetic vision of the mountain as the "Altar des lieblichsten Danks" (77) is juxtaposed with the attitude of "intuiting peoples" in the past.

Scheitel,
Den mit Geisterreihen
Kränzten ahndende Völker.

(79–81)

Perhaps the most economical way of characterizing the semantic relevance of these lines is to distinguish the threads of significance woven together in the verb "kränzen" ("to place a wreath on"). (a) First, the verb designates an act of religious meaning attribution or belief formation insofar as it alludes to the superstition that the "Brocken" provided the site for satanic festivities ("Walpurgisnacht"). (b) Second, the act of placing a wreath on something can be understood as exemplifying the sphere of 'naive, ritual actions' and thereby as connoting the domain of 'folk culture' conceived as an originary sphere of creative-imaginative production.[34] Needless to say, this path of reading is also suggested by the explicit mention of the "Völker" with the stanza's final word. (c) Finally, the verb implies 'poetic creation' by virtue of the conventional meaning of the wreath as a symbol of poetic accomplishment. The entire context of stanzas IX–X, which begin with the injunction "Umgib mit Wintergrün . . . Die feuchten Haare . . . deines Dichters!" (62–65) supports this interpretation. These three strands of significance—(a) the formation of religious belief/superstition, (b) the "Volk" as expressive collectivity, (c) poetic creation—evoke, in their synthesis, the idea of an archaic, religious-poetic act carried out by, and binding together, a communal subject.

The concept of the "Volk" as the collective subject of an originary mythopoetic production is, of course, by no means unique to this text of Goethe's. On the contrary, due primarily to the influence of Herder, whose views on the matter have entered into consideration at various points in Chapters 6 through 8 above, the notion earns general acceptance across the decade of the 1770's and comes to inform the literary-historical work of the Romantics. However, rather than tracing out these connections, I want to concentrate here on the functional significance of the concept within the system of the text. In this regard, of course, the most salient feature is the oppositional force the concept assumes in its juxtaposition with the poet's own 'vision'. How are these two actions—the archaic positing of poetic-religious significance and the poet's own act of meaning constitution—related to one another? An answer to this question is provided by the modifying participle "ahndend," which means both the intuition of some-

thing spiritual or noumenal behind normal appearances and the anticipation of a future event. The primitive surmise of the spiritual, even if
superstitious in character, is interpreted as a prefiguration of the poetic-
religious act embodied in the text of "Harzreise im Winter" itself. The
poet stylizes himself as the successor of the "ahndende Völker"; he repeats,
consciously, the creative insight of the archaic peoples and thereby overcomes the confusion and fear sedimented in the mythic figuration of that
insight. As in "Prometheus," the poetic vocation is conceived in relation to
an originary poetic-religious projection, but, rather than denigrate that
projection as deluded, the poet of "Harzreise im Winter" reformulates it in
such a way as to disclose its legitimacy.

This reading of the clause makes clear why it forms a bridge to the final
stanza, for the comparison of the poet's vocation with the mythopoetic
vision of the "intuiting peoples" introduces an element indispensable to
the achievement of closure in the tradition of high or publically oriented
poetry the text at once accepts and modifies. That element is the figuration
of a *collective subject*. Then, in stanza XI, with the phrase "astonished
world" ("erstaunten Welt," 84), a further collective subject appears, which,
like the archaic peoples, is defined by its attitude toward the mountain as a
figuration of the divine. As the 'universal' significance of the term 'world'
indicates, this subject embraces the entirety of mankind. To be sure, the
universal human domain was already alluded to in the second stanza, but
there it was characterized by disunity, the division between fortunate and
unfortunate. As has been emphasized several times, the task the poem sets
for itself is the elimination of this fateful sundering of humanity, which is
to say that one aspect of the poem's aspiration is the recovery, or disclosure,
of a unified human community. This is achieved through a sublime poetic
vision that repeats the originary poetic-religious act of the collective
subject "Volk," but repeats it in such a way as to overcome superstition and
terror.

Closure, of course, is a complex matter generally and in poetry in
particular,[35] but essential aspects of its workings in stanza XI can be
grasped, I believe, by examining three major operations through which it
is accomplished and which conspire, therefore, to constitute the finality of
the stanza's semantic gesture. The first of these is what I shall call *narrative
closure*, whose function is to take up intentions or projects mentioned in
earlier passages and to bring them to a conclusion. In this regard, the final
stanza stands at the end of two processes that define the overriding

structure of the text. On the one hand, it bears a clear relation to the ascent of the poet as related in the two antecedent stanzas (IX–X) and marks the conclusion of that movement. On the other hand, the positional markers indicating that the poet has reached the mountain peak recall the poetic aspiration articulated in the first stanza and indicate that it has been fulfilled. Thus, the eleventh stanza completes the two narrative itineraries associated with the figure of the poet, the movement from aspiration to fulfillment that covers the entire text and the actual topographical climb figured in stanzas IX–X. For this reason, the eleventh stanza must be read primarily as a poetological emblem in that it constitutes the final realization of the poetic project progressively unfolded across the text.

The completion of the action sequences, however, does not suffice to achieve textual closure. Even everyday narratives of personal experience include, as William Labov and Joshua Waletzky have shown, an evaluative dimension that facilitates their integration into broader contexts of relevance.[36] I call the operation which indicates the contours of this evaluative domain *cognitive closure*; its function consists in the circumscription of the knowledge produced in the course of the foregoing communication. As it were, the text must draw out its moral quintessence, announce the paths of generalization that radiate outward from its explicit claims. In "Harzreise im Winter" this operation is especially important because the goal of the poetic quest is to achieve a particular sort of knowledge vis-à-vis the Absolute, and a major task of the eleventh stanza, therefore, is to provide a pointed and compact formulation of this knowledge.

The formulation in question designs a complex arrangement in which two entities are related one to another: on the one hand the mountain (which also figures the 'divinity') referred to with the pronoun "Du," on the other hand the "erstaunte Welt" and thereby 'humanity' conceived as collectivity. This configuration is drawn with the poetic density that characterizes the earlier passages of the poem and therefore does not allow for easy paraphrase. However, a glance at the architecture of the entire stanza reveals how its overall composition contributes to the operation of cognitive closure. The stanza consists of three clauses, which designate the relationship between the just-mentioned entities with the three verbs "stehen . . . über," "schauen . . . auf," and "wässern," and all three of these verbs are employed in the present tense in such a way as to indicate atemporal states of affairs. That is, the knowledge conveyed in this stanza bears on the 'true and eternal' character of the relationship between the

Absolute and the human community. Precisely this knowledge, acquired by the poet in the course of his sublime ascent and vision, provides the solution to the problem of destiny.

Cognitive closure, then, is achieved *when the antecedent process of semantic transformation culminates in a tableau of stable and permanent relationships.* This point deserves special emphasis because prior interpretations of the poem have tended to focus exclusively on the mountain and to overlook thereby the network of relations posited in the three conjoined assertions of the stanza. Exactly this relationality, however, constitutes the cognitive content of the poet's vision. Consider, for example, the first of the three clauses:

> Du stehst mit unerforschtem Busen
> Geheimnisvoll offenbar
> Über der erstaunten Welt,   *(82–84)*

For the moment I shall bracket the two adjectives and the seemingly paradoxical adverbial construction in order to concentrate on the syntactic or propositional skeleton of the utterance: "Du stehst . . . über der . . . Welt." The spatial relationship which this nuclear sentence expresses applies so clearly to the situation of the mountain and the valley below that no critic has found it necessary, as far as I know, to comment on it. However, if, as I have maintained, the term "Welt" refers not merely to a particular piece of land, but to the entirety of mankind, then the configuration established with the verb of 'standing above' can no longer be interpreted merely in a topographical sense. The verb and the spatial configuration it designates can be read as an archaic gesture of social power and authority. To "stand above the entire world" means simply to rule over that world.[37] In this sense, the final stanza can be seen to recover the signification of 'sovereign power' that is a component of the first stanza and to integrate that signification into the poetic cognition that the poet presents as the result of his sojourn.

One might argue that the final stanza recapitulates, within its tableaulike arrangement of semantic values, the semantic process that has been worked through in the course of the poem. For what follows upon the initial clause of sovereign command—a connotation that recalls the terrifying features of the godhead—is first of all a perceptual-cognitive phase as signaled in the verb "schauen . . . auf," and then a phase of actual contact figured in the final clause of the stanza:

> Die du aus den Adern deiner Brüder
> Neben dir wässerst. *(86–87)*

Again I want to restrict my comments to the nuclear assertion: the mountain (apostrophized as "du") waters ("wässert") the "empires and glory" (grammatical antecedents of the relative pronoun), which, in turn, are aspects of the 'world'. In the first place, this statement can be interpreted as circumscribing an economic state of affairs, namely the fact that the Harz region yields important metals. No doubt a generic feature of the higher ode, namely a tendency to pronounce on the public issue of wealth and resources, makes itself felt here.[38] But Goethe's text, although it draws on this generic convention, can hardly be said to conform to it fully. On the contrary, the most essential function of the verb "wässern" here derives from its position within the series of terms evoking the schema of liquidity, one of the major semantic-cognitive structures of the text. In its previous activations, this schema was consistently employed as a figure of 'divine surabundance', as in this decisive passage bearing on the outsider:

> Öffne den umwölkten Blick
> Über die tausend Quellen
> Neben dem Durstenden
> In der Wüste. *(47–50)*

The verb of 'watering' designates a gift to the human community of far greater import and value than the raw materials of economic wealth. The 'mountain'/'divinity' is the source of the communal life itself, of its ethical substance. In this sense it quenches the thirst of religious despair with the overflowing of its inexhaustible bounty.

It would be possible, of course, to ramify this analysis of the operation of cognitive closure accomplished in the final stanza, but even the few observations made thus far suffice to underline what I take to be the crucial matter. The knowledge the concluding tableau codifies is essentially knowledge regarding the timeless relationships between the community and the Absolute. This knowledge, the object of the poet's quest, aligns within what might be called a *concord of opposites* the values of 'sovereign power' (as indicated in the archaic gesture of upright authority) and of 'liquid donation' (the 'watering' of the world). In this way, the vision achieved in the course of the poet's sublime ascent congeals into an enigmatic emblem in which the opposition between masculine and feminine values is resolved. The apostrophic "Du" holds together in co-reference *the severity of the paternal law and the liquid donation of the maternal breast.*

The third and final operation I want to consider here is that of *pragmatic closure,* whose function is to establish a particular set or orientation toward the poetic message on the part of the reader. Of course, neither in this stanza nor in any other passage of "Harzreise im Winter" does one meet with explicit directives for the reader. The only addressees of the poet's speech are the higher powers, apostrophized as "Vater der Liebe" (44), "Liebe" (65), and the "Du" of stanza XI, at once the mountain and the divine power it manifests. And yet these apostrophes, even as they suggest the total absorption of the poet in his vision, imply a public before which they are performed; this is the heritage of the higher poetic genres, in whose tradition Goethe's poem stands. In the eleventh stanza, perhaps due to the exigency of achieving pragmatic closure, traces of this otherwise invisible public—marks of its presence in and pressure on the text—become noticeable. Consider, for example, the participial adjective "erstaunt" in the phrase "Über der erstaunten Welt" (83). I earlier suggested that this word be interpreted by analogy to the narrative function of 'recognition' described by Propp, a function that involves public acknowledgment of the hero's achievement in bringing the 'object of value' to the community. So construed, the adjective "erstaunt" marks the attitude of a public internal to the diegesis vis-à-vis the poet and his accomplishment. Compare this usage of the term with that in the following text by Anna Luise Karsch celebrating the victorious Frederick the Great:

> Erstaunt wie ich: vernehmt und bebet,
> Ihr Länder, die mein König schützt![39]
>
> Be astonished as I am: hear and tremble,
> You lands that my king protects!

In this direct address to the public, typical of the high lyrical genres, the imperative "erstaunt" governs the response of the recipient. Goethe, of course, does not employ such an obvious tactic to influence his audience; rather, he locates the astonishment within an objective or diegetic scene, thereby offering his public a fictional model of the attitude it is to assume. With this shift in the array speaker/text/recipient, an aspect of the modification of the elevated lyric subgenres accomplished in "Harzreise im

Winter" as well as in other texts by Goethe becomes legible. The point to emphasize is that the traditional generic orientation toward a public is not abandoned for the sake of a sheerly autobiographical-expressive (*Erlebnis*-based) poetry, as earlier interpreters supposed. To be sure, the poem no longer simulates, as, for example, in the text by Anna Karsch, the communicative situation of public speech, but the orientation toward a public, hence toward 'universal' concerns, is preserved. The decisive difference lies in that the public no longer figures as the audience of oratorical address. Rather, it is conceived as a readership that silently accompanies and works through the process of poetic reflection.

From this analysis of the adjective "erstaunt," a general characterization of the operation of pragmatic closure in the final stanza can be derived. The position and orientation of the "erstaunten Welt" vis-à-vis the mountain provides a model of the attitude of the reader toward the poetic message. This also applies to the adverbial construction "geheimnisvoll offenbar" (83), which not only characterizes the way in which the Absolute reveals itself to the 'world' within the diegesis, but also the mode in which the Absolute manifests itself in the poetic text. The mountain, then, is not merely a transitive symbol of something (say, the 'divine' or the 'Absolute'), but is simultaneously located on a meta-level. *As the correlate of the poetic act of vision, the mountain is the symbol of poetic symbolization.* And if Goethe, echoing the earlier allusion to the revelation of the Lord to Hagar in the desert (stanza VII), qualifies the mountain's manifestation of the Absolute as "geheimnisvoll offenbar," then this paradoxical combination can be taken to mark the enigmatic quality of poetic symbolization as a concord of opposites. This observation makes clear why it was necessary to set the poet's vision in relation to the originary mythopoetic production of the "Volk." Just as the "Volk" constitutes itself as collective identity in the symbolic configurations that define its relation to the Absolute, so too does the poetic process worked through in "Harzreise im Winter" provide a medium in and through which a modern public or 'world' can constitute itself as a collectivity grounded in a poetic religion of gratitude.

This description of the operations of narrative, cognitive, and pragmatic closure leaves an important question unanswered: What is the position of the poet, the subject of the poetic utterance, as the text reaches its end? Due to a number of ambiguities that are built into the text, this question does not allow for an unequivocal answer. On the one hand, the use of the pronoun "Du" implies a speech situation in which the speaker is clearly distinguished from his addressee (the mountain). In this regard, one can infer that the poet is a member—perhaps a privileged member, but nonetheless one among others—of the human community that is designated by the expression "world." On this reading, the speaker would share the subjective perspective or attitude implied in the adjective "erstaunt" and in the paradoxical adverb "geheimnisvoll offenbar." Yet there are indications that the speaker assumes the position of the mountain he addresses or (more radically, but nonetheless within the realm of linguistic-rhetorical possibility) that the pronoun "Du" is used as a self-address. For example, the lines: "Und schaust aus Wolken / Auf ihre Reiche und Herrlichkeit" (84–85) suggest that the speaker's field of vision coincides with that of the apostophized "you." Moreover, if we compare the use of the expression "Brüder" in this and in the eighth stanza, it becomes clear that the poet and the addressee of stanza XI occupy homologous positions:

"Dichter" : "Brüder der Jagd" :: "Du" : "Brüder neben dir."

Both the poet and the "Du," as solitary representatives of an 'inner' (ethical-spiritual) value, are opposed to a group of "brothers," which influences 'external' aspects of human existence. The text allows for no clear determination as to whether the poetic voice here addresses an other or apostrophizes itself.

How is this systematic ambiguity regarding the position and status of the poet to be interpreted? In my view, it bears on the conception of poetry as a medium of reflection in which the community achieves its unity vis-à-vis the Absolute. That is, it is of the nature of high or sublime poetry to mediate between the community and the Absolute without itself belonging to one or the other. Indeed, these two poles are themselves brought forth in and through the oscillating movement of poetic reflection; *the 'community' and the 'Absolute' are moments of a religious consciousness that articulates itself in poetic discourse.* This final figuration of poetry as a medium of reflection points back to the poem's introit. The poetic aspiration expressed there is directed not only at the vertical superiority and visual-cognitive reach of the "Geier," but also at the peculiar hovering quality of the bird's flight: "Dem Geier gleich . . . Schwebe mein Lied" (1, 5). The verb "schweben," of course, is a conventional designation for the traditional notion of poetic flight.[40] Goethe's text, however, remotivates the conventional figure so that, in addition to its citational function as a generic marker, it acquires a function within the textual system. In this way, it initiates a process of semantic modification that, some twenty years after the composition of "Harzreise im Winter," enables the verb to serve as a figure for Romantic poetry generally. Thus, one of the key Romantic definitions of poetry as a medium of reflection reads:

> And yet it [Romantic poetry] can also best *hover on the wings of poetic reflection* [*auf den Flügeln der poetischen Reflexion in der Mitte schweben*] between the represented and the representing subject, free of all real and ideal interest, and can again and again potentialize this reflection and multiply it as in an infinite series of mirrors.[41] (Emphasis added)

The wings of poetic reflection Friedrich Schlegel here invokes in his famous 116th *Athenäum* fragment had their decisive trial flight in Goethe's reworking of the tradition of sublime poetry in "Harzreise im Winter." In this text, as in Goethe's lyric corpus of the 1770's generally, is to be located one of Romanticism's most productive and distinguished beginnings.

Notes

Notes

Chapter 1

1. Carlo Ginzburg, "Morelli, Freud and Sherlock Holmes: Clues and Scientific Method," *History Workshop* 9 (1980): 5–36.

2. *Gedichte 1756–1799*, 134–35. Goethe's authorship of this text has been disputed. See Eibl's note, ibid., 846. In view of the systematic connections that my analysis establishes between the poem and Goethe's other texts, the attribution of the text seems to me nearly certain.

3. Ibid., 129–30.

4. *H.A.*, I, 449–50.

5. The concept of *Erlebnis* designates the emergence of meaningful configurations out of the life process, the self-actualization and objectification of life as meaning. The concept received its most decisive formulation in Wilhelm Dilthey's study *Das Erlebnis und die Dichtung* (Berlin: Teubner, 1906) and has remained fundamental in the interpretation of Goethe's early lyric poetry, which is often referred to as *Erlebnislyrik*. See, for example, Gerhard Kaiser, *Geschichte der deutschen Lyrik von Goethe bis Heine: Ein Grundriß* (Frankfurt a. M.: Suhrkamp, 1988). For a trenchant, semiotically informed critique of this concept, see Marianne Wünsch, *Der Strukturwandel in Goethes Lyrik* (Stuttgart: Kohlhammer, 1975). Walter Benjamin's assault on the concept of *Erlebnis* (Benjamin, *Charles Baudelaire*, ed. Rolf Tiedemann, [Frankfurt a. M.: Suhrkamp, 1974], 106) is carried further by Philippe Lacoue-Labarthe, *La poésie comme expérience* (Paris: Christian Bourgois, 1986), 33.

6. The most recent published discussion of Goethe's Sesenheim lyric, despite a repudiation of the concept of *Erlebnis*, evinces the same tautological mode of explication. See Helmut Brandt, "Goethes Sesenheimer Gedichte als lyrischer Neubeginn," *Goethe Jahrbuch* 108 (1991): 31–46.

7. Michel Foucault, *L'ordre du discours* (Paris: Gallimard, 1971); English trans. "The Discourse on Language," appendix to Foucault, *The Archaeology of Knowledge*, trans. A. M. Sheridan Smith, (New York: Harper Colophon, 1976), 215–37. Friedrich A. Kittler, *Aufschreibesysteme 1800/1900* (Munich: Wilhelm Fink, 1985); English trans. *Discourse Networks, 1800/1900*, trans. Michael Metteer, with Chris Cullens, foreword by David E. Wellbery, (Stanford: Stanford University Press, 1990).

8. Salomon Geßner, *Idyllen von dem Verfasser des Daphnis* (Leipzig: I. G. Loewen, 1760), 45.

9. Ibid., 55–56.

10. The decisive methodological passage is the twelfth chapter of the second treatise of *Genealogy of Morals*. See Friedrich Nietzsche, *Sämtliche Werke, Kritische Studienausgabe in 15 Bänden*, ed. Giorgio Colli and Mazzino Montinari, (Berlin: Deutscher Taschenbuch Verlag and Walter de Gruyter, 1980), 5: 313–16. I have translated Nietzsche's term "Interpretation" as "reinterpretation" in order to stress that Nietzschean genealogy eliminates the notion of an original, noninterpreted text.

11. On the history of the idyll in Germany, see Helmut J. Schneider, "Die sanfte Utopie," Afterword to *Idyllen der Deutschen: Texte und Illustrationen*, ed. H. J. Schneider (Frankfurt a. M.: Insel, 1981), 353–418. The importance of the idyllic imagination in Goethe's work generally has been stressed by Gerhard Kaiser, *Wandrer und Idylle: Goethe und die Phänomenologie der Natur in der deutschen Dichtung von Geßner bis Gottfried Keller* (Göttingen: Vandenhoeck & Ruprecht, 1977).

12. See, for example, Moses Mendelssohn's notion of "naive expression" as developed in his essay of 1758 (slightly revised in 1771) "Über das Erhabene und das Naive in den schönen Wissenschaften," in Moses Mendelssohn, *Gesammelte Schriften*, Jubiläumsausgabe, ed. F. Bamberger, H. Bordianski, S. Rawidowicz, B. Strauß, L. Strauß, I. Ellbogen, J. Guttmann, and E. Mittwoch and continued by Alexander Altmann, 17 vols. (Stuttgart: Friedrich Fromann, 1971f.), 1: 493–94, esp. 83. For a range of eighteenth-century statements on the idyll, see *Deutsche Idyllentheorien im 18. Jahrhundert*, ed. Helmut J. Schneider (Tübingen: Gunter Narr, 1988).

13. Niklas Luhmann, *Liebe als Passion: Zur Codierung von Intimität* (Frankfurt a. M.: Suhrkamp, 1982); English trans. *Love as Passion: The Codification of Intimacy*, trans. Jeremy Gaines and Doris L. Jones (Cambridge: Harvard University Press, 1986).

14. By referring to these three concepts as quasi-synonyms, I am suggesting that a line of theoretical affiliation runs from Nietzsche to Luhmann. Nietzsche's influence on Foucault, of course, is well known. In a personal communication, Niklas Luhmann indicated to me that he had read Nietzsche quite thoroughly,

but was unaware of any direct influence. Interestingly enough, however, the title of Luhmann's study, *Liebe als Passion*, cites the title of a Nietzschean aphorism.

15. Obviously I draw here on the terminology (authentic, care, self) of Martin Heidegger's *Sein und Zeit*, 12th ed. (Tübingen: Max Niemeyer, 1972); English trans. *Being and Time*, trans. John Macquarrie and Edward Robinson (New York: Harper & Row, 1962). I do not mean to claim for Goethe's lyric poetry what might be termed an existential thematics. Rather, the cited terms seem useful to me in characterizing the enunciative position of the lyric subject as one who speaks of its *own* concerns, desires, anxieties, etc.

16. On the emergence of empathetic reading and listening in the second half of the eighteenth century, see Richard Alewyn, "Klopstocks Leser," in Bernhard Fabian, ed., *Festschrift für Rainer Gruenter* (Heidelberg: Carl Winter, 1978), 100–21. The theme is developed with regard to Goethe's *Werther* in Anselm Haverkamp, "Illusion und Empathie: Die Struktur der 'teilnehmenden Lektüre' in den *Leiden Werthers*," in Eberhard Lämmert, ed., *Erzählforschung: Ein Symposium* (Stuttgart: Metzler, 1982), 243–68. The reorganization of literary communication I am charting here parallels the paradigm shift from theatricality to absorption that Michael Fried discusses with regard to eighteenth-century French painting and art criticism. See Michael Fried, *Absorption and Theatricality: Painting and Beholder in the Age of Diderot* (Berkeley: University of California Press, 1980).

17. "When the effort is worth it, this vital reading, this divination [*Divination*] into the soul of the author, is the only true reading and the most profound instrument of self-formation," Johann Gottfried Herder, *Sämmtliche Werke*, ed. Bernhard Suphan, 33 vols. (Berlin: Weidmannsche Buchhandlung, 1877–1913), 8: 208. On Herder's theoretical innovation, see my study *Lessing's 'Laocoon': Semiotics and Aesthetics in the Age of Reason* (Cambridge: Cambridge University Press, 1984). Schleiermacher's use of the term can be followed out in the collection Friedrich Schleiermacher, *Hermeneutik und Kritik*, ed. Manfred Frank (Frankfurt a. M.: Suhrkamp, 1977). I note in passing that the cognitive operation of "Divination," according to Schleiermacher, is a "female strength." (See p. 169.) The notion that the ideal "diviner" of the speaking subject's internality and will-to-meaning is female will prove important in Goethe's lyric as well.

18. I use the notion of *Jetztzeit* (literally, "now-time"), which is common in phenomenological discourse, because it seems to capture the notion of a time that, rather than stretching out as duration, emerges as the actuality of a lived subjective position.

19. This is one of the central observations in Mikhail Bakhtin's analysis of the "idyllic chronotope." See M. M. Bakhtin, "Forms of Time and Chronotope in the Novel," *The Dialogic Imagination: Four Essays by M. M. Bakhtin*, ed. Michael Holquist, trans. Caryl Emerson and Michael Holquist (Austin: University of Texas Press, 1981), 224–36.

20. In view of the overburdened, ideological character of the notion of symbol in Goethe scholarship, it is worth pointing out that I am using the notion "symbolic," at least at this point in my inquiry, in the sense of Dan Sperber: symbolism is a loosely systematic array of values that organizes various experiential domains by correlating relations among terms drawn from one domain with terms drawn from another. Symbolism, then, is not the signification of a meaning through an individual sign, but the mapping of one set of relations in terms of another. Moreover, the domain-specific relations do not preexist this symbolic mapping, but rather are articulated in and through the establishment of the symbolic code. In the case at hand, the three domains brought into correlation, receiving thereby their symbolic articulation, hence their intelligibility, are Nature, Love, and, as we shall see, Art. See Dan Sperber, *Rethinking Symbolism*, trans. Alice Morton (Cambridge: Cambridge University Press, 1975).

21. This formulation is influenced by Philippe Lacoue-Labarthe's study of Paul Celan: "La voie que le poeme cherche à se frayer, ici, est la voie de sa propre source. Et cheminant ainsi vers sa propre source, c'est la source en general de la poésie qu'il cherche à atteindre" (*La poésie comme expérience*, 31). This discursive project, which Lacoue-Labarthe describes with respect to one of its latest, most troubled and difficult instances, has its beginnings in Romanticism and in particular in Goethe's lyric corpus of the 1770's.

22. On this point see Kittler's afterword to *Discourse Networks, 1800/1900*, esp. 369.

23. The term *Keimentschluß* (seminal decision, opening of the seed) in Schleiermacher's hermeneutics designates the ultimate reference point of the act of hermeneutic divination, the point of subjective emergence and creation that is the Origin of the text to be interpreted.

24. Pierre Macherey, *Pour une théorie de la production littéraire* (Paris: Maspero, 1966), 255.

25. Karlheinz Stierle has argued that this point holds especially as regards lyric texts, that the defining moment of the lyric is its "transgression of discourse." See Karlheinz Stierle, "Die Identität des Gedichts—Hölderlin als Paradigma," in Odo Marquard and Karlheinz Stierle, eds., *Identität*, Poetik und Hermeneutik 8 (München: Wilhelm Fink, 1979), 505–52.

26. On the paradoxical function of the frame, see Jacques Derrida, "The Parergon," *The Truth in Painting*, trans. Geoff Bennington and Ian McLeod (Chicago: University of Chicago Press, 1987), 37–83, esp. 97–98.

27. Klaus Weimar (*Goethes Gedichte 1769–1775: Interpretationen zu einem Anfang* [Paderborn: Schöningh, 1982], 32–39) has demonstrated that the peculiar difficulties of the lines reside in the use of the particle "wie," which differs here from its relatively transparent significance in other parts of the text. I am indebted, here and throughout, to Klaus Weimar's study, still the best on

Goethe's early lyric, and to Klaus Weimar himself for extremely suggestive discussions of this and other texts by Goethe.

28. On the envoi as a structural feature of the lyric, see Paul Zumthor, "On the Circularity of Song," in Tzvetan Todorov, *French Literary Theory Today* (Cambridge: Cambridge University Press, 1982), 179–91.

29. After completing this section of my study, I received a prepublication of Rüdiger Campe's discussion of "Maifest" in his study *Affekt und Ausdruck: Zur Umwandlung der literarischen Rede im 17. und 18. Jahrhundert* (Tübingen: Niemeyer, 1990), 537–54. Our readings complement one another especially with regard to two points. First, Campe discusses what he describes as a systematic "forgetting" of rhetoric in the production of this "hermeneutic" text. This parallels the strategy of effacement regarding the spatio-temporal articulation of the poem that my own reading focuses on. Second, Campe (following Weimar, *Goethes Gedichte 1769–1775*) sees the final two lines—with their aberrant "wie"-comparison—as the site where rhetoric returns, or at least leaves the trace of its suppression. My discussion of the same lines as an *envoi* that at once calls attention to the poem's textual status and compensates for this status by urging that the poem be returned to the 'loving Source' from which it originated strikes me as a cognate claim. In a suggestive comparison of the semiotics of Saint Paul, Luther, and Goethe, Manfred Schneider comes to analogous conclusions regarding Goethe's effacement of textuality. See Schneider, "Luther mit McCluhan: Zur Medientheorie und Semiotik heiliger Zeichen," *Diskursanalysen* 1 (1987): 13–25, esp. 22–24.

Chapter 2

1. The text on which I base my analysis is a composite: I have used the version published in the journal *Iris* in 1775, but have inserted in lines 9–10 formulations deriving from a manuscript of the first ten lines of the poem found among the papers of Friederike Brion. Thus, where the *Iris* version reads "seinem Wolken-hügel" in line 9, I have substituted "einem Wolkenhügel"; and where the *Iris* version reads "Schien kläglich" in line 10, I have substituted "Sah schläfrig." (Both versions are reprinted in *Gedichte 1756–1799*, 128–29. See also Eibl's editorial remarks, 837–38.) My reason for undertaking this contamination of two variants is that my analysis focuses on systematic features of the text. Structural analysis often uses variants (of myths, of texts, of genres, etc.) as an aid in developing hypotheses regarding patterns of signification, a procedure that, as it were, allows divergent formulations to illuminate one another. This methodological step has, of course, something decisionistic about it, but for that matter so does every determination of textual identity. To claim, as, for example, Eibl does (837), that it is questionable to contaminate the two variants as I have done

presupposes that the only legitimate analytic procedure is one that follows the different chronological phases of composition, a premise as decisionistic as any could be. Fundamental reflections on this question of textual identity are developed in Hans-Jost Frey, *Der unendliche Text* (Frankfurt a. M.: Suhrkamp, 1990).

2. The opposition "wild"/"mild" functions similarly in "Jägers Nachtlied" ("Hunter's Night Song"), *Gedichte 1756–1799*, 225.

3. Any reader interested in a detailed critique of the traditional scholarship on this poem, and, implicitly, on Goethe's early poetry generally, should consult David E. Wellbery, "The Specular Moment: Construction of Meaning in a Poem by Goethe," *Goethe Yearbook* 1 (1982): 1–41. The same article contains numerous references, likewise suppressed in this version, to the semiotic theories from which I draw methodological guidance. Since the publication of that article, two noteworthy discussions of the poem have appeared: Eckhardt Meyer-Krentler, *Willkomm und Abschied—Herzschlag und Peitschenhieb: Goethe—Mörike—Heine* (Munich: Wilhelm Fink, 1987); Peter Utz, "Das getrübte Glück des sprechenden Blicks: Wahrnehmung, Identität und Sprache in 'Willkommen und Abschied,'" *Das Auge und das Ohr im Text: Literarische Sinneswahrnehmung in der Goethezeit* (Munich: Wilhelm Fink, 1990), 100–10. Utz's discussion of the text unfolds as a dialogue with my article of 1982 and I shall return to this dialogue further on. Recent interpretations by Hiltrud Gnüg (*Entstehung und Krise lyrischer Subjektivität* [Stuttgart: Metzler, 1983]) and Helmut Brandt ("Goethes Sesenheimer Gedichte als lyrischer Neubeginn," *Goethe Jahrbuch* 108 [1991]: 39–41) fail to go beyond the traditional understanding of the poem.

4. Two points deserve at least marginal annotation here. First, by poetic convention, the 'moon' often functions as a stand-in for a beloved woman and therefore provides the poetic subject with a certain comfort despite the absence of that beloved. "Jägers Nachtlied"—a text I have already referred to because of its deployment of the opposition "wild"/"mild"—exemplifies this complex. Thus, the threat of absence the poetic subject here suffers through could be read as deriving preeminently from the absence of the beloved female figure to whom, in this dark night of the soul, not even her lunar representative provides a link. Second, the adverb "schläfrig" applied to the moon's regard could be read as a projection of the subject's own condition onto the things around him such that it is the speaking subject who is in fact "sleepy" here. I will return to this possibility in Chapter 4.

5. On the question of closure and on closure signals in general, see Phillipe Hamon, "Clausules," *Poétique* 24 (1975): 495–526.

6. *Gedichte 1756–1799*, 135. The connection of this text to "Mir schlug das Herz" has, as far as I know, not been noted. In an excellent reading of "Mir schlug das Herz," however, Marianne Wünsch has pointed out that the vision of the beloved in the third stanza might very well be considered a dream vision. (See

Marianne Wünsch, *Der Strukturwandel in Goethes Lyrik* (Stuttgart: Kohlhammer, 1975), 112. The cited poem lends support to this surmise.

7. Despite its abruptness, the transition to the third stanza is not without motivation. The echo of "zerfloß" (16) in line 18 ("Floß") indicates that the fluid, expansive emotion in 15–16 becomes in 17–18 the medium in which lover and beloved are united in their visual encounter. More precisely, the indefinite emotional *zerfließen* acquires the specific character of "joy" ("Freude," 17) exchanged between "ich" and "dich"; the "milde Freude" named here is, in fact, the fluidlike interchange and immediate reciprocity that joins the two figures.

8. I am reminded here of the terrifying multiplication of eyes in E. T. A. Hoffmann's *Der Sandmann*, a text I will return to in the following chapter. Utz (*Das Auge und das Ohr im Text*, 104) disagrees with my reading in terms of dismemberment, arguing instead that the first two stanzas evoke, through their interplay of visual and auditory elements, the totalizing structure of sense perception. I agree with Utz that stanzas I and II especially foreground aural features, but would interpret this fact in turn as evidence of a certain *disjunction* of the senses: eye and ear can no more be brought together than the "soughing" winds ("Ums*au*sten sch*au*erlich mein Ohr," 12) can be seen. Absence, which can't be seen, makes itself auditorily felt.

9. This, of course, is the famous definition of the poetic function put forth by Roman Jakobson, "Closing Statement: Linguistics and Poetics," *Style in Language*, ed. Thomas A. Sebeok, (Cambridge: MIT Press, 1960), 350–77.

10. I cannot help but remark, although it involves a tremendous anachronism, that Goethe's color theory, as developed in his *Farbenlehre*, introduces the term "trübe" as the mediating term between 'light' and 'darkness.' Could it be that his early poetic experimentation provided the (unconscious) schemata that organized his later scientific observations?

11. Utz (*Das Auge und das Ohr*, 298) criticizes my "fixation" on vision, but does not discuss my construction of the code of vision that provides the text with one of its major semantic armatures; nor does he offer an alternative hypothesis regarding the semantic organization of the text. Our differences, which I consider productive, derive from the different kinds of questions we raise regarding the poem. Utz's study is essentially a thematic analysis (the treatment of vision and audition) that runs across genres. My interest is in analyzing Goethe's lyric as such, a project which quite naturally passes through the reconstruction of particular textual systems. In addition, it seems to me that Utz works with a much more mimetic or referential notion of the poetic text than I do.

12. On narrative as the crossing of a topographic-semantic border, see Jurij M. Lotman, *Die Struktur literarischer Texte*, trans Rolf-Dietrich Keil (Munich: Wilhelm Fink, 1972), 329–40. I will return to this model in my analysis of "Mahomets Gesang" in Chapter 5.

13. I refer here to Hölderlin's note "Urtheil und Seyn" from 1795, in which—to summarize drastically—the judgment ("Urtheil") is interpreted as a primal severance ("Ur-teilen") within the undifferentiated unity of being ("Seyn"). See Friedrich Hölderlin, *Sämtliche Werke*, ed. Friedrich Beissner (Stuttgart: Kohlhammer, 1961), 4:216–17. I pick up this reference again at the opening of Chapter 3.

14. Although opposed to one another, these two semantic terms are similar by virtue of the absoluteness and undifferentiation they imply. Perhaps it is for this reason that the text passes so quickly from one term to the other. That the reversal can move in the opposite direction as well—that absolute presence in the eyes of the beloved can become absolute absence—is demonstrated by the narrative structure of *Werther*. Cf., for example, the following: "Hier, wenn ich die Augen schließe, hier in meiner Stirne, wo die innere Sehkraft sich vereinigt, stehen ihre schwarze Augen. Hier! ich kann dir es nicht ausdrücken. Mache ich meine Augen zu, so sind sie da; wie ein Meer, ein Abgrund ruhen sie vor mir, in mir, füllen die Sinne meiner Stirne" (*H.A.*, 6: 92). ("Here, when I close my eyes, here in my forehead where the internal power of seeing is united, stand her black eyes. Here! I can't express it. If I close my eyes, they're there; like a sea, an abyss they rest before me, within me, fill up the senses of my forehead.")

15. See Rodolphe Gasché's discussion of the infrastructure of the "remark" in *The Tain of the Mirror: Derrida and the Philosophy of Reflection* (Cambridge: Harvard University Press, 1986), 217–24.

16. To draw out the connotation of negativity in this gesture of looking to the earth one need only compare our text with the drama *Götz von Berlichingen*. There the gesture occurs in a context that unmistakably defines it as a response to death and that contrasts it with the enlivening "Blick" of a loved one: "Ach daß ich Georgen noch einmal sähe, mich an seinem Blick wärmte!—Ihr seht zur Erden und weint—Er ist tot—Georg ist tot.—Stirb, Götz—Du hast dich selbst überlebt, die Edeln überlebt" (*H.A.*, 4: 175). ("Oh that I might see Georg one more time, warm myself in his regard!—You're looking to the earth and crying—he's dead—Georg is dead.—Die, Götz—you've outlived yourself, outlived the noble ones.")

17. *Goethes Briefe*, ed. Karl Robert Mandelkow, vol. I, *Briefe der Jahre 1764–1786* (Hamburg: Christian Wegner, 1962), 91.

Chapter 3

1. *Briefe von und an Hegel*, ed. Johannes Hoffmeister, vol. I, *1785–1812* (Hamburg: Felix Meiner, 1952), 355.

2. This aspect of the Romantic project has been discussed most recently in the following contributions: Philippe Lacoue-Labarthe and Jean-Luc Nancy, *The Literary Absolute: The Theory of Literature in German Romanticism*, trans. Philip

Barnard and Cheryl Lester (Albany: State University of New York Press, 1988); Manfred Frank, " 'Intellektuale Anschauung'. Drei Stellungnahmen zu einem Deutungsversuch von Selbstbewußtsein: Kant, Fichte, Hölderlin/Novalis," in Ernst Behler and Jochen Hörisch, *Die Aktualität der Frühromantik* (Paderborn: Schöningh, 1987), 96–126; Winfried Menninghaus, *Unendliche Verdopplung: Die frühromantische Grundlegung der Kunsttheorie im Begriff absoluter Selbstreflexion* (Frankfurt: a. M.: Suhrkamp, 1987). Menninghaus's argument takes Walter Benjamin's dissertation of 1919 as its point of departure: Benjamin, *Der Begriff der Kunstkritik in der deutschen Romantik* (Frankfurt a. M.: Suhrkamp, 1973). For a critical review in English of the literature on Romanticism and self-consciousness (reflexivity), see Alice A. Kuzniar, "Reassessing Romantic Reflexivity—The Case of Novalis," *The Germanic Review* 63 (1988): 77–86.

3. *Gedichte 1756–1799*, 132–33. Eibl reprints as well the stanzas added to the poem by Lenz, which I have here omitted. The line numbering has been changed accordingly.

4. In a recent article, Manfred Schneider has used the poem to exemplify how the emergent literary discourse of the 1770's can be read as a kind of colonization of female readers through the implantation of a phantasm of the loving author. As interesting as I find Schneider's argument, I think he overlooks the fact that the poem is a citation of an earlier and, from the perspective of the poet, outworn lyrical mode; that the poem, in a sense, is about its own inadequacy and anachronistic character. See Manfred Schneider, "Wie man eine Frau programmiert," *Merkur* 490 (1989): 1055–68.

5. The pragmatics of the poem's address presuppose that the verses we hold before us are written down, that the poem, in other words, writes its scene of writing (absence of the beloved). Some of the contradictions Marianne Wünsch notes in the text (*Der Strukturwandel in Goethes Lyrik* [Stuttgart: Kohlhammer, 1975]) disappear when this is taken into consideration. If the maiden is posited as sleeping in the present, and if the poem says that she will now hear, as punishment, what the poem has rhymed, then this "now" can only refer to the moment of reading/recitation that follows upon the completed inscription and transmission of the text. Thus, "Erwache Friedericke" makes implicit the envoi structure that the concluding lines of "Maifest" veil: it predicts its own destination, its reading, with the difference, of course, that this reading can only be inadequate because the beloved's *Blick* did not sponsor the poem in the first place. "Maifest" succeeds where "Erwache Friedericke" fails because origin and destination are one.

6. Michel Foucault, *The Order of Things: An Archaeology of the Human Sciences* (New York: Vintage Books, 1973), 332.

7. Foucault's epochal construction (which is developed in terms of the three epistemological fields economics, language theory, and natural history) parallels

that set forth in the researches of Reinhart Koselleck, who has repeatedly designated the last third of the eighteenth century a "Sattelzeit" ("saddle period"), during which a fundamental mutation in the conceptualization and experience of history occurs. See esp. Koselleck, "Die Herausbildung des modernen Geschichtsbegriffs," in Otto Brunner, Werner Conze, and Reinhart Koselleck, eds., *Geschichtliche Grundbegriffe*, vol. I, E–G (Stuttgart: Klett Cotta, 1975), 647–717. For a consideration of the literary work of the young Goethe in the context of this discussion of epochal concepts, see Walter Falk, "Der epochengeschichtliche Wandel beim frühen Goethe," *Verhaltensformen in der industriellen Revolution*, ed. August Nitschke (Stuttgart: Kohlhammer, 1975), 118–35. The formation of a literary-political culture sustained by the medium of print and its associated institutions provides the focus of James J. Sheehan's masterly overview (note the dates of his title), *German History 1770–1866* (Oxford: Oxford University Press, 1989). See esp. 9–205, "Eighteenth-Century Background."

8. The reevaluation of Fichte has its starting point in Dieter Henrich, *Fichtes ursprüngliche Einsicht* (Frankfurt a. M.: Klostermann, 1967). Henrich's work and teaching form the basis of the so-called Heidelberg School. The most important contribution to the theory of self-consciousness to have emerged from this school is Ulrich Pothast, *Über einige Fragen der Selbstbeziehung* (Frankfurt a. M.: Suhrkamp, 1971). The Heidelberg theory has been trenchently criticized from the perspective of analytic philosophy in Ernst Tugendhat, *Selbstbewußtsein und Selbstbestimmung: Sprachanalytische Interpretationen* (Frankfurt: a. M.: Suhrkamp, 1981). Tugendhat has in turn been criticized from a neo-Romantic perspective by Manfred Frank, "Subjekt, Person, Individuum," in Manfred Frank and Anselm Haverkamp, eds., *Individualität*, Poetik und Hermeneutik 13 (Munich: Wilhelm Fink, 1988), 3–20. For a reading of Fichte's first principle that shifts focus away from questions of consciousness and attends instead to the aspect of linguistic-rhetorical performativity, see Werner Hamacher, "Der Satz der Gattung: Friedrich Schlegels poetologische Umsetzung von Fichtes unbedingtem Grundsatz," *MLN* 95 (1980): 1155–80.

9. Fichte, *Grundlage der gesamten Wissenschaftslehre* (1794), ed. Wilhelm G. Jacobs (Hamburg: Felix Meiner, 1970), 13.

10. Ibid., 14.

11. Henrich, *Fichtes ursprüngliche Einsicht.*

12. Fichte, *Versuch einer neuen Darstellung der Wissenschaftslehre* (1797–98), ed. Peter Baumanns (Hamburg: Felix Meiner, 1975), 39.

13. Ibid., 42. Fichte's phrase "in sich zurückkehrendes Handeln" is a nearly perfect description of what "Maifest" (Text 2) aspires to be: a song that in singing sings nothing but the singing that it is, that folds back upon its own origination out of the specular regard, the gift of the beloved maiden. This is why I referred to the project of the poem as that of a poetic cogito.

14. J. G. Fichte, *Gesamtausgabe der Bayrischen Akademie der Wissenschaften*, ed.

Reinhard Lauth and Hans Jakob (Stuttgart-Bad Canstatt: Fromann, 1962f.), 4/2: 49.

15. Ibid., 2/6: 169.

16. Fichte, *Sämmtliche Werke*, ed. I. H. Fichte (Berlin: Veit, 1846), 8: 462.

17. Novalis, *Schriften: Die Werke Friedrich von Hardenbergs*, vol. I, *Das dichterische Werk*, ed. Paul Kluckhohn and Richard Samuel, with Heinz Ritter and Gerhard Schulz (Stuttgart: Kohlhammer, 1960), 315.

18. Ibid., 135.   19. Ibid., 177.

20. Ibid., 110.   21. Ibid., 197.

22. Novalis, *Schriften: Die Werke Friedrich von Hardenbergs*, vol. II, *Das philosophische Werk I*, ed. Richard Samuel, with Hans-Joachim Mähl and Gerhard Schulz (Stuttgart: Kohlhammer, 1960), 104.

23. Ibid.   24. Ibid., 113.

25. Ibid., 106.   26. Ibid., 114.

27. *H.A.*, 3: 110. It is worth noting that Faust, in the same speech, evokes the specular moment ("Schau' ich nicht Aug' in Auge dir") as the occasion of such feeling.

28. Novalis, *Schriften*, 2: 105.

29. Ibid., 106.

30. I am referring, of course, to the poem "Wünschelrute":

> Schläft ein Lied in allen Dingen,
> Die da träumen fort und fort,
> Und die Welt hebt an zu singen,
> Triffst du nur das Zauberwort.
>
> A song sleeps in all things,
> Which dream there on and on,
> And the world begins to sing,
> If you just hit upon the magic word.
>
> *(Joseph von Eichendorff, Werke*
> *[Munich: Winkler, 1970], 1: 132)*

I cannot develop a reading of this text here, but note that the poet's "divining rod" ("Wünschelrute"), hence his desire, is pulled toward a transcendental song that unconsciously underlies (in "dream") the world of objects ("things"). The poet who can "hit upon" the magically evocative word, therefore, not only transforms the world of objectivity into its originary form, but also achieves in and through this poetic evocation an erotic union with his own (maternal) origin.

31. Joseph von Eichendorff, *Werke in vier Bänden*, ed. Wolfdietrich Rasch (Munich: Hanser, 1981), 1: 436–37.

32. See the excellent article by Raimar Stefan Zons, " 'Schweifen': Eichendorff's *Ahnung und Gegenwart*, in Hans-Georg Pott, ed., *Eichendorff und die Spätromantik* (Paderborn: Schöningh, 1985), 39–68.

33. Compare the poem "Verschwiegene Liebe," in Eichendorff, *Werke*, 4: 92.

34. I have in mind here the remarks of André Green in the section "L'hallucination negative de la mère," in his *Narcisissme de vie, Narcisissme de mort* (Paris: Minuit, 1983), 125–27.

35. E. T. A. Hoffmann, *Werke*, ed. Herbert Kraft and Manfred Wacker (Frankfurt a. M.: Insel, 1967), I: 7. The second translation I offer ("idealization and sexuality") draws its legitimation from the examples of irony in Callot's work that Hoffmann cites.

36. Ibid., 138–39.

37. Ibid., 129–30.

38. On this subgenre of the Romantic lyric see Alexander von Bormann, "Der Töne Licht: Zum frühromantischen Programm der Wortmusik," in Ernst Behler and Jochen Hörisch, eds., *Die Aktualität der Frühromantik* (Paderborn: Schöningh, 1987), 191–207.

39. I borrow this term from the study by Kaja Silverman, *The Acoustic Mirror: The Female Voice in Psychoanalysis and Cinema* (Bloomington: Indiana University Press, 1988). See esp. chapters 3 and 4 (72–140), which deal with the "fantasy of the maternal voice." Silverman's book develops a wide-ranging and perspicacious critique of the psychoanalytic literature on this aural phantasm.

40. My reading of the passage here follows closely that of Friedrich A. Kittler, *Aufschreibesysteme 1800/1900* (Munich: Wilhelm Fink, 1985), 83–114, esp. 84; English trans. *Discourse Networks 1800/1900*, trans. Michael Metteer, with Chris Cullens, foreword by David E. Wellbery (Stanford: Stanford University Press, 1990), 77–107, esp. 78. Kittler reads the song of the snakes as an aural hallucination of the Mother, who appears as a presignificant (asemantic) orality. This is not entirely accurate, since the song does exhibit a certain semantics. It sings, as I have argued, of its function: to fill in the *gaps between things* ("Zwischen-" dominates the song's beginning) and to suggest the *maternal presence* ("Blüten" as "Brüsten"). Furthermore, as we shall see shortly, the song also sings of the paternal law that circumscribes its space. Kaja Silverman's study of the phantasy of the maternal voice, and especially her critique of the psychoanalytic conceptualization of this phantasy, could have acquired a sharper historical focus had she consulted Kittler's study. Elsewhere ("Foreword" to Kittler, *Discourse Networks*, xvi–xxv) I have summarized Kittler's thesis on Romanticism with the formula: "Romanticism is the discursive production of the Mother as the source of discursive production." His description of the historically specific techniques and materialities of acculturation, esp. language learning, that render such discursive production of the Mother possible is something of an archaeology of the psychoanalytic theories Silverman reviews and criticizes.

41. Hoffmann, *Werke*, 1: 130.

42. *H.A.*, 6: 9.

43. Nicolas Abraham, "Le Symbole ou l'au-dela du phénomène," in Nicolas Abraham and Marie Torok, *L'Ecorce et le noyau* (Paris: Aubier-Flammarion, 1978).

44. André Green, *Narcissisme de vie*, 145: "I want to say that the love of the object is a transitive function in which the object is alternatively the mother and the infant. The infant becomes the object of the object within the illusory relation of the unity mother-infant." Green's studies on narcissism have been extremely suggestive to me throughout the preparation of this book. Perhaps it is useful to cite one definitional formulation that has proved to be especially productive: "Narcissism is the effacement of the trace of the Other in the Desire of/for the One" (127).

45. The sun is explicitly encoded as maternal in "The Golden Jar." See Hoffmann, *Werke*, 1: 139, where the text develops a mythic genealogy of the snakes that has its starting point in the sun's "mütterlichen Schoß" ("maternal womb").

46. Ibid., 131.

47. Ibid., 147. Perhaps it should be noted that the "illusory relation of the unity mother-infant" described by Green in the passage cited in note 44 continues, according to Green, "up until the point when this illusion yields to the disillusionment created by becoming conscious of the third figure, which is the father" (*Narcissisme de vie*, 145).

48. Hoffmann, *Werke*, 1: 204.

49. The fruitfulness of this notion for the analysis of late-eighteenth- and early-nineteenth-century texts has been demonstrated by Dorothea E. von Mücke, *Virtue and the Veil of Illusion: Generic Innovation and the Pedagogical Project in Eighteenth-Century Literature* (Stanford: Stanford University Press, 1991).

50. *Freud-Studienausgabe*, ed. Alexander Mitscherlich, Angela Richards, James Strachey, 4th corrected ed. (Frankfurt a. M.: S. Fischer, 1970), 4: 241–71.

51. See Samuel Weber, "The Sideshow: or, Remarks on a Canny Moment," *MLN* 88 (1973): 1102–33; Helene Cixous, "Fiction and Its Phantoms: A Reading of Freud's 'Das Unheimliche,'" *New Literary History* 7 (1976): 525–48; Friedrich A. Kittler, "'Das Phantom unseres Ichs' und die Literaturpsychologie: E. T. A. Hoffmann–Freud–Lacan," in Horst Turk and Friedrich A. Kittler, eds., *Urszenen: Literaturwissenschaft als Diskursanalyse und Diskurskritik* (Frankfurt a. M.: Suhrkamp, 1978), 139–66; Neil Hertz, "Freud and the Sandman," in Josué V. Harari, ed., *Textual Strategies: Perspectives in Post-Structuralist Criticism* (Ithaca: Cornell University Press, 1979), 296–321.

52. *Freud Studienausgabe*, 4: 256.

53. Hoffmann, *Werke*, 2: 34.

54. For the discussion of another example, see David E. Wellbery, "E. T. A.

Hoffmann and Romantic Hermeneutics: An Interpretation of Hoffmann's 'Don Juan'," *Studies in Romanticism* 19 (1980): 455–73.

55. Hoffmann, *Werke*, 2: 25.

56. *Freud Studienausgabe*, 3: 371–78, "Die Verneinung."

57. See *Freud Studienausgabe* 3: 59 ("On Narcissism: An Introduction").

58. *Freud Studienausgabe*, 7: 149–65.

59. Freud's misreading of the scene is pointed out by Samuel Weber, "The Sideshow: or, Remarks on a Canny Moment." See also Stanley Cavell, *In Quest of the Ordinary* (Chicago: University of Chicago Press, 1988), 156.

60. Hoffmann, *Werke*, 2: 38. Note also that it is Klara who calls attention to this "bush" just as it was she who had suggested climbing the tower in the first place. The entire scene could be read as her initiation of a sexual encounter with Nathaniel, or as Nathaniel's hallucination of such sexual forthrightness on her part.

61. Ibid., 39.

62. On the figure of the "Blick" in Dante, Petrarch, and Baudelaire, see Rainer Warning, "Imitatio und Intertextualität. Zur Geschichte lyrischer Destruktion der Amortheologie: Dante, Petrarca, Baudelaire," *Kolloquium Kunst und Philosophie*, vol. II, *Ästhetischer Schein*, ed. Willi Oelmüller (Paderborn: Schöningh, 1982), 167–205; on the figure of the lover's regard in Shakespeare, see Joel Fineman, *Shakespeare's Perjured Eye: The Invention of Poetic Subjectivity in the Sonnets* (Berkeley: University of California Press, 1986); on Celan's overcoming of the Romantic figure of reflexivity, see Werner Hamacher, "Die Sekunde der Inversion: Bewegungen einer Figur durch Celans Gedichte," in Werner Hamacher and Winfried Menninghaus, eds., *Paul Celan* (Frankfurt a. M.: Suhrkamp, 1988), 81–126.

63. Heinrich Heine, *Säkularausgabe*, ed. Nationaler Forschungs- und Gedenkstätten der klassischen deutschen Literatur, Weimar, and Centre National de la Recherche Scientifique, Paris, vol. I, *Gedichte 1812–27*, ed. Hans Böhm (Berlin: Akademie; Paris: CNRS, 1979), 65.

Chapter 4

1. *H.A.*, 3: 340. The lines are from *Faust II*, 11289–92.

2. Christoph Martin Wieland, *Geschichte des Agathon*, rpt. of 1st ed. (1767), ed. Klaus Schaeffer (Berlin: Akadamie, 1961), 15.

3. Even the ambiguous status of the specular moment (dream or reality?) alluded to above is anticipated by Wieland: "Was it a dream I encountered or did I really see her, did I really hear the sweet accent of her voice, did my arms really embrace more than a shade? If it was more than a dream, then why does there

remain to me nothing but a memory of the object that extinguished all others from my soul?" (Ibid., 22–23).

4. For a reading of the bildungsroman along these lines, see Friedrich A. Kittler, "Über die Sozialisation Wilhelm Meisters," in Gerhard Kaiser and Friedrich A. Kittler, *Dichtung als Sozialisationsspiel: Studien zu Goethe und Gott-fried Keller* (Göttingen: Vandenhoeck & Ruprecht, 1978), 12–124; Dorothea E. von Mücke, *Virtue and the Veil of Illusion: Generic Innovation and the Pedagogical Project in Eighteenth-Century Literature* (Stanford: Stanford University Press, 1991), chapter 5.

5. Here I am especially indebted to Dorothea von Mücke's reading of the novel in *Virtue and the Veil of Illusion.*

6. Wieland, whose reinterpretation of classical mythology is of immeasurable importance for German literature of the classical-romantic period, was, of course, well aware that Pythia, the priestess of Apollo's temple, was positioned over a chasm that gave forth poisonous gases and that she spoke the oracles in mysteriously ambiguous formulations.

7. Christoph Martin Wieland, *Sämmtliche Werke*, ed. Hamburger Stiftung zur Förderung von Wissenschaft und Kultur (Hamburg: 1984), I, 3: 417. Note that the passage describing the specular moment remains essentially unchanged in this edition.

8. Ibid., 424.

9. On this point, see Kittler, "Über die Sozialisation Wilhelm Meisters."

10. The decisive contribution to this research was undoubtedly Philippe Aries, *L'Enfant et la famille sous l'ancien regime* (Paris: Flammarion, 1973 [1st ed., 1960]). See also: Karin Hausen, "Die Polarisierung der 'Geschlechtscharaktere'—eine Spiegelung der Dissoziation von Erwerbs- und Familienleben," in Werner Conze, ed., *Sozialgeschichte der Familie in der Neuzeit Europas* (Stuttgart: Klett Cotta, 1976), 363–93; *Familie und Gesellschaftsstruktur*, ed. Heidi Rosenbaum (Frankfurt a. M.: Suhrkamp, 1978). The theoretically most sophisticated and historically most detailed investigation of the literary relevance of this shift is Friedrich A. Kittler, *Aufschreibesysteme 1800/1900* (Munich: Wilhelm Fink, 1985), English trans. *Discourse Networks 1800/1900*, trans. Michael Metteer, with Chris Cullens, foreword by David E. Wellbery (Stanford: Stanford University Press, 1990). See also the essays collected in Friedrich A. Kittler, *Dichter—Mutter—Kind* (Paderborn: Schöningh, 1991). For a very interesting sociohistorical study on a particular aspect of the literary encoding of familial life in the literature of Romanticism, see Michael Titzmann, "Literarische Strukturen und kulturelles Wissen: Das Beispiel inzestuöser Situationen in der Erzählliteratur der Goethe-zeit und ihrer Funktionen im Denksystem der Epoche," in Jörg Schönert, ed., *Erzählte Kriminalität* (Tübingen: Niemeyer, 1990), 123–69.

11. Of course, they are not predictions in the strict sense, since my reading of the poem preceded their formulation.

12. *Gedichte 1756–1799*, 220–21.

13. Sauder, in his commentary to the Munich edition of Goethe's works (*Münchener-Ausgabe*, I/1, 889) argues that the text is a parody of the fairy tales of the Countess Marie Catherine d'Aulnoy. Eibl notes the influence of French fairy tales in such words as "obligeant" (*Gedichte 1756–1799*, 942). Goethe considered the text significant enough to place it at the head of his collected poems in the 1789 edition of his *Schriften*, which suggests that the text is to be read as programmatic or exemplary.

14. *Münchener-Ausgabe*, I/1, 224–25.

15. See Niklas Luhmann, *Liebe als Passion: Zur Codierung von Intimität* (Frankfurt a. M.: Suhrkamp, 1982), 123–82; English trans. *Love as Passion: The Codification of Intimacy*, trans. Jeremy Gaines and Doris L. Jones (Cambridge: Harvard University Press, 1986), 129–44. Social historians have stressed the significance of the waltz as an innovative corporeal practice symbolizing the values of intimacy, freedom, and individuality. See Wilhelm Braun, "'The Invention of Tradition': Wilhelm II. und die Renaissance der höfischen Tänze," *Zeitschrift für Volkskunde* 82 (1986): 227–49, esp. 234–41; Henning Eichberg, "Der Umbruch des Bewegungsverhaltens: Leibesübungen, Spiele und Tänze in der industriellen Revolution," in August Nitschke, ed., *Verhaltenswandel in der industriellen Revolution, Beiträge zur Sozialgeschichte* (Stuttgart: Kohlhammer, 1975), 118–35.

16. Roland Barthes, *A Lovers Discourse*, trans. Richard Howard (New York: Hill and Wang, 1978).

17. *H.A.*, 6: 25.

18. Sophie von LaRoche, *Geschichte des Fräuleins von Sternheim*, ed. Fritz Brüggemann (Leipzig: Reclam, 1938), 166–67. I have parenthetically inserted the original German wording where it corresponds to the formulations in "Auf Cristianen R.," indicating, if not a direct borrowing, at least a shared set of perceptions. Another passage from La Roche's novel (55) indicates that even the rake Derby is driven to rage by the liberties the dance allows the Prince, although his eye is keen enough to note that Miss Sternheim struggles to resist. During his German sojourn, Coleridge perceived the waltz with the same moralistic abhorrence: "a most infamous dance called the Waltzen—There are perhaps 20 couple—the Man & his Partner embrace each other, arms around waists, & knees almost touching, & then whirl round & round, the whole 20 couple, 40 times round at least, to lascivious music." Cited in Hugh Kenner, *Historical Fictions* (San Francisco: North Point, 1990), 40.

19. *Freud Studienausgabe*, 4: 95–96.

20. On this convention, see Heinz Schlaffer, *Musa iacosa: Gattungsgeschichte*

und Gattungspoetik der erotischen Dichtung in Deutschland (Stuttgart: Metzler, 1971).

21. The transition from an *ars erotica* to a coupling of sexuality and truth is discussed, of course, in Michel Foucault, *The History of Sexuality*, vol. I, *An Introduction*, trans. Robert Hurley (New York: Pantheon, 1978). In an interview (the reference for which I have been unable to recover), Foucault once pointed to Goethe's *Faust* as a foundational text for the linkage of sexuality with the truth of the subject. And indeed, Gretchen is not merely a conquest in the domain of sensual pleasure, as female figures in the earlier versions of the Faust myth were, but rather something like Faust's means of access to the inner truth of nature.

22. See Michel Foucault, "Le 'non' du père," *Critique* 178 (1962): 195–209, from which I borrow this formulation.

23. *Gedichte 1756–1799*, 137–38.

24. Cf. *Freud Studienausgabe*, 5: 100–101 (section II, 5 of *Three Essays on the Theory of Sexuality*); 5: 243–251 ("The Dissolution of the Oedipus Complex").

25. For this poetic locus dominated by the function of 'seeing,' Otto Fenichel, "Schautrieb und Identifikationen," *Internationale Zeitschrift für Psychoanalyse* 21 (1935): 561–83, is extremely suggestive. See esp. 571: "There can be no doubt: the powerful drive with the goal of *seeing* the penis stands in relation to the equally powerful phantasy of being the penis." Fenichel's discussion of the equivalence between the most archaic forms of visual perception and the process of identification sheds considerable light on the insistence of the specular moment in Goethe's poetic texts.

26. In a richly speculative article, Georg Groddeck discusses the meaning complex "zeugen–erzeugen–bezeugen" ("procreate–produce/create–bear witness to") as centered on the symbolic function of the phallus. See Groddeck, "Vom Sehen, von der Welt des Auges und vom Sehen ohne Augen," *Psychoanalytische Schriften zur Psychosomatik* (Wiesbaden: Limes, 1966), 263–331, esp. 297–301. Samuel Weber's lucid and rigorous discussion of the notion of the "phallus" in Lacan's thought demonstrates that the phallic function entertains a strong relation to the field of visual phenomenality, and therefore to phantasy and to the phantasm. I am much indebted to Weber's discussion both of this aspect and of Lacanian theory in general. See Samuel M. Weber, *Rückkehr zu Freud: Jacques Lacans Entstellung der Psychoanalyse* (Berlin: Ullstein, 1978), esp. 114–24 ("Die Bedeutung des Phallus, oder: Was der Fall ist . . ."), and 123 on the relation between the phallus and visual phenomenality. The English translation of the later, expanded edition is: *Return to Freud: Jacques Lacan's Dislocation of Psychoanalysis* (Cambridge: Cambridge University Press, 1991), 139–51.

27. On this complementarity, see *Freud Studienausgabe*, 3: 59 ("On Narcissism: An Introduction").

28. Freud, "Das Medusenhaupt," *Standard Edition*, 18: 273.

29. *Freud Studienausgabe*, 6: 242.

30. Ibid., 279.

31. Ibid., 306.

32. Jean Laplanche, *Problematiques II / Castration-Symbolisations* (Paris: Presses Universitaires de France, 1980), 44–76. Laplanche has in general very important things to say about the link between castration and perception, a link established by virtue of the child's narcissism. See also Neil Hertz, "Medusa's Head: Male Hysteria under Political Pressure," *Representations* 4 (1983): 27–54, esp. 31.

Chapter 5

1. Immanuel Kant, *Kritik der Urteilskraft* (Frankfurt a. M.: Suhrkamp, 1974), 241 (par. 46). Kant's definition of genius reads as follows: "Genius is the talent (natural gift) which gives art its rule. Since talent, as inborn productive capacity of the artist, itself belongs to nature, then one could express oneself thus: genius is the inborn capacity of mind (*ingenium*), through which nature gives art its rule" (241–242). Nearly everything I have to say about the poem "Mahomets Gesang" later on in this chapter can be understood as a commentary on this Kantian definition of genius as the point of transition between nature and art. On French copyright law, see Heinrich Bosse, *Autorschaft ist Werkherrschaft* (Paderborn: Schöningh, 1981), 8, 145.

2. Jochen Schmidt, *Die Geschichte des Genie-Gedankens 1750–1945*, 2 vols. (Darmstadt: Wissenschaftliche Buchgesellschaft, 1985), 1: 224: "Für Goethe ist er [Genius] die alles vermögende Seelenkraft des schöpferischen Menschen."

3. *Münchener-Ausgabe*, I/2, 363. The text is from a review by Goethe published in the *Frankfurter Gelehrten Anzeigen*.

4. The reading of the term "Nachahmung" ("imitation" or "mimesis") in Text II as a potential site of mimetic rivalry was suggested to me, of course, by the works of René Girard. See in particular *Violence and the Sacred* (Baltimore: The Johns Hopkins University Press, 1972).

5. *Münchener-Ausgabe*, I/2, 416–17.

6. Ibid., 303.

7. See Wendelin Schmidt-Dengler, *Genius: Zur Wirkungsgeschichte antiker Mythologeme in der Goethezeit* (Munich: Beck, 1978).

8. "Unsre Häuser entstehen nicht aus vier Säulen in vier Ecken; sie entstehen aus vier Mauern auf vier Seiten, die statt aller Säulen sind, alle Säulen ausschließen, und wo ihr sie anflickt, sind sie belastender Überfluß." ("Our houses do not arise from four columns in four corners; they arise from four walls on four sides, which are there in place of all columns, exclude all columns, and where you sew them [columns] on, they are a burdensome superfluity"; *Münchener-Ausgabe*, I/2, 417–18.

9. Ibid., 415.

10. Horace, Ode IV, 2. The decisive passage reads:

> A river bursts its banks and rushes down a
> Mountain with uncontrollable momentum,
> Rain-saturated, churning, chanting thunder—
> There you have Pindar's style,
>
> Who earns Apollo's diadem of laurel
> In all his moods
>
> *(Horace,* The Odes and The Centennial Hymn, *trans.*
> *James Michie [Indianapolis: Bobbs-Merrill, 1963], 187)*

For Goethe's acquaintance with the passage, see his letter to Herder of July 10, 1772 (approximate date), in *Goethes Briefe,* 1: 131–34, esp. 131.

11. See Vinzenz Rüfener, "Homo secundus deus: Eine geistesgeschichtliche Studie zum menschlichen Schöpfertum," *Philosophisches Jahrbuch* 63 (1955): 249–91.

12. *Münchener-Ausgabe,* I/2, 415.

13. Ibid., 411–14.

14. See Reinhart Koselleck, "Die Herausbildung des modernen Geschichtsbegriffs," in Otto Bruner, Werner Conze, and Reinhart Koselleck, eds., *Geschichtliche Grundbegriffe,* vol. I, E–G (Stuttgart: Klett Cotta, 1975), 647–717. Also relevant is Niklas Luhmann, "Temporalisierung von Komplexität: Zur Semantik neuzeitlicher Zeitbegriffe," in his *Gesellschaftsstruktur und Semantik,* vol. 1 (Frankfurt: a. M.: Suhrkamp, 1980), 235–300.

15. Cf. *Münchener-Ausgabe,* I/2, 350–51, 422–23. The last reference is to the concluding passage of "Von deutscher Baukunst."

16. See Eibl's editorial remarks, *Gedichte 1756–99,* 911–14.

17. Ibid., 193–95.

18. *Münchener-Ausgabe,* I/1, 516–19.

19. My discussion of this text in terms of the problem of supplementarity assumes that Goethe's is a cognate endeavor to that of Rousseau. Here, of course, I am indebted to Jacques Derrida, *Of Grammatology,* trans. Gayatri Chakravorty Spivak (Baltimore: The Johns Hopkins University Press, 1974), esp. Part Two, "Nature, Culture, Writing," 95–316.

20. *Münchener-Ausgabe,* I/2, 380. The sentence is from a review of some etchings published in the *Frankfurter Gelehrten Anzeigen.*

21. My reading of the figures of parasitism that dry out the streams as a cultural death, which may seem forced on the basis of the single sentence I cite in confirmation of it, is lent strong support by Goethe's reflections on the language of religious inspiration. In a text devoted in part to the miracle of Pentecost, Goethe equates the speaking in tongues with a stream in order to mark its point

of dissipation: "Sucht ihr nach diesem Bache; Ihr werdet ihn nicht finden, er ist in Sümpfe verlaufen, die von allen wohlgekleideten Personen vermieden werden. Hier und da wässert er eine Wiese ins Geheim, dafür danke einer Gott in der Stille. Denn unsre theologische Kameralisten haben das Prinzipium, man müßte dergleichen Flecke all einteichen, Landstraßen durchführen und Spaziergänge darauf anlegen." ("Look for this stream; you won't find it, it has run off into swamps that all well-dressed people avoid. Here and there it waters a meadow secretly; one can silently thank God for that. For our theological cameralists have the principle that one should dam up all such spots, build a road through them and lay out walking paths on them"; *Münchener-Ausgabe,* I/2, 442–43). The "theological cameralists" who "dam" what is left of the waters of divine inspiration represent the dessicating legalism of a religious orthodoxy of the letter, the cultural deadening of the very divine force that makes culture (religion) possible in the first place. I shall return to this text (entitled "Zwo wichtige bisher unerörterte biblische Fragen" ["Two Important, Previously Unexplicated Biblical Questions," 1773]) in Chapter 6 in connection with Goethe's conception of poetic language.

22. The structure of reflexive supplementarity that links 'nature' and 'culture' in the genius of religious foundation is rendered explicit in Hölderlin's thoughts on the relation between nature and art in his "Grund zum Empedokles" ("Foundation of Empedocles"): "Die Kunst ist die Blüthe, die Vollendung der Natur, Natur wird erst göttlich durch die Verbindung mit der verschiedenartigen, aber harmonischen Kunst, wenn jedes ganz ist, was es sein kann, und eines verbindet sich mit dem andern, *ersetzt den Mangel des andern,* den es notwendig haben muß, um ganz das zu seyn, was es als besonderes seyn kann, dann ist die Vollendung da, und das Göttliche ist in der Mitte von beiden." ("Art is the blossom, the completion of nature, nature first becomes divine through its connection with the heterogeneous, but harmonious [sphere of] art, when each is entirely what it can be, and one joins itself with the other, *supplementing the lack of the other,* which it must necessarily have in order to be entirely what it can be as an individuated [entity], then the completion [perfection] is there, and the divine is in the middle of both"; *Sämtliche Werke,* ed. Friedrich Beissner [Stuttgart: Kohlhammer, 1961], 4: 152, my emphasis.) I am not, of course, arguing for Goethean influence on Hölderlin. The point is that the depth of thought achieved in the poem discloses epochal possibilities of reflection. Hölderlin's thought leads him to a concept of religious foundation (for Empedokles is also a religious founder, like Mahomet) organized according to the reflexive supplementarity of nature and art. The point where the two domains are joined is for Hölderlin the divine, for Goethe the genius.

23. The logical matrix of contrary and contradictory terms is discussed in Gottlob Frege, *Begriffsschrift* (Halle: Nebert, 1879). A. J. Greimas has transformed

this set of logical relations into a flexible tool of semiotic analysis. See, for example, the essays collected in A. J. Greimas, *On Meaning: Selected Writings in Semiotic Theory*, trans. by Paul J. Perron and Frank H. Collins, foreword by Fredric Jameson, Theory and History of Literature 38 (Minneapolis: University of Minnesota Press, 1987). I have found Jameson's Foreword (vi–xxii) especially useful in thinking about the application of Greimasian method to my own subject matter.

24. See the analysis of Marcel Detienne, *The Gardens of Adonis: Spices in Greek Mythology*, trans. Janet Lloyd (Atlantic Highlands, N.J.: Humanities Press, 1977).

25. Goethe developed a veritable myth of the cedar tree in his text "Salomons Königs von Israel und Juda güldene Worte von der Zeder bis zum Issop" ("The golden Words of Solomon, the King of Israel and Judea, on the Cedar and Ysup"; *Münchener-Ausgabe*, I/2, 446–48.)

26. I have profited especially from the interpretations of Klaus Weimar (*Goethes Gedichte 1769–1775: Interpretation zu einem Anfang* [Paderborn; Schöningh, 1982], 66–86) and Jochen Schmidt (*Die Geschichte des Genie-Gedankens 1750–1945*, I: 224–54. From the earlier scholarship on the poem, Heinrich Henel's discussion (*Goethezeit* [Frankfurt a. M.: Insel, 1980], 221–51) is to be recommended.

27. See "Zwei Gedichte von Friedrich Hölderlin" in Walter Benjamin, *Gesammelte Schriften*, ed. Rolf Tiedemann (Frankfurt a. M.: Suhrkamp, 1977f.), 2: 105–26. I have commented on this text in "Benjamin's Theory of the Lyric," in Rainer Nägele, ed., *Benjamin's Ground: New Readings of Walter Benjamin* (Detroit: Wayne State University Press, 1988), 39–60.

28. *Gedichte 1756–1799*, 195. Since I shall be citing this text only selectively, all the passages reproduced here should be understood as bearing the same number (16). This will facilitate later cross-references to the poem.

29. I owe to Klaus Weimar the insight that the allusion to Parnassus in 15 establishes the imaginary topography of the entire text. See Klaus Weimar, *Goethes Gedichte 1769–1775*, 66–86.

30. The hermetic associations of such terms as "Mittlepunkt," which Rolf Christian Zimmermann (*Das Weltbild des jungen Goethe*, vol. 2, *Interpretationen* [Munich: Wilhelm Fink, 1979], 103–4, 108–9) adduces in his interpretation of this passage, would require a more extensive critical discussion than is possible here. In my brief commentary, I am concerned solely with the delineation of the fundamental conflict providing the dominant structural tension of the text and cannot attend in detail to such connotational and intertextual relations as those discussed by Zimmermann in his excellent study. I would note, however, that Zimmermann's interpretation seems to me to play down the agonistic element of the text.

31. Niklas Luhmann and Peter Fuchs, *Reden und Schweigen* (Frankfurt a. M.: Suhrkamp, 1989), 146–51.

32. From this perspective, Harold Bloom's contention that Goethe did not suffer from the "anxiety of influence" must be deemed untenable. See Harold Bloom, *The Anxiety of Influence*, (New York: Oxford University Press, 1973), 51.

33. See the decisive contribution by Rainer Nägele, "*Götz von Berlichingen*," in Walter Hinderer, ed., *Goethes Dramen: Neue Interpretationen* (Stuttgart: Reclam, 1980), 65–77.

34. Asked if his son should be summoned to his deathbed, Götz, in his penultimate speech of the drama, replies: "Laß ihn, er ist heiliger als ich, er braucht meinen Segen nicht.—An unserm Hochzeittag, Elisabeth, ahndete mir's nicht, daß ich so sterben würde.—Mein alter Vater segnete uns, eine Nachkommenschaft von edeln tapfern Söhnen quoll aus seinem Gebet.—Du hast ihn nicht erhört, und ich bin der Letzte." ("Let him be; he's holier than I; he doesn't need my blessing.—On our wedding day, Elisabeth, I didn't suspect that I would die this way.—My old father blessed us, and a progeny of noble, brave sons should have flowed from his prayer.—You didn't hear him, and I'm the last"; *H.A.*, 4: 175). Because the female figure fails to hear the paternal word, thereby interrupting its procreative transmission, the issue of Götz's and Elisabeth's marriage is the feminized Karl. Compare this failed fatherhood with the successful paternity of Erwin von Steinbach, whose tower, as we have seen, perpetually engenders (Text 14).

35. *Gedichte 1756–1799*, 146.

36. Ibid., 199–201.

37. Hans Rudolf Vaget, comparing the passage from Homer alluded to with Goethe's text, has demonstrated that the text involves a conflict in which Apollo plays the role of antagonist. I am much indebted in what follows to his reading. See Hans Rudolf Vaget, "Eros und Apoll: Versuch zu 'Künstlers Morgenlied'," *Jahrbuch der deutschen Schillergesellschaft* 30 (1986): 196–217.

38. *Greek Lyric Poetry*, ed. C. M. Bowra (Oxford: Oxford University Press, 1936), 204.

39. *Iliad*, 16: 817–22. Homer, *The Iliad*, with an English trans. A. T. Murray, The Loeb Classical Library (Cambridge: Harvard University Press, 1985), 2: 225.

40. See Reinhart Meyer-Kalkus, "Werthers Krankheit zum Tode: Pathologie und Familie in der Empfindsamkeit," in Freidrich A. Kittler and Horst Turk, eds., *Urszenen: Literaturwissenschaft als Diskursanalyse und Diskurskritik* (Frankfurt a. M.: Suhrkamp, 1977), 76–138.

41. *Münchener-Ausgabe*, I/2, 357. The review was originally published in the *Frankfurter Gelehrten Anzeigen*.

42. *H.A.*, 6: 81.

43. This reference to debt, which designates a structural feature of the complex

I am analyzing here, is a permutation of a poetic statement by Goethe. In an epistolary poem written to his sister Cornelia in 1765, Goethe finishes by conveying his greetings to their mother:

> Grüß mir die Mutter, sprich, sie soll verzeihn,
> daß ich sie niemals grüsen ließ, sag ihr
> Das was sie weiß,—daß ich sie ehre. Sags,
> Daß nie mein kindlich Hertz von Liebe voll,
> Die Schuldigkeit vergist. Und ehe soll
> Die Liebe nicht erkalten eh ich selbst,
> Erkalte.

> Give our mother my greetings, say, she should forgive
> That I never send her greetings, tell her
> What she [already] knows,—that I honor her. Say
> that my childlike heart full of love never
> Forgets its obligation. And before
> My love grows cold I will myself
> grow cold.

> *(Gedichte 1756–1799, 31)*

I cite this early passage not in order to demonstrate Goethe's personal (idiosyncratic or even pathological) attachment to his own mother. On the contrary, the passage clearly indicates a strategy of distancing: Goethe inserts his sister into a position of mediation between himself and his mother. What interests me, rather, is that the text documents a figure of thought: that the male subject is bound to the mother by a debt, that this debt has its expression in love, that this love is essential to the subject's life, and that the subject, therefore, perpetually has, by virtue of its affective bond to the mother, the heart of a child. One of the central claims of this study is that this figure of thought is insistent in Goethe's poetry of the 1770's.

44. *Münchener-Ausgabe*, I/2, 402.

45. Ibid., 422–23.

46. Ibid., I/1, 745.

47. Hans Vaget, "Eros und Apoll."

48. Recall in this connection "Der neue Amadis" (Text 8), with its association of "Mutterleib" and "Phantasie."

49. See Hans Robert Jauß, "Fr. Schlegels und Fr. Schillers Replik auf die 'Querelle des Anciens et des Modernes'," in H. R. Jauß, *Literaturgeschichte als Provokation* (Frankfurt a. M.: Suhrkamp, 1970), esp. 72–95.

50. Wilhelm von Humboldt, *Gesammelte Schriften*, ed. Albert Leitzmann et al. (Berlin: Behr, 1903–36), 2: 202.

51. Ibid., 203.

52. Ibid., 202.

53. Karl Phillip Moritz, *Götterlehre oder Mythologische Dichtungen der Alten* (Bremen: Carl Schünemann, n.d.), 7. I shall return to Moritz's treatise in Chapter 8.

54. Humboldt, *Gesammelte Schriften*, 2: 137.

55. Ibid., 179.

56. Compare the article "Einbildung, Einbildungskraft" in Joachim Ritter, ed., *Historisches Wörterbuch der Philosophie* (Darmstadt: Wissenschaftliche Buchgesellschaft, 1971f.), 2: 346–58. In his study *Das Fiktive und das Imaginäre: Perspektiven literarischer Anthropologie* (Frankfurt a. M.: Suhrkamp, 1991), Wolfgang Iser repeatedly stresses that the conception of the imagination as an autonomous productive instance is belied by the fact that imaginative activity requires external incitement. Iser's historical sketch of prominent theories of the imagination (292–410) provides an excellent contextualization for the argument I am developing here.

57. My explication here is guided by Heidegger's Kant interpretation, in which the transcendental imagination ("transcendentale Einbildungskraft") is read as the pure self-affection of time. See Martin Heidegger, *Gesamtausgabe*, section I, vol. 3, *Kant und das Problem der Metaphysik*, ed. Friedrich-Wilhelm von Hermann (Frankfurt a. M.: Klostermann, 1991), par. 34 ("Die Zeit als reine Selbstaffektion und der Zeitcharakter des Selbst"), 188–95. The notion of transference, of course, is foreign to Heidegger. It is interesting to note, however, that in his lectures on Kant in 1927–28, in which the main outlines of the Kant book were worked out, Heidegger discussed the pure synthesis of the ego through the transcendental imagination as an act of *Versetzen*, that is, as a kind of displacement or transport that seems to me to bear some relation to the idea of transference I am stressing here.

58. *Münchener-Ausgabe*, I/2, 499.

Chapter 6

1. See Wilfrid Sellars, "Empiricism and the Philosophy of Mind," in his *Science, Perception, and Reality* (New York: Humanities Press, 1964), 127–96, here 196.

2. In his study of Paul Celan's translation of Shakespeare's Sonnet 105, Peter Szondi adapts this notion from Walter Benjamin's translation theory in order to designate the historical specificity of a linguistic artifact (Peter Szondi, *Celan-Studien* [Frankfurt a. M.: Suhrkamp], 18–20). I have rendered the notion (in German "Intention auf die Sprache") as "orientation toward language" in order to produce a certain interference with Roman Jakobson's definition of the poetic principle as "orientation toward the message." (See Roman Jakobson, "Closing Statement: Linguistics and Poetics," *Style in Language*, ed. Thomas A. Sebeok

[Cambridge: MIT Press, 1960], 358.) The point of this interference is to lend Jakobson's concept a historical inflection. Whereas "orientation toward the message" may characterize poetry in general, this orientation will be nuanced differently according to variations in the historical being of language itself. The fact that he fails to consider this historical variability is the reason for the disappointing thinness of Jakobson's (nevertheless brilliant and ground-breaking) analyses of individual poetic texts. That is, since he does not take into account the cultural specificity that inflects noetic attitudes toward language, the metalanguage he employs in his analyses is always the same, the language of post-Saussurian structural linguistics. It is possible, I want to claim, to preserve the precision of Jakobson's work and avoid its historical abstractness. Szondi's adaptation of Benjamin seems to me to show how this might be done.

3. Paul Valéry, *Cahiers*, ed. Judith Robinson (Paris: Gallimard, 1974), 2: 1090.

4. Johann Gottfried Herder, *Abhandlung über den Ursprung der Sprache: Text, Materialien, Kommentar*, ed. Wolfgang Proß (Munich: Hanser, 1978), 49.

5. Ibid., 53–55. On this aspect of Herder's theory, see Jürgen Trabant, "Vom Ohr zur Stimme: Bemerkungen zum Phonozentrismus zwischen 1770 und 1830," in Hans Ulrich Gumbrecht and K. Ludwig Pfeiffer, eds., *Materialität der Kommunikation* (Frankfurt a. M.: Suhrkamp, 1988), 63–79.

6. Johann Gottfried Herder, *Sämmtliche Werke*, ed. Berhard Suphan (Berlin: Weidmannsche Buchhandlung, 1877–1913), 8: 412.

7. For an excellent overview and a thorough bibliography, see Helmut Kiesel and Paul Münch, *Gesellschaft und Literatur im 18. Jahrhundert: Voraussetzungen und Entstehung des literarischen Markts in Deutschland* (Munich: Beck, 1977). See also James Sheehan, *German History 1770–1866* (Oxford: Oxford University Press, 1989), 144–206.

8. For such an interpretation, see Heinz Schlaffer, "Einleitung," in Jack Goody, Ian Watt, Kathleen Gough, *Entstehung und Folgen der Schriftkultur*, trans. Friedhelm Herborth (Frankfurt a. M.: Suhrkamp, 1986), 12–13.

9. Herder, *Sämmtliche Werke*, 25: 314–15.

10. For Goethe's Werther, too, the Homeric epics function like a lullaby ("Wiegengesang"; *H.A.*, 6: 10).

11. Compare Herder, *Sämmtliche Werke*, 8: 433: "A poet is the *creator* of a people about him: he gives them a world to see and has their souls in his hand to lead them there." A page later the metaphor of the stream is used to express the same idea: "The true poet is a god on earth, like streams of water he holds the heart of the people in his hand."

12. Herder, *Abhandlung über den Ursprung der Sprache*, 88.

13. The term "natural economy" ("Haushaltung der Natur") is Herder's own. Cf. ibid., 86.

14. Ibid., 89.

15. Ibid.

16. Cited in Friedrich A. Kittler, "Lullaby of Birdland," *Der Wunderblock* 3 (1979): 10.

17. Theodor Bohner, *Philipp Otto Runge: Ein Malerleben der Romantik* (Berlin: Frundsberg, 1937), 131.

18. See Klaus Weimar, *Versuch über Voraussetzung und Entstehung der Romantik* (Tübingen: Niemeyer, 1968).

19. See Herder, *Abhandlung über den Ursprung der Sprache*, 49.

20. On this development, see: Helmut Müller-Sievers, "Verstimmung: E. T. A. Hoffmann und die Trivialisierung der Musik," *Deutsche Vierteljahrsschrift für Literaturwissenschaft und Geistesgeschichte* 63 (1989): 98–119; Wolfgang Scherer, " 'Aus der Seele muß man spielen': Instrumentelle und technische Bedingungen der musikalischen Empfindsamkeit," in Hans Ulrich Gumbrecht and K. Ludwig Pfeiffer, eds., *Materialität der Kommunikation* (Frankfurt a. M.: Suhrkamp, 1988), 295–309.

21. C. F. Michaelis, *Über den Geist der Tonkunst mit Rücksicht auf Kants Kritik der Urteilskraft* (1795), cited in Müller-Sievers, "Verstimmung," 105.

22. See Scherer, " 'Aus der Seele muß man spielen'."

23. Roland Barthes, "The Romantic Song," *The Responsibility of Forms*, trans. Richard Howard (New York: Hill and Wang, 1985), 288.

24. *Münchener-Ausgabe*, I/1, 671 (ll. 96–99). Subsequent references to other portions of the *Prometheus* fragment will still count as Text 20. Line numbers refer not to the cited passage, but to the numeration of the entire drama.

25. See Jacques Derrida, *Speech and Phenomena, and Other Essays on Husserl's Theory of Signs*, trans. David B. Allison (Evanston, Ill.: Northwestern University Press, 1973); Derrida, *Of Grammatology*, trans. Gayatri Chakravorty Spivak (Baltimore: The Johns Hopkins University Press, 1974).

26. See Derrida, *Speech and Phenomena*, 75–76.

27. Here an insight of Derrida's seems especially pertinent. In *Speech and Phenomena*, he writes: " 'presentation' is a representation of the representation that yearns for itself therein as for its own birth or its death" (103). This applies to the passage from *Prometheus* under discussion insofar as that text represents a presence-to-self in the pure self-affection of primary orality that is the "birth" of both subjectivity and language. Moreover, the second act of the *Prometheus* fragment, which I cannot discuss here in any detail, establishes an equivalence between the embrace of 'love' and 'death' and concludes by sending Prometheus and his "daughter" Pandora offstage to experience this *Liebestod*.

28. Ibid., 84.

29. See *Münchener-Ausgabe*, I/1, 516.

30. Ibid., I/2, 441–42.

31. The concept of poet as translator appears, for example, in Herder: "There-

fore the truer, the more recognizable and stronger the impress of our sensations is [on tones, language, gestures], that is, the more it is true poetry; the stronger and truer is the impression it makes, the more and longer it has an effect. Not poetry, but rather nature, the entire world of passion and action that lies in the poet and that he strives to bring out of himself—this is what has an effect. Language is merely a channel, the true poet merely a translator, or, more literally, the bringer of nature into the soul and the heart of his brothers. What had an effect on him and how it affected him, that continues to take effect, not through his, not through arbitrary, sewn-on, conventional forces, but through the forces of nature" (*Sämmtliche Werke*, 8: 339–40; the bracketed portion is a variant of the published version). What qualifies a poet as truly a poet, in this conception, is his capacity to translate the force and effectiveness of a more primordial language, a language of nature. But this raises the question as to how such translation is possible when the target language of the translation process is characterized precisely by a conventionality and arbitrariness that are deadeningly antithetical to the natural language of the original. Herder suppresses this question through his emphatic notion of the *true* poet, a figure who, like Homer in a passage previously discussed, bears a remarkable similarity to the genius-stream of "Mahomets Gesang." True poetry would be a poetry without difference. But when Herder takes up the task of rendering an original text in German, he cannot but sense the alterity endemic to the process of translation. In connection with his own translation of the "Song of Songs," he writes: "An additional factor is that nothing *is so different as Oriental poetry, language, and love from ours*" (8: 534). This difference makes accurate translation impossible, an impossibility Herder expresses with the following revealing comparison: "I would sooner claim to render the lalling of my child and the cooing of the turtle dove in the oratorical language of Cicero such that both would remain what they are—" (ibid.). Successful and complete translation from the language of the origin—be this the language of nature, of the Orient, of the child, or of the birds—is impossible, except, of course, in the case of the true poet. But no poet attains to this 'truth'. The 'true' poem, the perfect translation, is a fiction. Goethe makes this clear in a passage from *Wilhelm Meisters Lehrjahre*. After reproducing Mignon's first song in the body of the text—and Mignon is, as Friedrich Schlegel recognized, the figure of "Naturpoesie"—the narrator recounts how Wilhelm first heard the song accompanied by the tones of a zither, how he then asked Mignon to repeat it and explain it to him, and finally how he translated it. This translation is the text the novel's reader has just read. The narrator's comment repeats the Herderian motif of impossible translation: "Aber die Originalität der Wendungen konnte er nur von ferne nachahmen. Die kindliche Unschuld des Ausdrucks verschwand, indem die gebrochene Sprache übereinstimmend und das Unzusammenhängende verbunden ward. Auch konnte der Reiz der Melodie mit nichts verglichen werden." ("But he could only imitate from afar the originality of the turns of phrase. The childlike innocence of the expression disappeared in that the broken language was made to agree internally and the disconnectedness was bound together. Also the charm of the melody had no equivalent"; *H.A.*, 7: 146.) The point of the passage, of course, is that there is no archaic Italian original to Mignon's song, that the primal song prior to translation exists only as the empty reference of the fiction, and that the poem itself—Mignon's "Kennst du das Land," one of the supreme achievements of the German language—is, qua language, already a translation marked by the alterity that separates it from the primal orality ("Mignons Stimme") out of which it originates.

32. The hermeneutic narrative par excellence. Cf. Jean-Luc Nancy, "Sharing Voices," in Gayle Ormiston and Alan Schrift, eds., *Transforming the Hermeneutic Context: From Nietzsche to Nancy* (Albany: State University of New York Press, 1990), 211–60, esp. 214: "In this way, the hermeneutic circle is suspended in the supposition of an origin: both the origin of meaning and the possibility of participating in it, the infinite origin of the circle in which the interpreter is caught always already. The circle can be nothing other than the movement of an origin, lost and recovered by the mediation of its substitute. Insofar as it renders possible the right direction for interpretive research, this substitute implies a mode for the conservation and preservation of the origin up to and through its loss. Hermeneutics requires—very profoundly, very obscurely perhaps—that the 'participation in meaning' is unaware of the absolute interruption. On account of this profound continuity, hermeneutics represents the process of historicity which is valued both as suspension and as revival of the continuity. It designates in the most accentuated fashion the *history* of a *permanence* and a *remanence*, that is to say, the possibility of returning from (or to) an origin."

33. *Gedichte 1756–99*, 645–46.

34. Ibid., 233.

35. Herder, *Abhandlung über den Ursprung der Sprache*, 26 ("Mangel"), 32–33 (the scene of the lamb).

36. On the storm as a figure of an aggressive conscience, see Heinz D. Kittsteiner, *Die Entstehung des modernen Gewissens* (Frankfurt a. M.: Insel, 1991).

37. In an early text, Jacques Lacan discusses the "complex of severence" as arising out of the infant's most primitive—that is, oral-proprioceptive—relation to the mother. Two features distinguish the "maternal imago" at this stage: it does not appear as a visual object, and it is inherently ambivalent. This ambivalence expresses itself as a bidirectional "cannibalism": the experience of sucking in and eating oscillates with the sense of being swallowed and eaten. My contention is that "An den Geist des Johannes Sekundus" draws its resources from this ambivalent cannibalism. See Jacques Lacan, *Les complexes familiaux dans la formation de l'individu* (Paris: Navarin, 1984), 28–30. For an examination of

orality in another text by Goethe, see my "Morphisms of the Phantasmatic Body. Goethe's *The Sorrows of Young Werther*," in Veronica Kelly and Dorothea E. von Mücke, eds., *Body and Text in the Eighteenth Century* (Stanford: Stanford University Press, 1994), 181–208.

38. See Freud, *Studienausgabe*, 4: 227–34 ("The Antithetical Meaning of Primal Words," *S.E.* 11: 153f.).

Chapter 7

1. This title stems from Herder's widow Karoline, who brought out the 1807 edition. In replacing Herder's earlier and simpler title *Volkslieder*, Karoline relied on a sketch her husband had given Johannes von Müller, which bore the superscription "Stimmen der Völker." See Johann Gottfried Herder, *Sämmtliche Werke*, ed. Berhard Suphan (Berlin: Weidmannsche Buchhandlung, 1877–1913), 25: x–xi.

2. See Max Kommerell's comparison of Herder's orientation with that of Arnim and Brentano in "Das Volkslied und das deutsche Lied," in Kommerell, *Dame Dichterin und andere Essays*, ed. Arthur Henkel (Munich: Deutscher Taschenbuch Verlag, 1967), 7–64. The essay first appeared in 1933.

3. Cf. *Herders Sämmtliche Werke*, 25: x: "the living voice of the peoples, indeed of humanity itself, as it could be heard here and there under all sorts of conditions, tender and terrible, joyful and sad, joking and serious."

4. *H.A.*, 12: 270: "Würden dann diese Lieder nach und nach in ihrem eigenen Ton- und Klangelemente von Ohr zu Ohr, von Mund zu Mund getragen, kehrten sie allmählich belebt und verherrlicht zum Volke zurück, von dem sie zum Teil gewißermaßen ausgegangen, so könnte man sagen, das Büchlein habe seine Bestimmung erfüllt und könne nun wieder als geschrieben und gedruckt verloren gehen, weil es in Leben und Bildung der Nation übergegangen." Goethe's hesitation here seems particularly motivated by the concept of "Volk" as source. This is evidenced by his awkward qualification, "zum Teil gewissermaßen," as well as by the implicit juxtaposition of the concepts "Volk" and "Nation."

5. Ernst Beutler, " 'Der König in Thule' und die Dichtungen der Lorelay," in *Essays um Goethe* (Berlin: Deutsche Buchgemeinschaft, 1957), 332–86, here 349–55.

6. Cited in ibid., 349–50.

7. *Gedichte 1756–1799*, 278.

8. Herder's remark accompanies his printing of a version of the text, first in a contribution on archaic poetry ("Extract from a Correspondence on Ossian and the Songs of Ancient Peoples") in *Von deutscher Art und Kunst* (1773), then in his edition of *Volksliedern* (1779). For Herder's presentation of the poem, see *Gedichte 1756–1799*, 124.

9. *H.A.*, 6: 16.

10. This reading of the poem as dramatizing the return of a haunting memory approaches Geoffrey H. Hartman's discussion of Goethe's "Erlkönig" in *The Fate of Reading and Other Essays* (Chicago: University of Chicago Press, 1975), 189–97.

11. *Poetics*, 1457b. I have consulted the edition *Aristotle's Theory of Poetry and Art*, trans. S. H. Butcher, 4th ed. (New York: Dover, 1951), here 67.

12. In the *Ausgabe letzter Hand* of Goethe's works, the grammatical impropriety is corrected. According to Eibl (*Gedichte 1756–1799*, 830), this correction was probably undertaken by the printer.

13. On the potential aggressivity of the virgin and the threat of castration the figure poses, see Freud *Studienausgabe*, 5: 211–28 ("The Taboo of Virginity," *S.E.*, 11: 191f.).

14. *Gedichte 1756–1799*, 1222.

15. That the prenatal union of mother and child is a component of Goethe's poetic universe is demonstrated by the text "Ich saug an meiner Nabelschnur," *Gedichte 1756–1799*, 169. Also relevant, of course, is the line from "Der neue Amadis": "Wie in Mutterleib" (Text 8, 5).

16. Max Kommerell notes in his discussion of the text that this is the single word that "betrays" the poet, who otherwise completely disappears behind the impersonality of the ballad or romance genre ("Das Volkslied und das deutsche Lied," 14). This is an admirable observation, but it applies solely to the lexical plane of the text and ignores the narrative function of such elements as 'giving' or 'drinking', elements that intertwine in manifold ways in Goethe's poetic universe. Precisely because he ignores the text's meticulous narrative logic, Kommerell's attempt at semanticizing the cup remains on the level of helplessly vague intuition. "What is the cup? Something that everyone yearns for and no one has. Not love, beauty, youth, poetry, and yet all this together, so eerily, sweetly together that no one could bear it" (Ibid.).

17. Letter to Lavater, September 20, 1781, in *Goethes Briefe*, 1: 325.

18. See Niklas Luhmann, "The Individuality of the Individual: Historical Meanings and Contemporary Problems," in *Reconstructing Individualism*, ed. Thomas Heller, Morton Sosna, and David E. Wellbery (Stanford: Stanford University Press, 1989), 313–28.

19. Martin Heidegger, *Sein und Zeit* (Tübingen: Niemeyer, 1972 [1927]), 82.

20. *Gedichte 1756–1799*, 302–3.

21. Kant, *Kritik der Urteilskraft*, 259 (par. 51): "Der *Dichter* kündigt bloß ein unterhaltendes *Spiel* mit Ideen an, und es kommt doch dabei so viel für den Verstand daraus, als ob er bloß dessen Geschäft zu treiben die Absicht gehabt hätte." Kant's definition, it should be noted, opposes the poet to the rhetorician, who announces a project for the intellect, but offers nothing more than a play of ideas. Hence the essentially deceptive nature of the rhetorician's art. Goethe's

text, as we shall see, does not allow for such a neat distinction, but rather situates deceptiveness—suggestion, temptation, seduction—at the center of aesthetic semblance. The female figure who emerges from the water is, among other things, a rhetorician.

22. The verb *laben* (to quench or refresh, primarily through oral intake of liquid or food) may also introduce a semantic nuance of 'cleansing' or 'purification' (cf. Latin *lavare*), a point to which I shall return.

23. I have received methodological guidance for these remarks on the phonic texture of Goethe's lines from: Kenneth Burke, "On Musicality in Verse," *Perspectives by Incongruity* (Bloomington: Indiana University Press, 1964); Geoffrey H. Hartman, "The Voice of the Shuttle: Language from the Point of View of Literature," *Beyond Formalism: Literary Essays, 1958–1970* (New Haven: Yale University Press, 1970), 337–55; Garrett Stewart, *Reading Voices: Literature and the Phonotext* (Berkeley: University of California Press, 1990).

24. See Goethe's remark to Eckermann from November 3, 1823: "Es ist ja in dieser Ballade bloß das Gefühl des Wassers ausgedrückt, das Anmutige, was uns im Sommer lockt, uns zu baden." ("In this ballad merely the feeling of water is expressed, the charm that in the summer beckons us to swim"; Johann Peter Eckermann, *Gespräche mit Goethe* [Munich: Deutscher Taschenbuch Verlag, 1976].) Note that Goethe's formulation, however reductive it may appear to be, does center on the verb *locken* (to attract, tempt, beckon), which is one of the poem's key words.

25. See Emil Staiger, *Goethe*, Vol. II, *1786–1814* (Zurich: Artemis, 1956), 305.

26. Similar claims were made regarding the refrain of "Heidenröslein" as dramatizing the return of poetic phantasy. Again I find myself in the neighborhood of Geoffrey Hartman's reading of "Erlkönig."

27. My rephrasing of this theoretical point in terms of the phenomenological concepts of noesis (structure of intentional act) and noema (structure of intended object) follows the analysis of Nicolas Abraham, "Esquisse d'une phénoménologie de l'expression poétique," in *Rythmes: De l'oeuvre, de la traduction et de la psychanalyse*, ed. Nicholas Rand and Maria Torok (Paris: Flammarion, 1985), 9–72; English trans. *Rhythms: On the Work, Translation, and Psychoanalysis*, trans. Benjamin Thigpen and Nicholas T. Rand (Stanford: Stanford University Press, 1995), 5–63. Abraham's "Esquisse," still unsurpassed in its precision, dates from 1948.

28. With these considerations in mind, Goethe's remark to Eckermann cited above (n. 18) can be considered as more than a deflection of hermeneutic urgency. The poet was referring to an artist's attempt to illustrate "Der Fischer." Since a visual representation thetically intends a noematic world, we can say, in the terms of the argument developed here, that the illustration reads the poetic narrative as fictional narrative. It is precisely such a reading that Goethe's deflective remark

seeks to block. The poem, in other words, is not about something visualizable, but is the expression of an alluring charm that takes effect this side of vision.

29. See the chapter "Sehnsucht und Ruhe," in which the polarity is played out in various registers. I have consulted the illustrated edition, Friedrich Schlegel, *Lucinde* (Munich: Dietrichs, 1918), here 124–27.

30. Freud *Studienausgabe*, 4: 241–74, here 249–50 ("The Uncanny," *S.E.*, 17: 219–52).

31. Georg Groddeck, "Der Symbolisierungszwang," *Imago* 8 (1922): 67–81, reprinted in Günter Clauser, ed., *Psychoanalytische Schriften zur Psychosomatik* (Wiesbaden: Limes, 1966), 114–30. The citation is from the latter edition, 118. Groddeck's partial justification of his reading in terms of grammatical gender loses force when one considers that in the eighteenth century "Angel" could be employed as either a masculine or feminine noun. Thus, Groddeck's significant anomaly is in fact grammatical correctness. On the other hand, Groddeck's interpretation of the "Angel" might be considered a motivating factor for Goethe's preference for the masculine alternative in this context.

32. Ibid., 119.

33. This factor of reification and material particularity, I note in passing, generates the often comic or grotesque tonality that accompanies 'phallic' significations. The elements foot and (especially) fishpole seem to me faintly to reverberate with this comic tone.

34. This reading of the combination "nach dem" as a shadow version of the word "nackten" occasions a further observation. The line in question—"Sah nach dem Angel ruhevoll," (3)—is the first metrical anomaly in the poem. Between the initial accent on "Sah" and the second accent on "Ang-," the two unaccented syllables ("nach" and "dem") elicit a voicing that feels rushed, that catapults forward toward the point where metrical regularity is again achieved. This rhythmical gesture can be read as the index of a liminal anxiety, a slightly desperate urgency. This anxiety is stilled only when the "looking toward" ("Sah nach dem") finds its object ("Angel"), at which point a slight pause for breath occurs, after which the intonation again becomes calmly regular, precisely at the point where "calm" is thematized ("ruhevoll"). The rhythmical gesture performed by the line, then, enacts the tenuousness, the precariousness of the fisherman's self-control. The fact that the locus of the rhythmically conveyed anxiety proleptically echoes the sexualizing term "nackten" suggests that the threat to composure is sexual in character.

35. *Gedichte 1756–1799*, 229.

36. Ibid., 300.

37. A further similarity links the two hunter poems to "Der Fischer." Addressing his beloved, the hunter asks: "Und ach mein schnell verrauschend Bild / Stellt sich dir's nicht einmal?" ("And oh my quickly disappearing image / Doesn't it at

least once pose itself to you?"; *Gedichte 1756–1799*, 301.) The verb "sich stellen" ("to pose oneself") is a hunting term designating the presentation of the prey to the hunter's shot. That is, the erotic metaphorics of hunting moves through a role reversal in which the hunter becomes the hunted. Similarly, in "Der Fischer" the verb of "luring" ("locken," 10) that designates the fisherman's cunning attraction of the fish likewise designates the pull of temptation that draws him into the water (21). I'll have more to say about this verb subsequently. The point to be made here is that the shared movement through a reversal of directionality (hunter/hunted vs. fisherman/fished) indicates that the hunter poems and "Der Fischer" participate in the same erotic-poetic universe.

38. Rhetorically speaking, this difference derives from the fact that in the hunter poems the 'weapon', a metonymy of the subject, is metaphorized, on the one hand via the verb and the pun ("Rohr"/"Ohr"), on the other hand by the participle ("Gespannt"), which applies equally to the musket and to the subject. The "Angel," by contrast, remains a metonymy by proximity. I shall take up this metonymic structure subsequently.

39. *Gedichte 1756–1799*, 242.

40. The insertion of this time marker is accompanied by a shift in verb tense from the imperfect to the present of narration, a shift that on the one hand heightens the immediacy of the event (past action narrated as if it were occurring in the present), on the other hand suggests a certain interference between the event narrated and the present of narration. This latter function can be read as an indirect thematization of the text itself. The emergence of the sprite, that is to say, occurs not only before the fisherman, but also in the experienced present of the poem. The text ironically alludes to the magic of its own evocative power by calling attention to the fact that now, as the reader is sitting and listening, the sprite makes her appearance. This is important because the corresponding (that is, opposed) lines of the fourth stanza (29–32) likewise allude to the magic of poetry, this time thematizing the 'disappearance' of the figure. The semantic nuance of 'emergence into visual presence' carried by the prefix "hervor" (8) thus has its counterpart in the concluding line of the text: "Und ward nicht mehr gesehn" (32).

41. Perhaps this is why the title of the ballad includes no reference to the sprite. "Der Fischer" suffices for the reason that the text is about what happens in, for, and to him.

42. After completing this chapter, I came across the article by Rainer Wild, "Der Narziß und die Natur: Bemerkungen zu Goethes Ballade 'Der Fischer'," *Lenz Jahrbuch: Sturm-und-Drang-Studien* 1 (1991), 168–87. There are considerable differences between our readings, but Wild and I are in agreement in construing the sprite as a projection of the fisherman. Moreover, Wild places considerable emphasis on the importance of the Narcissus tale in Ovid's *Metamorphoses* for Goethe's poem, a matter I take up subsequently.

43. A possible source for Goethe's thematization of this contradiction, in all its logical and affective intricacy, is Rousseau's *Pygmalion*, whose hero declares at one point: "Heavens! What am I saying! If I were she, I would no longer see her, I would not be the one who loved her! No, I would that my Galathea lived and that I were not she. Ah, let me always be another that I may always desire to be she, that I may see her, that I may love her, that I may be loved by her." (Jean Jacques Rousseau, *Oeuvres complètes*, 4 vols., ed. M. Raymond and B. Gagnebin [Paris: Gallimard, 1959–69], 2: 1228). Goethe, of course, knew the text.

44. If we add to this series of "w"-words the two instances of the particle "wie," the entire alliterative chain can be seen to form a chiastic figure: "wüßtest"– "wie"–"wohlig"–"wie"–"würdest." The extreme points of the sequence are verbs applying to the fisherman, the axial word of the chiastic figure the adjective that modifies the little fish's state of being. One could say that the figure highlights the word "wohlig," centers it, and thereby intensifies its affective charge.

45. My employment of the term "rhetoricity" here is continuous with the usage of the term "rhetoricality" in a previous, collaborative essay. See John Bender and David E. Wellbery, "Rhetoricality: On the Modernist Return of Rhetoric," in Bender and Wellbery, eds., *The Ends of Rhetoric: History, Theory, Practice* (Stanford: Stanford University Press, 1990), 3–39.

46. I am indebted here to Jacques Derrida's discussion of the concept of auto-affection and temporalization in *Speech and Phenomena and Other Essays on Husserl's Theory of Signs*, trans. David B. Allison (Evanston, Ill.: Northwestern University Press, 1973), esp. 79–85. By demonstrating that the auto-affection of the phenomenological voice ("the possibility for what is called *subjectivity* or the *for-itself*," 79) involves temporalization, and that temporalization is a process in which "the same [self-same] is the same only in being affected by the other, only by becoming the other of the same" (85), Derrida introduces otherness into the self-same as its condition. Derrida's use of the term "auto-affection" seems to me to involve a twofold reference, on the one hand to the texts of Husserl which are his object of analysis, on the other hand to Heidegger's discussion of temporality and the transcendental imagination in *Kant und das Problem der Metaphysik*. If I diverge from Derrida's usage by employing the term hetero-affection, it is in order to stress my agreement with the results of Derrida's analysis.

47. The passage is cited near the end of Chapter 5.

48. I have consulted the Loeb Classical Library edition: Ovid, *Metamorphoses*, with an English translation by Frank Justus Miller (Cambridge: Harvard University Press, 1916). Subsequent references are given in parentheses, citing book and line.

49. See, for instance, Hartmut Böhme, "Eros und Tod im Wasser—'Bändigen und Entlassen der Elemente': Das Wasser bei Goethe," in Hartmut Böhme, ed., *Kulturgeschichte des Wassers* (Frankfurt a. M.: Suhrkamp, 1988), 208–33, here 212.

50. I have attempted a reading of the complex voice/echo/quotation in "Morphisms of the Phantasmatic Body: Goethe's *The Sorrows of Young Werther*," in Veronica Kelly and Dorothea E. von Mücke, eds., *Body and Text in the Eighteenth Century* (Stanford: Stanford University Press, 1993), 181–208.

51. *H.A.*, 6: 114.

52. *Goethes Briefe*, 1: 248.

53. Ibid.

54. As we have seen, this movement from dual subjects to a singular subject is prepared in the lines bearing on the reflection of sun and moon, in which the two heavenly bodies are united in a single face governing a singular verb.

Chapter 8

1. *Gedichte 1756–1799*, 329–30.

2. For recent work on the poem, see: Klaus Weimar, *Goethes Gedichte 1769–1775: Interpretation zu einem Anfang* [Paderborn; Schöningh, 1982], 87–94; Jochen Schmidt, *Die Geschichte des Genie-Gedankens 1750–1945*, 2 vols. (Darmstadt: Wissenschaftliche Buchgesellschaft, 1985), 1: 254–69; Karl Otto Conrady, "Goethe: 'Prometheus'," in Wilhelm Große, ed., *Zum jungen Goethe* (Stuttgart: Klett Cotta, 1982), 81–91 (republication of a text from 1956); Horst Thomé, "Tätigkeit und Reflexion in Goethes 'Prometheus'," in: *Gedichte und Interpretationen*, vol. 2, *Aufklärung und Sturm und Drang*, ed. Karl Richter (Stuttgart: Reclam, 1983), 427–35; Bernhard Sorg, *Das lyrische Ich: Untersuchungen zu deutschen Gedichten von Gryphius bis Benn* (Tübingen: Niemeyer, 1984), 62–68; Ulrich Gaier, "Vom Mythos zum Simulacrum: Goethes 'Prometheus'-Ode," *Lenz-Jahrbuch: Sturm-und-Drang-Studien* 1 (1992), 147–67. The relationship between the ode and the drama fragment *Prometheus*, a segment of which I discuss in Chapter 6 above, is thoroughly, and definitively, explored in Rolf Christian Zimmermann, *Das Weltbild des jungen Goethe*, vol. 2, *Interpretationen* (Munich: Wilhelm Fink, 1979), 119–66. The centerpiece of Hans Blumenberg's study of the Prometheus myth and its reception (*Arbeit am Mythos* [Frankfurt a. M.: Suhrkamp, 1979]) is a long section on Goethe (433–604), which, however, is more concerned with the biographical background and the reception of the ode (see 438–503) than with its poetic structure. Similar interests in biographical matters and questions of reception guide the recent article by Hartmut Reinhardt, "Prometheus und die Folgen," *Goethe Jahrbuch* 108 (1991): 137–69.

3. This comparison of "Prometheus" and "Mahomets Gesang" bears a certain polemical edge. A predominant tendency in the secondary literature at least since World War II is to view the "Prometheus" ode together with the poem "Ganymed." See in this connection Herman Meyer, "Goethes Prometheusode in ihrem zyklischen Zusammenhang," *Revue des langues vivantes* 15 (1949): 222–34. In-

deed, this pairing of texts has come to assume such canonical status that nearly every discussion of the "Prometheus" ode contains the proviso that this poem expresses only half of Goethe's worldview, the other half being embodied in the "Ganymed" poem. The worldview in question here is the conceptual polarity of "Verselbstung" ("self-concentration") and "Entselbstung" ("self-expansion"), of inward-directed isolation and outward-directed fusion, with which Goethe himself, in the retrospective account of *Dichtung und Wahrheit* (book 8), characterized the structure of his early thought. In his commentary to the *Hamburger Ausgabe* of Goethe's works (see esp. *H.A.*, 1: 472), Trunz insists on this polarity as central to the reading of Goethe's poetry, and Zimmermann (*Das Weltbild des jungen Goethe*, vol. 2) has developed, on the basis of extensive research into Goethe's possible sources, a rich interpretation of several early works that rests entirely on the notions of "Verselbstung" and "Entselbstung." Even the most recent publications on the "Prometheus" ode (e.g., Gaier, "Vom Mythos zum Simulakrum"; Reinhardt, "Prometheus und die Folgen") are informed by this perspective. In view of this consensus, I feel compelled to make explicit my own standpoint. First of all, I see no reason *not* to read the texts "Prometheus" and "Ganymed" together. Their juxtaposition in Goethe's 1789 edition of his works, in fact, suggests such a reading. But (and this is the force of my comparison of "Prometheus" and "Mahomets Gesang") other cross-readings are possible and, to the degree they prove to be internally coherent and illuminating of the texts, equally relevant. Moreover, any comparison of "Prometheus" with "Ganymed" must meet the same criterion of pertinence with regard to textual structures, a criterion no text-external factor (neither site of publication nor autobiographical comment) can replace. Second, in my view the conceptual opposition of "Verselbstung" and "Entselbstung" does not provide an adequate basis for reading either "Prometheus" or "Ganymed." Not only does the use of the polarity as an interpretive schema lead to identifiable misreadings regarding particular passages, the concepts themselves are far too nebulous to serve adequately as descriptive instruments. Implicit in my reading of the text, then, is the negative claim that the poetic texture of the "Prometheus" ode (exactly the object my analysis endeavors to capture) is not reducible to a single global concept ("Verselbstung"), even if that concept is authorized by the poet himself. Finally, I detect in the insistence on a balanced treatment of both sides of Goethe's worldview—in the cautionary proviso that "Prometheus" does not represent the whole of Goethe's thought—an endeavor to defuse the explosively anti-religious potential of the text. In a manuscript sent to me by Prof. Bernath Arpad of the Jozsef Attila University, Szeged, Hungary, ("Goethe-Strukturen. Goethe-Interpretationen. Einführung in eine vergleichende Untersuchung der Texte: Ganymed, Die Leiden des jungen Werthers, Stella, Erlkönig und Faust"), I find my reservations regarding the interpretive schema "Verselbstung" vs. "Entselbstung" as well as my sense that textual comparisons should be based on identifiable text structures (and not global connotative values) confirmed.

4. The version I have cited, however, is that published by Goethe in the 1789 edition of his *Schriften*. Earlier versions will be referred to subsequently.

5. The conversation between Lessing and Jacobi is reported in Jacobi's *Über die Lehre des Spinoza in Briefen an den Herrn Moses Mendelssohn* (1785), which is also the first publication of the text. The entire exchange is reproduced in Eibl's commentary on the poem, *Gedichte 1756–1799*, 922–23, from which my citation is taken. The comment, as reported by Jacobi, is followed by an avowal of pantheism (which is to say, Spinozism) on Lessing's part, a scandalous declaration that initiated the heated "pantheism debate" between Jacobi and Moses Mendelssohn. See *Die Hauptschriften zum Pantheismusstreit zwischen Jacobi und Mendelssohn*, ed. H. Scholz (Berlin: Reuter and Reichard, 1916). As a result of these circumstances, interpretations of the poem have often centered on the question of its Spinozistic or pantheistic content, with rather unsatisfying results. For recent discussions of the issue, see Blumenberg's subtle account, *Arbeit am Mythos*, 442–66; Reinhardt, "Prometheus und die Folgen," 157–69.

6. See John Bender and David E. Wellbery, eds., *Chronotypes: The Construction of Time* (Stanford: Stanford University Press, 1991).

7. The exception is Weimar, *Goethes Gedichte 1769–1775*, in which structural issues are always central.

8. Schmidt, *Die Geschichte des Genie-Gedankens 1750–1945*, 1: 266.

9. The juridical *dispositio* that determines the text's overriding rhetorical organization betrays a degree of calculation and strategy that such characterizations of the verbalization as a "hurling" of words ("entgegenschleudern," Sorg, *Das lyrische Ich*, 65) miss altogether. The general tendency among interpreters of the text is to see its unity as a function of sheer emotional intensity that holds from beginning to end.

10. On the figure of emancipation in Enlightenment philosophy of history, see Odo Marquard, *Schwierigkeiten mit der Geschichtsphilosophie* (Frankfurt a. M.: Suhrkamp, 1973), 14–19.

11. The concentric movement from "earth" to "hut" to "hearth" betrays what I would call the experiential anchorage of the text, its egocentric perspective. That is to say, the term 'earth' here does not refer to an astronomical or geological entity, but to that upon which the perceiving subject stands and over which it looks, to a ground and field of activity. This experiential anchorage of the text conforms to the speaker-perspective Herder attributed to the account of creation in the Book of Genesis. In his commentary on the first chapter of the Bible (*Aelteste Urkunde des Menschengeschlechts*, 1774), Herder makes a good deal of the experience-bound semantics of terms such as 'heaven' and 'earth', emphasizing that the account of creation is formulated from the standpoint of the "Erde-

Mensch," for whom the term 'earth' signifies a kind of primary certainty. See Johann Gottfried Herder, *Sämmtliche Werke*, ed. Berhard Suphan (Berlin: Weidmannsche Buchhandlung, 1877–1913), 6: 213. The pertinence of this reference to Herder will become clear in the course of my reading.

12. Among the poem's interpreters, Sorg (*Das lyrische Ich*, 67) stresses the compositional centrality of the phrase "heilig glühend Herz" most forcefully, without noting, however, the link to the 'glowing hearth' as the initial, still mythical figuration of the principle of centrality.

13. Among the most important contributions of Gaier's analysis ("Vom Mythos zum Simulacrum") is that it shows to what degree Goethe's allusions to the myth draw on texts by Lucian, in particular his *Prometheus* and *Zeus elenchomenos* (both available in the Loeb Classical Library edition: *Lucian*, trans. A. M. Harmon [Cambridge: Harvard University Press, 1955], vol. 2). The tendency of Gaier's reading of the poem's allusive network, however, is to demonstrate that the poem conflicts with (and is therefore wrong about) the mythological tradition. See in this regard esp. 155–59. But this argument rests on the dubious assumption that the task of the poem is accurately to reproduce the givens of the mythologeme. On the other hand, Gaier's reading does have the merit of taking seriously the question of what this text is actually doing with the mythological material it draws on. Most interpretations fail to raise this question at all, remaining content with the assertion that the poem focalizes the aspect of the mythologeme that ascribes the creation of mankind to Prometheus.

14. My terminology—observation of observation—alludes to Niklas Luhmann's notion of "second-order" observation. For an application of this notion to the domain of art, see Luhmann, "Weltkunst," in Niklas Luhmann, Frederick D. Bunsen, and Dirk Baecker, *Unbeobachtbare Welt: Über Kunst und Architektur* (Bielefeld: Cordelia Haug, 1990), 7–45.

15. Cf., for example, Trunz's commentary, *H.A.*, 1: 472; Conrady, "Goethe: 'Prometheus',᾿" 88; Schmidt, *Die Geschichte des Genie-Gedankens 1750–1945*, 1: 265. Since it would be absurd to command Zeus to perpetrate the violent acts the utterance calls for, both Conrady and Schmidt construe the command as a kind of banishment, an expulsion of Zeus from the earthly domain and a confinement to the heavenly sphere. Schmidt's construction: "In blasphemous reversal of the traditional hymnic invocation, Goethe's Prometheus commands [*auffordern*] Zeus to disappear into a transcendent sphere experienced as irrelevant." Of course, in order to make this claim, Schmidt must ignore the fact that the acts Prometheus apparently calls on Zeus to perform would occur in the earthly domain (e.g., mountain tops, oaks, but even the clouds that cover over the heavens). Conrady does not ignore these earthly elements, but in order to save his interpretation reads them as signifying an upper region belonging to heaven: "The upper region belongs to Zeus: heaven, the clouds, the mountain peaks, he

can even vent himself on the tips of oak trees." Both critics fail to note that what is being ordered here—parodistically, I argue—is the natural, and that is to say, worldly phenomenon of a violent thunderstorm. Only when this fact is taken into consideration is it possible to avoid the hopeless contradiction that on the one hand Prometheus addresses Zeus and on the other hand he argues for the nonexistence of the father-god. The interpretations of Conrady and Schmidt (and others as well) are hampered by this contradiction insofar as they attribute a certain sphere of authority to Zeus and nevertheless claim that the text denies his existence. Reading the opening illocution as a parodied command that discloses hermeneutically the precise character of the god—namely, a figuration produced out of the child's fear of such natural phenomena as thunderstorms—provides a way out of this contradiction. The precondition of such a reading is an accurate appraisal of the illocutionary structure of the opening stanza.

16. This is where my reading, as mentioned at the outset, crosses that of Jochen Schmidt (note 8 above). See also Sorg, *Das lyrische Ich*, 64, and Eibl's note in *Gedichte 1759–1799*, 927, for statements that come close to Schmidt's concept of projection. It should be remarked that the poem's second and third stanzas provide the reference point of the cited interpretations. As far as I am aware, the thematization of a mechanism of linguistic projection in the simile, as well as the implications of the illocutionary structure of the parodied command, have not been discussed in the secondary literature.

17. The figure of the boy beheading thistles cites a line from Macphearson's *Ossian* forgery: "Warriors fell by the sword as the thistle by the staff of a boy." See Sauder's commentary, *Münchener Ausgabe*, I/1, 871. Since the *Ossian* poem was held to exemplify the concrete figural language of primitive poetry, the citation supports a reading of the simile as a thematization of an originary poetic-metaphorical process. The full relevance of this connection between primitive poetry and religious belief will become clear subsequently.

18. Another line of connection between the two stanzas appears in the lines: "Ich kenne nichts ärmers / Unter der Sonn' als euch, Götter!" (12–13). The isolation of the term "Götter" here bends the usage of the term away from a strictly vocative function ("you gods!") and lends it a parodistic accent. Just as the parodied command quotes the content of an antecedent threat, the term "Götter" likewise suggests the quotation of a false claim to a title. To draw out this suggestion, one might translate the lines as: "I know nothing more impoverished / Beneath the sun than you, so-called gods!" In the course of my reading I shall point to other examples of this citational-parodistic strategy. From a rhetorical point of view, of course, there is no better way to deflate an opponent than through a practice of insistent, parodistic citation, as one can learn, for example, from Mark Antony's funeral oration for Caesar.

19. This point is misunderstood by Zimmermann, *Das Weltbild des jungen Goethe*, 2: 163, who finds it hardly intelligible that the poem, as an expression of

complete individual self-concentration ("Verselbstung"), mentions "beggars" and "fools" at all. This mistake is interesting because it reveals that Zimmermann's interpretive schema, based on the opposition "Verselbstung" vs. "Entselbstung," is a Procrustean bed to which the poem can be made to fit only by chopping off, or declaring nonsensical, certain of its elements. In general, Zimmermann's remarks on the text fail to grasp its historico-philosophical dimension, a dimension that includes reference to a humanity held in thrall to a deity whom its deluded worship constitutes ("Kinder und Bettler"), as well as to a humanity to come, which, as we shall see, is the implicit addressee of the text. The same criticism can be made with regard to Sorg's interpretation, in which the poem is characterized as an "apotheosis of self-love" (*Das lyrische Ich*, 68).

20. This is not the only similarity between the ode and the dialectic of lordship and bondage as described by Hegel in the *Phenomenology of Spirit*. One could also call attention to the fact that Hegel's Lord establishes his rule through a simulation of the power over life and death that strikes fear in the self-consciousness destined to become the slave as well as to the fact that the slave works his way out of his inadequate consciousness by discovering his own formative capacity objectified in the products of his labor, much as Prometheus can rely on the self-certainty he has acquired by producing, independently of Zeus, the hut.

21. Oskar Walzel, *Das Prometheussymbol von Shaftesbury zu Goethe* (Darmstadt: Wissenschaftliche Buchgesellschaft, 1985, rpt. of the 1910 ed.).

22. Sauder, for example, adduces Shaftesbury's definition of the artist as a "second Maker, a just Prometheus under Jove" in his commentary on the poem, *Münchener-Ausgabe*, I/1, 869. And in the most recent article on the poem, Reinhardt writes: "The internal image [*Inbild*] of his ode is productive artistic activity, which reflects itself in the Prometheus myth and is reflected by it. Thus, Goethe enters into a tradition of poetological doctrine [*Dichterlehre*] that was decisively informed by Shaftesbury and which already in 1770 neither an aesthetician of genius nor a genial poet could do without" ("Prometheus und die Folgen," 139).

23. The relevant texts are Rousseau's first Discourse (1750), Wieland's "Traumgespräch mit Prometheus" (1770), which involves a critique of Rousseau, Herder's *Abhandlung über den Ursprung der Sprache* (1770), to which I shall return, and Goethe's "Zum Schäkespears Tag," "Von deutscher Baukunst," and, of course, the drama fragment *Prometheus*. On Goethe's various early references to the Prometheus figure, see Blumenberg, *Arbeit am Mythos*, 492–99; Karl Eibl, "'. . . mehr als Prometheus . . .': Anmerkung zu Goethes Baukunst-Aufsatz," *Jahrbuch der deutschen Schillergesellschaft* 25 (1981): 238–48.

24. I am grateful to Inca Mülder-Bach for calling my attention to the fact that my recontextualization of the "Prometheus" ode has an important precedent in

the "Prometheus" chapter of Wolfdietrich Rasch's study, *Goethes 'Iphigenie auf Tauris' als Drama der Autonomie* (Munich: Beck, 1979), 55–70. Rasch emphasizes especially the significance of Voltaire's opera libretto *Pandore* (1740) as an Enlightenment redaction of the Prometheus material.

25. Frank Manuel, *The Eighteenth Century Confronts the Gods* (Cambridge: Harvard University Press, 1959).

26. Pierre Bayle, *Pensées diverses sur la comète*, ed. A Prat (Paris, 1911), 1: 170, cited in Manuel, *The Eighteenth Century Confronts the Gods*, 35.

27. None of these texts are mentioned in connection with Goethe's "Prometheus" in Hans Blumenberg's study *Arbeit am Mythos*. Thus, rather than seeing the ode in terms of the theory of mythology, which, after all, is his theme, Blumenberg discusses the text as a kind of immanent product of the poet's individuality, going so far as to adduce a remark of the six-year-old Goethe on the Lisbon earthquake of 1755 (468f.). However intriguing Blumenberg's commentary might be as a biographical construction or speculative fiction, it contributes little to an understanding of the poetic specificity of the text. The neglect of the connection between "Prometheus" and the eighteenth-century discourse on mythology seems to me to derive from the method of Blumenberg's study, which ignores the solidity of historical formations of discourse for the sake of what might be called transhistorical configurations of thought. This configurational approach (as well as the immanentist view of Goethe) causes Blumenberg on one occasion to overlook an important clue. Jacobi's publication of the poem, Blumenberg remarks, is accompanied by a note that associates it with the atheism of Hume, Diderot, Holbach, and the Lucian translations (455). This grouping, I would contend, is not fortuitous; rather, it identifies the discursive context most immediately pertinent to Goethe's text, a context that was in all likelihood as perceptible to Lessing as it was to Jacobi. Note that this is the only reference to Hume in Blumenberg's book and that the work of Frank Manuel goes entirely unmentioned.

28. As demonstrated by Gaier, "Vom Mythos zum Simulakrum." Gaier does not, however, remark the positional significance of references to Lucian in eighteenth-century mythographic discourse.

29. Manuel, *The Eighteenth Century Confronts the Gods*, 132.

30. Giambattista Vico, *The New Science*, trans. T. G. Bergin and M. H. Fisch (Ithaca: Cornell University Press, 1948), 105–6.

31. I cite from the edition of the "Natural History of Religion" contained in David Hume, *Writings on Religion*, ed. Anthony Flew (La Salle: Open Court, 1992), 107–82, here 107. Subsequent page references are indicated in parentheses in the text.

32. A reference in a review written for the *Frankfurter Gelehrten Anzeiger* demonstrates awareness of Hume's significance within the discursive context sketched out here: "Wir müssen es einmal sagen, weil es uns auf dem Herzen

liegt: Voltaire, Hume, la Mettrie, Helvetius, Rousseau und ihre ganze Schule haben der Moralität und der Religion lange nicht so viel geschadet als der strenge, kranke Pascal und seine Schule." ("We have to say it finally, because it has weighed on our heart for a long time: Voltaire, Hume, la Mettrie, Helvetius, Rousseau and their entire school have done less damage to religion and morality than the strict, sick Pascal and his school"; *Münchener-Ausgabe*, I/2. (See Rasch, *Goethes 'Iphigenie auf Tauris' als Drama der Autonomie*, 61.) Perhaps this is the point to mention that the negative evaluation of fear and hope is also a feature of Spinoza's discussion of the emotions (see *Ethics*, part 4, prop. 47). In this sense, the ode could be considered Spinozist, but Spinoza's psychology and not his metaphysics would be the source of influence.

33. Hume's authority is Dionysius of Halicarnassus; Goethe's, in all likelihood, Lucian.

34. Herder, *Sämmtliche Werke*, 32: 193–97.

35. Ibid., 85–140.   36. Ibid., 123.

37. Ibid., 106.   38. Ibid., 108.

39. Hume, "Natural History," 117.

40. Herder, *Sämmtliche Werke*, 32: 110.

41. Ibid., 113. Vico, of course, is an exception to my claim that such a statement is foreign to the discourse on mythology.

42. Ibid., 118.

43. Cf., in this connection, Herder's text "Fragmente einer Abhandlung über die Ode," ibid., 61–85.

44. Ibid., 148–52.   45. Ibid., 148.

46. Ibid., 151.   47. *Sämmtliche Werke*, 6: 193–511.

48. The "Versuch einer Geschichte der lyrischen Dichtkunst" also concludes with a demonstration that the Humean thesis applies to the earliest stages of the Jewish religion (cf. *Sämmtliche Werke*, 32: 126–40). Another relevant text from the same complex, of course, is the fragmentary commentary on the biblical account of creation, "Das Lied von der Schöpfung der Dinge" ("The Song on the Creation of All Things"), ibid., 163–65. Traces of the Humean thesis are still perceptible in the published version of *Aelteste Urkunde*. Commenting on the notion that in the beginning everything was chaos and night, Herder writes: "Whoever has, on the desolate world-sea, covered by night and fear of death, hoped for dawn, will have felt this scene" (see *Sämmtliche Werke*, 6: 215). Precisely this trace of Humean thought, however, reveals the distance between Hume and Herder. It is no longer a matter of identifying the mechanism of misrepresentation, but rather of "feeling" the immediate affective experience that has shaped itself in the biblical text. The hermeneutic task is to disclose the moment within the "history of the feeling of all mankind" (ibid., 216) the text articulates, and this task is achieved through empathetic reenactment.

49. This designation is also suggested by Reinhardt, "Prometheus und die Folgen," 138 ("Antihymne"), but without reference to the discursive context I have constructed here.

50. Karl Phillip Moritz, *Götterlehre oder Mythologische Dichtungen der Alten* (Bremen: Carl Schünemann, n.d.).

51. Ibid., 7.

52. Friedrich Wilhelm Joseph Schelling, *Philosophie der Mythologie* (Darmstadt: Wissenschaftliche Buchgesellschaft, 1957, rpt. of the 1856 ed.).

53. Another major difference, of course, is that Moritz's essentially cyclical conception (from night through form and back to night) is replaced by a historico-philosophical conception that charts a progressive line.

54. Schelling, *Philosophie der Mythologie*, 1: 482.

55. Hans Blumenberg, *Arbeit am Mythos*, 633.

56. *Gedichte 1756–1799*, 203. The version is from Goethe's first Weimar collection of his poems (1778).

57. Or perhaps the purpose of the alteration was to demote the personal pronoun referring to Zeus. In the two-line version, a parsing in which the "du" is stressed seems probable: "Die du nicht gebaut." The merged line, however, can (but need not) be read with the stress falling on the negative particle: "Und meine Hütte, die du nicht gebaut."

58. Note that another, still earlier version of the poem found among the papers of Goethe's friend Johann Heinrich Merck divides stanza I (in the version I am citing) into two stanzas of seven and five lines respectively. See *Münchener-Ausgabe*, I/1, 229–31. This version, then, supports my construction of stanza I as a combination of a five-line unit and a seven-line unit. However, I prefer to see the division of stanza I as falling between line five and line six, a caesura that makes more semantic and illocutionary sense than that in the Merck manuscript. Thus, the correlation between beginning and end that seems pertinent to me involves a parallelism of two 5 + 7 groups and not an inversion (beginning, 7 + 5; end, 5 + 7). But the major point, of course, is that the Merck manuscript supports a reading of the twelve-line stanza as a fusion of two smaller units.

59. In his judicious commentary on the manuscript of the poem from the papers of Johann Heinrich Merck (see previous note), Sauder parses the eight stanzas of that version as follows: stanzas I–III (present situation), stanzas IV–VI (past); stanzas VII–VIII (return to present). See *Münchener-Ausgabe*, I/1, 869. This division differs from my own in that it characterizes the last stanza (VII in the version I have cited, VIII in the version from Merck's papers) as a return to the present. To be sure, the stanza is spoken out of the present, but its semantic orientation, in contradistinction to the opening two (or three) stanzas, is clearly toward the future. The stanza articulates Prometheus's *intention* to create a humanity that will not respect Zeus just as he does not. But this is a minor

difference. What I find especially interesting about Sauder's grouping of the stanzas is that he joins stanzas VII and VIII (or VI and VII in the version used here) in a single unit. Of course, his justification for this grouping doesn't hold: stanza VII (or VI) is not, as he claims, directed toward the present (cf. "Wähntest," "reiften"); semantically, it still belongs to the past-oriented, narrative portion of the poem. My suspicion is that Sauder overlooked the tense of the verbs because the numerical correspondence (7 + 5 and 5 + 7) so strongly suggests a parallelism between beginning and end. The point, of course, is not to decide for one or the other of the two possible arrangements, but rather to see that the text allows for both. Semantically (in terms of tense) and rhetorically (as rhetorical question), stanza VI (VII in the Merck manuscript) belongs in a group together with the preceding stanzas; numerically (and also rhetorically, as we shall see) it belongs together with the final stanza. The composition of the text operates simultaneously with both arrangements.

60. This holds for other texts by the young Goethe often taken (mistakenly) to lack rigorous compositional order. For an especially revealing example, see Arlene Teraoka, "Submerged Symmetry and Surface Chaos: *Götz von Berlichingen*," *Goethe Yearbook* 2 (1981).

61. My argument for the paradigmatic character of the gesture of turning the eye toward heaven is supported by the use of the identical gesture in eighteenth-century texts on the origin of religion. In the *Aelteste Urkunde des Menschenge-schlechts*, Herder identifies the gesture of "looking upward" ("Hinaufschauen") as the primordial experience of divinity in primitive man ("Wilden"). See *Sämmt-liche Werke*, 6: 216. The act that Prometheus recalls, then, embodies a decisive moment within what Herder designates "the history of feeling of all human beings" (ibid.), inaugurates the childhood of man. I have already called attention to the use of the same figure by Hume: "The absurdity [of anthropomorphic projection] is not less, while we cast our eyes upwards" ("The Natural History of Religion," 118). The most famous instance of the look toward heaven (although it was not well known in the eighteenth century) is Vico's account of the *giganti*, who, aroused by the rumble of thunder, for the first time look upward toward the sky and in and through this gesture constitute the gods. See Giambattista Vico, *The New Science*, 105–6. In view of the epitomizing character of the gesture, the claim that "Prometheus is speaking only of himself" (Conrady, "Goethe: 'Prometheus'," 89) is a massive foreshortening; he is speaking here of himself as exemplary of a phase in the history of mankind and this historical status is internal to the poetic significance of the figure. Reinhardt's interpretation of the stanza as a "piece of Goethe's authentic history" ("Goethe und die Folgen," 150) involves a similar, but more grievous, restriction of poetic significance.

62. Note that the nominalized participle "des Bedrängten" bears a semantic nuance of 'typification'. Prometheus, that is to say, characterizes himself not

merely as distressed on this or that particular occasion, but as the representative of the human condition of distress. The nominalized participial form ensures the generalization of the Promethean situation, marks it as a universal human condition. The identical effect is achieved through the use of the same grammatical form in stanza V: cf. "Beladenen" (39), "Geängsteten" (41). Once again, a reading of the text as expressive of an insular individuality proves inadequate.

63. The semantic nuance of 'spatial disorientation' is connoted as well by the qualification of the 'eye' that turns toward the sun as "mein verirrtes Auge" (23). The eye, that is to say, is confused; it can find no bearings in a world in which "aus" and "ein" are indistinguishable. At the same time, the word "verirrt" indicates that the turn toward the sun is an error, the belief that turn constitutes deluded. It should also be remarked that the phrase "Nicht wußte wo aus noch ein" can be read in a second way. The sort of ignorance marked here, that is to say, could be ignorance of the causal relations that obtain in the world, ignorance, for example, regarding the causes of thunderstorms. Recall that for Hume and the Enlightenment mythographers generally precisely such nonknowledge regarding the natural causes of prodigious, hence frightening, phenomena actuates polytheistic belief. This reading, which I find suggestive, but uncertain, does not, of course, conflict with my construction in terms of spatial disorientation. Indeed, the two readings fit together well, as the sentence by Hume cited above—of which Goethe's stanza almost seems to be a citation—shows: "And in this disordered scene, with eyes still more disordered and astonished, they [men] see the first obscure traces of divinity" ("The Natural History of Religion," 116).

64. Ibid., 117.

65. Conrady, "Goethe: 'Prometheus'," 89.

66. One of the major insights of Sorg's interpretation (*Das lyrische Ich*, 67) bears on the status of the "Herz" as the authentic addressee of the text.

67. Once again, the ambiguous status of stanza VI, its determination according to two patterns of composition, stands out. In terms of the parallel deployment of rhetorical questions, stanza VI coheres with the foregoing two stanzas (IV, Questions *A A B C*; V–VI: Questions *A A B C*). In terms of line count, however, stanza VI stands outside the two nine-line stanzas it follows. This position exterior to the group IV–V allows stanza VI to be combined with stanza VII to form the concluding stanzaic pair, consisting of a five-line and a seven-line component.

68. This, of course, is the thesis of Roman Jakobson's essay "Closing Statement: Linguistics and Poetics," *Style in Language*, ed. Thomas A. Sebeok (Cambridge: MIT Press, 1960), 350–77. Note also Herder's use of the concept in his *Aelteste Urkunde des Menschengeschlechts*, in *Sämmtliche Werke*, 6: 213, a text exactly contemporary, of course, with the "Prometheus" ode. Reading the "Prometheus" ode from the standpoint of Herder's theory of parallelism, one could

say that the text claims for itself the status of a poetic *Urkunde des Menschenge-schlechts*, that it institutes a symbolic universe much as the first Book of Moses does, but a symbolic universe that no longer relies on a transcendent deity. That Goethe's text cites Genesis in its final stanza, then, is coherent with its overriding strategy.

69. To claim that the intonational arc is the same in both series simplifies matters slightly. In fact, both the *B*- and *C*-components of the second series involve a quantitative expansion of the corresponding components in the first series.

70. Cf. Conrady, "Goethe: 'Prometheus'," 89: "dieses gefühlsgeladene Sprechen."

71. See my remarks on the rhetorical questions employed in "Der Fischer" in Chapter 7. Without going into the matter in any detail, I would note a distinction between the "Yes!" elicited by the *B*-questions, a "yes" of affirmation, and that called for by the *C*-questions, which is a "yes" of admission or concession.

72. Cf. Sauder's annotation, *Münchener-Ausgabe*, I/1, 871. In *Prometheus Bound*, Zeus does, of course, protect Prometheus from the Titans' revenge. The reader aware of this fact must therefore see Prometheus's implicit claim that no one helped him as a retraction of his own mythological story.

73. As far as I know, this allusion to the mythological element of punishment has not been noted in the secondary literature. In support of my reading I would point out that the trigger of the allusion, the word "geschmiedet," recalling the 'forging of the chains,' is employed by Hederich, Goethe's principal source, in his account of this episode. Cf., Benjamin Hederich, *Gründliches Mythologisches Lexikon* (Darmstadt: Wissenschaftliche Buchgesellschaft, 1986, rpt. of the 2d ed., Leipzig, 1770), 2092–93 ("angeschmiedet"). With Prometheus's reinterpretation of this element, the intimidating story of punishment is exposed as a misunderstanding: it was not a punishment at all, but the necessary and, in the sense that it shapes one into manhood, purposeful experience of suffering that is a natural component of human life. The retraction of the particulars of the mythologeme coincides with the disclosure of the universal human significance those particulars metaphorically designate.

74. Herder, *Sämmtliche Werke*, 6: 216.

75. Hederich notes this fact at 2093 and 2097 (there the use of the term "Schmiedekunst").

76. Although the most obvious (hence indisputable) allusion carried by the line "Hat nicht mich zum Manne geschmiedet" bears on the metallurgical significance of the Prometheus mythologeme, it has gone unnoticed in the interpretation of the poem. With the following remarks on the inner unity of the poem's two peak lines (33, 42) and the autological structure of self-fashioning they instantiate, then, I depart from the secondary literature on the text.

77. "Zeit" and "Schicksal," which the text names as the grammatical subjects of the act of forging, would, on this reading, be the instruments—the hammer blows, perhaps—with which the act is performed. The attribution of agency to these instruments would thus amount to a metonymic substitution that places them in the subject position in fact occupied by Prometheus. Recalling that the participle "geschmiedet" also alludes to the punishment of Prometheus, one could say that what is accomplished in the interpretation of the anguished past is an instrumentalization of pain. My suffering is that with which I purify and shape myself. In support of the reading of "Zeit" and "Schicksal" as metonymies (instruments for agent) of Promethean agency, I note the fact that the finite verb they govern is singular.

78. Far from being indulgent wordplay, this association, in addition to being motivated from within the figural context of metallurgy, is supported by the text's most obvious paronomastic series. That is, the paronomastic slide from "Erde" (6) to "Herd" (9)—the locus of "Glut" (10)—to "glühend Herz" (33) suggests a relation between the first and last terms of the chain. And, of course, "Erz" ("ore") comes from, is even a kind of, "Erde."

79. Goethe probably drew the notion that Zeus is ruled by destiny from a text by Lucian. For details, see Sauder's commentary, *Münchener-Ausgabe*, I/1, 869. The fact that Zeus does not control destiny is interpreted in Lucian's dialogue (*Zeus elenchomenos*) as a reason for not worshipping him. Hence the relevance of the allusion here, where the question "Ich dich ehren? Wofür?" has set the frame for the rhetorical questions. As noted above, Hume likewise calls attention to the notion that the gods are subject to destiny. The import of this notion for Hume is that polytheism does not consider the gods in terms of the concept of creation. This fits well with Goethe's text, in which the idea of human self-formation is being worked out. And this idea, as we shall see, is polemically opposed in the final stanza to the Judeo-Christian idea of a divine creation of man.

80. See *Gedichte 1756–1799*, 204. Apart from a single comma, this version is indistinguishable from that found in Merck's papers. See *Münchener-Ausgabe*, I/1, 231.

81. Perhaps it is not superfluous to decode this compound. Its nominal center is the word "Träume" ("dreams"), which is modified according to the agent who produces the dreams ("Knabe"), the time of their production ("morgen," which is to say, 'early,' from the standpoint of 'inexperience'), and their content ("Blüten," a flowering or blossoming which would be the fulfillment of the dreams). The "Knabenmorgen-/Blütenträume" are wishful anticipations of a future made by the youth on the basis of his metaphorical projection of the god. The fact that these dreams did not ripen is thus equivalent to the fact that the youth's wishful projections are not confirmed in the process of maturation. This disappointment is nothing other than the process that is worked through in the

tragically cathartic phase of the narrative culminating in the demonstration that the god doesn't exist. Typically, the compound is glossed as characteristic of the drastic tendency of Goethe's Sturm-und-Drang style. This is true enough, but the point that should be emphasized is that the very monstrosity of the compound serves to ridicule what it figures: belief (to which the cautionary word clings) is denigrated by a metaphor that, across all four of its components, demonstrates its insubstantial, puerile, naively wishful character.

82. This reading of stanza VI diverges from that offered by Schmidt, who interprets the notions of hating life and fleeing into deserts as connoting a Christian asceticism: "Hate of life and flight into the desert mean the Christian-ascetic withdrawal from the world and disdain for life" (*Die Geschichte des Genie-Gedankens 1750–1945*, 1: 265). Schmidt's interpretation rests on the specification of the "deserts" mentioned in line 48 as an allusion to the legendary type of the god-seeking anchorite, an attribution of meaning he supports by adducing the conclusion of *Faust II*, where a chorus of "heiligen Anachoreten" appears in the Dantesque ascent of Faust toward the eternal feminine. But it is obvious that this reading cannot be made to fit with the overall syntactic context, which clearly defines the hatred of life and the flight into deserts as resulting from the fact that the "Knabenmorgen-/Blütenträume" have failed to ripen. Now these dreams are nothing other than the belief in god constituted in Prometheus's youthful act of imaginary projection, a belief that, at this point in the text, has been demolished. Thus, Schmidt's reading is caught in the contradiction that it claims as an aspect of belief what is in fact a response to the loss of belief, to disillusionment. Far from being an allusion to the ascetic practice of the anchorite, the idea of hating life and fleeing into deserts figures a pathological condition (melancholy): the rejection of and retreat from life that follows upon disappointment or disillusionment. The appropriate intertext from Goethe's work for this passage is not *Faust II* (which, after all, is separated from the "Prometheus" ode by more than fifty years!), but the poem "Harzreise im Winter." There we encounter a disappointed lover who has retreated into a desolate landscape ("Wüste"!) and who lives there in a kind of self-consuming hatred for mankind. I shall return to this figure in the following chapter.

83. Again Hume's text provides an interesting point of comparison: "Good and ill are universally intermingled and confounded; happiness and misery, wisdom and folly, virtue and vice. Nothing is pure and entirely of a piece. All advantages are attended with disadvantages. An universal compensation prevails in all conditions of being and existence. And it is not possible for us, by our most chimerical wishes, to form the idea of a station or situation altogether desirable" ("Natural History of Religion," 180). Hume's insistence on a healthy acceptance of the mixture of happiness and misery endemic to existence corresponds to the affirmation of a life that includes both suffering and enjoyment in the final stanza

of the ode. And the "chimerical wishes" of a life free of this mixture have their counterpart in the "Knabenmorgen-/Blütenträume." Note that Hume's remark occurs in the final chapter of his "Natural History," that it bears, in other words, the force of a concluding appraisal and that the corresponding passages in the poem likewise function in a conclusionary manner. Hume's tone of cautionary skepticism and stoical acceptance of human limitations differs from Goethe's more emphatic gesture of affirmation, of course.

84. This is the point at which to mark the most significant difference between my reading and Ulrich Gaier's interpretation of the text ("Vom Mythos zum Simulacrum"). To my knowledge, Gaier is the only interpreter of the poem to have thematized the contradiction between the address to Zeus, which *seems* to presuppose his existence, and the argument of the poem, according to which Zeus does not exist. To this degree we are in agreement. But Gaier interprets this contradiction as the final statement of the poem; he views the poem as the dramatization of an absurdity (see esp. 158). He can maintain this position, however, only so long as he ignores (as indeed he does throughout) the parodistic structure of Prometheus's speech. Once this structure is taken into account (along the lines of the previous two paragraphs), the absurdity Gaier attributes to the poem falls into the lap of his own interpretation. Much the same holds for Gaier's interpretation of the Prometheus figure. According to his view, Prometheus, by making statements that contradict the mythic context in which he figures, carries out a kind of self-negation, removes the very basis of his own existence (see 158–59). Thus, the "result" ("Ergebnis") of Gaier's reading is that the poem which sets out to demolish the god and affirm Prometheus's "titanic selfhood" ends up by confirming the god in his preeminence and destroying Prometheus (159). This result, which strikes me as patently wrong, is nevertheless indicative of the fact that Gaier, to a greater degree than any previous interpreter, has perceived some of the intricacies involved in what I have been calling the autological structure of the Promethian speech act, intricacies that, in the final analysis, point to paradoxical figures as the ground of the text.

85. As far as I can see, only two critics have offered explicit alternatives to the expressive model: Weimar (*Goethes Gedichte 1769–1775*), who views the text as an experiment in role playing, and Gaier ("Vom Mythos zum Simulacrum"), who views the text as a process of self-nullification, a rendering absurd ("*ad absurdam führen*," 163) of the mythological figure.

86. *Arbeit am Mythos*, 440–41.

87. "One can see his formation of human beings, along with various other representations, on an ancient monument. He sits there with a cloak wrapped around his body, which covers his lower body in a peculiar way. Next to him he has a basket with clay, and in front of him an already completed human figure stands. With his left hand he holds in front of him a second figure and seems to

have given it its finishing touches with the chisel he holds in his right hand. Minerva stands behind this figure and places a butterfly on its head, signifying its endowment with a soul" (Hederich, *Gründliches Mythologisches Lexikon*, 2092). The ode dispenses with the aspect of the mythologeme according to which the soul or life of the statues is given them by Minerva, an element that in the drama fragment *Prometheus*, as we have seen in Chapter 6, remains central. The reason why the Prometheus of the ode can animate his human creations without Minerva's aid will become clear subsequently.

88. Conrady, "Goethe: 'Prometheus'," 90.

89. See Eibl's commentary, *Gedichte 1756–1799*, 926, which summarizes the consensus in the research.

90. In Herder's first sketch of an interpretation of the creation story in Genesis ("Das Lied von der Schöpfung der Dinge"), he likewise interprets the theologeme of man's likeness to God along projectionist lines: "*Man in our image.* Oriental idol of the ruler as god, and of man therefore as God's image. Not our dogm. [atic] explan[ation]" (*Sämmtliche Werke*, 32: 165). This remark preserves the critical edge of the Enlightenment discourse on religious origins that is smoothed over in Herder's later, affirmative account in *Aelteste Urkunde des Menschengeschlechts*. It seems important to me to remark that Goethe's "Prometheus" remains faithful, in this respect, to the spirit of Enlightenment criticism, although in other respects, of course, it breaks new ground.

91. Ovid, *Metamorphoses*, I, 83; Lucian, *Prometheus*.

92. Again, see Eibl's commentary, *Gedichte 1756–1799*, 926.

93. The reading of the line: "Hier sitz' ich, forme Menschen" as descriptive of the act of writing is also suggested by Reinhardt, "Prometheus und die Folgen," 148. The only other interpreter of the text who holds this view, as far as I know, is Carl Pietzcker, "Goethes Prometheus-Ode," in Pietzcker, *Trauma, Wunsch und Abwehr* (Würzburg: Konigshausen and Neumann, 1985), 9–64. The difference between my reading of the line and those developed by Reinhardt and Pietzcker is that they view the lines as a description of an external fact whereas I see them as autoreferential to the poem itself. This is the point in the text where the poetic act remarks itself as a poetic act formative of humanity.

94. Recall that "Mahomets Gesang" likewise operates with a paradoxical structure, the figure of self-fathering or poetic auto-engenderment.

95. See Roman Jakobson, "Shifters, Verbal Categories and the Russian Verb," *Selected Writings II* (The Hague: Mouton, 1957), 130–47.

96. See Karl Bühler's concept of the "ich-nun-hier origo" in his *Sprachtheorie* (Stuttgart: Fischer, 1965).

97. *Münchener-Ausgabe*, I/2, 412.

98. Ibid., I/1, 413.

99. Ibid., I/2, 413–14.

100. The idea that Prometheus has internalized the primordial donation achieved within the specular exchange is supported by a textual detail common to the ode, "Wandrers Sturmlied," and "Künstlers Morgenlied": the use of the term "Neid" ("envy"). In "Wandrers Sturmlied," the speaker calls on his own inner "Glut" to sustain him in the mimetic competition with Apollo, noting that, if his capacity to "glow against" the god is insufficient, the god's princely regard ("Fürstenblick," Text 16, 65) will glide past the speaker and settle "neidgetroffen" (67) on the cedar tree. The failure of the poetic project in "Wandrers Sturmlied," then, is equivalent to the inability to attract the envy of the solar deity. But precisely this attraction of the god's envy is what the speaker of "Künstlers Morgenlied" accomplishes when he summons the gods to witness his erotic union with the beloved and "Beneiden unser Gluck" ("envy our bliss," Text 18, 78). The reason the speaker of "Künstlers Morgenlied" succeeds where the speaker of "Wandrers Sturmlied" fails is that the former withdraws from the epic scene of Homeric battle (analogous to the wanderer's attempt to equal Pindar) and grounds his artistic production in the sphere of specular love. The specular donation of "Glut," then, is sufficient to excite envy in Apollo. This constellation allows us to make sense of Prometheus's claim that Zeus "envies" ("beneidest") him because of the "Glut" that dwells within his "Herd" (9–11). The "Heilig glühend Herz" (33), which is the truth of this glowing hearth has received into itself the dual gift of love and language stemming from the Minerva of the *Prometheus* drama. And just as the specular donation of "Künstlers Morgenlied" provides the matrix of a modern, lyric art that supplants the ancient, epic model of Homer (and Apollo), the "Heilig glühend Herz" of the "Prometheus" ode becomes the principle of a poetic discourse that displaces the mythic address to Zeus.

101. *Abhandlung über den Ursprung der Sprache*, 42. My translation of the passage attempts to do justice to Herder's use of the term "Merkmal" by rendering it as "feature of recognition."

102. Shaftesbury is cited by Sauder in his commentary to *Münchener-Ausgabe*, I/1, 868, by Conrady ("Goethe: 'Prometheus'," 91), by Sorg (*Das lyrische Ich*, 66), by Reinhardt ("Prometheus und die Folgen," 139). Shaftesbury's concept of genius, however, is a theological and mimetic notion grounded in a deist view of the universe as created according to rational-moral principles which it is the task of the artist to imitate. I have not found any references in the secondary literature to Herder's allusion to the Prometheus figure in connection with the origin of language.

Chapter 9

1. On April 6, 1773, Goethe writes to Kestner: "Ich wandre in Wüsten da kein Wasser ist, meine Haare sind mir Schatten und mein Blut mein Brunnen." ("I

wander in deserts where there is no water, my hair is my shade and my blood my spring [i.e., source of water].") In July of that year, he writes with reference to his work on the *Prometheus* drama: "Was das kostet in Wüsten Brunnen zu graben und eine Hütte zu zimmern." ("What it costs to dig springs in the deserts and to fashion a hut.")

2. *Gedichte 1756–1799*, 322–24.

3. I do not intend to structure my reading of "Harzreise im Winter" as a dialogue with the interpretive tradition, but a brief note on the secondary literature is nevertheless required. The present chapter is a reworking of a previous publication, "Poetologischer Kommentar zur 'Harzreise im Winter'," in David E. Wellbery and Klaus Weimar, *Harzreise im Winter: Eine Deutungskontroverse* (Paderborn: Schöningh, 1984), 45–78. The contribution by Klaus Weimar to that volume ("Goethe's 'Harzreise im Winter': Zur Auslegung sprachlicher Bilder," 15–44) includes a critique of the tradition of biographical interpretation. The areas of consensus and disagreement between Weimar and myself are likewise discussed in that volume (79–86). What might be termed the culmination of the tradition of biographical interpretation is represented by Albrecht Schöne, "Auguralsymbolik: Goethe, Auf dem Harz Dezember 1777," *Goethe-Jahrbuch* 96 (1979): 22–53, rpt. in Schöne, *Götterzeichen, Liebeszauber, Satanskult: Neue Einblicke in alte Goethetexte* (Munich: Wilhelm Fink, 1982), 13–52, a contribution that Weimar discusses in detail. Just before the publication of Weimar's and my joint volume, an essay by Jochen Schmidt appeared, in which the reduction of the text to an autobiographical document is also criticized: Schmidt, "Goethes Bestimmung der dichterischen Existenz im Übergang zur Klassik: 'Harzreise im Winter'," *Deutsche Vierteljahrsschrift für Literaturwissenschaft und Geistesgeschichte* 57 (1983): 613–35. A slightly reduced version of the article is included in Schmidt, *Die Geschichte des Genie-Gedankens 1750–1945*, 2 vols. (Darmstadt: Wissenschaftliche Buchgesellschaft, 1985), I: 282–309. The most decisive break with the schema of biographical interpretation in the older literature is Heinrich Henel, *Goethezeit: Ausgewählte Aufsätze* (Frankfurt a. M.: Insel, 1980), 76–101. I wish to acknowledge that my own interest in this text derives from conversations with Heinrich Henel during the period of my studies at Yale University.

4. One of the major differences between the reading proposed here and that of Jochen Schmidt (see note 3) should be marked at this point. In Schmidt's view, the outsider is an essentially negative figure, the representative of an inadequate consciousness which the text rejects as such. This seems to me to miss the point that the poet's ascent involves an exact reversal of the situation of the outsider, that the poet's vocation is to redeem that figure from its self-consuming spiritual desolation.

5. The courtiers are not merely the beneficiaries of destiny, they transform fate, in the guise of the goddess Fortuna, into an object of religious reverence. But the

abjuration of the courtiers also carries a poetological signification. The parade accompanying a regent's entry into a city ("des Fürsten Einzug") was one of the more grandiose ceremonies of ideological legitimation in absolutism. Goethe, who witnessed such a ceremony in Strasbourg, alludes to the practice in the Shakespeare speech: "Auf die Reise, meine Herren! die Betrachtung so eines einzigen Tapfs, macht unsere Seele feuriger und größer, als das Angaffen eines tausendfüßigen königlichen Einzugs." ("Onward in our journey, gentlemen! the contemplation of a single such trace [the footprint of the wanderer Shakespeare] makes our souls grander and more enflamed than gaping at a royal procession of a thousand feet"; *Münchener-Ausgabe*, I/1, 411. One reason for contrasting, as both the Shakespeare speech and "Harzreise im Winter" do, witnessing a royal procession with participation in the wanderings of poetic genius is that such processions included, as an instrument of ideological legitimation, poems written to celebrate the regent. A representative example of such poetry is "Den Vater des Vaterlandes Friedrich den Grossen bey triumphierender Zurückkunft besungen im Namen der Bürger von A. L. Karschin" (To the Father of the Fatherland, Friedrich the Great, on His Triumphant Return, Sung on Behalf of the Townspeople by A. L. Karschin; Berlin: Georg Ludwig Winter, printed March 30, 1763). By saying that it is easy to follow Fortuna's wagon, then, the poet is contrasting his poetic aspiration and poetic path with the epideictic grandiloquence of such singers of the king.

6. Karlheinz Stierle, "Die Identität des Gedichts—Hölderlin als Paradigma," in Karlheinz Stierle and Odo Marquard, eds., *Identität*, Poetik und Hermeneutik 8 (Munich: Wilhelm Fink, 1979), 517.

7. See Charles Fillmore, "Topics in Lexical Semantics," in Roger Cole, ed., *Current Issues in Linguistic Theory* (Bloomington: Indiana University Press, 1977), 76–138. The extremely interesting model of the poetic text as a "texte polyisotopique," which has been developed by the Belgian *Groupe mu* (*Rhétorique de la poésie* [Brussels: Editions Complexe, 1977]) is obviously closely related to the model employed here. It seems to me, however, that the concept of schema, as developed in American pragmatic and cognitive theory (with reference, on occasion, to Kant), is to be preferred to the concept of isotopy because of its greater structural variability and proximity to empirical experience. These features make the mediation between text and cultural context easier to grasp. In his classical study "La Geste d'Asdiwal," Claude Lévi-Strauss employs a concept of schema that is close to my own usage. Especially pertinent to my argument is Lévi-Strauss's notion that the sequence of mythical narrative is crossed by several schemata, whereby each schema operates at a specific level of abstraction and with regard to a particular domain (e.g., geology, economy, social relations, cosmology). See Claude Lévi-Strauss, *Structural Anthropology II* (New York: Basic Books, 1976), 146–98.

8. On the concept of encyclopedia, see Umberto Eco, *A Theory of Semiotics* (Bloomington: Indiana University Press, 1976), 98–100.

9. The path schema is certainly one of the most deeply rooted in our culture and often serves as a grid for the organization of mythological, literary, and argumentative texts. See, in this connection, the brilliant article by Michel Serres, "Language and Space: from Oedipus to Zola," in Serres, *Hermes: Literature, Science, Philosophy,* ed. Josué Harari and David Bell (Baltimore: The Johns Hopkins University Press, 1982), 39–53.

10. For a general theory of schemata that includes all levels of the text from the graphic to the semantic-conceptual, see David Rumelhart, "Toward an Interactive Model of Reading," *Attention and Performance VI,* ed. S. Dornie (Hillsdale, N.J.: Lawrence Erlbaum, 1977).

11. This term is introduced by Stierle ("Die Identität des Gedichts," 514) in order to characterize the subversion of discursive regularities that characterizes the lyric.

12. Phonological echoes also link the peasant to the outsider figure of stanzas V–VII. Compare: "*Zehrt* er . . . auf / Seinen eigenen *Wert*" (40–41); "*Wehrt* mit Knütteln der Bauer" (59).

13. Thus, "Harzreise im Winter" bears a trace of the earlier poem "Ganymed" (*Gedichte 1756–1799,* 205). Another indication that the text absorbs complexes from earlier poems into its texture and reworks them is the use of the verb "beizen," which we have already encountered in the text "An den Geist des Johannes Sekundus": "Ach gesprungen weil mich, Öden, Kalten, / Über beizenden Reif, der Herbstwind anpackt" (Text 24, 21–22). In this passage, the "biting" or "searing" frost that cuts into and wounds the poet's lip does not bear the connotation of seizure by the bird of prey. Note, however, that a poetic problem is being worked through in both texts in terms of harsh meteorological conditions (the figure of the "meteorological other" so prominent in Goethe's poetry). The decisive difference between the two texts is that in "Harzreise im Winter" the poet is aided in his trek through the wintry landscape by the force of 'love' (a matter to be discussed in greater detail); in "An den Geist des Johannes Sekundus," by contrast, poetic failure coincides with the 'absence of love'. Thus, "Harzreise im Winter" discloses the positive, Ganymede-related potential of the verb "beizen." Finally, I would note that in the vocabulary of Pietism, the hunter's sudden seizure of its prey is a standard metaphor for the inrush of religious faith upon the subject. In the lines: "Mit dem beizenden Sturm / Trägst du ihn hoch empor" (73–74), the schemata of the hunt, poetry, and religion achieve maximal condensation.

14. I don't recall that any interpreter of the poem has noted the jarring effect of the mixed metaphor: "bittre Schere" = 'death'. The snip of Atropos' scissors brings death and death is conventionally bitter, but the fusion of the two terms is

disturbingly dissonant. The model of the text I am developing here accounts for this dissonant combination. The term 'bitter' refers to a quality of 'beverages' and therefore evokes the liquid schema. One drink that is particularly noted for its—literal and metaphorical—bitterness is poison. And poison is taken up in the account of the outsider figure: "dem Balsam zu Gift ward" (36).

15. Hegel's definition of experience is as follows: "This *dialectical* movement which consciousness exercises on itself, both on its knowing and on its object, *insofar as the new, true object emerges for consciousness* out of this movement, is actually what is called *experience*" (Georg Wilhelm Friedrich Hegel, *Phänomenologie des Geistes* (Frankfurt a. M.: Ullstein), 62–63. Likewise, in the introduction to the *Phenomenology* (passim) Hegel characterizes the itinerary of consciousness as a passage through various "configurations of consciousness." Experience, in the Hegelian sense used here, designates the transformative movement from one configuration to the next.

16. This connotation of 'wild exteriority' as applied to the winter landscape of the Harz mountains seems ridiculous today, but in the late eighteenth century the idea of climbing the "Brocken" in winter seemed extremely audacious. The idea that the poet must depart from the enclosed social sphere in order to find the song that articulates the fundamental values of the social group is common to many cultures. See, in this connection, James W. Fernandez, "Moving Up in the World—Transcendence and Social Anthropology," *Stanford Literature Review* I/2 (1984): 201–26. On the figure of the hunter as mediator between untamed nature and culture, see Jacques Le Goff and Pierre Vidal-Naquet, "Lévi-Strauss en Broceliande," in Raymond Bellour and Catherine Clement, eds., *Claude Lévi-Strauss* (Paris: Gallimard, 1979), 274–97, esp. 284.

17. Goethe's commentary on the poem was occasioned by the publication of a text by Karl Ludwig Kannegießer, *Über Goethes Harzreise im Winter* (Prenzlau, 1820, rpt. in *Goethe* 24 [1962]: 228–35). The most significant passages of the commentary are reprinted in the apparatus to *Gedichte 1756–1799*, 1035–39.

18. In his *Morphology of the Folktale* (Bloomington: Indiana University Research Center in Anthropology, Folklore, and Linguistics, Publication 10, 1968), 62, Vladimir Propp identifies this applause, or as he calls it, recognition of the hero, as one of the basic narrative functions of his generic tale. A trace of this function appears in "Harzreise im Winter" in the phrase "erstaunten Welt" (84).

19. That the minimal requirement for personification is the semantic marker 'animate' is demonstrated in Paolo Valesio, "Esquisse pour une étude des personnifications," *Lingua e Stile* 4 (1969): 1–21.

20. The melancholy condition of the outsider bears, as has often been noted, a similarity to Werther's desolate state of mind. For a discussion of the complex orality-liquidity in *Werther*, see my article "Morphisms of the Phantasmatic Body: Goethe's *The Sorrows of Young Werther*," in Veronica Kelly and Doro-

thea E. von Mücke, eds., *Body and Text in the Eighteenth Century* (Stanford: Stanford University Press, 1994), 181–208. For a discussion of melancholy in the later novel *Wilhelm Meisters Lehrjahre*, see my article "Die Enden des Menschen: Anthropologie und Einbildungskraft im Bildungsroman (Wieland, Goethe, Novalis)," in Karlheinz Stierle and Rainer Warning, eds., *Das Ende*, Poetik und Hermeneutik 16 (Munich: Wilhelm Fink, 1995).

21. Letter of December 10, 1778.

22. One might say that what is being figured here is *sublime rapture*, recalling that "rapture," in the sense of ecstasy, is related etymologically to the idea of seizure (Latin *rapere*) and to birds of prey (Latin *raptores*). Of course, the idea of violent erotic seizure suggested by the relation of the figure to the Ganymede myth likewise belongs to this etymological field, as evidenced by English "rape."

23. *Der Göttinger Hain*, ed. Alfred Kelletat (Stuttgart: Reclam, 1967), 194. Stolberg's poem was composed during a journey to Switzerland in 1775 on which he was accompanied by Goethe.

24. See Chapter 5, note 11.

25. Friedrich Leopold Graf zu Stolberg, *Frühe Prosa*, ed. J. Behrens (Stuttgart: Reclam, 1970), 41.

26. Johann Peter Uz, "Theodizee," *Deutsche Dichtung des 18. Jahrhunderts*, ed. Adalbert Elschenbroich (Munich: Hanser, 1960), 77.

27. For a discussion of the concepts 'imaginary' and 'symbolic' that maps very well onto the problematic of "Harzreise im Winter," see Shoshana Felman, *Jacques Lacan and the Adventure of Insight* (Cambridge: Harvard University Press, 1987), 109–17.

28. One encounters the same condensation in the famous sentence from Hegel's analysis of lordship and bondage in the *Phenomenology*: "For consciousness did not sense anxiety for this or that particular thing, nor during this or that particular moment, but for its entire being: it sensed the fear of death, the absolute Lord" (*Phänomenologie des Geistes*, 119). This correlation implies the possibility of reading Hegel's dialectic of lordship and bondage as a development of the poetry of the sublime.

29. See Immanuel Kant, *Kritik der Urteilskraft* (Frankfurt a. M.: Suhrkamp, 1974), 185.

30. Ibid., 188–89.　　　　　　　31. Ibid., 195.

32. Ibid., 194.　　　　　　　　33. Ibid., 194 and passim.

34. One can catch a glimpse of the popular or "folk" culture still quite vital in the Harz region at the time of Goethe's journey by consulting the description of the annual wreath festival published by a certain Prorektor Nachtigal in his "Bruchstücke aus Briefen über den Harz," in *Deutsche Monatsschrift* (Leipzig: Sommersche Buchhandlung, 1795), 64–65. There one can read that "a wreath is

attached to the highest oak on the highest mountain in the area so that it can be seen from far and wide" (65).

35. On poetic closure, see Phillipe Hamon, "Clausules," *Poétique* 24 (1975): 495–526, and the book-length study by Barbara Herrnstein Smith, *Poetic Closure* (Chicago: University of Chicago Press, 1968), which Hamon discusses at length. A. J. Greimas examines important aspects of narrative closure in his *Maupassant: La sémiotique du texte* (Paris: Seuil, 1976), 252–62.

36. William Labov and Joshua Waletzky, "Narrative Analysis: Oral Versions of Personal Experience," in June Helm MacNeish, ed., *Essays on the Verbal and Visual Arts* (Seattle: University of Washington Press, 1967), 12–44.

37. Support for this reading can be drawn from Elias Canetti's remarks on "standing" and on the position of the orchestra conductor in *Masse und Macht* (Frankfurt a. M.: Fischer, 1980), 433–35, 442–44.

38. Compare the following lines from Stolberg's poem "Der Harz" (cited from *Der Göttinger Hain*, 177): "Dein wohltätiger Schoss, selten mit goldenem / Fluche schwanger, verleiht nützendes Eisen uns, / Das den Acker durchschneidet, / Und das Erbe der Väter schützt!" ("Your beneficent womb, seldom pregnant / With the golden curse, gives us useful iron, / That cuts through the fields, / And defends the inheritance of our fathers!")

39. "Den 3ten November 1760 gross durch den Sieg des Königs bey Torgau, beschrieb Anna Louise Karschin gebohrene Dürbachin aus Glogau" (Magdeburg: Johann Christian Pansa, 1761).

40. Compare the opening stanza of Stolberg's "Mein Vaterland" (*Der Göttinger Hain*, 187): "Das Herz gebeut mir! Siehe, schon schwebt, / Voll Vaterlandes, stolz mein Gesang!" ("My heart commands me! See, already hovers, / Full of the Fatherland, proudly, my song!")

41. Friedrich Schlegel, *Schriften zur Literatur*, ed. Wolfdietrich Rasch (Munich: Hanser, 1972), 37–38.

Index

In this index an "f" after a number indicates a separate reference on the next page, and an "ff" indicates separate references on the next two pages. A continuous discussion over two or more pages is indicated by a span of page numbers, e.g., "57–59." *Passim* is used for a cluster of references in close but not consecutive sequence.

M E R I D I A N

Crossing Aesthetics

David E. Wellbery, *The Specular Moment: Goethe's Early Lyric and the Beginnings of Romanticism*

Edmond Jabès, *The Little Book of Unsuspected Subversion*

Hans-Jost Frey, *Studies in Poetic Discourse: Mallarmé, Baudelaire, Rimbaud, Hölderlin*

Pierre Bourdieu, *The Rules of Art: Genesis and Structure of the Literary Field*

Nicolas Abraham, *Rhythms: On the Work, Translation, and Psychoanalysis*

Jacques Derrida, *On the Name*

David Wills, *Prosthesis*

Maurice Blanchot, *The Work of Fire*

Jacques Derrida, *Points . . . : Interviews, 1974–1994*

J. Hillis Miller, *Topographies*

Philippe Lacoue-Labarthe, *Musica Ficta (Figures of Wagner)*

Jacques Derrida, *Aporias*

Emmanuel Levinas, *Outside the Subject*

Library of Congress
Cataloging-in-Publication Data
Wellbery, David E.
    The specular moment : Goethe's early lyric and the beginnings of
romanticism / David E. Wellbery.
        p. cm. — (Meridian)
    Includes bibliographical references and index.
    ISBN 0-8047-2618-3 (cl) ISBN 0-8047-2694-9 (pbk)
    1. Goethe, Johann Wolfgang von, 1749–1832—Criticism and
interpretation. 2. Romanticism—Europe. I. Title. II. Series:
Meridian (Stanford, Calif.).
PT1898.L8W45 1996
831′ .6—dc20
95-36711   CIP   REV

⊛ Printed on recycled paper

Typeset in Adobe Garamond and Lithos by
Keystone Typesetting, Inc.

Original printing 1996
Last figure below indicates year of this printing:

05   04   03   02   01   00   99   98   97   96

5